The Public Record Office 1838–1958

own copyright 1991

published 1991

0 11 440224 8

Library Cataloguing in Publication Data
P catalogue record for this book
ilable from the British Library

ISO

SO publications are available from:

SO Publications Centre
l and telephone orders only)
Box 276, London, SW8 5DT
ephone orders 071–873 9090
eral enquiries 071–873 0011
euing system in operation for both numbers)

SO Bookshops
High Holborn, London, WC1V 6HB 071–873 0011 (counter service only)
Broad Street, Birmingham, B1 2HE 021–643 3740
they House, 33 Wine Street, Bristol, BS1 2BQ 0272–264306
1 Princess Street, Manchester, M60 8AS 061–834 7201
Chichester Street, Belfast, BT1 4JY 0232–238451
Lothian Road, Edinburgh, EH3 9AZ 031–228 4181

MSO's Accredited Agents
Yellow Pages)

through good booksellers

inted in the United Kingdom for HMSO
291120 8/91 C8 GP488 CCN 20249

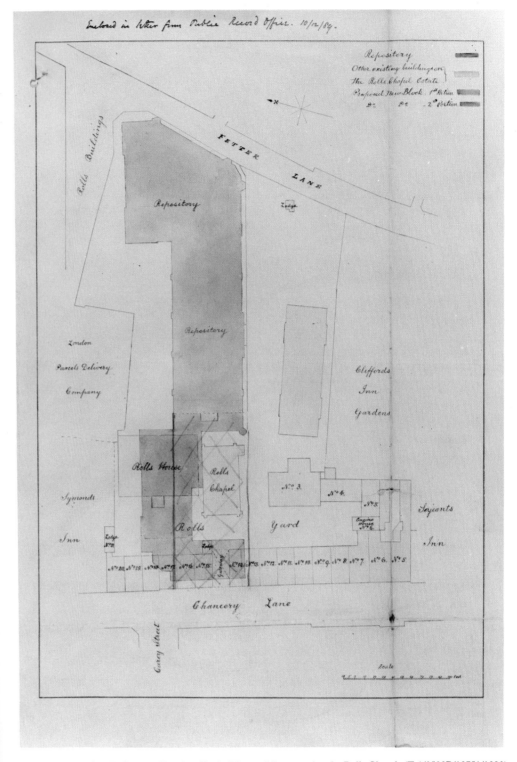

An abortive plan of 1889 for extending the office buildings while preserving the Rolls Chapel. (T 1/8538B/18751/1890)

Sir James Pennethorne's drawing of the proposed repository as seen from the Rolls House c. 1850. (MPD 177, f 65)

THE PUBLIC RECOR
1838–1958

By John D. Cantwel

London : HMSO

Contents

Foreword

In commending this history, I am very conscious that the Lord Chancellor is a comparative newcomer to the field of public records, having been responsible for the Public Record Office only since 1959, the point at which this book ends. It deals with the preceding 120 years, when the Office and its records were in the charge of the Master of the Rolls and its day-to-day operations were carried out under the Deputy Keeper of the Records and a succession of assistant keepers, clerks and workmen. Much of this history concerns those people and how they discharged their duties in ensuring the preservation of the records and in making them available to those members of the public who were interested in them. It tells the story of an institution which throughout the period covered by this book had a dual identity as the repository of legal memory and as the fount of historical knowledge, with the latter role gradually becoming the more dominant. The great popularising role of the Office in family and local history still lay ahead.

As long ago as 1888 a reader, T. C. Noble, told the Master of the Rolls that one day he hoped to write the history of the Office. Nothing came of his intention or of the official design, half a century later, to produce a similar work to mark the first centenary of the Record Act of 1838. It was the interest aroused in the sesquicentenary of the Office in 1988, marked by a celebratory conference and other events, which led to the writing of this history. Its author, a former inspecting officer and later an assistant keeper, is one of the relatively few people still active who have long memories of the Office in the days before the 1958 Public Records Act, which has been both the instrument and the vehicle of the many changes which have taken place during the last three decades. He writes with sympathy not only of the major figures of the Office's history, but also of others of less exalted rank, such as the loyal band of nineteenth-century workmen and the supplementary clerks of the early twentieth century. The work is not, however, a mere panegyric, and it does not pass over awkward events in silence. Readers may thus judge for themselves how far the Office succeeded in fulfilling the high ideals of its founders: whether John Pym Yeatman, one of its fiercest critics, was justified when he referred to it in 1875 as a 'nest of corruption'; or whether the truth lies rather with the great legal historian Frederic William Maitland, who described the Office as 'the greatest store of material that has ever been gathered in one place'.

What is certain is that countless historians and other researchers from both this country and overseas have drawn, and continue to draw, upon its riches. For them, for students of public administration, for archivists and records managers and I hope, for many ordinary members of that public whom the Public Record Office is designed to serve, this history will be of great interest.

Mackay of Clashfern
C

Lord Mackay of Clashfern,
Lord High Chancellor of Great Britain

List of Illustrations

Introduction

The power possessed by successive deputy keepers during the first 120 years of the Public Record Office's existence, tempered though it was by the keepership of the master of the rolls and Treasury control, was still decisive, and the arrangement of this work in the order of their administrations was almost automatic. Equally important was the absence of any great themes of policy apart from the constant quest for better and more secure accommodation for the records. Accordingly, the story in these pages might seem to some as much a chronicle as a history. To the practising archivist of today the absence of a formal professionalism in the office's grading structure may seem surprising, particularly as Sir Francis Palgrave, the first deputy keeper, was in no doubt 'that the Record service, requiring as it does a knowledge of law, of languages, and of general history, must if it is to be rendered efficient, be treated as a distinct profession'. But in fact the assistant keepers and the various associated and support grades were no less archivists and conservators for not being labelled as such. For much of the time the theory of the well-educated generalist held sway, and there was a justifiable fear that to stray too far from the haven of the general Treasury grades of the Civil Service would adversely affect pay. Even today that remains broadly true although the burgeoning of the record world in this country outside the Public Record Office in the past 30 years means that 'archive science', much of which the office traditionalists might look upon as the codification of common sense, has come into its own.

On the other hand, for Sir Hilary Jenkinson, whose *Manual of Archive Administration* first appeared in 1921, none of that would have been surprising, although he might have looked askance at the extent to which the new profession has developed its role, independently of Record Office tutelage. But it was 1947 before Jenkinson finally came into his kingdom, by which time his autocratic ways did not fit easily into the post-war world, and it was not surprising that he should choose to resign at the age of 71 in 1954. The last of the old-style deputy keepers was his successor, Sir David Evans, an altogether more accommodating personality. Indeed, there is a sense in which Jenkinson was really the last of the line of supremos, although not all of them chose to exercise the full power of their office.

By drawing the line at 1958 I have had regard not only to the 30-year rule, but to the passage during that year of the new Public Records Act, which thereafter placed the office on a quite different footing and enabled it, not before time, to begin to tackle the problem of twentieth-century record-keeping along the lines recommended by the all-important Grigg Committee on Departmental Records of 1952 to 1954.

Throughout my researches I have been fortunate to have had discussions with very many serving and retired members of the office's staff about events with which they were familiar. I am deeply grateful to them all. In particular, I must single out Dr Roy Hunnisett, who as director of publications read my manuscript when in draft, and whose advice and helpful criticism has been of inestimable value in getting it to its final form.

I wish to acknowledge also the support received from Dr John Post, who succeeded Dr Hunnisett in the latter stages of the preparation of this work, and to Derek Burr for seeing it through the press. Patricia Marron and Beryl Saddington must also be warmly thanked for deciphering my handwriting and producing the typescript for the printers.

Outside the office much helpful information about the Grigg Committee came from Sir Kenneth Clucas, who was its secretary. I have also been greatly assisted by the kindness of Mr Christopher Palgrave-Barker in granting me access to the Dawson Turner Papers and for his permission to quote from them. For permission to quote from the Henry Cole Papers in the Victoria and Albert Museum I am indebted to Mrs Elizabeth Bonython, who was ever ready to place at my disposal her vast knowledge of this great Victorian and his contemporaries. Crown copyright material from records within the Public Record Office itself is quoted with the permission of the controller of HM Stationery Office.

Thanks are also due to the staffs of the Bodleian Library, British Library, Chetham's Library and the University of Newcastle upon Tyne for their help and co-operation. I must also record my sincere thanks to Eric O'Dell and Ray Street, foremen of the repositories at Chancery Lane and Kew, and to their staff for handling so efficiently my many demands for documents from my base in the Romilly Room. I am sure that Sir John Romilly, the begetter of the Round Room and always conscious of the needs of searchers, would have approved.

Finally, I should explain that in 1984 I wrote two articles covering, in rather different form, many of the events described in the opening chapters. Consequently, I have not always felt it necessary to repeat the references provided earlier. Interested readers are referred to 'The 1838 Public Record Office Act and its Aftermath: a New Perspective' (*Journal of the Society of Archivists*, VII (1984), 277–86) and 'The Making of the First Deputy Keeper of the Records' (*Archives*, XVII (1985), 22–37).

John Cantwell
June 1988

Chapter I

Origins of the Public Record Office Act 1838

. . . nothing but the moral influence of your Lordship united to your official station can put down the agitation and put an end to the bickerings and jealousies which have disgraced the record offices.

(Sir Francis Palgrave to Lord Langdale, 20 April 1837: PRO 1/1)

'An Act for keeping safely the Public Records', the first of its kind, became law on 14 August 1838. It was known formally as the Act 1 & 2 Vict. c 94, but it was usually called the 'Record Act' or the 'Public Records Act'. Not until 1877, when an act was passed to regulate the disposal of public records, was it officially styled the 'Public Record Office Act 1838' which, although a little misleading, reflected the original limited aim of the measure, to place the government record offices under one authority. However, it was 1840 before a Public Record Office began to emerge as a distinct entity, and 1851 before the first stone of the new building was laid. The main reason for the slow development was that the government was a reluctant legislator, forced to act in response to pressure from the master of the rolls, Lord Langdale, who had assumed, somewhat unwillingly, the temporary superintendence of the record vote in March 1837. A year later, with new arrangements still awaited, Langdale's threatened resignation persuaded the government that it could procrastinate no longer. Even after the act was passed progress was slow: complications arose about the appointment of a deputy keeper of the records, the working head of the office; and the assimilation of the staff of the existing record offices, for which provision was made by the act, took nearly two years. The received version that the Public Record Office emerged, almost inevitably, from the report of a parliamentary select committee in 1836, fits the notion of the age of reform, but implies a vision and sense of purpose, which were almost entirely absent, except in the minds of three or four persons actively engaged in record affairs.

Foremost among them was Henry (later Sir Henry) Cole, who was to serve in the Public Record Office as an assistant keeper of the first class from 1840 until 1850. He left to take up duties in connection with the Great Exhibition, under the patronage of the prince consort, and went on to become the secretary of the Department of Science and Art. Cole joined the record service straight from Christ's Hospital at the age of 15. From 1823 until 1832 he worked for Sir Francis Palgrave, who became the first deputy keeper of the records in 1838. At the time of Cole's engagement Sir Francis was Francis Cohen, but shortly afterwards he married Elizabeth Turner, daughter of Dawson Turner, the East Anglian banker, botanist and antiquary, and changed his name to Palgrave, the maiden name of his wife's mother. A year earlier he had left the law to take up an appointment as a sub-commissioner with the Record Commission, the forerunner of the Public Record Office. Believing much light would be thrown upon the foundations of the English constitution and the origins of the common law from the records of Parliament, Palgrave persuaded the commission to underwrite his editorship of *Parliamentary Writs*.[1] For this he regularly received well in excess of £1,000 annually, comprising a fixed salary of £500 with further sums varying according to the number of folios of transcripts made and the number of sheets passed for press. On his own account he employed a small number of young men, Cole being one, whom he trained to assist him. Some of them also held clerkships at the Tower Record Office, the repository of the older records of Chancery, and were paid by Palgrave on a piece-work basis, working out of office hours. In 1826 separate payment for transcribing ceased and it was undertaken thereafter by directly-employed clerks, whose salaries were reimbursed to Palgrave by the commission. The former Tower transcribers included Thomas (afterwards Sir Thomas) Duffus Hardy, his brother William (afterwards Sir William) Hardy and Charles Roberts. All three were to have distinguished careers, the first two becoming the second and third deputy keepers of the records, and Roberts the secretary of the Public Record Office from 1857 until 1866.

Cole left Palgrave in 1832 under a cloud, having become involved, possibly unwittingly, in a campaign against him led by Sir Nicholas Harris Nicolas, the formidable antiquary, aided and abetted by Charles Purton Cooper, who had not long taken over the secretaryship of the Record Commission from John Caley, the keeper of records of the Treasury of the Exchequer at the Chapter House, Westminster. The expense involved in Palgrave's work on the *Parliamentary Writs* had been singled out by Nicolas for particular censure in his *Observations on the State of Historical Literature*, which he had submitted to Lord Melbourne, then home secretary, in 1831. Both Nicolas and Cooper thought the work could be undertaken much more economically, even if it should retain the high priority it enjoyed over other projects. Nicolas believed the difficulty to lie in the inadequate control exercised by the Record Commission. Largely due to the exertions of Charles Abbot (later Lord Colchester) that body had been set up in 1800 as a result of a report from a parliamentary select committee. It started with excellent intentions, but lacked adequate powers and, as it contained many eminent men with other claims on their time, Nicolas thought it imperative to reconstitute it on more professional lines. Cooper, on the other hand, had no particular quarrel with the Record Commission in which he had an obvious stake; but he was anxious to meet some of Nicolas's criticisms, which extended to the way the record offices were run and the high fees exacted for searches. It so happened that at that time Cole was becoming

---

1. *Parliamentary Writs and Writs of Military Summons with Records and Muniments relating to Suit and Service to Parliament etc.*, 2 vols in 4 (Record Commission, 1827–1834).

2

increasingly frustrated about his pay and prospects with Palgrave, and Thomas Hardy was seeking editorial work to supplement his pay as a clerk at the Tower. Realising the opportunity this presented to displace Palgrave, Cooper and Nicolas resolved to utilise the evident talents and natural ambitions of these two gifted young men in a remodelled and more economical publications programme.

Thanks to his friends in the ruling circles of the Whig Party and his own deservedly high historical reputation – his *Rise and Progress of the English Commonwealth* had been published in 1832 – Palgrave, who was knighted in the same year, was at first able to fend off the attacks on *Parliamentary Writs*. For all that, the project ground to a halt in 1834, although a year earlier, by way of compensation, the Record Commission had placed Palgrave on a fixed annual salary of £1,000. He was also permitted to serve on the Municipal Corporations Commission, which he did from 1833 to 1835,[2] and in 1834 he succeeded in obtaining the keepership at the Chapter House on the death of John Caley. Paradoxically, Cooper was partly responsible for the latter appointment, although his motive was as much to relieve the Record Commission vote as to advance Palgrave, who remained bitter, particularly about the conduct of Hardy and Cole. There had been ill-feeling between Hardy and Palgrave ever since 1823, when Hardy and his younger brother William were in dispute about their rate of pay when making transcripts for him. In 1831 they thought their reputations had suffered when Palgrave told a committee of the Record Commission of his preference for directly-employed transcribers; and in April 1832, when the manoeuvres against Palgrave were coming to their climax, a physical clash occurred at the Tower between him and the young Thomas. The following month matters were made even worse when Palgrave was lampooned in a penny broadsheet, the *National Omnibus and General Advertiser*, and said to have received two black eyes.[3] As for Cole, Palgrave never really forgave him for what he saw as his disloyalty, and his feelings of resentment were rekindled when his former apprentice became the driving force behind the Select Committee Inquiry of 1836 into the management of the record service. On leaving Palgrave in 1832 Cole had taken up work with the Record Com-

---

2. But he disagreed with his colleagues' findings, declined to set his name to their report, and published his own views separately: 'Protest of Sir Francis Palgrave' (*Parliamentary Papers*, 1835 (135) xl). Sidney and Beatrice Webb later described it as 'an able and instructive document by the most distinguished of the Commissioners': *English Local Government*, III (London, 1908), 772n.

3. J. C. Jeaffreson, *A Book of Recollections* (London, 1894) II, 75–79, ascribes the verses to the Reverend Richard Harris Barham, but Frederic (later Sir Frederic) Madden in his journal for 1832 (now in the Bodleian Library) says they were written by Charles (later Sir Charles) George Young of the College of Arms, which seems more likely. Eight years later the verses were still circulating, as W. H. Black records being shown them by Frederick Devon, although he was obviously unimpressed, describing the '*National Omnibus*' as 'an absurd ephemeral paper': PRO 1/121/8, p 35.

mission, but in 1835 he suffered the indignity of arbitrary dismissal, after a bitter quarrel with Cooper over a claim for payment for additional work undertaken at the Augmentation Office. Through his friendship with the parliamentary radicals, and particularly Charles Buller, Liberal MP for Lis-keard, who was appointed chairman of the Select Committee, Cole fought back. In his campaign against the Record Commission, which he also carried to the press, Cole was strongly supported by Nicolas and Hardy, both by that time having also fallen out with Cooper. Cole also had the ear of Edward Protheroe, one of the record commissioners and a former MP, who returned to the House as member for Halifax in 1837. Another critic of the Record Commission was Patrick Fraser Tytler, the Scottish historian. He had little love for that body, partly, perhaps, because he had been narrowly beaten by Palgrave for the keepership of the Chapter House in 1834. Palgrave himself, although no out-and-out defender of the Record Commission, was highly apprehensive of the consequences of change, believing his opponents to be unscrupulously seeking to advance their own cause at his expense. He refused to acknowledge any public-spirited element in the reformers' campaign, likening them to 'Kilkenny cats', who would 'soon eat one another up to the tips of their tails'.[4]

An equally determined opponent of change was the learned antiquary, the Reverend Joseph Hunter, who in 1833, late in life, moved from Bath to London to take up an appointment as a sub-commissioner with the Record Commission. He clashed bitterly with Cole and Hardy during the course of the parliamentary inquiry, and his fears for the future were finally set at rest only when appointed an assistant keeper in the Public Record Office in 1840. Ranged with Hunter was a Record Commission colleague, William Henry Black. He saw the 'cloven foot of that devil Cole' in the Select Committee's findings, and, on being told that Buller seemed so ill it was not thought he would last the session, commented 'He were better in his grave than in Parliament'.[5] Black, too, later joined the Public Record Office, but only as an assistant keeper of the second class, mainly because as a Seventh Day Adventist he refused to work on Saturdays, which limited his usefulness to the office and, coupled with his inability to attend regularly, eventually led to his enforced resignation in 1853. But all that was in the future, and with Hunter he now helped Cooper prepare his case against the critics. Assistance was also rendered by John Bruce, a lawyer, whose later efforts to join the

---

4. PRO 36/31: Sir F. Palgrave to W. H. Black, 6 January 1837. The allusion must be to the limerick which, as I was reminded by my colleague John Walford, runs: There once were two cats from Kilkenny – Each thought there was one cat too many – So they fought and they fit – They scratched and they bit – Till instead of two cats there weren't any.

5. PRO 36/31: W. H. Black's note of 6 January 1837 on a pamphlet concerning the Select Committee and his comment about Buller in a letter of [2] March 1837 from F. Montagu.

Public Record Office were of no avail, but who eventually became an editor of the *Calendar of State Papers*. Palgrave played no part in the proceedings, having no confidence in Hunter and Bruce, whom he thought to be behind a 'virulent attack' against him which had appeared in the *Gentleman's Magazine* in the previous year. However, his informant, Charles Devon, a clerk at the Chapter House, was hardly disinterested, as both he and his younger brother Frederick had fallen foul of Hunter somewhat earlier in connection with their editorial work.

In spite of its attempted defence, the commission stood condemned in the eyes of the Treasury by its failure to control its expenditure. Since 1800 the bulk of its money had been spent on payments to editors and the printing and publication of historical texts when, in the view of the Select Committee, it should have been used to house properly, conserve and arrange the records. Consequently, the Select Committee was convinced that the building of a new repository was a matter of the first importance and it therefore wanted control of the record service to be vested in a new commission under the full-time direction of, at most, three commissioners. The record commissioners countered this by pointing to the bill they had drawn up in 1833 for the building of a general record office on the Rolls Estate. They contended that until it was built control of the various record offices could best be exercised by an inspector-general responsible to them rather than by a new commission. Always the man of action, and having no confidence in the existing state of affairs, Cole decided to force matters by drafting a bill of his own. Although the Select Committee had recommended that the older state papers might be transferred to a new repository when built, his measure was confined to the existing record offices and the records of the courts. That accorded with the contemporary distinction between public records, which had a legal character, and other public documents. Cole thought that the proof they gave of some public or private right, stemming from legislative, judicial or executive proceedings, was the primary justification for their preservation. He conceded their value for historical purposes, which he thought grew with age, but was always incidental and subordinate,[6] an opinion he was to modify at a later stage of his career when he became an assistant keeper.

At the time, however, he saw his measure as designed to improve the administration of justice, especially for poorer litigants. To achieve that, he proposed the abolition of search fees and the provision of better access to the records in a new repository under a keeper general, empowered, subject to the consent of the judges, to rid himself of 'worthless records'.

---

6. H. Cole, 'The Record Commission', *Law Magazine*, XVII (1837), 80.

In drawing up his bill, Cole was in close touch with friends, such as Thomas Hardy and John Mitchell Kemble, the philologist and historian, as well as Charles Buller, who introduced it in the Commons where it received its first reading on 24 February 1837.[7] Shortly afterwards Buller was told that the government was willing to introduce its own measure but thought that the master of the rolls, who was chairman of the now-doomed Record Commission, should become keeper general. Consequently, the home secretary, Lord John Russell, persuaded the master of the rolls, Lord Langdale, in March 1837 to undertake the superintendence of record affairs by assuming responsibility for the £5,000 voted for them until new permanent arrangements could be made. A short bill, drafted by Black and Stacey Grimaldi, an antiquarian, for the immediate amendment of the 'principal grievances complained of respecting the Public Records', which limited itself to the question of access and fees, failed to get beyond its authors,[8] but in May 1837 J. E. Drinkwater Bethune,[9] parliamentary counsel to the Home Office, was told to draw up a government bill upon instructions from Langdale.

Meanwhile Palgrave, having strongly objected to the suggested appointment of a 'deputy', under Langdale, to undertake the practical direction of the record keepers – a proposal which was to re-emerge in the 1838 act – was further alarmed when told by C. P. Cooper of the possibility of a place being found for Kemble as 'chief archivist or the like'.[10] Palgrave had already asked Langdale for permission to submit an alternative to Buller's bill, and this he now did on his own account, hoping it would prove effectual against what he thought the disreputable behaviour of the reformers, some of whom were regrouping in a newly-formed English Historical Society. Ostensibly, Palgrave told his father-in-law, 'Tytler, Stevenson, Kemble, Hardy and John Miller (who ought to keep better company)'[11] had as their purpose the publication of the old English historians, but really it was to oppose the

---

7. In bringing in his bill, Buller was supported by Benjamin (later Sir Benjamin) Hawes and Sir Charles Lemon, MPs for Lambeth and Penryn respectively. Both had served on the Select Committee.

8. PRO 36/31: Draft of a Short Act, 17 March 1837. See also letter from W. H. Black to Stacey Grimaldi: BL Add. MSS. 34189, ff 134–135.

9. Bethune, known at the time as John Elliott Drinkwater, had also been a member of the Municipal Corporations Commission with Palgrave. After the abandonment of record legislation in 1837 he was again told to take consultations about the form of a bill in March 1838 ahead of the main proposals in the following June.

10. BL Add. MSS. 52187: Palgrave to John Allen, one of the record commissioners. Referring to Kemble, Palgrave wrote: 'I can only say as before that however painful it may be to abandon the studies and pursuits of a whole life, I would rather do so than to submit or act under any person of that age or class – and the job would be rank in the extreme.'

11. Dawson Turner Papers (in private hands): Palgrave to Dawson Turner, 27 May 1837. The society was dissolved in 1849.

Record Commission. Palgrave's bill, unlike Black's, was a full-scale affair, and provided for the record service to be placed under the master of the rolls within the Court of Chancery, with salaries payable from the Suitors' Fund. The keeperships at the Chapter House, the Tower of London and the Rolls Chapel were retained, and provision was made for the appointment of a secretary of records. More radically, the measure would have extended, by stages, to the State Paper Office, Privy Council Office, and other public departments; it was also clear from the 'interpretation' clause that Palgrave wanted a substantial broadening of the traditional use of the term 'record'. All these matters were, however, thrown into the melting pot with the death of William IV in June 1837 which automatically resulted in a six-month period being placed upon the continued existence of the Record Commission. As the government's main interest in the matter was to dispatch that troublesome body, it was now quite content to wait, although the Rolls Estate Act, which could be seen as a long-term planning measure for the proposed new record office in Chancery Lane, became law in July 1837. When the Record Commission at last expired in December 1837, Lord John Russell once again prevailed upon Langdale to continue his oversight of record business, which was proceeding on little more than a care and maintenance basis. Publication work was almost at a halt, but a place had been found in the service for Henry Cole at the Exchequer of Pleas. Charles Buller had used his influence with Langdale, whose Benthamite sympathies inclined him towards the reformers' cause, to secure Cole's reinstatement. C. P. Cooper, who was continuing as secretary for record affairs, could hardly have welcomed the return of his late adversary, but consoled himself with the thought that his critics were still not much further forward in their careers than before the setting-up of the Select Committee Inquiry in 1836. Hardy was now chief clerk at the Tower,[12] but his editorial work was more or less at a standstill, as was that of Nicolas, who was to make his peace with Palgrave after a fashion during the early part of 1838.

Palgrave himself knew that all now rested on his own efforts. He had failed to persuade the ageing Henry Petrie, the keeper at the Tower, to make common cause with him, not surprisingly as they had often clashed in the past and there was a sense in which Petrie, who had beaten Palgrave for the Tower post in 1819, was Hardy's protector. Neither was anything to be gained by seeking support from Thomas Leach, the keeper at the

---

12. The former chief clerk, John Bayley, was an incidental casualty of the earlier campaign against Palgrave by Cooper, Nicolas and Hardy, who during the course of their investigations uncovered irregularities in his editorial charges. Madden, who had an eye for a keepership at the time, revealed some of the underlying aspects of the affair in an entry in his journal for 23 May 1832, in which he wrote: 'I think Bayley one of the greatest knaves breathing and Palgrave as great a Jew as when he was first circumcised'.

Rolls Chapel,[13] whose interest barely extended beyond the fees of the place, the main responsibilities devolving upon the clerks, Thomas Palmer and Henry Holden, whose service stretched back to 1796 and 1810 respectively. Palgrave therefore concentrated upon making his own views known to Langdale at every opportunity, to ensure that when changes came he would not be the loser. His position was of particular delicacy because, although he was receiving £1,000 a year from public funds, only £400 was in respect of his Chapter House keepership, the balance coming from the Record Commission vote. With the demise of the commission that £600 was under threat, and Palgrave knew that unless he could secure acceptable compensation or the senior place in the new order – for he was not prepared to serve under anyone else in the record sphere – his future was bleak indeed. Others in the record service, such as Hunter and Black, were equally concerned, as were the clerks at the Chapter House. Moreover, the workmen employed to clean and repair the records were getting restless and seeking an increase in wages from 25 to 30 shillings a week, trusting that 'in naming this sum we shall not be thought rude but actuated by very humble and moderate desires'.[14]

Determined that the uncertainty should not be allowed to continue indefinitely, Langdale made it plain to the Home Office and the Treasury during the early months of 1838 that unless matters were placed upon a regular footing he was no longer prepared to shoulder responsibility for record affairs. One response to his pressure was the replacement in April 1838 of C. P. Cooper by F. S. Thomas as Langdale's secretary for record business. Thomas was seconded specially for the purpose from his clerkship at the State Paper Office. He had the advantage over Cooper that he had not been involved in any of the 'bickerings and jealousies' which had, in Palgrave's words, 'disgraced the record offices'. Langdale had suggested in March 1838 as a first step that the offices should be united under a new authority. Treasury approval was given in May 1838, although it reserved its position on the building of a new repository and took the opportunity to question the basis upon which Palgrave should continue to be paid. It was eventually

---

13. He owed his appointment in 1831 to his brother, Sir John Leach, then master of the rolls. A year earlier Henry Gawler had been given the post in succession to the long-serving John Kipling. On that occasion Palgrave had made an unsuccessful bid: see his letter of 7 September 1830 to John Allen, one of the record commissioners, in PRO 30/26/109.

14. Although the men complained of 'very severe privations' due to their low wages, Langdale's room for manoeuvre was limited and nothing came of their petition. Dated 5 March 1838, it is in PRO 1/1, followed by a letter to C. P. Cooper from their spokesman, Henry Mogford, dated 9 March 1838, giving details of wage rates in similar trades. Palgrave thought that if Langdale was given the conservancy of the records the foreman, Charles Gay, 'a very able and deserving person', and all the workmen employed in repairing records should be placed under the Stationery Office. For his letter of 1 March see pp 63–64 below.

agreed that that should remain unchanged until March 1839 or until new arrangements were introduced, if earlier. No special provision was made for W. H. Black, who much to his disgust, was left without record employment. On the major issue of unification, Lord John Russell was unsure about getting the necessary legislation through Parliament before the end of the session, but the solicitor general, Sir Robert Rolfe, was instructed to take the appropriate steps. By mid-June 1838 Langdale had the first draft of a bill drawn up by J. E. Drinkwater Bethune, whose interest in the subject, as mentioned earlier, went back to May 1837 when the government had detailed him to prepare an alternative to Buller's bill. In form and content the proposed new measure was very similar to Buller's. The main difference concerned custody which was given to the master of the rolls instead of a keeper general, but only after the establishment of a suitable repository. Fees were also left to his regulation rather than being abolished altogether. The bill differed more obviously from the one drafted by Palgrave as the places of the keepers in post were not expressly retained and no call was proposed upon the Chancery Suitors' Fund, a proceeding to which Langdale was strongly opposed. Neither did it extend beyond the courts of law and the existing record offices. However, unlike both the Palgrave and Buller bills, it made no provision for the disposal of 'valueless records'. For all that, the three bills had much in common as will be seen from a summary of their salient points in Appendix I.

Bethune's first draft bill, submitted to Lord Langdale on 14 June 1838, included a proviso giving the judges power to defer transfers to the Public Record Office beyond the normal period, which he suggested should be 50 years. Langdale was willing to accept the judges' veto, but thought that records should usually be transferred after 20 years. He also thought that the absence of a power to remove records from their existing places of deposit, many of which were wholly unsuitable, rendered the clause enabling him to make orders for the preservation and arrangement of the records meaningless. He also considered that he should have power to order the cleaning and repair of the records, and, more fundamentally, he wanted the legal charge of them given to some person immediately, without waiting for the provision of a suitable repository. To that end he suggested that the several buildings in which the records might be deposited should be constituted branch offices. With the lesson of the Record Commission in mind, he did not want anything to do with publication or distribution except by way of recommendation to the Home Office or Treasury. He was puzzled to find he was given power to appoint a keeper of records, subject to crown approval, as he had been advised as recently as 6 June 1838 that that appointment was to be made by the first lord of the Treasury. To Langdale's surprise, when Bethune circulated a revised draft on 23 June 1838, the chief record keeper post was again placed in his gift, subject to crown approval, but it was now styled deputy keeper of the rolls. Langdale immediately pointed out that this could not remain in the bill without the express authority of Lord John Russell. Previously, the master of the rolls had had the patronage of the keeperships at the Rolls Chapel and at the Tower, but in the latter case the appointment was made 'with the approbation of His Majesty under his sign manual'.[15] It was later suggested that Langdale insisted upon the nomination of the deputy keepership to compensate for his loss of patronage, but the official papers do not support that assumption.

On the question of titles Langdale considered that record keeper for the chief, and assistant record keepers for the other senior officers, would be preferable. However, in other respects, the revise – which now extended the bill's provisions to the Court of the Palatinate of Durham although describing it, wrongly, as 'lately abolished' – attempted to meet most of his original objections. In particular, legal custody of the records was vested in him immediately, but, not wishing to assume responsibility for non-Chancery records unless he could be sure of housing them properly, he argued that until they were formally transferred to the Public Record Office, or one of its branches, they should be committed only to his 'charge and superintendence'. This last key alteration was, at his insistence, made at the bill's committee stage when the traditional link of the master of the rolls with the records of Chancery was also confirmed and they were placed in his custody on enactment.

The bill, as introduced in the Commons on 10 July 1838, differed from the previous versions by specifying among the records covered those of the Admiralty Court. It also included a clause for the recovery of records in private possession and provided for the extension of the act by order in council to records other than those named. This last clause was to be used in 1852 to embrace departmental records, but in 1838 the primary intention of the law officers was to provide for the transfer at a later date of any judicial or quasi-judicial records, such as those of the Offices of the Duchies of Lancaster and Cornwall, which might be temporarily excepted.[16] The Office of Woods also sought exemption for land revenue records, which, like the records of the Pells of the Exchequer, were taken out in the Commons but later reinstated in the Lords after strong representations from Langdale. The power to compel private persons to deliver up records in their possession was also dropped in the Commons as the law officers concluded that recovery could be effected by means of an action of trover or detinue. Also dropped were the provisions concerning the giving in evidence of printed calendars, catalogues and indexes, about which Joseph Hunter in particular had been expressing misgivings because he regarded the existing texts as inadequate. Concerning staffing, the bill differed from the June drafts by providing for the appointment of a fit person, duly qualified by his knowledge of records, to act as chief record keeper with the title deputy keeper of the records. Power of appointment remained with the master of

---

15. *HC Accounts and Papers*, 1825, XIX, 297 (Courts of Justice Patronage).
16. Appendixes to the *First Report of the Royal Commission on Public Records*, I, pt III (Cd. 6396), 181.

the rolls, subject to crown approval. Provision was also made for the appointment by the Treasury of similarly qualified persons as assistant record keepers, to be selected, in the first instance, from among those already in the record service who might otherwise be entitled to compensation for loss of office. Further changes in committee saw the inclusion of the records of the late Court of the Palatinate of Ely – a provision which was never used – and a new clause enabling records in the Baga de Secretis of the Queen's Bench, which mostly concerned state trials, to remain under the keys of the same officers by whom they were kept formerly. This early attempt at secrecy, which, as Cole pointed out, meant that the master of the rolls could take the Baga but not open it was removed in the Lords at the committee stage on 3–4 August 1838. At the same time, at Hardy's suggestion, the definition of records as 'Rolls, Records, Writs, Books, Papers, and Documents whatsoever of a Public Nature belonging to Her Majesty' was expanded by the insertion of the words 'Proceedings, Decrees, Bills, Warrants, Accounts'. Another Hardy suggestion, to destroy at 20-year intervals documents 'preserved as of Record', but considered 'of no public or private utility', was not taken up. A clause concerning the control of salaries by the Treasury and the fixing of an upper limit to the deputy keeper's salary by Parliament was taken out, but the most important change concerned the requirement for the provision by the Treasury of 'an additional building in London or Westminster for keeping the public records in the custody of the Master of the Rolls which shall be called the Public Record Office'. Back in June, Langdale had thought this could scarcely be approved by the Treasury as it stood, and so, at his suggestion and at the continued urging of Palgrave, it was now modified to read: 'shall provide such suitable and proper or additional building or buildings as may be required'. To add substance, a Public Record Office was to be established, under the direction of the master of the rolls, as soon after the appointment of a deputy keeper of the records as convenient. The bill, thus amended, returned to the Commons on 7 August 1838 and was agreed there on 10 August. Royal assent followed on 14 August and so, in spite of the fierce controversies concerning the management of the records since the beginning of the decade, its parliamentary passage was completed in little more than a month.

During the bill's progress through Parliament, Langdale was in consultation about its provisions with Palgrave, Thomas Duffus Hardy, Henry Cole and Joseph Hunter, all of whom were to take up senior posts in the new record department. He received comments also from Rowley Lascelles, the Irish antiquary, a long-standing critic of the former Record Commission and friend of Cole and Hardy. When Bethune first drew up his draft he had the benefit of the earlier bills prepared by Cole and Palgrave. Consequently, when the matter again became active in June 1838, a framework had already been established. While a number of points, mainly of detail, were raised by the records men after the bill's introduction in the Commons in July 1838, their observations did not greatly alter its general structure. In so far as the act differed from the bill as first conceived – as in the 'charge and superintendence' clauses and the speedy establishment of a new office – it was due to Langdale, earning him the title of 'Father of the Records'. Although the act came to be seen as something of a curiosity, that was because it was expressly designed for the needs of the time. That it ultimately became inappropriate – particularly in respect of the problems posed by departmental records – cannot be denied, but the responsibility for that does not rest with Langdale and the others who helped shape it, but with those whose indifference allowed it to remain on the statute book for no less than 120 years.

Chapter II

The First Appointments

His policy in the great Record struggle of this year has been to keep as quiet as possible; that is, to have others to fight the battle, the chief gain of which will be his.

(From a biographical notice by the Reverend Joseph Hunter on Sir Francis Palgrave, 29 November 1836: BL Add. MSS. 36527, f 192)

On 14 August 1838, the day royal assent was given to the new act, Lord John Russell wrote privately to Lord Langdale asking to be told when he had found a fit person to be deputy keeper. Langdale replied next day that before asking anyone to accept the office he wished to know the salary and whether he ought to communicate with Russell or the Treasury as to expenses, but he presumed he was subordinate to Russell in establishing a plan of management. Neither of the letters is in the official records and we know of their existence, but not their precise content, from a summary of correspondence prepared by F. S. Thomas, the secretary of the Public Record Office, in which he set out Langdale's connection with the care and management of the public records during the period 1837 to 1839.[1] The letters and the subsequent sequence of events, unremarkable in themselves, are nevertheless of interest because of the later allegations, eventually to be repeated in the *Dictionary of National Biography*, that Thomas Duffus Hardy was promised the deputy keepership by Langdale, only to be deprived of the appointment due to ministerial pressure which resulted in the selection of Sir Francis Palgrave instead. In compiling his summary – which was placed at Hardy's disposal, when gathering material for his *Memoirs of Lord Langdale* in 1852 – it is clear that Thomas had access not only to the official papers but also to those accumulated by Langdale in a private and semi-official capacity. The latter were last seen by the Royal Commission on Public Records 1910–1919 at a firm of solicitors in 1912 and their present whereabouts, or indeed whether or not they still exist, is not known in spite of many inquiries. From the surviving material among the public records, all the evidence suggests that Palgrave was the first and only choice, and it is significant that Thomas – no lover of Palgrave – does not suggest otherwise, saying that the appointment resulted from the Treasury's desire to avoid payment of compensation to him for the loss of his keepership at the Chapter House. It is true that at about the same time that Langdale was exchanging letters with Russell he was also in touch informally with Alexander (later Sir Alexander) Young Spearman, the equivalent of the modern-day permanent secretary of the Treasury, although then called assistant secretary. The full

---

1. PRO 36/54.

extent of their discussions will never be known, but they certainly revolved around the need to determine the deputy keeper's salary and the question of any expenditure resulting from a possible survey of the Rolls House, Chancery Lane, which Langdale considered a convenient centre for record administration. The manner in which record business was to be regulated by the government was also discussed, and Spearman gave it as his opinion that in order to confine it to a single channel all correspondence should, in the first instance, pass through Russell, the home secretary.

The result was that on 17 August 1838 Langdale wrote officially to Russell, saying that, although he would not be in a position to submit a general plan for record management for some time, he hoped he might be excused for requesting his attention to certain points without delay. In particular, he emphasised his need to know the salary he might offer the deputy keeper; the need to appoint a place to house the arranged and most useful records, and to accommodate an officer to deal with record enquiries from the public; and the need to save from destruction or embezzlement a large quantity of records currently without proper protection, especially those of the lately-abolished Welsh courts which were reported to be greatly neglected. For the last purpose, Langdale suggested that the Welsh records should be examined to see how far it might be appropriate to bring them to London and the probable expense of so doing. Subject to survey, he thought the Rolls House might be a convenient centre because, if the Queen's Bench records then housed there were sent to the Tower and replaced by documents in greater demand, a nucleus would be formed for the intended general record office. As for the deputy keeper's salary, he proposed to ask the Treasury the amount he was authorised to offer, and sought Russell's approval accordingly.

Not long after the dispatch of this letter Langdale received a letter from Spearman, dated 20 August 1838, in which he explained that he had been unable to speak to the chancellor of the Exchequer, Thomas Spring Rice, until the Saturday, which was the 18th. The joint secretary, Francis Baring, had then been consulted and the conclusion was that £600 a year, increasing to £700 after five years' service and to £800 after ten years, was a suitable salary for the deputy keeper. The chancellor also approved the proposed survey of the Rolls House and agreed with Spearman that record business should be conducted through the Home Office to ensure that there was a single line of communication. Next day Langdale wrote to Spearman that he thought the scale suggested for the deputy keepership was sufficient and now felt able to name it to anyone to whom he proposed the acceptance of the office. Meanwhile, he said, he had received from Palgrave a compensation claim for £687 18s 4d for losses due to the recent act. However, before he was able to offer the post to anyone – significantly, Palgrave was in Wales at the time – he was dismayed to get a letter from Russell, dated 24 August, in which he said he had forwarded Langdale's letter 'containing the details of a Plan for the management of the public records' to the Treasury, calling its attention to the several points mentioned in it and recommending a salary which he thought might properly be paid to the deputy keeper, but he left Langdale in ignorance of the sum – it was £800 – he had in mind.

Naturally enough, Langdale thought he was being quietly rebuked for rushing matters, and, as he told Spearman privately on the 25th, he considered it fortunate that he had not communicated to anyone the scale he had previously thought settled. At the same time, seeking to make amends to Russell, he wrote to explain that he had done no more than submit some particulars which he thought needed immediate attention. If, as he inclined to think, he had been guilty of a mistake, he begged him to excuse it as due to his desire that something which he considered clearly beneficial to the public should be done without delay. He did not wish to withdraw from any responsibility imposed upon him by the act, nor to form or execute any plan without Russell's approbation, and did not intend to incur any expense without government authority. He reminded him that the £5,000 already granted for record business for 1838/1839 sufficed only for the work carried out by the late commission and allowed nothing for the record offices now placed under his superintendence or for the additional expense which the new system would entail. Consequently, the government should fix an annual sum for all these purposes, taking account of the extent and importance of the work which was greater than persons who had not 'minutely attended to the subject are apt to think'. Provided he was given this information, Langdale said, it would then be proper for him to submit an estimate of its appropriation. He was willing to suspend active proceedings until the total sum was decided, although if Russell thought some other course more convenient he would try to comply. His letter was accompanied by an unofficial one in which, according to the summary, Langdale told Russell that he had addressed an official letter to him and that when he knew the whole sum to be allowed he would 'be able to suggest an appropriation etc. etc.' Russell replied, also unofficially, on 28 August, postponing the consideration of record matters. The summary gives no further details, but presumably the delay was due to the holiday season. At any rate, realising that early progress was unlikely, Langdale decided to leave for Tunbridge Wells, although he made arrangements for any communications from the Home Office to be forwarded and also any outstanding returns from the various record offices concerning their establishments which Thomas had previously requested on his behalf.

When Langdale returned from the country at the end of September there was still no news about the deputy's salary, although there was a letter from Russell telling him that the Treasury wished to know how the balance of the record service grant for the half year ending 31 March 1839, namely £2,500, was to be spent. In his reply on 2 October Langdale said that he was unable to prepare a satisfactory estimate without the help of a deputy keeper. But presuming that he would soon be able to make such an appointment, and that the Treasury would continue to make payments to the record officers at the Tower and at the Chapter House, he thought the service might continue as formerly, not because this was good in itself but to provide for its continuation until he was able to propose a better system. Accordingly, he set out his requirements as in the following table:

Chapter House [2a]

	One quarter		
	£	s.	d.
Sir Francis Palgrave	150	0	0
J. T. Jowett	17	10	0
J. Burtt	17	10	0
F. Devon	27	6	0
C. Devon	25	0	0
C. Beavan	13	0	0
Binding, etc.	70	0	0
	320	6	0

Augmentation Office (Records of the Queen's Remembrancer)

Rev. Jos Hunter	112	10	0
E. Bond [2b]	25	0	0
W. Nelson	15	0	0
F. L. Hunter	12	10	0
H. Hertslett	12	10	0
T. M. Green	12	10	0
J. Redington	12	10	0

2a. The chief clerk, J. W. Clarke, was borne on the Treasury vote, receiving £170 a year, attending from 10 a.m. to 1 p.m. daily. Additionally, Palgrave received £400 a year, Charles Devon £140, Frederick Devon £110 and Beavan £40 from the same source. Charles Devon, who also practised as a record agent, was responsible for paying a salary of £100 a year to his clerk, John Kentish. Frederick Devon also worked at the Duchy of Cornwall Office from 1 to 4 p.m. for which he received £120 a year, it being understood that he would have to give up that appointment if required to work at the Chapter House after one o'clock.

2b. Young Edward (later Sir Edward) Bond, who was related to Cole, resigned in December 1838 to take up an appointment in the Manuscripts Department of the British Museum. He succeeded Sir Frederic Madden as head of that department in 1866 and became principal librarian in 1878.

Workmen

C. Gay (Superintendent)	28	16	0
R. Hanney	17	2	6
H. Barber	17	2	6
J. Blainey	17	2	6
R. Toovey	17	2	6
W. Y. Finley	17	2	6
H. Mogford	17	2	6
P. Paul	17	2	6
W. Goodenough (Carlton Ride)	16	5	0
J. Trickey for attending to open and shut Carlton Ride	6	10	0
	373	18	6

Tower Record Office

Salaries borne on Treasury vote	–	–	–

Rolls Chapel

One workman, H. Gay	17	2	6
(Other salaries payable from fees)			

Exchequer of Pleas

H. Cole	87	10	0
W. Lascelles	17	10	0
	105	0	0

Secretary's salary, stationery, repair materials, contingencies and incidentals	433	13	0
	1250	0	0

In forwarding his estimate, which it will be seen was for three months only, Langdale assured Russell that, once established on a sound footing, the record business need not and ought not to give the government any trouble whatever, but it could not be brought into active operation without some attention and some expense. He suggested either that a sum should be fixed, which would enable him, with the assistance of a deputy keeper, to submit an estimate of appropriation; or that he should be permitted, with like assistance, to propose a proper plan for carrying the Public Records Act into effect, and the probable expense. He went on to say, somewhat tartly, that, if neither course was approved, perhaps he could be told what other course he might with propriety follow in order to bring into execution the new act, which for the present remained inoperative. That had the desired effect, for on 9 October Langdale was told that as soon as Russell could obtain Treasury authority for a salary for the deputy keeper he would like a plan submitted for the future management of the records. Two days later, confident that positive action would now be taken, Langdale instructed Thomas to send to Palgrave copies of the official correspondence with Russell and the returns obtained since the passage of the act from the various keepers of records concerning their establishments.[3] Thus ended for Palgrave, now clearly deputy keeper designate, the suspense he had long endured about his future, although he could have had little idea of the trials ahead. As early as June he had prepared for Langdale some 'Observations upon the plans to be adopted for the management of the records' (Appendix II, i), and as soon as he knew the shape of the proposed new Record Act he had submitted the following application for the deputy keepership:

My dear Lord Langdale

In the event of your Lordship being empowered to appoint a Deputy Keeper of Records it is with the greatest submission that I venture to lay before you what I may term my chronological qualifications for such an office. I mean as to the quantity of time during which I have had an opportunity of becoming acquainted with business – and from which your Lordship may in some measure judge whether you will be pleased to admit me upon the list of candidates for a situation of so much confidence and trust.

In 1805 I was articled to Messrs Loggen & Smith Solrs., Basinghall Street, City – and after my articles had expired, I continued with them in the capacity of managing clerk, superintending the conveyancing and chancery departments. Upon Mr. Loggen's death, Mr. Smith offered to take me into partnership upon payment of a sum adequate to the value of the business which was very large. Not being able to raise the money, he proposed that I should continue with him and with the gentleman (Mr. Rickards) who become his partner, receiving an increased salary, and I continued to conduct their

---

3. Later reproduced in the *First Report of The Deputy Keeper* (1840), Appendix I, 17–24.

business until 1822, when having obtained the Sub-Commissionership of
Records, I quitted their service, and entered myself at the Inner Temple
where I was called to the bar in 1827. My intention was to have entered into
Parliamentary & Equity practise, but the record employment so gained
upon me as to render that course impracticable and since that period, i.e.
1822, I have been wholly devoted to records though still keeping up my
legal reading, as a matter of amusement.

Should I be honoured with the appointment I should, of course continue to
perform all the duties of Keeper of this office; and therefore *one* assistant
keepership *would be saved* – and I hope I should be enabled to execute the
task according to your wishes and in such a way as to give you satisfaction.

I have the honour to remain, my dear Lord Langdale, with the greatest
respect, Your Lordship's ever obedient & faithful servant

Francis Palgrave

Chapter House
7 July 1838

At that time Palgrave was deeply concerned that what he termed the 'vile
intrigues' arising out of the late commission might yet deprive him of the
appointment, which, not without justification, he thought his by right. He
was not prepared to accept what he saw as the 'subordinate situation of an
assistant keeper', but he feared that, under the bill, failure to do so could
compromise the payment of compensation. He told his old friend John
Allen, who had been a member of the former Record Commission, that he
saw no degradation in being called deputy keeper in place of keeper, but
there would be insufferable degradation 'if I were to be compelled to sit at
the same desk with Mr. Cole and take orders from Mr. Hardy'. He thought
the contest was being conducted with 'unexampled malignity', and his apprehensions must have been increased by Langdale's willingness to receive
comments on the bill, then going through Parliament, from both the younger
men. In the past his Whig connections had served him well, and so, through
the agency of John Allen, he sought the backing of Lord Holland, who sat
in the Cabinet as chancellor of the Duchy of Lancaster. It is debatable if
that was really necessary, for by early August all the signs were pointing to
Palgrave, who was helped by the view, long held by Langdale, that the
interests of the existing record officers should be respected in the new
organisation. That was bound to tell against the outside candidates of whom
the most considerable were Patrick Fraser Tytler and John Mitchell Kemble.
Moreover, of the keepers, Petrie was elderly and in indifferent health, while
Leach had already signified his wish for compensation for loss of office. If,
but only if, Palgrave chose to decline the post, both Hardy and Cole had
obvious claims, and Hunter could also have come into the picture. As it
was, during the crucial period the younger men seemed to be persuaded
that if Palgrave were to be stopped, the challenge had to come from those

outside, whose social and political connections could rival his in a way theirs could not.

Palgrave had, in fact, previously been asked by Henry Hallam, the historian, who was also promoting his interest, whether 'Kemble may not be exercising some sinister influence with Lord John Russell and Spring Rice'. For his part, Palgrave, while 'loth to think ill of Beowulf', was sufficiently alarmed to wish to guard against it by any 'fair and allowable method', and that accounted for the letter he wrote to Lord Holland. However, although Kemble was in touch with Cole and Hardy, it seems unlikely that Langdale would have been impressed by his formal application, which was strangely diffident, and perhaps explains why the writer was no more successful in his bid for the deputy keepership than he was when he joined contest with Anthony Panizzi for the principal librarianship of the British Museum in 1856. His letter to Langdale, dated 25 July 1838, reads:

My Lord,

I earnestly hope that there is no impropriety in my addressing your Lordship on a subject of mere private and personal interest; on almost any occasion but the present, I should feel that there was: but as it is currently reported that your decisions will be final respecting the appointments under the new Public Records' Bill, I venture to take a step which I should otherwise adopt with great reluctance.

My hope is to move your Lordship to place me in a situation where I can carry on my researches under more favourable circumstances than at present. The studies to which I have devoted myself are neither profitable (rather indeed expensive), nor do they hold out the rewards to which an honourable ambition may aspire. Yet they are very necessary, not only for the interests of History, but even of that noble Profession to which I have the honour of belonging in common with your Lordship.

They are also absorbing in their nature, and requiring those favourable circumstances which cannot be found where the mind is distracted by the necessity of undertaking other labours for the sole object of gaining a subsistence. Of my own qualification it little becomes me to speak; but the learned men both of our own country and the continent, will I believe bear witness to them.

As I write this in entire ignorance of your Lordship's powers or engagements, I trust that I shall meet with your favourable construction, and your pardon should I have been guilty of an indiscretion in this application.

I am My Lord with profound respect Your Lordship's most humble & obedient Servant

John M. Kemble

In contrast, Tytler's application for the post, dated 8 August, had the merit of displaying his willingness 'to exert myself to the utmost to fulfill its important duties'. It was also accompanied by a plan (Appendix III) setting out succinctly his views for the better arrangement and preservation of the records. By 22 August, fearing he had been unwise not to give Langdale the names of some influential persons who could speak on his behalf, Tytler gave as referees Lord Glenelg and S. M. Phillipps, under-secretary of state at the Home Office, who could speak from personal knowl-edge as 'to those qualifications of temper, manners and general deportment which are essentially requisite in any gentleman to whom such a responsible charge is committed'. Evidently not seeing Thomas Duffus as a contender, he concluded: 'I have the pleasure also of being intimately known to Mr. Hardy, Deputy Keeper of the Records [sic] at the Tower, whose learning, experience and judgement must give value to his opinion'. These represen-tations followed hard on a letter, which had been written to the prime minister two days earlier by the Hon. Charles Augustus Murray, master of the Royal Household:

Buckingham Palace
August 20/38

My dear Lord Melbourne,

I send these two lines to remind you of your promise to submit the name of Mr. Patrick F. Tytler for Lord Langdale's consideration as a fit person to fill the office of Deputy Keeper, in the event of the new Record Commission being regularly established:- Mr. Tytler is doubtless known, both to your Lordship and to Lord Langdale, as the author of a History of Scotland, and of several biographical works, in which he has shown much patient industry and antiquarian research; and his evidence before the House of Commons committee on the subject of the late Record Commission proves how thoroughly conversant he is with that branch of learning: I should add that Mr. Tytler begged me to say that he had no claim to your Lordship's favour but that believing it was Lord Langdale's intention to bestow the office in question upon the applicant best qualified to fill it, he respectfully entreated to be called to Lord Langdale's memory as a person who had devoted many years to the study of the ancient records of the kingdom, and who is most willing, whether he receives the appointment or not, to lend his services in any way that they may promote the objects contemplated in the new commission.

Believe me, my dear Lord, faithfully yours

Ch. A. Murray

Melbourne forwarded the letter to Langdale on 28 August in fulfilment of a promise, but observed, significantly, that he left it to his lordship to act upon it as he thought proper. By now, though, the die had been cast. As early as the first week in August C. P. Cooper, who through his Chancery practice was still in touch with Langdale, had no doubt that Palgrave, 'who always comes on his legs', would become deputy keeper. Outwardly Palgrave was certainly maintaining a fine show of confidence. As far back as 20 July he had told Langdale that during the whole vacation he would always be within call at a day's warning. On 13 August, the day before the bill became law, he reiterated his availability and told Langdale that he supposed the Treasury would take the lead in the new arrangements, thereby possibly contributing, no doubt unintentionally, to the subsequent misunderstanding between Langdale and Russell. On 18 August Palgrave wrote that he would be leaving town on the 21st or the 22nd and would be in Wales until the 29th before travelling cross-country to stay with his father-in-law at Yarmouth. He had not previously visited the principality, although he had long wanted to, and in now taking his two older boys there (his urchins as he called them)[4] he proposed, knowing Langdale's interest, to take the opportunity to inspect the Welsh records. He was, perhaps, thereby making it clear that he was not to be outdone by the ever-alert Cole, who early in July had drawn Langdale's attention to the state of those documents, having been acquainted of their poor condition by John (later Sir John) Jervis, MP for Chester. Palgrave sent a short report on them to Langdale from Chester on 22 August, having earlier indicated that he intended to return to town at the end of September, or sooner if required under the new order of things, hoping then 'to be able to resume employment in such a way as may be satisfactory to you'. By 11 September, having had no word from Langdale, his underlying anxieties were revealed when he wrote to Thomas, enquiring if any progress had been made in the arrangements for carrying the act into execution and now saying that he expected to be in town in the first week of October, but emphasising once again that he could, of course, come up whenever required. Thomas replied that Langdale had done all in his power to facilitate the new arrangements, but, everybody being out of town, his lordship had taken the same course and was quite prepared for active measures as soon as the means were afforded him. Langdale subsequently told Thomas that his reply was quite right, and that the delay was disagreeable, but that until he had proper sanction he would adopt no proceedings that would incur increased expense.

On 26 September, learning from 'Mr. Devon' that Langdale would be back in town on the 29th, Palgrave wrote to him that he would now, owing to the arrival of friends, be in Cromer from 5 to 9 October, but expected

---

4. The trip gave great pleasure to Palgrave's eldest son, Francis, the future editor of the *Golden Treasury*, who described in his journal the visit to Chester and Conway with his father and brother Gifford: *Francis Turner Palgrave: His Journals and Memories of his Life*, Gwenllian F. Palgrave (London, 1899), 19.

to return to London on the 10th. He also gave this information to Thomas, telling him at the same time not to make any payments in respect of the Chapter House establishment until he returned. It was, perhaps, a sign of squalls to come that this was over-ruled by Langdale, who did not think the clerks at the Chapter House should be made to wait that long for their salaries. Nevertheless, in spite of his occasional high-handedness, Palgrave was at that time enjoying a reasonable relationship with his clerks, although some had once been, in his words, 'actively engaged in the war carried on against me by my opponents'.[5] Probably he had the Devon brothers, Charles and Frederick, particularly in mind. They had been skirmishing on the fringes of the various record quarrels throughout the decade, and in 1831 it was Frederick's eavesdropping that had resulted in the fierce altercation between the Hardy brothers and Palgrave over directly-employed transcribers. They had entered the record service through the influence of Caley to whom they were related, and had Treasury contacts, which C. P. Cooper was accustomed to exploit when in need of information. They did not get on at all with Cole, but managed to keep on good terms with Hardy. However, they had an uneasy relationship with Hunter, who was highly critical of their editorial competence. Charles, the elder, had already intimated that he would be seeking compensation under the new arrangements, but Frederick was hoping to be accommodated in some way and was probably the 'Mr. Devon' who was keeping Palgrave abreast of events. At any rate, as already seen, no sooner had Palgrave returned from the east coast than he was acquainted by Langdale of the efforts being made to implement the provisions of the act. Over the next few days he wrote briefly to Langdale on record plans, and on 23 October submitted a 14-page memorandum setting out his 'Observations upon the mode of carrying the Record Act into execution' (Appendix II, ii). This added flesh, as it were, to the plan he had produced in June. Seemingly, his opening remarks about 'the necessary elapse' of time before the unification of the records in a newly-built repository were too cautious for Langdale who pencilled 'Why?' in the margin. Langdale also sidelined Palgrave's suggestions concerning the appropriation of search fees for record purposes, and the charging of certain expenses to the Suitors' Fund as though to indicate his disagreement. In general, however, he must have felt reassured by the degree of thought that Palgrave had evidently given to establishing the new organisation.

Meanwhile, the Treasury Board had met on 19 October and decided that the deputy keeper's pay scale should be the same as that suggested by the chancellor of the Exchequer in August, which Langdale had already indicated he thought sufficient. This decision was notified to Russell on the 23rd and passed on by him to Langdale on the 29th. The next day Langdale

---

5. PRO 1/1: Palgrave to Langdale, 14 June 1838: 'None liked the charge of "a resident" master over them instead of being their own masters – yet I am thankful to say we have gone on as good friends'.

wrote formally to Palgrave to offer him the appointment and to tell him the salary scale proposed. The latter must have been a bitter disappointment to Palgrave who lost no time in seeking better terms, setting out his reasons in a letter of qualified acceptance, dated 31 October:

My Lord

I have the honour to acknowledge the receipt of your Lordship's letter of the 30th instant, whereby your Lordship is pleased to communicate to me that 'the public record Act imposed upon your Lordship the duty of recommending a proper person to be Deputy Record Keeper, and that your Lordship is desirous to name a Gentleman on whose knowledge of records and zeal for the service reliance can be placed' – also 'that the salary of the Deputy Record Keeper has been fixed by Government in the first instance at £600 a year, to be increased to £700 a year after five years service, and to £800 a year after ten years service as such'. Your Lordship is further pleased to state, that, 'looking upon me as possessed of the qualities required for the due performance of the duties your Lordship requests me, as soon as I have had time for consideration, to inform your Lordship whether it will be agreeable of me to accept the office of Deputy Record Keeper'.

Honoured, as I thus am, by your Lordship's approbation, being the most valuable testimony as to my past conduct which I could possibly receive, I should at once thankfully declare my unconditional acceptance of the important office which you are pleased to offer to me, and without any further remarks, were it not that the immediate salary proposed by Government, is less than the sum which I am entitled to claim as a compensation for the losses which I sustain by the passing of the Act in question, such sum amounting to £687:18:4 per annum as appears by the statement delivered to your Lordship (pursuant to the Act) on the 15 Aug last; and in which my services are set forth; and if I should live until the period when the proposed salary would be raised to £800 per annum I should then, after *twenty-six* years continuous and laborious employment as a public servant, be placed upon a lower scale of remuneration than I now receive. I do not come before Government as a new man and an untried candidate, but as one who has, by long service, acquired much experience in the business of the department; – It has been the occupation of an entire life, and the proposed remuneration would deprive me of the advantages which I have fairly earned.

With respect to the amount of salaries, viz. £1,000 per annum of which I am now in possession, I shall only remark that such amount was, after much enquiry and deliberation, fixed by the Treasury in 1833. And as their Lordships were then pleased to estimate my services in connection with the records of the country at that amount (Lord John Russell having also recently approved of it) I venture to hope that, now that I have the great additional recommendation of your Lordship's approbation, the Government will not consider it as an unreasonable request that I may be continued in active employment at a rate not lower than my present rate of remuneration.

Thus much for my own particular case; but, may I presume to add, that upon general grounds the salary is not adequate to the responsibility of the office, or to the utility and importance which it will possess when managed according to your Lordship's views. The Deputy will not be a mere curator of an Antiquarian Museum, but the Chief Manager under your Lordship of a Department of practical and encreasing business. Your Lordship has intimated that you expect that the Deputy shall consider himself as the general servant of government in the record department, that he shall, when required, make all searches and perform all business which may be required for the service of the Crown. For these purposes, the Solicitors of the Treasury, Land Revenue, Duchy, &c employ record agents by which considerable expence is frequently incurred, and which will be saved by the duties which your Lordship annexes to the Office of Deputy Keeper: and when this circumstance becomes known to the government, I trust it will have its due weight in enducing them to accede to the request which I have preferred.

Lastly, let me be allowed to add that I trust I shall be always able to satisfy both Government and Parliament, should any enquiry be instituted, that the larger salary will have been fully and fairly earned by the labour and exertion bestowed by me in the discharge of the duties of the office.

I have the honour to remain, My Lord, With the greatest respect,
Your Lordship's ever obedient & faithful servant

Francis Palgrave

The next day Langdale sent this letter on to Russell, indicating his disagreement with Palgrave about compensation, and asking whether in view of Palgrave's arguments about his salary the matter might be reconsidered as 'if not, I shall consider it to be my duty to require from him an immediate and conclusive answer to my proposal'. Langdale's comments arrived at a particularly harrowing time for Russell, whose wife, Adelaide, the former Lady Ribblesdale, died on the very day it was written, having caught fever following childbirth. Despite that, and many more pressing and weighty problems, such as the future of Canada where there was much discontent, Russell still found time to attend to the matter. A barely legible pencilled draft letter to the chancellor of the Exchequer, Thomas Spring Rice, indicated that he differed from Langdale, thinking Palgrave to be entitled in equity to his claim, 'but you will be able to judge of his case better and according to your practice in other retiring salaries. It would be a pity to lose Sir F. P.'s services for a few pounds and if he were remunerated at the sum he claims £687:18:4 and encrease as their L[ordship]s propose it would make little difference to the public'.[6] Replying to Fox Maule, parliamentary under-secretary of state, on 9 November 1838, Russell being away from his desk, the chancellor explained why, under Treasury rules, Palgrave could not claim compensation for his temporary employment with the Record Commission; he thought that he was entitled to consideration as keeper at the Chapter House, but wondered if he would be continued there. The following day the chancellor wrote to Langdale to say that he agreed with him about compensation and that he thought it had been right 'both on the principles of economy and justice, to give Sir Francis Palgrave the first offer of the appointment'. As a result of these exchanges Russell wrote again to Langdale on 15 November to ask whether the keepership at the Chapter House would be abolished, merged or retained as a separate office. On 17 November Langdale replied:

In answer to your Lordship's letter dated the 15 inst., I have the honor to inform your Lordship that in my opinion the office now held by Sir Francis Palgrave ought to be abolished.

If he should accept the office of Deputy Record Keeper he might for a time perform the duties attached to his present office, but before long it would become necessary to place the Records in the Chapter House under the care of an Assistant Record Keeper to be appointed by the Treasury.

If the office of Deputy Record Keeper had not been tendered to Sir Francis Palgrave, I apprehend that under the Act it would have been incumbent on the Treasury to offer him the office of an Assistant Record Keeper. I conceive it to be a duty to avoid the obligation to give compensations, by employing persons already engaged in the service who are competent and would be entitled to compensations if not employed and in the case of Sir F. Palgrave I have acted accordingly.

Unwilling to give up the fight, Palgrave also wrote to Russell on 17 November. His letter, which vividly conveys his anguish, reads:

My Lord

Having been informed by Mr Bethune that official business is now brought before your Lordship, I venture to call your Lordship's attention to the correspondence relating to my intended appointment as Deputy Keeper of the Records, transmitted to your Lordship by Lord Langdale.

---

6. Written on reverse of Langdale's letter of 1 November 1838 to Russell in HO 39/12.

When your Lordship shall have fully reconsidered the nature and terms of the appointment I cannot but hope that the great length of time which I have [been] employed in this branch of the public service, will weight with your Lordship in recommending my continuance at my present rate of salary. Unless this be conceded, the promotion that Lord Langdale so kindly offers to me, will, in fact, be a most serious misfortune. After having been *reduced* by the Record Commission to my present rate of remuneration I fully understood and believed that Lord Grey's minute assured its continuance during good behaviour. I viewed it as a species of contract, and having now the additional testimony of Lord Langdale's approbation, the proposed reduction would place me under great difficulties for besides the encreasing expenses of a large family, I effected heavy insurances upon my life at a period when my official salary fully warranted me in so doing: and if my advance in station to the head of the department is to be accompanied by the reduction of salary, it would be equally ruinous to me to continue them or to abandon them.

In my letter to Lord Langdale, which I presume is before your Lordship, I have adverted to the nature of the Office and to the duties which I shall have to perform. Upon these I will not enlarge as they are there sufficiently stated. I shall only venture to add that I would not expose your Lordship to the Parliamentary responsibility of fixing the higher salary if I did not feel reasonably confident that, if I have health, I shall be always able to satisfy a Parliamentary committee that I have given the public a full equivalent in attendance and labour.

I have the honour to remain, my Lord, With the greatest respect, Your Lordship's ever obedient & faithful Servant

Francis Palgrave

Obviously wishing to do what he could to help Palgrave, particularly as he had no difficulty in approving his selection, but recognising Treasury primacy in matters of the purse, Russell wrote once more to Langdale on 19 November:

I should wish the Lords of the Treasury to be consulted in the question of the future salary to Sir Francis Palgrave. Perhaps on considering his long services and devotion to this subject they may think themselves justified in allowing him to commence at the highest rate of £800 a year – it is a question entirely for their decision.

Langdale passed this letter on to the Treasury the next day, but had to wait until 7 December for its reply, which made it clear that the most it was willing to concede was to allow Palgrave to reckon his Chapter House service for increment, which meant he might move to the £700 point in May

1839. It also indicated its willingness to appoint F. S. Thomas to a situation on the new establishment as soon as it was formed despite a request by the State Paper Office for his return. That must have been most welcome to Langdale who had come to value Thomas and made it clear to the Treasury that he could ill afford to lose him. Above all else, however, Langdale was determined to dispose of the long-outstanding matter of the deputy keepership, and, in addition to writing formally to Palgrave on 8 December to convey to him the unwelcome news, he also wrote privately in the following terms:

I am afraid that the answer of the Treasury as to the salary of the Deputy Record Keeper will disappoint you and I am sorry for it – But considering the decision final, I must request you to give me a conclusive answer to the proposal which I made to you.

I intended to make you an offer, the acceptance of which might be useful to the Public and gratifying to yourself and as the two objects must be in great measure concurrent, I am induced to say that if the amount of salary now settled is such that you cannot be contented with it and feel yourself in a situation to perform the duties of the office with cheerfulness and with satisfaction to yourself, it will in my opinion be better to decline it at once and I shall think you intirely justified in doing so – as on the other hand, if you accept the office, I shall rely, as I think I have reason to do so, on the constant performance of the duties of the office with diligence, attention and zeal and shall not think you justified in making any further reclamation or shewing any further marks of dissatisfaction.

Choosing to ignore the somewhat peremptory tone of Langdale's letter and his insistence upon a conclusive reply, Palgrave, responding the same day, sought more time:

My dear Lord Langdale

Whilst the matter was still open, I did not think it proper to communicate with any one on the subject – but as the terms are now fixed, I should wish to be permitted to consult my Father-in-law Mr Turner on the subject – as by his opinion, I shall be mainly guided. I write to him by this night's post – but as it is *just* possible that I may be under the necessity of seeing him in person, I hope you will, considering the difficulty of my position, permit me to have next week for deliberation in the event of my not receiving such a written answer from him as may settle my mind.

I am most thankful to you for your kind and considerate private letter – and be assured that if I am soliciting time for consideration, it is with the sole intent of enabling me to ascertain whether I can accept the trust you intend to confide to me, in such a manner as may be conformable to your wishes.

I have the honour to remain, My dear Lord Langdale, With the greatest respect, Yours ever faithfully

Francis Palgrave

But hardly had he written this letter than he felt obliged to come to a decision because, as he told his father-in-law on 15 December, 'Lord Langdale wrote (after I had despatched my letter to you) in such pressing terms for my answer I was compelled at once to signify my acceptance of the office for which as you may suppose there are plenty of applicants'. The only record of a further letter from Langdale is the official one, also dated 8 December, notifying Palgrave of the Treasury decision, but this does not seem to be the communication in question. At any rate, on 10 December Palgrave sent an undated letter to Langdale:

My Lord

In reply to your Lordship's letter of the 8th Inst, I have the honor to inform your Lordship that I am willing to accept the office of Deputy Record Keeper under the Act 1 & 2 Vict c.94 upon the terms therein mentioned.

And remain, with the greatest respect, Your Lordship's ever obedient & faithful servant

Francis Palgrave

Crown approval followed within a matter of days, and Palgrave, concerned for appearances, suggested that a suitable notice about his appointment should be inserted in the *London Gazette*. The Home Office refused to deal with this, saying it was not usual in such cases, and when Palgrave drew up a short paragraph for insertion by Langdale he declined to send it.[7] But Palgrave persisted and an amended notice appeared on 25 January 1839. The first draft had indicated that pursuant to the act the master of the rolls, with the approval of her majesty, had appointed Palgrave, whereas the insertion merely said that 'Her Majesty has been pleased to approve of the appointment of Sir Francis Palgrave, kt., to be Deputy Keeper of the Records'. This suggests that Langdale was already distancing himself somewhat from the appointment. On this unhappy note was concluded a business which, far from taking, as it should have done, a few days to settle, dragged on for several months. Cole, for example, was not told of the appointment until 18 December, although his diary records that on 21 November Thomas 'seemed to admit that Palgrave was to be Deputy Keeper'. Throughout the

---

7. PRO 2/85, p 339.

period speculation must have been rife, and it is not surprising that Hardy, in particular, came to feel he had been cheated. Early in January 1839 he told Cole that Langdale had 'once proposed himself as Deputy', although it is not clear from Cole's diary if this statement was based upon Hardy's own knowledge or upon information passed to him by one of the Devons, who were great gossipers. If Langdale ever had such an intention, one possibility, perhaps the most likely in view of the use by Hardy of the term 'once', is that it went back to 1837 when Langdale first took responsibility for the record vote and there was talk of a 'deputy' or similar officer to superintend the practical side of the business. Even under the reformers' original plans it was apparent that they envisaged an executive of one head with a deputy.[8] Certainly Palgrave's apprehensions reached their peak at that period because, as he told Langdale, 'to be placed under a Deputy would be a situation which I could not assume with any degree of comfort or respectability'. That letter must have brought home to Langdale the difficulty he would have in accommodating Palgrave, who saw immediately that the designation of a 'deputy' would place that officer favourably vis-à-vis the existing keepers, including himself, when the new organisation took shape. For that reason Palgrave suggested the appointment of a secretary of records, as such a post was not open to the same objection. Moreover, by 1837 Hardy must have seen himself as the heir-apparent to the ailing Petrie, whose keepership at the Tower was in the gift of the master of the rolls, although subject to crown approval.

When the Irish Record Bill was under consideration 30 years later, George Ward Hunt, financial secretary to the Treasury, told Lord Derby that 'it also appears that the late MR was told that the Crown's right of veto would be exercised in the event of his making an appointment he contemplated'.[9] But Hunt's remarks were based upon a letter written six days earlier to the chief secretary in Ireland by George Alexander Hamilton, permanent secretary of the Treasury, who evidently confused the appointment in 1838 with that of Petrie at the Tower in 1819 when Sir Thomas Plumer was master of the rolls. Hamilton, whose remarks seem to have been based upon a misinterpretation of information given to him by Hardy, wrote:[10]

As regards the patronage of the proposed office of Deputy Keeper of the Records, it is true that by the 1 & 2 Vic. c 94 the Master of the Rolls in this country has the appointment of the Deputy Keeper of Public Records

---

8. See Cole's 'Lord Brougham's Record Commission' in which he indicates that this arrangement might cost £2,000 annually: *Frasers Magazine*, XV, no. LXXXVI. According to Cole this article, which appeared in February 1837, was 'written with much feeling': see his *Fifty Years of Public Work* (London, 1884), II, 64.

9. T 1/6757B/20123/1867: Hunt to Derby, 25 January [1867].

10. T 1/6757B/20123/1867: Hamilton to Naas, 19 January 1867. The letter is also entered in Hamilton's private letter book: T 168/3, pp 178–179.

subject to the approval of HM – but the reason appears to have been that previously there had been 2 officers of Deputy Keeper of certain documents at the Tower and elsewhere which were under the patronage of the Master of the Rolls, and that the then MR made it a condition that he should have the appointment in consideration of giving up the patronage of these 2 officers – but the view of Government and Parliament was marked by the restriction of the appointment being subject to the Queen's approval, and it is curious that when a vacancy occurred Sir [T] Plumer, then MR, proposed to appoint his son, when it was intimated that HM's approval would not be given – and Mr Hardy tells me that there was an understanding that a clause was to be introduced into any suitable Bill to the effect that hereafter (after the vacancy of the present MR) the appointment should be vested in the Crown. This I think settles the question of patronage.

As for the ministerial pressure alleged to have been exercised upon Langdale, it must be said that if there were any the ministers went about it in a most peculiar way. Not only did they release the nomination to Langdale when they might have kept it to themselves, as originally intended, but they drove such a hard bargain on the salary scale that they would have had no one but themselves to blame had they lost Palgrave altogether. Palgrave had Russell's backing, but a year earlier – in rather different circumstances – Thomas's summary for 18 August 1837 notes that Russell wrote that if Langdale 'would be generally head of the Records the Clerk Assistant of House of Commons [John Rickman] would save him nearly all the trouble'. Six years later Cole recorded in his diary for 9 May 1843 that Palgrave told him that Russell wanted the appointment of Rickman – better known as the census statistician – in order to save his retiring salary. It was also known that upon the passing of the act Charles Lechmere, deputy keeper of state papers, was approached by Phillipps at the Home Office about the possibility of some employment but declined the offer.[11] The very ambivalence of ministers can also be seen in the attitude of Langdale, who must have realised that the handling of a man of such exceptional talent as Palgrave would demand much skill and patience. The suspicion remains that, had Palgrave refused the appointment, Langdale might not have been particularly displeased. As it was, their official relationship got off to a bad start and never fully recovered. Little wonder, therefore, that Langdale may have regretted his choice and implied to Thomas, who knew him better than most, that the question of compensation was paramount. If, in the event, Langdale and Palgrave had managed to work harmoniously, the chances are that we should have heard no more of the matter. The fact that that was not the case, coupled with the many difficulties that had gone before, meant

---

11. T 1/6008A/13821/1856: Lechmere to Trevelyan, 2 August 1856. Lechmere's sister Mary was married to Thomas.

that the belief that there had been malign influences working against Hardy
gained a ready acceptance and persisted until well into the second half of
the present century. Although he could have had no personal knowledge,
they were stated in their extreme form by Hardy's friend John Cordy
Jeaffreson in his 'Quarrel of Two Authors', which appeared in his *Book of
Recollections*, published in 1894. With his tale of malcontent and importunate
ministers, together with the 'manifest distress' of Langdale, relieved only
when Hardy freed him from his promise and urged him to appoint Palgrave
instead, it is evident that Jeaffreson's work owed more to a lively imagination
than historical fact. But along with a colourful account of the fracas at the
Tower in 1832 it made a good story, and, although it must now be dismissed,
it is uncertain if the exact truth has yet been established or, indeed, ever
will be.

Chapter III
The Shaping of the Organisation

Your difficulty will be to make the government understand that a record office ought to be a species of college.

(Sir Francis Palgrave to Lord Langdale, 14 June 1838: PRO 1/1)

In November 1838 Palgrave followed up his draft plan of management for the public records by suggesting to Langdale a number of amendments to the Record Act. Palgrave thought that office copies might be certified by qualified clerks, as well as by assistant keepers, so that higher-grade posts might initially be kept to a minimum. He also thought that fees should be retained for general departmental expenses instead of being surrendered to the Exchequer. He wanted the deputy keeper to be given power to accept corporation archives because 'the Town Clerks who can rarely read these documents have generally much neglected them'. Finally, he wanted stronger powers for the recovery of public records in private hands, alleging that the original clause in the bill was dropped at the instance of a 'celebrated collector'.[1] Perhaps Palgrave had Sir Thomas Phillipps in mind, particularly as the latter's evidence to the 1836 Select Committee suggests there was friction between the two men. However, Langdale thought it far too soon to alter the act, especially as he wished to concentrate his efforts on settling the organisation of the new department. Consequently, Palgrave had no alternative but to confine his views to how the new record arrangements might be implemented, and he set them out in a letter to Langdale on 23 December 1838. Most of his points were taken up by Langdale when he submitted his own proposals to the government in a letter to Russell on 7 January 1839.

Langdale, whose letter was later reproduced by Palgrave in his *First Report* as deputy keeper, emphasised that, although 'The Records have justly been called the Muniments of the Kingdom and the People's Evidences', many of the same kind, and forming different parts of the same series, were to be found in two or more places of deposit. In some such places no one attended regularly to look after them, different regulations obtained in the several offices, and there was no general repertory or catalogue. The bulk of the records brought under the act were scattered in large collections in the Tower of London, Chancery Lane, Lincoln's Inn, the Temple, Somerset House, Carlton Ride, Whitehall Yard, Spring Gardens, New Palace Yard and the Chapter House. To remedy this Langdale wanted a new general

---

1. PRO 1/1: Palgrave to Langdale, 8 November 1838.

repository built on the Rolls Estate without delay. Immediately, he wished to establish the headquarters of the new Public Record Office at the Rolls House and to provide a general reference service there for the benefit of the public. He wanted to have the records properly catalogued and to have holdings outside London surveyed, particularly those in Wales. Given the consent of the courts, he wished to investigate the possibility of moving to the Rolls House and the late Cursitor's Office in Rolls Yard the ancient rolls of Chancery from the Tower and 'arranged' records from other repositories. To make room for them he proposed to move out to the Tower the Queen's Bench records, which were less consulted. In drawing up his proposals and detailing how the office might be managed, Langdale acknowledged the advice and assistance he had received from Palgrave, whose outward display of interest and concern for the new service disguised the deep unhappiness he felt on entering it at a lesser salary than he had previously enjoyed. He had hoped to supplement his pay by undertaking legal work for government departments but Langdale had ruled against that. An added trial for Palgrave was that in forming his establishment he knew he had to accommodate Hardy and Cole, upon whose loyalty he could scarcely rely. He was well aware of their talents, but unsure how to fit them in. Knowing that, and distrustful of his motives, both men were staking out their positions with some care. Hardy was the more apprehensive because, unless Petrie chose to retire, he could not count upon a place at the Tower at a senior level, especially as Langdale, at Palgrave's prompting, had told Russell that no officer ought to be allowed to consider himself as permanently attached to a particular duty or place. Cole was better situated since, besides having sole charge of the records of the Exchequer of Pleas, his stock was rising due to his vigorous support for the Penny Post campaign. In February 1838 he had secured Langdale's permission to become involved in the movement for a more efficient postal system, and soon after the deputy keepership was settled he was told by Langdale that he might expect an assistant keeper appointment when the new establishment was formed.[2] On 25 January 1839 he noted in his diary that 'T. D. Hardy called and stayed till 3 discussing his plan which he was about to propose to Ld. Langdale'. Hardy's plan, really a series of general suggestions, was as follows:[3]

All Records ought to be deposited in places secure from fire, damp and any casualties.

Any Records so exposed ought to be removed to the Tower where there is ample room for the same.

2. Cole Diary, 26 December 1838. Sir Henry Cole's diaries are in the National Art Library (Victoria and Albert Museum) in 43 volumes: 14117–1934 to 14159–1934.
3. PRO 36/54.

All Records deposited in places inconvenient for public consultation, such as those in the vaults of Somerset House ought to be removed to a more eligible situation.

No Records to be removed from their present place of deposit until they have been stamped with the seal of the Public Record Office and an inventory or list made of them.

All Records which have been arranged and catalogued, such as those in the Exchequer of Pleas and Kings Remembrancer's Offices, ought to be removed to the Rolls House or Tower for public consultation.

Catalogues of the contents of every office ought to be immediately made.

The number of Membranes and schedules in each Roll ought to be ascertained, and all loose documents sorted, numbered and stamped, and a minute made of their state of preservation.

No calendars ought to be commenced, and those now in the course of formation should be suspended, until all the Records are catalogued.

All calendars and indexes ought to be removed forthwith to the Rolls House, and placed under the charge of some responsible person, whose duty should be to superintend and assist applicants in their searches whether for legal or historical purposes, and to keep an account of all searches made &c.

All persons whether engaged in legal or historical enquiries ought to be allowed gratuitous access to all Record Calendars and Indexes; or they may have a general search made by the Office through all the Manuscript Calendars upon any specific subject upon the payment of £5 5s 0d.

All persons whether engaged in Legal or Historical enquiries to pay the sum of one shilling for every Record they inspect, and to be allowed to make in pencil any extract they please without any additional charge.

All persons searching the original Records to which there is no calendar, such as the Placita Rolls, Bundles of Fines, to pay the sum of one shilling for every Roll or Bundle searched.

A Book to be kept in which is to be entered the name & address of every person consulting a Record and a list of the Records so consulted.

Any person to be allowed to compound for the sum of £2 2s 0d to inspect all Records for a specific enquiry.

The Master of the Rolls to reserve to himself the power of remitting the fees for inspecting Records.

Office copies to be furnished at 6d per folio to any person requiring them whether for Legal or Historical purposes.

Office Copies for legal purposes to be stamped with the Seal of the General Record Office, after they have been examined by the Assistant Keeper or chief Clerk, for which the sum of two shillings is to be paid.

Any person may also have an office copy attested by the Assistant Keeper in addition to the Office stamp for which one shilling will be charged.

Reading between the lines one can see that Hardy was trying to keep the Tower material intact, adding to it if possible. It was obvious that he was strongly opposed to any special concession to historical searchers, in contrast to Palgrave who was urging that the deputy keeper should be empowered to remit their fees in suitable cases. Hardy clearly wished Langdale to treat his proposals as confidential, and was content to let Cole, who was of much the same mind as himself, submit formal proposals. On 11 February Cole recorded in his diary that he had 'Called on Hardy at the Tower to discuss Records Scheme which I agreed to send in my own name'. Three days later, with due deference, he sent the following letter to Langdale:[4]

> Whitehall Yard
> 14 Feb 1839

My Lord

The encouragement I have always received from your Lordship, to express any opinions I may entertain respecting the management of the Public Records appears to me to warrant the transition of the accompanying notes, which have suggested themselves in considering how the Public Records Act might be carried into effect. In order to be precise, I have found it impossible to be very brief. Should it seem, that I am hereby overstepping my proper position, I trust your Lordship will overlook the indiscretion & bear in mind that I am sincerely zealous for the good of the Service.

I have the honour to be, My Lord, Your Lordship's very faithful Servant

> Henry Cole

---

4. PRO 1/2. At the beginning of 1838 Cole had been approached by Charles Buller, MP, to accompany him to Canada for service with the governor-general there, and early in 1840 he was offered an engagement with the Anti-Corn Law League, but he decided against both these undertakings in favour of record employment: see *Fifty Years of Public Work* (London, 1884), I, 16, 34–35, 57–58.

In his 'notes' Cole proposed the establishment of a Public Records (*sic*) Office at the Rolls House, where all business should originate. Under this head office he envisaged six branches which, he suggested, should be manned during the same hours each day and organised as follows:

Branches	Contents Records of	Custodes	Clerks	Workmen	
1 The Tower	Chancery		2	3	To work at the Tower
	Pipe		1	2	
	Lord Treasurer's		1	2	
	Exchequer of Pleas		1	–	
	Custos Brevium (Common Pleas)	1		1	
	Welsh				
	Durham				
	Ely				
2 Chapter House	Present contents of Chapter House	1	3	3	
	Pell Office				
3 Carlton Ride	Exchequer	1	3	4	Workmen to work at 3 Whitehall Yard
	Common Pleas		1	1	
4 Augmentation	Augmentation	1	1	1	
	Land Revenue		1	1	
	First Fruits		1		
5 Rolls Chapel	Chancery	1	3	3	To work at Rolls House
6 Rolls House	Queen's Bench		1	2	

Additionally, Cole proposed that all finding-aids should be kept at the Rolls House and made available to the public free of charge, no distinction being made between legal and historical enquirers. A superintendent of searches should be appointed there, who would be required to give general assistance to callers, and make searches of the indexes, etc, for those unable to do so themselves. This officer would also be responsible for issuing warrants to branches to produce documents for inspection. It would also be his duty to examine and authenticate all office copies. The charge for such copies, which would be made at the branches, would be 6d a folio, and for translations twice that amount, but searchers might, if they wished, make their own copies or notes, provided they used a pencil. The fee proposed for inspections for one or more records of each class was 1s, for a general inspection for one purpose 10s. Such arrangements, said Cole, meant that searchers would save time in travelling as the whereabouts of documents could readily be discovered, and there would be a considerable reduction in charges for consulting the records and for obtaining copies of them.

Cole also wanted an office established at 3 Whitehall Yard for arranging (i.e. sorting, packing and labelling) and repairing the records from the various branches. It should be placed under a superintendent, who would also be responsible for removals, the aim being, subject to the over-riding need for security, to concentrate the records in fewer repositories and unite dispersed classes and series. Every effort should be made to ensure that no expenditure was incurred which would be wasted when a new general record office was provided. For that reason it was questioned whether the expense was warranted of changing the whole system of gas lighting and flue-warming at the Rolls House in order to make it fireproof, for the reception of records, such as Domesday Book and the ancient rolls of Chancery, which were already securely housed. If moves were to be made – and all the time the Rolls House was used for the purposes of the Rolls Court there would be an element of insecurity there – the most that might be justified would be the transfer of 'arranged' records from repositories, such as the Augmentation Office, where security was even worse. To prove he wished to be constructive, Cole set out fully a plan of transfers to illustrate how the records might be logically rearranged when accommodated within his six proposed branches.

The question of the physical arrangement of the records was dealt with at length (see Appendix IV), emphasis being placed on giving priority to the most valuable. To carry out the necessary cleaning, repairing, packing, stamping, etc., a very considerable increase in the number of workmen would be required. Measures should also be taken to improve the make-up of modern records. Their shape and size, material, binding, stitching and handwriting, all required attention. Lists or memoranda of every document should be made or started at every office. When completed, 'a synthetical compendium exhibiting a chronological view of the Records existing for every year should be compiled on the plan suggested by his lordship the Keeper General'. Discussion of the sort of catalogue most suitable for each class of records should be delayed until the lists were completed. Lithography might be useful in reproducing copies of the calendars. A survey and report should be made forthwith of the Welsh, Durham and Ely records.

All officers should be required to make progress reports at prescribed intervals, and be acquainted with their conditions of service and prospects. The establishment should comprise: the deputy keeper, assistant keepers, clerks – first, second and third classes, three head workmen and workmen. Finally, there should be periodic increases in salary, a provision for super-annuation, and prospects of promotion for such as 'shew themselves superior in diligence, proficiency and merit'.

Langdale lost no time in acknowledging Cole's work, writing on 15 February 1839:

> I have received and have already hastily read your valuable notes on the
> execution of the Public Records Act. It is very gratifying to me to observe
> the careful attention which you have paid to the subject and you may be
> assured that such of your suggestions as differ from the views to which I now
> incline, shall be carefully considered.

He also told Thomas 'to request Sir F. P. to give his attention to Mr Cole's notes'. Three days later Palgrave replied:

> Pursuant to your Lordship's instructions of the 15th Inst I have perused and
> considered Mr Cole's notes relating to the mode of carrying the Act into
> effect. Many of them are worthy of consideration – and his opinions as to
> the number of persons required on the new Establishment are particularly
> useful. Your Lordship will be pleased to consider, whether it may not be
> expedient to obtain similar information from other Gentlemen (at the Tower
> or elsewhere) capable of affording it?
>
> I have discussed with Mr Thomas and Mr Cole the plan of the books to be
> kept at the several offices, shewing the work performed, and have prepared
> a specimen accordingly. Is it your pleasure to take the same now into
> consideration, or shall I postpone bringing it before you?

Evidently thinking that Palgrave had not given the matter the attention it deserved and that his enquiry about obtaining information from other gentlemen was not so innocent as it sounded, Langdale minuted:[5]

> I hope to receive from Sir Francis Palgrave a full Statement of his opinion
> upon the several points referred to in Mr Cole's notes. The duty of preparing
> the details of the plan when approved by Government will principally devolve
> on Sir F. P. – and it is important that his attention should be most carefully
> addressed to the subject – and that I should be acquainted with his views
> upon those points which require most consideration. When the plan has been
> matured it must before it is finally adopted, be submitted to the consideration

---

5. PRO 1/2.

of all the officers whose interests may be affected by it or who may be thought capable of affording useful advice and assistance; I should be much obliged to any of them who would like Mr Cole, afford voluntary assistance in framing the plan, but I cannot take the liberty of requiring them to do that which appears to me to be the peculiar duty of the Deputy Record Keeper. I should be glad to see the specimen of the plan of Book-keeping which is referred to.

In reply, Palgrave commented fully on Cole's notes in a letter to Langdale, dated 26 February 1839.[6] He agreed that searches for records and the authentication of office copies should form a separate department, but he did not think that one officer, as suggested by Cole, would be sufficient. In his view authentication and searches should be devolved to the assistant keepers at the branches. He did not believe that translations were proper to the public business of a record office, and he held to his opinion that a distinction should be made between legal and historical inquiries. Overall, he thought the fees suggested by Cole too low, and referred to a letter he had written to Langdale about a scale of fees earlier that month. Among other things he had then argued:

Whilst on the one hand it is unjust to fix so high a rate as to impose an oppressive tax upon those who have occasion to use the Records, or to view the Fees as a source of revenue, and therefore to be raised to the highest practicable amount – it is on the other hand equally undesirable to fix them at so low a rate as to encourage idle or unnecessary applications, by which the public time of the officers will be broken up and wasted. That this result may be expected if the scales be too low is certain. It frequently happens that individuals (generally of the lower classes of society) imagine that they are entitled to property or peerages which have descended to them from some remote ancestor. People of this description applying without professional aid, have of course no accurate idea of the evidence which such a claim requires. Labouring under this delusion such individuals give the greatest possible trouble by their indiscreet demands, and without any benefits to themselves for I need hardly remind your Lordship that when claims of this nature have been brought into Court, there is hardly an instance known of their having been sustained. Other persons being professional men would use the Records simply for the sake of vexatious litigation, particularly concerning charities and corporate rights – and if the Records could be used for a small outlay of money, the privilege would be exceedingly abused by such practitioners. I have also found that when persons not acting dishonestly, yet without judgement, have been permitted to have gratuitous access to the Records in the Chapter House, they also abuse the concession, in one instance

6. PRO 36/54.

the party required the production of so many Fines, that it would have occupied a Clerk during a fortnight to look them out for him.

That as a matter of theory or abstract principle a party whether in claiming or defending his rights, ought not to be put to expence in obtaining justice, may be admitted, but the same remarks would extend to every branch of legal administration, and the answer is, that under existing circumstances the theory is not practicable. All that can be done is to bring the fees within their proper limits . . .

Palgrave went on to propose that instead of searchers being granted free access to calendars, etc., as suggested by Cole, they should be charged 1s a day. As against Cole's suggested 1s for an inspection, he thought 2s 6d should be charged, although it might be deducted subsequently from the cost of an office copy.

Concerning removals and transfers, Palgrave said he broadly agreed with Cole, but that he could not give a final opinion until the Treasury gave its answer to Langdale's proposals about a central office at the Rolls, although he still believed that the removal to that office of the rolls at the Tower was highly desirable. Regarding 'arrangement', he thought the plan adopted by Cole for the records of the Exchequer of Pleas in his care was well calculated to afford the readiest means of reference and admirable for their preservation and security. He was against interfering with records already tolerably well arranged, and had reservations about a topographical arrangement if it would break up existing series. He doubted the use of lithography, but was in general agreement with Cole on the question of the office establishment.

Although the two men greatly differed in temperament and outlook, in practice they were not all that far apart, Cole being no more likely to suffer an idle or impertinent applicant than was Palgrave to turn away a genuine request for help. While making plain his objection to undertaking searches for those unable to do so themselves, Palgrave also made it clear that he considered search-room officers should render every assistance in their power to inquirers. All these matters inevitably placed Cole at the centre of events, and on the day, 26 February, on which Palgrave was commenting on his notes Cole's diary provides ample evidence of his key role:

Club: met there Mr J. Jervis who asked me to be the bearer of a letter to Lord Langdale about the Welsh records. Called on Sir F. Palgrave about Calendars, etc., – met there Lady Palgrave. Whitehall. Called on Ld. Langdale who expressed himself highly pleased with my notes on Record Act – Met T. D. Hardy there.

Throughout this period Palgrave must have been well aware of Hardy's collaboration with Cole behind the scenes, but it did not prevent him from offering what could be seen as an olive branch, when he wrote to his old adversary on 25 March 1839 in the following terms:[7]

My dear Sir

Upon considering the plans for making general tabular inventories of the Records a task upon which we must all be speedily simultaneously engaged, I find some difficulty in ascertaining what would have appeared to be an easy point, vizt the beginning of the *legal* year of Edw. III.

His peace having been proclaimed 24 Jan 1326/7 I conclude there is no doubt but that such is the commencement of his regnal years – and for the first year of his reign the Rolls of the Terms of the Common Pleas proceed in the following order

Pasch   1mo
Trin   1mo
Mich   1mo
Hill   1mo incipiente 2^{ndo}

and continue in the same cycle during the remainder of the reign.

So far, therefore, there is no difficulty, but in the King's Bench, I cannot *from the Rolls*, make out with certainty whether the Hilary Term of 1328 was reckoned as belonging to the first or to the 2nd years – or in other words when the King's Bench of Edward III began its functions – and the subject being one both of importance and curiosity, I shall be much obliged to you if you will let me have from the Rolls copies of the Writs or Patents appointing the Justices & Barons of the K.B. C.P. & Exchequer (for I wish to compare them all) upon the accession of Edward III – as well as any proclamations (if there be any) for the opening of the courts, together with any other matter which may bear upon the question – and which I have no doubt but that you will follow up with your usual tact and knowledge.

I have the honour to remain, Dear Sir, Your Obedient & faithful servant.

Francis Palgrave
The Deputy Keeper of the Public Records

Hardy acknowledged this by return and next day sent the following reply:[8]

---

7. PRO 2/85.

8. PRO 1/2. When he became deputy keeper, Hardy put in hand a Table of Law Terms from the Norman Conquest to 1 William IV. It was prepared by A. T. Watson, a transcriber, and was appended to the *Twenty-eighth Report of the Deputy Keeper of the Public Records* (1867).

My dear Sir

I have always considered that the *Legal* year (until 1753) commenced on the 25th March, and as the First day of Hilary Term always fell either on the 23rd or 24 of January, that Term was then the last instead of as at present the first, term in the year.

Edward the Third having commenced his reign on the 24th of January 1326 Legal style, the first day of Hilary term in that year was during the inter-regnum between his accession and his Father's deposition – the first day of Hilary Term 1327 Legal style would then of course be the last day of Edward's first Regnal year, and so on. This computation perfectly agrees with the Rolls of the Common Pleas referred to in your letter, and with the Essoine Rolls at the Tower.

I have not copied the Patents appointing the judges of the Courts of Exchequer, King's Bench, and Common Pleas, as I found that they did not elucidate your point, but I have sent the dates of their patents, which I conclude will answer your purpose. The Patents themselves however shall be copied if you require them.

Believe me to remain Your faithful & obedient servant

Thomas Duffus Hardy

Within a few weeks Palgrave was asking Hardy to call concerning some editorial work at the Tower, but nothing positive was resolved, and so if these moves represented a tentative attempt by Palgrave to mend fences they did not get very far.

On the records front generally, great uncertainty still prevailed, three months having elapsed since Langdale placed before Russell his proposed scheme of management for Treasury approval. Langdale was well aware of governmental indifference to his problems, and shortly after Palgrave became deputy keeper he told him 'it was impossible to describe the aversion which is entertained at the Treasury to the word "Record" '.[9] His underlying irritation came to the surface in April when Russell told him that the Treasury had approved the provision of office accommodation at the Rolls House for Palgrave and Thomas, and the survey of premises there for possible record storage, but wanted more information about the proposed establishment. This request provoked a strong rejoinder from Langdale, who minced no words when he told Russell on 25 April:

---

9. Dawson Turner Papers: Palgrave to Dawson Turner, 1 January 1839.

It seems therefore to be intended that the business should be conducted in this provisional and unsatisfactory manner for another year. I presume to think that there is no ground whatever on which this delay can be excused – and although I am aware I have no means of preventing still further delay, I must take the liberty of expressing my opinion that the public service is injured and great anxiety to individuals is unnecessarily occasioned by the neglect with which the Record business is treated.[10]

Langdale would not have reacted as he did, had he known of a Treasury minute of 8 April respecting future records management which was not sent on to him as intended due to a bureaucratic mix-up. Russell hastily tried to make good the damage by forwarding it on 6 May. This minute, which was to be reproduced in the deputy keeper's *First Report* a year later, placed on record the deep obligation the Treasury considered the public owed to Langdale for attending to a subject not directly connected to his judicial functions. Admitting that the present arrangements were unsatisfactory, it agreed that one general record office, properly managed, was essential for a perfect system. But it thought that much expense might be avoided if the Victoria Tower of the new Houses of Parliament could be adapted for the establishment of such an office. Accordingly, the Works Department, which then formed part of the Office of Woods and Forests, should be asked to investigate its practicability as compared with the cost of a new building on the Rolls Estate. Although some years would necessarily elapse before any new office could be prepared and fitted up, the Treasury thought it would be highly objectionable if any steps were taken in the interim which might be inconsistent with the ultimate decision. Unless, therefore, some very conclusive reason could be shown, it could not approve the proposed exchange of records between the Rolls House and the Tower. It favoured the involvement of the Stationery Office in the work of cleaning, binding and repairing the records if suitable arrangements could be made, and concurred in the suggested survey of the Welsh records and those of Ely and Durham. It also conveyed general approval for the proposed cataloguing of the records, but warned against doing too much indexing and calendaring in case by entering upon it prematurely time, labour and expense might be wasted. To enable an establishment to be approved, it wished to know the number of persons it was felt expedient to employ, and to be furnished with a statement of fees it was intended to sanction and continue.

In passing on this Treasury minute Russell, anxious to avoid future misunderstanding, suggested that Langdale should communicate direct with the chancellor of the Exchequer concerning the matters to be settled and inform him when he had done so. Langdale lost no time in referring the questions to Palgrave whose reply on 10 June 1839 expressed great satisfaction that

---

10. PRO 1/2.

the Treasury had given general approval of the proposed plan of management, subject only to further consideration as to the siting of the new general record office and the removal of records during the intermediate period. He thought the act ought now to be brought into operation for the following offices and classes of records:

1. Record Offices and records in the Tower of London, Rolls Chapel, and Chapter House.

2. Records of the Court of Queen's Bench in the Rolls-house.

3. Records of the Common Pleas in the Carlton-ride – in the house, No. 3 Whitehall-yard (the latter being Records of the suppressed office of the Custos Brevium) – and in the basement story of the Common Pleas Office, Serjeant's-inn, being Records of the suppressed offices of the Filacers, Secondaries, &c.

4. Records of the late Chirographer's Office, in the custody of the Registrar of Acknowledgments, partly in his office in Serjeant's-inn, and partly in the old Alienation Office in the Temple.

5. Records of the Court of Exchequer, or offices of the Exchequer, vested in the Remembrancer, the clerks in court, or any persons appointed by or under them, in the vaults of Somerset-house – the Stone Tower, Westminster-hall – the Augmentation Office – and the house No. 3, Whitehall-yard.

6. Records of the First Fruits and Tenths, in the office of the Governors of Queen Anne's Bounty, in Dean's-yard, except any required for current business.

7. Pell Records, and all other ancient Records in the custody of the Comptroller of the Exchequer, Whitehall-yard.

8. Records of the Courts of Great Session of Wales, Chester, and Flint, and the County Palatine of Durham.

9. And (probably) such records of the Land Revenue Office as are not required for current business but which cannot yet be specified, no return having been received from that office.

Palgrave went on to say that the dispersal of the records meant that a larger establishment would be needed than if they were concentrated at one place. The making of office copies presented particular difficulty as their examination and certification by an assistant keeper was a statutory requirement. Great care and attention were required as the administration of justice, the proof of private rights, and the credit of the office depended upon such copies which, when sealed,[11] were equivalent to the original for legal purposes. Necessarily, earlier records had to be examined by individuals possessing much experience and skill. In some cases, however, and especially for comparatively modern records, less experience was needed. Therefore, in order to prevent the wastage of senior officers' time, the assistant keeper grade should be divided in two, the second being, in Palgrave's words, 'only superior clerks'. A similar division was also necessary for those actually styled clerks, whose grade ought to be split into two, or perhaps even three classes, according to proficiency and seniority. Writing or copying clerks would also be wanted to avoid the continued employment of law stationers, and messengers or house-keepers would be needed at each office. Having regard to the extra burden created by the examination of copies, the increase in the number of records to be managed, and the fact that calendaring and indexing would be of increased importance, Palgrave did not think operations could be begun efficiently with fewer than 30 assistant keepers and clerks as against 22 keepers and clerks at present. This number should consist of 6 assistant keepers of the first class and 6 of the second, together with 18 clerks, 6 first class and 12 second.

Palgrave did not think it his province to comment upon salaries, but suggested they should be increased periodically and that some allowance should be made for early attendance and the quantity of work performed. He also drew attention to the words of the act, which required assistant keepers to be 'skilled in records'.

Concerning the cleansing, binding and repairing of records, he thought the workmen should be managed and paid by the Stationery Office, their work being superintended by an assistant keeper or other record officer. He also thought it possible that the vaulted or basement storey of the Rolls House might be used as a workshop. He concluded by hoping that the Treasury would not object to occasional transfers of records on a small scale where obvious advantages would result.

On 18 June 1839 Langdale sent Palgrave's letter on to the Treasury, and subsequently began negotiations in which C. P. Cooper was unofficially involved and which resulted in the appointment of W. H. Black to survey the Welsh records at a fee of £200 to cover remuneration and expenses. This enabled Langdale to go some way towards placating Black, who had been refusing to surrender books and papers of the former Record Commission and generally behaving awkwardly ever since his employment in the record service had been terminated in June 1838. With the resolution of these difficulties the way was cleared for his appointment which was welcomed by Palgrave, who held a high opinion of Black's abilities. In other circumstances

---

11. William Wyon, chief engraver at the Royal Mint, was responsible for the Public Record Office's first seal.

the choice might well have fallen upon Cole, who had long been concerned about the state of the Welsh records. However, he was still heavily engaged in the postal reform campaign and had been successful in a Treasury competition for the best method of implementing the form of the Penny Post, sharing the award with three others. In October he was given permission to help Rowland Hill in drawing up the new scheme, going to the Treasury each day after finishing work at the Exchequer of Pleas repository in White-hall Yard. All this activity was placing much strain on Cole, who also had the misfortune to fall sick with an abscess on his thigh, which kept him at home for a fortnight.

A little earlier a smoky office fire had done nothing to help his humour, leaving him, as he complained to Thomas, 'in a dusty, dusky, and invisible condition'.[12] Unwisely, he brought his younger brother, Charles, along to the office as a general assistant, much to the alarm of William Lascelles, son of Rowley Lascelles and later an assistant keeper, who had served there as a junior clerk since the beginning of 1838 and now suspected, rightly or wrongly, that Charles was being groomed to replace or be set in authority over him. Shortly before Christmas 1839, Lascelles's misgivings reached their peak when he refused to receive a message from Cole through his brother and was suspended from duty. On Langdale's instructions Palgrave was detailed to examine the facts. In the event, although Lascelles's conduct was found highly improper, Langdale was reluctant to take extreme measures, and so Palgrave wrote on 18 December to tell him that, provided he 'engaged to behave with proper respect and submission to Mr. Cole as your official superior and with proper decorum to your inferiors', he could return to his duties, but any repetition would render him liable to immediate removal. The next day Cole asked whether he need apply officially to employ his brother as his amanuensis, but was soundly rebuked by Palgrave, who told him he was to make no such proposal and his brother was to be withdrawn from the office.[13] Evidently, the young Lascelles, who in the words of Thomas 'seems to require a little management', had done himself no lasting harm with Palgrave.

Black, who had been in Wales since September, was making good progress there, although he partly spoilt the effect when he became involved in a newspaper controversy in Caernarvon and Bangor concerning the fate of local records, which earned him a stern reprimand from Langdale.[14] At the Chapter House, Frederick Devon, fearing there was to be little for him in

---

12. PRO 1/2: Cole to Thomas, 4 November 1839.

13. PRO 2/86: note appended to Cole's letter to Palgrave, 19 December 1839.

14. PRO 2/86: Thomas to Black, 5 November 1839. This conveyed Langdale's express command that no person connected with this service be allowed to write any paragraph in a newspaper. 'And I have his Lordship's directions to request that as long as you are acting under his orders you will refrain from interfering with the Public Press'. For Black's notes on the matter see PRO 1/121/6.

the new organisation, was hoping he might be allowed to retire on an allowance of £200 a year and told Palgrave that a medical examination he had undergone for insurance purposes revealed his lungs to be in a bad state, and since there 'was no doubt I have not long to live: under these (to me) melancholy circumstances I have to request you will transmit my application to the Lords Commissioners of HM Treasury'.[15] Langdale ruled against that as inappropriate in the still unsettled state of affairs, but he was, once more, becoming restless about the Treasury's dilatoriness in dealing with Palgrave's proposals sent to it in June. In an attempt to get action he contacted Lord Normanby, now at the Home Office in succession to Russell who had moved to the Colonial Office. This bore fruit for early in the new year the chancellor of the Exchequer told Langdale of his general approval of the proposals, and official confirmation followed in a letter dated 17 January 1840. A complement of 30 assistant keepers and clerks was agreed, but the Treasury thought that they should be split into three classes, with not more than 6 officers of the first class, 6 of the second class, and 18 of the third class. Only officers of the first class would be considered assistant keepers, but if it was ever thought necessary for the purposes of the act to designate an officer of the second class as an assistant keeper that might be done, although there would be no consequential adjustment of salary. The pay scales of these officers, all of whom were to be covered by the Superannuation Act 1834, were fixed as follows:

First class: £400 a year, to be increased to £450 after five years' service and to £500 after ten years' service.
Second class: £250 a year, to be increased to £300 after five years' service and to £350 after ten years' service.
Third class: £80 a year, to be increased to £100 after five years' service and to £140 after ten years' service. Thereafter, to increase £10 annually to a maximum of £200.

As a result of the Treasury letter Palgrave wrote to the keepers at the Tower and the Rolls (Henry Petrie and Thomas Leach) to ask how they wanted to be treated under the 1838 act. Both said they wished to claim compensation for loss of office, being unwilling to accept appointment under the new arrangements. That opened the way for the nomination to the senior grade by Langdale of T. D. Hardy at the Tower and Thomas Palmer at the Rolls. Although Hardy had already served 21 years, Palmer, whose service went back to 1796, was the most senior of the four nominees to the first class, the other two places going to Henry Cole and the Reverend Joseph Hunter. Much to his dismay no room was found in the class for Frederick Devon. His chances of having his case reconsidered had not been helped by

---

15. PRO 1/2: F. Devon to Palgrave, 26 November 1839.

a scandal concerning the destruction and sale of Exchequer documents at Somerset House. They had been carted away from the vaults there as waste by a fishmonger at £8 a ton, and subsequently some had found their way on to the open market. Devon had no responsibility for that, but between 1835 and 1838 he had been working nearby on Pells Office records and had given casual and unauthorised advice to the Exchequer clerks reviewing the material. Although examination suggested very little of the condemned portion was of great value, a complaint to the Treasury by the British Museum in 1838 resulted in some of the odium attaching itself to Devon. There may well have been feelings of guilt at the Exchequer as Devon later told the Select Committee of the House of Lords, which investigated the matter between April and July 1840, that at the time he had reported his misgivings to the comptroller general. However, the effect was spoilt when it appeared his reason for doing so was to secure the superintendence of work for himself. All this was surfacing at quite the wrong moment for Devon, who, in default of a senior post, remained anxious to retire on pension. On the other hand, Black, who was obsessive about embezzled records, and who was also summoned before the committee, was emerging virtuously, telling its members how between 1836 and 1838 he had been concerned in tracking down strayed public records and 'it has been my habit and my constant endeavour to recover them for the Public Service. I must say that in this Cause I have acted with a great deal of self-denial for I have deprived myself of my own comfort many a Day and many a Night to go in search of Records sometimes in Disguise. I have gone to Workshops and Cellars, to Public Houses and other Places with Keys and other [Bow Street] Officers to trace or identify Public Records'.[16] Langdale's view on all these matters was that if Devon was to continue to be paid from public funds he had to work for it, and the best he might expect was an appointment to the second class. Had he wished to remain in the service Devon's brother, Charles, might have been equally unfortunate, but as his record agency practice was already yielding him some £600 per annum he had no wish to stay and was seeking compensation. Also intended for the second class were Charles Roberts and Henry Holden, long-serving clerks at the Tower and Rolls respectively. A place had also been reserved in the same class for J. W. Clarke, but he died early in 1840. Clarke, who had worked at the Chapter House since 1810, was the son of Dr Adam Clarke, the much-criticised editor of the Record Commission edition of the *Foedera*. According to Frederick Devon, still bristling with anger at his own treatment and no lover of Hunter and Cole, Clarke's death was accelerated when he saw a clergyman (not of the established church) and a 'discharged clerk' about to be brought in over his head.[17] An assistant keeper post was also intended

---

16. *House of Lords Sessional Papers* (1840), XXII, 463. Black's account is entered in his memoranda book for 2 July 1840: PRO 1/121/8, ff 12–13.
17. PRO 1/4: F. Devon to Langdale, 1 July 1840.

for Black, but his absence in Wales meant the offer could not be finalised. All the clerks taken over from the Record Commission were offered appointments. Eight in number, their posting and suggested starting salary was as follows:

Henry James Sharpe	Tower	200
Walter Nelson	Augmentation Office	100
John Thomas Jowett	Chapter House	100
Joseph Burtt	Chapter House	100
William Lascelles	Whitehall Yard	80
Henry Charles Hertslett	Augmentation Office	80
Joseph Palmer Redington	Augmentation Office	80
Thomas Moses Green	Augmentation Office	80

All four clerks at the Augmentation Office had been attached to Black's 'School of Transcribers',[18] and Burtt and Jowett had worked for Palgrave for some years. Cole represented to Palgrave, following a conversation with Langdale, that in view of this the 'old servants' now re-employed, including his own clerk, William Lascelles, should receive more than 'new hands' who would enter at the minimum of the scale. To a limited extent some allowance had already been made for service and no alterations were made. Sharpe's salary, for instance, reflected his many years at the Tower where, although slightly junior to Hardy and Roberts, he had served since 1821, having been introduced there by Henry Petrie, his uncle. Additionally, posts were found for John Edwards, John Kentish and Charles Cole. Edwards had been giving occasional assistance at the Rolls since October 1838 and had proved a great help in the Secretariat. Kentish had been employed by Charles Devon who secured the place for him, and in spite of Palgrave's earlier rebuff, the irrepressible Cole had managed to persuade Langdale to fit in Charles, stressing his brother's classical and mathematical attainments. Little of this was to Palgrave's liking. Far from feeling elation at the prospect of a more settled state of affairs, he told his father-in-law: 'I continue employed upon the very disagreeable task of making out the lists of the new establishment'.[19] Fearing squalls ahead, he wondered whether to push for a retiring allowance and attempt to start a parliamentary agency. This was in complete contrast

---

18. A paper concerning this 'School' was laid before the 1836 Select Committee by C. P. Cooper: *Report from the Select Committee on the Record Commission*, Appendix B, 743–744.

19. Dawson Turner Papers: Palgrave to Dawson Turner, 19 February 1840. Another sour critic, W. H. Black, recorded in his memoranda book for 2 September of the same year meeting 'Charles Cole, a brother of the notorious Henry Cole!!!, a young man lately appointed who knows nothing of records': PRO 1/121/8, f 29.

to his outward bearing, as in his *First Report*, written three months later, which concluded:

> I venture, with all humility, to observe that your Majesty's Public Records constitute a series of unparalleled completeness and antiquity. No other European state possesses consecutive archives commencing at so early a date or extending over so long a period of time. They exhibit the full development of the laws and institutions of your Majesty's realm, and are evidences of the progress of society in the various changes which the policy of the nation has sustained. And it is hoped that the endeavours which may be made by those who are entrusted with the charge of rendering these most valuable muniments conducive to the dignity of your Majesty's Imperial Crown, the preservation and defence of your Majesty's rights and prerogatives, and the general benefit and advantage of your Majesty's subjects, will not be entirely incommensurate with the importance of the objects which the Legislature has sought to obtain by the statute pursuant whereto this my first Report is most humbly submitted to your most Excellent Majesty.

Neither would it have been possible to divine from the *Report* the growing discontent of the office workmen. Realising that changes were afoot, they decided it was time to make their bid, although past experience could hardly have encouraged them to entertain much hope.

On 24 February 1840 they wrote to Palgrave and Langdale from the Augmentation Office, setting out their case for better pay on the basis of fair comparison with men at the British Museum, and in other occupations similar to their own (Appendix V). They also submitted an estimate of 'the weekly necessaries for a Man, Wife and Two Children'. Applying their figures to the workmen's weekly wage of £1 5s resulted in such a family, having paid 4s for its rent, met the cost of basic food and drink, including two pints of beer daily, and seen to the supply of coals, candles and soap was left with a mere 3½d. Yet this sum was expected to cover such items as 'Medicine, clothes, shoes, shoe-mending, wear and tear of furniture, table and bed linen, domestic utensils, pepper, salt, etc., vegetables, cheese, fruit, flour, firewood, schooling for children, etc., etc., etc.'. To emphasise the point the eight signatories added that between them they had no fewer than 24 children to support.

Two days later their foreman, Charles Gay, whose services went back to the Caley era and whose activities had figured prominently in the evidence given before the Select Committee in 1836, wrote to Thomas:

> Sir
>
> On Monday last I wrote to Revd J. Hunter stating that I have never received any answer to the letter I placed in his hands (August 1838) addressed to Lord Langdale, relative to my claim for some remuneration for my long services more fully explained in that letter to which he yesterday answered me that he placed the same into your hands.

The time now having arrived when his Lordship is taking steps to carry the Act of Parliament into execution allow me to remind you of this letter and to add that my present wages was fixed to teach the repairing and superintend the Workmen with a promise of a rise in proportion with them, this has never been carried into execution with me, and during the last five or six years the whole responsibility has entirely rested with me relative to the classing together (to make perfect documents preparatory to their being Calendared) the disjointed membranes of the various Records that have undergone reparation and taking this duty with my long Services into consideration I hope you will use your kind endeavours to obtain with his Lordship the favourable consideration of my claim.

I am, Sir, Your obedient Servant

Charles Gay

The next month the men's spokesman, Henry Mogford, wrote to ask if there was any information about their memorial as 'up to the present they have not had the slightest notice taken of it'. Towards the end of June all eight of them, together with William Bradley, wrote again to Palgrave, pointing out that as they had been refused extra hours they had 'the painful perspective of seeing the long days vanish fruitlessly in waiting for an answer which they begin to fear they are not justified in expecting from the humble position they are unfortunately destined to fill in the Record Service'.[20] While the harsher side of the age was exposed by official indifference to the men's grievances, the fact remained that, because of the shorter hours worked by the office staff who were required to supervise the premises, the workmen were at a disadvantage compared with others in similar occupations, whose working day might stretch to ten hours or more. The desire to rid himself of a troublesome problem was one of the reasons why Palgrave hoped to have the men managed by the Stationery Office. When it became clear that agreement on this was not going to be secured before the consolidation of the Public Record Office's establishment on 1 July 1840, Hunter was asked by Thomas to tell the men that 'proper inquiries having been made it is not intended to increase their wages'.[21] However, it was arranged for them to work an additional hour daily and so increase their earnings by 3s 6d a week. Although Palgrave made no reference to any of this in his annual report, his review was otherwise wide-ranging, occupying, with appendixes, 146 pages. It outlined the inquiries that had been made in order to bring the act into effect, and it detailed the various proceedings in connection with the management of records. The latter revealed that

20. PRO 1/3: the workmen at the Augmentation Office to Palgrave, 25 June 1840. The earlier correspondence during February and March is also in this volume.
21. PRO 1/3: Thomas to Hunter, 30 June 1840.

Palgrave was already working towards the introduction of some kind of classification, which, while keeping, or restoring, the documents to the administrative group of which they formed part, distinguished such grouping on the shelves from what he called their literary or theoretical classification on paper. In illustration, he referred to the inclusion of the Coronation Rolls under the title 'The King, Royal Family and Household' in the table prepared at the turn of the century by Alexander Luders for the Select Committee established by the House of Commons to look into the record problem. While accepting the propriety of noting these rolls under that head, Palgrave pointed out that they were, and always had been, records of the Court of Chancery. For that reason, he said, they should always continue physically among the records of that court. More generally, he thought that except in a minority of cases the mechanical and theoretical arrangements would not coincide. He may have been making the point to emphasise that the methods used by Cole at the Exchequer of Pleas were not necessarily applicable elsewhere. Differences in treatment, according to the nature of the records, were already evident in the reports made by Hunter on the huge mass of unarranged Exchequer documents, filthy, crumpled, fragmentary or worse, contained in 751 sacks at Carlton Ride and the Augmentation Office. Hunter's reports were among the appendixes to Palgrave's *Report* and show the meticulous way in which he tried to apply some kind of scientific method to his work, so that the awesome mass might eventually be made – as it was – intelligible to searchers. No general archival theory held sway, as on the continent, but the regard for provenance displayed by the staff of the Public Record Office in its early years meant that in practice the record 'groups', with very few exceptions, have continued to reflect both the organisation of the parent courts and departments and, incidentally, the French concept of 'fonds'.

The deputy keeper's *First Report* also included reports from Cole on his work at the Exchequer of Pleas, and a lengthy series of reports from Black detailing his survey of the Welsh records. On completing this work, Black complained that all but a few pounds of the £200 allowed him had been swallowed up in expenses. He was partly soothed when offered employment on the Pells Office records of the comptroller of the Exchequer, and more so on receiving confirmation that in view of his practice of keeping Saturday holy he would not be required to work on that day. His pay was consequently fixed at the rate of £1 a day which placed him, theoretically, in the second class, thus excluding him from what might be described as the board of management of the Public Record Office, consisting of Langdale, Palgrave, F. S. Thomas, and the four senior assistant keepers. Langdale looked to this group for policy guidance, and its existence, although not formalised, explains why Palgrave, as chief executive, felt so unhappy about the position in which he found himself. It was in this forum that the suggested rules for the new organisation were discussed, and Cole's diary for 11 April 1840 notes:

T. Hardy called & we went together to Ld. Langdale's to discuss proposed regulations for New Office. Dined there (Hunter, Palmer, H., Self, Thomas, & Palgrave). Ld. Langdale pressed Pal: very hard for his reasons wh: he tried to shirk but was not allowed.

Afterwards Cole left for the opera where he met his wife, Marian, and his cousin, Charlotte, just in time for the last act of *Lucia di Lammermoor* and to see Fanny Elsler in *La Tarentule*. Travelling home in the Kensington omnibus he must have been in good heart compared with Palgrave, who now seemed embarrassingly exposed. Palgrave did ultimately succeed in getting search work delegated to the branches, and a fee of 1s was fixed for a general search in all the calendars and indexes in each office, as opposed to the free access for which Cole and Hardy had been pressing. Much to his dismay, however, no provision was made for remitting fees to historical enquirers, and the fee for an inspection, which for most records was also fixed at 1s, was less than Palgrave, or for that matter Palmer, wished.

Otherwise the rules were not controversial. Each office was to open daily to searchers from ten until four, except on Sundays and certain public and other holidays. Intending searchers were required to enter personal particulars in an attendance book and were at liberty to make pencilled extracts or copies from the records. No officer was to act as a record solicitor or record agent other than in discharge of his official duties. Access by the public to the records was forbidden except in the presence and under the inspection of an assistant keeper or other officer. No officer was to take any fee or gratuity from any person consulting the records, although the customary fees for the inspection of Kipling's indexes might be received by the assistant keeper at the Rolls Chapel until new arrangements were made. Langdale wished to purchase these for public use but, as the right to them was in contest between Palmer and the executors of Kipling's estate, negotiations were in suspense. Since to forbid payment for their use might obstruct searchers at the Rolls, Langdale, with reluctance, excepted them temporarily from the general regulations, which received Treasury approval on 9 July 1840. Eight days later they were formally signed by Langdale and laid before Parliament in accordance with the act. In a letter circulated by the secretary to the assistant keepers, dated 30 June 1840, they were reminded of their responsibility for the care and custody of the records under their superintendence and their obligation to give every information and assistance in their power to searchers, not merely from the calendars and indexes but also from their own knowledge of the records. Any time not required in attendance on the public was to be 'sedulously and unremittingly employed' in the making of inventories, calendars and catalogues and sorting and arranging the records, it being the particular wish of the master of the rolls that the preparation of calendars, etc, should be considered as one of the most important duties of the grade and 'amongst the best tests of your efficiency and good conduct therein'.[22]

Nearly two years had passed since Parliament had authorised the creation of a Public Record Office, but, although it was now in being, past rivalries and personal discontents attached many question marks to its development. A later deputy keeper, Sir Henry Maxwell Lyte, used to say of the first batch of assistant keepers that they 'loved each other like cold boiled veal'.[23] That was broadly true, although Hardy and Cole were good friends, and Cole actually named one of his sons Henry Hardy Cole. Roberts and Holden kept low profiles, but among the others, although open conflict may have ceased, there was little more than an armed truce, symbolised in the uneasy relationship of Palgrave and his former apprentice, whose diary for 3 July recorded that in dealing with the deputy keeper 'I intend to be very official with him for if not I dare say he will be fidgety and fractious, he is no gentleman but full of wild conceits'. If that were not enough, Palgrave had the mortification of knowing, as he lamented to his old friend, John Allen, that, while all the assistant keepers were better off than formerly, he was actually worse off.[24] Fortunately for the Public Record Office, his understandable bitterness in no way weakened his professionalism, which meant that he could do no other than strive to establish it on a sound footing.

22. The regulations and circular letter are printed in the *Second Report of The Deputy Keeper* (1841), Appendix I, 14–16.
23. Charles Johnson, 'The Public Record Office', in *Studies presented to Sir Hilary Jenkinson*, ed. J. Conway Davies (Oxford, 1957), 182.
24. BL Add. MSS. 52188, 8 July 1840.

Chapter IV

Rolls House and its Branches, 1840–1843

*At the Tower, Mr. Petrie, the late highly respectable keeper, retires on a
pension, and Mr. Thomas Duffus Hardy, for many years chief clerk,
and very popular with all searchers at the Tower, succeeds him as the
new assistant keeper. Mr. Roberts, of the same office, is also appointed
an assistant keeper. Mr. Leach, the late keeper at the Rolls Chapel, gives
way to Mr. Palmer, who practically has administered the business of the
office almost time out of mind. Mr. Frederick Devon is the assistant keeper
at the Chapter House. The records of the Common Pleas and Exchequer
of Pleas are placed under the assistant keepership of Mr. Henry Cole.
The Rev. Joseph Hunter, employed on the highly important business of
arranging the 4,000 bushels of miscellaneous records of the Queen's
Remembrancer Office, is also an assistant keeper, though at present
unattached to an office.*

(H. Cole, 'The New Record System', *Law Magazine*, XXIV (1840), 362)

Shortly after the consolidation of the Public Record Office on 1 July 1840,
a warrant was issued by Langdale authorising Palgrave to take over the
records at the Chapter House, Westminster, but as he was the outgoing
keeper there that was no more than a formality. Warrants were also issued
to him to take possession of the records at the Tower of London, the Rolls
Chapel, the Rolls House, Carlton Ride and 3, Whitehall Yard. A similar
warrant for the records of the queen's remembrancer of the Exchequer was
held over until the transfer of the Exchequer's equity jurisdiction to Chancery. That was later dealt with under the Court of Chancery Act 1841, but
an attempt by Petrie to exclude the Chancery records at the Tower was
unsuccessful. He maintained that the 1838 act did not apply to them, but
Palgrave had little difficulty in persuading Langdale that there was not much
in that argument, and so the documents were handed over by Petrie on 18
July 1840, with Hardy as official witness. Twenty years had passed since
Palgrave, and his clerks, boarded the London Bridge wherry from Westminster daily for the Tower Record Office, which among its former keepers
boasted the name of William Prynne, the celebrated puritan pamphleteer.
Palgrave's many visits there in connection with the ill-fated *Parliamentary
Writs*, and his fierce clash within its walls in 1832 when, in his own words,
'[Hardy] flew upon me as the children say'[1] meant that each of the principals
present at the handover had private, possibly unsettling, memories to recall.

---

1. PRO 30/26/109: Palgrave to John Allen, 25 April 1832.

Certainly Palgrave had not been anticipating the event with any sense of triumph or pleasure, and he told his father-in-law two days later that he found the whole business most unpleasant. Not the least of his worries was that Hardy, now in command at the Tower, showed no sign of giving him whole-hearted co-operation. In particular, the demands of searchers, increased by the reduction in fees, prevented Hardy from doing as much editorially as Palgrave wished. In an attempt to ease that Palgrave recommended to the Treasury in August 1840 the appointment to a junior clerkship of William Basevi Sanders, who was working at the Tower unofficially, having been admitted by Hardy at the instance of the boy's father. Sanders senior, besides being a personal friend of Hardy's, was also Langdale's chief clerk. Palgrave subsequently criticised the way the young man, who suffered from lameness but was otherwise healthy, was introduced before it was clear that a permanent place could be found for him, but that was not foreshadowed in the letter he wrote to Hardy on 5 August:[2]

My Dear Sir,

I have great satisfaction in being able to say that I have anticipated your wishes. Yesterday, by Lord Langdale's directions, I wrote to the Treasury requesting that Mr. Sanders might be appointed a Junior Clerk upon the ground that the Public Service would be benefited thereby. I thought this was the most effective testimony I could give and I am sure I can always do it in favour of anyone who has had the advantage of your instructions.

  Yours ever faithfully

Francis Palgrave

Sanders's appointment was subsequently sanctioned by the Treasury, which had earlier authorised a similar clerkship for John Bond, a relative of Cole, thanks to the influence of Protheroe. Meanwhile, Frederick Devon, still sulking about his exclusion from the first class, felt the full force of the deputy keeper's displeasure when found in possession of some information concerning the accounts of the office, which he could only have obtained irregularly. Palgrave and Thomas were convinced that it resulted from the unofficial contacts Devon was known to have at the Treasury, and Palgrave represented to Langdale the need to put a stop to them. To add to his woes, Devon had been refused permission to leave an hour early each day, and so

---

2. PRO 2/87, p 271. But in the following year, when the Treasury complained about the way in which certain clerical posts in the office had been filled, Palgrave told Langdale that 'Mr Sanders jun. was taken into the Tower by Mr Hardy upon his own responsibility and without consulting me and I was not aware of the fact until he came forward as a candidate': PRO 2/89, p 404.

had to abandon the £120 he had drawn annually for his record work at the Duchy of Cornwall Office, Somerset House, where he had previously attended every afternoon. At much the same time the office withdrew Cole's dispensation to leave for the Treasury at three o'clock each day, rather than allow Devon to allege discrimination. That did not prevent Cole from continuing to assist Rowland Hill after office hours, but left Devon in a thoroughly disgruntled mood, telling Langdale that he was not concerned for himself but for his family, who would be the ones to suffer from his loss of income. To soften the blow, and realising that dignity as well as money was involved, Langdale decided not to place one of the first-class men in formal authority over Devon, for which they were probably more than grateful. 'Mr Caley', as Devon was soon to tell Cole, 'he had more sense in his little finger than you all put together'.[3] While relieved at the concession, Devon chose to interpret it as placing him on much the same footing as the class I men, but without the pay, compelling Langdale to minute ruefully: 'I have never given Mr Frederick Devon the least reason to suppose that he is to remain at the head of an office. His future rank and employment will entirely depend on the mode in which he performs the duties assigned to him whatever they may be'.[4]

Another problem for Langdale was that Palmer, whose legal dispute concerning his right to Kipling's indexes was eventually to be settled amicably, was disappointed at the office's reluctance to acquire them at the sum he thought fitting, and was jangling with Thomas about the terms upon which he was continuing to occupy apartments at the Rolls Chapel Office. That left Langdale no alternative but to remind Palmer that he continued in occupation on sufferance, was not entitled to any allowance of coals, and was responsible for the payment of rates, taxes, etc while he continued to live in them.[5] Elsewhere, Hunter was concerned at the strain the new regulations for public access might impose upon him at the Augmentation Office where so much material remained unarranged, while Black, now working on Pells Office records, was awaiting the formalisation of his appointment. Cole, still smarting at the criticism by the Devons and their friends of his (and Hunter's) appointment, decided it should not pass unremarked, and in an unsigned article on 'The New Record System'[6] countered, arguing:

The act provides that the new appointments shall in the first instance be

---

3. Cole Diary, 12 December 1840.

4. PRO 2/87, p 291. In fact, the Duchy of Cornwall granted Devon a small pension and he continued to do some work there after 4 p.m. as is clear from a letter he wrote to Palgrave on 19 March 1852 in PRO 1/16.

5. PRO 2/87, p 309: note from Langdale appended to letter from Thomas, 26 August 1840.

6. *Law Magazine*, XXIV (1840), 357–370.

given to officers of the record office entitled to compensation who shall be thought 'fit', and some complaints have been made that Mr. Hunter and Mr. Cole, not being legally entitled to compensation, though employed for many years by the Record Commission, should have been appointed. The complaint seems frivolous, unless it can be shown that some 'fit' person has been unjustly passed by.

But Cole's main theme was the improvement in record affairs since he last wrote on the matter in the same journal in 1837. He alluded scornfully to John Allen's evidence before the 1836 Select Committee about the 'hazardous experiment' which a change in the system would involve, and attributed most of the gains since then to the appointment of Langdale, 'the first and only one to superadd action to conviction'. He reminded his readers how all searches at the Rolls were made by the record officers, who told applicants the result of their inquiries after two or three days, and charged 1s for each year of a calendar or index searched for one name. As there were often several grantees in a deed, only one of whom might be indexed, searches were frequently lengthy and expensive. In 1836 Stacey Grimaldi, the record solicitor, had told the Select Committee of one such case where his client could not afford the £15 required for the search, let alone the inspection and copies, and so went to trial without it. Now, wrote Cole, every public calendar and index could be searched for the whole day at the cost of 1s and 'poverty may enjoy the luxury of establishing its rights'. But the greatest relief at the Rolls was the right to take notes or copies of the records in pencil. That was not allowed under the old system and as copies had to be ordered at full length, extracts not being permitted, much cost was often involved.

A further boon under the 1838 act was the provision for the issue of certified copies, which were then admissible as evidence in legal proceedings. Previously proof of authenticity had to be supplied orally in court, but now, as Cole pointed out, if a civil case was heard at a provincial assizes, 'instead of sending a record agent from London . . . at three guineas a day, all the ends of justice will be met by dispatching an authenticated copy of a record by the penny post'. Cole's prediction that this provision would also be of great use in making copies of records which in a few years would be 'altogether illegible' was to prove wide of the mark, but he applauded the deputy keeper's emphasis upon describing the contents of the various record offices as his priority. To facilitate that Cole thought the records must first be mechanically well arranged, and strongly advocated the engagement of a large body of workmen for that purpose. He referred with approval to Black's survey of the Welsh records as appended to Palgrave's *First Report*. He considered there could be no doubt about the need to move them to London, revealing in the process his growing enthusiasm for the railways – he later became a regular contributor to the *Railway Chronicle* – by saying that it would soon be easier for someone from Swansea to travel by train to London to make a search than to get to Caernarvon at present. Cole had never been slow in the past to use the press, often anonymously or through his friends, to further record reforms and other causes, and evidently felt in no way inhibited from continuing to do so by reason of his new status. While in full agreement on the need for a new repository, Cole, unlike Langdale and Palgrave, favoured the Treasury's preference for the Victoria Tower, Westminster, partly because the office would, he argued, then have the benefit of the genius of Charles Barry, the first architect of the day. Cole also thought that some classes of records, such as coast bonds, were utterly useless and ought to be sent to the glue makers without delay. He also thought a safe test of worthlessness would be found in allowing the British Museum, or any museum, to make selections from the condemned lots for curiosity's sake.[7a] He finished by hoping that Langdale might 'live to see the reformation of the record system, so well begun, completed, or at least carried safely into port'.

Whereas the course of future progress was being charted by Langdale, the tangled affairs of the Record Commission had still to be wound up. It took Thomas until 1842 – and only after much difficulty – to clear its accounts, and it was not until 1844 that an outstanding claim by John Sherren Brewer for payment for editorial work was finally settled by the Treasury; there was also a problem about the commission's outstanding publications. In April 1840, therefore, Langdale asked Ellis, the principal librarian at the British Museum, to suggest what might be done about the dozen or so suspended works, held largely or partly in printed proof form. Ellis reported in July and the following month Palgrave gave his opinions in a long letter, marked 'private and confidential', taking up 16 closely-written foolscap sheets of the Public Record Office letter book. In nearly half the cases the two learned men were in direct disagreement (see Appendix VI) and it was not until January 1841 that Langdale made his own recommendations to Normanby, the home secretary. He agreed more with Palgrave than with Ellis, but the reason for the long delay remains something of a mystery for Langdale was normally very prompt in despatching business once all the facts were before him. The suspicion must be that he was unsure about the course he should recommend concerning Petrie's massive work upon the early sources of national history. Significantly, Ellis, in his report, said he understood from Langdale that no doubt existed but that the volume would appear. He entirely concurred, being convinced of its value to the

---

7a. But Cole would not have been so sanguine had he known of a conversation between Madden of the British Museum and the bishop of Llandaff, noted in the former's journal for 4 January 1839: 'He seriously said he wished a person of discretion could be appointed not as a preserver but as a destroyer of records, which now grew so voluminous as to impede research and render less valuable those which might be of value. If reports be true the Exchequer officers have spared the government the trouble of such an appointment as they have been destroying by cartloads all documents not considered by them of a legal character. Pretty mischief!'

historical world. Palgrave, on the other hand, thought the work was intrinsically defective because grounded upon the methods of Dom Bouquet, the French historian, which involved much selection from the ancient chronicles and subsequent dispersal of the chosen extracts in chronological order over many volumes instead of printing the original texts entire.[7b] For full measure Palgrave, whose critique took up almost a third of his long report, also took issue with Petrie's treatment of the national saints and Roman inscriptions. While he felt the work, so far as it had progressed, possessed some value, he objected to its continuance and thought no more should be done than to publish it as it stood with a short preface, without incurring the additional expense of an elaborate introduction or an index. Some of Palgrave's objections – such as those about the Dom Bouquet method – had previously been aired before the 1836 Select Committee, which nevertheless concluded that the work was sufficiently important to justify its completion with the employment, as necessary, of an increased number of editors and literary assistants. Although it had been started in 1823 under Petrie's direction, with the assistance of the Reverend J. Sharpe, his brother-in-law, as co-editor, progress on it slowed from 1832 when Petrie's health began to deteriorate. The Record Commission therefore put it in suspense in 1834, but the sections concerning the Anglo-Saxon laws and the Welsh laws were taken out of Petrie's hands, and it was arranged that they should be published separately under the respective editorships of Benjamin Thorpe and Aneurin Owen. Their volumes continued under Langdale and by 1840 were about to come out, but there was still a problem about Petrie's texts. Realistically, Petrie must have known that the chances of completing them as originally conceived were remote, but he must also have been anxious to see something salvaged, and certainly had the scheme been written off entirely it would have been a devastating blow. As it happened, he was to die in March 1842, his death being 'brought on', according to Hardy in his introduction to Petrie's *Monumenta*, 'by anxiety and disappointment', which was something of an exaggeration since his health had been poor for many years.

Hardy also presented a problem for Langdale, not only on account of his great loyalty to Petrie, which automatically placed him on his side, but also because his work on the Close Rolls was strongly criticised by Palgrave, who thought the proposed volume might be judiciously abridged and reduced to about a quarter of its size. Ellis, on the other hand, thought that it had been executed by Hardy with ability and care, and should be extended from 11 to 56 Henry III, the end of the reign. In the event, apart from the Record Commission edition of the *Foedera* and Cole's Exchequer catalogues, Langdale decided that all the outstanding works at the printers were to be printed and published, but no further volumes were to be undertaken in the same

---

7b. In 1841 Palgrave carried his criticisms to a wider public in an article in the *Edinburgh Review*, 73, 108–109.

'series'. Any decision to go further would certainly have been unpalatable to Palgrave, who remained as resentful about the abandonment of his own *Parliamentary Writs* as when, at his request, his remonstrance was read into the record of the final board meeting of the Record Commission on 4 December 1837,[8] concluding:

> Had the Parliamentary Collections been completed . . . they would when added to the already published Journals of the Lords & Commons have formed a work affording materials without parallel in historical Literature – materials elucidating the uninterrupted progress and complete development of the Constitution from the Middle Ages to the present day. No other Country in Europe can offer such Materials because in none other does there exist so unbroken a series of Records as those we possess – and the work would not only have become the sole authentic foundation for the constitutional History of this Country but would also have thrown light upon the constitutions of Estates, Diets and other legislative bodies in the various portions of the Medieval Common Wealth of Latin Christendom.

While the outcome of the publications issue proved no further irritant to Palgrave, the year 1841 began unhappily for him as he suffered a succession of setbacks, which must have added to his discontent. Ever since the public records had last come under critical scrutiny in 1836, Palgrave had considered the funds of the courts should be charged for record services performed on their behalf. The huge and continuing accessions from the Court of Common Pleas and the Court of Exchequer were, in particular, imposing great strains upon the office as their records were being taken over in an extremely poor condition, unaccompanied by proper finding-aids. In Palgrave's view had the courts discharged their clear responsibility for their own records, there would have been no need for a separate organisation, such as the Public Record Office. As it was, the full burden of cleaning, arranging, repairing, listing, etc. these neglected records fell upon the office, and so Palgrave asked the Treasury if those services might be shown in his accounts as a charge against the appropriate law courts. This idea failed to impress C. E. Trevelyan at the Treasury, which was, perhaps, just as well because Langdale, who had always opposed the use of court funds for such purposes, was much put out when he discovered what had been suggested, and on 7 January 1841 observed with great regret:[9]

> Sir Francis knowing that I disapprove of his proposal to charge upon the

---

8. PRO 36/12. For an assessment of Palgrave's role in nineteenth-century historical writing see P. B. M. Blaas: *Continuity and Anachronism: Parliamentary and Constitutional Development in Whig Historiography and in the Anti-Whig Reaction between 1890 and 1930* (The Hague/Boston/London, 1978), especially Chapter II.

9. PRO 2/88, p 217.

Funds of the Law Courts the expences of the custody of their Records would have done better if he had stated the fact in his letter. As the Treasury has rejected the proposal I am relieved from the necessity of taking further notice of it.

At the same time, Langdale, having conferred with Cole, ruled decisively against Palgrave about the organisation of the workmen grades, having concluded that their employment had to come under the sole authority of the department, and could not be left to the Stationery Office. Since the consolidation of the office in July 1840, the number of workmen employed had steadily risen, and by early 1841 it had more than doubled to 26, although a few of them were boys, one of whom (E. Mogford) was only 11 years of age but said to be able to write and to be 'useful in dusting and removing records'. The increase was mainly due to continuous agitation by Cole, who realised that without such a force for portering at one extreme to repairing at the other it would be impossible to make any impression upon the mass of the records, which occupied at Carlton Ride alone nearly sixty thousand cubic feet. The Common Pleas rolls were in a particularly bad condition: one with a large hollow space had, apparently, served as a rat's nest. In appearance, these rolls were said by Cole to resemble 'Cheshire cheeses' and many were too heavy to be lifted by one person. Cole also argued the case for workmen on economic grounds as their labour was both cheap and plentiful. Additionally, he wanted them to have a graduated pay scale, which would enable the more skilled to be better rewarded. Palgrave was more cautious, fearing that clerical labour, which was also needed, would be squeezed out. Neither did he relish responsibility for the workmen grades and had long looked to the Stationery Office for relief. Even before the act he had set out his views for Langdale in a letter, dated 1 March 1838:[10]

> Should your Lordship accept the conservancy of the records . . . trouble
> would be much diminished by placing Gay & all the workmen employed in
> repairing records under the Stationery Office. Gay, as he well deserves, might
> be appointed foreman or managener [sic] and then all the disburse for the
> repair & binding of the records would pass through one proper official
> channel, just as all the disburse for the repairs of the building containing
> said records passes through another proper official channel – your Lordship
> upon the report of the Keepers would authorise the Stationery Office to
> expend a given sum upon the records of each repository – and whilst you
> could thus regulate the amounts of the expense, the pecuniary accountability
> would devolve upon the Controller of the Stationery Office, who for this
> purpose would be your officer. The Record Commission had no more right

---

10. PRO 1/1.

to *pay* the expenses of repairing the inquisitions in your Lordship's chapel than they would have had to pay the expenses of mending the roof or cleaning the gutters – for the latter purpose had they been required to interfere they would have applied to the *Board of Works* – and for the former they ought to have applied to the Stationery Office. Gay is a very able and highly deserving person and if the Stationery Office were to create a record repair and binding department and place Gay at the head – he would then train up a school of workmen who could be permanently useful.

By apportioning expenditure in that way and limiting the Public Record Office's own vote, Palgrave believed there might then be a better chance of obtaining sufficient funds for record services as a whole. Always something of a patrician, he may also have feared that if the new office was seen to be staffed predominantly by manual grades, it would be insufficiently esteemed to attain first rank as a national institution. That view was not shared by Langdale, who thought that any benefits from juggling the accounts were more apparent than real, and accompanied by other drawbacks. Had Palgrave succeeded in contracting out work to the Stationery Office as he wished, women would probably have entered the office's practical activities a full century earlier than they did as the controller of the Stationery Office thought that 'a good deal of the lighter work may be done by women, and, if so, a considerable saving may be expected'.[11] However, the Treasury seemed quite happy for the grade to remain a male preserve, accepting the office's proposal that it should be split into a number of classes paid hourly as follows:

Foreman (Augmentation Office)	1s
Foreman (Carlton Ride)	9d
Workman, first class	7d
Workman, second class	6d
Workman, third class	5d
Youth, first class (above 17)	4d
Youth, second class (above 14)	3d

At much the same time as Palgrave was suffering these organisational reverses, he also became involved in a wrangle about the stamping of documents on which he had to give ground. He favoured overstamping the

---

11. PRO 2/88, pp 249–250: J. R. McCulloch to C. E. Trevelyan, 6 January 1841. Palgrave had already indicated that accommodation could be found for the women if the contractor wished to employ them, but he hoped that some of the existing men might be retained as 'it would be rather hard to discharge them suddenly from their employment': PRO 2/88, pp 135–136, 277–278, 344.

writing on the face of a document, believing that to be the best way to protect it from embezzlement. Hardy did not think it could be too strongly condemned, and but for Cole, who did not see the issue quite so starkly, would have carried his case in person to Langdale.[12] Eventually dissuaded from that course, Hardy protested in writing, telling Langdale as the 'Guardian of the Public Records of the Kingdom' that very many records were of so much importance that not one word should be sacrificed as the context could never supply the word or words obliterated. If, he said, he were to deface a document in the manner proposed, he would be guilty of breaking the oath he had taken before the then master of the rolls on first entering the record service in 1819, and answerable in law for his misdemeanour.[13] Thinking it best to leave the matter to the records men to settle, Langdale referred it back to Palgrave, who was now looking for a way out. Sensing some disagreement among the assistant keepers, Palgrave asked Cole to investigate and report. That was a shrewd move as Cole believed strongly in stamping and his expert knowledge of postal franking methods made him well qualified technically for the task. After examining the Privy Seal document at the Tower which Palgrave had stamped at the outset of the controversy to illustrate his favoured method, Cole tactfully reported that he had been able to determine the wording on the bill as he knew the context, but in many cases that would not suffice. Realising he had overplayed his hand, Palgrave deftly changed course by allowing Cole to turn the inquiry to the subject of stamping generally and the type of stamps which might be employed. Cole's experiments suggested that none of the inks used hitherto was indelible, and he therefore proposed a 'tattooing' stamp which would leave small perforations on the document. Early in March 1841 he sent his report to Palgrave, who circulated it immediately to the assistant keepers for comment. Holden at the Rolls and Roberts at the Tower agreed with their respective masters, but the others held a multitude of opinions, although Palmer, Hunter and Hardy were all opposed to puncturing documents, and, in varying degrees, hostile to the stamping concept. The only one to give Cole whole-hearted support was Black, who pointed to the strong recommendation in favour of stamping made the previous summer by the House of Lords Select Committee which had investigated the sale of Exchequer documents, and before which he had given evidence. Palmer was in no doubt that stamping would do much mischief, and was sceptical about the assumed dangers from embezzlement, saying that the only case of which he was aware was from the Six Clerks' Office where bills and answers had

---

12. Cole Diary, 20 January 1841: 'Chapter House: T. D. Hardy whom I had not seen for months called in on his way to the Rolls with a complaint against Palgrave abt. stamping the Records: I persuaded him at last not to see Ld Langdale until he sent for him. I felt rather opposed to his sending the letter, thinking it better that Palgrave should introduce the subject than himself'.
13. PRO 2/88, pp 258–261: Hardy to Langdale, 20 January 1841.

been converted into drumheads for which the party concerned was prosecuted and transported. Devon, to whom the paper was sent last, said he had the advantage of reading the remarks of two practical and two theoretical men. With ill-concealed glee, he said Black had weakened his case by attacking Hardy rather than the argument,[14] and pointed out that the English word 'tattooing' meant 'beating the drums for battle', perhaps the drumheads alluded to by Mr Palmer. What Palmer thought of such levity is not recorded, but he made it clear he was unwilling to 'submit or approve of any plan'. Neither Hardy nor Hunter proved so obdurate, acquiescing when Palgrave insisted that stamping was imperative, although making it plain that that was subject to no injury being done to the document. Hardy thought stamping alone was unlikely to provide security, but that it was useful as an indication of provenance, particularly when the records were united in a new building. The cause of the dispute was quietly forgotten when all accepted that the face of the record should not be stamped, a practice said by Hunter to be inexpedient and inadmissible. As regards 'tattooing', Cole thought that those opposed should submit their own proposal, and when none was forthcoming, Palgrave wound up the debate by saying that it might be worthwhile to find out if an indelible printer's ink could be made, or, failing that, one which could not be removed without injuring the parchment. It was his intention to contact Brande of the Royal Mint or Faraday of the Royal Institution, but whether or not he did so is not known, although stamping thereafter became commonplace.[15]

If Palgrave had hardly covered himself with glory in the stamping episode, elsewhere in the archival field he was proceeding with much firmer tread. Since the early autumn of 1840 he had been making a comprehensive survey of the current and accruing records of the courts, and of certain quasi-legal offices, such as the Land Revenue Record Office, which had still to be brought under the act. Rather like a twentieth-century inspecting officer, he visited the offices in person, examined the various classes of records, and drew up reports upon them, setting out their salient features. However, unlike those later officers, he had no discretion as to what might be preserved; neither had a code of practice been established about the preparation of records for transfer, and it was evident that Palgrave's visits were far from welcome to the clerks and others concerned. In reporting to Langdale, Palgrave argued that the overloading of the office with worthless material

---

14. Black and Hardy were old foes and their first meeting in the new service at Rolls House did nothing to improve matters. In his memoranda book for 10 November 1840 Black notes that 'Hardy came in and would scarcely notice me when I saluted him after 3 years' absence: and refused to shake hands': PRO 1/121/8, f 36.

15. For Cole's report and the comments of the other assistant keepers see PRO 1/5 and PRO 2/89, Appendix pp 1–26. The Privy Seal bill overstamped by Palgrave, which gave rise to Hardy's protest, still survives as C 81/83/2564. There is an impression of Cole's 'tattooing' stamp on p 16 of his report of 5 March 1841 in PRO 1/5.

would inevitably be at the expense of other records whose value was undoubted. For that reason he attempted to get the lords chief justice of the Queen's Bench and the Common Pleas and the lord chief baron of the Exchequer to say after what period their records might be safely destroyed and what ought to be preserved. Unfortunately, the judges, while accepting the desirability of the eventual disposal of worthless documents, did not think they had power to destroy any records under existing legislation. Palgrave also indicated ways in which he thought court business might be recorded so as to reduce the accumulation of documents. He reported in detail upon a wide range of common law and equity records, and took the opportunity to draw attention to Hardy's concern about the difficulty in cataloguing the ten thousand or so bundles of bills and answers at the Tower. Each bundle contained Chancery proceedings in sixty or seventy suits, and there were almost as many bundles of depositions. Their arrangement was much confused due to the method of filing. Sometimes the early bills and answers were assembled under the name of the first plaintiff, or the first name to catch the eye of the sorter, and then bundled under the initial letter, although not chronologically. From the reign of Charles II to 1714 they were even more confusedly arranged, being divided into six divisions bearing the names of the six clerks in Chancery, but each division was arranged differently from the others, and even within each division there was no consistency. As it was evident that with existing resources it would take many years even to establish the title of each bundle, and count and stamp the number of bills and answers within it, it was essential to establish a better order and arrangement for the future. When he came to write his *Second Report* in the middle of May 1841, Palgrave set out every one of these matters at very great length. In all, his findings and recommendations took up some three-quarters of his 79-page *Report*, with a further eight pages of related correspondence among the appendixes. If nothing else, that highlighted the problem and the responsibility of the courts although, reading between the lines, one can see that they possessed neither the will nor the capacity to do much about it. Additionally, while Langdale thought the department had a legitimate interest in the make-up of the records, he was disposed to be far less interventionist than Palgrave.

Viewing the huge mass of records awaiting proper classification in the branch offices, and taking into account those due to arrive, Palgrave was naturally anxious to build up his clerical complement. Although he did not succeed in expanding it to the same degree as the workmen grade, the number of clerks still rose from 11 in July 1840 to 18 in March 1841, the largest single block – six in all – working at the Rolls. Among the latter was William Lascelles who had, once again, fallen foul of Cole, and been removed from Whitehall Yard after a clash with another clerk there, Joseph Garnier. Cole thought quite well of Garnier and was sorry to see him resign after just two months due to dissatisfaction with his pay. Cole's good opinion was not, however, shared by Hunter, who told him at a later date that he did not consider Garnier a very clever person as he had alluded to Palgrave's Jewish origin.[16] In fact, since all the clerks at that time were entering by nomination, it was difficult to be sure how well qualified they were. To rectify that, at the end of 1840 Palgrave secured Treasury approval for the examination of all nominated clerks on their first entering the office. The test was designed to find out the state of their knowledge so that they might be told the further skills they had to acquire before they might expect to be confirmed in their appointment. Because the offices were dispersed Palgrave thought it necessary for the clerks to undertake, under the direction of the assistant keeper, any of the business carried on in them. Consequently, until the records were united in one repository, he did not think suitable employment could be found for those who did not possess sufficient knowledge to cope with the older documents. For that reason he expected his clerks to have good handwriting, a sufficient knowledge of Latin and Norman French and the ability to read the ancient material, and to be skilful and neat in arranging and sorting records. For good measure he considered it was also desirable for them to have a knowledge of other foreign languages, to be aware of the forms of ancient and modern legal proceedings, and to possess a knowledge of English history. Only exceptionally did he favour the recruitment of anyone over 21 as he thought it difficult to bring older persons into training. In any case, whatever their age, such paragons had, first and foremost, to be of good moral conduct, diligence and application.[17]

Not surprisingly, the first unfortunate to submit himself to this ordeal, the 23-year-old Percy Bysshe Shelley Leigh Hunt, son of Leigh Hunt, the poet, was found so deficient by Palgrave in Latin and French that the Treasury was told he could not expect to be confirmed for 18 months instead of the normal 12 months. As the young man had previously served satisfactorily for four years in the office of the South Australian Emigration Office, the Treasury made it clear to Palgrave that Hunt's probation should not extend beyond the usual period. Separately, the Treasury told Palgrave that however desirable the qualifications he sought in his clerks, it was unlikely that they would be met in any person disposed to accept a clerkship in the Record Office at £80 a year. Neither, it said, was any department of the public service known where so much would be expected on first admission. In the Treasury it was the practice for the chief clerk to certify at the end of a young man's probationary period that he was diligent and attentive and there was reason to suppose he would eventually be qualified for the higher duties of the office.[18] Realising it was pointless to push the matter further, Palgrave contented himself with suggesting there was not really all

16. Cole Diary, 15 February 1841. Racial innuendo was a cross Palgrave had long borne, one example, among many, being a reference by the hardly unintelligent C. P. Cooper to 'Mr Cohen Palgrave' in a letter to C. H. B. Ker, dated 2 June 1832: PRO 30/10/15.

17. PRO 2/88, pp 229–231: Palgrave to Langdale, 12 January 1841.

18. PRO 2/88, p 298: E. J. Stanley to Palgrave, 30 January 1841.

that much difference between his and the Treasury view, as he accepted it was unlikely that his desiderata would all be found in one individual, but those most qualified would stand highest and have the best claims to promotion. A little earlier, Palgrave had obtained full reports from the assistant keepers on the work and conduct of the clerks and workmen under their superintendence, making it clear that the clerks already in post were expected to attain the same standard as new entrants before they could expect to be confirmed. That hardly seemed much of a problem as most of them were said to have a good knowledge of the ancient records, while their Latin and French ranged mainly between moderate and good. Their average age was 24 to 25 and they were nearly all thought diligent and steady, some also being described as docile.

A similar set of good reports was also made on the workmen, most of whom possessed some skill or aptitude – such as binding, repairing or arranging – which made them valuable members of the staff.[19] Without exception the assistant keepers greatly valued their men. At the Rolls, Palmer was full of praise for Henry Gay, senior, and Henry Gay, junior, saying that their sobriety, diligence and obedience were everything that could be wished in father and son. Hunter, too, thought himself fortunate, and, like Palgrave, had a great admiration for Charles Gay, the foreman, who, although without any pretension to scholarship, had much general knowledge of the records, particularly those of the Augmentation Office, and was able to assist searchers and make transcripts. Hardy knew his workmen's worth, while Cole made no secret of his belief in the importance of the grade, and once or twice obtained approval for their wives to assist on a piece-work basis with the sewing of labels on bags, etc. Perhaps the feeling that Cole was carrying his enthusiasm too far was responsible for the warning, conveyed to him by Thomas shortly before Christmas 1840, that he was not to incur any further expense in buying beer for the men or in any other way pay them extra.[20] Possibly the men still had their beer, but, while Cole was always quick to praise and reward, he operated a system of fines for late-comers and for minor infractions of regulations and he could be very sharp with those who incurred his displeasure. For instance, early in 1841 Henry Mogford (probably the father of the 11-year-old), whom he had previously thought had the makings of a foreman and who had been employed since 1835, fell into his bad books for unpunctuality and for failing to exercise sufficient control over the young boys on the pay-roll. A more prudent man than Mogford would have taken the rebuke to heart and tried to make amends. Instead, he asked for a transfer to the Augmentation Office, and was unwise enough to make some remarks about his successor, Peter Paul, which got back to Cole. Paul had previously worked in the record service between

---

19. PRO 2/88, pp 232–235.
20. PRO 2/88, p 138: Thomas to Cole, 19 December 1840.

1827 and 1839 when he resigned; his wife was connected with the Cole household, and so when Cole discovered that Mogford was reported to have said that Paul owed his re-appointment to 'petticoat influence' he was very angry. According to Paul, Mogford – who was the men's spokesman – was always exciting them in one way or the other and was given 'to speak ill of all whether high or low'. Palgrave, who was advised of Mogford's 'improper conduct' by Cole,[21] declined to take note of the complaint, thinking it was largely based on hearsay, but within a matter of weeks the matter resolved itself with Mogford's departure from the service, apparently by his own decision. At much the same time that this unhappy little incident took place, Palgrave seemed to have had Cole in his sights when he told his father-in-law, in reference to the government's intention to give £10,000 to the schools of design and twice as much to the National Gallery, that there would be 'fine pickings for the future jobbers, great and small'.[22]

Difficulties with Cole – and Hardy – were no more than Palgrave expected, but his sense of isolation must have greatly increased when he also found himself at odds with Black whose irregular attendance was causing him concern. That was a particular disappointment for Palgrave who had been instrumental in obtaining Treasury approval for Black's appointment as an assistant keeper II, with official recognition of his right not to work on Saturdays when he had obligations as minister of the congregation of Seventh Day General Baptists at the Mill Yard, Whitechapel.[23] Hunter, too, was causing Palgrave problems as the demanding nature of his work on the Exchequer accounts, still under arrangement, meant he did not welcome troublesome enquiries from searchers. His tardiness resulted in a bruising encounter with Palgrave's former foe, Sir Nicholas Harris Nicolas, which was only settled after an appeal by the latter to Langdale and the intervention of Palgrave, involving a prolonged correspondence.[24] Furthermore, Thomas was proving far too close to Langdale for Palgrave's comfort, while Palmer was hardly an easy colleague. In his case matters were not improved when he was given notice to quit his apartments, adjacent to the Rolls Chapel, by

21. PRO 2/89, pp 78–79: Cole to Palgrave, 26 April 1841. Cole's diary for 13 November 1840 suggests that Mogford was responsible for the drawing of the decayed roll at Carlton Ride (Plate 3) because it records that Palgrave 'extolled Mogford's drawing of the roll'.

22. Dawson Turner Papers: Palgrave to Turner, 23 April 1841. Cole struck up his long friendship with Richard Redgrave, the painter, at this time, and joined forces with him to improve the schools of design.

23. Black refused to be styled 'Reverend' and shortly after his ordination on 19 November 1840 told Palgrave of his old 'remonstrance against others and my belief that it would be injurious to the service': PRO 1/121/8, f 37.

24. My colleague Dr David Crook first drew attention to this episode in 'The Reverend Joseph Hunter and the Public Records', *Hunter Archaeological Society Transactions*, XII (1983), 1–15. By that time Palgrave had forgiven his old adversary, telling Turner on 29 May 1841 'would that I could put him in my situation that is all the harm I wish him'.

Lady Day 1841. He was allowed an annual sum of £40 as compensation, but as he had claimed twice that amount he was far from satisfied. At the same time compensation for loss of office was awarded to Petrie and Leach in the sum of £500 per annum each, while Charles Devon was given an annual award of £110. As for Palgrave, his annual compensation, which was merged in his salary, was fixed to his intense indignation at £300, less than half the amount he had claimed. Coupled with his difficulties with his senior colleagues, and his uneasy relationship with Langdale, his sense of helplessness and bitter frustration at this time may be judged from a letter to his father-in-law in which he alluded to the poor prospects in the record offices and went so far as to say: 'I would sooner see a child behind a counter than entering them, they are wretched'.[25] His failure to secure any improvement in his compensation allowance in spite of an appeal to the Treasury added to his misery, and in October 1841 he once again opened his heart to his father-in-law:[26]

> I have not the slightest expectation that Lord Langdale will do anything to improve my situation unless he is compelled and therefore as soon as I have any reasonable prospect of any employment to the amount of £400 or upwards I shall tender my resignation. This may bring him to his senses – nothing else will – and I am quite certain that if I had had sufficient courage to refuse the £700, in the first instance, I should have gained my point. I have now two negotiations in foot and if (DV) either turn out well I shall adopt the course of resigning or at least of tendering my resignation.

Another matter troubling Palgrave was that since 1836 he had been a member of the board of the London Joint Stock Bank, which eventually became part of the Midland Bank. It did not make great demands on Palgrave's time and when he was first offered the place C. P. Cooper, then secretary of the Record Commission, raised no objection. However, the Treasury was now in no doubt that such an appointment was incompatible with Palgrave's position as a public servant and so, although the bank wanted him to continue, he decided he must resign. Quite how Palgrave saw the future does not appear from the official records, but on 2 December 1841 the two Hardys called upon Cole, whose diary records:[27]

---

25. Dawson Turner Papers: Palgrave to Turner, 21 June 1841.
26. Dawson Turner Papers: Palgrave to Turner, 26 October 1841. The Treasury papers are in T 1/4603/15940/1841. Baring, then chancellor of the Exchequer, thought Palgrave's pretensions ridiculous.
27. The C. E. Trevelyan letter books in the University of Newcastle upon Tyne throw no light on the matter, but it may be relevant that William Hardy then held the post of record keeper to the Duchy of Lancaster, and was allowed to undertake private record agency work. It is possible that Palgrave drew the attention of the Treasury to that arrangement, particularly if he was seeking some loosening of the ties binding the deputy keepership.

> T. D. Hardy called to see the arrangement of the Common Pleas writs. Wm.
> Hardy came too. The former said Palgrave had proposed to the Treasury
> to take the appointment of Deputy Keeper in their own hands, always to
> appoint a barrister, & to give him £1,000 a year.

If there was any truth in that, it seems possible that Palgrave saw himself in this new guise, or perhaps he was trying to forestall Hardy's or Cole's succession in the event of his resignation. In any case, such an alteration required an amendment to the 1838 act, and could hardly progress without Langdale's acquiescence, both of which were most improbable. Whatever Palgrave intended – for there is no independent confirmation of the Hardy story – he must have realised it was impractical or unlikely to improve his position, for no change took place.

To add to Palgrave's concerns Frederick Devon was continuing to make difficulties about the running down of the Chapter House branch. He was also blaming Palgrave for the presence of mildew on certain Common Pleas rolls there. Some time earlier his brother Charles had written to Langdale on the matter, alleging that that was due to Palgrave's decision to store the rolls in paste-board boxes and pointing to the ill results of certain repair practices such as 'washing' the records. The Devons' case was strengthened when Cole, who had originally dismissed their boxing theory, was obliged to concede that there was some force in their argument so far as those particular boxes were concerned, and a fresh impetus was given to their complaints when at the beginning of 1842 Langdale, alarmed at the state of many of the affected records at the Chapter House, insisted upon Palgrave instituting a thorough investigation into the problem of mildew generally. Much to Devon's amusement Hunter, who had at first reported that the documents at the Augmentation Office were all in good condition, had to admit that he was mistaken when some of them were also found to be tainted. While Hunter's report on the problem, and those of the other assistant keepers, revealed nothing further, a fresh awareness of the danger meant that particular care was now being taken to guard against it, the main remedy being seen as the free passage of dry air and the thorough drying out of any documents dampened during the course of repair. However, Palgrave was not prepared to abandon boxing just because a particular type of box was found unsuitable, especially as boxes gave protection against dust and dirt and greatly facilitated the identification of records on the shelves and their production and return.

Meanwhile, Cole, whose work at the Treasury with Rowland Hill came to an end in January 1842, was looking for some activity to fill the gap. He had just written a short article on the 'History of the Public Records' for the *Penny Cyclopaedia*[28] and now decided that, as the government was unlikely to

---

28. Reproduced in *Fifty Years of Public Work* (London, 1884), II, 36–50.

resume record publication in the near future, a Record Society ought to be formed for the purpose. He persuaded Edward Bond, who was still at the British Museum, to act as secretary, and put in hand the printing of his proposals for circulation to those who might be interested. On obtaining Langdale's blessing – 'he considered me one of the least irritable of the record folks' – Cole issued the following prospectus:[29]

RECORD SOCIETY

For the Publication of Selections From

RECORDS AND STATE PAPERS

Although several Societies have been formed for the purpose of publishing materials elucidatory of our National History, there is not one which has exclusively directed its attention to, and derived evidences from the Public Archives. It will be the aim of the Record Society to supply this deficiency, by selecting and classifying the experience of the past, and applying it to the many questions which are constantly exciting public interest, in a form disburthened of the technicalities of Records, and made accessible to all readers.

The importance of these Venerable Muniments can hardly be exaggerated; by their means the improvements and discoveries in the Arts and Sciences may be traced, and valuable information connected with the social condition of the people made available. At the present day there is hardly a question of moment which may not receive considerable light from the public documents. An illustration or two of the objects proposed to be attained by the Record Society will not be out of place.

Public attention is directed to early decorative art in connexion with the New Houses of Parliament, and though much evidence on that subject may be found in our Ecclesiastical Structures, and much may be gleaned from the writings of Vertue and others, yet it is from our Public Archives alone that the most perfect information, so far as it can be conveyed by description, is to be gathered.

The science of Statistics would receive valuable contributions from the Public Muniments, which afford unerring data on the subject. Not only are the numbers of inhabitants of the various towns of England, their trades and occupations, the wages and conditions of the labouring classes to be found,

---

29. Copies of this and an earlier draft are in the Cole Collection in the Victoria and Albert Museum, Misc III, ff 27–28 (55 AA47). They are dated 1838, but that cannot be right.

but also the ages of certain classes are detailed with accuracy sufficient to form an average of the duration of life compared century by century.

From the series of fiscal records accurate tables may be formed of the revenue and expenditure of the Crown; and the rise of commerce is materially elucidated by the same authorities. From another species of documents we obtain the political orations of Sovereigns or their Ministers at the opening of successive Parliaments from the reign of Edward the Second to that of Henry the Eighth. Materials for the early history of the English Army and Navy, are more abundant than is generally supposed. The subjects above enumerated, all of which would be embraced in the Works of the Society, are perhaps, sufficient for the limits of a Prospectus, and will show that their interest will be equal to the Historian, the Politician, and the Artist.

The Right Honourable the Master of the Rolls, Keeper General of the Public Records, has signified his approbation of the Proposed Society, and his intention to become one of its Members.

Any who may be willing to become Members of the Record Society are requested to signify their intentions to Mr. Edward Bond, of the British Museum, and when a sufficient number of names shall have been collected, a meeting for the establishment of the Society will be called.

Unfortunately for Cole his enthusiasm was not shared by his colleagues, even Hardy, while willing to join the society, making it clear he did not wish to serve on its proposed governing council. Hunter refused point-blank, while Palgrave had many objections, the chief, as he told Cole, being the disagreement among the records staff on the matter of publication. Privately, he was far from sorry to see the enterprise founder as it did, and as he anticipated – regarding the proposed society, probably unfairly, as little more than a 'rallying point for many of the heroes of the Record Commission battles'.[30]

Apart from this ill-fated scheme, there was much tension between Palgrave and Cole at this time. Some of it arose from another Cole project, a short guide to Westminster Abbey which he was writing under the *nom de plume* Felix Summerly, a name he had adopted for a number of his private ventures. One of the illustrations in the little handbook was actually drawn by Lady Palgrave – with whom Cole always got on well – and Palgrave had himself discussed its general outline with Cole, and was willing to give advice. Cole, however, made the mistake of referring to the housing of Domesday Book in the adjoining Chapter House, indicating that it could be seen there by members of the public on payment of a shilling. In theory,

---

30. Dawson Turner Papers: Palgrave to Turner, 15 March 1842.

that was correct, but it greatly displeased Palgrave, who feared it would then be exposed to the merely curious, and so he asked for the paragraph concerned to be recast. He may also have been put out because some six months earlier he had turned down a suggestion from Cole for Domesday and other valued documents to be placed on display at the Chapter House, following the queen's example in throwing open to the public the apartments at Hampton Court Palace and elsewhere. In principle, Palgrave had no objection to that, but he doubted if it was possible with the resources available and he probably thought that Cole was now attempting to achieve his ends through the back door. However, as the work was far advanced at the press, Cole was most reluctant to amend it, but finally yielded on learning that on this matter, at any rate, Palgrave seemingly had the backing of Langdale.

Another area of conflict between the two men concerned the pay, hours and grading of the workmen at Carlton Ride where Cole wished to extend the men's working day from seven to ten hours, and to secure improvements in the pay of certain men, including the foreman, Peter Paul. Palgrave agreed to the men working a nine-hour day as an experiment, subject to Cole answering 'for the strenuous performance of the duties during the extended period',[31] and approved two minor grading adjustments, but he was unwilling to alter Paul's pay, thinking that to advance it from 8d to 9d an hour would, by narrowing the differential, be unfair to Charles Gay, who was then receiving 1s an hour. He also thought that to improve the rate of two of the first-class men, then receiving 7d an hour, would be prejudicial to the junior clerks. That was all too much for Cole who retorted:[32]

With respect to the assumed analogy between the situation of a Junior Clerk and that of a Workman, I would point out that the first has a permanent office, is entitled to superannuation, with a prospective certainty of increased remuneration, which may possibly reach 6 or 7 times its original value. The Workman, on the contrary, is engaged by the week, has no claims in case of sickness, and no prospect of provision in old age excepting from himself, cannot rise beyond a certain limited amount and is dependent for his subsistence wholly on his labour, and I do not hesitate to say that there are cases in which the labour of a Workman is both positively and relatively of greater value than that of a Junior Clerk.

The next few months saw much friction between the two men, and there was also a fierce clash between Thomas and Cole about the latter's miscellaneous accounts, mainly because Cole took strong exception to direction from an officer of equal rank. It was hardly surprising, therefore, that

---

31. PRO 2/90, p 332: Palgrave to Cole, 13 April 1842. The experiment did not last long for in May 1842 the Treasury ruled against payment for extra hours.
32. PRO 2/90, pp 334–335: Cole to Palgrave, 14 April 1842.

when Cole offered to survey the records at Durham for a fee during his summer holidays, taking a junior clerk with him, his proposal was brusquely rejected by Palgrave. Nevertheless Palgrave did not doubt Cole's ability, and knew that he could rely upon him to carry out his orders, unwelcome though they might be to him personally, which was more than he could say of Devon. He was also impressed by Cole's management of his clerks, and when the pay of Manners Fenwick, who had worked in the office since November 1840, was frozen until he was able to deal effectively with the older Latin records, Palgrave went out of his way to commend Cole, saying:[33]

> The Deputy Keeper does not wish this opportunity to pass without
> expressing his satisfaction at the general care which Mr Cole takes in
> rendering his clerks useful and efficient officers.

That was all part and parcel of Palgrave's keen interest in the development of the younger men. He thought that Joseph Burtt at the Chapter House, who had first joined him in the 1830s, was progressing well, and he held a good opinion of Lascelles at the Rolls Chapel and Bond at Carlton Ride. He also greatly valued the services of John Edwards, who was proving a tower of strength to Thomas and himself on the secretarial and accounting side of the office. Although, privately, he thought the clerks' prospects miserable, the arrival of promising recruits gave him much satisfaction, and he told Hardy on 18 October 1842: 'You will hear with pleasure that the second son of our friend Sir Henry Ellis has obtained an appointment in the Record Service and by his Father's wish, and with Lord Langdale's assent, he will be placed in your department, where I don't doubt he will be very serviceable for you'.[34] If the young men fell ill he quite often made it his business to contact their parents, partly from genuine concern and partly, perhaps, as a check on possible malingering or other misconduct. Jowett's absences from duty at the Chapter House, for example, had seemed excessive to Langdale until Palgrave's enquiry of the young man's father revealed the seriousness of the tuberculosis from which he was suffering, and which was to lead to his death in 1846.[35] On another occasion the receipt of a medical certificate from William George Cooper at the Rolls stating he was confined to bed by 'severe inflammation of the testes' aroused Palgrave's suspicions and resulted in the return of the certificate for the doctor to add his address and to say when Cooper might be expected back at work. Thomas, at Palgrave's request, also wrote in much the same vein to the boy's father, who was the clerk to the attorney general, and a few days later a further certificate arrived, signed by another doctor, in rather more general terms and saying that Cooper was gradually recovering and should be able to resume in a week or

---

33. PRO 2/91, p 239: Palgrave to Cole, 17 November 1842.
34. PRO 2/91, p 167.
35. PRO 2/90, pp 134, 144–145.

ten days.[36] Unhappily for Cooper, soon after his return Palmer reported adversely on his work, telling Cole he thought him 'idle, talkative, disobedient, and unpunctual'. The outcome was that Palgrave, who did not consider Palmer so skilful as Cole in managing his clerks, gave Cooper some six months to qualify himself as a good copying clerk of English records, but, like Fenwick, not to expect any rise in salary until he obtained a knowledge of Latin records.

Overall, however, Palgrave was unhappy about the way the clerks were recruited and organised, but he had not been successful in persuading Langdale of the need for change. Writing to him on 14 February 1842 he had argued that the clerical grade should be split into higher and lower divisions, the maximum salary of the lower being limited to £140. Unless that were done Palgrave feared some clerks would rise automatically to the existing maximum of £200, which might be more than they deserved; while others of greater ability, but less service, would receive much less. To effect a proper division of labour he thought promotion to his proposed higher division and from that division to assistant keeper II should be by examination. Similarly, future assistant keepers II ought not to be promoted to the first class without passing a further examination. Palgrave also set out the regulations and proceedings of the 'Ecole des Chartes' in France for the study of palaeography, saying it provided an example which ought to be taken into account in considering the future development of the system he had in mind.

Until the branch establishments were brought together in one repository, Palgrave accepted it was not practicable to effect his scheme, but after consolidation he thought the office should be organised in four departments. Its general business, including correspondence and accounts, would be supervised by himself with the assistance of the secretary. This department, to be known as the Deputy Keeper's Department, might also undertake some editorial work under his special direction. All dealings with the public would be carried out by assistant keepers in Search Department. Some of them would need to be capable of helping searchers wishing to consult the older records. Others would deal with enquiries concerning the more modern records and would examine and authenticate office copies. There would also be a Binding Department to handle the cleaning and binding of the records and their arrangement on the shelves. Although much of such work was mechanical, Palgrave thought that its general superintendence required a considerable degree of literary knowledge if serious mistakes were to be avoided. For that reason he proposed that an assistant keeper should be placed in charge and also given managerial responsibility, under himself, for the Museum. Finally, there should be an Archival Department to perform what he described as 'the literary labour of the Office', making inven-

---

36. PRO 2/91, pp 137–138, 147.

tories, catalogues and calendars of the records. It would be staffed by assistant keepers, assisted by competent clerks.

Langdale was not, however, impressed and when he came to reply on 2 April 1842, pointed out that periodical increases of salary depended on certificates of good service. He also rejected the idea of internal examinations, saying:

> I have little faith in set examinations as tests of merit. They are sometimes
> resorted to as a means of relieving those who ought to decide upon merit
> from responsibility or trouble, and they seem peculiarly unnecessary in an
> Establishment in which the constant course of business affords the means
> of testing the proficiency of all who are engaged in it.

Langdale also picked up many of Palgrave's expressions and points by writing critical comments upon them in the margin of his letter. One of the most significant arose from a reference by the deputy keeper to 'When your Lordship formed the present Establishment' which was glossed 'When the present Establishment was formed'. Another example was that where Palgrave had written 'it may be thought expedient to form a species of Historical & Palaeographical Museum in which some of the more curious articles may be exhibited to the Public, such as Domesday, the Red and Black Books of the Exchequer', Langdale, apparently alluding to Cole's earlier initiative, wrote 'has been suggested that it might be expedient and practicable to afford to the Public an easy means of inspecting as curiosities some of the most interesting of the ancient Records'. But quite the most revealing was Langdale's comment about the suggested Deputy Keeper's Department: 'A slight indication of this sort is perfectly useless. If I had to describe what I conceive to be the duties of the Deputy Keeper & Secretary, I believe I should fill more paper than is occupied by the whole of this letter'.[37a] Clearly, the relations between Langdale and his senior officer were now at a deplorably low ebb, but irrespective of where the blame for that lay, it was a pity that Palgrave's suggestion of splitting the clerical class, which anticipated the executive and clerical structure of the following century, was not given greater consideration because the all-purpose grade of third-class clerks was ill-designed for the office's needs. The fundamental flaw, however, lay in the method of first entry, dependent in the yet unreformed Civil Service upon patronage and influence. No amount of training, examining or sifting would do if the material was wrong in the first place. Fortunately for the office there was no immediate crisis because most of the junior clerks had been taken over from the former record service, and some of the others, such as John Bond, Charles Cole, Peter Turner, and, a little later, Frederick Ellis, Sir Henry's son, and William Glover, son of the queen's librarian,

---

37a. PRO 1/125.

owed their positions to their families' acquaintance with the field, which generally meant they knew what further knowledge they needed to acquire if they were to have a successful record career. Others, while well connected politically – Bolton Lennox Peel was such a case – did not always fit in quite so well, and so there was a fair amount of wastage from that source, posing, as Palgrave realised, serious difficulties for the future.

With all these mounting administrative and staffing problems it was a wonder that Palgrave still found time for record work, but no less than 55 pages of his *Third Report* were taken up with his inventory and calendar of the hitherto closely guarded Baga de Secretis which consisted mostly of records relating to state trials, including those of Anne Boleyn, Sir Thomas More, and John Fisher, bishop of Rochester. It was also customary for Palgrave to incorporate in his *Report* the inventories etc. prepared during the year by the assistant keepers or under their direction. The year reported on, 1841, was no exception, and Palgrave took the opportunity to mention specifically the amount of time spent by Hardy in attendance upon the public, which inevitably reduced his editorial output. As that was coupled with an objection to Hardy's treatment of the Inventory of Inquisitions Post Mortem – thought too detailed to be appended to the *Report* – the implied rebuke was fairly evident. In fairness to Palgrave, however, Hardy was allowed to give his reason for shaping his inventory as he did and his letter was also reproduced in the *Report*.[37b]

Both Palgrave and Hardy pointed out the damage done to the inquisitions in the past by the use of tincture of galls and other treatment, which had resulted in many of them gradually becoming darker. As further deterioration was expected it was intended to make certified copies of the worst affected before they became wholly illegible. Palgrave also referred to the discovery in the Tower of an important mass of Chancery records, previously unsorted and unexamined. As an indication of their nature, Hardy abstracted a number of them – such as fourteenth-century 'proofs of age' and letters from Cardinal Pandulph, the papal legate and bishop of Norwich, who died in 1226 – and they were included by Palgrave in his *Report* together with extensive inventories of holdings submitted by the assistant keepers at the Augmentation Office, Carlton Ride, and the Rolls Chapel. An inventory made by Black of the books of the Pells Office, which had been moved to the Rolls House from the vault at Somerset House in June 1841, was also reproduced. Black's main concern at this time was with the Pells records, but he had not lost his interest in Welsh material, and it was due to him that a defect in the legal processes involving the recording of assurances to titles in Wales was to be corrected in the Fines and Recoveries Act 1842. Palgrave thought highly of Black's inventories of the Pells records – 'constructed with extraordinary precision and diligence' –

37b. Appendix I, 14.

especially as they were providing a groundwork for a history of the Exchequer and proving useful to those with pecuniary claims against the crown or as proof of payments by former debtors.

All that was in stark contrast to the criticisms levelled during the Record Commission period against the like work of the unfortunate Devon, whose past slips were not overlooked by Black when making out his reports. Devon was, in fact, being buffeted on all sides, not only by his colleagues but also by many of the learned users of the office, so much so that Elizabeth Strickland, sister of the better known Agnes, felt impelled to rally to his defence, telling Sir Thomas Phillipps of the great benefit she had derived from his work on the Issue Rolls.[38] Devon remained resentful about his lesser position, especially as an appeal to the Treasury had been turned down in spite of his claim that Spearman, who had been succeeded by Trevelyan, had promised him a first-class post. Moreover, he was bitterly aware of his vulnerability, particularly as Palgrave made no secret of his desire to close down the Chapter House branch office as soon as possible. That was mainly because, with the early provision of a new building receding, Palgrave was anxious to concentrate his holdings in as few repositories as possible. He also wished to unite dispersed series of documents, and, in the case of the Chapter House, was concerned about the fire risk and the dilapidated state of the building. In accordance with this policy a warrant for the removal of the Common Pleas records from the Chapter House to Cole's custody at Carlton Ride was issued early in 1842. Both Frederick Devon and his brother Charles, who frequently used those documents in his record agency business, particularly for proving title to property, were greatly put out by this transfer, which was one of the reasons why they had renewed their efforts to embarrass Palgrave with their allegations about mildew. In a fit of rage, Frederick told Cole 'that he hoped that anything would be sent to the Chapter Hse. even coast bonds, that he wd. like to be the "useless keeper" of the "useless records" '.[39]

Throughout 1842 Frederick Devon's relations with Palgrave, whom he continued to taunt for changing his former opinions about a central repository and for allegedly throwing the Chapter House into 'confusion', steadily deteriorated. Matters were not helped when in July of that year a hundred roll at the Chapter House could not be found and Palgrave recalled Devon from Herne Bay where he was on leave. As Devon's credit fell Cole's began

---

38. The original of this letter, dated 31 October 1841, is among the Phillipps-Robinson Manuscripts in the Bodleian Library, but there is a photocopy in PRO 22/86. It seems that the Strickland sisters visited the Chapter House on 15 October 1841 to see Domesday Book: PRO 2/89, p 278. I am indebted to Dr Philippa Levine of the University of East Anglia for drawing my attention to this correspondence.

39. Cole Diary, 29 December 1841.

to rise, and on 28 October Palgrave, commenting on the removal of records from the Chapter House to Carlton Ride, told Langdale:

the difficulties raised by Mr Devon (and he always has pursued this course) in the execution of anything which I direct, renders it needful that I should speak by your Lordship's authority; and I have no doubt that Mr Cole, who fully and cheerfully enters into my views, will, under my direction, bring the whole Chapter House into order in a short time if I can be authorised so to employ him.

As the year drew to an end Palgrave was indignant when he was told by Langdale that Devon had written a letter of complaint in which he had said:

I mentioned all the circumstances to one of my superiors that happened to be here, but he was not at all astonished, and only said he 'had served the public many years but could not serve Sir Francis'.

When Devon declined to say who it was, Palgrave decided not to press the matter, observing that it reflected 'little credit on Mr Devon or the individual to whom Mr Devon alludes'. A little earlier, on 10 January 1843, Palgrave had told Langdale:

After much, and I may add, anxious consideration I believe that if Mr Frederick Devon will conduct himself with decency and propriety he may be retained in the Service with advantage to himself, and in a department in which, if he will apply himself to his duties cheerfully and honestly, he may be sufficiently effective.

That resulted in Devon telling Langdale that Palgrave was wrong in thinking he wished to be a 'record martyr', but he was sorry to have caused displeasure and promised to 'turn over a new leaf'. He also apologised to Palgrave, saying 'For the future you will find me a different (but I fear not a better) man'. For his part Langdale wondered whether he might have done Devon an injustice in not appointing him to the first class, but was reassured when Cole, on being asked for his opinion, said 'more than justice'. 'Then', said Langdale, 'injustice to the public'.[40]

Apart from the moves from the Chapter House the concentration of the records in fewer repositories led to the closure in 1842 of 3 Whitehall Yard,

---

40. For reference to the difficulties between Palgrave and Devon see PRO 2/91, pp 195, 302–303, 328–329, 351, 354–356. For Langdale's misgivings see Cole Diary, 7 January 1843. The missing hundred roll was found out of place with the Assize and Quo Warranto Rolls in 1888, happily too late for further recriminations this side of the grave, Palgrave and Devon being long since dead.

on the site of the old Whitehall Palace. A similar fate was intended for the record premises at the former Augmentation Office, opposite St Margaret's Church. Although Hunter was in favour, particularly as his repository was at great risk from fire due to the new method of warming adjacent apartments by flues, he was worried in case it might lead to his downgrading. In the event, however, when amalgamation took place at Carlton Ride in 1843, he retained his post alongside Cole with responsibility not only for the trans-ferred records and staff but also for records remaining in the Stone Tower, adjoining Westminster Hall. Referring to the transfer of these Exchequer documents and Hunter's editorial work, Palgrave pointed out in his *Fourth Report* that they 'appear to have been the favourite objects of attention of preceding keepers; and in particular they had the advantage of having been subjected to the care of Madox, one of the most useful and laborious legal antiquaries of the last age'.

In the same report Palgrave referred approvingly to the arrangement of the records by Cole at Carlton Ride. In many cases – such as the uncoiling and flattening of Common Pleas rolls, previously little more than 'huge twists' – some two-thirds of the space formerly occupied had been saved. That had led to the prince consort remarking, after a visit to the repository in March 1842, that if ever he wanted to pack the greatest number into the smallest space he would look to Cole. The prince's visit had been suggested by C. E. Trevelyan, who, knowing he was to inspect certain royal regalia at the Ride, thought he might take the opportunity to see 'the great collection which has already been made of the old records and the ingenious processes by which those in an imperfect state are restored'.[41] Palgrave thought Carlton Ride an ideal model for the new general repository when built, pointing to the colouring of the presses by Cole – red for the Common Pleas and blue for the Exchequer – as an aid to the replacement of documents, and the clear labelling of the rolls and books by tickets printed on site. Similarly, commenting upon Hardy's report on operations at the Tower, Palgrave praised his work, particularly his treatment of the royal letters and the inquisitions post mortem. He also referred, with approval, to the device contrived by the two men to protect the Chancery rolls from injury and crumpling during the course of rolling and unrolling. Both men's stock also remained high with Langdale to whom Hardy had just dedicated a *Catalogue of the Lords Chancellors, Keepers of the Great Seal, Masters of the Rolls and principal officers of the High Court of Chancery*, a work which drew, not surprisingly, a highly favourable review from Cole in the *Law Magazine*.[42]

At much the same time, in March 1843, the caretaker's place and house fell vacant at the Tower, and Palgrave agreed to appoint Hardy's nominees,

---

41. C. E. Trevelyan Letter Book 2, 23 February 1842.
42. XXIX (1843), 22–35, 'Officers of the High Court of Chancery'.

Mr and Mrs Kirk. He need not have done so, especially as he had been canvassed earlier, much to Hardy's annoyance, by Langdale's porter, who sought the place for his son, William Bradley, another workman at the Tower. The Bradleys secured the position four years later when Mrs Kirk was discovered using lucifer matches to light the office fires in contravention of strict orders and resigned in order to avoid dismissal. Signs of an improved atmosphere were also to be seen in the spring of 1843 when it was arranged for Cole to spend a week in Norfolk to examine Palgrave's father-in-law's collection of documents and paintings. It was also noticeable that when Cole reviewed the *Deputy Keeper's Reports*, 1841–1843, for the *Law Magazine*,[43] the coded barbs were absent, apart from an apparent dig at Charles Devon in a reference to record agents who fattened on the old system and now sought to maintain their business by discrediting the validity of office copies. Cole welcomed the consolidation of records and offices, although acknowledging it as temporary and incomplete 'until a general public office is erected, that grand and indispensable panacea for all past mismanagement, and the only certain guarantee for permanent good'. With high good humour, Cole referred to the recent transfers to Carlton Ride of the records of the late Offices of the Pipe and the Lord Treasurer's Remembrancer from the 'gloomy vaults in Somerset House, famous for their generation of stalagmites, stalactites, and the rheumatism'. He pointed also to the advantage for searchers of the unification in the same repository of the judgment rolls from the three superior courts of common law, writing:

It is but a year or two since, that a search for a judgment in the three Courts might have imposed upon the inquirer, at least, six journies to as many different parts of the town: to Lincoln's Inn Old Square and Whitehall Yard for the Exchequer of Pleas; to Serjeant's Inn or Carlton Ride for the Common Pleas; to Chancery Lane and the Temple for the Queen's Bench. Beside the journies, there was all the risk of non-attendance, for even where attendance was given, its period was usually most uncertain. After tedious and patient toil in treading a labyrinth of courts and alleys, you by chance came to a rough black door on which the various tickets of 'gone,' – 'return directly,' &c. were eternally suspended, – or you were informed that the record keeper's private residence was some miles off in an unknown region. But the vexation of all this is abolished, and you may now for a shilling spend a whole week, if necessary, in examining every docket book of every Court without removing from your seat. The amount of fees will never be a safe index, however, of the popularity or utility of the new system; for though the tendency of the system itself is to promote an increase of business, the alterations in the law is a much more preponderating cause of decrease.

43. XXX (1843), 379–393.

Although searches were roughly sixty per cent up on the old system, the large reduction of eighty per cent in fees meant that revenue from this source was well down. Exact comparisons cannot be made because payment of a single fee could result in several documents being consulted, but by twentieth-century standards the use of the records was comparatively light. During the whole of 1842 inspections numbered no more than 4,000, searches a mere 2,400, and £1,100 was received in fees, mainly from 1,250 copies. While no figures were published of the number of searchers, they could rarely have exceeded 20 or so persons a day. The Chancery records at the Rolls Chapel were the most frequently consulted, Palmer stating that about 3,000 persons had visited that office during the course of the year. Expanding on this, Palgrave said in his *Fourth Report*:

> They consist of persons of all professions and various conditions, not merely
> persons practising in the different branches of the law, but other individuals
> searching for information for historical purposes, for evidence of title, or for
> matters connected with arts and manufactures. Many of the latter are
> common workmen; and it may be remarked, that many of the unprofessional
> persons so making searches have acquired the habit of prosecuting them with
> great patience, intelligence, and perseverance.

Equally praiseworthy was the stoicism of the public whose facilities were no more than makeshift. It was just as well, therefore, that more persons were not seeking to use the office. At Carlton Ride, for example, the search room was only eleven feet by twelve and had to accommodate two clerks as well as up to five or six applicants at any one time.[44] Gradually, however, the records were being made more accessible, as may be seen by Palgrave's account in his *Fourth Report*, of the improvements at the Rolls Chapel due to ticketing the shelves of the racks in the 'dark passages under the galleries' where the Patent, Close, and Confirmation Rolls were kept:

> the Rolls were heretofore taken out almost at hazard, the persons taking
> them out being only guided by their general knowledge of the position of
> the Records, and putting them back again in the same manner. Hence they
> were liable to constant displacement. The Records can now be found by a
> common workman with ease and security.

The credit for this went to Lascelles, who was settling down well at the Rolls, and whose willingness to assist the public drew special praise from Palmer in his report for the six months to the end of December 1842. Palgrave could not, however, resist saying:

---

44. PRO 2/91, p 103.

When the Documents shall be removed to a General Repository, this arrangement, though much required and very useful, will have become useless; and I venture to submit this fact to Your Majesty, as one of the numerous disadvantages under which the service at present labours, of performing a great deal of work and incurring a great deal of expense in temporary arrangements, which will be in a manner turned to waste when the Central Repository shall be erected.

A further cause of expense was the need to take additional precautions against fire at all the repositories, none of which was wholly secure. Evidence of the danger was provided by the King's Silver Books at Carlton Ride, containing entries of fines, which had suffered grievous damage in March 1838 because of a fire in the chambers in the Inner Temple where they were then kept. Some were beyond repair, but over 700 volumes had been treated, mainly by careful separation of the 29,000 stuck or, in Cole's words, agglutinated pages.

To lessen further risks, the water supply at the Rolls and at Carlton Ride had been improved, and two night-watchmen were engaged at Carlton Ride, each working eight-hour shifts between four o'clock in the afternoon and eight o'clock the following morning. As a further precaution so-called tell-tale clocks were installed to check their attendance. At the end of 1843 that arrangement was supplemented by the Metropolitan Police, four constables being placed at the disposal of the record service, two of whom kept constant watch on the Carlton Ride repository during the silent hours. The superintendent of the London Fire Brigade, the redoubtable James Braidwood, also installed an engineer on the premises. Concern also continued to be felt for the safety of the records at the Tower due to the presence of ammunition there. The Ordnance Office was responsible for the site, but there had been a serious fire in the Bowyer Tower on the night of 30 October 1841, which led to Black, who lived nearby at Magdalen Row, Goodman's Fields, hastening to the White Tower where the records were kept in order to superintend precautions to prevent the spread of the blaze. As it happened, the records were unharmed, which allowed Black to point out how seven years earlier, while living at Lambeth, he had performed a similar service when he was first on the scene 'to clear the way and save the records' at the burning of the Houses of Parliament.[45]

The building of the promised central repository would have greatly reduced fire risks, but it still seemed as distant as ever, although the Public Record Office itself was now firmly established and by the end of 1843 its staff had increased to 78, distributed as follows:

---

45. PRO 2/90, pp 72–73. Palgrave and Cole were also present and active at the fire in 1834.

	Deputy Keeper	Secretary	Assistant Keepers	Clerks	Workmen	Total
Rolls House	1	1	1	2	2	7
Rolls Chapel			2	3	4	9
Tower			2	4	5	11
Chapter House			1	2	1	4
Carlton Ride			2	9	36	47
Total	1	1	8	20	48	78

Although well over half of the office's manpower was committed to the arrangement and repair of the records taken over under the 1838 act, the department was also involved with the older holdings of the Admiralty and the Treasury, and had taken on charge material from expired commissions, such as the Charity Commission and the French Claims Commission. Editorial work was proceeding on a wide front, and included among the inventories printed in the appendixes to Palgrave's *Fifth Report* for 1843 was his own of the final section of the Baga de Secretis, and another, prepared under Hardy's direction, of the records of the forfeited estates commissioners, which had languished at the Tower unexamined since their transfer by Treasury direction from the former State Paper Office building in 1819. Further inventories of Pells Office records were also printed, although progress was not as rapid as Palgrave wished, partly due to the amount of time spent by Black in dealing with searchers wishing to consult Exchequer records at Rolls House. The absence of adequate indexes to these compounded the problems, and resulted in many unnecessary productions, specific reference being made to the examination of 20 to 50 documents a day by Nicolas arising from his research into the life of Chaucer. Black's health was also troubling him – he had been away sick from June to August 1843 – and his 'severe and continued illness' was mentioned by Palgrave in his *Report*. Palgrave had also hoped to report the first accession from the Land Revenue Record Office, but was thwarted by strong opposition from the Office of Woods to such a transfer. Although Palgrave would have liked to publish the correspondence his certainties were not shared by Langdale, which led to the Treasury preventing him from doing so, Trevelyan thinking it should be omitted because it revealed differences of opinion between public departments. Much as he may have regretted the Treasury veto, Palgrave probably took even greater exception to its subsequent rejection of an application by all six chief officers for an improvement in their salaries. Originally, Palgrave wanted to proceed independently of the others, but Langdale insisted upon one application as a condition of his support. Their first submission in June 1843 failed to impress him, but as a result of further correspondence and discussion they made a fresh approach on 10 November 1843:

My Lord

We the undersigned Chief Officers of the Public Record Establishment, beg leave most respectfully to solicit your Lordship's attention to the amount of the salaries paid to this service.

We bring the subject before your Lordship under a full, though respectful conviction, that the salaries are an inadequate remuneration to the officers, considered in relation to the difficulty, extent, & importance of the duties performed, and the qualification which they require.

The superintendence which your Lordship exercises over the Establishment appears to render it superfluous to enter into any detail of the nature of those duties, or the qualifications.

We venture to suggest to your Lordship the possibility that in the arrangement of the salaries of the Officers, upon the first formation of the Establishment, the Lords of Her Majesty's Treasury were influenced by the circumstances out of which the new system sprung, rather than by a full knowledge of the duties to be performed under the operation of the Act and of Your Lordship's superintendence, but supposing in this we are mistaken, we still prefer our request on the broad principle that the salaries are inadequate to our services, which we may perhaps be permitted to remark are felt to be more responsible & onerous than was contemplated at our first appointment – and are peculiarly heavy under the present state of the records.

We would further beg leave to remark, that the Chief Officers have been on an average in the Public Service about twenty-four years, and have all brought considerable experience and knowledge to bear upon the performance of their several duties.

With respect to the Clerks also we would submit to Your Lordship that the rates and principle of progressive increase do not appear to be such as to bind them permanently to the Service – and this is shewn by Clerks who had been placed here entirely without experience having sought and obtained removal to other Departments for the sake of better payment and prospects after considerable pains and labour had been bestowed in training them – and your Lordship will perceive that such a system tends to deprive the Establishment of officers properly trained for the higher branches of the Service, for owing to the peculiar and technical nature of the record duties, there is perhaps no public Office which has so strong an interest in insuring the retention of practised officers as this.

We trust that we may be permitted to refer as an evidence of the manner in which our duties have been discharged to the increased and increasing use of the Records by the Public, and to the state of the Records themselves. We hope that these results have created favourable impressions in the minds of Her Majesty's Government & of your Lordship.

In conclusion we beg your Lordship to give this statement your consideration – and if your Lordship should be of the opinion that our application for an increased remuneration is warranted by the circumstances of our case we solicit your Lordship to transmit the same to the Lords Commissioners of Her Majesty's Treasury, accompanied with such a recommendation as may seem fit to your Lordship.

We have the honour to be, My Lord, Your Lordship's most obedient humble servants.

Francis Palgrave, Thomas Palmer, T. Duffus Hardy, Henry Cole, Joseph Hunter, F. S. Thomas

Within a fortnight Langdale forwarded his chief officers' letter to the Treasury, although he omitted, presumably with their agreement, the paragraph concerning their length of service. In his accompanying letter Langdale made it clear that their request had his support, saying:

considering the nature and importance of the duties which these officers have to perform, the education & attainments which are required to qualify them for the due performance of those duties, the advantage of exempting them from strong temptations to undertake employment unconnected with the Office, and the great expediency of providing for the superior officer such a remuneration as may probably afford to steady & well-educated youths an inducement to enter the Office, and to the younger officers an inducement to remain there for the chance of promotion, it has appeared to me that it would be right on public grounds to make some increase to the salaries now allowed – and being of this opinion, I have considered it to be my duty to communicate to their Lordships the Memorial which has been presented to me, and which I now enclose.

The Treasury proved unsympathetic and in its reply on 8 December 1843, expressed regret[46]

that they cannot give any encouragement to a proposal which has your Lordship's recommendation, but as it appears that the amount of the salaries of the several officers of the Record Department was well considered at the

---

46. A copy of the application and the Treasury reply will be found in PRO 1/7. In the original in T 1/4880/24218 Palgrave inserted after his signature the words 'the Deputy Keeper of the Public records'.

period of its first establishment on its present footing, & that the nature of the duties to be performed was fully understood, my Lords do not feel that they should be justified in holding out to the Memorialists any expectation of a compliance with their request.

The Treasury's firm rebuff must have greatly disappointed all those concerned and Palgrave was inclined to blame Langdale for failing to take their petition in person to Sir Robert Peel, the prime minister, at the outset. Cole, who had rested his hopes in the expansion of legal business, now realised that the office had to broaden its base if it hoped to obtain a more sympathetic hearing. It was because of that that he favoured the centralisation of the records at Westminster, believing that to house them there was much more likely to stimulate public interest than if they were in Chancery Lane. The value he had once attached to the records as legal instruments was also in course of modification, for he now argued:[47]

> The use of the Records in the administration of justice is only one of their uses, and though perhaps that use is of the highest importance to individuals, it is of the narrowest interest to the public at large. In viewing the venerable Domesday Book, one of the last aspects in which it interests, is its utility in determining the boundaries of a manor, but this would be its sole aspects as a legal document.

As for Palgrave, he was deeply pessimistic about an improvement in his personal position, particularly as he felt that since Lord Holland's death in 1840 he had little influence in government circles. As he had left it too late to risk outside employment he had to consider making economies in his personal and household expenditure. A handbook he had written on Northern Italy[48] had not long been published, and had any suitable editorial work been in prospect he would have welcomed it. The completion of Petrie's work attracted him, but there were many obstacles, not the least being Hardy's involvement with the executors of Petrie's estate, and the interest of the English Historical Society in the same material. As 1843 drew to its close, therefore, he must have known he had little option but to make the best of his predicament, concentrating upon the challenge of the many records problems still awaiting settlement.

---

47. *Law Magazine*, XXX (1843), 393.
48. *Handbook for Travellers in Northern Italy* (London, 1842).

Chapter V

Rolls House and its Branches, 1844–1851

Called on Lord Langdale who said he did not doubt he took more interest in the Records than was pleasing to a 'certain person'.

(Cole Diary, 2 January 1844)

Of those concerned in the campaign for record reform in the 1830s none was more feared by Palgrave than Nicolas, whom he thought was motivated by a virulent, though unprovoked, hostility directed at him personally. With the demise of the Record Commission Nicolas's interest in record reform waned, and he did not take part in the shaping of the new legislation. The result was that the tension between the two men began to ease, and following the establishment of the Public Record Office and the smoothing out by Palgrave of the difficulties encountered by Nicolas in his dealings with Hunter, their relationship – which had originally been fair – was again tolerable. When Nicolas's life of Chaucer appeared, Palgrave wrote on 7 February 1844, drawing attention to a factual blemish which must have caused him much irritation:[1]

My dear Sir Harris,

In your very excellent life of Chaucer you speak of Mr. Hardy as Deputy Keeper of the Records in the Tower. As I need not remind you of the importance of giving official designations correctly you will excuse me in requesting your reference to the Act by which you will find there is only one Deputy Keeper of the Records and that the other officers are his Assistants.

I am truly glad that you have been enabled to collect such very valuable information from our Records and I can only hope you will be enabled to continue your researches in which I shall always be glad to afford you every assistance in my power.

   Yours ever truly

Francis Palgrave

---

1. Palgrave's draft and Nicolas's reply are in PRO 1/8. The same confusion arose some 13 years later when Mrs Everett Green, an editor of the *Calendar of State Papers*, was corrected by Palgrave for referring to Lemon as deputy keeper of the State Paper Office, a post that had been occupied by his father, and after him by Lechmere, but which was abolished when the State Paper Office was merged with the Public Record Office in 1854.

A good-natured reply was despatched by Nicolas on the same day:

My dear Sir Francis

Many thanks for your obliging letter. I assure you I had no intention of
attributing your title to a subordinate officer, nor of raising him to your
dignity. In truth I was ignorant, or at least forgetful, whether the 'Deputy'
assisted the 'Assistants' or whether the 'Assistants' assisted the 'Deputy' but
I shall know better in future, and as I deal somewhat largely in Honours, I
ought to have been more careful in the instance to which you are good enough
to call my attention – I fear I cannot cancel the page, impressed as I am with
the importance of my error.

I am glad you are pleased with the life of Chaucer. Most assuredly I am
gratified by the present state of the Record System: first, because it is nearly
perfect; and, secondly, from the egotistical feeling that it has been the result
of my own labours and plans when 'Record Reform' had awful horrors for
'ears polite'.

I think, however, the shilling fee a petty nuisance (for literary inquiries)
which ought to be abated. It produces little and does act as an impediment
to inquiries.

I readily believe in your desire to assist my researches and I shall not hesitate
to ask your aid if I find difficulties (which very rarely happens); or to
complain of anything that ought to be remedied.

   Yours very faithfully

                              N. Harris Nicolas

Palgrave must have been cheered by Nicolas's views on literary search
fees, remission being dear to his own heart, but he was far too close to the
realities to accept the somewhat complacent assessment of the happy state
of record affairs. He also knew that, except on editorial matters where he
still held sway, it was Hardy's writ that ran in the Tower, irrespective of
official designations. That was broadly true also of Palmer at the Rolls
Chapel. Both these long-serving officers headed branches with an established
past, and, although since the 1838 act public access to their holdings was
less restrictive and costly, the day-to-day running of their repositories continued much as before. Palmer took his responsibilities so seriously that,
when Palgrave removed some Charity Commission volumes from the Chapel
to the Rolls House Library, he wrote an indignant letter of protest at what
he felt was an unlawful intrusion. He saw his custodianship in the nature
of a sacred trust and on one occasion, when Hunter asked to see a document,

charged him for doing so. If Palmer is to be believed, Hunter's approach left something to be desired, but, when Langdale was told about the matter by Palgrave, he ruled that all the assistant keepers were entitled as of right to inspect and study the records wherever they might be and Hunter got his money back. However, all the assistant keepers were highly conscious of their personal accountability, and according to a note in Black's journal, when Palgrave produced some records he had taken from the Rolls before a Lords' Secret Committee on the Post Office in July 1844, they agreed that Langdale's opinion should be taken on any future attempt to encroach upon their duties and responsibilities.[2] Hardy himself enjoyed the additional protection of a cordial relationship with Langdale and wide-ranging contacts outside the office. A pointer to his dominance in his own sphere was that two of the three clerks appointed to the Tower since 1840 had been introduced due to his friendship with their fathers and the third was the cousin of Charles Roberts, his trusted second-in-command. When in 1844 the Reverend Sydney Smith solicited a similar place there for the young Alfred Kingston, Palgrave felt obliged to advise Langdale of his misgivings, saying there was 'serious objection to permitting an assistant keeper to establish a species of popular reputation, which, by rendering his Division more desirable, would necessarily give him an undue preponderance over his colleagues'.[3] Palgrave emphasised that he was not saying that anything of the kind had yet taken place, but he thought it very necessary to guard against it. Regardless of that, Kingston, whose family had fallen from its former affluence in the West Indies, was still admitted at the Tower, but Palgrave made it clear that at some future time he expected Hardy to give up one of his existing clerks for duties elsewhere.

At the newly-established Carlton Ride it was a different story. A room was reserved there for the deputy keeper, who exercised oversight over the many new works required and the requisitioning of supplies from the Stationery Office for packing and repair. He took an almost proprietorial pride in Cole's achievements, telling Langdale that he believed Cole had 'acquired the proficiency which he now possesses mainly by having been employed when young, very constantly, to the indexing of the *Parliamentary Writs*'.[4] At times Cole must have found Palgrave's superintendence irksome, but he had not, perhaps, ever quite broken free from the spell of his first master, resentful of it although he might often be. In default of a new

---

2. Black's journal for 1844 to 1846 is in Chetham's Library, Manchester: MS Div. B, Shelf 4, 43.

3. PRO 1/8: Palgrave to Langdale, 20 May 1844. Smith's letter to Peel commending Kingston 'an excellent lad, understanding and speaking French and German', and mentioning Hardy's friendship with the family is printed in Nowell C. Smith's *Selected Letters of Sydney Smith* (Oxford, 1981), 226.

4. PRO 1/8: Palgrave to Langdale, 10 December 1844. But the 19-year-old Cole did not know what was good for him because his diary for 7 May 1827 records 'At Parliament St. continuing that most horrible index'.

repository, Palgrave's first intention was to concentrate upon the development of Carlton Ride, but it soon became apparent that, despite Cole's skill in bringing the place to order, the rickety old building was quite unsuitable for long-term record storage and there was a grave risk from fire. Referring to the premises there and at the Rolls House, James Braidwood, the superintendent of the London Fire Brigade, minced no words, stating in June 1845 that no measures short of rebuilding would make them safe. It was also apparent that until more racking was provided the office could not deal properly with the accruals from the courts, aggravated, as it was, by the wretched condition in which they were invariably received. Consequently a stop was put on transfers in 1846 and 1847 and steps were taken to ease the problem of accommodation by expanding at the Tower and by the adaptation of the Stone Tower, adjoining Westminster Hall, where coast bonds and other little-consulted records were already stored. Partly baulked at Carlton Ride, Cole was already turning his mind to other things, and during the course of 1844 he formed a plan to publish privately an ecclesiastical directory, but he pulled back when he learned that Palgrave objected. However, Palgrave did not want to veto the project on his own responsibility, preferring to leave the decision to Langdale, who since the rejection of the assistant keepers' pay claim was disposed to permit their outside engagements, provided that they were not incompatible with their position as civil servants and did not interfere with their record duties. Palgrave himself had become a director of the Legal and Equitable Life Assurance Society (later Equity and Law) in nearby Lincoln's Inn Fields on its formation in 1844, but resigned at the end of 1846 when the time of board meetings was changed to 1 p.m. and he was no longer able to attend without a clash with office hours. Presumably such business was seen differently from his earlier banking connection which he had been obliged to sever in 1841, and although he was offered directorships on at least three railway companies Palgrave was in no doubt that his deputy keepership prevented him from accepting business commitments of that kind. As to Cole's directory, Langdale was not clear how it differed from Hardy's publication on the lord chancellors, but, when Palgrave explained that the latter was an original literary work whereas Cole's was a rearrangement of an official calendar from the Office of First Fruits and Tenths, Langdale decided not to sanction it.

In spite of that Cole went ahead with another of his schemes, to publish a weekly *Historical Register*.[5] This time he had a more favourable response, even Palgrave telling him 'I think your Journal will be of great utility and importance if carried on in the manner you propose'. Although Cole intended to include an ecclesiastical section in his publication covering much the same

---

5. Most of the papers concerning the *Historical Register* are among the Cole Collection in the Victoria and Albert Museum, catalogue reference 329E.

ground as his banned directory, Palgrave did not object to that because the paper itself was intended to range over the whole area of social and public life. Cole aimed to concentrate especially on the publication of notices of births, deaths and marriages, believing that the *Historical Register* would then become the recognised channel for the announcement of such events and of great value for genealogists and the protection of hereditary rights. He proposed to make a charge for this service not exceeding 2s 6d, and as a guarantee of authenticity had arranged with the General Register Office for all entries to be checked with the various registrars before publication. Cole also proposed to include biographies of well known persons and to record matters of interest concerning public health, probates of wills, divorce, changes of name, deaths from accidents, fires, life insurance and legal proceedings. With the co-operation of public departments, including the Treasury, he also aimed to document Civil Service appointments and promotions in much the same way as changes in the military establishment were regularly published in the *Army List*.

It was not Cole's first experience of the newspaper business because in 1837, in company with Charles Buller, Sir William Molesworth and others, he had published a radical weekly, *The Guide*, which ran for only eight issues, leaving him seriously embarrassed financially. This time he took care to arrange for the main risk to be taken by Longman, the publishers, and to ensure that the publication should be strictly non-political. Hardy, who had also lost money in the earlier venture, but not to the same extent, told Cole that he thought the *Historical Register*, which first appeared on 4 January 1845 at the price of 6d post paid, 'would have a brilliant success or fall dead'. The second prediction proved the more accurate for it had to be abandoned on 8 March after only ten issues. If the number of stamps issued by the Board of Stamps and Taxes be taken as a guide, its circulation averaged no more than 1,000 copies weekly. One of its contributors was none other than Black, whose past quarrels with Cole did not prevent him from accepting 11s for writing two articles. One concerned a lawsuit by the king of Hanover for the recovery of certain crown jewels and the other an account of a visit to the Public Record Office by the French ambassador.

An unwelcome diversion for Cole at this time was an unhappy dispute in which he became involved with Charles Lipsham, one of his workmen. In 1834 Lipsham, then 17, had been engaged by the Record Commission for industrial duties and sent to the Chapter House under Palgrave. According to Lipsham, Palgrave gave him copying work and arranged for him to have Latin tuition in the hope that he might eventually improve his position. Those arrangements were upset when Lipsham was transferred to the Augmentation Office as a 'duster' under Cole. Soon afterwards, being found away from his work bench without permission, he was dismissed. Lipsham then had two periods of clerical employment in solicitors' offices, but by 1840 was unemployed. In November of that year, by then married with two children, he wrote to Palgrave seeking another chance, admitting that he had 'formerly hindered much of my time by joking and nonsense'. Early in

1841 Palgrave agreed to take him back on probation, placing him with Cole at the very low wage of 10s a week. Lipsham soon proved useful as he was able to help the clerks by sorting documents and making office copies, and in Palgrave's *Second Report* as deputy keeper Cole mentioned that Lipsham had spent part of his time in calendaring some seventeenth-century rolls from the Exchequer of Pleas. By the end of 1844 Cole, who had originally opposed Lipsham's re-engagement, thought sufficiently well of him to recommend that his pay, which had risen to 24s a week, should be increased by a further 4s.

However, Lipsham was looking for something more than an increase in pay and was disappointed that a scheme of Cole's in 1843 to regrade some of the workmen as 'searchers' seemed to have got nowhere. He thought his workmates 'extremely ignorant and of all trades such as cheesemongers, shoemakers, hatters, ostlers, gentlemen's servants, printers, etc., etc.', whose only qualification for repair work was that they could be hired at a cheap rate of pay. Neither did he take kindly to Cole's strict regime, alleging that such a system of rules and fines was more appropriate for 'a parcel of schoolboys than for men employed in a Government Office where it is generally supposed more liberality exists'. Since he harboured such sentiments and had little prospect of advancement, the only surprise was that he was able to keep his feelings under control for nearly three years. At any rate, on the morning of 3 February 1845, unable to contain himself any longer, he openly defied an order from Paul, the foreman, to assemble with the other men so that a new rule made by Cole about unauthorised absence during working hours might be read to them. To make matters worse he had a further altercation with Paul in the afternoon about the distribution among the men of certain Christmas boxes. The next day, realising that his behaviour was to be reported, he went up to the loft and put his ear to the speaking pipe there in order to listen to the conversation between Cole and Paul in the office below. Immediately after that he went off sick and it was not until his return on 17 February that Cole sent for him to answer the charge of insubordination, which he admitted but gave no apology. Cole said that as it was not the first or second occasion on which there had been complaints about his conduct, he would be fined a day's pay and would be required to make a written apology which would be read to the assembled men. In default, he would be suspended and the matter would be referred to Palgrave for determination, accompanied by any answer he might care to make. In other circumstances, Cole, who sympathised with the workmen's aspirations, might have seen Lipsham privately to try to dissuade him from acting rashly, but tact was not his strong point and his domestic ties with the Pauls – which had caused trouble with Mogford in 1841 – may have compromised his position.

On 19 February Lipsham sent a long letter to Palgrave in which he justified his conduct because of what he regarded as the tyrannical nature of the regulations at Carlton Ride, citing the fining of a man for warming himself at the fire and another for not maintaining a certain average output.

Unimpressed, Palgrave told Langdale that he thought Cole's rules (see Appendix VII) 'needful for the good regulation of so large an establishment'. He also said he had given Lipsham every opportunity to apologise, or to express contrition, or to promise to obey the rules in future, but because he refused to do so he felt, with great regret, that he must recommend dismissal, as it would otherwise be impossible for Cole 'to maintain a proper degree of subordination amongst the workmen'. Langdale, who already knew from Cole that Lipsham had shown considerable talent and might be worthy of promotion, having read all the papers and relying on Palgrave's inquiries, said he saw no reason to object to Lipsham's dismissal although he expressed much regret that the office should be compelled to deprive itself of so useful a workman.

Langdale also instructed Palgrave to enquire further about the Christmas boxes, which he supposed to have come from searchers. If that were so, he said, such practice must be discontinued as he thought it improper. Cole, however, assured Langdale that these consisted of a gratuity given to the men by the clerks apart from one given by the person who supplied the paste to the Repair Department. Cole had not previously been aware of the latter and had immediately given instructions forbidding any tradesman to give any gratuity in future. Cole was, however, further embarrassed when Lipsham wrote to Langdale on 28 February complaining bitterly about the way Palgrave had conducted the inquiry a day earlier and making a number of charges against Cole of employing the workmen for his private purposes and taking office furniture and materials for his own use. He also alleged the wrongful distribution of wood by Paul. Once again Palgrave made inquiries and he told Langdale on 8 March that 'charges brought by a person in the situation of Lipsham must be received with great distrust and assuming Mr Cole's explanations to be correct, which I have no reason to doubt, I think they are satisfactory'. That was not good enough for Langdale, who, while in no doubt as to Cole's probity, minuted: 'This is not satisfactory. I required Sir F. P. not to assume but to inquire & to give me his opinion on the result of the inquiry'. Consequently on 11 March Palgrave reported yet again, saying that he thought Cole's explanations were satisfactory but that the manner in which the workmen had been allowed to use the refuse wood for firewood was improper. He also took the opportunity to comment upon the folding of the *Historical Register* at Carlton Ride by candlelight after office hours. Official attention had been called to that following an anonymous complaint sent to Thomas a month earlier. Palgrave had no doubt that the use of the office premises for that purpose was very irregular and said that 'generally speaking, Mr Cole has by mixing up his private transactions with those of the Office exposed himself to misconception and remark'. Subsequently, he told Cole that Langdale agreed with his opinion and desired him to use more caution in future. But that was not quite the end of the matter for, although Treasury approval was obtained for Lipsham's dismissal, he wrote to Langdale again on 15 March with a long list of complaints against Cole, dating back to his first entry to the record service in 1834, and making further allegations about him. This time, however, Langdale chose to ignore the charges and the unfortunate Lipsham – as much the victim of the inelasticity of the grading system as his own folly – was left to his own devices.[6]

Ever cynical in staffing matters, Palgrave must have allowed himself a wry smile about the embarrassment the Lipsham episode had caused Cole, although the latter's diary entry for 11 March 1845 suggests little change in his standing with Langdale:

> Rolls House: Palgrave showed me his Report. Saw Ld Langdale. He inquired about the Firewood, sd he hoped I wd not allow the charge to trouble me. He had not the slightest doubt there had been no abuses. His manner was very kind & he markedly shook me by the hand. Hardy came & was very hot abt his Clerks being removed from the Office. He cooled and we went away together.

Cole's comments also indicated the calming influence that he often exercised on the more excitable Hardy. Palgrave was probably never aware of that, yet of the many services Cole rendered him during those early years it was among the more useful. Even so, due to a last-minute change of mind by Langdale, Hardy was allowed to keep his clerks. Although Hardy's objection was no more than Palgrave anticipated, he was much put out by it, particularly as, when Kingston was posted to the Tower against his wishes in the previous year, he told Hardy he would be expected to give up one of his clerks at a later date. The reason for that was that Palgrave intended to set up a small Calendaring Department at the Rolls House under his personal supervision. To get it off to a good start he decided to withdraw Lascelles from the Rolls Chapel, but, being unable to replace him by a clerk from the Tower, he now filled the vacancy by moving Fenwick from Carlton Ride instead. Lascelles had previously worked part-time for Palgrave, calendaring patent specifications, and he now gave his undivided attention to that work, which Palgrave thought of great value as showing the progress of mechanical science and as a stimulus to would-be-inventors. In his work Lascelles was assisted by Berkely Buckingham Stafford, a newly-appointed clerk. Palgrave expected much of Stafford, who was well educated and a nephew of Fraser Tytler, but he resigned after little more than a year. However, the work made good progress and the calendar was published by Palgrave in appendixes to his *Reports*, the first portion appearing in the sixth.

Throughout 1845 Palgrave was plagued by staffing problems. That year began inauspiciously when Sir Robert Peel's young relative, Bolton Lennox Peel, fell from a punt while fishing during the Christmas vacation 1844 and

---

6. Lipsham's letter of 12 November 1840 seeking re-employment is entered in PRO 2/87. Most of the papers concerning the affair are in PRO 1/9.

was away from his desk at Rolls House for many months, much to the vexation of Black whose own record of attendance hardly entitled him to criticise. Peel's absences and the general poor state of his health eventually resulted in Palgrave persuading him to resign, and he was succeeded in November 1845 by Frank Scott Haydon, the son of the painter. Haydon, a Cambridge graduate, rapidly proved his worth, although his services were broken for several months in 1846 when he took up a Customs appointment, which he later relinquished. At Carlton Ride Percy Hunt, despite difficulties with his 'Norman French', was proving satisfactory, but his close friend there, Peter Turner, was causing concern by his frequent sick absences. Palgrave told Cole to keep a strict watch on him and when his elder brother, T. Hudson Turner, the antiquary, complained that Palgrave had imputed dissipation, Cole told him that 'his brother's conduct had given some colour to the notion'.[7] Nevertheless, Palgrave eventually satisfied himself that Turner was genuinely suffering from the after-effects of pleurisy and so succeeded in getting Treasury approval for the doctor's recommendation that he should spend the winter in Teignmouth to restore his health. However, in February 1846 Turner was seen in London by Holden, who lost no time in reporting the news to an alarmed and astonished Palgrave, who immediately launched an investigation, blaming Cole for not keeping an eye on Turner's movements. The explanation that the invalid had been too unwell to travel was, nevertheless, accepted by a sceptical office, relieved at not having to report the matter to the Treasury. Feeling let down, Cole was reluctant to take Turner back but was made to do so. In fact, when Turner resumed in the spring his work and conduct proved so satisfactory that he was given his periodic increase in the usual way. By the time Turner came to marry two years later, he had so redeemed himself that Palgrave, after some hesitation, supported Cole in seeking four weeks' special leave for him almost as a mark of the office's approbation. However, Langdale was not willing to consent to that, although he allowed Turner to anticipate a fortnight from his allowance for the following year.

A less happy outcome awaited William George Cooper at the Rolls, whose work continued to be reported as unsatisfactory, and he was to leave in 1846. On the other hand, after a very full enquiry by Palgrave, it was agreed in December 1845 that Manners Fenwick should have his increment. Whether that provided the ease it ought to have done proved debatable as two years later Fenwick was misguided enough to apply to the Treasury to receive his salary weekly instead of quarterly. In response, Trevelyan told Thomas that he would be doing Fenwick an act of kindness by advising him to withdraw his application as otherwise it would be brought to the official knowledge of the Treasury that he was an embarrassed man and therefore unfit for public trust.

---

7. Cole Diary, 6 November 1845.

Customarily, the office took a serious view of laxity by its staff in money matters. A workman owing money to a tradesman was liable to have the debt recovered from his wages, and in 1843 one of Hunter's clerks, J. E. Gibson, had been severely censured for accepting a bill payable at the office, which led to an official regulation strictly forbidding such practice. Two years later Gibson was still far from settling down and a question mark hung over his future, particularly as Palgrave thought there was a degree of boyish unsteadiness in his character which made it necessary to watch him with vigilance.

Palgrave's varying experiences with his clerks reinforced his belief that their method of recruitment was ill suited to the office's needs. He thought the clerks consisted of those who were waiting for something better to turn up and those without hope, and he no longer expected wide-ranging educational attainments. Provided, he said, a clerk had 'good handwriting and a tolerable knowledge of Latin and French, and if to these industry and a proper disposition of mind be conjoined, nothing further is required'. To secure that he wanted the Treasury to sanction the entry of young men by arrangement with public schools, such as Christ's Hospital. Although Trevelyan seemed agreeable, Langdale would have none of it, arguing that 'If two or three bad clerks were rejected, as they ought to be without scruple, it would soon be understood, to the credit of the Record establishment, that we would not keep stupid and ignorant fellows who could not write properly – & they would not be sent'. If such persons had been retained in the past, he thought the fault lay with the office itself. He told Palgrave that it was not good enough for him to rely upon the reports of the assistant keepers because he expected him to inquire personally into the way the clerks performed their work, reporting where remedial action was required as 'the heads of the Office cannot divest themselves of the responsibility and throw it upon the assistant keepers'. Langdale's lofty tone infuriated Palgrave, who defended himself by saying that in no case had an assistant keeper complained during a clerk's probationary period and that he could not 'conceal from your Lordship that the successful opposition afterwards made to my proposition for the removal of a clerk from the Tower to the Rolls had diminished that authority and influence which for the good management of the Establishment I ought, as Deputy Keeper, to possess'. However, he seized the opportunity to turn the tables on Langdale by saying that in future he intended to keep every new clerk for some part of the year at the Rolls House so that he might be able to judge him.[8]

Much of Palgrave's time was also taken up with problems arising from the management of the workmen. One of the consequences of the Lipsham affair was the drawing up by Cole of a unified grading structure, placing

---

8. The Langdale/Palgrave exchanges on this matter are among the papers for October 1845 in PRO 1/9.

them in one of four classes, irrespective of their place of work. Although that provided for an increase in the number of first-class posts at 8d an hour from four to six, Palgrave was not anxious to fill them quickly, fearing it would lead to what he termed 'importunity'. He favoured eventual promotion on the length-of-service principle, but was forced to give way in May 1846 following continuous pressure from Cole and instructions from Langdale. One of those promoted was Robert Logsdon at the Tower. He was said by Hardy to be 'fully qualified to make inventories and catalogues and to perform that class of business which in our service is called clerks' work'. Logsdon had come to Treasury notice in 1843 when he had been awarded £10 for helping to convict a Stationery Office employee of theft. Unhappily for him his intervention proved two-edged for it led to new regulations, which obliged him to give up the trade of a stationer, which he was then combining with his workman's duties. Soon after his promotion confidence in him was badly shaken when he was found drunk on duty, which led to a severe caution from Hardy.

Rightly or wrongly, Logsdon blamed a fellow workman, William Cusack, for his exposure. In August 1846 a chance to get his own back arose when he noticed Cusack leaving the Tower with two sheets of the office's brown paper in which were wrapped his working clothes. Taking advantage of Hardy's absence on leave, Logsdon had Cusack committed to prison for stealing official property. Hardy and Roberts were appalled at what had taken place, and were much relieved when Langdale made arrangements for Cusack's defence, despite his belief that Cusack ought not to have taken the office's paper. When the case went to the Old Bailey the charge was dismissed by the jury. Everyone at the Tower, but Logsdon, was relieved at the outcome, and doubly so when Logsdon chose to resign, coupled although that was with a threat to call for a parliamentary inquiry into the management of records business at the Tower.

Apart from leading to a new grading structure for the workmen, the Lipsham case led to a review of Cole's rules. They were left broadly unchanged, but those governing the grant of additional leave were actually tightened up and such days over and above the normal six days and public holidays were restricted to one or two for 'meritorious' service. Palgrave, who was behind the move, thought the Treasury exceedingly liberal on establishment matters, and in October 1845 expressed alarm at an apparent increase in the sick leave taken by the men. Non-attendance owing to illness needed to be supported by a medical certificate and was paid at the rate of six hours a day only. After a fortnight in any year each case was judged on its merits. Prolonged absence was reported to Palgrave, who now told Cole and Hardy to give their workforces an 'intelligible hint', otherwise, while it would give him great pain, he would be compelled to apply to the Treasury to discontinue the privilege. Cole responded vigorously, producing figures indicating that any increase was slight and due to special factors, such as the unhealthy environment at Carlton Ride. However, Palgrave remained suspicious, but when in March 1847 he went so far as to suggest that certain medical certificates might have been fabricated, Cole countered so effectively that he had no option but to withdraw.

Later that year Cole's management of his men again came under scrutiny when Thomas drew Palgrave's attention to the payments at Carlton Ride for beer, which were running at roughly one-third more than in the previous year. Palgrave thought that they had grown to such an extent that it was necessary to reduce them or get rid of them altogether. Cole reacted fiercely, arguing that the object of what he called the stimulus, usually amounting to a pint a day, was to encourage the men when undertaking unwholesome work and so get value for money. Palgrave doubted whether beer should be allowed merely because the work was disagreeable:

> The men take the good and the bad. The wages, the vacations, and holidays and the permanence of the situation affords very sufficient compensation.
> Items of this description are looked upon with jealousy by the Treasury, extras of any description being discouraged by the Board.

Nevertheless, he agreed that payments might be made occasionally, subject to a certificate that the work concerned was out of the ordinary routine or involved special factors. Cole, now very angry, refused to comply, alleging that he had been left for seven years to institute a system of management without any instruction or assistance whatever and, as his judgment was being called in question, he asked for the whole subject to be referred to Langdale. Palgrave agreed, but insisted it should be set in the context of the rules as a whole. Accordingly, on 27 November 1847 Cole furnished a summary, in the form of a profit and loss account for 1846, setting out the value of the men's labour in relation to their benefits:

	£.	s.	d.		£.	s.	d.
Wages	2034	14	6½	Holidays	118	7	6
less				Illness	32	18	5
Fines, etc	75	5	0	Beer	6	5	9
	1959	9	6½		157	11	8

Cole pointed out that sickness amounted to less than three days annually a man and that fines for unpunctuality, unauthorised absence etc, totalling 3,615 hours, had resulted in some saving of expenditure. Palgrave viewed the matter rather differently, noting that benefits exceeded penalties by £82 6s 8d, but three days later, evidently thinking he had provoked Cole enough, contented himself by telling Langdale:

> Mr. Cole's system works so well as a whole that I should deprecate any material alteration in it and I therefore waive some minor objections and in

particular I do not see any objections to the allowance of beer being continued under the instructions contained in mine of the 19th instant.

This time, for a change, he clearly got the better of it, Langdale minuting:

I see no objection to an allowance of beer made on special occasions only, discreetly, impartially and sparingly; but great care should be taken to prevent it being considered an ordinary perquisite.

Probably little changed until 1851 when Palgrave forbade the payment of beer or refreshment money without his prior approval, but by that time Cole had left the office. A more fundamental setback for Cole occurred in October 1847 when he argued that no one over 18 should be engaged for repair work without special qualifications. Young recruits would then undergo training in the same way as for any other handicraft. Palgrave disagreed, saying that any able-bodied workman who could read and write, and particularly if he had experience of similar work, could soon acquire the necessary skills, under the guidance of an assistant keeper. Palmer, Thomas and Black all differed from Cole and even Hardy backed Palgrave, maintaining that he had had ten times more trouble in teaching boys than men. Hunter gave Cole vague support but did not favour a general rule. He also thought boys might increase the security problem. Palgrave, summing up for Langdale, introduced another factor, providing an insight to his fears about the popular and industrial unrest of the time:

It will be very inexpedient to encourage amongst the workmen such an opinion of their own work and importance as might enable them to combine for the purpose of a strike, which they might be induced to do if supported in the belief that a long training was necessary, however useful such training might be in a particular case.

Usually Langdale was well disposed towards Cole's suggestions but this time he told Thomas verbally that he was not prepared to make a new rule, probably having no wish to upset the broad consensus among the assistant keepers.[9]

In practical terms the internal security problem mentioned by Hunter was far less serious than the office's inability to recover public records once they had strayed from official custody. That became plain in 1842 when the crown lost its action to recover a Common Pleas filacer's roll from Thomas Rodd, the well known bookseller. Rodd entered a spirited defence, issued a pamphlet arguing his case, and was ultimately successful in getting the

---

9. PRO 34/5: Thomas's note to that effect, dated 23 November 1847, is in this index under the entries for 'Workmen'.

Treasury to concede his claim for costs. Rodd himself was willing to part with the roll for 25s and Palgrave admitted that no charge was brought against his character or general respectability. But Langdale deplored the crown's failure to assert its absolute right of property in public records and thought the case had been mishandled.

There was also a scandal involving Marcham John Thorpe, a clerk in the State Paper Office, who had bought certain Exchequer documents privately and then put them up for resale. Although the bookseller concerned surrendered the documents and Thorpe was reimbursed the money he had laid out, the Treasury did not want the case to constitute a precedent, saying it thought the purchase and sale of public records by civil servants for speculative purposes extremely objectionable. However, following the settlement Robert Lemon, senior clerk at the State Paper Office, who had been in the habit of buying Exchequer documents in small lots as they came on the market, surrendered his collection to the government and was awarded £100 by the Treasury. Palgrave looked upon all such proceedings with distaste which hardly made him popular with the trade. Recording a conversation with W. H. Carpenter, the bookseller and publisher and later keeper of prints in the British Museum, Black wrote in his journal for 26 July 1844:

Mr. Carpenter told me that Pickering met FP & asked him whether he intended to seize records whenever he cd. find them, in private hands. Sir FP said 'yes' he did. 'Then', said Pickering 'go to Mr. Dawson Turner's and you'll find plenty of them'. Mr. T is Sir FP's father-in-law!

Black was obviously much amused by that and some restraint must have been placed upon Palgrave on that account for he later warned Turner, a great collector:[10]

For the assistant keepers bring these things before me, and I am compelled to take measures against the parties. I only hope you will not mix yourself up in any transactions of the kind. The documents are trash but I am bound to look after them. The only value of such things is when they form a continuous series.

At much the same time Palgrave was writing to William Wynne, the antiquary, to thank him for the preservation of a seventeenth-century subsidy roll for Merioneth, which had been in his family's possession. In delivering the roll to Hunter, Palgrave told him not to note it in such a way as to indicate it had been out of official custody. That would hardly have been approved by a later generation of archivists, but evidently Palgrave wished to avoid any publicity which might deter other donors. On the other

10. Dawson Turner Papers: Palgrave to Turner, 20 February 1845.

hand, everything possible was done to publicise inventories, catalogues and calendars by printing them at length as appendixes to the *Deputy Keeper's Reports*. Palgrave justified that not only by the value of the information itself but by the proof it gave of a particular leaf or membrane being in official custody. That was one of the reasons for his objecting most strongly in 1848 when Langdale yielded to pressure from the Stationery Office and the Home Office to drop the appendixes on economy grounds. A tentative inquiry from Sir Thomas Phillipps about the prospect of printing them privately failed to progress, and so the publication of calendars and inventories then came to a standstill. In 1852 Phillipps was to try again by having copies of calendars and indexes made at his own expense. By using special paper and ink, he hoped that the copies would serve as 'masters' to facilitate reproduction. But that scheme also failed to prosper as most of the assistant keepers were unenthusiastic, either because they were opposed in principle or because of the disruption they thought it would cause to normal working.

Langdale would have liked Palgrave's *Reports* to have conveyed a rather sharper impression of overall progress since the 1838 act and of the obstacles still to be overcome, but he accepted that the dispersed state of the office made it difficult to bring together the various threads. By way of remedy it was arranged for the assistant keepers to prepare summary reports on their branches over the entire period of their custodianship.[11] However, the truth was that Palgrave wrote his *Reports* not just for administrative purposes but to highlight those projects and activities likely to have most interest for users or potential users of the office's facilities. Besides detailing accessions, work on documents arising out of the Reformation, such as the acknowledgements of supremacy and church goods, was prominently featured, and information concerning past record practices was often supplied, as in the explanation of the ancient Chancery usage of bundling its files under 16 main heads. The names of certain of these – such as the privy seals, purse, staple and gallows bundles – spoke for themselves, but others were arbitrarily designated under pictorial signs. In that latter category fell the stool, horn, pit, and arrow bundles. Precedents for that were drawn from other offices, as, for example, the ancient records of the Custos Brevium, which, as late as 1732, were arranged under the divisions of the heart, the crow, the ladder, the buckle and the bell. Palgrave also used his *Reports* to draw attention to the work being undertaken to repair and conserve seals. They had not always received the care they deserved and particular reference was made by Palgrave to the work in 1845 on the loose but valuable seals previously appended to the barons' letter to Pope Boniface VIII during the reign of Edward I.

Above all else, however, Palgrave constantly argued the need for a central repository. His tactical opposition to that at the time of the controversies of

---

11. These reports are in PRO 34/3.

1836 to 1837 and to the union of what he called the 'ancient or dead records, down to the abolition of Latin and of the court hand', with the 'modern or living records' had given way to a belief that the Public Record Office should, as he stated in his *Second Report*, be 'the Treasury not only of your Majesty's Legal Records but of the Archives in the most extended application of the term'. In view of that it is strange to find the office agreeing in 1839 to release to the English (later the Royal) Agricultural Society certain records of the former Board of Agriculture which had been at the Tower since 1822.[12] The only dissenting voice was that of Petrie, who refused to surrender them until the opinion of the law officers was obtained. But despite the apparent contradiction the office was already looking to the time when its responsibilities might be expanded to embrace the State Papers. The office's particular fear was that if it failed to stake a claim the British Museum most certainly would, which was why Langdale rejected a request by the museum in 1839 to have certain transcripts, then in the State Paper Office, which had been made by M. D'Anisey for the former Record Commission. The 1836 Select Committee had proposed that the older state papers might be sent to the new record office it had in mind, by which, it said, somewhat contradictorily, was meant those 'not later than the Peace of Utrecht (1713) and probably as late as the accession of George III (1760)'. But that recommendation was something of an afterthought, having been included at the instance of Philip Pusey, a member of the Conservative minority on the committee. At any rate, no provision was made for state papers in the Public Records Bill drawn up for Buller in 1837 by Cole. Commenting on the powers given in that bill to the judges, the *Morning Chronicle* in its parliamentary column of 15 March 1837 showed its awareness of the problem, saying 'Surely all the records are not legal merely . . . the scheme is applicable enough to legal, but not to general records of other kinds, even supposing those which are placed in the State Paper Office to be excluded'. Consequently it thought a more comprehensive view would be required, and the draft measure drawn up by Palgrave in May 1837 included a clause providing for the eventual deposit of documents from the State Paper and other offices. Although the order in council proviso was inserted in the 1838 act to catch legal and quasi-legal documents which might escape the net its eventual extension to other records may well have been in Langdale's mind. Thomas thought that to be the case as regards the State Papers and his raising of the matter in the office's early days allowed Palgrave to set out his own views for Langdale on 25 January 1839.[13]

The terms 'Records' and 'State Papers' as employed in our ordinary language, convey mistaken ideas – they are generally understood as if they designated

---

12. Now in the Royal Agricultural Society's archive at the Institute of Agricultural History and Museum of Rural Life at the University of Reading.
13. PRO 2/85, pp 354–356.

two genera of documents having distinct characters, whereas in some of the most essential points their character is identical, forming only two classes of the Public archives – their separation arose from collateral causes and not from any variation in principle. The ancient Chancellor was the general Secretary for all departments for affairs of State as well as for legal proceedings. The fact that the document proceeded from the King was authenticated not by his Sign Manual, signatures not being yet in use, but by the Great Seal. The document was written upon parchment because paper was not commonly employed – and it was entered upon the Roll of Chancery as the King's letter book, because such was the accustomed mode of preserving the needful information. Subsequently, the business of the Royal correspondence passed out of the Chancellor's hands into other departments – the Privy Signet or Sign Manual became the mode of authentication, and paper was adopted instead of parchment; – but the essential character of the documents arising from their connection with the crown or its officers continued unchanged. The same remarks mutatis mutandis apply to Treaties, Proclamations, and other similar State instruments, all of which were entered upon the Chancery Rolls; – and if the so called State Papers be separated from the so called Records, and the first placed in the Museum, and the second in the General Repository, we shall entirely destroy the unity of character which should distinguish the great repository of our national archives.

No early action was taken to resolve the problems posed by the State Papers, but it was not long before the office's attention was directed to difficulties concerning the records of departments other than those of the secretaries of state. In 1841, for example, Hardy was told by a friend, R. P. Cruden, author of the *History of Gravesend*, of a large quantity of Navy Board records lying at Deptford Dockyard neglected, except by those who, in Palgrave's words 'probably made solutions from them'.[14] Due to Hardy's initiative, and with the backing of Langdale and Palgrave, those records, among which were found documents of much historical importance connected with the Dutch War during the Commonwealth, were taken in at the Tower that year. Other transfers of Admiralty material were planned on the understanding that the records remained under its direction and no reference to them was to be allowed except with its consent. Palgrave justified the accession on the precedent established by pre–1838 transfers to the Tower from the High Court of Admiralty, but that was hardly analogous. Meanwhile, the Treasury was considering what it ought to do with its own records. Trevelyan wondered if it should follow the practice of the secretaries of state in sending documents to the State Paper Office, but in January 1842 Palgrave persuaded him against that course. That decision, coupled with the transfer

---

14. Dawson Turner Papers: Palgrave to Turner, 10 March 1841.

of material from certain expired commissions and the completion by Black of a comprehensive survey of the Treasury's older records, led to Langdale writing a letter to it of crucial importance on 8 August 1845. It read:[15]

> I beg leave to state, for the information of their Lordships, my view that in the management of any Documents and Papers which may be transferred from the Treasury or any other Government Office, the General Record Office ought to be merely auxiliary or subservient to the respective Offices to which the Documents and Papers respectively belong; and for that purpose that it would be the duty of the General Record Office:–
>
> To take charge of such Records and Papers as each Office might think proper to transfer, either because they were not required for the current business of the Office, or because they could not be conveniently accommodated within the Office:
>
> To keep the Records and Papers belonging to each Office distinct from all other Records and Papers:
>
> To arrange them, and cause proper calendars and indexes of them to be made:
>
> To hold them for the special use of the Offices to which they respectively belong:
>
> To make searches and transcripts whenever required for the use of Government or Parliament:
>
> To transmit the originals to the Office from which they came, if and whenever required for the use of the Office:
>
> And to afford access and inspection to the public or to individuals, only in pursuance of Orders given by the Head of the Office from which they came, of some person authorised by him; or in pursuance of general or special rules approved by him.

An added and vital reason for the clarification attempted by Langdale was because, although the State Paper Office had moved to new premises in Duke Street only in 1833, they were now seriously overcrowded, and to his alarm it was seeking to enlarge its accommodation. That, he knew, could well be at the expense of the long-awaited 'General Record Office'. By now

---

15. Printed in the appendixes to the *First Report of the Royal Commission on Public Records*, I, pt II (Cd. 6395), 10–11.

spelling out the terms upon which government papers might be held by the Public Record Office he hoped to pave the way for the acceptance by the secretaries of state for home, foreign and colonial affairs of his eventual charge of their papers, because he knew that they would not agree to that unless assured of retaining control. He objected strongly to the indefinite perpetuation of two departments when it was obviously more convenient and economical to have one. But his main argument was that any extension of the State Paper Office would run counter to the intentions of Parliament as expressed in the 1838 act.[16] It may be doubted if that was so, but it suited the Treasury to agree with Langdale, particularly as it favoured his arguments on organisational grounds. Accordingly, in November 1845, following consultation with the offices concerned and further correspondence with Langdale, it was decided that once state papers had reached an age sufficient to confer an historical character upon them they should be transferred to the Public Record Office, where they would be managed on the same principles as those proposed by Langdale for departmental papers generally. The Treasury saw that as the first step in uniting the two offices, but the State Paper Office was far from resigned to its fate. Palgrave strongly favoured consolidation, believing that the Public Record Office would then attract wider public interest and support as its users would no longer be drawn mainly from the legal profession. It would, he thought, also result in better facilities for readers and the possibility of a logical record publication programme as activities would no longer be split between the State Paper Commission and the Public Record Office. But he did not underestimate the difficulties, telling his father-in-law on 24 October 1846:

> It is in contemplation ultimately to bring the state papers into my Department but this must not be mentioned as Hobhouse and the State Paper Commission are putting all their strength the other way; but this cannot be done until we have a new Office and that is a distant prospect which I may never live to see realised.

However, in June 1848 the Treasury's hand was strengthened when the amalgamation of the two offices was recommended by the Select Committee on Miscellaneous Expenditure, although only after the Liberal chairman, Robert Vernon Smith, later Lord Lyveden, had used his casting vote. By Treasury design it was the blunt and direct Cole, and not Palgrave, who gave evidence to the committee when it considered the Record Office vote. As with most such committees, the questioning was often of a tedious and detailed kind and it seems probable that the Treasury did not think it worth bothering Palgrave with such matters. In fact, and quite properly, Cole made it clear to the committee that he was not to be taken as speaking for

---

16. PRO 1/9: Langdale to Trevelyan, 21 July 1845.

108

the deputy keeper or the secretary, who could supply information regarding the general business of the office. The question of the State Paper Office was raised briefly and Cole indicated his belief in the desirability of union. Subsequently he submitted a paper in response to certain questions concerning progress since the 1836 Select Committee report, having first cleared his answers with Langdale.[17] The next move came on 8 August 1848 when the Treasury issued a minute saying that as 'Parliament has made provision for the whole of the State or Public Records of the Country being brought under one central management', the State Paper Office should become a branch of the Public Record Office on the retirement of Henry Hobhouse, the elderly and ailing keeper of state papers. The Treasury decision was taken after consultation with Langdale and was thought by Palgrave likely to prove the greatest boon ever conceded by any government to historical literature. Less loftily, he hoped to make it the basis of a claim for increased pay. However, his fears were re-aroused when early in 1849 the British Museum again applied for certain Record Commission transcripts. Its proposal was forwarded to the Home Office and the Treasury in the name of the trustees by Ellis, which might have been embarrassing for his son had he not resigned from the Public Record Office in 1846. More ominously, the trustees suggested that in the event of any changes being contemplated in the disposition of the public records they should be informed. The interests of historical research would best be served, they thought, if such records were deposited in the National Library, except for those which were of legal importance or contained matters of state policy which needed to be retained by the government. The moving spirit behind these proposals was Madden, who enjoyed the support of Lemon of the State Paper Office, a long-standing opponent of the planned link. Palgrave was well aware of the scheming taking place and thought it imperative to obtain an order in council under the 1838 act to secure the State Papers and legalise the transfers of departmental records that had already taken place. Unless that was done, he feared there could be no security.

Although Langdale strongly disapproved of the museum's proposals, he was not willing to go so far as Palgrave at that stage. He may also have felt that, as a trustee of the museum and as a member of the commission then inquiring into its constitution and management, he was well placed to counter any moves not to his liking. To maintain his independence on the Inquiry Commission he had decided that while it was sitting he would not attend trustees' meetings, which might explain why the museum's proposals had got as far as they had. At any rate, lest there was any doubt as to his views he set them out in a powerful letter to the Treasury on 20 April 1849, in which, after agreeing with the trustees about the need for increased facilities

---

17. *House of Commons Sessional Papers* (1847–1848), XVIII, pt I, 45–46, 311–318, 337–339; Cole Diary, 10 May 1848.

for the consultation of documents, he flatly denied their assumption that the records would be better arranged and managed in the museum.[18]

As a general rule Langdale favoured great publicity and easy access to records of all kinds. But he realised that government departments might wish to restrict the public's access to certain records. Such limits depended mainly upon the dates and subjects concerned, but no formula could be devised to cover every case. For that reason he did not believe that the government could allow its records to be transferred to a non-crown body, like the British Museum, where deposits were constitutionally vested in its trustees. The difficulty about the recovery of strayed public records already there ought to serve as a caution for parting with documents which might be wanted later by the government for public purposes. As regards the transcripts for which application had been made, he thought that they should remain in the Public Record Office where they had already been put to good use. It was also his hope that the time might come when the government, for its own credit and the good of the public, would sanction the resumption of record and historical publications despite 'the distaste occasioned by the imprudences of the late Record Commission'.

Apparently concluding that Langdale's letter effectively disposed of the matter, the Treasury did no more than forward it to the trustees. That suited Langdale, for he was not anxious to oblige Palgrave by seeking an order in council until he knew he was in a position to meet the additional responsibilities it would entail. He was also conscious of the office's many outstanding commitments not only in respect of the accruing records of the superior courts but also for those of the outlying records at Durham and Ely and in Wales. Action was also pending to place under his charge the records of the Palace Court and the Court of the Honour of Peveril, which was later effected when those courts were abolished under the County Courts Act 1849.

Isolated pockets of Welsh records had been transferred to the Rolls House during 1845 and 1846 and Palgrave himself had visited Ely in 1840 while on vacation at Cromer, but with no obvious result. At Durham, the librarian and keeper of the records of the dean and chapter, Joseph Stevenson, who had formerly worked for the Record Commission as a sub-commissioner and was a close friend of Hardy, offered to prepare his records for removal to London in 1844, but that was turned down by Palgrave who preferred to postpone action until he could spare a member of his own staff. In Wales the position was rather better as, following Black's mammoth report of 1839 to 1840, there was a regular correspondence with the local authorities, particularly on questions of custody and the provision of suitable accommodation. In all Welsh matters Palgrave looked to Black, the acknowledged expert. Moreover, it was not unusual for him to seek Black's advice on the

---

18. T 1/5459/8817/1849. For text see Appendix VIII.

interpretation of records generally. He did so partly because Black also worked at the Rolls House, but mainly because he had a great respect for his learning. Black's knowledge of Exchequer records and procedures was publicly displayed when he assisted in the discovery of an outstanding debt connected with the rebuilding of London Bridge, resulting in the payment to the government by the City of London of £1,250 in 1846, 16 years after it fell due. On another occasion, Black's appreciation of the value of certain slave compensation material saved from destruction records which subsequently enabled trustees to administer funded property, in one case amounting to more than £23,000.

Black was at his best when given a specific task. In 1842 he was instructed to report on the older records of the Treasury, a job that took him three years to complete. Both Palgrave and Langdale felt that too long a time, yet the thoroughness of Black's work drew their admiration, as it did Trevelyan's at the Treasury. The evidence of his labours was eventually seen in over one hundred printed pages containing his survey and the related correspondence about it appended to Palgrave's *Seventh Report*. The completion by Black of his long investigation provided a welcome day out for him which he detailed in his journal for 19 June 1845:

> Left home 8 o[clock] in cab for Rolls, got the two great portfolios and went
> by Richmond omnibus to East Sheen for Roehampton (whither I went
> across the fields) reached Lord Langdale's at 10.50 and left at 11½. Delivered
> both copies of my Report and he promised I should not be a loser for
> expenses in this Treasury business. Walked to Putney and dined at Star and
> Garter, returned by 'Lightning' steamboat 1 o[clock].

Cab	1.0
Omnibus	1.6
Dinner	2.8
Boat	6
Omnibus	6
	6.2

> Called on Mr. Cox 2–3½. Returned to Rolls and reported verbally the day's
> business to Sir F.P.

Despite Black's excellent work, relations between him and Palgrave were very strained, largely because of his poor timekeeping, irregular attendance and frequent failure to render reports punctually. Black also considered himself underpaid and that more was required from him by Palgrave than was reasonable. His religious scruples also led him to resent being disturbed on a Saturday, although that did not prevent Palgrave sending messages to Mill Yard on that day if he thought business required it. By the end of 1845 matters had come to such a pass that Palgrave thought that Black should resign, but Langdale was not anxious to force matters. Thomas, a most diligent man, was highly critical of Black's shortcomings and was particularly annoyed that the *Docquets of Letters Patent, Charles I*, which Black had edited for the Record Commission but which needed a little more work to complete, was still outstanding. Cole, Black's one time bête-noire, thought the best plan was to pay him by piece work. Part of Black's defence was his poor health – especially his eyesight – which he thought had suffered from his record work. He attributed his eye trouble to the events arising from a freak storm which swept London at the beginning of August 1846. That downpour was so intense that all the fanlights at the barn-like Carlton Ride were broken and but for the efforts of Cole and his staff the records there would have been extensively damaged. Even at the more solid Treasury Chambers nearby some of the fanlights were shattered, but, worse still, its vault was flooded when a drain burst, soaking the records stored there with foul water from the common sewers. Over the next few weeks Black and some of the workmen toiled to salvage what they could, but the working conditions were so unpleasant that he became ill and had 'to go two days into the country in consequence of inhaling the effluvia'[19] and subsequently his eyes became much inflamed. Those records, which included American and East Florida claims and accounts of the groom of the Stole, were said to have a 'peculiarly offensive and foetid odour' and were covered in a deposit of a 'saline, pungent and irritating character'.

On transfer from the Treasury in 1846 they were put in the Rolls House basement, but the following summer they were placed in the garden under a tarpaulin as their presence in the building was thought to be a hazard to health. A brick structure – described by Cole as a 'temporary shed like a navvies' hut'[20] – was later built in the garden for them and they remained there until the site was cleared in 1850 for the new repository. They were then moved to the loft in the engine house in the Rolls Yard and in 1853 William Lascelles was detailed to work upon them. His association with them proved even more ill-fated than Black's for in his *Fifteenth Report* Palgrave stated that 'in consequence of his [Lascelles's] labours amongst these damp and filthy papers his right eye has been so severely attacked by inflammation that the sight had been entirely destroyed'.

Lascelles's tragic misfortune would not have surprised Black, who had by then ceased to work for the office. But in 1846 Black's constant wrangles with Palgrave placed him very much at the centre of events and he was particularly forthright about his lack of clerical support. In May of that year an attempt was made to ease his difficulties when he was given the full-time services of a new recruit, George Knight, the son of a Scottish professor. Further relief came in September 1846 when Langdale sent him to Ireland

---

19. *Eighth Report of the Deputy Keeper* (1847), Appendix I, 29.
20. *Fifty Years of Public Work* (London, 1884), II, 57.

to report on problems concerning the Exchequer records there, after a plea from the Treasury for assistance. Noting that the Treasury wished to see 'the present efficient state of the Record Department thus turned to extended public use', Langdale drily recorded his pleasure at being able to help 'a neighbour in still greater distress than ourselves'.[21] Black's absence for just over a month, which included an inspection at Caernarvon on his return journey, provided no more than a respite in his clashes with Palgrave, but it did result in his becoming the Irish expert in the same way that he was already the Welsh. Young John Edwards told him he was now the travelling assistant keeper and wondered where he might go next. Although Black's first report was many months in the making, the Treasury was well pleased with it and awarded him £30 in addition to meeting his expenses. That report, and later reports by Black in 1848 and 1849 when he gave assistance to the commissioners on public records in Ireland, may be seen as a real contribution to the process which was to result in the eventual passage of the Public Records (Ireland) Act 1867. But when Irish record reform became a live issue in 1849, it was not helped by the fact that all was not yet well in England. Regretting that the master of the rolls in Ireland had not been consulted about the suggested changes, Langdale told Trevelyan on 11 August 1849:

But if the Repository in Ireland is to be subject to the procrastination and idle controversies, which have delayed the Repository in England and if at the end of 10 years the prospect of obtaining any Repository at all, is to be found in Ireland as remote as ever, as it now is in England, I beg leave to state my decided opinion that having regard to the Public interest the Office of Superintending the Records ought not to be imposed upon a judicial officer charged with duties so important and attended with so much labour and anxiety as fall to the share of Master of the Rolls.

Before commenting formally, however, Langdale told Trevelyan he intended to wait until Palgrave returned from leave so that he might have his opinions. That enabled Palgrave to draw attention to a section of the Common Law Offices (Ireland) Act 1844, which required the Irish judges to inspect their records personally at the beginning of each term to ensure that they were in good condition. Palgrave thought the Irish practice might usefully be employed in England, although acknowledging that deficiencies in the English system had been offset to a considerable extent by Langdale's own 'vigilance and exertions'. Edwards had pointed the same clause out to Black when he first went to Ireland in 1846, but apparently it was honoured as much in the breach as in the observance. In Palgrave's opinion a power was needed in any Irish scheme enabling the officers to destroy 'useless'

---

21. PRO 1/10: Langdale to Trevelyan, 5 September 1846.

records. Attention should also be paid, he thought, to the way legal proceedings were recorded so as to limit documentation. Palgrave also believed that the make-up of the records should be considered and he suggested that the secretary of the Irish Record Commission of Inquiry, J. F. Ferguson, should visit England to see the methods employed at Carlton Ride to pack, label and arrange the records. Finally, he expressed doubts about the proposed adaptation of the English Record Act to Ireland on the basis of the alterations proposed to it by Black, concluding:

> But with every respect for Mr. Black's zeal, learning and knowledge it must
> be recollected that his services have been confined to certain special
> departments, and that he has never had any opportunity of becoming
> acquainted with the affairs of the Record Department, so as to be enabled
> to judge of the general working of the system.

Writing to the Treasury on 23 October 1849, Langdale forwarded Palgrave's letter along with another from Thomas and reiterated his belief that if it was intended to provide a general repository in Ireland it was important that the master of the rolls there should be consulted. Like Palgrave, he thought the courts should be obliged to attend to the way their records were made up and kept. All officers seeking record employment or compensation should also be required to surrender any indexes in their possession. Langdale thought that when the 1838 act was framed it had been wrongly assumed that there was, or might be, a private right to such indexes. Langdale obviously had Palmer's indexes in mind, particularly as some three years earlier both he and Palgrave had been much put out on discovering that Palmer had inserted a note about them in the *Law List* where he was listed as a record agent.

Langdale also suggested that there should be an effective power to recover public records in private hands. He shared Palgrave's concern about the office's inability to secure these and as recently as February of that year, in thanking William Salt, the Staffordshire antiquary, for the presentation of certain tellers' bills had said: 'If the like justice and liberality were found in other quarters the Public would recover many valuable documents which through some misconduct and mismanagement have escaped from their proper place of deposit'.

Because of the importance of having efficient practical men to direct the Irish record establishment Langdale thought it might be appropriate to name two or three of the higher officers in the act. Provided such men could also manage staff he thought all would go well, because while their knowledge of ancient records might not be great that could be acquired, whereas 'men admirable for antiquarian learning if they have not early learnt to be men of business cannot (at a certain time of life) become such & no business or Office can prosper under their guidance'. Thomas, in his letter written at the beginning of August, concentrated on the need to give priority in any new establishment to the arrangement of the records before any calendaring was begun, pointing to the bad experience of the reverse process in the State Paper Office. Honouring an earlier promise, Thomas indicated Hardy's readiness to serve the government in Ireland if required. He went on to say that it would be a very bad policy to appoint a man as deputy keeper (or secretary) simply because he would be entitled to large compensation rather than because he was the best man for the job. That had the appearance of a tilt at Palgrave whose own view was that the new chief officer should be styled 'comptroller of the public records' rather than 'keeper' and should have power to inspect records and enforce compliance with his orders.

As 'deputy keeper' Palgrave's sensitivity about titles was understandable. Langdale's warning against antiquarians may have been directed at him, but more probably it was a caution against the likes of Black, who certainly fell into that category. Black himself had disclaimed any intention of seeking an Irish appointment, while as for Hardy's interest, it seems likely that Langdale had him in mind when he advised the Treasury:[22]

> If their Lordships should not determine to erect a general record Office in Ireland forthwith, I very much incline to think that it would not be useful to appoint a general Keeper of all the Records of Ireland but to appoint an Inspector of the Records of every Court & Office – giving him sufficient authority to inspect all the records and to require the several Officers whose duty it is to take care of them to do all such acts as may be necessary for their due preservation & to make them properly accessible to the public, giving the Inspector power to lay complaints before the Chiefs of the Courts and Offices and giving the Chiefs power to hear & decide upon such complaints & to inflict such punishments as may be proper to secure obedience to their orders.

Langdale's proposal for an inspector of the records of Ireland resembled the suggestion made at the height of the controversies in 1837 that an inspector general or working deputy should be appointed to oversee the English record offices and their keepers. It is possible, if not probable, that on each occasion Hardy was Langdale's candidate. If so, Hardy was twice unfortunate for the Irish plan was no more successful than the English one. In fact, it was not until after Hardy's appointment as deputy keeper in 1861 that fundamental Irish record reform was again attempted.

That failure must have been a considerable disappointment for Hardy because there seemed little prospect of advancement at home while Palgrave remained in post, and Cole's diary for 12 November 1849 records him as saying that he would go to Ireland if he could. He had not long completed the first volume of Petrie's *Monumenta Historica Britannica* with the added

---

22. Most of the papers concerning the possible reform of the record-keeping system in Ireland are in PRO 1/13. Some of Black's papers are in PRO 1/121/5.

satisfaction of the grant of his petition to dedicate it to the queen. For this task, for which J. M. Kemble had also, but unsuccessfully, applied, Hardy was awarded the sum of 200 guineas by the Treasury. However, following its publication in 1848 Hardy's further proposal that work on these 'Materials for the History of Britain' should be continued on the lines of Petrie's plan was hanging fire, and so Petrie's manuscripts remained in official custody under Palgrave. Any personal ambitions that Palgrave still entertained concerning them he kept to himself, but it had been the policy to lend out particular sections to approved applicants such as the Camden Society and the Society for Printing and Publishing Ecclesiastical Documents. On Palgrave's recommendation Dr John Allen Giles, the Anglican scholar, had also been allowed to borrow some of them in connection with his life of Becket and other works. As Giles was also seeking official approval to publish Petrie's material on his own account, Hardy was worried in case it might wreck his own design to continue the work, which he hoped to pursue in association with Stevenson and Brewer. As it happened, Giles's plans came to grief when it was found that certain of the transcripts he had borrowed had been mutilated as a result of his foolishness in letting them out to his printer.

At one time Hardy believed that Palgrave was actively promoting Giles's cause, and was relieved to find that he had, in fact, been behaving quite neutrally. Consequently Hardy felt able to show Palgrave his own preface to the *Monumenta* and to seek his comments, although he knew Palgrave to be a long-standing critic of the Bouquet editorial method followed by his former master. Explaining his reasons for doing so, Hardy told Stevenson:[23]

> Whatever my anxiety may be to defend Petrie through thick and thin I do not think I ought to peril the success of our great work by any injudicious defence especially as my conviction does not go the whole length. I perfectly, therefore, agree with you in thinking that it would be better to advise a modification of the plan – I have seen Palgrave since he wrote his letter to me and I told him I thought he would *approve* of what I had said, and I offered to let him see the sheets before they were worked off. He said he would read them over with much pleasure. I therefore send those pages to you which contain an exposition of the plan. You can make it harmonise as much as possible with Palgrave's views so that it does not reflect on poor Petrie whom I so dearly love and venerate.

Although the great personal distrust that existed between Palgrave and Hardy was never far from the surface, they had a genuine respect for each other's professional competence. When Devon launched yet another attack at the end of 1847 against Cole and Palgrave concerning the casing of an

---

23. PRO 1/124: Hardy to Stevenson [February 1848].

indenture of Henry VII and the state of the records at the Chapter House, Hardy expressly excluded Palgrave from his characteristically forthright condemnation of 'the criminal neglect of duty of the several Keepers of the Records in the Chapter House'.[24] Prudently, however, he refused to allow his opinion to be made known to Devon.

Since 1846 Hardy's relations with Palgrave had been relatively good. In April of that year Palgrave agreed to appoint as a workman at the Tower a young man, Edward Charles, at Hardy's personal recommendation, and in August, again at his request, allowed him the services of the 18-year-old James Gairdner, a clerical recruit of obvious promise. Two years later Palgrave took issue with the Tower officers about whether there should be a single index for persons and places mentioned in the Patent Rolls or, as he preferred, a separate index for each. Roberts took the main fire and the exchanges, in which Hardy and Brewer joined, were conducted without acrimony. To settle the matter Palgrave referred it to Edward Smirke, the lawyer and antiquary, and accepted the position when he ruled against him. The following year, however, serious differences broke out when Palgrave suggested he had been misled by Hardy concerning the amount of time needed to complete the repair and arrangement of the inquisitions post mortem and ad quod damnum. Somewhat self-righteously, Hardy denied that, emphasising the efforts he had been making to accommodate Palgrave in a letter dated 14 May 1849:[25]

My dear Sir,

. . . with respect to my not making any remonstrance when you desired the Privy Seals & Royal Letters to be pushed on, I think it due to myself that *twice* when I felt it my duty to object to certain orders you had given it created unpleasant differences between us & I determined for the future merely to follow your directions, hoping thereby to prevent any collision of opinion between us which might end in bringing the matter before Lord Langdale – I have but one object, which is to do my duty as pleasantly as I can to others as well as to myself, so that whenever a misunderstanding takes place I may have the satisfaction of knowing it did not commence with me.

Believe me to be very truly

T. Duffus Hardy

Because Hardy had few interests outside records he felt deeply when differences occurred within the office, whereas Cole, whose relations with

---

24. PRO 1/11: Hardy to Cole, 22 December 1847.
25. PRO 1/13.

Palgrave were, in many ways, infinitely more turbulent, was rarely upset for long as he was always able to turn his mind to other things. In 1846 and 1847 Cole was a regular contributor to the *Railway Chronicle* and held a retainer from the London and North Western Railway Company to promote their case in favour of the uniformity of the gauge. In 1846 he also branched out commercially with his Felix Summerly Art Manufacturers and became actively involved in the work of the Society of Arts, taking a particular interest in the organisation of exhibitions. The management of schools of design also interested him and in September 1848 he was given a commission by the Board of Trade to report on the production of designs for government departments and the workings of the act for the regulation of the copyright of design. That work and patent reform also brought him into contact with Charles Dickens who 'wondered at the flocks of sheep that had been partners in the Records'.[26]

In the autumn of 1848 trouble flared up between Palgrave and Cole when his brother Charles took a cab from Carlton Ride to the Tower with certain records and copies in order to get them authenticated by Hardy, when they might just as well have been certified at the Rolls Chapel which would have meant a shorter journey and less expense. Shortly afterwards Cole took some papers and reports of James Pennethorne, the future architect of the new repository, to Langdale at Roehampton and was furious when Palgrave refused to pay his railway fare of 2s 5d without more information. To make matters worse, the claim was returned to Cole, unenclosed, through Paul, his foreman. An indignant Cole was told by Langdale that he thought Paul should not have been involved, but 'he had better excuse Sir FP jealousy and frailty'.[27] Palgrave may well have been irritated by Cole's activities for the Board of Trade and by his close links with Langdale, but when Cole, ignoring Langdale's advice, protested vigorously to Palgrave about his want of confidence in him, a skilful attempt at pacification followed.[28]

My dear Sir,

Your explanation is entirely satisfactory, but when Mr. Thomas sent your memorandum into me for my sanction, I could not on the face of it give any other answer as that which he noted.

You must be aware that it is one of the peculiarities of my situation as Deputy Keeper that I am compelled frequently to take the ungracious side

---

26. Cole Diary, flyleaf, 1847. Cole's conclusions and reports on designs were later laid before the Select Committee on the School of Design before whom he also gave evidence: *House of Commons Sessional Papers* (1849), XVIII, 208–247, 337–347, 376, 392–409.

27. Cole Diary, 6 November 1848.

28. PRO 1/12: Palgrave to Cole, 8 November 1848.

in making objections etc, but I do so with great regret, whilst at the same time I am happy to add that there are few occasions on which it is ever needful for me to do so, & particularly with respect to yourself.

We are beginning, I hope, to recover from the disrepute in which all Record concerns have been so long involved, but it is only by strict attention even to small particulars that we shall acquire a good character.

Yours truly

F. Palgrave

Whereas Cole saw the record ructions of the 1830s as the precursor of the millenium, Palgrave thought them responsible for bringing discredit on the record service and thought it unlikely that the ill effect of those quarrels and recriminations would be removed within his lifetime. But for all his bitterness and resentments – 'we are doing all the dirty work (not metaphorically but literally)', as he once told George Cornewall Lewis at the Home Office[29] – by the mid–1840s he was beginning to feel less personally burdened as his two older sons, Francis and William Gifford, were coming to the end of their studies at Oxford with every prospect of promising careers. For a short time a place was found for Francis in Gladstone's Private Office and Trevelyan kept an eye open for a more permanent posting. That led to an appointment in the Education Department, but it was as an anthologist, especially for *The Golden Treasury*, once widely used as a poetry book in schools, that Francis was to earn fame and is best remembered. 'Giffy', as Palgrave called him, became a Jesuit and went to the Middle East as a missionary. He later left the order and had a distinguished diplomatic career.[30a] Besides family concerns, Palgrave took a lively interest in the world around him. Although he no longer mixed in political circles, he followed closely the great controversies of the day. When the Corn Laws were repealed, he told his father-in-law:[30b]

The Tories are stark staring crazy. Their first opposition to Peel brought in the Reform ministry – their present dogged personal antipathy will bring in *radical* reform.

---

29. PRO 1/12: 20 June 1848. Needless to say nail brushes and clothes brushes for officers were a stock issue, at least until 1860 when the Office of Works began to make difficulties about supplying them and they had to be bought, when required, out of the vote for contingencies. Palgrave thought them 'absolutely necessary for ordinary decency', but as late as 1927 Works needed persuading before authorising supply.

30a. See M. Allen's *Palgrave of Arabia: The life of William Gifford Palgrave 1826–1888* (London, 1972).

30b. Dawson Turner Papers: Palgrave to Turner, 30 June 1846.

Two years later he wrote:[31]

The new revolution is ever more portentous than the first. That was directed
against the landed proprietors – this against the capitalists. I think it may
possibly take a fearful ravage. The 'communists' have many partizans in this
country – what say you to Cobden as Premier?

Shortly afterwards, as the Chartist troubles came to a head, Palgrave
feared for the safety of the record offices, thinking that they might, as on the
Continent, become the object of popular attack as they contained documents
establishing aristocratic rights and title to land. Early in April 1848 the staff
of the office were sworn in as special constables, but on the day of the great
demonstration the riots that even Cole expected did not materialise and all
passed peacefully.

Although distrustful of the radicals, Palgrave was enough of a politician
to trim when necessary. When Charles Buller initiated a brief parliamentary
debate in June 1846, proposing the establishment of a select committee to
report on the best means to provide a general record office, Palgrave wrote
to him shortly afterwards offering office assistance and enquiring about
progress. Little came of that, however, as Buller's appointment to the post
of judge advocate general in Russell's new ministry meant that he was unable
to pursue the matter. He was to die tragically young in 1848. It was intended
that Edward Protheroe MP, the former record commissioner, should take
over but, although he succeeded in getting a motion in the House on 25
August 1846 calling for the building of a new record office without delay,
which led to the matter being referred to the metropolitan improvement
commissioners, he was to leave Parliament in the following year. Buller's
friend Richard Monckton Milnes (later Lord Houghton) attended to the
matter but fitfully thereafter.

Buller's suggested select committee investigation had arisen from the
failure of the original Treasury proposal to house the records in the Victoria
Tower. That scheme came to grief in 1844 when Cole's calculations revealed
that the Tower was not large enough to accommodate the quantity of records
involved. In 1845 a makeshift plan by Barry to utilise the roof space in the
new Houses of Parliament instead was also dropped following an inspection
and unanimous condemnation by Palgrave, Thomas and the four senior
assistant keepers. Despite Treasury reluctance to accept the final abandonment of the Victoria Tower and the Palace of Westminster site, by 1847
hopes of progress rested with the metropolitan improvement commissioners
whose *Sixth Report*[32] proposed the building of a record office on the Rolls

---

31. Dawson Turner Papers: Palgrave to Turner, 28 February 1848. The term 'com-
munist' was used in the 1840s to describe those who believed in the equal distribution
of property.
32. *House of Commons Sessional Papers* (1847), XVI, 349–400.

Estate as part of a grand plan for a new street running roughly from Long Acre in the west to Cheapside in the east. But the government displayed no enthusiasm for the ambitious designs of the commissioners or for an alternative in 1848 from Henry Robert Abraham, architect to the Westminster Improvement Commission, by adapting and extending Westminster Prison for record purposes. The one surviving hope lay in a resolution urging that the question of a new building should be speedily resolved, which had been approved by the same Select Committee on Miscellaneous Expenditure that had recommended the fusion of the State Paper Office and the Public Record Office. However, a proposed addendum suggesting that such a building might permit the destruction of a great portion of the records failed to win support.[33]

In all these schemes and discussions Langdale and Palgrave were much involved. Most of the executive work detailing the office's exact requirements was, however, delegated to the practical Cole. Furthermore, there was a sense in which he acted almost as Langdale's 'roving ambassador' to Westminster and Whitehall. But by 1849, in spite of all efforts, progress seemed as distant as ever. Langdale's disgust was made known to Trevelyan when he wrote to him about the Irish records on 11 August in a letter which has already been quoted. A few months earlier Palgrave had commented, sourly and pessimistically:[34]

the erection of a Public Record Office is a matter in which no one takes any interest, except the individuals belonging to the Department. I am tolerably certain that, so far as the Public Press is a token, not a line was ever inserted, excepting by individuals connected with the Record Department. Nor do I believe that a word ever yet has been said in their favour in Parliament, except when suggested by one of the very few who feel a personal interest therein. It is a matter about which no one cares except ourselves.

As for Cole, he was beginning to realise the limited opportunities the office had to offer and was becoming increasingly involved in the affairs of the Society of Arts. That association brought him into close contact with Prince Albert and the early planning for the Great Exhibition. At first it seemed that Cole assumed he might combine his official duties with his promotional work on behalf of the great event, particularly as he knew that Langdale had come to think that the salaries of the assistant keepers were too low and that they could not be blamed for doing other things. In October 1849, when Cole applied for six days extra leave for Exhibition purposes, a doubtful Palgrave asked Langdale for a ruling, only to be told:[35]

---

33. *House of Commons Sessional Papers* (1847–1848), XVIII, pt I, 48.
34. PRO 1/13: Palgrave memorandum, 27 March 1849.
35. The exchanges between Langdale and Palgrave about the grant to Cole of additional leave are in PRO 1/13.

What endeavours are proper? Is it clear whether extra employments are more or less inconvenient or dangerous to the service in proportion to their being more or less connected with the public or official employments. Writing histories, or dissertations or reviews on subjects of history as shewn or illustrated by Official documents in charge of the Officers, will by some be thought more fitting, & by others be thought most likely to seduce the officer from the strictly official line of duty – plausible reasons may be given for very different opinions.

Cultivating – or even teaching – abstract science or painting – drawing – music etc – or exhibiting specimens of art – will by some be thought particularly eligible, because the subjects are in general remote from those which are the special object of official consideration.

Palgrave, who was working on his *History of Normandy and of England* at the time was much upset by Langdale's letter, having no doubt it was aimed at him. Indicating that irrespective of the principle involved, no harm would be done to the office if Cole's request was granted, Palgrave's reply, dated 5 October 1849, ended bitterly:

The general question presents difficulties to your Lordship, but far greater to me. I have felt its stringency to my great pecuniary loss, first in relinquishing employment, & next in abstaining, according to your Lordship's intimation (*under circumstances which you may perhaps recollect*) from seeking another profitable employment to add to my income. Therefore as a party concerned, I will not give any opinion upon the general subject, now or hereafter. In the present case, I did not seek to obtain any other decision, except such as might exonerate me from official liability. I have brought the matter before your Lordship, & there it rests.

An angry Langdale replied on the next day to express his disapproval of Palgrave's letter, and to remind him of his duty to answer any question properly put to him, and 'that you cannot, so easily as you seem to imagine, be exonerated from official liability'. But by now Cole was so busy with Exhibition planning that it was obvious that something more than a few days' extra leave would be required, and the severance of his long connection with the record service became inevitable when he accepted an appointment in December 1849 to the Executive Committee of the Royal Commission for the Exhibition. Palgrave watched developments with a critical, if not envious, eye and Cole's diary for 18 December indicates an unedifying scene in which Palgrave gave vent to his frustrations, blaming everyone from the prime minister downwards for his discontents:

Sir F.P. called & sd. he thought I must retire – that he might live in the Country and take professorship of History: that indeed Ld. J Russell had proposed to appoint a blind man to the Dy Keepership etc. – very jealous.

However, a letter written by Palgrave that same day to his father-in-law conveys a rather different impression:

Cole is about to quit this service – and the vacancy will, as is often the case, draw on considerable changes and I am in communication with the Board of Works concerning the erection of a general repository in the Rolls Gardens. I have been employed for many weeks in calculating and details. I hope we can start with £30,000, a large sum, but not more than the extreme importance of the building will warrant. Previous estimates were £140,000 which of course frightened the Chancellor of Exchequer out of his wits – but this included official houses and a vast lot of superfluity and much architectural magnificence. My belief, or rather certainty, is that from £40,000 to 45,000 will do all that can be really wanted and required.

Nevertheless, it was clear from a letter written by Palgrave to his father-in-law three days later that he was under much strain for he complained that although he hoped to spend Christmas with him, his stomach continued to be 'incessantly delicate and feeble – and roast turkey and mince pies and plum pudding will be taboo as long as I live'. Resentment may well have contributed to Palgrave's indigestion, but more important was the renewed zest with which he was tackling the question of a new repository. One of Cole's last acts concerning that matter was to go over Palgrave's plans with Pennethorne on the final day of 1849. Palgrave, subordinating any personal preferences, was determined upon a purely functional structure, realising that any suggestion of extravagance would lead inevitably to a Treasury veto. A fresh proposal had also emerged in a pamphlet from James Ferguson, the architect, to remove the Sculpture, Antiquities and Natural History Departments from the British Museum, and to replace them by the records, but his plans, which also envisaged a new National Gallery, failed to attract official backing.[36]

Immediately, however, the terms upon which Cole was to take up his new duties had to be settled and the New Year saw much wrangling on the matter between Langdale and Palgrave, illustrated by Langdale's refusal to receive a letter from Palgrave headed 'private and confidential' until that marking was removed. In Palgrave's opinion Cole had to make a clean break, but he was willing to reinstate him if he chose to return when the Exhibition was over. Privately, Palgrave thought that unlikely and by 4 May 1850 was telling his father-in-law of the 'great *sconvolgimento* in our Office in consequence of Mr Cole's secession' and going on to say: 'I don't expect he will ever return to this humdrum department. Prince Albert swears by him, as folks say'. Palgrave's reconciliation to Cole's good fortune had not taken long to assert itself, and on 25 February 1850 Cole wrote in his diary:

---

36. James Ferguson, *Observations on the British Museum, National Gallery, and National Record Office, with suggestions for their improvement* (London, 1849).

At Rolls. Sir F.P very courteous: thought I shd. be celebrated over the world. Ld. Langdale had written answer to the Treasury himself.

Throughout the negotiations about Cole's future status Langdale had been hoping to keep some kind of link with him, but he was much put out on realising that that was not possible, and when Cole called upon him shortly before taking up his new appointment on 1 April 1850 he referred to him as 'Mr. Stranger Cole'.[37] That autumn Cole tried to restore the old relationship, but on going to the Rolls House found Langdale 'too much engaged' to see him. That must have upset him rather more than Palgrave's insistence that he 'must not go in before him'. The next day Cole walked over to Templeton House, Roehampton, only to find that Langdale had gone to town. Lady Langdale tried to make amends by showing him round the garden instead.[38] But Cole's great respect for Langdale remained undiminished and when he and Marian christened their fourth daughter a few weeks later, on 23 September 1850, they named her Isabella Langdale.

In fairness to Langdale, it was apparent by 1850 that official burdens were affecting his health and his customary urbanity. Quite apart from his exacting judicial work and his Public Record Office and British Museum responsibilities, he had the daunting task of attempting to unravel the appalling complexities of the land transfer system through his chairmanship of the Registration and Conveyancing Commission, a post he had held since 1847. Little wonder that the various strains were beginning to tell and that he was determined to resign in 1851. That resolve was not at first generally known, but he indicated as much to Palgrave in the summer of 1850 and also told him that Sir John Romilly, the attorney general and MP for Devonport, would probably succeed him if the Whig/Liberal government remained in power.[39]

Langdale's lessening involvement in office affairs allowed Palgrave a freer hand in settling the succession to Cole than might otherwise have been the case. That proved a complicated matter when Holden, the senior class II man, refused to move from the Rolls, much to Palgrave's annoyance. The next in line was Devon, who was lobbying hard, but Palgrave knew that Hunter was vehemently opposed to having him as a colleague at Carlton Ride. Cole also retained sufficient interest in the office to express his strong disquiet at the possibility of Devon succeeding him, and as Cole's clerks shared his feelings Palgrave knew that to move Devon to the Ride would invite trouble. Nevertheless, Palgrave had decided, not without hesitation, to give Devon a chance, but only after he had been made to apologise for

---

37. Cole Diary, 27 March 1850.

38. Cole Diary, 19 and 20 August 1850. Templeton House is still standing and is now used as a college of education under the Froebel Institute. It is situated in Priory Lane close to the Roehampton Gate, Richmond Park.

39. Dawson Turner Papers: Palgrave to Turner, 27 July 1850.

past disrespects. Consequently Devon, who had been doing good work on records of the Courts of Wards and Requests at the Chapter House, was upgraded there in post, and Roberts was transferred from the Tower to take Cole's place at the Ride on the implied promise that he might expect the next class I vacancy. To complete the moves, Petrie's nephew, H. J. Sharpe, the senior clerk, was promoted to the second class to succeed Roberts. Ideally, Palgrave would have liked to move Sharpe to the Ride, but his lack of experience in controlling staff hardly fitted him for the management of the large force of workmen there.

Black was excluded from the field of promotion for Cole's post as Palgrave had told Langdale that as soon as the office reorganisation was completed he proposed to raise with Black the question of his continued employment. Accordingly, on 20 April 1850, he told Black:

> In other words the yoke which the situation of an assistant keeper of records imposes is too heavy for you and your continuance in the employment will only compel me to be continually animadverting upon your deficiencies and you to continue in unavailing efforts to supply them. The exact causes whether physical, mental or arising from other engagements I cannot ascertain, but such is the result . . . I am glad, however, that the delay [arising from Cole's retirement] has ensued for it will give you the opportunity (which I *most* earnestly hope you will embrace) of resigning your situation . . . and if any arrangements can be made by which you can be employed upon special missions or inquiries connected with the records or public papers generally, such inquiries not needing continuous attendance during Office hours in an Office, the arrangement would, I believe, be very useful to the public service.

Luckily for Black, three days before Palgrave wrote to him, he had submitted an application for special leave because of his continued eye trouble so that Langdale felt obliged to express reservations about the course favoured by Palgrave, when he wrote to him on 24 April, in a tactful letter which also indicated the growing pressure of business upon him:[40]

> It is unfortunate that this discussion with Mr Black should have arisen upon an application by him for leave of absence on the ground of ill health – I know it to be otherwise – but it will bear the appearance of taking advantage of the occasion & this much the rather, if he has observed the conditions imposed when I last saw him in your presence. I am glad to notice the kind and considerate tone in which your last letter to him is expressed – but it would unavoidably seem very hard if any new irregularities have been forced upon him by infirmity & ill health & could not [be] attributed to his old fault.

---

40. PRO 1/14.

It is very difficult for me to find a time in which I can see you at present but if you can be here at 3 – I shall be able to give a few minutes today.

Thanks to Langdale, Black's request for leave was granted, but it was accompanied by a stern warning from Palgrave that 'should the necessity occur, which I trust it will not, of acting up to the intimation contained in mine of the 20th April, the conduct I should then have to pursue, would be scarcely less painful to you than to me'. The possibility of further upheavals in the staffing of the office was now very much in Palgrave's mind and the lesson of Sharpe's unpreparedness for work other than that of an editorial kind had not been lost upon him. At one time Palgrave had thought it unwise for a young man to attach himself to what he considered a 'lean' concern, but he now realised that prospects were brighter than formerly. On the whole he had a good opinion of his more senior clerks, particularly Edwards, Lascelles and Burtt, and recognised the need to increase their responsibilities in readiness for higher duties. Of the 11 clerks installed at the time of consolidation in July 1840 no fewer than 9 remained in post, and all enjoyed good health apart from Moses Green under Hunter at Carlton Ride. The position of the clerks nominated subsequently was very different: although 21 had been sent from the Treasury since that time 9 had ceased duty, mainly at their own request. Of those remaining, Bond, Gairdner and Kingston were thought generally satisfactory and Turner, after his uncertain start, also fell into that category. Palgrave thought Haydon very able and Sanders, Knight, Hunt and May were considered good at their work, but all of them had poor sickness records. Question-marks continued to hang over Fenwick and Gibson, while Yonge had insufficient service to be judged although by early 1851 Palgrave considered that he was behaving well and possessed very good abilities.

But life for the young clerks in those grim unlit offices must have been singularly unattractive, especially as much of their time was spent making copies of the records for searchers. They also undertook calendaring and other editorial work, but there was not much scope for individual initiative, although Palgrave made it clear that it was in that field that they could best demonstrate their record knowledge and show that their hearts were in the work. Some idea of the conditions at that time can be gained from the testimony of James Gairdner when he came to give evidence to the Royal Commission on Public Records over sixty years later:[41]

As a young man I thought myself very wise and that I could improve things very much; but my duty was laid down for me and I could not discuss it with people. I felt I was set to do work and could not even talk over the system and the way of doing it. I have since found by experience that the plan laid

---

41. *First Report of the Royal Commission on Public Records*, I, pt III (Cd. 6396), 68.

down by Sir Francis Palgrave for the Calendar of Patent Rolls was really not a bad one but there was a difficulty in getting explanations sometimes.

If the lot of the young gentlemen was unenviable, that of the rest – collectively styled 'workmen' – was infinitely worse as the only recognised avenue of promotion open to them at that time was within their own ranks. The more experienced were engaged in repairing and binding, while others undertook a certain amount of transcribing, sorting and listing work of a fairly straightforward kind. But many of them were engaged on general repository duties, such as packing, stamping and ticketing, as well as work connected with the production of documents for officers and searchers, and the movement of records within the building and cleaning. Inevitably, Cole's departure led to Palgrave exercising more control over them, and in November 1850 he decided to stop them using pre-printed medical certificates with the Carlton Ride address, which they were accustomed to take to their doctor for completion if they were away sick. Palgrave had long thought that such forms might be used fraudulently and considered that their official appearance could result in medical men filling them in almost as a matter of course. Always inclined to be suspicious, he told Roberts on 16 November to report specially on all sick cases, because 'I am sure you will not grudge any trouble in preventing the abuses which might deprive the deserving workmen of the charitable aid which our present practice allows'.[42]

While Roberts did not have Cole's flair, he was by no means in thrall to Palgrave and contested matters with him when he considered that necessary. Like Cole, he thought the rule restricting the men's daily holiday pay to six hours most unjust. Consequently, when they petitioned in June 1850 to be paid at the rate of the eight hours they normally worked, he gave them his full support. Hardy joined with him in that, but Palgrave was unimpressed, calling some of the men before him to reject their request. He felt his stand vindicated when he read in the *Quarterly Review* at the beginning of 1851 that the workmen at the British Museum were not paid at all for illness or holidays and urged the office workmen to avoid 'any conduct which may tend to any abuse of the great indulgences granted to them or any encroachments upon the consideration which has been extended to them'.[43] Palgrave was a strange mixture and on one occasion in April 1850, while visiting Carlton Ride, mentioned to Bond and Paul that a kitchen or mess-room might be provided for the workmen in the new building. That suggestion, coming from such a source, persuaded Paul to circulate it to the men at the Tower, which upset Hardy, as it was the first he had heard of it, and led Palgrave to tell him that Paul had no authority to put himself forward in the way he had done and that although 'I will assume that he has done so

---

42. PRO 1/14.
43. PRO 1/15: Palgrave to Roberts, 15 January 1851.

inadvertently, still I consider the proceeding very improper and will take care to express my disapprobation'.[44]

Apart from his staffing problems, Palgrave's main concern during the early months of 1850 was to obtain official clearance for the building of the new repository and he was in close contact with Pennethorne, whom he thought 'very clever', about the practical details. For the first time the signs looked favourable and by the beginning of April Palgrave was sufficiently sure that funds would be forthcoming to insert a note to that effect in his *Eleventh Report* for 1849. However, instead of joining in the jubilation, the best Langdale could do was to question the propriety of Palgrave's action, thinking it 'odd – to say the least of it – that it should become the office of the Deputy Keeper of Records – to inform HM of what has been determined by the LC of Her Treasury'. But Palgrave, scenting success, was not prepared to be put off quite so easily and on 16 May told Langdale:[45]

On Tuesday Lord Seymour sent for me, he also saw Mr Pennethorne, & I believe that the communications made to & with the Treasury amount virtually to an approval. But I agree with you as to the apparent oddity of the information given to Her Majesty by the DKR and therefore perhaps some slight expression of hope entertained will answer the purpose better than the statement now inserted.

Langdale made no further objection, and so a general statement appeared from Palgrave expressing extreme satisfaction at the intention of the Treasury 'to commence the building of the Repository so emphatically urged by his Lordship the Master of the Rolls, and so long desired'. In July 1850 Parliament voted the sum of £30,000 in part of the estimated total cost of £45,320 and a delighted Palgrave wrote to his father-in-law on 27 July, rejoicing at what, in the light of past disappointments, was a startling turn of events, symptomatic of the growing national confidence in its future:

But of course I can never see its completion. It will be one of the first of its kind and even Joseph Hume will be satisfied with the economy exerted. No ornamentation or decorations of any sort and indeed they would be quite out of place in a structure of which the beauty ought to result from strength and utility.

The correspondence about the new building from the time Palgrave had drawn up fresh proposals in December 1849 was laid before the Commons with the 1850/1851 estimates in July 1850.[46] Those papers, which were accompanied by a plan, made it clear that above all else Palgrave wanted

---

44. PRO 1/14: Palgrave to Hardy, 16 April 1850.
45. PRO 1/14.
46. *House of Commons Sessional Papers* (1850), XXXIV, 485–501.

the new record office to be fireproof. For that reason it was proposed to break the building down into a large number of strong rooms so that any outbreak of fire could be isolated. For the same reason central heating was ruled out, Palgrave quoting the views of Braidwood about the fire risks then associated with such systems. Moreover, Palgrave, like many others at the time, thought artificial warming of the air responsible for much bad health. Neither did he think it necessary for the preservation of the records, citing many notable repositories where its absence had not led to harm and in proof of his contention referring to Domesday Book, which from its first deposit at Winchester in the reign of the Conqueror 'certainly never felt or saw a fire, yet every page of the vellum is bright, sound and perfect'. More mundanely, he pointed to the way the condition of the damaged Treasury records had remained stable from the time of their deposit in the unheated building in the Rolls Garden. He also called in aid the testimony of Sir William Hooker, director of Kew Gardens. Hooker, who was married to Lady Palgrave's older sister, expressed full agreement with Palgrave, based upon his experience of the preservation of vegetable matter in the Herbarium. With parliamentary sanction assured, Palgrave was in high hopes that the building might be roofed within two years, but that proved over-optimistic. Even at the outset the clearance of the site and necessary excavations, scheduled to begin in October 1850, were a month late in starting.

Meanwhile, Palgrave was calling the attention of the assistant keepers to the importance of directing all their operations 'consentaneously' to the task of preparing the records for transfer to the new building. But once again Black was causing him concern. His absence for 19 weeks during the first nine months of the year led Palgrave to warn him on 26 October 1850 that 'I am therefore driven into the necessity of making this unpleasant communication to you, wishing to preserve to the Establishment the advantages of your talents and to yourself the advantages the situation affords'. To aggravate matters, a few weeks later Black took part in a deputation to the home secretary from the Whitechapel Association for promoting habits, leading to cleanliness, health and comfort of the industrious classes and when Palgrave read of it in *The Times* of 19 November he told Black his action was not right or proper and 'I must request that any such attendances may in future be discontinued, unless you are preparing to retire from the Service'. Black responded the same day with vigour, demanding to know if he was to understand Palgrave's letter as a threat. That resulted in Palgrave handing him a memorandum on 20 November explaining his views:[47]

It is most disagreeable and abhorrent to my feelings to exercise any species
of espionage over the Gentlemen of this Department, or in any way, directly
or indirectly, to interfere with them in their private capacities . . . Except

---

47. PRO 1/14.

with the express permission of the Master of the Rolls, I do not consider it
as consistent with the public duty of an Officer in this Department that he
should form part of any Deputation to the Secretary of State for the Home
Department or any Government or Public Functionary whatever; and that
it is a great impropriety so to do . . . With respect to Mr. Black's reference
to my letter of 26th October, Mr. Black, if he think fit, may do as he says,
'answer every word of it': though I would strongly advise him as a friend
to consider that any relapse into those negligences which for so many years
have been the subject of incessant remonstrance must certainly terminate in
his being speedily requested to resign his situation.

The following month Black produced a report upon a large quantity of
Audit Office documents relating to expenditure in the Peninsular War. On
13 November 1848 the Treasury had asked Langdale to have them inspected
and state whether there was any objection to their destruction. By his letter
of 21 November 1848 Langdale concluded he had no authority to say what
documents ought to be, or might not improperly be, destroyed. At the same
time he thought it would eventually be necessary to give the Record Office
power to destroy 'useless' records. But that power should be accompanied
by strict regulations the object of which would be:

(i)   to secure the greatest caution in its exercise

(ii)   to preserve short lists, abstracts or indications of the nature or effect of
       the destroyed documents; and

(iii) to preserve distinct evidence of what had been done, and by whose
       order.

Langdale thought that 'we are, perhaps, all too apt to suppose that things,
of which we do not ourselves immediately see the use, cannot be turned to
use by others',[48] a notion which, he believed, had led to the destruction of
many documents it would have been much better to preserve. Because he
did not think it clear that the documents mentioned were without any
historical, military, statistical or economic value he arranged for Black to
examine them. In his report of 5 December 1850 Black specified the classes
which he thought should be kept on account of their historical, biographical
and topographical value and for their Portuguese interest, but indicated that
a much more detailed examination of the entire assembly was necessary
before final decisions could be taken. He also recommended that rules should
be drawn up for the disposal of official papers. The outcome was a decision
to release him to undertake the work as soon as he could be spared, on the

---

48. PRO 1/12.

understanding that clerical and other support would be provided by the Audit Office.

It seems likely that Palgrave was seeking something in the nature of a secondment, but in the event other matters intruded. In fact, Black's main concern at the beginning of 1851 was his pay which had remained at £260 per annum since his engagement. The other assistant keepers of the second class had started at £250 but were now at their maximum of £350, having had two five-yearly increments of £50. Black thought the value of his services would bear comparison with those of the assistant keepers of both classes and said that he had never been wanting in times of greatest difficulty and danger 'as all night at the two great fires at Westminster and at the Tower'. He also thought it necessary to state his case, as he had been 'frequently informed by the Deputy Keeper that your Lordship contemplates an early retirement from your high and important Office'.

In a memorandum on Black's application, dated 10 February 1851, Langdale pointed out that pay was not a matter over which he had any control, but he was prepared to give his opinion to the Treasury if required. He thought Black had eminent qualifications and was not aware that 'they are, or are likely to be, surpassed by the qualifications of any other officer in the Department'. Black's reports would, he thought, provide lasting proofs of his talents and information. He noted that Palgrave was suggesting an increase to £290, which was roughly one-sixth less than the maximum of the class II scale, whereas he thought that if an increase was granted the new rate might be somewhat higher than that because in the first instance Black's pay had been set at £10 more than the class II minimum. Summing up, he did not think Black's religious objections to working on a Saturday ought to deprive him of such periodical increase as the government might approve, had not his irregular attendance created so serious a difficulty.[49]

An even more significant claim was also pending from Palgrave, who had petitioned the Treasury on 30 January 1851 for his salary to be increased from £800 to £1,000 per annum. On 6 February he wrote privately to Trevelyan to tell him that he had also written to Langdale to acquaint him of the matter in the hope that he might have his support. On 10 February he wrote again to Trevelyan to complain that it was illustrative of Langdale's *manière d'être* that he had not taken any notice of his letter. There is no trace of that letter to Langdale in the Public Record Office's own registers[50] and so whether Langdale acted on it at all is unclear, but in view of subsequent developments it seems probable that he did not. However that may be, time was now running out for him and almost his last act as keeper was to write to the Treasury on 24 March 1851 to urge the publication of the pioneering *Guide* which Thomas had been preparing to the records and

49. The papers concerning Black's application for an increase in pay are in PRO 1/15.
50. The Treasury papers concerning Palgrave's claim are in T 1/5690B/22687/1851.

which Palgrave in his *Twelfth Report* considered 'so to speak, as an Index-map to the whole assemblage of documents concentrated under the custody of the Master of the Rolls'. Within a few days of that letter Langdale laid down the burdens of his office, Hardy recalling:[51]

On Tuesday the 26th of March, I saw Lord Langdale for the last time: he came to take his leave of the Record Department, which, it may be truly said, he had created, and which he regarded with parental affection: he felt an individual interest in the members of the establishment, and, perhaps, with some solitary exception, he was beloved and idolized in return.

My parting with him will never be effaced from my mind. Through all the trials of my official life, which were not a few, he was the friend on whom I could rely for support and assistance. 'Come to me', he has often said when I have been harassed and vexed, 'let me hear all about your grievances, and if you are right, I will be your safety-valve; if wrong, I will always advise you for the best'.

Two days later all the assistant keepers attended a meeting at the Rolls Chapel with Palmer in the chair, and on Hunter's proposition, seconded by Hardy, carried the following motions unanimously:[52]

That it is our duty to convey to the Right Honourable Lord Langdale an expression of the great regret which we feel on his retirement from the Office of Master of the Rolls which involves his retirement from the General Custodiship [sic] of the Public Records – our sense of the extreme value of the attention which he has given to this department of the Public Service and of his personal kindness to each of us individually – and our earnest hope that he may enjoy health and happiness in the years which remain to his useful and honourable life, and

That Sir Francis Palgrave, the Deputy Keeper, be respectfully requested to concur with us in this Address, and that he will be kindly pleased to draw up such an Address as he, the Secretary, and the assistant keepers may think suitable to the occasion.

It was then proposed by Black, seconded by Roberts, and unanimously agreed that Hunter and Hardy should present the resolutions to Palgrave. What happened then is not recorded, but Hardy said later that Palgrave refused to place his signature with the rest. Whether that was on account of personal dignity or because he was still smarting from Langdale's indiffer-

---

51. *Memoirs of the Life of Henry, Lord Langdale* (London, 1852), II, 189.
52. PRO 1/15.

ence to his claim for an increase in pay, and felt it improbable that he could subscribe to the kind of address likely to be acceptable to the assistant keepers, is not clear. Perhaps it was a combination of many factors. At any rate, on the following day, 29 March 1851, which was a Saturday, he wrote to Palmer:[53]

> My dear Sir
>
> It is truly both a pleasure and a privilege to me, to promote any measure desired by or agreeable to our Department.
>
> I have the honour to acknowledge the receipt of the resolutions of the 28th instant, and thank you very sincerely for the kind manner in which you permit me to advise with you, & I venture to submit that the following course be pursued, viz:–
>
> That the headings & the first resolution be fairly transcribed – and signed, either by yourself as Chairman – or, by such of the Gentlemen of the first and second class of Officers as may desire to concur in the testimonial and;
>
> that, being so signed, you do request me to transmit the same to his Lordship as the expression of the feelings of the Department over which he has so long presided.
>
> I have, etc.
>
> F Palgrave

It was a skilful attempt by Palgrave to extricate himself from his dilemma, but it was nothing like good enough for the assistant keepers, who lost no time in deciding to proceed independently. Black must have been given the job of drafting an address, but on 1 April Hardy, who clearly played the key role, asked Hunter to revise it.[54] The next day all the assistant keepers again gathered and it was moved by Black, seconded by Roberts, and resolved unanimously:

> That the Address this day agreed upon be fairly copied and signed in duplicate and that, when signed, the Secretary be requested to transmit one copy to the right honourable Lord Langdale, and to preserve the other among the official papers in his own Office.

One copy of that address remains in the Public Record Office archives,[55] testimony to Langdale's great services, yet evidence of the deep and continu-

---

53. PRO 1/15.
54. BL Add. MSS. 24869, f 27.
55. PRO 1/15.

ing rift between Palgrave and his senior colleagues. The other copy, signed by all the assistant keepers and the supernumerary Cole, was despatched on 2 April 1851. It read:

May it Please Your Lordship

We, the undersigned, being Officers of the Public Records, who have so long enjoyed the benefit of your Lordship's vigilant superintendence, and just and prudent direction of the affairs of our department, feel that we should be wanting in respect, and deficient in our duty, if we did not venture to express in a few words the deep regret with which we have received the information that the time has arrived when that superintendence and direction will no longer be continued to us.

We cannot but recall, each of us for himself, instances of your Lordship's kind consideration. We cannot but collectively feel that we have received essential benefit from the firm and temperate manner in which this department of the Public Service has, when need were, been protected by your Lordship, and its reasonable claims supported.

We cannot but regard your Lordship with the deepest respect and veneration, as having been the author of a new system of management of the Public Records of this nation; by which provision is made for their better security and more extended usefulness; a system, the value of which will be better understood as time passes on; so that distant generations will feel how much they are indebted to you. Nor can we forbear on this occasion to speak of our concern that it has not been permitted to you to witness the complete development of all that your Lordship has contemplated in respect of the invaluable muniments of which, at so much personal sacrifice, you undertook the charge.

May your Lordship, therefore, be pleased to accept this expression of sincere feeling from persons whose situation enabled them to form a just appreciation of your Lordship's eminent services in this department, and their most earnest wishes that, with renovated health, you may enjoy all comfort and happiness in the years which remain of a useful and honourable life.

We are, with profound deference and respect, your Lordship's most faithful and devoted servants,

F S Thomas	Fred. Devon
Thomas Palmer	Henry George Holden
T Duffus Hardy	Chas. Roberts
Joseph Hunter	Willm. Henry Black
Henry Cole	H J Sharpe

On 5 April Langdale replied from Roehampton to Thomas:

My Dear Sir

I request you to convey to the Record Officers who have favoured me with
so kind an address, the high gratification which I have received from this
proof of their regard and good opinion.

It will always be a great pleasure to me, to remember that in using my best
endeavours to lay the foundation of a system of Record management, which
I hope will, in due time, be productive of great benefit, I have for so many
years been associated with men of so much learning, ability and industry.

I remain, my dear Sir,

Very truly yours

Langdale

But Langdale was a broken man and on 14 April, with Sir John Romilly
now installed as master of the rolls, Palgrave somewhat unkindly and contradictorily was writing to his father-in-law:

He [Romilly] can stand work but Lord Langdale has sunk under it. On
Saturday a telegraphic message notified that he was struck with the palsy. He
has lost use of one side and is very ill. The stimulus of business kept him
up but a collapse was immediately visible as soon as that stimulus was
withdrawn.

On 18 April 1851 Langdale was dead and the Public Record Office, which
until his decline he looked upon as one of his 'pets', had lost its first keeper.
Pace the address of the assistant keepers, it seems unlikely that 'distant
generations' have hitherto entertained feelings of indebtedness to him, any
more so than the readers who have thronged the appropriately named Langdale Room at Kew since its opening in 1977. But hopefully this History
makes clear his enormous contribution to the development of the Public
Record Office during its formative years, which assures him an honourable
place in its annals.

Chapter VI

The New Repository and its New Keeper, 1851–1855

Yesterday was a day of events. I was sitting at my desk in my working jackett when the Housekeeper, Mrs Bradley, rushed in, in a most stunningly fine cap, exclaiming that she had heard Sir John and his lady were coming to see their House and accordingly I had the honour of receiving my new Master and Mistress – he will not enter upon his duties till term-time. He is [a] most greable and kindly-mannered person.

(Sir Francis Palgrave to Dawson Turner, 29 March 1851: Dawson Turner Papers)

The heat was so great yesterday that the workmen were forced to pour water on the bricks of the new building before they could handle them.

(Sir Francis Palgrave to Dawson Turner, 2 July 1851: Dawson Turner Papers)

The appointment of the 49-year-old Sir John Romilly, son of the famous Sir Samuel, as master of the rolls in succession to Langdale and therefore ex-officio keeper of the records came as no surprise. Almost 19 years younger than Langdale, he had not been involved previously in record matters, but his appointment as a member of the Cambridge University Commission in 1850 had already directed his attention to the Public Record Office's holdings and activities, because that commission and the similar commission for Oxford University had been making heavy demands upon the office for searches and copies of documents in connection with their inquiries. Unlike Langdale he was an active politician, being Liberal MP for Devonport and serving successively as solicitor general and attorney general in Russell's ministry from 1848. He was the last master of the rolls to have a seat in the Commons: he was defeated at the general election in 1852 and did not stand again; and the right of the master of the rolls to sit as an MP was removed under the Supreme Court of Judicature Act 1873.

The immediate effect of the change in keepership was to strengthen Palgrave's position considerably, for Romilly decided that all official communications to him as keeper from the Treasury and other government departments on record matters should be sent under cover to the 'Deputy Keeper at the Rolls House'.[1] That decision gave to Palgrave an authority he had never enjoyed under Langdale, whose record business went, in the first instance, through Thomas as secretary. That had been a source of irritation to Palgrave, but the reason for it was largely historical as when Thomas first

---

1. PRO 1/15: circular letter from Palgrave to Treasury and other departments, 8 April 1851.

joined Langdale in April 1838, in succession to C. P. Cooper, he handled all his record correspondence automatically, and Langdale, having become accustomed to that procedure, saw no reason to change when the Public Record Office was established later in that year. On occasions the practice had led to some blurring in the chain of command, but it was now clear that Romilly intended a single line of communication through Palgrave. To Thomas's dismay that meant his privileged role, almost as private secretary to the master of the rolls, was at an end, although he retained his place as secretary of the department. Like Langdale, however, Romilly did not look upon his record responsibilities as a mere formality and made it plain that he wished to be fully briefed on departmental affairs. He also sought to revive life at the Rolls Chapel by joining the congregation there, as was described by Palgrave in a letter to Turner, dated 17 April 1851:

> Sir John Romilly has entered upon the discharge of his functions and on Sunday last he, Lady Romilly and their family, attended divine service in the Chapel, an attendance disused for very many years. There is a private passage from the Oriel in the Chapel which later had been turned into a lumber closet and the housekeeper had to make a wonderful clearance of mops and brooms and pails and rolls of rugs and carpets.

The following month, on the Queen's Birthday, Saturday 24 May, at 1.35 p.m. an even more notable ceremony occurred when the 'first stone of this treasure house of the Public Records and Archives' was laid by Romilly at the north-west corner of the proposed building. Two days later Palgrave told Pennethorne he wished the lettering on the inscription recording the occasion to be of the 'lapidary character' by which he meant:[2]

> the plain Roman characters as they are seen in ancient inscriptions of the 16th century in Italy, i.e. not imitated from printing press types according to the vulgar fashion of the stone mason's yard with upstrokes and downstrokes, but square bold and deep and *not* to be coloured. I should wish to see it written upon the face of the stone before it is chiselled.

> Sir John is much interested in our proposed scheme of ornamentation and has given some useful hints for carrying [it] out, he quite approves of the general idea and repeated the expression he used [when] he laid the stone – that whatever is worth doing is worth doing well.

Sadly, Langdale was not there to see the beginning of the repository for

---

2. PRO 1/15: Palgrave to Pennethorne, 26 May 1851. Two biblical texts were also incorporated: on the north face of the stone 'Except the Lord build the house they labour in vain that build it'; and on the west 'Let the beauty of the Lord our God be upon us and establish thou the work of our hands upon us yea the work of our hands establish thou it'.

which he had struggled so long. Neither was his passing remarked upon by Palgrave when he came to give his *Thirteenth Report* for 1851. It might have been otherwise had the assistant keepers allowed him to forward their address as he suggested, but even after making allowance for that and the many slights he had received at Langdale's hands, the absence of any acknowledgement of his services leaves an unfortunate impression of pettishness which can never be removed. Certainly the omission could have done nothing to improve Palgrave's credit with his senior colleagues. There had been some change in their ranks in the autumn of 1851 when Palmer retired on health grounds after 55 years' service. The class I vacancy thus created was filled by the upgrading of Roberts at Carlton Ride, who received his reward for transferring from the Tower a year before. Holden had first claim on seniority grounds and petitioned accordingly, but Palgrave brushed that aside, persuading Romilly that Holden should pay the penalty for his earlier refusal to leave the Rolls. The second assistant keeper post there was then filled by moving Sharpe from the Tower, while Joseph Burtt, the senior clerk, was promoted to be an assistant keeper of the second class, remaining at the Chapter House, probably because Palgrave, who trusted him, still wanted an eye kept on Devon. Although Holden must have been deeply disappointed by his failure to succeed Palmer, his co-operation and assistance in the new arrangements were favourably noted by Romilly as was his promise to abandon the practice of advertising Palmer's indexes, in which he now had an interest, in the *Law List*. Palmer's retirement also meant that Holden was required to take the lead in bringing into the Rolls Chapel the first accessions from the Signet Office, when that department was abolished under the Great Seal Act of 1851.

Palgrave's attitude towards the workmen remained difficult, as instanced by his tightening up on the payment of 'beer money' and his refusal to modify the rule by which payment for annual or sick leave was restricted to six hours a day. During the summer of 1851 he indicated his willingness to allow a day's leave to any workman wishing to attend the Great Exhibition, but only at the six-hour rate. On behalf of the men at the Tower, Hardy thanked him for the permission, but said that as they were family men they were not prepared to give up two hours' pay for their own pleasure. However, Palgrave remained unmoved, telling Hardy on 24 June that the indulgences extended to the men were extremely liberal and 'the best advice you can give them is to let well alone'. On the other hand, when Palgrave satisfied himself that a workman at Carlton Ride with ten years' service, James Cheshire, was genuinely suffering from a serious eye complaint, he succeeded in getting the Treasury to extend their 'humane and favourable consideration' to him by granting him a further three months' sick leave. Thereafter, Cheshire continued fitfully in post until 1853 when he finally retired. Although Palgrave thought the men had little of which to complain, he was not unappreciative of their efforts and in his *Thirteenth Report* for 1851 specially commended one of them, William Palmer, for his cleverness in constructing two large wooden boxes with cedar trays for storing and protecting valuable and ancient seals which had become detached from records in the Chapter House.

The establishment matter which was foremost in Palgrave's mind during 1851 was the question of his own pay. Langdale had left that unresolved, which was, perhaps, just as well for Palgrave because in June of that year the Treasury referred the papers to Romilly, who proved much more sympathetic. As a result of his opinion the Treasury agreed in December to increase Palgrave's salary from £800 to £1,000 annually, but ruled that the increase was personal to him and that the deputy keeper pay scale should remain unchanged.[3] Relieved and heartened by the decision as he was, Palgrave's satisfaction was tempered by his growing concern about the failing health of Lady Palgrave, with whom he had always enjoyed a warm and loving companionship. Nevertheless, as he told her father on 18 December 1851, 'with my dear bedridden wife's expenses this help is very providential'. Unhappily, the additional support was not long needed: to Palgrave's great distress Lady Palgrave died in August 1852. Fortunately Palgrave had an excellent relationship with his four sons. He was closest to Francis, who was still at home and generally spent holidays with him, but he kept in touch with 'Giffy' who was still in the Middle East, Inglis who was on the staff of the Turner family bank at Yarmouth, and Reginald, now a lawyer, who was to obtain a clerkship in the House of Commons in 1853.

The other matter which had long concerned Palgrave was the question of fees for literary searches. Langdale, backed by Hardy and Cole, had always maintained that all classes of searchers should be treated equally and, when the matter was first considered in February 1839 and the table of fees settled the following year, it was that view that carried the day. Palgrave had never accepted that decision as final and lost no time in urging a change of course upon Romilly. But he was not prepared to advocate abolishing fees altogether as he thought some expense inseparable from legal proceedings and that the existing charges for such searches and inspections were moderate and equitable. More dramatically, he considered it almost an act of charity to discourage misguided persons, generally in humble circumstances, from pursuing imaginary claims to property or titles because such endeavours frequently led to insanity or beggary. The news that Romilly was well disposed towards Palgrave's desire for some modification soon became known and those interested decided that the time was ripe for a concerted attempt to obtain free access to the records for literary searchers. John Bruce of the Camden Society took a leading part in the campaign, and, having secured the signatures of no fewer than 83 distinguished persons including Thomas Carlyle, Henry Hallam, Thomas Macaulay, Charles Dickens, William Harrison Ainsworth and Charles William Dilke, wrote to Palgrave on 7 July enclosing a memorial (Appendix IX) on the matter, telling him that

---

3. T 1/5690B/22687/1851.

the memorialists hoped they might enjoy his powerful support as no other man was so well able to vouch for the literary value of the records or had done so much to make that value known to the world. A rather different stand was taken by Cole, who, when he heard what was afoot, expressed his misgivings to Romilly the same day:

Dear Sir

Although I am at present only an Honorary Assistant Keeper of the Public Record Office, I hope you will allow me the opportunity of seeing you when convenient on the policy of permitting literary persons to consult the records without payment of fees, which I hear is under your consideration. It was Lord Langdale's opinion which I confess seems to me impregnable that if any Class of persons ought to have exemptions from fees, it is those who have the misfortune to be obliged to consult the records to defend their rights rather than those who consult them to promote their own profit or fame. Practically my whole experience has been that the present low fees administered on the discretion of the assistant keepers do not prevent the consultation of the Records at all by any persons literary or otherwise and I would submit to you that if remitted on behalf of one Class, it would be fair to give all Classes the same benefit.

I have the honour to be, Dear Sir, your faithful Serv[ant]:

Henry Cole

But Romilly's mind was already made up, and not wishing to see Cole, he told his chief secretary to reply on his behalf:

Dear Sir

I am directed by the Master of the Rolls to acquaint you that his numerous duties prevent him from giving you an interview but that the arrangements for facilitating the inspection of the Records for literary purposes have been considered a month ago between Sir Francis Palgrave and himself, and a Memorial having subsequently been received by the Master of the Rolls from Lord Mahon and other literary characters upon the subject an answer will be given as soon as possible to the Memorialists: with respect to the general remission of fees for searches and inspections to which you seem to allude the Master of the Rolls cannot at present entertain the question, but should any general revision of the fee system take place in this and other departments he will be prepared to consider the subject.

I am, Sir, Your obedient Servant

W G Brett

Meanwhile, Romilly was busily engaged in drafting a reply to the memorialists, and after consultation with Palgrave wrote to them on 31 July 1851 saying that he was willing to free literary searchers from fees, subject to certain restrictions. His letter and Mahon's reply of 2 August, thanking him warmly for the concession, were both printed subsequently in the appendix to Palgrave's *Thirteenth Report*.

Regulations were then drawn up, approved by the Treasury in November 1851, and issued the following month. Apart from laying down that all applicants were to state the reason for their search in writing and give the deputy keeper personally such further explanation as might be required, they also ruled that all applications were to be reported to the master of the rolls and entered in a book kept for the purpose. Each branch office was also to maintain registers of all productions along the same lines as those kept for manuscripts in the British Museum. The regulations, signed by Romilly, also stated the need to explain to literary inquirers

> that the time of the various officers and other persons employed in the Public
> Record Office is so wholly ingrossed by the performance of their present
> duties, that it will not be possible for the officers to assist any literary
> inquirers beyond the production of the documents, and giving a general
> explanation, if needed, of their character and nature. No applicant ought to
> present himself who is not sufficiently acquainted with the handwriting,
> abbreviations, and language of ancient documents, so as to be able to read
> and decipher their contents.

In accordance with previous practice searchers were allowed to make copies only in black-lead pencil to prevent the records being injured by blots of ink or the risk of a fraudulent entry. Fresh impetus was also given to the task of stamping the records, this time without the arguments that had bedevilled the matter when it was last considered in 1841.[4]

Another decision of great importance was made in 1851 following a letter to the Treasury from the registrar general about the disposal of documents relating to the 1841 census. According to Palgrave, the registrar general wondered if it was any longer necessary to keep them as much of the information they contained had been published in statistical form. But Palgrave had no doubts, telling Romilly on 10 July:

> In such opinion I do not coincide. It appears to me that these books are of
> great national importance and fit to be preserved. The particulars which they
> may furnish as to the identity, residence, occupation and age of all the
> enumerated inhabitants of the United Kingdom on the Census Day will
> hereafter be invaluable for Historical and Legal purposes.

---

4. Romilly's directions of 4 December 1851 concerning stamping and the comments of the assistant keepers are in in PRO 8/28.

The same arguments applied, thought Palgrave, to the 1851 census. Similarly, he recommended that a small collection of documents concerning the enumerations of 1821 and 1831 should be kept as they had been earmarked for preservation by John Rickman whose 'judgment may be depended upon as to their value and utility'. The registrar general offered no objection as his main concern was finding accommodation for them from his own scarce resources. He was also anxious to store birth, death and marriage registers in part of the new repository when built and at the beginning of December 1851 made a request to Romilly to that effect. However, space for those registers became available in Somerset House in 1853, enabling the registrar to withdraw his request. In 1859, when the Chapter House repository was being emptied, the registrar took back the census returns although they were retransferred later.

Romilly's willingness to meet many of Palgrave's views led to the submission of two other important matters to him during December 1851. One – to regulate more strictly the production of original records in court under *subpoenas duces tecum* – failed to get very far, but the other was to result in the issue of an order in council placing all government documents under the 'charge and superintendence' of the master of the rolls. In a memorandum to Romilly of 19 December, Palgrave argued for an order to legalise the transfers of departmental documents that had already taken place and to bring the State Paper Office under the 1838 act, otherwise the master of the rolls was merely a 'storekeeper' of departmental documents. Believing the British Museum still wished to obtain the State Papers, he thought it essential to counter any such attempt by an order as the Treasury minute directing the consolidation of the Public Record Office and the State Paper Office could be rescinded at any time by another Treasury minute. Some provision should also be made for other accruing records to be transferred at regular intervals as was already the case for records of the courts. The expense connected with the management of the records also concerned him, and he argued that it should be borne by the departments by whom they were transferred. Finally, he maintained that the title 'Public Record Office' conveyed a false idea and that the new building should be designated 'The General Repository of Her Majesty's Public Records and Archives'.

Romilly did not take up all of Palgrave's points, but on 17 February 1852 he wrote to the Privy Council Office seeking an order in council to sanction the departmental transfers that had already taken place and to bring the State Paper Office under the act of 1838. However, the law officers did not think it was possible to cover previous transfers by an order, but instead of seeking further clarification from Romilly they went ahead with an order, wrongly described as placing certain records in the 'custody' of the master of the rolls, which actually placed all records then in government offices under his 'charge and superintendence'. The consequence of the order as drawn was that it was theoretically possible for him to take such records into his custody without the prior approval, or even knowledge, of the head of the department concerned. As the Royal Commission of 1910–1919 observed, it became lawful 'for the Master of the Rolls, by a stroke of the pen, to dislocate the whole executive machinery of the State'.[5] Palgrave immediately saw the absurdity of what had been done, but his and Romilly's efforts to obtain a supplementary order providing for transfers only on the direction of the Treasury, Admiralty or head of the department concerned, and subject to the lord chancellor's approval, were of no avail. Realising it was essential to maintain the informal understanding that had already been reached with departments, Palgrave, having cleared the matter in person with the Council Office, took the occasion of his *Thirteenth Report*, issued on 3 June 1852, to emphasise that the order would be called into effect only on the command of the department concerned, thus continuing the existing practice. For working purposes, therefore, Langdale's letter of 8 August 1845 concerning the management of departmental documents by the office remained the authority for transfers from government establishments. Conversely, although the order remained non-operative, its existence gave the Public Record Office the legal title for which Palgrave had been pressing and assured its position, name notwithstanding, as the national archive. In the words of Palgrave's *Thirteenth Report*:

> The scope of the authority given to the Master of the Rolls by the Record Act is now considerably enlarged. Your Majesty's Order in Council renders him the Keeper, not merely of the Records in a legal or historical sense, but all of Your Majesty's Public Documents and Archives whatever, and the Repository will ultimately become (if the expression may be allowed) the strong box of the Empire.

On the staffing front 1852 began with a startling and unwelcome incident, reminiscent of a scene from Trollope's *The Three Clerks*, when the hapless Manners Fenwick was arrested in the office for debt. That could have resulted in most serious consequences for him as his poor handwriting and spelling had attracted strong censure from Palgrave the previous summer, and it was only Holden's special pleading and assurance that Fenwick's Latin had improved that had allowed him to move to the £150 point on the clerical scale in November 1851. Once again Holden must have come to the rescue. Although his letter has not survived in the office's records, it is clear that he did his best to shield Fenwick, whose solicitor managed to secure his release from his creditors' clutches. A very stern warning followed from Palgrave who told Fenwick that he was never to allow the office to be a place of appointment for his private affairs again. Less fortunate was James Gibson at Carlton Ride. During the summer of 1851 he also fell into debt and a shoemaker sued him in the county court. That was bad enough, for

---

5. *First Report of the Royal Commission on Public Records*, I, pt I (Cd. 6361), 4. The relevant correspondence is printed in I, pt II (Cd. 6395), 8–11.

any kind of moral weakness was anathema to Palgrave, but it was made worse by Gibson's many past lapses and poor sick record. Hunter, while conceding that Gibson's work gave no cause for complaint, had frequently found him troublesome and was not disposed to rally to his defence, especially as he had tried unsuccessfully to have him dismissed in 1849. When Gibson again went sick, therefore, in November 1851, Palgrave obtained Romilly's approval to sack him. Gibson's whereabouts proved difficult to establish, but he was eventually traced and in February 1852 tendered his resignation in lieu of discharge. At much the same time another clerical vacancy was created when Arthur May, who had started at the Chapter House in 1846, decided to leave the office, having failed to settle down at the Rolls Chapel where he had been transferred, against his wishes, at the beginning of 1852. Although the office was not particularly sorry to lose May, who had been causing difficulties for Holden, the clerical complement was under some strain because George Knight, Black's clerk, had fallen sick. His health had never been robust and in 1851 he had been allowed to spend six months in the south of France. While Palgrave thought well of Knight he was hesitant about again submitting his case to the Treasury but, with Romilly's blessing, eventually did so and succeeded in obtaining two months' leave of absence for him. Faced with these problems and the expected expansion in office business, Palgrave took the opportunity in February 1852 to place before Romilly the views he had long held concerning the inadequacies of the existing system of recruiting and managing the clerks.

Without the introduction of a stricter and longer period of probation and some system of reward for good performance, Palgrave was pessimistic about the prospects of improvement, prefacing his remarks with Trevelyan's comment:[6]

> If Hope and Fear be, as has been truly observed, the influences through
> which men are excited to do their duty, no Establishment can be more
> destitute of these means of exercising authority than the Public Record
> Office.

Immediately, however, the problem was to fill the posts vacated by Gibson and May. The first went to William Beattie Kingston, the younger brother of Alfred. Although the use of the family connection to secure clerks had not always succeeded in the past – an application for A. Tytler had gone awry in April 1850 – it was not unknown and the real surprise was the wholly unprecedented appointment to the other post of the 26-year-old John Ringwood Atkins, one of the office's workmen. Palgrave carefully kept his

---

6. Palgrave reminded Trevelyan of those words when he wrote to him informally on 19 June 1852. Both that letter and his long memorandum to Romilly on the subject of the clerks' qualifications are in T 1/5852/25790/1853.

intentions to himself until almost the last moment, but among the Treasury's records will be found the application he made to Romilly on Atkins's behalf on 3 April 1852:[7]

My Dear Sir John

I venture to appeal to your kindness and liberality of feeling, on behalf of a very humble individual, employed in this department as a workman, J R Atkins whose letters and testimonials I enclose. Atkins entered this service, being then a boy, 8th Oct. 1841 at the rate of 4d per hour now raised to 6d per hour, his wages are paid weekly, and they will continue at this rate until he can be raised to 7d per hour, which rise, according to the Treasury Regulations, and the rules of seniority, he will not be able to attain for many years. There are 16 men in the *sixpenny* class, thirteen of whom are ranked as his seniors and who, according to the custom of our workshop, will be entitled to promotion before him. Moreover they cannot be promoted until vacancies occur in the superior classes of operations, the sevenpenny, eightpenny, & ninepenny which contains 16 men.

Mr Atkins is stationed in the Rolls House Branch Office where he works under my observation flattening and arranging papers – writing and pasting book tickets, cleaning and bundling documents, making lists of volumes and bundles, and occasionally transcribing reports, and, in his turn answering the bell. In such capacity I always found him diligent, careful, and attentive, but I had no idea of his various talents, nor of the laudable manner in which he devoted himself to the cultivation and utilization of such his talents during his spare hours, until towards the beginning of this year, when he applied to me for that which it was not in my power to grant, an increase of wages.

He produced to me upon this occasion, and the transactions which grew out of it, various testimonials which he had obtained for the purpose of procuring engagements as a private teacher of languages during his spare hours (see copies enclosed) and also specimens of his translations from the Latin, French and German (a specimen from Schiller is also enclosed) and also two lectures on the English Constitution, delivered at a Metropolitan institution (also submitted to you). He has a good knowledge of the before mentioned three languages, and his historical knowledge is as sound as could be expected from his age and opportunities.

Not having any other means of helping him, I applied to Sir Robert Inglis to use his influence at the British Museum, where Atkins would be

---

7. T 1/5745A/16450/1852. Atkins actually commenced duties at the Tower on 10 October 1842 on Hardy's recommendation.

excellently well calculated for the Library department. Sir Robert, most kindly, immediately applied to the Abp of Canterbury, but the answer given by his Grace does not give any sanguine hope of success – in fact as nearly next to none as may well be.

Now, a vacancy amongst the clerks (or officers of the third class) of this Office has just arisen by the resignation (which I enclose) of Mr Arthur May and under the circumstances I am sure you will excuse the liberty which I take in earnestly requesting you to recommend the Treasury to nominate Mr Atkins as his successor. Besides the satisfaction of rewarding merit, you will promote the good of the public service in every way. Mr Atkins, if appointed, will come in, not as a raw probationer, but as one fully acquainted with the business of the office: and I have every reason to believe that he will prove an efficient officer. Our workmen are an intelligent and respectable set of men – and the elevation of one of their own body to a superior official rank, – so far from exciting jealousy amongst them, will be accepted as a tribute of respect to the whole class, and encourage them to the better performance of their duties and, as far as the fact may become public, it will shew that when the higher classes of society inculcate upon the inferior grades, the advantages of the acquisition of useful knowledge, they, on their part will, when opportunities offer, give some reward to those who obey the exhortation.

I have the honour to remain, My dear Sir John, with the greatest respect, your most obedient & faithful Servant

Francis Palgrave

Forwarding Palgrave's letter to the Treasury, Romilly emphasised how struck he was by Atkins's case, and stressed the great advantage the department would obtain from his appointment. The Treasury must have been similarly impressed for they lost no time in agreeing to nominate Atkins, who took up his new duties on 23 April 1852. He received further recognition in 1866 when he was promoted to the grade of senior clerk, the equivalent to assistant keeper II, a rank he held until his death in 1878.

Within a fortnight of Atkins's promotion the workman grade again came into prominence when one of the men at Carlton Ride, Henry Le Dieu, reported that his wife had bought some articles at a grocer's shop off Leicester Square, which were wrapped in a leaf of paper apparently torn from a Common Pleas docket book of posteas and inquiries. His prompt recognition and report resulted in the recovery of a considerable fragment of a strayed volume, the shopkeeper, who had bought it as part of a consignment of waste paper, being content to surrender it for 1s 6d. No formal inquiry followed, although there was no doubt that the blame rested with the courts. In his *Fourteenth Report* for 1852 Palgrave made particular reference to the difficulties encountered in that area, citing the long-standing

146

practice whereby the officers of the Court of Exchequer retained records in their own desks or even in their private houses. Palgrave was in no doubt that the fact that many Exchequer rolls and Household books had been lost or put up for sale stemmed from that lack of control. He also reported, with obvious scepticism, the queen's remembrancer's claim that certain of his records, such as the Red Book of the Exchequer, could not be released as they remained in constant use.

Although Palgrave first drew his increased salary in 1852 and found Romilly much more understanding than Langdale, neither factor compensated for the loss of Lady Palgrave or for his own deteriorating health, which towards the end of that year obliged him to take medicine daily. His digestion was especially troublesome, perhaps not helped by his usual lunch, which was a mutton chop boiled in broth. He was also painfully aware of the lack of goodwill towards him on the part of his senior colleagues. His refusal to sign the address to Langdale still rankled with them, and the issue was given a fresh twist when Hardy pointedly alluded to it in his *Memoirs of Lord Langdale*, which was published in July 1852. Among Hardy's papers[8] concerning his book is an assembly of what is described as 'Langdaleana', apparently prepared for him by John Edwards, in which the expediency of printing the record officers' memorial and Langdale's reply is tactfully queried. But that caution was disregarded by Hardy who had enthusiastically flung himself into the work on being asked by Lady Langdale to undertake it in November 1851. When Romilly heard about it, he said he rejoiced at the project although having no papers in his possession which were likely to help. But before many months had passed Lady Langdale was pondering the wisdom of her invitation to Hardy as he unearthed what might have turned out to be an embarrassing episode in Langdale's past concerning money he had drawn, and later repaid, from a foundation for fellows at his Cambridge college, Gonville and Caius. Hardy's further investigations vindicated Langdale, but not before Lady Langdale's blood had risen to 'boiling point' when Dr B. Chapman, master of Caius, insinuated that Langdale must have known he was acting wrongly.[9]

Elsewhere, Hardy was busily gathering in recollections from Langdale's contemporaries, and although he reported to Lady Langdale[10] that he was having difficulties in securing assistance officially, he received much help from G. W. Sanders and T. Le Dieu of the Rolls Court staff as well as from Thomas and Edwards, the record colleagues who knew Langdale best.

---

8. PRO 1/120/2.

9. C. N. L. Brooke, *A History of Gonville and Caius College* (Boydell and Brewer, 1985), 201–202.

10. PRO 1/120/2: Lady Langdale to Hardy, 10 March 1852. When told of the difficulties, Lady Langdale said: 'It had never occurred to me that you might have some difficulty in procuring material from the Rolls House – but your allusion to it carried instant conviction to my mind'.

Thomas, who prepared a paper for Hardy as 'rather a clue for you than anything else', told him that in order to effect a saving to the government Langdale had waived his right in the matter of the deputy keepership in 1838 and appointed Palgrave who would otherwise have been entitled to compensation. That resulted in Hardy stating in the *Memoirs* that Langdale had given the post 'up to the Treasury for the purpose of effecting a saving in the retiring allowance of the gentleman who was appointed to it'. Perhaps significantly, Hardy dropped the important qualification 'on being assured by the government that their recommendation was a proper one' which he had originally included in his draft. Nearly one hundred years later another assistant keeper, Dr Buckland, relying on Hardy's entry in the *Dictionary of National Biography*, which said that Langdale had been compelled by ministerial pressure to withdraw his offer of the deputy keepership to Hardy, nevertheless thought that the appointment of Palgrave, although apparently forced on Langdale, was a wise, if political, one. Noting Hardy's silence on that aspect of the matter in the *Memoirs*, he described his work as 'otherwise naive'.[11] That judgment, although harsh, contains more than an element of truth, for Langdale was not nearly so guileless as Hardy depicted.

However, although the contemporary reviews were mixed – the *Quarterly Review* being particularly scathing – Lady Langdale was well pleased and the Public Record Office's own copy is the one she presented to it in August 1852. For his labours Hardy received £150 from Richard Bentley, the publisher, which was not particularly generous. But Hardy was glad to do it, although it put back his revision and continuation of Le Neve's *Fasti Ecclesiae Anglicanae*, which eventually appeared in 1854.

Among those whom Hardy approached for information about Langdale was Cole, who took the opportunity to reveal to him his intention to take up a post in the Board of Trade in connection with the schools of design. However, as it was not clear whether that situation would prove permanent, the Treasury subsequently told Romilly that Cole's absence from his assistant keepership was to be extended for a further year. Both Romilly and Palgrave were vexed by that decision because of the uncertainty it created, and Romilly represented to the Treasury that it would be best for all concerned if Cole severed his connection with the Public Record Office entirely and continued in 'the career he has opened for himself and in which he is eminently fitted to excel'. To no one's surprise that is exactly what happened, and within a year Cole was joint secretary of the newly established Department of Science and Art. Thus was ended his attachment to the record service, stretching back to 10 April 1823 when, straight from school, at the age of 14 he had presented himself, as his diary records, 'in an Oxford mixture suit with tailed coat at Mr. Cohen's office'.

Of the eight original assistant keepers six now remained in post, but that

---

11. PRO 1/565: Buckland to Flower, 23 July 1943.

number fell to five in 1853 when Black's services were terminated. Throughout 1852 the familiar pattern of conflict between Palgrave and Black had continued unabated. For much of that time Black was working upon Treasury records, including papers of the commissariat service in Ireland arising from the terrible famine during the second half of the 1840s. Those papers had the distinction of being the first to be taken into the office by the master of the rolls under the order in council of 1852. Black also spent nearly three months at Chester in connection with the possibility of establishing a local repository in the castle for the records of the palatinate. His reports on these assignments were inordinately delayed, and in the case of the Audit Office records, for which he had been given responsibility in 1851, he failed to make any progress at all. By early 1853 Palgrave, knowing Black of old and despairing of improvement, decided he could tolerate his shortcomings no longer, telling Romilly:[12]

> I have never acted spy upon Mr. Black but during 6 weeks I went upstairs into his room 12 times never earlier than an hour and a half after 10 o'clock upon business which had occurred or which he had to do, for the purpose of speaking to him and I never found him at his post . . . yet the licences taken have already been the cause of much relaxation of discipline in the Office and I am afraid that any stipulated concession made to him will only increase the price. His talent is very great but we cannot afford to purchase the price.

Palgrave was determined upon that course despite the fact that in August 1852 the Treasury had approved his recommendation that Black's pay should be increased to £291 13s 4d, five-sixths of the maximum of an assistant keeper II. For that, however, he received little thanks from Black, who was quick to point out that when he had first petitioned for an increase in January 1851 Langdale, noting that he had started at a point £10 above the class II minimum, had concluded that, subject to Treasury sanction, his pay might properly have been increased to £312 after five years and to £364 after ten. But Palgrave had no qualms on that score. He knew that Black was hardly in straitened circumstances as he occupied a good house in his capacity as minister of the Mill Yard Chapel and also received the tithes of Little Maplestead, Essex, of which he was the rector.

Because Palgrave thought that Black was well placed compared with the other assistant keepers he had no compunction about telling Romilly of Black's constant involvement in litigation and referring to a case some two years earlier in which heavy damages had been awarded against him for a libel upon a brother Baptist minister for which he was rebuked by the judge. On Trevelyan's suggestion Romilly told Black that he thought he must

---

12. PRO 2/2, pp 92–114: Palgrave's notes and observations are entered with Black's letter to Romilly of 8 February 1853, rebutting the charges made against him.

retire, but that if he could produce medical evidence to show that his failure to carry out his official duties was due to his health the Treasury would consider awarding him a pension under the Superannuation Act. That gave Black no trouble because he was able to produce certificates to prove that he was suffering from ophthalmia. He had, of course, long complained that his eyesight had been harmed as a result of his record work and part of his defence of poor time-keeping was that he was unable to get up in the morning until his eyes had become accustomed to the light. However, Palgrave's tardiness in submitting a superannuation claim to the Treasury, coupled with uncertainty about any future employment of Black within the public service, meant that it was not until May 1854 that he was finally awarded a retiring allowance of £68 per annum.

Nevertheless, as far as the Public Record Office was concerned Black was regarded as having resigned at the end of March 1853, but that was denied by Black who argued that he had done no more than agree to Romilly's wish that he should retire upon an allowance. Originally, Trevelyan had thought that when Black left the Public Record Office he might be set to work upon the papers of the Treasury solicitor, which were in urgent need of attention. However, it was decided that it would be better to give that work to Joseph Burtt at the Chapter House, at least in the first instance, and for Black to continue to work upon the domestic records of the Treasury itself where much still needed to be done. Meanwhile, Black submitted a petition for a retiring allowance, setting out at length the many services he claimed to have rendered in the record field, including the remarkable suggestion that he had 'been mainly instrumental in procuring the defeat of Mr. Charles Buller's Record Bill and preparing the way for the system of custody and management of the Records which was brought about by Lord Langdale's Record Act'.[13] The same Langdale he had reviled in 1838 and 1839 was now Black's 'late honoured and beloved Master', whereas Palgrave, who had sympathised with his predicament at that time, had become the object of his unbounded animosity. Palgrave himself was much distressed and bothered by the entire episode. He retained great respect for Black's gifts, but he was convinced that the course he had chosen was the only one open to him. He was, therefore, greatly disconcerted when Trevelyan suggested during the summer of 1853 that, as Black's exact status had still to be settled, he might be regarded as a supernumerary assistant keeper while employed at the Treasury. Palgrave persuaded Romilly that such an arrangement was unacceptable, but on Trevelyan's authority Black's pay at his former rate continued to be issued from the Public Record Office vote until March 1854 when his work at the Treasury ceased. That almost marked Black's severance with the record service, which was a disappointment to

---

13. T 1/5852/25790/1853: Black to Trevelyan, 21 March 1853, enclosing his petition to the Treasury of 17 March 1853 for permission to retire on an allowance.

Romilly, who was reluctant to lose him altogether and would have been content to see him placed in charge of the branch record office which had been mooted for Chester.[14] But as such an appointment would have had to be made by the local authorities and the cost borne by them, and as there were thought to be legal obstacles because of the 1838 act, that course was not pursued. Black's unfinished Record Commission work on the *Docquets of Letters Patent, Charles I*, which had long troubled Thomas, remained outstanding until after his death in 1873. As late as 1870, Hardy, by then deputy keeper, was attempting to get Black to clear it up, urging him in November of that year not to 'let an hour elapse before taking the matter in hand'.

The assistant keeper vacancy created by Black's removal presented a problem for Palgrave and Romilly, the claims of three or four of the more senior clerks being nicely balanced, but they eventually decided that the promotion should go to Walter Nelson, who was the most senior and who had received a sound education at Merchant Taylors'. Furthermore, Nelson had served Hunter at Carlton Ride faithfully for many years, having first entered the record service in 1834, paradoxically through Black's so-called 'School of Transcribers'. The hard-pressed Roberts saw Nelson's appointment as an opportunity to rid himself of some of his certification work, but that idea drew strong opposition from the testy Hunter and was only resolved in Roberts's favour after reference to Romilly. To balance matters, Hunter's clerical complement was augmented by the transfer of the gifted Haydon from the Tower.

It was unfortunate for the office's reputation with the Treasury that just before the difficulties with Black came to a head an application was submitted to it by Palgrave at the end of 1852 for special leave for Peter Turner, who had again fallen sick. Although the Treasury sanctioned Turner's absence until the spring, it restricted him to half pay and took the opportunity to point out that since 1845 the number of such cases from the Public Record Office, amounting to nine, exceeded the usual proportion and indicated the existence of some special cause. It wished to know, therefore, what steps were taken to ensure that, on entry, clerks were fit enough to perform their duties adequately. Both Romilly and Palgrave were much disturbed by the Treasury's response which they saw as an expression of displeasure and censure. To counter that, a detailed return was sent to the Treasury in explanation of the cases that had occurred.[15] The existing rules were also documented and fuller guidance sought for the future. In May 1853 Trevelyan gave his general approval to the office's rules, but said that, if unfair

---

14. PRO 2/2, pp 518–522: Romilly to Sir John Hanmer, 18 June 1853. For an account of the Cheshire records see Dorothy Clayton 'An early Cheshire Archivist, Faithful Thomas (c. 1772–1844) and the records of the Palatinate of Chester', *Archives*, XVII, no. 76 (1986), 3–26.

15. T 1/5852/25790/1853: Romilly to Trevelyan, 9 February 1853.

advantage was taken of the usual indulgence in cases of illness, a corresponding deduction was to be made from an officer's annual leave. Before appointment, new entrants were to produce a certificate of medical fitness and be examined in such manner as the master of the rolls might think fit to check that they had enjoyed a liberal education and were sufficiently competent in Latin and French to undertake record work. If qualified on all these counts and of a suitable age, they might be admitted on a year's probation, but were liable to removal before the end of that time if the master of the rolls reported them for irregular attendance or for unsatisfactory performance.

As an indication of how the office's rules might be enforced against those who deliberately flouted them, Trevelyan referred to the case of Charles Cole, which had recently been reported to the Treasury by Romilly and which had resulted in his periodic increase in salary being stayed. Cole was able enough at record work, but although he had high pretensions he lacked the flair and drive of his older brother Henry. Perhaps the strain of trying to keep up with Henry began to tell upon Charles, who by the early 1850s was beginning to show signs of the mental instability which ultimately wrecked his career. During 1852 he was burdened with a family executorship and also became involved in a number of business activities outside the office. They resulted in such irregularity in his attendance that by March 1853 his relations with Roberts had deteriorated to the point where the latter was no longer prepared to have him at Carlton Ride, and he was transferred to the Rolls Chapel, exchanging places with Fenwick. No sooner was he there than he caused a stir by calling for a workman to clean his boots and upsetting searchers by his loud manner. Within a matter of days he fell sick, alleging that it was due to the poor furnishing of his new office, particularly the lack of any carpet or rug,[16] and subsequently produced a certificate to say that he was suffering from an acute inflammation of the testicle. His behaviour immediately brought him into conflict with Holden, for whom he made no attempt to disguise his contempt, writing to Romilly on 12 April to say 'though to his credit he may have raised himself to his present position – I hope I am not out of propriety in supposing – naturally conserves the habits in which he was educated and which are not evidently of the same description of my own'. When Holden, not surprisingly, asked for Fenwick's return, Cole again wrote to Romilly on 15 April reflecting on the competence and character of the luckless Manners. But Palgrave and Romilly were unimpressed by Cole's outbursts and did not think his illness genuine. However, as he was not prepared to resign, which Palgrave thought might be best, Romilly decided to make an example of him by withholding his increment and reported him to the Treasury. On 16 June Romilly followed this up by issuing a circular instructing the assistant keepers to report all

16. PRO 2/2, p 278: C. Cole to Holden, 18 March 1853. Later correspondence concerning Cole's irregularities will also be found in this letter book.

future absences by the clerks to him and to indicate how they should be dealt with.[17] During the late summer of 1853 the new system claimed its first victim when Percy Hunt forfeited two days from his 1854 leave allowance, having exhausted his current entitlement. As for the revised entrance arrangements for clerks, they proved too much for the first candidate, Robert Tabrum, who failed his medical examination and was replaced by his younger brother Edward in November 1853. However, Charles Cole, thanks to a satisfactory report from Holden, had his increment restored in the spring of 1854, but shortly afterwards he took a day off without permission to attend the opening of the Crystal Palace at Sydenham in order to make a report for the press. That nearly resulted in his dismissal, but Romilly relented at the last moment, letting him off with a severe reprimand on his written assurance, as a gentleman, to behave properly in future. Naturally the tightening up of office discipline was far from welcome to the clerks, and on one occasion Henry Yonge was rash enough to voice his feelings, which led to Palgrave telling him bluntly:[18]

> I am very sorry that you should have felt annoyed at my letter particularly
> as you know that every endeavour is made to enforce the needful regulations
> with as much delicacy towards those who are the object of them as is possible
> and unless you are able to restrain this tendency you will never have any
> comfort in any Public Department.

Apart from penalising possible malingerers, the new measures were part and parcel of a concerted effort by Romilly and Palgrave to improve office efficiency by obtaining more precise information from the assistant keepers about the work going on in their branches.[19] They also aimed to increase their knowledge of the clerks by examining their diaries weekly. The sketchiness of that knowledge was shown in 1854 when Palgrave discovered for the first time that not only was Thomas Moses Green, one of the long-serving clerks at Carlton Ride, of limited usefulness in dealing with the older Exchequer records but that he also carried out business as an ironmonger. Perhaps as a counter-thrust, Hunter remarked that he had been told that Edwards carried out business as a coal merchant, but on that he was misinformed as Edwards had given up that activity as far back as 1841.

At much the same time as this review of administrative business was taking place the pay and grading of the workmen came to the fore when they submitted a memorial, signed on their behalf by the senior man at each branch, drawing attention to the better pay said to be enjoyed by men in the British Museum, the Stamp Office and Marlborough House. In the past

---

17. PRO 2/2, pp 514–515.
18. PRO 2/3, pp 249–250: Palgrave to Yonge, 8 June 1854.
19. PRO 2/2, pp 812–814, 817–818: Palgrave to the assistant keepers, 30 November and 2 December 1853.

such approaches had been given short shrift, but Romilly took a more conciliatory line and on 23 November 1853 Palgrave informed the assistant keepers:

His Honour has pleasure in observing that the memorial is very properly and temperately worded. He is also of the opinion that the remonstrances of the Workmen are not without some foundation, but it is out of his power to take the subject into consideration as an isolated question or otherwise than in connection with the alterations in the existing regulations of the Operative Department, which will be needed when the establishment of workmen, now divided in the several Branch Offices, will have to be consolidated in the new Repository.

In addition to the question of the workmen's pay, Palgrave was concerned about their complement as he had not attempted to fill vacancies for many years. The most recent had been caused by the death of Charles Gay, the long-serving and highly respected foreman, who could, according to Palgrave, judge with marvellous accuracy the date and class of a document by the mere look of the parchment and the form and colour of the writing. Realising that substantial strengthening was needed to prepare the records for transfer to the new building, he persuaded Romilly to agree to the engagement of ten more men, having explained to him fully the history of the grade which stretched back to its first establishment early in the century under John Caley, then secretary of the Record Commission.[20a] Palgrave thought there should be an upper age limit of 30 to 35 and that all new recruits should be able to write. There should also be a preference for anyone with a special talent, such as bookbinding, or for children or relatives of the more deserving workmen. Of the first six newcomers recruited, half fell into the latter category, while one of them, William Woolby, aged 27, was Palgrave's servant, having been with him since 1849. Evidently the office did not lose by the arrangement: Woolby was competent enough, although his appointment could be seen, and probably was by Palgrave's detractors, as a hidden subsidy towards his household expenditure. Nevertheless, the discipline under which the men laboured remained strict as was shown in September 1854 when one of them had his wages reduced by 2s a week for three months after an altercation with Lascelles, who had accused him of stealing a portion of his pennyworth of pease pudding and greens, which the man had been sent out to fetch for him.[20b]

The most important and obvious aspect of the changing record scene was

---

20a. PRO 2/2, pp 741–750: Palgrave to Romilly, 27 October 1853.

20b. When the man concerned, Henry Broughton, retired in 1875 the stoppage was recorded on the claim form for superannuation sent to the Treasury on his behalf, Hardy giving it as his opinion that the punishment had certainly been too severe: PRO 2/39, p 13.

at the Rolls where the shell of the huge new repository now stood in place of the flowers and fruit trees of the master's garden. The staff, watching the building develop day by day, could not escape its looming presence, although it was already evident that the new accommodation would barely provide for existing needs and the planned second and third blocks would be needed sooner than originally thought. The building was also badly behind schedule, Palgrave's belief, some 18 months earlier, that it would be ready to receive records by the end of 1852 proving wildly over-optimistic.[21] The delay sprang mainly from the highly specialised nature of the office's requirements and the absence of sufficiently detailed planning to enable the repository to be rapidly fitted up. These difficulties were aggravated by the fact that the repository, which was connected at its first floor to the Rolls House by a tubular bridge, was broken down into a large number of comparatively small strong rooms about 25 feet long, 17 feet wide and 15 feet high. Each was to be self-contained to minimise the risk from fire, if not eliminate the danger entirely. However, early in 1852 Braidwood, who had been involved in the earlier planning, was disturbed to find that, contrary to previous understanding, there were communicating doorways between the strong rooms. Although Braidwood was still superintendent of the London Fire Brigade, he discovered what had been done quite unofficially and so decided to write to Henry Cole, knowing how closely he had been concerned in the original negotiations. Cole lost no time in passing Braidwood's letter on to Thomas so that it might be laid before Romilly and Palgrave. The latter was furious at Braidwood's intervention, which he thought impertinent, and doubly so when a critical paragraph appeared in *The Times* of 18 March. Nevertheless, the upshot was a decision to brick up the openings, but not before Palgrave, who had asked for them for convenience of working, had blamed Pennethorne who, he thought, should have warned him if there was a fire risk. Pennethorne declined to take the blame and seven years later, when Palgrave complained about the appearance of cracks in the walls, turned the tables on him by attributing them to the bricked-up doorways,[22] while pointing out their structural unimportance.

Early in 1853 Pennethorne was again in hot water when Palgrave and Romilly believed that he was dealing directly with the assistant keepers, and steps had to be taken to ensure that all communications went through the deputy keeper to prevent confusion. That did not debar Palgrave from treating with Perkins, Pennethorne's able clerk of works, when he thought that necessary, but although Palgrave held very decided opinions he was willing to take other views into account and went to considerable lengths during 1853 to achieve a consensus with his record colleagues. One of his

21. PRO 1/14: Palgrave to Hardy, 2 August 1850.
22. PRO 1/23: Austin to Palgrave, 30 May 1859, enclosing Pennethorne's letter of 27 May 1859 to the first commissioner of works, to which Palgrave, rather defensively, has added a footnote 'Urged by Mr. Cole'.

hopes was to provide a study in the basement for officers and 'sufficiently qualified' workmen to work upon the records after office hours for literary purposes or for their own pleasure and information, keeping the room open until ten o'clock in the evening so that 'the public service will derive all the benefit of an "Ecole des Chartes" without the expense and display of such an establishment'.[23] Other needs pushed out that imaginative idea, but on the general question of the internal arrangement and fitments of the repository Palgrave sent out two detailed questionnaires to the assistant keepers during 1853, seeking their views on a wide range of matters, including the fitting-up of the search rooms and workshops. In order that all points might be fully considered, the answers were collated and re-circulated for further comment. Each assistant keeper received two copies, one of which he returned with any additional comments or suggestions and the other he retained among his own papers. As a matter of convenience, Palgrave arranged for the replies to be specially printed, getting the Treasury to sanction such a course after the Stationery Office had objected. Palgrave also promised to let the assistant keepers have a copy of the conclusions when finalised.

In all these matters Roberts, Hardy and Holden played leading roles, with Palgrave as co-ordinator-in-chief and John Bond from Carlton Ride providing valuable support in planning the removal of the records from the branches to their appointed place in the new repository. At times, Penne-thorne, who still saw the Record Office as but one feature of the larger metropolitan improvement he had in mind, must have been sorely tried by Palgrave's insistence upon being acquainted with every last detail of the new building. Inevitably, that insistence meant a price was paid in terms of progress, and further delay ensued when Palgrave, never completely at ease with plans and drawings, refused to give clearance for the fitting-up of the repository until one room was racked as a model. All the fixtures were to be of iron or other incombustible materials, and it was intended that each room should have two tiers, access to the upper storey being by means of a circular staircase in the corner. It was not until well into 1854 that the model was provided, but Palgrave's attempt to hammer out agreed proposals immediately ran into difficulty when the assistant keepers, with the exception of Burtt, offered strong objection to his proposal to fit iron shelves. They argued for wood, pointing out that it could be fire-proofed and was already used for boxing certain classes of records. Palgrave was backed by Romilly whose alternative choice was slate, which was eventually chosen although only after much argument. On security grounds Romilly also supported Palgrave's view that every division of the racking should be lockable and that no workman should produce a record from a strong room without an assistant keeper being present. The assistant keepers greatly doubted the

---

23. PRO 2/2, pp 84–85: Palgrave to Romilly, 5 February 1853.

need for such precautions or their likely efficacy, although accepting that any records in the search rooms, where the public might be present, should not be on open shelves. Summing up his own and Romilly's conclusions, Palgrave suggested that the views of the critics would not have had Langdale's support telling Hardy:[24]

The Plan of the Building was fully examined in all its stages by Lord Langdale who besides his general knowledge of books and libraries, was very fully acquainted with the existing Record Repositories and well possessed of all the principles and leading details required in a Building intended for the reception and use of the Records and the accommodation of the Record Officers. Nor would he in the last stage sign the plans, until Mr Pennethorne had attended him at Roehampton for the purpose of fully explaining them. Lord Langdale was in constant communication with Mr Cole and yourself, and had every means of discussing any point which might be considered as questionable, and you in particular had peculiar knowledge of the interest which he took in the Building and of his anxiety to see it completed according to the plans of which he approved.

Never since we have known anything of the History of Architecture was there any public or private building which escaped criticism or censure, or which has *fully* answered its purpose. Did ever any gentleman raise a mansion, in which however carefully the designs were prepared, there was not found something to amend or supply or alter, when the family and their Establishment came to inhabit it?

In the present case, it will be essential to bear in mind that inasmuch as no Archival structure of equal magnitude and solidity has ever yet been erected, the chances of involuntary error may be somewhat above the usual average, and it was for this reason that Sir John Romilly determined that no continuation should be erected until the present portion of the Structure should have been actually used for a sufficient time to afford the means of judging whether any improvements might be suggested by experience. At all events we may be certain that even the fragment so far as it extends, will always afford a most honourable testimony of Mr Pennethorne's judgement, taste, and constructive talent; and when we recollect how all the inconveniences of the present crowded and ill adapted Repositories have been mitigated by the exertions, attention, diligence, and talent of the Officers, it cannot be doubted but the same intelligence, assiduity, and conscientiousness continued in the New Repository, will much more than counter balance any slight mistakes in the structure. I do not offer these observations controversially or for the purpose of calling in judgement any

---

24. PRO 2/3, pp 268–276: Palgrave to Hardy, 19 June 1854.

opinions which may differ from mine, but simply for the purpose of showing
that every pains have been taken to come to right conclusions and that if
any of such conclusions should prove erroneous they have at all events not
resulted from haste or pertinacity.

Despite the disagreements, on 19 July 1854 Hardy, Roberts and Holden
signed the plans showing the allocation of space in the new repository[25] and
they were countersigned by Palgrave the next day. Of the 87 rooms, those
on the top and first floors, known as A and B floors, were given over to the
records, while those on the ground floor and certain of those in the basement,
known as C and D floors, were reserved for officers, searchers, workmen,
stores, laundry and a guard room. The rest of the basement space and
that in the tower was also set aside for records, especially those awaiting
arrangement. In fact, the basement was pressed into service almost immediately as a temporary storage area for the Welsh records, the earlier plan to
establish a branch office at Chester having been abandoned. By the end of
1854 the bulk of those records had been sent to London, filling five North
Western Railway luggage vans and three Great Western horseboxes. Their
weight was nearly twenty tons, and ten large waggons were needed to get
them from the railway terminus to the new repository. A further four tons
were removed during 1855. All these operations were entrusted to Roberts,
whose experience on the road between Dolgellau and Caernarvon, described
to Thomas on 10 September 1854, was typical of the troubles he encountered:[26]

the expenses of yesterday were far beyond my calculation. I had no idea of
the difficulty of conveying a heavy load across these mountains nearly 50
miles from Dolgelley to this place. We were at it from 9 in the morning till
nearly 7 – and I was obliged to get a stage coach and put on 4 horses most
of the road – and such jabbering in Welsh was never heard – at one time
they swore they would not bring us on, and I thought we should spend the
night in the hills.

Besides accommodating the transfers from Wales, the new repository had
to receive a small block of records from the former Court of the Honour of
Peveril. They were brought from Nottingham in August 1854 by Hardy on
his way back from Durham where he had been sent a fortnight earlier to
report upon the records of the palatinate. Hardy found the Durham records
in great confusion and was obliged to send for William Cusack to help him.
Even with his assistance and in spite of working ten hours daily, Hardy felt
he had not been allowed enough time to do the job properly. However, the

25. MPI 299/11–16.
26. PRO 2/4, pp 46–47.

full account he gave of the extent, condition and history of those records greatly impressed Palgrave, who had no hesitation about appending it to his *Sixteenth Report*. Hardy's notes on the origins and history of the Peveril Court were also appended, as well as Roberts's detailed report on his activities in Wales where, despite the physical problems caused by the removals, he said that he had met with the greatest courtesy and attention and did not find any disinclination to part with the records. Further material did, in fact, come up from Ruthin in 1859 and 1860. However, because space was precious, Palgrave made no attempt to call in the records from Durham or to deal with the other outlying block in respect of the Isle of Ely, which was believed by the bishop's secretary to be in the strong room at Ely House, London.

In addition to problems arising from the fitting-up of the new repository and the transfers of records to it, Palgrave had to consider how the work should be organised. With Romilly's support he believed that it should be by function, and on that matter he was also backed by all the assistant keepers, apart from Hunter and Devon who favoured separate departments corresponding broadly to the previous branches. By establishing distinct Search, Operative and Calendaring Departments and centralising copying work, Palgrave aimed to broaden the staff's knowledge of the records as a whole. That was needed because under the branch organisation someone familiar with Chancery records at the Tower might know next to nothing about common law material at Carlton Ride and *vice versa*. Palgrave and Romilly were also unhappy about leaving the workmen in a separate workshop in the new building under the sole supervision of a foreman drawn from their own ranks and thought they should be under the constant surveillance of a gentleman recruited for that purpose. The assistant keepers did not believe such an arrangement necessary or proper, but in any case were all agreed that repair and similar work had to come under their general direction. That particular problem was circumvented when James Hood, a skilled bookbinder, was brought in from outside in April 1855 as superintendent at the same rate of pay of 1s an hour enjoyed by Charles Gay, and Henry Gay was appointed second foreman alongside Peter Paul at 9d an hour. The assistant keepers were also unhappy about the system introduced at Henry Cole's insistence during the early years of the office, whereby the workmen worked two hours extra daily in order to bring their wages up to a sufficient amount. They thought that little was done during that time and there would be no real loss if the men were required to work only the normal office hours from ten to four. Immediately, however, no fundamental changes in the organisation were in prospect as it was clear that the union of all the branches under one roof was going to take much longer than originally thought.

The blame for that rested largely with the unforeseen requirements of the service departments arising from the Crimean War. In February 1855 troubles came to a head when the Board of Ordnance sought to repossess for storage purposes the rooms in the White Tower where the Admiralty records were stored. Those records were considered of comparatively little importance, at that time, and Palgrave had intended that they should remain where they were until the second block of the new repository was ready to receive them. Any idea of storing them in the new repository, even as a temporary measure, was out of the question as great difficulties were already being experienced there due to an emergency demand from the War Office to accommodate a large quantity of documents from its depot in Whitehall Yard, which was urgently required by the Army and Ordnance Medical Board. Although Palgrave and Romilly regretted the War Office request, which completely disrupted the fitting-up of the strong rooms and the planned removal of the records from Carlton Ride, they reluctantly agreed to assist in the national interest, but pressed the Treasury to consider extending the building and, possibly, increasing the establishment. During February and March 1855 Holden and Lascelles were given the task of bringing in the displaced War Office records, often working 14 hours a day until the entire mass, exceeding one hundred and fifty tons and over one hundred van loads, was installed temporarily in the corridors of the new repository. Because the records were still liable to be wanted officially, they were stored as nearly as possible in their original order in the presses in which they had been kept at Whitehall, which were also moved for that purpose. For their labours Holden and Lascelles were each awarded £25 by the Treasury, Romilly making the point in recommending the extraordinary payment that Lascelles had already lost the sight of his right eye in the public service.

That still left the problem of the Admiralty records at the Tower, which was partly relieved by the pulping of a great number of them following an inspection by Hardy and Sir John Liddell, director general of the Medical Department of the Navy. To accommodate those it was decided to preserve, and to provide for the War Office records cluttering up the corridors of the new repository, the Office of Works took steps to obtain possession of nine houses in Chancery Lane. Although the houses were far from suitable for record storage, the Public Record Office's occupation began on a gradual basis from November 1855. Meanwhile, the charge of the new repository, where the fitting-up of the strong rooms was incomplete, had been given to Holden in December 1854. He also continued to manage the Rolls Chapel branch office and attended the master of the rolls as clerk of the Chapel in connection with judicial business when recognizances etc. were vacated. He was officially described as caretaker of the new repository and the adjoining buildings, although he was not resident but continued to live in Kentish Town. As such, he had special responsibility for superintending the policemen assigned to patrol the new repository and its surrounds, numbering four during the silent hours and one during the day. Their value was soon proven when in July 1855 a large quantity of rain penetrated the roof of the repository and, while damage was caused to some Treasury and Exchequer records, its discovery during the early hours of the morning prevented worse injury. To add to Holden's heavy labours, besides dealing with any searches into the Chester and Welsh records he was much involved in attending on

Bennet Woodcroft, superintendent of patent specifications, and his staff, who were engaged daily upon the copying of specifications for the commissioners of patents for inventions and the queen's printers.

It was fortunate for Palgrave, whose age was beginning to tell on him, that he had at his disposal the services of so many gifted and hard-working colleagues. He was well aware of that and, despite personal differences, never lost an opportunity to point out to the Treasury his strong belief that they were inadequately rewarded and that there were insufficient incentives for good performance. Romilly was in full agreement, as he stressed to the Treasury in February 1854 in forwarding to it a memorial for an increase in pay, signed by all the assistant keepers and clerks. Eighteen months were to pass before that matter was settled. Thomas had succeeded in obtaining an increase of £100 in his annual salary from 1 October 1853, but, like Palgrave, only on a personal basis. That award resulted partly from his work, much of it in his own time, on the *Handbook to the Public Records*, which was published that year at the price of 12s; and in writing a short preface to and seeing through the press Rowley Lascelles's long-outstanding work for the Record Commission *Liber Munerum Publicorum Hiberniae*. It also counted in Thomas's favour that his earlier works on the history of public departments and of the Exchequer had proved of great utility in the Treasury. In all his activities Thomas received sterling support from Edwards, who was, nevertheless, unsuccessful when he petitioned the Treasury in January 1853 for a salary increase based upon his services in the office Secretariat and as Palgrave's confidential secretary.[27] In the latter capacity Edwards was Palgrave's only official intimate apart from Romilly, who always treated his deputy keeper with great consideration. Outside the office, and particularly since Lady Palgrave's death, Palgrave was even more isolated. Writing from Hampstead to Turner on 11 March 1855 he explained:

Except Hallam and Sir Robt Inglis I see no one. I have been compelled to give up all dinner parties and merely vibrate between this place and the office, riding both ways.

But worse was to come: within two months Palgrave was at Inglis's funeral, mourning the loss of his old friend, the ultra-conservative MP and godfather to his third son. Over a hundred years later the then keeper, Stephen Wilson, who also lived in Hampstead, customarily drove daily to the office in his car, taking much the same route that Palgrave rode on horseback. Wilson also had staffing problems and serious accommodation difficulties, but scarcely worse than those with which the ailing Palgrave had to contend in 1855. In many ways, however, that year was a milestone in

---

27. T 1/5852/25790/1853. Besides Edwards's memorial, this piece also contains papers concerning the increase in Thomas's pay. The Treasury papers relating to the assistant keepers' petition are in T 1/5909B/26957/1854.

the office's development for it marked the completion of the process of the long-awaited amalgamation with the State Paper Office, which had begun the previous year and which was to establish the broad pattern of working for over a century.

Chapter VII
Palgrave's Closing Years, 1854–1861

The archives of France, the most abundant and perfect beyond the Channel, do not ascend higher than the reign of Saint Louis, and compared with ours are stinted and jejune; whereas in England, taking our title by Domesday, the documents which by the Records Act, the Order in Council, and the incorporation of the State Paper Office with the Public Record Office, are or will be placed in the charge of the Master of the Rolls, contain material for the religious, legal, and political history of England and Wales, in every branch and in every aspect or relation, civil, political, social, statistical, moral, or material from the Norman Conquest, without any material interruption, to the present day.

(*The Seventeenth Report of the Deputy Keeper* (1856), 28)

Time had done nothing to reconcile the State Paper Office to the prospect of its absorption by the Public Record Office. The Treasury was convinced of the case for amalgamation, but there were many doubters. In 1852 *The Athenaeum*[1], reviewing Palgrave's *Thirteenth Report*, was critical of the extension of the Public Record Office's activities under the order in council of that year, sensing an element of 'empire building'. The State Paper Commission, which had been established in 1825 to print and publish the State Papers, was also much opposed to any change and, all its previous attempts to prevent the union having failed, it made a last-minute approach in January 1853 to Palmerston, then home secretary. As foreign secretary he had half-heartedly acquiesced in 1848 to the proposed merger, but he now told the Treasury that he saw many objections, the most important being that documents would no longer be so accessible to the secretaries of state, and that no saving worth making would be obtained. He also had misgivings about public access, but the Treasury was in no mood to compromise, although before replying it sent the papers to Romilly for comment. The result was a mammoth report on the entire issue by Palgrave, which, even with Edwards's assistance, took him six months to prepare and was not finally submitted to the Treasury by Romilly until January 1854.[2] Palgrave's report, which was printed and ran to over one hundred pages, set out in great detail the negotiations that had already taken place and the work the

---

1. *The Athenaeum*, no. 1288 (3 July 1852), 721–722. The writer may have been John Bruce because the arguments were not very different from those in an earlier article of his, 'The public records – what they are and what is to be done with them', *Gentleman's Magazine*, IX (1838), 15–21.
2. PRO 1/18.

office had done since 1839 for government departments and other public bodies. It also specified the assistance given to literary readers, and the subject of their researches, since the new regulations governing free access had been introduced, and summarised the correspondence from 1838 with public libraries and similar bodies for grants of printed publications. By now it was evident that the secretaries of state, preoccupied with the all too real hostilities in the Crimea, had more important things to do than to engage in a war of words with Palgrave. Consequently, Lemon, secretary of the State Paper Commission, reading the signs correctly, decided the time had come when prudence required that he should make his peace with Palgrave and on 16 January 1854 he wrote to him privately:[3]

Dear Sir Francis

I have been exceedingly interested in reading your Report, and I presume I shall have it officially communicated to me by the Secretary of State to whom the Memorial was addressed. It is very desirable each of our Commissioners should have a Copy, and as it is far too long to make several transcripts of, may I beg the favour to be furnished with copies for that purpose, if you have a sufficient number to spare. Our Commissioners are

The Foreign Secretary	Lord Mahon
The Home Secretary	Mr Hallam
Mr Hobhouse	Sir David Dundas
Lord John Russell	Mr [T] B Macaulay
Lord Monteagle	

As I presume the two Secretaries are furnished, and I know Mr Hobhouse to be so, that leaves Six Copies to the other Commrs if so many can be spared.

Permit me Sir to say a few words to you – *confidentially* – I am placed in a peculiar position. Whatever my private opinions may be, I am bound to execute the orders of the Commission under which I serve, faithfully and zealously. I have endeavoured to do so to the best of my ability; but in doing so I trust and hope that I have not in any instance given personal offence to any man.

If the current of events shall place this collection under other regulations, I

---

3. PRO 1/18. In spite of his protestations Lemon had always strongly opposed the union, although it is worth noting than when the 1838 act first became law he had put himself forward for the post of 'treasurer or receiver of fees' without success: PRO 1/1: Lemon to Langdale, 24 August 1838.

shall in the same manner and I trust with equal zeal and fidelity, endeavour
to carry out the principles of those to whose management it may be consigned.

I am, etc.

Robt. Lemon

Romilly thought that Lemon's letter was very satisfactory, but Mahon
(later Viscount Stanhope), the most active of the state paper commissioners,
took strong exception to Palgrave's report, saying that he had read a great
part of it and it seemed to him 'for an official document a pretty sharp attack
on some of our recent proceedings at the State Paper Office' and that he
was urging Palmerston to convene a special meeting of the commission.[4]
However, nothing came of that due to the death of Henry Hobhouse, keeper
of state papers, in April 1854, which led to a request to Romilly from the
Treasury on the 22nd to propose without delay a scheme for carrying on the
business of the State Paper Office in accordance with the recommendations of
the Select Committee of the House of Commons on Miscellaneous Expenditure, 1848, while having regard to the various reservations previously
expressed by the departments concerned. The reactions of the secretaries of
state, particularly Clarendon at the Foreign Office, to Romilly's response
that henceforth the State Paper Office should be a branch office of the Public
Record Department was one of grudging acceptance,[5a] despite the fact that
Romilly made it plain that no material, even if purely historical or of an
innocuous character from the point of view of public access, would be
removed to the new repository without their consent. Clearly, it was their
hope that apart from the nominal substitution of Romilly for Hobhouse
nothing much would change. That was to underestimate Palgrave, who was
never content to be a mere cipher, although the letter he wrote to Turner
expressing his satisfaction at the outcome indicated that much of his old
sparkle had vanished:[5b]

The State Paper Office will, by the directions of the Treasury, pass into my
charge. The measure has been long contemplated, but such a strenuous
opposition was raised against it by powerful interests that I did not think it
would be carried into effect. As a mark of confidence it is gratifying . . .
Twenty years ago I should have enjoyed the prospect of such an unbounded

---

4. SP 45/88: Mahon to Lemon, 20 January [1854].

5a. Clarendon's letter to the Treasury is printed in the appendixes to the *First Report
of the Royal Commission on Public Records*, I, pt II (Cd. 6395), 118–119.

5b. Dawson Turner Papers: Palgrave to Turner, 24 April 1854; printed in *The
Collected Historical Works of Sir Francis Palgrave, K.H.*, ed. R. H. Inglis Palgrave
(Cambridge, 1919), I, li.

store of information being opened to me, but now I can only think of gathering up my fragments during the remaining years.

Once the secretaries of state's assent had been obtained, steps were taken to revoke the State Paper Commission, which was formally wound up on 14 August 1854. A further five months elapsed before Romilly was able to submit proposals to the Treasury for the assimilation into the Public Record Office of all 13 members of the staff of the State Paper Office, ranging from Charles Lechmere, its deputy keeper, to Mrs Scutt, the housekeeper. In the interim the staff were paid as previously, with an appropriate allowance to those who had formerly been permitted to undertake record work privately. It was also arranged that from the beginning of 1855 the hours should be increased from five to six daily to bring the State Paper Office into line with the other branches. Inevitably, the introduction of so many newcomers to the Public Record Office had disturbing implications for the assistant keepers and clerks already there, whose existing prospects were poor and whose petition to the Treasury in February 1854 for an improvement in pay still remained unanswered. Romilly and Palgrave strongly favoured an increase in order to attract and retain competent officers, and Palgrave continued to urge the payment of 'early' and 'bounty' money, believing that a good brain was worthless unless backed by hard work and regular and punctual attendance. The Treasury appreciated that there was a problem and decided to give priority to improving the career structure by raising the number of assistant keeper posts from 8 to 14 and substituting annual increments for the previous five-yearly ones. The clerks' minimum was also increased from £80 to £100, but their maximum remained unchanged as did that of the assistant keepers. On the other hand, the maximum salaries of the deputy keeper and secretary posts were lifted by £200 to £1,000 and £700 respectively. The Treasury also made it clear that in the event of a vacancy in either post it expected it to be filled by the best qualified internal candidate.

Although Romilly recognised that the Treasury's proposals were a move in the right direction, he was irritated because he had not been consulted about them beforehand and he objected strongly to what he saw as Treasury interference in his right, under the 1838 act, to nominate a deputy keeper if a vacancy occurred. In such a case he thought it would be his duty to choose the best person he could find, and he told Trevelyan on 25 May 1855[6] that his conclusion was that in most instances the public service would be best served by choosing a gentleman with no previous connection with the department as the qualities most necessary for a deputy keeper were not the same as those required for an assistant keeper. He considered it wrong, therefore, to hold out to the assistant keepers an illusory hope of succession to that office as a reward for good service. He objected also to the separation

---

6. T 1/5968A/19558/1855.

of the secretary's pay scale from that of the first class assistant keepers with which it had been formerly associated. The opening up of a gap of £200 was, he thought, tantamount to the creation of a 'species of 2nd Deputy Keeper' – a phrase which sounded like, and may have been prompted by, Palgrave – which, Romilly believed, would lead to a conflict of authority and have injurious consequences. At the same time, Romilly was glad that Thomas, who already received £100 more than the assistant keepers on a personal basis, was to receive a further increase as he believed he deserved it. Nevertheless, he much lamented that the same consideration had not been extended to the assistant keepers despite his strong recommendation in their favour. He also pointed out that he was receiving £1,000 less than Langdale and the saving in Hobhouse's salary of £1,200 as a result of the amalgamation with the State Paper Office meant that the superintendence of the new establishment was being discharged for £2,200 less than previously. He stressed also the difficulties the assistant keepers faced in their job and the talents required of them, drawing special attention to the case of Holden upon whom had fallen the extra labour of superintending the new repository. He also argued that the considerable benefits given to the officers senior and junior to the assistant keepers had the appearance of a slight and he feared this could have a depressing effect on morale. Summing up, he said:

There is no Department in which zeal and willingness to work are more required than in the Record Department, because from the nature of the duties they have to perform it is almost impossible from the amount of the work done, to measure the degree of labour necessary for that purpose.

Another consideration ought as it appears to me to weigh with their Lordships in the consideration of this subject: the Office is no ways connected with Politics – no influences of that description have affected the appointments which have taken place in it, but it is one of the very few establishments in this Country which affords some promise of reward to literary men and literary inquirers and which it cannot but be useful to encourage. My great and principal reason however for pressing this matter on the attention of their Lordships is my belief that the public service will be prejudiced unless the claims of these officers be more favourably considered; and I beg to suggest to their Lordships as the very lowest measure of justice due to them, that the maximum salaries of the assistant keepers of the First Class ought to be raised to £600 and that of the Assistant Keepers of the Second Class to £400. I beg to say that I earnestly press this upon their Lordships not only as my sincere conviction of what is the least that is due to the gentlemen themselves but also as the least sums by which persons fully competent for the efficient discharge of these duties for the public service can be obtained.

However, Trevelyan was not to be moved, and he told the chancellor of the Exchequer, Sir George Cornewall Lewis, on 4 June 1855:

considering all the circumstances of their employment, and especially the fact that they are relieved both from money responsibility and from the anxiety and wear and tear which belongs to the Offices charged with the current business of government and looking to the general rate of remuneration in public and private employment I entertain a sincere conviction that the scale of salaries in the Record Department should not rise above £500 except in the case of the Deputy Keeper and the Secretary.

Lewis, anxious to avoid giving further offence to Romilly, thought it best to invite his comment upon Trevelyan's views before taking a decision, and Romilly replied privately and with great force on 9 June. He repeated many of his former arguments, and poured scorn on what he believed was Trevelyan's failure to appreciate the intricacies of the assistant keepers' duties, owing to his regarding them in the nature of a pastime. He also attacked Treasury policy on public service pay, which he thought depended upon the views of its secretary for the time being. As regards the office's own tensions, he revealed Thomas's jealousy of Palgrave's increased influence since Langdale's death. He also mentioned Thomas's boasting of having the Treasury's ear, and Palgrave's belief that that was so. Four days later, Trevelyan, stung by Romilly's onslaught, assured Lewis that there had been no prior consultation with Thomas about the proposed arrangements. He also vigorously defended his contention that the officers of the Public Record Office were already well paid. Uppermost in his mind at that time was his and Northcote's plan for Civil Service reform. In his eyes Romilly's intention to appoint an outsider as deputy keeper if a vacancy occurred must have numbered him among those heads of departments hostile to any change in the former system of patronage. Yet Romilly's right to do so under the 1838 act could not be challenged. But that act also required that the deputy keeper should be a 'fit person duly qualified by his knowledge of records'. Taking that into account, along with the general principle of promotion on merit, Trevelyan considered it probable that the other qualities required of a deputy keeper would be 'developed in some of the numerous well educated and intelligent gentlemen composing the Establishment'. Notwithstanding those advantages, however, he admitted that if a better qualified person could be found the master of the rolls should exercise his power to appoint him.[7a]

Lewis, caught between the crossfire, passed Trevelyan's letter to Romilly, who replied on 21 June, saying that no personal reflection upon Trevelyan was intended and denying that he thought Thomas involved. But Romilly pointed out that the review ought not to have been restricted to the union of the two departments as the memorial from the record officers about their

---

7a. Romilly's and Trevelyan's letters are reproduced in Appendix X. The originals are in T 1/5968A/19558/1855.

pay ought also to have been considered. If it was correct that they were liberally paid by comparison with other offices he did not wonder that complaint was made of the working of the entire system. Impressed by Romilly's advocacy, Lewis decided some concession was necessary and on 26 June it was agreed that three of the assistant keepers of the first class might be allowed to rise by annual increments of £20 to £600 and four of those of the second class by £15 increments to £400. The improvement, the Treasury said, was 'to provide a reward for those who are distinguished by their constant attention to their official duties and by the exertions they have made to qualify themselves for the full performance of them'.

As a result of the chancellor's decision Lechmere and Lemon were appointed to the first class and Hans Hamilton, also of the State Paper Office, a most accomplished man, who had previously worked under Stevenson for the Record Commission, was appointed to the second class. The remaining three places in that class were filled by the promotion of Lascelles, Edwards and Bond. The four existing men of the second class, Holden, Burtt, Sharpe and Nelson, were all allowed to proceed to the new £400 maximum, while Hardy, Hunter and Lechmere were placed on the scale for the new maximum of £600 fixed for the first class. Lechmere, however, was far from happy, as he was started at the minimum of the scale at £400. That equated roughly with the amount he had been receiving at the State Paper Office although he was allowed to retain his apartments there. Five years later he was still not reconciled to his treatment, but failed to secure Romilly's support for the reconsideration of his case by the Treasury. Lemon was placed at the £500 point on the scale because in addition to his post of second or chief clerk at the State Paper Office he had been secretary of the State Paper Commission and he had also received certain fees as a literary agent. The remaining clerks of the State Paper Office were not at all pleased with the outcome because, although they were placed at various points on the clerical scale to reflect their previous service, they nearly all suffered some reduction in pay, the Treasury argument being that any loss was more than offset by the permanence of their new situation and the better prospects it offered. Of their number, William Noel Sainsbury was perhaps the most unfortunate as at one time Romilly had proposed to make him an assistant keeper, but the Treasury did not think that he had enough service and so he was placed near the head of the clerical scale at £192. The Treasury also decided that those assistant keepers on the extended scale had to serve a full year before getting their increment, a decision which led Palgrave to tell Trevelyan that 'your Treasury rules are felt to be grudging and ambiguous'. Palgrave also felt aggrieved that his personal salary remained unaltered and that no allowance had been made for the many years he had served at a lesser salary than that to which he believed he was entitled. Overall, however, the assistant keepers and clerks of the old establishment were delighted about the improvements obtained and, apart from Charles Cole, lost no time in drawing up a letter, which Thomas forwarded to Romilly on 15 August 1855, to thank him for the efforts he had made on their behalf, without which they were convinced that their application would not have been favourably received by the government.[7b] In thanking the officers and expressing his great satisfaction at their letter, Romilly told them he thought his success was due to the fair and candid spirit in which the chancellor of the Exchequer regarded their 'mental acquirements and capacities'. Cole did himself no good not only by declining to sign but also by writing to Romilly to protest about the promotion of John Bond, alleging that because of his own non-selection he would be less able to look after his sick father. Joseph Redington, who was senior to all three promoted Public Record Office men and who enjoyed a good reputation at Carlton Ride under Hunter, was more circumspect, writing a dignified letter of protest. Romilly responded very civilly, leading Redington to suppose that he might expect promotion on the next vacancy.

The extension of the office's activities to the State Papers provided Palgrave with the opportunity he had long been seeking to resume publication. Romilly was of like mind and as early as the beginning of 1853 had broached the matter with Trevelyan, who thought that provided the scandal of the Record Commission could be avoided there was every reason to suppose that the confidence of the government and of the public could be secured. The curtailment of the calendars previously appended by Palgrave to his *Reports* had long rankled with him and in his seventeenth for 1855 he took the opportunity presented by the resumption of publication to enter a full-scale apologetic of the former practice. Refuting the argument that no calendar should be undertaken until a perfect classification was effected, he tellingly maintained that each generation ought to provide for its own needs, avoiding any 'long-winded' plan incapable of completion until the compilers were lying in their graves. He believed it a national duty to make the contents of the office widely known: it was impossible to exaggerate the importance of expanding facilities for home study because a quiet hour spent by a student at his own desk was, in his opinion, worth a day in any public library.

With Romilly's support, Palgrave decided that because of public interest priority ought to be given to publicising documents from the time of Henry VIII. He believed that, although to employ his own staff on such work was highly desirable as it encouraged competition between them without awakening jealousy or rivalry and gave them the satisfaction of publication, their efforts should be supplemented by the appointment of outside editors engaged solely for that purpose and paid in accordance with the quantity of work passed for press. The first such person selected was Mrs Mary Anne Everett Green. Back in 1843 Palgrave had noted the excellence of her work – she was then Miss Wood – and compared her researches in the records for the *Lives of the Princesses of England* very favourably with those of Agnes

---

7b. PRO 1/125.

170

Strickland for her *Letters of Mary Queen of Scots*. Good humouredly, he had wondered at that time whether they would at last 'come to the royal birth and wet nurses'.[8] In fact, Mrs Green's progress was to be altogether more stately. She managed to combine her family responsibilities with those of a leading editor of the domestic state papers, completing by the time of her death in 1895 no fewer than 41 volumes. Her appointment in 1855, which she accepted dutifully, saying she had Mr Green's permission to do so, was followed by that of John Bruce and Markham John Thorpe. Mrs Green, who was fortunate in being able to call upon some assistance from her sister, started work with the domestic correspondence of James I in continuation of Lemon's calendar, still in progress, for the preceding period. Bruce set to work on the domestic papers for the reign of Charles I, while Thorpe, who had lived down the earlier episode arising from his purchase of strayed public records and who had been working for William Salt, the Staffordshire antiquary, since resigning from his clerical post at the State Paper Office in 1848, was engaged at a slightly lesser rate of pay to perfect the calendar of Scottish and Border Papers down to the accession of James I. The existence of draft calendars made earlier by State Paper Office clerks was thought to provide a sound basis for the editor's work, but Bruce soon ran into difficulties as those for his period proved grossly defective, which led to Romilly securing Treasury approval to pay him the sum of £400 in 1856 instead of the £8 8s for each sheet of 16 pages previously agreed. It was also arranged to pay him £200 plus £5 5s a sheet during 1857 and to allow two of the clerks, W. Impey and W. D. Hamilton, to assist him. Mrs Green was originally engaged at £10 10s a sheet but that was later reduced to £8 8s and she was left free to negotiate her own fee with Longman, the publishers, for any introduction she might write. The association of Longman with the series was a new development, the former Record Commission publishers, Butterworth, much to their chagrin, having been displaced by them. In submitting Bruce's case to the Treasury, Romilly indicated that he might be asking for some additional payment for Mrs Green, evidently intending to ensure that her remuneration should not get out of line.

On Palgrave's recommendation Romilly added a fourth member to his team in 1856 by appointing the Reverend John Sherren Brewer, the former Record Commission editor and friend of Hardy, to edit a series of *Letters and Papers of Henry VIII*. As Brewer lectured for eight hours a week during term at King's College London where he was professor of the English language and literature and lecturer in modern history, it was agreed to pay him £350 per annum. He was held in high esteem by Romilly, who later appointed him reader and then preacher at the Rolls Chapel. Brewer's task was made immensely more difficult by the way that so much of the original

---

8. Dawson Turner Papers: Palgrave to Turner, 18 October 1843. On 17 May 1845 Palgrave sent Turner the young lady's autograph, saying 'her knowledge of ancient records etc. is truly wonderful'.

material had been dispersed, obliging him to carry his researches beyond the Public Record Office to the universities of Oxford and Cambridge, the British Museum and Lambeth Palace. But he was a determined and single-minded man, and with the able assistance of young James Gairdner he performed wonders in managing to bring together in his calendar the various documents for the history of Henry VIII's momentous reign. Interested as he was in all periods that of Henry VIII had an especial fascination for him and it was said that when sorting documents he classified them as 'Henry VIII', 'Not Henry VIII', 'Trash' and 'Rubbish'.[9]

The union of the Public Record Office and the State Paper Office greatly facilitated publication despite squabbles, which still broke out from time to time between the State Paper branch and the others as to where particular papers should be held.

Palgrave took the view that as far as possible the original arrangement should be kept and was opposed to the break-up of distinct series such as those of the Court of Requests or the Augmentation Office. However, where material was already hopelessly confused, as in the case of many of the state papers brought into the general repository from the branches for Brewer's use, different considerations applied. There was little alternative but to re-arrange them chronologically, but that was easier said than done: many of them were undated or fragmentary, and extensive research was often required before they could be placed in their correct order. Although Brewer's main record concern was with his calendar he was also involved with another great editorial project, the Chronicles and Memorials of Great Britain and Ireland during the Middle Ages, which became known as the Rolls Series. The roots of that enterprise lay in Petrie's *Monumenta Historica Britannica*. As seen earlier, the first part of that work, covering the period before the Norman Conquest, had appeared in 1848 under Hardy's editor-ship, and immediately after its publication he had submitted a plan for its continuance, in which he was supported by Brewer and Stevenson. Nothing came of their proposal at that time, but in November 1856 Stevenson, by then vicar of Leighton Buzzard, wrote to the Treasury, arguing that as it had been decided to publish the documents from the time of the Reformation the moment had come to revive the earlier intention, first determined in 1822, to print the early sources of British history. He indicated his willing-ness to undertake such a project, particularly as he believed Hardy and Brewer to be occupied on other important tasks. Stevenson's timing was good because in Lewis the country had a chancellor of the Exchequer sympathetic to historical pursuits, who had even found funds from the normally tight-fisted lords of the Treasury to send a palaeographer to the monasteries in the Levant. Romilly needed little persuasion, especially as

---

9. Charles Johnson, 'The Public Record Office', in *Studies presented to Sir Hilary Jenkinson*, ed. J. Conway Davies (Oxford, 1957), 179.

172

Hardy was as enthusiastic as ever about any enterprise which might further the work Petrie had begun. Hardy's hand, as well as Palgrave's, can be seen in the letter that Romilly sent to Trevelyan on 26 January 1857.

In his letter Romilly argued that Great Britain lagged behind other nations in making its historical treasures known to the world, and pointed to the extent of the ancient manuscripts and other extant material remaining partly or wholly unpublished. He agreed with Palgrave, Brewer and other critics about the unsuitability of the Dom Bouquet editorial method, adopted by Petrie, of bringing material together in a chronological arrangement and favoured instead the publication of each work in its entirety. For that reason he did not believe Petrie's design should be continued, as suggested by Stevenson, but thought the task should be given to those literary gentlemen who had shown themselves competent to undertake such work, aided by officers of the Public Record Office itself. Subject to Treasury approval of each work and its editor, he thought that an expenditure of £3,000 a year for ten years would accomplish most of what was required. He believed it would also be useful to have a chronological catalogue of all the historical annals and pieces connected with English history, but did not think the general scheme should be delayed on that account. Romilly mentioned that Hardy had already assembled much material for that purpose and thought some special payment ought to be made to him in recognition of the work he had done and was willing to continue. Romilly also indicated his intention to publish medieval documents in the Public Record Office, such as the royal letters, as circumstances permitted as well as the state papers from the time of Henry VIII. It was clear that he had carefully prepared his ground because a fortnight later the Treasury gave its broad approval to his proposals and so enabled him to push ahead with his ambitious project without delay.[10a]

At the outset Romilly invited Palgrave, Hardy, Stevenson and Brewer to draw up lists of works for inclusion in the series. Differences between Palgrave and his colleagues were soon manifest and he gradually withdrew into the background, apparently content to leave the general direction to Romilly and Hardy, whose position was further strengthened in June 1857 following a conference with Lewis and Trevelyan.[10b] However, Palgrave's advocacy of the publication of records of the Corporation of London did result in the inclusion in the series of the *Munimenta Gildhallae Londoniensis* under the editorship of Henry Thomas Riley, later an inspector of the

---

10a. The correspondence was laid before Parliament and ordered to be printed in March 1857 (*HC Accounts and Papers*, 1857, Sess I, XIII, 43–52). The subsequent development of the Rolls Series was elegantly described by the Reverend M. D. Knowles in his presidential address to the Royal Historical Society in 1960: *RHS Transactions*, Fifth Series, II (1961), 137–159. See also L. J. Cappon 'Antecedents of the Rolls Series: issues in historical editing', *Journal of the Society of Archivists*, IV, 358–369.

10b. PRO 37/73: minutes of a conference between the master of the rolls and the chancellor of the Exchequer in Downing Street, 1 June 1857, in the presence of Sir Charles Trevelyan and Mr Hardy.

Historical Manuscripts Commission. In addition to the engagement of out-side editors, it was also agreed that Brewer, Gairdner, Haydon and Charles Cole might undertake certain works out of office hours for which they might be given a gratuity. Hardy's close involvement was greatly helped by the fact that during the early part of 1856 he had moved to the Fetter Lane Repository, as it was then known, although for several months thereafter he still spent some of his time at the Tower, ceasing to attend there only when the bulk of the records had been moved out. While Hardy must have appreciated the closer contact with Romilly as a result of his transfer, it also meant an increase in his dealings with Palgrave, which could hardly have been welcomed by either. According to Maxwell Lyte, who came to know a number of those who had been on the staff during Palgrave's deputy keepership, the two men were not on speaking terms. Jeaffreson went even further, alleging that by reason of Palgrave's unbending hostility Hardy treated him as though he were a 'mere piece of official furniture' when approaching him on business.[11] That there was still great tension and sus-picion between Palgrave and Hardy and that they were always prepared to believe the worst of each other cannot be doubted, but the degree to which their animosity was openly displayed at this period may well have been exaggerated. It was certainly not obvious from Palgrave's *Eighteenth Report* covering 1856, in which he included Hardy's views on calendaring and the best way to provide for the needs of the 'inquirer living at a distance'. Privately, however, Palgrave undoubtedly found Hardy's closer presence disturbing and that may explain why in April 1856 he asked the elderly Turner for the return of the letters he had written to him over many years, apparently fearing they might otherwise fall into unfriendly hands. In particular, he stressed that 'in relation to the Record Department (which I am aware abounds with those who wish me no good) such disclosures of private affairs would be in the highest degree detrimental to my position and character'. He mentioned his concern about his dealings with official persons relating to his appointment as deputy keeper and letters illustrating his relations with Langdale and the Treasury. He was also worried about correspondence arising from the Record Commission controversies with 'Cooper, Hardy, Nicolas, Devon, etc.'.[12] Turner duly obliged, seemingly enabling Palgrave to obliterate an odd passage or two concerning his banking and other activities about which he may well have felt a sense of guilt. It is also possible that one or two letters may have disappeared altogether, but so much has survived, creditable and not so creditable, that it seems more probable that Palgrave, historian and archivist, wished merely to conceal them in his own lifetime, leaving it to his family, as appears from his will, to determine their disposal thereafter. Understandably, when 'Inglis'

11. PRO 8/47 (Sources and General bundle, Pt 2): J. R. Crompton's notes of an interview with Lyte, *c.* 1936–1937; and Jeaffreson's *Recollections*, 83–84.
12. Dawson Turner Papers: Palgrave to Turner, 19 April 1856.

Palgrave came to write an introduction to his father's collected works, which were published in 1919, he drew a veil over the various record controversies, but the survival of Palgrave's own accounts of those bitter events enables posterity to form its own judgment, besides providing a valuable supplement to the official documents for the record historian.

Even by 1856, when Palgrave recovered his letters, he had not finished battling with his colleagues, but he had the consolation of knowing that the government wished to appoint him a trustee of the proposed National Portrait Gallery, an honour he was to accept in December of that year. Against that, he was becoming increasingly depressed about his failure to make better progress with his Norman history and his health continued to give him problems. Although 68, he still rode to the office on horseback in all weathers, which must have taken pluck, particularly in March 1856 when a neglected blow on the heel ulcerated and he could barely manage the journey. One of his problems at that time was the serious difference between the assistant keepers and himself on the question of security and the need to accompany workmen to the strong rooms. Furthermore, his, and Romilly's, insistence upon wire or glass doors for the presses had resulted in such large additional expense – nearly £25,000 – that the programme had to be spread over three years, delaying still further the fitting-up of the repository. By 1859 the operation was still not complete and some £3,000 of equipment had to be put in store at Somerset House when a change in the storage arrangements in the rooms in the basement made it senseless to hang wire doors in them because the presses were not deep enough to enable the doors to be shut on the bundles of Chancery proceedings stored there. With so much locking and unlocking there was also an immense problem looming concerning the 3,000 or more keys which would be required. Originally, Palgrave had thought that, under his general direction, the problem of the day-to-day control of the keys and the access to the strong rooms might be overcome by charging the officer appointed caretaker with the responsibility. But that, too, failed to satisfy the assistant keepers who felt it constituted an interference with their personal responsibility for the records in their charge. Consequently, it was agreed that the caretaker was to have four master keys, one for each floor, but they were to be sealed for use in emergency only. However, when Hardy became deputy keeper in 1861 and assumed personal responsibility for all the records, he decided to simplify matters by sanctioning the opening of strong rooms by the masters as a matter of course and vested their charge in three of the workmen, with assistance, as necessary, from four others, all seven being specially named for the purpose.

The question of the caretaker post had itself also aroused controversy because in 1844, when detailed consideration was first given to the building of the new central record office, Cole and Hardy were agreed that two official residences ought to be provided for assistant keepers, but their suggestion was strongly opposed by Palgrave. Cole, who had fought unsuccessfully for some such provision at Carlton Ride, mainly as a precaution against fire, even went so far as to suggest that it would also give some protection against popular tumults and riots, possibly thinking that that might appeal more to Palgrave. In fact, when he drafted his own Public Records Bill in 1837 Palgrave had inserted a clause to enable official residences to be provided in the new central record office he envisaged, but as deputy keeper he took a rather different tack, believing that the permanent presence on the site of a senior officer or officers might lead to a conflict with his own authority and that any such post should be filled from the class of domestics. Langdale disagreed, thinking a superior officer should be appointed, but that one such post was enough. In the early months of the new repository Holden acted as non-resident caretaker, but as the building began to fill up Palgrave, on Hardy's recommendation, replaced Holden by Alfred Kingston, who was willing to accept as the promised provision of accommodation enabled him to marry. That was fortunate for the office, which would otherwise have been hard pressed to find anyone willing to take the job. It was well into 1857, however, before Kingston was able to take up residence at 12 Chancery Lane, an earlier idea to utilise certain rooms in the central tower in the new building having been abandoned. Some furniture was provided for his house but not to the extent that Palgrave thought appropriate, which resulted in his being granted an additional £1 a week allowance. Thomas much disliked the use of the word 'caretaker', thinking 'resident officer' more appropriate. He also maintained that, provided a responsible officer was on the site, patrolling by the police was unnecessary. His view was not shared by Palgrave who was, nevertheless, anxious to ensure that Kingston should not gain undue preference over his clerical colleagues. His duties were, however, of a very different nature from theirs because he was made responsible for the good order of the building, the issue of furniture, stores and the like, and the general control of the workmen, as directed by the assistant keepers. In fact, he carried out many of the duties which eventually came to be undertaken by the office keeper grade.

Although Kingston's stock stood high at that time, all had not been going well for a number of his clerical colleagues, including his younger brother William who was under a cloud and in April 1856 decided to resign. In July Moses Green, who was in the process of trying to restore his reputation with Palgrave, died unexpectedly. A little earlier Fenwick, who was rarely out of trouble for long, had the misfortune to lose the key of Westminster Hall where certain records were still in the Stone Tower. That caused a frightful commotion, relieved only after handbills were posted in the area offering a 10s reward to the finder and the key was eventually returned by a small boy, who claimed to have found it in St Margaret's churchyard while playing ball there. Another unfortunate was Frederick Hohler, a former State Paper Office clerk, who had lost his increment and been moved to the Rolls House under Lascelles. Hohler, whose father was an Anglican clergyman, but was himself something of a bohemian, was also concerned in a bizarre episode involving George Knight, whose delicate health had caused Palgrave so much worry some years earlier, William Hart, a Palgrave protégé, and the long-serving John Kentish. The trouble arose from the circulation within the office of the following notice:[13]

Mr. George Knight of the Public Record Office, Instructor to the Presbyterian Sunday School of the Camden Town District, who is well experienced in the profession of religion, has, from purely conscientious motives, and from a hearty desire to forward the interests of the Gospel, undertaken, at great personal inconvenience, pecuniary loss and denial and in many cases at the risk of serious bodily injury, to reform the indecent and blasphemous language which is constantly carried on in all Government Offices, to the evil example of others.

Mr. Knight's efforts have, the Lord's name be praised, been successful in reclaiming from paths of vice and immorality the Officers in the Treasury and Exchequer of Receipt Division of the Public Record Office, namely, Messrs Hart & Hohler, whose language has hitherto been of the grossest description, indeed to such an extent did this practice prevail with them, that Mr. Knight, though most unwillingly, was forced to appeal to the Deputy Keeper for redress but unfortunately, without success, such is the pitch which the evil has reached.

Yet the Gospel was at work, the mustard seed which Mr. Knight had sown in their hearts above a year ago, had, unperceived by them, took root, it started from the ground, it increased, Yea, from the least of all seeds it became the greatest among herbs, (Matt. 13.32.) and came to maturity even yesterday; then did Mr. Hart and Mr. Hohler rejoice, and exclaim with a loud voice that they were converted, then did they praise the name of the Lord and say "I will arise, and go to my Father, and will say unto him, Father I have sinned against Heaven and before thee and am no more worthy to be called thy son" (Luke 15.18.).

In testimony of this Messrs Hart and Hohler will be happy to furnish testimonials of Mr. Knight's success in their conversion.

In order fully to carry out his intentions Mr. Knight proposes to call on Mr. Kentish on Wednesday at three o'clock in order to remonstrate with him on the evil practice which Mr. Knight has made it his business to reform, and in the mean time he hopes that the perusal of the enclosed tract will pave

---

13. PRO 1/21. In 1852 Hart was undertaking research into the history of Hatcham, Deptford, where he was then living. He came to Palgrave's notice at that time, being one of the first searchers granted free access to the records, and later undertook record-agency work. Although he qualified as a solicitor, he decided against following that profession, and, on Palgrave's nomination, joined the office as a clerk in January 1855. The tract said to be enclosed with the circular has not survived.

the way to the softening of his heart, and turning of his ways, which none
but an experienced spiritual adviser can effect.

An early answer is requested.

P.S. Gentlemen in spiritual difficulties waited upon at their own
residences.

Rolls House
January 19. 1857

The copy bound with the office correspondence seems to be the one which
was sent to Kentish. It is set in litho apart from the words 'Mr. Kentish',
which have been inserted, apparently in Hart's hand, in a space left blank
for the purpose. The names of other recipients may well have appeared on
the copies sent to them, suggesting that the whole affair was an elaborate
jape, in extremely poor taste, at Knight's expense.

Needless to say the incident did not pass unremarked, and the assistant
keepers at Carlton Ride sent an angry letter of protest to Palgrave on 22
January 1857.[14]

Sir

A circular letter in the name of Mr. Knight having been addressed to the
several gentlemen in our Departments which they consider of a highly
offensive and insulting description and derogatory to the character of the
Office (in which opinion we cordially co-incide) we are requested by them
to call your attention to the subject, and to express the disgust they feel on
this occasion.

As we understand the circumstances are specially reported to you for the
information of his Honour the Master of the Rolls by Mr. Lascelles who
has charge of the Department in which it occurred, we will not trouble you
by entering into detail, but only express our hope that such steps will be
immediately taken as this very inexcusable and mischievous act demands.

We have etc,

Joseph Hunter, Charles Roberts, H J Sharpe

Although not requested by the Clerks in my department to report this
transaction, I beg leave to state that I entirely concur in the sentiments
expressed in this letter.

T Duffus Hardy

---

14. PRO 2/9, p 513.

Palgrave, a regular churchgoer, could hardly have been best pleased by the inference that he, too, had been touched by the evil, but he acted skilfully to defuse the situation, as was apparent from the letter he sent to Hardy and Roberts five days later:[15]

Dear Sirs

Nothing could be further from my mind than the apprehension that the destruction of the letter signed by yourselves and other Officers of the Establishment could be construed as a token of disrespect to you. But I had previously destroyed the Papers sent in to me by Mr. Hart upon the full conviction (a conviction which I shall entertain until over-ruled by superior authority) that I could not consistently with my official obligations take official notice of such a transaction and that it was consequently inexpedient to keep any documents relating to the matter. I have however unofficially and for the purpose of restoring good feeling advised Mr. Hart to apologize to the Gentlemen he has offended.

   Much regretting the involuntary vexation I have caused to you.
   Believe me, etc.

F Palgrave.

Plainly, the issue of the circular, even if taken at its face value, was highly imprudent, but, however that may be, it was not surprising that within weeks Palgrave moved Knight, who had never got on well with Lascelles, to the State Paper Office where he was put to work on the calendar of state papers of Charles I. Shortly before the circular appeared, another scandal had erupted when one of the workmen at Carlton Ride, William Yorke Finley, was made bankrupt. Foolishly, and contrary to Treasury rules, he had been dealing in stationery, trading under his wife's name as a bookseller, newsvendor and tobacconist. He had previously borne a good character and his record service went back 23 years, but his business failure meant that, with the loss of his furniture and with a wife and seven children to support, his distress was dire. However, Romilly and Palgrave brushed aside his plea for clemency, believing that to accede would undermine office discipline, and so he was dismissed. Nevertheless, it is difficult to believe that his activities were not known, unofficially, at Carlton Ride, but evidently his mistake was to fall into debt and so make public what was going on.

Finley's dismissal brought to light some similar activities by S. A. Mowels, the highly skilled bookbinder at the State Paper Office. He revealed that he had recently bought a bookshop and stationers in Sloane Street for £600,

---

15. PRO 2/9, p 516. Although Palgrave said he had destroyed the papers sent in to him, he may not have realised that copies of the correspondence were entered in the letter books at the Rolls House and Carlton Ride.

claiming to have done so in ignorance of the regulations. As he had been in the service for 14 years and was an extremely valuable man to have on the staff, Lechmere and Lemon thought an attempt should be made to obtain exemption for him. Romilly was unwilling to approach the Treasury but gave Mowels six months' grace to dispose of his business or resign. Unable to sell without an unacceptable loss, Mowels resigned at the beginning of 1858, being replaced by Thomas Beall, Hood's son-in-law.

If those who broke the rules received short shrift from Palgrave, it was also true that he would go out of his way to help those he thought deserving. For instance, while not prepared to authorise holiday or sick pay to short-service workmen, he made it clear that if they were seriously ill he was always prepared to use his influence to obtain advice for them or admission to a public hospital. He had much admiration for those men on the staff who tried to extend their knowledge, for example H. A. Mealy, a third-class workman and nephew of Gay, who was seeking a better position at the British Museum. Writing about him to Panizzi in May 1857, Palgrave said: 'I never knew of a more honest, firm and steady desire of self improvement than in him'.[16] Palgrave was also reluctant to see the men diverted to purely menial tasks, such as lighting fires and sweeping floors, thinking that such work should be undertaken by part-time charwomen. However, when it became clear that some general portering and cleaning work had to be carried out on a full-time basis, he agreed to engage a workman for that purpose, grading him in the fourth class at 4d an hour. Necessarily, the preparation and movement of records into the new repository involved the workmen in much physical labour, leading to the reaffirmation of the grant of 'beer money' or the issue of beer in exceptional circumstances. In November 1859, after the movement of records in bulk was at an end, Palgrave issued a regulation forbidding the bringing of beer into the office except between 12 noon and 2 p.m. In the repository it was allowed only in the kitchen in the basement where all cooking and serving of meals took place. Spirits were not allowed except in case of illness, and then only with the sanction of an assistant keeper. Any case of drunkenness was to be reported immediately to the deputy keeper and secretary and was punishable by 'reduction or suspension of wages, degradation to a lower class or dismissal'. However, a change occurred in October 1861 when Hardy authorised a dinner break for the men of half an hour, but forbade cooking or the consumption of beer and spirits in the office. His prohibition remained in force for a further five years, when the workmen's hours were changed from 8 a.m. until 4 p.m. to 9 until 4.30, but they were obliged to take lunch on the premises.

Apart from the slowness in fitting-up the strong rooms, an added difficulty was the failure of the Office of Works to supply ladders and steps. After

---

16. BL Add. MS. 36718, ff 99, 103.

one or two accidents resulting from men clambering on the shelves, a stop was put on removals, but it took many months and a special appeal to the Treasury before a sufficient supply was authorised. The gradual build-up of the complement of workmen at the new repository meant that it was now the centre for the office's repair and binding work, and led to an attempt by Hardy and Roberts in January 1857 to have the men's hours reduced to bring them more or less into line with the office's opening hours, from ten to four o'clock. No change, however, took place, even when in April 1857 all but one of the senior staff in each branch were allowed to leave at two o'clock on a Saturday afternoon. Hardy and Roberts also advocated that the post of superintendent or senior foreman of the workmen should normally be filled by internal promotion.

Hardy's and Roberts's pleas were by no means premature: the wide disparity of treatment between the workmen and the clerical grades, which Henry Cole had deprecated during the office's early years, had barely changed since that time. Furthermore, the £3,500 voted annually for the wages of the 55 workmen and the seven charwomen contrasted starkly with the £3,000 allowed for the handful of part-time editors of the Rolls Series and the £1,500 set aside for the calendaring of the State Papers. Yet Palgrave's *Reports* regularly detailed the vast quantity of repairing, binding, sorting, packing and labelling undertaken each year, which, slowly but surely, was effecting a remarkable improvement in the physical condition of the office's holdings, besides facilitating identification and production. Much of the credit for that progress, which was to lay the foundation for the emergence of the twentieth-century record service, was due to the workmen whose lowly status reflected the social and class prejudices of the age rather than the true value of their labour. The more highly skilled repairers had a particular grievance, as did those men who undertook clerical work, such as the making of office copies of modern records. When one of the latter, G. W. Thompson, who was paid no more than 5d an hour for a 48-hour week, complained, the best answer Romilly could give him was to regret his inability to improve matters as the Treasury would say that the workmen knew their conditions when they accepted the job.[17] The truth was that cheap labour was at a discount and the men had no trade union to speak on their behalf. Moreover, they thought themselves fortunate to have relatively secure employment, and such wastage as there was came mainly from age and sickness. However, it may not have been a coincidence that, at the same time as the Thompson case, consideration was given by the office to the creation of a 'draughtsman' post to make copies of plans and drawings, perhaps because it was hoped to nominate a qualified workman to the Civil Service Commission for such an appointment.[18] But the

---

17. PRO 2/14, p 376: Romilly to Thompson, 25 April 1860.
18. PRO 2/14, pp 378–384: J. Edwards's memorandum, 25 April 1860.

completion by the patent commissioners in 1858 of their huge task of copying specifications of inventions had reduced the demand for such work and so no action was taken, particularly as a private firm of patent agents was available to undertake it. One important improvement affecting the workmen grade did take place during 1860, because the retirement on health grounds of Robert Hanney, a repairer whose service went back to 1821, called in question their unsatisfactory position as regards superannuation. In theory, Hanney had no entitlement, but Palgrave, as in other cases, had no hesitation in recommending him to the Treasury for a retiring allowance on compassionate grounds. The uncertain nature of that process led to a Treasury review, resulting in an agreement with Romilly that future entrants to the workmen grade should be engaged through the Civil Service Commission in order to enjoy the benefits of the new Superannuation Act of 1859, which might then be extended to men already in the service.

The age of admission of boys and workmen was fixed as 14 to 25 and it was arranged that they should be examined by the commission in reading, writing and simple arithmetic. Romilly had thought that any examination might have been left to the deputy keeper, but on further consultation with the Treasury agreed to the scheme when he was assured that his right of nomination remained unaltered. Unfortunately, the first case under the new system went awry because, although the candidate, William Swain, passed his examination in February 1860, inquiries proved him to be under age. Romilly and Hardy were anxious to keep the lad, who had come to their notice through St Dunstan's School in nearby Fleet Street, and so it was decided that he should remain in the service without pay until his fourteenth birthday in the October, when he would be formally established. That was a good bargain for the public purse, but Swain's parents were anxious to settle him and raised no objection. The boy himself was also keen and when he first knew he was to be nominated had written a letter of thanks hoping 'it will please God to keep me a honest and truthful boy, from bad company and from them which may try to displace me'.[19] The acceptance by the office of the commission's role cleared the way for an award to Hanney of a yearly pension of £47 6s 4d, which he did not long enjoy because he died in August 1861. The new arrangements were subsequently gratefully acknowledged by the workmen in a memorial which they sent to Palgrave, through Hood, on 22 May 1860, expressing also the hope that men already in post might be favoured in the same manner as Hanney should a similar case arise in future.

Despite the provision of the central block of the new repository, the office's accommodation problem remained acute throughout the 1850s and would have caused even greater difficulties but for the requisition of the old houses in Chancery Lane. These houses backed onto the Rolls Yard and effectively precluded direct access to the new block, which was normally

---

19. PRO 2/14, p 20: Swain to Romilly, 9 January 1860.

approached via Fetter Lane although it was possible to get to it through the Rolls Chapel Office. There was also the walkway at first-floor level connecting Rolls House to the repository, but that was reserved for official use. One of the requisitioned houses provided accommodation for the caretaker, but the rest contained records, including those of the Admiralty, formerly at the Tower, and those from the War Office, which had been cluttering up the corridors of the new building. It was estimated that some six hundred tons of records were stored in the houses, and that figure would have been greater had not Lascelles and a representative of the War Department succeeded in destroying as waste some twelve tons after a joint examination over four months. Palgrave's *Twentieth Report* for 1858 made no attempt to conceal the unsuitability of those premises for record storage, emphasising the expense involved in shoring them up and general repairs. Being without any form of heating, they were also most unpleasant places in which to work during the winter months. In 1856 the office had secured a small amount of relief when the new charity commissioners withdrew their predecessors' records, but that was more than offset by accessions, such as those from the Treasury solicitor and the registrar of metropolitan buildings. A peculiar feature of transfers at that time was the inclusion in Palgrave's *Reports* of details of the location in the repository of all deposits even down to the very shelf. In spite of the constant emphasis upon security and the fact that the possibility of the abstraction of documents by search-room readers was recognised, little danger was seen from outside intrusion to the repository itself, perhaps because members of the public were confined to the ground-floor search rooms at the south-eastern end of the building and would have had to penetrate the locked entrances to the corridors on the other floors before they could even get to a strong room, let alone enter it.

In the course of time, however, information concerning the location of records in the strong rooms came to be restricted, but it has to be remembered that in the office's early years control on the movement of searchers presented little problem. Even when plans for the new building were first drawn up it was not thought necessary to provide more than 30 places for searchers. Throughout the 1850s it is doubtful whether that number was ever reached despite the lifting of fees and expansion in the office's holdings. Initially, the legal or business searchers were accommodated in a separate room from the literary readers, but in 1858 both classes of user were brought together in the one search room. Between 1852 and 1860 the number of literary inquirers was 939 and they made 11,609 visits. By the end of that period the number of literary readers using the office was about 150 a year, each making, on average, 15 or so visits. Most attendances were at the new repository, but use was also made of the facilities at the State Paper Office where the accommodation had been re-arranged to provide for up to 12 searchers a day. There were roughly two or three times as many legal as literary searchers, but their attendance was generally for a shorter period and they consulted fewer documents. From 1858 the secretaries of state allowed unrestricted access to papers earlier in date than 1688, relinquishing the control they had formerly exercised over all such searches. Where permission was given for readers to see documents of later date any copies or notes taken were vetted; and when the Foreign Office asked for this task to be undertaken, in the first instance, by officers in the search room, they were told to mark up papers which might be thought politically or personally sensitive, such as:[20]

i) papers bearing on current negotiations with foreign governments;

ii) papers whose publication might damage foreign relations;

iii) accounts of the domestic lives of members of the English or foreign royal families;

iv) names of English persons who may have been involved in foreign political intrigues, the disclosure of which might wound the feelings of their relatives or descendants.

Some two years earlier the assistant keepers had been consulted about the possibility of some change in the regulations for literary searchers, and a new set was issued in July 1858 after the rules for access to the State Papers were revised. However, apart from the dropping of the express prohibition on the use of ink by searchers making their own copies or notes from the records, they were little different from those which had come into effect at the beginning of 1852 when fees were first lifted. In practice, the assistant keepers appear to have insisted upon pencils only, and some of them seemed to have believed that Palgrave issued readers' tickets too readily, particularly as the tickets, which remained valid for a year, were normally renewable as a matter of course. In 1859 a new table of fees was issued, the main alterations being that all office copies were to be authenticated under the official seal or stamp and to consist of a maximum of 72 words instead of 90 as previously.

An incidental effect of the accommodation pressures was to squeeze out Palgrave's proposed study room for the use of the staff after office hours.[21]

---

20. PRO 2/10, pp 336–339: Hammond to Romilly, 21 January 1858. PRO 6/325 contains details of the permits issued between 1800 and 1877 to readers wishing to inspect state papers. Even when all state papers had to be seen under permit the number of searchers was very small. During the 1830s the annual average of admissions was only 18 although there was a gradual increase thereafter.

21. PRO 2/6, pp 579–581: Hart, Gairdner, Knight and Atkins to Palgrave, 24 November 1855. The clerks wanted an apartment set aside in the Rolls House, but Palgrave told them that, although he wished to help, nothing could be done until the records were completely located in the new building. But even by 1860, when the new repository was fully operational, Palgrave felt unable to allow Atkins to remain behind for an hour or two to transcribe some letters of Edward II, when prince of Wales: PRO 2/14, p 187.

Plans for a second block at the eastern end of the building had been drawn up by Pennethorne and approved as early as October 1856, but the Treasury showed no disposition to authorise the necessary funds. Langdale, whose marble bust, sculptured by Baron Marochetti, had been specially commissioned by Lady Langdale and now stood in the main entrance hall, would have understood his successor's impatience but might have wished to have achieved even half as much within the space of six years.

From the standpoint of office administration the biggest change since the Langdale era was the reduction in the influence of the secretary, although that post was now better paid than formerly. One consequence was to allow Thomas to press ahead with a collection of *Historical Notes*, which he had been compiling over many years and which were finally published, under Treasury authority, in 1856. Romilly thought the *Notes*, which appeared in three volumes, were likely to be of great value within the office for reference purposes, particularly for officers and editors calendaring the State Papers. During the summer of 1857 it became clear that Thomas, who was then in his early sixties, was no longer wholly fit, but his death at his home at Broad Green, Croydon, on 27 August still came as a great shock. Palgrave was abroad at the time, but when Romilly, who was on holiday at Bangor, was told he wrote immediately to Mrs Thomas, Charles Lechmere's sister, to express his high sense of her husband's merits and the loss the office had sustained by his death. He also wrote to Edwards on 1 September asking him to undertake Thomas's duties until more permanent arrangements could be made and telling him until Palgrave returned to refer to Hardy any letters addressed to him as master of the rolls which were not mere routine.

At the same time Romilly wrote to Hardy, mentioning that Edwards had applied for the secretaryship and saying:[22]

> With regard to yourself considering your situation in the Record Office I should hardly have thought it was a place that you would have wished to occupy yourself, offering as it does no increase of emolument to you or of station & being a position which is generally considered as final it being of great importance having regard to the nature of the duties to be performed by the Secretary that there should not be a rapid succession in that office.
>
> I have too great a regard for your opinion and for the assistance you have been continually affording me to take any decisive step in this matter without conferring with you on the subject.

By return Hardy wrote to point out tactfully that he would like the post and to correct Romilly's impression that it would mean no increase in pay. On 5

---

22. PRO 1/122: Romilly to Hardy, 1 September 1857. Other correspondence on the matter between the two men is in the same box.

September Romilly advised Hardy confidentially that Palgrave was urging Edwards's appointment, and subsequently Hardy must have alluded to the succession to the deputy keepership because on 13 September Romilly told him:

> Still with all this I must take the course which on the whole I think would be most beneficial to the public service of the Record Department. I well remember the observations to which you refer respecting the office of Deputy Keeper my principal object was as you understood to prevent any fetter being placed on the freedom of selection of myself or my successor in the event of that office becoming vacant. At that time I certainly had no one in mind but if the office were now vacant which I should much regret I do not think that I should do wisely in appointing a stranger to fill it.

That seemed remarkably like a broad hint to Hardy of better things to come irrespective of any decision concerning the secretaryship. In fact, Hardy's standing probably handicapped him because Romilly may well have felt that if Hardy became secretary it would result inevitably in the creation of a second deputy keeper, the very situation he feared would arise from the Treasury reorganisation in 1855. In the circumstances, Palgrave's views were crucial and Romilly seemed to accept that to be the case when he explained to Hardy on 26 September that he would do all in his power to prevent an outside appointment to the vacancy, but added:

> The only point on which I feel a difficulty is this whether the opinion of the Deputy Keeper on a question of this nature, *viz.*, the officer who shall be promoted to fill the vacant place, ought not to be preponderating.

Hardy, supported by most of his senior colleagues, took strong exception to the prospect of being passed over in favour of Edwards. The result was that on 13 October all the first-class men, except for Hunter, waited on Romilly to present a memorial to him, objecting at length to the suggested appointment. Separately, Lemon, Devon and Hardy also wrote to Trevelyan at the Treasury.[23a] Lemon and Devon thought Edwards's appointment would cast a slur on the first-class men and that Palgrave's wishes ought not to be paramount. Hardy, who sent his letter through Romilly, said he objected because he felt his services could not have been satisfactory if he was passed over, and that he did not wish to appear indifferent, especially as he understood others had applied for the vacancy. He also said that he understood Romilly felt a difficulty in the matter and presumed he would be letting the Treasury know the reason for his embarrassment. But Romilly was not prepared to allow that to pass unremarked, telling Hardy on 17 October: 'I frequently feel embarrassment in making up my mind, but once

---

23a. T 1/6097A/19023/1857.

186

made up I consider it settled & I express no embarrassment whatever in the communication of my decision'. Very fairly, however, Romilly forwarded to the Treasury the memorial from the senior men, while recommending Edwards as the most suitable candidate. But the Treasury was not prepared to sanction Edwards's promotion if there were more senior officers qualified to fill the post and asked Romilly to name the fittest person among the first-class men to succeed to the vacancy.

The Treasury request placed Romilly in a quandary because he knew Palgrave did not want anyone other than Edwards. Hunter was ailing and not interested and Romilly must have decided that the objections to Hardy's appointment were insurmountable. Devon had long wished to retire, and, in any case, had indicated that he would be content to see Hardy or Lechmere get the job. Lechmere and Lemon were handicapped by their limited knowledge of the department, and, although Lemon had originally put himself forward for advancement to the upper section of the first class in the event of a vacancy, which raised a few eyebrows at the Treasury, he had later withdrawn, somewhat transparently, in favour of Devon. That left the dependable Roberts, formerly Hardy's trusted second-in-command at the Tower, but the least unacceptable of all of them to Palgrave. Accordingly, it was Roberts whom Romilly recommended to the Treasury on 28 October 1857 as Thomas's successor. Consequentially, Holden was promoted to the first class and Redington to the second. Lascelles was also advanced to the higher section of the second class in place of Holden. Paradoxically, Edwards, the intended beneficiary, continued exactly as before, but supported Roberts with good grace and continued to act as Palgrave's private and confidential secretary.

How upset Hardy really was about not getting the job is uncertain, but Palgrave must have been disappointed at not securing for Edwards the promotion he thought he had earned. One other person less than pleased about the outcome was J. W. Pyecroft, a searcher, who had the reputation of being difficult. He wanted the post for himself, and, when told by Romilly that an internal appointment was intended, sent him a long letter, alleging office maladministration comparable in scale to that which had toppled the Record Commission.[23b] But Pyecroft's poor opinion of the office and his view that the secretaryship should be reserved for a legal antiquary were not widely shared by his fellow users, although trouble still broke out with them from time to time. One such unhappy incident had blown up at Carlton Ride in June 1857 when William Hardy, who had been commissioned to edit a volume in the Rolls Series and who had not long returned from Paris in that connection, threatened Hunter with legal proceedings for refusing

---

23b. Pyecroft continued to use the office for many years and in May 1874 was at the centre of a minor storm when a number of searchers complained of his offensive and obtrusive behaviour in the room set aside for refreshments. A little earlier he had suffered the indignity of expulsion from the Society of Antiquaries.

to allow him to take his bag into the search room. Mercifully, such disputes were rare and generally the office tended to defend its staff, but this time Romilly decided that Hunter had behaved unreasonably and he was told that he was not to display rules for the regulation of searchers unless first approved by the deputy keeper.[24]

The Thomas connection with the office did not end with his death: his 18-year old son, Francis Charles, was nominated to fill the clerical post vacated by Redington's promotion. The young man, who owed his nomination to Romilly, got off to an unfortunate start when Hardy arranged to put him in Palgrave's room in the new building at the north-western end of the ground floor corridor. Hardy thought that it would benefit from a fire because it was not often occupied, but when Palgrave, who was very possessive in such matters, heard, he immediately forbade it, reacting in much the same way as he had done earlier in the year when it was suggested that the room set aside for him at the State Paper Office might be used by members of the public. Despite that, Palgrave wanted to smooth Thomas's entry into the office, but there was a difficulty because under the Northcote/Trevelyan report of 1853 the Civil Service Commission, which had been established in 1855, needed to be satisfied that he possessed the ability to undertake the work required. No clerks had entered the Public Record Office since the introduction of the new system, and so it was agreed with the commission that before being granted a certificate of qualification Thomas and all subsequent candidates for clerical appointments should sit papers in handwriting (text hand, round hand, running hand and printing) and orthography; arithmetic (including vulgar and decimal fractions); bookkeeping by single entry; geography; history of England; Latin translation; French translation; and précis. No previous knowledge of ancient handwriting was required because Romilly was told by Palgrave that he had never found a clerk who could not read or copy records of average difficulty within a month or five weeks.[25] That may sound dismissive, but has to be set in the context of a sufficient understanding of Latin and French, and the existence of many facsimiles, accompanied by printed texts, among earlier record publications. Unfortunately, perhaps because Thomas did not know what to expect or because he was nervous, he failed to satisfy the commissioners in respect of his spelling, arithmetic, Latin and précis. His history was also marked as indifferent. Palgrave was very upset and tried, without success, to obtain an early re-examination, keeping Mrs Thomas closely informed.

With Romilly's approval Palgrave subsequently arranged for the young man to work with Brewer as an unpaid 'improver' to learn something of record work. Poor Thomas, who had a stammer, must have been overawed by the attention of these eminent and sobersided gentlemen to his future,

---

24. PRO 2/9, pp 504–508; PRO 2/10, pp 4–5.
25. PRO 2/10, pp 216–218: Romilly to J. G. Maitland, 27 November 1857.

kindly meant although it was. Before long, however, Mrs Thomas decided to withdraw him so that he might be coached in earnest for his next examination. At a guinea for an hour's tuition daily from a Cambridge man for five days a week, that involved much sacrifice on her part because there was no regular scheme for widows' pensions in the Civil Service at that time. But Palgrave thought the money spent would be amply repaid if all went well, which happily proved to be the case when young Francis passed his examination in March 1859 by beating one other candidate, a third having withdrawn. His success was a relief to Palgrave, who had tried to have the entrance requirements modified but met resistance from Sir William Jolliffe, then secretary to the Treasury, who insisted that the examination should be competitive because:[26]

> Though the duties of the Office in the junior branches may be easily
> performed, yet it is precisely one of those Offices where considerable ability
> and high attainment may most avail and become of the greatest value to the
> public service.

Mary Thomas, who must often have been told by her husband and brother of their difficulties with Palgrave, may well have wondered if he was quite so black as painted. At any rate, she was prepared to risk placing her son under him. On the other hand, Palmer's daughter, Ellen, had no doubt about Palgrave's villainy, and after her father's death in January 1857, when his indexes, in which Holden held a one-third share, were again offered for sale to the office, she made it plain that she blamed Palgrave for the failure of the previous negotiations to purchase them, which had been initiated in 1840. Her strictures were hardly fair on Palgrave as Langdale was equally, if not more, responsible. However, because Miss Palmer was unwilling to accept Palgrave's assessment of the value of the indexes, Romilly asked Roberts, William Hardy and H. G. Hewlett, the well known record agent, to determine a price for them, and as a result of their recommendation the indexes were acquired for £1,200 in 1858. They proved a valuable acquisition for the office. In more than half the cases in which the indexes were used, searchers found the references they wanted, which they would not have done had they consulted the official calendars; and Palgrave appended a catalogue of them to his *Twentieth Report* in which he acknowledged their usefulness.

In the same *Report* Palgrave recorded that 'Mr. Devon departed this life on the 30th December, having made a Report of the business for the year'. Despite his readiness to pay off old scores and his attachment to the former system of fees, Devon was a card, and although he had to endure much

---

26. PRO 2/12, pp 21–22; Jolliffe to Palgrave, 3 December 1858. The age for admission of candidates was fixed at 17 to 30 years. For table of results see PRO 2/12, p 341.

criticism of his editorial efforts under the Record Commission, later generations of scholars have not been quite so scathing. He was 58 at the time of his death, but as in 1840 he told Langdale he had not long to live he survived remarkably well. It was typical of him that even in his final year he was unable to resist a dig at Rolls House, chiding Roberts concerning a bill for the Chapter House water rate which the Office of Works had left unpaid, saying:[27]

> Perhaps you will see it settled or they will cut our Cock off and we shall be
> obliged to go unwashed & become a dirty set of fellows, made dirtier by
> our dirty vocation.

He was a constant thorn in Palgrave's flesh, but his attitude towards the office is best summed up in a report on his proceedings at the Chapter House during 1846 in which, while taking a side-swipe at Cole, whom he detested, he said:[28]

> One of my superiors used to say he 'had everything to gain and nothing to
> lose by agitation' and well it succeeded . . . I am not given to party, but think
> a man not tamely subservient to the body with which he acts, but judging
> it impartially, criticising it freely, bearing testimony against its evils, and
> withholding his support from wrong, does good to those around him and at
> the same time promotes the public service.

Record storage at the Chapter House had a long history but, as Palgrave pointed out in his *Thirteenth Report* for 1851, magnificent though the building was as a monument of ecclesiastical architecture, it was wholly unsuitable as a record repository. For that reason Palgrave had placed it at the forefront of his list of closures, but partly through circumstances, partly through Devon's manoeuvring, it was the last of the original branches to be cleared, the first removals commencing only in 1859, shortly after Devon's death. Most of the records there were removed at that time, although some, including common law writs, were not transferred until 1861. Domesday was Devon's prize possession and he managed to retain it in his custody throughout his assistant keepership despite plans made at various times to move it, first to the Rolls Chapel, where a special press was actually fitted up for the purpose, and then to the Stone Tower. It finally entered the Rolls Estate, being brought over in person by Burtt on Palgrave's special instructions in July 1859 and kept by him in his own office facing the main entrance on the ground floor of the new repository.

Devon's decease was followed in November 1859 by that of Holden, who

---

27. PRO 1/22: F. Devon to Roberts, 10 April 1858.
28. PRO 4/2: F. Devon's report for 1846, p 4.

had resigned on health grounds in the previous June. The original band of assistant keepers was now dwindling, but Cole and Black, although no longer on the office's staff, were still alive. Black continued to minister at Mill Yard and Cole remained at the Department of Science and Art, having returned there in 1859 from Italy, where he had been sent to convalesce for six months after a breakdown in his health from over-work associated with the establishment of the South Kensington Museum. Hunter was still in post, but with the closure of Carlton Ride in 1858 was stationed at the new repository although he was no longer able to give regular attendance on account of failing health. Palgrave struggled to attend regularly but his health was indifferent and was aggravated by problems with his sight, which required a rim to be affixed to his side-table to prevent him placing pens, knives, seals, etc. too near the edge and so knocking them off. That left Roberts and Hardy, both of whom remained active. As Roberts was under-pinned by Edwards on the secretarial side, he was able to undertake much useful record work, concentrating particularly upon the sortation and arrangement of the Welsh records in which he was assisted by Turner. Hardy was increasingly prominent in all matters affecting the management of the office and its publications, and it was a mark of the special esteem in which he was held by Romilly that early in 1860 he was invited to succeed Holden as warden of the Rolls Chapel.[29] His relations with Palgrave were also much calmer: he could enjoy a quip at the expense of his old foe but his attitude towards him was altogether more relaxed.

The burden shouldered by Hardy in connection with the Rolls Series, although very much a labour of love, was very considerable, and during the spring of the previous year, when the Treasury appeared to be questioning the continuance of the project and the elderly Benjamin Thorpe was causing much concern because of the inadequacies of his work on the Anglo-Saxon Chronicle, Hardy's health almost gave way, as was clear from a letter he wrote to his bosom friend, Joseph Stevenson:[30a]

> Thanks for the letter: the plot thickens. I have compared his text with the facsimiles and found innumerable errors & some of them of the gravest kind. The MR has seen them and is determined to cancel all that has been printed – about 200 pages – so slovenly has he done his work that he allowed the lithographer to choose his own plates. The man accordingly has chosen one which has nothing to do with the Chronicle. The MR is very angry indeed and has written to him (Thorpe).

> This anxiety and some others today pressing on me have quite knocked me up and my medical man has advised me off to the sea for a week and I am

---

29. PRO 1/122: Romilly to Hardy, 2 February 1860.
30a. Farm Street (Jesuit) Archives: Hardy to Stevenson, Wednesday [27 April 1859].

not to look into a book or use my mind at all – he says I have had a slight attack of congestion of the lower brain – but all will go right if I can keep quiet for a little. God bless you old fellow, ever affectionately yours.

T. Duffus Hardy

Hardy was soon restored to his usual healthy self, but what almost proved disastrous for him was a fierce attack launched in the summer of 1860 by the Protestant Alliance upon William Barclay Turnbull, a Roman Catholic convert then engaged upon the calendaring of the foreign diplomatic papers, commencing with the reigns of Edward VI and Mary. Turnbull had already successfully edited *The Buik of the Croniclis of Scotland*, published in the Rolls Series in 1858, and had been specially recommended to Romilly by Hardy to undertake the calendar. The extent to which he had become part of Hardy's circle is shown by a jocular letter he had written at the beginning of 1860. In it Turnbull told Hardy, light-heartedly, about the practice of suspending 'a good-sized bladder (old Palgrave's if you can get it!)' in a flue to prevent smoke blowing down the chimney, and to there being no difficulty about executing the plan because a sweep could certainly be found in the State Paper Office.[30b] Very much more than smoke was soon to blow Turnbull out of the office altogether because the Protestant zealots were in no doubt that his appointment was wholly inappropriate on account of his Catholicism and avowed Jesuit sympathies. Bowing before the storm, Palmerston concluded that the appointment had been unfortunate because the events of the period to be documented were so intimately connected with the national break from Rome. He thought some other employment ought to be found for Turnbull, but before the matter could be put to the test Turnbull decided to resign. His case was subsequently taken to the Lords by the marquess of Normanby, who unsuccessfully petitioned for a select committee on the issue, and a memorial was organised by Charles Pearson, professor of modern history at King's College London and by Henry Coleman Folkard, a barrister, calling upon the master of the rolls not to accept Turnbull's resignation. Among the 800 signatories appeared many notable names, including Edward Freeman, James Froude, F. D. Maurice, Benjamin Jowett, Dean Stanley, A. V. Dicey, Thomas Hughes and T. H. Green. In addition to Hardy and Brewer, the Public Record Office signatories included Palgrave, Hunter, Roberts and Edwards. But matters had gone too far to be reversed and within a short space of time Turnbull was succeeded by Stevenson, who, as it turned out, was soon himself to embrace the very faith which had led to his predecessor's downfall.[31] Perhaps the Turnbull controversy partly explains why, soon after

---

30b. PRO 1/129: Turnbull to Hardy, 13 January 1860.

31. The Public Record Office's papers on the Turnbull controversy are in PRO 1/129, and the Treasury's in T 1/6323A/16560/1861.

Stevenson's conversion in 1863, his work on the Foreign Calendar for Elizabeth I's reign was limited by Romilly to papers within the office, where the task could be pushed on without undue publicity, although the official reason of the greater expense and difficulty of compiling a comprehensive calendar was an obvious factor.

Devon's death and Holden's resignation resulted in the promotion of Sharpe and Burtt to the first class and the elevation of Edwards and Bond to the upper section of the second. Gairdner and Sanders joined the ranks of the assistant keepers, the former after an internal examination devised by Romilly in which all the clerks were invited to participate. After the examination the papers were sent to law stationers for copying to preserve the anonymity of the candidates and then passed to Hardy and Brewer for marking. Romilly thought that while conduct, industry and seniority should all be given weight it was necessary to ensure that any clerk promoted should be able to perform the full range of duties of the higher grade and be acquainted with the work of the different branches of the office. His scheme differed from that which Palgrave had submitted to Langdale without success in 1842 only in so far as Romilly did not consider a further examination necessary for promotion from the second to the first class of assistant keeper. In a letter to Palgrave, dated 10 January 1859, Romilly explained that those sitting the examination would:[32]

> Be required to give a précis of a document on each of the undermentioned Rolls and to write out in extenso a few lines of the same document, vizt.
>
> A Patent Roll of the reign of Hen. III [Plate 14]
> A Crown Roll of the court of King's Bench of the reign of Edwd. I
> A Plea Roll of the court of Common Pleas of the reign of Edwd. II
> A Memoranda Roll of the court of Exchequer of the reign of Edwd. III
>
> He will also be required to give a précis of three undated State Papers – one in Latin – another in French – and another in English; and he will have to fix the dates of each of those documents either from his knowledge of the history of the period with which it is connected or from its internal evidence.

Romilly thought that one of the virtues of his system would be to encourage the clerks to familiarise themselves with the workings of the office as a whole, and to assist that process he proposed to introduce an interchangeability scheme to circulate the clerks around the branches. In any future competition he also proposed to include questions on the public records generally. Palgrave was, however, given the assurance that the system for circulating the clerks would not apply to those who assisted him, for it was

---

32. PRO 2/12, pp 110–116.

recognised that administrative and accounting skills were of a different order from those required on the editorial and search sides of the office.

Romilly's scheme was not generally popular with the clerks. Although 13 out of 20 of them agreed to take the examination, which was topped by Gairdner, at least two, Turner and Hart, took part reluctantly. Turner later petitioned the Treasury about non-selection, saying he had sat only because of Romilly's assurance that seniority was to be given proper weight.[33] Fenwick, Hunt and Tabrum declined to sit, as did all of those at the State Paper Office branch, apart from W. D. Hamilton, younger brother of Hans, and Knight. The State Paper men had the full backing of Lechmere and Lemon, whose separatist tendencies were illustrated by their constant feuding with Palgrave about the use of the term 'State Paper Office' instead of 'State Paper Branch Record Office' and who believed that two of their clerks, Sainsbury and Impey, were fully entitled to promotion to the assistant keeper class on merit. The State Paper clerks also believed that their work, consisting of calendaring and searching, was superior to that of the record clerks generally, claiming that much of the latter's work consisted of making office copies. They argued also that, in view of the understanding at the time of amalgamation, their specialist duties for the secretaries of state should mean their exclusion from the interchangeability scheme proposed by Romilly, and they petitioned the Foreign Office, Colonial Office, Home Office and Treasury over their grievances. They maintained also that the next two promotions should be reserved for them, as the proportion of assistant keeper posts to clerical posts at the State Paper branch office was markedly below that at the central repository.

The secretaries of state sympathised with the clerks whose treatment reinforced their earlier misgivings about the merger, Malmesbury at the Foreign Office being particularly forthright in his condemnation of what had taken place. The Treasury, too, thought the clerks had some reason to feel aggrieved, but believed their attitude smacked too much of insubordination to be encouraged and so no action was taken on their memorial. However, the Treasury made it clear to a discomfited Romilly that, while it approved of Gairdner's appointment, it believed that promotion ought normally to be given on the basis of ability and industry in carrying out official duties. It emphasised that, although the power to read ancient manuscripts might be necessary in certain departments of the office, the power of reading and writing English was equally necessary in others. It also took the view that competitive examinations for promotions within an office were, as a general rule, of less value than those for first appointment.[34] Although Romilly made a spirited defence of his actions, pointing out that it was want of knowledge

---

33. T 1/6206A/15923/1859: P. Turner's petition, 29 January 1859.

34. Most of the papers arising from the memorials of the State Paper Branch Record Office clerks to the secretaries of state and the Treasury response are in T 1/6206A/15923/1859 and HO 45/6837.

of the different records in the office that had compelled him to employ external editors to make calendars of state papers, it came as no surprise that no further examination took place when Holden retired in June 1859, the appointment going to Sanders, who was third most senior after Kentish, Charles Devon's former clerk, and Charles Cole.

Shortly after Sanders's promotion Kentish, one of the old school, whose habits had been targeted for reform in the circular purporting to come from Knight, went sick for nine weeks. His failure to provide medical certificates to cover the whole of that period earned him Palgrave's severe disapprobation and the loss of 12 days from his 1860 leave allowance. Again in disgrace at that time was the more flamboyant Frederick Hohler, who had fallen into debt and was saved only by the intervention of his father. Hohler, a sergeant in the volunteer artillery, was now working for the more tolerant Hardy, but his long-term prospects seemed even worse than those of his former colleagues at the State Paper Office, two of whom, W. D. Hamilton and W. Impey, were particularly restive. Unfortunately for them, their earlier temporary service with the State Paper Commission, 8 and 14 years respectively, was not reckonable and placed them at a considerable disadvantage in terms of seniority. For that reason, when the clerical grade was reorganised in 1860, Romilly made a particular effort to obtain special treatment for them but failed to move the Treasury. Fortunately for Impey the post of deputy keeper of the land revenue records and enrolments fell vacant shortly afterwards, and with Romilly's backing he succeeded in obtaining the appointment. Romilly, who was now evidently anxious to placate the State Paper men, also persuaded a reluctant Palgrave to restore to another clerk there, Frederick Wilson, 15 days' leave which had been deducted from his allowance because of unapproved absence in 1857; approved the appointment of Sainsbury to edit a *Calendar of State Papers, Colonial*; and when Palgrave placed before him Lechmere's and Lemon's continuing refusal to describe their office as the State Paper Branch Record Office, he decided it wisest to avoid further dissension by ruling:[35]

> I still think that we had better not attempt to compel Mr. Lechmere and
> Mr. Lemon to add the words *Branch Record Office*. It will be sufficient if we
> always use them ourselves & if we prevent their acting as an independent
> Office and compel all applicants to come through your Department.

Romilly's staffing difficulties were, however, no more than a minor irritant compared with his continuing accommodation problem. In an effort to secure relief he wrote a long letter to the Treasury at the end of 1858 – included by Palgrave in his *Twentieth Report* – setting out the events leading to the building of the first block of the new repository and urging that

---

35. PRO 8/29, p 265: Romilly to Palgrave, 29 October 1859.

another be built without delay. He laid stress upon the unanticipated influx of documents from government departments and their unsuitable storage in the requisitioned houses in Chancery Lane, which had drawn a protest from the Admiralty whose documents were among those kept there. The Treasury refused to make any early provision, pleading more pressing demands elsewhere and querying the need to preserve permanently all the material transferred by departments. Accordingly, on 8 January 1859 it issued a minute establishing a committee to make recommendations concerning the disposal of departmental documents which had been received at the office during the previous few years and to indicate what arrangements might be made to keep suitable specimens or abstracts of those which it was decided to destroy. The committee was to consist of three members drawn from the Treasury, the Public Record Office, and the department whose documents were under investigation. In the first instance, it was decided that the papers of the War Office and Admiralty should be reviewed and the committee started work on 8 February 1859. Romilly nominated Lascelles, who had been called to the bar in 1855, as the Public Record Office member, and P. G. Julyan, assistant commissary general, represented the Treasury until May, when he was succeeded by G. F. Parratt. But as quick results could not be expected from the committee, the expedient was adopted of adding to the motley collection of outbuildings by securing from the Office of Works the use of further houses at 6 and 7 Chancery Lane and fitting them up for records which continued to flow in.

Although Romilly was by no means as hesitant as Langdale about the destruction of material thought to have no long-term value, he looked upon the committee as no more than a device by the Treasury to buy time. Lascelles's nomination meant that he had the distinction of becoming, in effect, the Public Record Office's first inspecting officer, although Hardy had some time earlier been involved in particular operations concerning the disposal of documents belonging to the Admiralty, Inland Revenue and the Ordnance Office. Despite his nomination, however, Lascelles was out of favour with Romilly, who believed he had given support to those clerks who were opposed to the system of a competitive examination for promotion. To make matters worse, the new committee decided to style itself the 'Committee on Public Records' to which Palgrave and Romilly took great exception, and it required the intervention of a policeman before an offending notice to that effect could be removed from the door of the room at 2 Rolls Yard where the committee was examining documents. Romilly lost no time in sending a stern rebuke to Lascelles on 23 February 1859, making it clear that he was not willing to tolerate what he regarded as insubordinate conduct and that unless he received a suitable assurance from him as to his future behaviour one of them had to go. Realising who would have to depart, Lascelles immediately sent a penitential letter, pointing out that he was but one of a committee of three and denying any part in the clerks' protest apart from having sympathised with his own clerk, Hart, who felt at a disadvantage, having been confined to one section throughout his service. Fortunately

196

for Lascelles, Romilly was not the man to split hairs and he accepted the explanation offered, saying that he now intended to dismiss the matter from his mind.[36] The committee, now known as the Committee on Government Documents, continued its work on reviewing War Office papers apace. By the end of 1859 some estimated forty tons had been sent to the Stationery Office as waste, and four officers from the War Office were engaged upon the weeding of certain classes which needed to be examined piece by piece.[37] Particular concern was felt about the destruction of documents sent to the Stationery Office for pulping, but Comptroller McCulloch was unwilling to vary his usual arrangements, which had Treasury approval, observing tartly that the operation 'which may take place in some distant part of the Empire' might, nevertheless, be subject to some additional superintendence if Romilly cared to appoint his own officer for that purpose.[38] Lascelles was at the centre of all these events, but he was not the easiest of men and, besides upsetting Romilly, also crossed swords with George Renwick, the Admiralty representative on the committee, by refusing to search for a reference to a ship's log he wished to consult. He was subsequently overruled by Romilly who told him that if he was unable to get on with Renwick he should make way for someone who could, a suggestion that was not taken up.

Renwick's service on the committee did not prove happy for him as during the course of its work he had the misfortune to be afflicted with a serious eye infection, which the committee attributed to the filthy state of the records he had been examining. The dangers from that source were emphasised by the committee in its report to Romilly upon the Admiralty records, in which it drew attention to Black's resignation from eye trouble at the age of 46 in 1853 and the loss by Lascelles of the sight of one eye later in the same year.[39] On the main question, the most significant of the committee's recommendations was a suggestion that records of the accountant general of the Navy to the year 1760 should be opened to the public, a proposal to which the Admiralty gave its consent in 1861. Apart from that, the committee's deliberations resulted in the destruction of some 165 of the 400 tons of Admiralty papers reviewed. Although there was no formal response to the committee's complaint about the hazards to which they thought themselves exposed, the limited protection available at the time to the staff from industrial disease and injury must have been a constant source of concern and seemed to be responsible for the very strong line taken by Palgrave with the

---

36. PRO 2/12, pp 287–294. But despite Romilly's assurance, the incident was held against Lascelles when a class I vacancy occurred in 1861.

37. Minutes of the committee's proceedings are in PRO 39/1/1–3. In dealing in this and later chapters with nineteenth-century records disposal matters, I wish to acknowledge the help received from notes supplied to me by my colleague, John Walford.

38. PRO 1/23: McCulloch to Roberts, 28 May 1859.

39. PRO 2/15, pp 42–338: third report of the committee appointed to examine etc. the papers of the administrative departments of the government deposited in the Public Record Office, 20 July 1860.

Office of Works in June 1860 concerning a dangerous crane used in the new repository to hoist documents, an odd contraption which was finally removed only in 1956. The office's worry about injuries generally was also shown by its compilation of a return in November 1860 listing accidents sustained by its workmen during the course of their employment, but not, apparently, for any specific purpose other than to indicate possible dangers.[40]

The year 1860 also saw an important change in the organisation of the office, arising from the increasingly unsatisfactory position of the 20 clerks. The 18 most senior had served on average for no less than 14 years and six of them were on their maximum salary. Apart from the creation of six additional assistant keeper posts at the time of the union with the State Paper Office, there had only been five vacancies among the assistant keepers since consolidation in 1840 and the clerks' promotion prospects remained poor. Moreover, their salary maximum of £200 compared unfavourably with that enjoyed by officers of the same class in other public departments, which was generally £100 more. For that reason Romilly wrote to the Treasury early in 1860 arguing for an increase in their maximum to £300, explaining that a Record Office clerk:[41]

> Must understand ancient French & medieval Latin. He must be able to decipher every form of handwriting from the earliest to the latest period, an acquirement not easily gained. He must make himself perfectly acquainted with obsolete law terms and with the usages existing in the management of Public business. He must understand the ancient method of dating documents, their proper titles and descriptions, and a variety of technical details not to be mastered without much labor and reference to expensive works. This variety of acquirements is as indispensable for his advancement in this Service as reading and writing English is in other departments.

The Treasury recognised that the clerks had a legitimate cause for complaint, but it did not favour increasing their maximum because it felt that some would then receive more than they were worth, while there was the added disadvantage that their pay scale would, if increased as proposed, exceed the minimum of the assistant keeper II scale by £50. Its favoured solution, therefore, was to increase the second class posts from eight to twelve with a corresponding reduction in the number of clerks. Romilly offered no objection to the suggested change, but in a further letter told the Treasury that it was also desirable to restyle the second class as clerks,

---

40. PRO 2/15, pp 446–449. The earliest incident recorded is that of a corroded pin running into Rowland Hart's finger in 1840 while he was sorting documents. The list also includes details of two fractures and two ruptures. No case of eye infection is listed although the workmen were just as much exposed to any occupational hazard of that kind as the assistant keepers.

41. T 1/6252B/10390/1860: Romilly to G. A. Hamilton, 3 February 1860.

pointing out that in 1840 the Treasury had itself proposed that grading and explaining:[42]

> The title of Assistant Keeper as applied to Officers of the Second Class was rendered necessary by the dispersion of the Branch Record Offices in various localities. Owing to the limited number of First Class Officers (then only four), it was found necessary to give the title of Assistant Keeper to those officers of the Second Class to whom was entrusted the management of a Branch Office or to those who were to act in the absence of the Chief Officer; but as all those Branch Offices are now united in the General Record Office the necessity for so many Chief Officers no longer exists. At present an Assistant Keeper of the second class is no longer under the control of the [sic] Assistant Keeper of the First Class; by reason of the title he considers himself, and is treated as, a superior and not as a subordinate. Unless the alteration in the title be made, and should the present proposition of their Lordships be adopted simpliciter, there will be 18 Chiefs besides the Deputy Keeper and Secretary (each acting, according to the present state of things, independently of the other, if not upon his own responsibility) and only 16 Clerks to act under them. Upon the inconvenience and the necessary delay and interruption of the Public Service that would result from such a state of things it is hardly necessary for me to enlarge.

The upshot was that Charles Cole, Turner, Kingston and Haydon, respectively second, fifth, seventh and eighth in the seniority list, were raised to the second class as senior clerks, but the existing officers in that class were allowed to retain their title of assistant keeper, which was greatly prized. Dr Levine has shown how the assistant keepers at that time already saw themselves as a select band of highly qualified professionals.[43] Certain of them, notably Hunter and Sharpe, had little patience with readers they regarded as mere amateurs, such as those seeking to draw up their pedigrees. When Romilly launched an inquiry in 1860 into the wisdom of continuing to make the records freely available to literary searchers, there was a strong feeling that more stringent tests should be applied before any concession was granted. Hardy stood out from his assistant keeper colleagues in favouring the encouragement of searchers of all kinds by abolishing fees entirely, a view that was shared by Brewer. However, apart from a decision to stamp all state papers before production, no changes resulted from that inquiry, which had been prompted by Romilly's fear that the security of the records could be endangered by unscrupulous searchers. The immediate cause of his concern was a claim by John Payne Collier, the Shakespearian critic, to have seen certain documents in the State Paper Office which could no longer

---

42. T 1/6252B/10390/1860: Romilly to G. A. Hamilton, 27 February 1860.
43. Philippa Levine, 'History in the Archives: the Public Record Office and its Staff, 1838–1886', *English Historical Review*, CI (1986), 20–41.

be found. Much controversy surrounded Collier's allegations, which had also persuaded Romilly to mount a special investigation into the authenticity of a petition to the Privy Council among the records in the State Paper Office, which purported to come from the players at Blackfriars, requesting that the Blackfriars Theatre be allowed to remain open. That inquiry, which was conducted by Palgrave, Hardy and Brewer, assisted by Madden and N. E. S. A. Hamilton of the British Museum, pronounced the manuscript to be spurious, a conclusion that was later challenged by Lemon.[44]

Although the members of the inquiry co-operated well enough with each other for that limited purpose, relations between them were strained at the time because the British Museum, and Madden in particular, believed that it should have had the Conway Papers which had been deposited in the State Paper Office by the Home Office in 1857. The museum's claim was fiercely resisted by Romilly, and ultimately the Home Office decided in his favour, although it was agreed to release to the museum certain papers in the collection which were of a private character.[45]

With more than enough material of a public kind to contend with and limited accommodation, Romilly was not anxious to expand his holdings beyond the limits laid down by the 1838 act and the order in council of 1852, but the bulk of the Conway Papers, while formerly considered as private property, could properly be seen as having strayed from official custody. Romilly thought that the publicity given by the office to the existence of documents previously unknown, resulting in particular from its publication programme, was responsible for the widespread support given by literary men and others prominent in public life to a memorial presented in July 1859 to Palmerston, then premier, by George Harris for an inquiry into historical manuscripts held in private collections. In December 1859 Romilly wrote to the Home Office saying that he believed the memorialists' fears to be overstated because in his opinion most of the material held was of little public interest except to the families concerned, consisting for the most part of private deeds relating to their estates. But accepting that some valuable papers existed concerning the administration of public affairs, he doubted whether the idea of a separate body of paid commissioners and inspectors as proposed by the memorialists was the right way to make their existence better known and their future safeguarded, particularly as a number of archaeological and other societies were already active in that field.

---

44. N. E. Evans, *Shakespeare in the Public Records*, PRO Handbooks, no. 5 (London, 1964). A transcript of the document in question appears in this publication, which also discusses the controversy surrounding it. It remains in the office as SP 12/260, no. 117. Romilly later placed on record that Lemon's opinion that the document was not spurious, as expressed in a note appended to it, was added without his knowledge or sanction: PRO 2/26, p 16.

45. HO 45/6442 contains the official correspondence arising from the dispute.

The Home Office considered the proposed scheme 'a very wild project',[46] but Lewis, who had by that time left the Exchequer and was home secretary, wondered if any steps ought to be taken to accomplish any of the objects contemplated. Consequently, Romilly, who had intimated his willingness to submit an alternative plan, wrote again in January 1860 to say that in view of the high standing of so many of those who had signed the memorial he thought some attempt should be made to meet their wishes and proposed that inspections might be made under his auspices, embracing collections held by ecclesiastical and lay corporations as well as by private individuals. If the papers surveyed were reported to be valuable, he thought they might be arranged and listed by a member of the Record Office staff on condition that they were then made available to the public. He believed the latter work might be undertaken with a very small addition to the office complement, probably one junior clerk in the first instance. That estimate was not put to the test because the government decided against action. Nearly ten years were to pass before the matter again became active and the Royal Commission on Historical Manuscripts was established in 1869.

At the outset of the 1850s Palgrave had been the force behind the drive for the new repository, but by the end of the decade, at the age of 72, he no longer had the energy to battle for the further building needed. Trevelyan had been succeeded at the Treasury by G. A. Hamilton, who now held the rank of permanent secretary there. When negotiations took place with him about the administrative workings of the office the main burden was shouldered by Romilly. Similarly, Romilly took the lead in all publication matters, a remarkable new feature of which was the appointment of Gustav Bergenroth, a German scholar, to research the Simancas Archives for documents relating to English affairs of the Tudor period. Hardy, who had now completed over forty years' record service, remained Romilly's right-hand man on the editorial side, besides dominating the search room and repository. While no longer so active as formerly, Palgrave occasionally displayed his old vivacity, for example, urging the presentation to New Zealand of certain record publications in August 1860 because 'taking the matter in a broad point of view, historical feeling furnishes a strand in the bond between the mother country and her children'. When Burtt, whose early training had been at Palgrave's hands, told him of the pending visit of the London and Middlesex Archaeological Society to the Chapter House in October 1860 Palgrave went to great pains to remind him of the features there most likely to be of interest to the visitors. As a fellow of the Royal Society he took great interest in the progress of physical science, but was cautious about its

---

46. HO 45/6836: endorsement on Romilly's letter to Waddington of 22 December 1859. For a fuller account see R. H. Ellis's article in the Royal Commission on Historical Manuscripts publication *Manuscripts and Men* (HMSO, 1969), 1–39 and another concerning the commission's 'Origins and Transformation' in the *Journal of the Society of Archivists*, III (1969), 441–452.

application to the records. Nevertheless, he had approved an application by Cosmo Innes in March 1860 to send a photographer into the office to photograph certain seals attached to Scottish documents and offered no objection to a project which led to the filming of some maps in the State Paper Office for the Irish Office. However, when Burtt proposed the rebinding of Domesday, although his first reaction was to sanction it, he had second thoughts and decided to forbid it for the present because 'mischief enough has been done already'.[47] It was only with reluctance that he finally acquiesced in the experimental scheme, under the direction of Sir Henry James, the director of the Ordnance Survey, to reproduce at Southampton the Cornwall section of the great survey by his new photozincographic process.[48]

In November 1860 Palgrave had apparently decided to get his personal affairs into order and he made a new will. On the occasion of an earlier will in 1845, Black and one of the workmen had been summoned into his office to witness it, but this time two of the office juniors, Edward Tabrum and Alexander Ewald, were called in for that purpose.[49] Further indication that Palgrave was pondering his future came in January 1861 when he gave up the room in the new repository reserved for his personal use, agreeing that it might be racked up for documents from the Colonial Office. Even more significantly, in March 1861 he presented the faithful Edwards with a medallion likeness, engraved in December 1860 by Thomas Woolner, the sculptor, 'as a token of my thankfulness for your kindness in helping me in my work during a period now running on to the conclusion of a quarter of a century'. Shortly after Palgrave's death Edwards gave it to the office[50] and on Romilly's order it has been on display at Chancery Lane ever since. On 25 April 1861 Palgrave wrote a touching letter to Romilly thanking him for his kindness in continuing him on the 'free list' for record publications and acknowledging Thorpe's much-criticised edition of the Anglo-Saxon Chronicle which had finally been allowed to appear. Palgrave, never a pedant, thought the work a great addition to the Anglo-Saxon library, but noted the numerous mistakes, largely occasioned by Thorpe's, and his predecessors', misreading of the 'minims', the short perpendicular strokes used in the ancient manuscripts for the letters i (or j), m, n and u (or v). Palgrave also thought the rule of publishing rare works existing only in manuscript ought to be relaxed. He said he had never had the time to make

---

47. PRO 2/14, p 310: Palgrave's note, 11 April 1860.

48. Elizabeth M. Hallam, *Domesday Book through Nine Centuries* (Thames and Hudson, 1986), 154.

49. IR 59/63. The main beneficiary under Palgrave's will, which was proved in 1862, was his sister Rosa, for whom an annuity was purchased by his executors. His sons were already well provided for and, in any case, he did not die a wealthy man as he rented his house at Hampstead and his estate was valued at just over £2,900. Ewald, a son of Dr Ewald, the Hebrew scholar, had been in the office for only three months, having entered through a competitive examination with Charles Jelf in August 1860.

50. PRO 1/25: Edwards to Romilly, 19 July 1861.

use of any public repository and was compelled to buy the collections of the old English historians such as Twysden and others, as they became available. 'In this way', he said, 'I saved my bacon', but because such books had disappeared from the market he believed that they should be reprinted.[51]

A fortnight after writing that letter Palgrave received the melancholy news of Hunter's death at the age of 78 on the morning of 9 May. He lost no time in urging Romilly to appoint Edwards to the first class, but appreciative although he was of Edwards's services, Romilly decided that it would not be right to pass over Nelson. He, besides being the senior, had also been standing in for Hunter, who had been attending but fitfully during his final years. Hunt was promoted to the grade of senior clerk, which led to an unsuccessful appeal to the Treasury by Kentish, who pointed out that he had sat Romilly's examination in 1859 in contrast to Hunt who had declined. But Kentish's absence from duty on a plea of sickness after Sanders's promotion had not been forgotten, still less forgiven, and Sharpe found himself rebuked by Romilly for having given a certificate in Kentish's favour, which had accompanied his petition to the Treasury. Although Sharpe was evidently sympathetic to Kentish, who had a wife and seven children to support, his benevolence did not extend to Hohler, whose conduct was again under scrutiny, and it was following an adverse report from Sharpe to Hardy upon him that he was interviewed by Palgrave and a stop again placed upon his increment.

Despite indifferent health and signs of a contemplated withdrawal, Palgrave attended the office regularly throughout the first five months of 1861, issuing his twenty-second and final *Report*, which was rather briefer than usual, on 5 March. But in June his constitution began to give way and he was absent for eight days. He was in the office on 1 July but again fell sick on the 3rd, and on Saturday, 6 July, the news came of his death that day. His sons arranged for his burial, like Lady Palgrave before him, at Irstead in Norfolk. *The Times* carried no more than a formal announcement of his decease, but an appreciative obituary appeared in October 1861 in the *Gentleman's Magazine*. A tribute to him written many years before by Charles Knight, the author and publisher, in reference to his work as keeper at the Chapter House reveals the indebtedness of the record profession to him:[52]

No man has laboured more assiduously in this field than Sir Francis Palgrave;
and he has especially shown that a true antiquary is not a mere scavenger
of the baser things of time, but one whose talent and knowledge can discover
the use and connection of ancient things, which are not really worn out,

---

51. PRO 37/63: Palgrave to Romilly, 25 April 1861.
52. *Old England: A Pictorial Museum of Royal, Ecclesiastical, Municipal, Baronial and Popular Antiquities*, ed. Charles Knight, (London, n.d. [c. 1844]), I (Book II, Chap I), 114.

and which are only held to be worthless by the ignorant and the unimaginative.

His deputy keepership will always be a matter of controversy, but the last word can safely be left to Sir Henry Cole, who in his old age, all anger spent, reflecting upon the former record quarrels, tersely recorded that 'Sir Francis Palgrave, after peace was concluded, took the office of Deputy Keeper of the Public Records', discharging 'the duties from 1838 to 1861, with ability'.[53] Only a bold man would question that assessment.

53. *Fifty Years of Public Work* (London, 1884), I, 14.

Chapter VIII
Thomas Duffus Hardy, 1861–1869

We have in Mr. Duffus Hardy, who is the Deputy Keeper of Records, a man who appreciates and thoroughly understands the value and mode of utilising public records.

(G. A. Hamilton, permanent secretary of the Treasury, to Lord Naas, chief secretary for Ireland, [August] 1866: T 168/3)

By 1861 the 57-year-old Hardy's pre-eminence within the Public Record Office was such that his succession to the deputy keepership was something of a formality, although all might have been ruined for him at the last moment had Romilly been raised to the Woolsack on Lord Chancellor Campbell's death in June of that year. But Romilly remained at the Rolls and, having long since abandoned his one-time resolve to choose an outsider as deputy keeper in the event of a vacancy, told Hardy two days after Palgrave's death, Sunday having intervened, that he had named him to the home secretary for the post. Hardy, an emotional man, was deeply moved by the news, telling Romilly:[1]

12 Park Village West
[Regents Park]

8th July 1861

Sir,

This afternoon when you so promptly announced to me the fulfilment of your long cherished kind intention, I had not sufficient command over myself to express how deeply grateful I felt.

Pray now accept my warmest and most heartfelt thanks.

I need hardly assure you that during the time I may hold the office, I shall devote myself earnestly and entirely to my duties and to you.

In seven years (if I am spared so long) I shall have completed my fifty years of public service, and shall be entitled to retire on full pay. Nevertheless I consider that I only hold the place in trust, and nothing would give me so

---

1. PRO 1/122: Hardy's letter, and that from his wife, are in this box in the bundle for 1861.

much real happiness as to assist in instructing a successor of your own choosing. If you would give me such a task it would be a true labour of love.

I feel that in saying this I touch on delicate ground, but I am sure you will understand my feeling and forgive me if I have done wrong.

Even in writing this I am conscious that I express myself coldly and badly but I am so excited and overcome that I can neither command my pen nor my speech.

Once more, dear Sir, accept my thanks and gratitude and believe me to be, Sir, your most faithful and obedient servant.

T. Duffus Hardy

The next day Hardy's second wife Mary, the novelist, whom he had married in 1846, also wrote to 'the author of his good fortune' to express her thanks and to say that, although her husband valued his promotion more for the position than the increased income, she took a more 'matter of fact' view and rejoiced that their wordly anxieties would be lessened and their enjoyment increased.

It was not until Wednesday, the 10th, that Hardy's close friend Stevenson read in *The Times* that 'P., poor old soul, died on Saturday'.[2] Stevenson, who was hoping to succeed the unfortunate Turnbull as editor of the *Calendar of State Papers, Foreign* (which he eventually did in December 1861), while not allowing himself to doubt the result as it affected Hardy and the deputy keepership, could not conceal his anxiety and begged to be told as soon as the matter was decided. In fact, an announcement was not long delayed: crown approval of Hardy's appointment was given on 15 July and official notification from Lewis to Romilly followed three days later. In truth, there was no rival to Hardy among the assistant keepers, and had he not been available Romilly's choice might well have been Brewer.

Romilly could have had no doubt about the outcome because on the very day of the decision he took Hardy and Roberts with him to the Commons to give evidence to the Select Committee on the Courts of Justice Building (Money) Bill. His purpose was to oppose the plan to move the Rolls Court from the Rolls House to a site between Carey Street and the Strand where it was intended to concentrate the courts. Romilly told the committee that 'Hardy is practically Deputy Keeper at present', and referred to 'the death of Sir Francis Palgrave, a very eminent and learned person, whose loss, I

---

2. PRO 37/59: Stevenson to Hardy, Wednesday morning [10 July 1861]. That was probably the kindest remark that Stevenson ever made about Palgrave in the course of his extensive correspondence with Hardy.

am sure, everybody will deplore'.[3] Although the site proposed was nearby, Romilly thought that any move would greatly disrupt record business and reduce the hour or so a day during which he was able to confer with his chief officers, normally at 4 p.m. after the completion of his judicial business. Hardy and Roberts gave loyal support, but the committee was not impressed by the special pleading and by five votes to two declined to recommend that the Rolls Court be exempted from the move. Over twenty years were to pass, however, before the Royal Courts of Justice were brought together on the one site. By then Romilly was dead and the business of the Rolls Court had been transferred to the other judges of the Chancery Division of the High Court of Justice under the Supreme Court of Judicature Act 1881, when the master of the rolls became a full-time judge of appeal, a change which left him with still less opportunity for record work.

One of Hardy's first acts as deputy keeper was to issue an office notice abolishing the customary deduction of two hours' pay from the workmen's daily wages when they were away as a result of illness, holidays, births, bereavement or the like. Hardy ruled that such absences, if authorised under office regulations, were to be paid at the normal rate of eight hours, and also announced that half the work force might be allowed to leave the office at two o'clock on Saturdays. The workmen lost no time in sending him an address, signed by them all, thanking him warmly for the 'great boon' and congratulating him upon his appointment. Responding, Hardy asked Hood to tell the men that 'so long as they do their duty they will find in me an unfailing friend'.[4] As though to emphasise that a completely new chapter had opened in office administration, Hardy also allowed Hohler to have his increment with effect from 1 July. But official benevolence had its limits as the workmen assisting the government papers committee found when they failed to secure extra payment for their labours, although four years later one of them, Thomas Steward, succeeded in getting a gratuity of 2s 6d a week, backdated from the time of his commencement in 1859, and was again successful in getting an extra allowance in 1868. However, the first-class assistant keepers were told by Romilly in November 1861 that he did not think the time opportune to forward to the Treasury a memorial for better pay which they had presented to him detailing the higher salaries enjoyed by the senior grades in other departments. A year later they tried again, but although Romilly, somewhat half-heartedly, gave them his support their case was firmly rejected by the Treasury. The outcome was predictable because, while the Treasury conceded the valuable and expand-ing work undertaken by the office in managing the non-current records of government departments, including its own, and recognised that it could not ignore the growing esteem in which the office was held in academic and

---

3. *HC Committee Reports*, 1861, XIV, 202.

4. PRO 1/25: Hardy to Hood, 22 July 1861. The office notice and the workmen's address are also in this volume.

literary circles, it did not believe that the duties of the higher branches of record work were sufficiently onerous to justify the same pay as that enjoyed at the senior levels of the Civil Service generally. The satisfaction the record men were thought to get from their work was also seen by the Treasury as an argument against granting them more.

The Treasury was also reluctant to commit funds for the further record accommodation urged by Romilly in 1858 and again at the end of 1861. It was on its guard because the cost of the central block at £88,490 was almost double the £45,320 originally estimated, and much of it had stemmed from Palgrave's and Romilly's insistence, on security grounds, on wire doors to the presses, the need for which already seemed fanciful. Furthermore, Palgrave had thought that the new building would provide for at least twenty years' accruals and the Office of Works had gone even further, estimating fifty years. Not surprisingly, the Treasury was now treating the matter with caution, but it was unable to refute Romilly's assertion that what seemed a miscalculation about future needs could be explained by the unforeseen and huge accessions from the War Office and the Admiralty at the time of the Crimean War. By the end of 1861 it was also clear that, although the review of those records undertaken by the Committee on Government Documents had led to the scheduling for destruction of 220 out of 560 tons, that was not enough to offer any hope of giving up the unsatisfactory Chancery Lane houses where they were stored, unless an extension to the main repository was authorised. Moreover, of the remaining 200 tons of government documents awaiting review it was thought that only about one-third could properly be destroyed.

Had that been the only problem the Treasury might have remained unmoved, but the accommodation crisis had become more acute during 1861 when the government itself decided to pull down the State Paper Office in Duke Street to make way for new offices in Whitehall. The reaction of the Office of Works was to suggest the removal of the State Papers to the Victoria Tower, but Romilly firmly rejected that idea after an inspection by Hardy and Roberts, which revealed that there was no suitable room there for searchers and access was by means of a narrow, winding staircase of 170 steps to the first floor and a further 266 to the top. It was next thought that the Chapter House, which had by then been cleared, might be pressed back into service. Initially the Foreign Office gave its consent, but changed its mind on discovering that it was not intended to man the building after four o'clock each day. It was particularly concerned about the security of its secret diplomatic papers and wanted to ensure that any records it needed to consult could be speedily produced, both during and out of office hours. As a compromise it eventually agreed to a proposal to store in two houses in nearby Whitehall Yard its correspondence from 1760 and ratifications of treaties, and consented to the removal to the new repository of material earlier than that date. That agreement necessitated many expedients as regards storage at Chancery Lane and added to the difficulties there for searchers, now once more segregated in Legal and Literary Search Rooms.

Conditions were particularly unpleasant in the small Literary Search Room, measuring 25 by 16 feet, and led to complaints in April 1862 from the Reverend W. W. Shirley of Wadham College, Oxford, a Rolls Series editor, and other readers. An anonymous correspondent, writing to *The Times* of 11 March 1862, had earlier protested:

> There is scarcely a room in any one of our clubhouses set apart for consulting the files of the daily papers of the last five years which is not ample compared with that provided at the Record Office for consulting the files of the last 10 centuries.

The Treasury still wondered whether the Victoria Tower might be used for documents of lesser importance but could scarcely have been surprised when it was brusquely ruled out by Romilly. In July 1862 it agreed, reluctantly, to the building of a portion of the eastern block to provide two search rooms and office accommodation, including a copying office on the first floor, 60 feet long and 26 feet wide, in what was eventually to become the Rolls Room.[5] Despite the urgency, the foundations for the new works were not started until June 1863, the hope being that they would be completed by Lady Day 1865. Interestingly, one of Palgrave's firm prejudices lingered on, for when the staff were asked whether they wished their rooms to be warmed by hot-water pipes they were almost unanimous in opposing it. But when the new wing came to be built, the officers' rooms and the public search rooms were partly warmed by such means.

In so far as the demolition of the State Paper Office was to lead to the partial building of the long-desired extension to the central block, it proved to be a blessing in disguise. But to the staff there it was most unwelcome, finally confirming their union with the Public Record Office. The senior men, Lechmere and Lemon, each with more than forty years' service, were particularly aggrieved. To add to Lemon's discontent he was being made to wait a year before receiving his increment on the higher assistant keeper scale to which he had been admitted on Hunter's death, although he had already been on his maximum for several years. In a bitter complaint to the Treasury he said that Hunter[6]

was suffered to retain office till he was 79 years of age with what actual

---

5. The correspondence between Romilly and the Treasury about the extension was laid before Parliament and printed: *HC Accounts and Papers*, 1862, XLIV, 363–392. The Treasury's own papers are in T 1/6379A/15256/1862. The Foreign Office's letter of 1 August 1861 expressing its misgivings about the Chapter House proposal is printed in the *First Report of the Royal Commission on Public Records*, I, pt II (Cd. 6395), 119–120.

6. T 1/6323A/16560/1861: Lemon to Hamilton, 20 September 1861. Although Romilly thought the incremental rule should be changed, the Treasury refused to make any alteration. It was not until 31 May 1862 that Lemon was told.

benefit to the public service may be conjectured, but certainly with most injurious effects to those immediately below him. Such a case as this justifies the consideration of a period of age at which retirement should be compulsory.

Romilly and Hardy thought Lemon's remarks, which could hardly have helped the office's standing, were in very bad taste, but chose to ignore them. They also tried to soften the blow involved in the transfer from Duke Street by agreeing that Lechmere, Lemon and certain other staff might move to the houses in Whitehall Yard, which were being commandeered for the records which the Foreign Office wished to retain. In the event that was not possible, and Lemon reluctantly accepted his move to the Rolls Estate while Lechmere succeeded in obtaining permission to retire. If anything, his position had seemed worse than Lemon's because the disappearance of the Duke Street building meant the loss of his residential accommodation there. In that connection the Treasury, while refusing to acknowledge that he had any claim for compensation, finally conceded an annual addition of £100 to his salary. But rather than face the upheaval which the transfer involved, Lechmere, who was then 61, decided he wished to be superannuated. With Romilly's backing that was allowed and he was awarded a pension of £485 13s 4d, which he drew until his death in 1878. The change in his fortunes meant that he parted from the office on better terms than had once seemed likely. Quite gratuitously, he agreed to stay on at Duke Street for some weeks after his formal retirement to supervise the removal to the houses in Whitehall Yard of the material which the Foreign Office had insisted should be held back. As a final gesture, he also presented to the Public Record Office his private collection of maps and his Diplomatic Index. Rather less fortunate was the 74-year-old Mrs Scutt, the Duke Street housekeeper, for whom no place could be found at Rolls House and whose loss of accommodation hardly seemed compensated by the £25 pension awarded, which she received until her death in March 1865.

A number of staff changes at the central repository stemmed from Hardy's appointment as deputy keeper. Romilly recommended to the Treasury Edwards's promotion to the vacant class I post and that of Fenwick to the second class with the title of senior clerk. Because neither man was the senior in his grade the Treasury asked for more information, which greatly annoyed Romilly who resented his judgment being questioned. He also felt it left him no option but to reveal the trouble he had had two years earlier with the senior men, Lascelles and Kentish, which had contributed to his decision to pass them over. In view of Romilly's explanation the Treasury accepted his recommendation in favour of Edwards, but it did so reluctantly, having only a short while before awarded a gratuity of 100 guineas to Lascelles for his work on the Committee on Government Documents. However, it was not prepared to authorise the promotion of the 53-year-old Fenwick, who had been passed over five times before, especially as Romilly admitted that Fenwick was no more able to perform the full range of duties of the second class than Kentish, whom he described as incompetent but whose disqualification was attributable to his past misconduct. On the other hand, Romilly did not think it was in the best interests of the office repeatedly to pass over long-serving and hard-working men such as Fenwick because that was eventually bound to affect adversely their willingness to work. The Treasury had no patience with sentiment of that kind, which it thought placed a premium upon inefficiency, and insisted upon the submission by Romilly of one name only when, somewhat petulantly, he tried to throw the onus of selection upon it by naming no less than six of the clerks as qualified to undertake the duties of the higher grade. Ultimately an unenthusiastic Romilly forwarded the name of the most senior of the qualified men, none other than Knight, the purported evangelist of 1857, and the Treasury approved his promotion accordingly. Hardy gave his full backing to the stand which Romilly had taken, and grieved for the luckless Fenwick, who he believed to have the sympathy of the whole office at the way he had been denied promotion by the Treasury.

The fact remained that the Treasury had a duty under the 1838 act to appoint the assistant keepers and other staff and was concerned that the power of the master of the rolls as head of the department should be exercised wisely. Any doubts it may have had on that score could only have been reinforced in February 1862 when, to its astonishment, Kentish, so recently reported as incompetent, was named by Romilly for promotion to senior clerk. The Treasury marvelled that Kentish should pass from 'ignorance to bliss' in such a short space of time,[7] but finally accepted the recommendation when Romilly pointed out that Kentish had been receiving special tuition from Kingston to improve his Latin and French and confirmed that his ability to cope with the older manuscripts had been tested by Hardy with satisfactory results. Kentish had tried hard to redeem himself and his promotion came when Lascelles was promoted to the first class in place of Lechmere, an appointment which presented the Treasury with no difficulty. Trouble might have occurred again in August 1862 when Walter Nelson, then in charge of the Literary Search Room, died unexpectedly. His replacement by John Bond, the senior class II man, was uncontroversial, but friction about who should fill the vacant place for a senior clerk was avoided only because Romilly bowed to the Treasury's continued objection to the promotion of Fenwick. Instead the appointment went to W. Noel Sainsbury, whose reputation stood high as a result of his editorial work on the *Calendar of State Papers, Colonial* and who thus had the distinction of being the first clerk to be promoted from the original establishment of the State Paper Office since the time of the merger. Of the four clerks from that office still in post, Temple and Wilson were handicapped by their lack of Latin and

7. The extent of Treasury disquiet comes out in its internal memoranda in T 1/6395A/18140/1862 and in its earlier papers in T 1/6323A/16560/1861.

French while question marks remained against Hohler. W. D. Hamilton was able enough and had done well in the internal examination in 1858, but it was his misfortune to stand at a lowly position in the seniority list.

From 1861 the departure of a number of senior men and the death in 1863 of Yonge at the age of 31 inevitably resulted in a quickening of the recruitment of clerks from the Civil Service Commission by means of competitive examination. During those three years E. H. Rhodes, C. T. Martin, A. J. Crosby, L. O. Pike and E. Lethbridge joined the office, all of them graduates of obvious talent. In order to sit their examination a nomination was required, and the distinguished nature of the influences necessary even to compete was made plain in a letter written to the office secretary in 1913 by the then Sir Roper Lethbridge, Conservative MP for North Kensington from 1885 until 1892, in which he described his happy memories on entering the department:[8]

> I was nominated for the limited competition by Mr. Gladstone himself, on the recommendation of the late Profr. Goldwin Smith who knew my work at Oxford, in the spring of 1863 and after winning the competition, offered for, and passed in, a large number of voluntary subjects of examination. On joining the Department, I was placed by the then Deputy Keeper Mr. Hardy (afterwards Sir Thomas Duffus) in the office of his own Private Secretary Mr. Tabrum for the first few weeks to learn the ways of the Office and to come under his own observation and thereafter he was always my kindest and most generous friend. He then appointed me to be an Assistant to the late Professor Brewer, who was editing Giraldus Cambrensis and the Henry VIII State Papers. At that time also I joined the Rolls Chapel Choir – and sometimes sang solos in the Rolls Chapel, with Mr. A. Kingston, an Assistant Keeper. After that, I became an Assistant to Mr. Peter Turner, an Assistant Keeper who was highly skilled in the reading of ancient documents. That work I greatly loved – and I would never have left the Office but for the fact that in 1867 (just when I was ready to be called to the Bar) my wife was declared to be consumptive and to need a hot climate. A distant relative (Sir Stafford Northcote) was at that time Secretary of State for India – and he, on the joint recommendation of Professor Goldwin Smith and the Deputy Keeper with some other friends, appointed me to the then vacant Professorship of History and Political Economy in the State Colleges of the Calcutta University. I once made part of a tour in Normandy with Sir Thomas Duffus Hardy, and he was at all times my very kind and good friend, for whose vast knowledge of Records, and generally of the materials for British History, I had the most unbounded admiration.

It was not surprising that some of the clerks already in the office felt at

---

8. PRO 8/55, p 81: Lethbridge to Roberts, 20 January 1913.

1 *A view of the interior of the Chapter House Branch Record Office as reproduced in the* Illustrated Times *of 25 February 1860*. (PRO 8/61, p 98)

2 *The 'White Tower' at the Tower of London in which the records were housed*

3 *A sketch of one of the many decayed Common Pleas rolls at Carlton Ride.* (PRO 1/4)

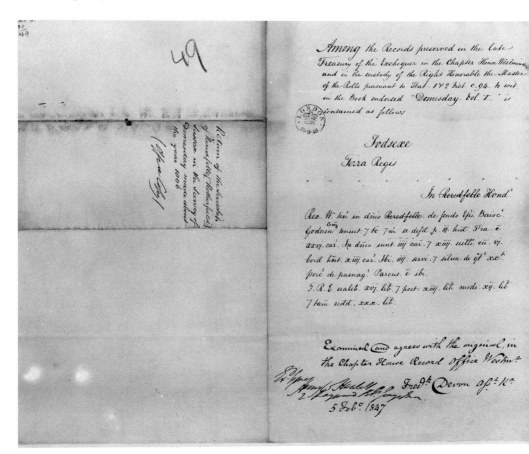

4 *Until the introduction of photostat copies during the Second World War much of the time of the office's clerks was spent in making office copies. The one shown here, an extract from Domesday Book, was made in 1847 for Henry Hewlett, a leading record agent. It was certified by Devon, then in charge of the Chapter House branch.* (LRRO 67/190, no 49)

5 *Bust of Lord Langdale in*
   the main entrance hall
   at Chancery Lane

6 *Bust of Lord Romilly in the*
   Public Waiting Room at
   Chancery Lane

7 *Sir Francis Palgrave,*
deputy keeper 1838–1861

8 *Sir Thomas Duffus Hardy,*
deputy keeper 1861–1878

9 *Sir William Hardy,*
deputy keeper 1878–1886

10 *Sir Henry Maxwell Lyte,*
deputy keeper 1886–1926. (By
kind permission of the British
Academy)

11 *Henry Cole at the time of the Great Exhibition from an engraving in* The Illustrated London News, *1851*

MR. BLACK MAKING UP HIS MIND NOT TO ASCEND THE TOR.

THE MEETING OF THE BRITISH ARCHÆOLOGICAL ASSOCIATION AT BRIDGEWATER AND BATH.

12 *Black's antiquarian interests ranged well beyond the office. He is shown here in company with members of the British Archaeological Association on an outing to Glastonbury Tor.* (PRO 8/56)

13 *Lascelles's notice which caused such offence to Romilly and Palgrave, who thought it called in question their over-riding authority for the public records.* (PRO 1/23)

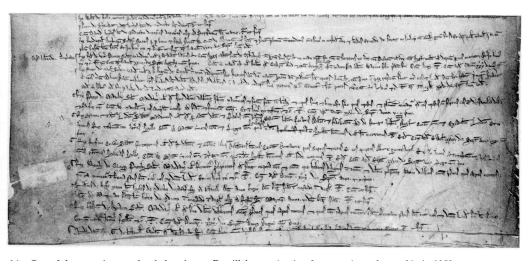

14 *One of the tests given to the clerks who sat Romilly's examination for an assistant keepership in 1859 was to transcribe and give a précis of an extract like this from a thirteenth-century patent roll. Gairdner was the successful candidate.* (C 66/17, m 3)

PUBLIC RECORD OFFICE.

Regulations as to Workmen.

1   A Workman is not to leave the Public Record Office, between 8 and 4, unless sent by the Deputy - Keeper, Secretary, an Assistant - Keeper, or the Care - Taker; or passed out by the Senior Foreman on duty, for some special reason. Any breach of this Regulation to be reported as speedily as is convenient, to the Secretary.

2   BEER is not to be brought in for the Workmen, except between 12 and 2; and, in the Repository, into the Kitchen (D. 12) only, where all cooking, meals, &c., for the Repository is to take place: - SPIRITS are not to be introduced at any time, except in case of illness with the sanction of an Assistant - Keeper.

3   The Officers of the Service, the Foremen, and the Policemen are requested and empowered to enforce these Regulations, and to report immediately to the Deputy - Keeper or Secretary any infringement thereof, or any case of Drunkenness; *which will be punished by Reduction or Suspension of Wages, Degradation to a lower Class, or Dismissal from the Service.*

(*Signed*) FRANCIS PALGRAVE, D. K.

18 *November,* 1859.

15 *The nineteenth-century workmen were strictly regulated. This notice of 1859 sets out the penalties for absence from duty or being the worse for drink.* (PRO 8/29, p 285)

a disadvantage compared with the newer men. Even Gairdner, who could hold his own with any of them, was to say many years later to the Royal Commission of 1910:[9]

In my time also Civil Service examinations were first instituted – a reform which I heartily welcomed, for we had not all of us received a first-rate education, and the framers of the Public Records Act seem to have been of opinion that a staff consisting of a few old Record agents and a few copying clerks was all that was required. I did not think so myself, but, as the literary use of records was looked upon only as a subordinate matter, there were really no means of proper training for those duties for which we ought to have qualified ourselves. From this cause I feel I have myself been a sufferer.

Gairdner went on to say that the first generation of assistant keepers, some of whom had been record agents, possessed a general knowledge of the records which their immediate successors often found it hard to acquire. Palmer, Devon, Lechmere and Lemon all operated in that field, but perhaps Gairdner had Hardy particularly in mind because he had combined record agency work with his clerkship at the Tower before making over the business to his brother William. Gairdner's apprehensions may also have been shared by Hart, a qualified solicitor and a fellow of the Society of Antiquaries, whose literary competence was not to be judged by the circular of 1857 which had caused so much offence to his colleagues. At any rate, in 1862 he made an application for five months' special unpaid leave for each of three years to take a degree at Magdalene College, Cambridge. Romilly was willing to release him, but the Treasury refused its sanction. Shortly afterwards, however, consolation came for Hart when Romilly and Hardy gave him the editorship of the *Historia et Cartularium Monasterii S. Petri Gloucestriae* in the Rolls Series. Hart's introduction to that work was later subject to some criticism, possibly reflecting prejudice against his approval of many of the practices of the medieval church. However, he was promoted to the senior clerical grade in 1868, although disappointed when a project to publish a definitive edition of ancient charters, which he proposed to Romilly in December of that year, was squeezed out by other claims on the office's resources. In 1869, quite out of the blue, Hart announced that a change in his personal circumstances enabled him to give up his job and he resigned in June. Frustration at being denied the editorial work he wanted may have played a part in his decision because within a comparatively short time he was seeking re-employment within the record service. Although, as will be seen in the next chapter, his attempt failed and produced much ill feeling, he continued to press his case and was eventually appointed, jointly with the Reverend P. A. Lyons, to edit the *Cartularium Monastereii de*

---

9. *First Report of the Royal Commission on Public Records*, I, pt III (Cd. 6396), 67.

Rameseia in the Rolls Series, the third and final volume of which was published in 1894, six years after his death in 1888.

At a less exalted level a significant change was heralded in 1862 by the introduction of a transcriber grade to assist Brewer, Bruce and Mrs Green in their calendaring work. After a special examination conducted by Lemon, involving the transcription and abstraction of a selection of state papers, six workmen were nominated by Romilly to the Treasury in October that year for appointment. One of them was G. W. Thompson, whose unsuccessful attempt to obtain an increase in pay from Romilly in 1860 has already been mentioned. Thompson had also managed to live down an incident in September 1861 when Hardy had declined to receive a letter from him because it had not been sent through the proper channels. In it Thompson not only asked for special payment for his work on government documents but also employed language in his comments upon Lascelles which was described by Tabrum as 'very disrespectful'. If Thompson entertained extravagant hopes they would have been dashed because, although the changes introduced represented a definite step forward, the pay scale authorised by the Treasury of 24s a week for the first three years' service, 28s for the next two years, and a maximum of 32s was modest and still left the transcribers well short of the £100 minimum starting salary of the clerks. Hardy reported that the class was 'to consist of persons accustomed to abstract ancient documents, familiar with ancient handwritings, and otherwise qualified',[10a] but that was a little misleading because the domestic state papers with which the original transcribers were principally concerned, while often extremely difficult to read, were generally in English and mainly of the sixteenth and seventeenth centuries. Furthermore, much of the transcribers' work consisted of making fair copies of the editors' calendars for the printers and assistance in seeing proofs through the press, besides the sortation and arrangement of papers. Their value to the office was, however, undoubted and not unlike certain of the duties exercised by the junior executive grades a century later. Recognition of their worth came in 1864 when their leave allowance was doubled to 12 days and their daily working hours reduced to six and a half. Hardy himself was never loth to utilise their services, and on more than one occasion when visiting collections outside London took a transcriber with him. Among the appendixes to his *Reports* will also be found the occasional list or calendar prepared by a transcriber. By 1867 the office, looking to the future and hoping, ultimately, to be able to undertake all calendaring work itself without the help of external editors, obtained Treasury authority to increase the number of transcribers from six to eight, one of the workmen promoted in consequence being none other than Woolby, Palgrave's former servant. The other, Tyler, rapidly proved his worth, so much so that within six months Romilly had taken him into his

10a. *The Twenty-fourth Annual Report of the Deputy Keeper* (1863), xvi.

own chambers as an assistant clerk and he was succeeded by W. Tolfree, another workman. In default of getting Treasury approval for the extra transcriber posts he considered necessary, Romilly feared he would be obliged to seek an increase in the number of clerks because the transcribers were also performing work previously given to the clerks, who were fully employed upon other pressing business.[10b]

Hardy's first *Report* as deputy keeper had appeared early in 1862. The twenty-third in the series, it is easily recognised on the shelves, being the first published in octavo format compared with Palgrave's foolscap-size pages. In his opening paragraph Hardy referred to the office's great loss in the death of Palgrave to whom, he said, it was

> indebted for many of the advantages it possesses, and the permanent benefits
> conferred by his zeal and labours, not only on those who have occasion to
> consult the Records of this Kingdom, but on Historians in general, cannot
> be too highly estimated and will not easily be forgotten.

In the aftermath of his old adversary's death Hardy had arranged for his papers to be sorted for the family. Among them were found some documents which had been borrowed many years before from Yarmouth Corporation. They were eventually sent back there, but not before Hardy had emphasised that they must have been overlooked because Palgrave was scrupulous in avoiding anything resembling a private collection. In his *Report* Hardy singled out Palgrave's great achievement in uniting at the Rolls Estate the contents of the different offices and his exertions in connection with the building of the first block of the repository. He also reported that, subject to the higher jurisdiction of the master of the rolls, his own first act as deputy keeper had been to assume the custody and control of the records, formerly spread among the assistant keepers in their branches. Secondly, he had ordered 'a Chronological Inventory to be prepared of all the Public Muniments in the Office', which was strangely reminiscent of the type of index at one time favoured by Langdale, and, as it was to turn out, equally unrealistic to compile, given the limited resources available. Hardy also referred to the arrangements for the making of a facsimile of Domesday Book by the photozincographic process at the Ordnance Survey Office at Southampton. Originally Burtt had been sent there to supervise the work, but to his annoyance his services at the repository were found by Hardy to be so urgently required in connection with the use of the Exchequer records as to lead to his recall and replacement by Sanders. Burtt thought the need for his presence had been exaggerated and blamed Knight for not coping better with searchers and others in his absence. But the problems encountered emphasised the drawback of the old branch organisation, in which a

---

10b. T 1/6757A/20078/1867: Romilly to Hamilton, 19 June 1867.

clerk might know next to nothing of records outside his own sphere, and suggested that it would be some while before services in the new repository were fully integrated.

Much of Hardy's *Report* was given over to a full-length account of the work carried out to that time upon the calendaring of the State Papers, the object of which, he said, was to make the contents of the office known especially to the imaginary 'inquirer living at a distance'. He also reproduced in full the instructions issued by Romilly to editors of calendars. Many years later Professor Sir Charles Firth, in a reasoned critique of the editorial policy of the Public Record Office for the Royal Commission on Public Records, drew attention to inconsistencies in Hardy's views, as expressed in the twenty-third and later *Reports*, about the necessity or otherwise for inquirers to consult the originals of calendared documents. Firth also pointed to apparent contradictions in Romilly's instructions, but it must be said that they seemed to be understood by editors, and appreciated by readers, well enough at the time. Undeniably, however, calendars grew fuller with successive volumes, which, as Firth pointed out, led inevitably towards the situation against which Tytler, giving evidence to the 1836 Select Committee, had warned so memorably, as 'the substitution of an unfathomable sea of *print* for an unfathomable sea of *manuscript*'.[10c]

Rather more briefly, Hardy had referred in the same *Twenty-third Report* to the work upon the Chronicles and Memorials of Great Britain and Ireland during the Middle Ages, which, he explained, was intended to fill the chasms existing in the printed materials of English history. He also set out the general directions issued to their editors, soon to include among their number William Stubbs, but only after three previous rejections.[11] No fewer than 25 volumes had now been issued in the Rolls Series, and Hardy reported that a further 16 were in the press or in progress including his own *Descriptive Catalogue of Manuscripts relating to the Early History of Great Britain and Ireland*, the first volume of which was to appear in 1862, prompting Romilly to tell the Treasury that when, as he expected, Hardy's work came to be fully recognised in the learned literary world, he hoped some special mark of honorary distinction might be conferred upon him by the queen.

Another notable work reported by Hardy as being in the press was Gustav Bergenroth's *Calendar of Letters, Despatches and State Papers . . . Preserved in the Archives at Simancas and Elsewhere*, centring upon the correspondence of the Spanish ambassador in England with his own court. Bergenroth's undertaking had been accompanied by extraordinary difficulties, in deciphering the documents and in coping with the adverse living conditions at Simancas. Both were to be graphically described in his introduction. Too

---

10c. *First Report of the Royal Commission on Public Records*, I, pt II, 103–104.

11. PRO 2/18, p 130: Romilly to Hamilton, 23 January 1862. Stubbs was entrusted with a work illustrative of the life and reign of Richard I and his wars in the Holy Land. See also Levine's 'History in the Archives', 30.

late for Hardy's *Report* came a petition to the Treasury from Earl Stanhope and others seeking the appointment of Rawdon Brown to carry out similar work upon the archives relating to England at Venice. After initial hesitation, his engagement was approved by the Treasury and he started work in 1862. On the other hand, a suggestion by Hardy that records relating to state and criminal trials might be published officially was turned down by the Treasury, which thought it should be left to private enterprise.

The completion of Thorpe's much-chequered edition of the Anglo-Saxon Chronicle was also reported by Hardy, but nothing was said of Thorpe's proposal to publish a collection of Anglo-Saxon charters. Thorpe believed that Hardy's hostility towards him personally had persuaded Romilly to turn down that project and subsequently he issued a pamphlet setting out his dissatisfaction. Nothing came of his efforts to have his case reviewed, although he managed to raise sufficient funds to have his work published privately in 1865. A year before his death in 1870 he petitioned the Treasury for a grant to continue his work, again without success. Romilly was a hard taskmaster when it came to editorial matters, and his decision owed less to Hardy than to his loss of faith in Thorpe's competence and to the fact that certain of the charters had already been published by Kemble for the English Historical Society. The work of the young Reverend F. C. Hingeston, a one-time suitor of Stevenson's eldest daughter, had also attracted Romilly's critical eye. Hardy's *Report* mentioned that the second volume of Hingeston's *Royal and Historical Letters During the Reign of Henry IV*, was in the press, but when Romilly, suspecting the worst, subsequently arranged for its collation, mainly by Riley, it received such a savaging that he decided to suppress it. But the unfortunate Hingeston's work was not entirely wasted because a century later, in 1965, it was published by Kraus Reprint, complete with his tormentors' amendments.

Few realised the drama behind the making of the office's publications, the publicity aroused by the Turnbull affair being exceptional in that respect. Hardy said nothing in his *Report* about that disturbing episode, apart from recording the engagement of Stevenson as Turnbull's successor. In practice, however, it meant that where religious susceptibilities were concerned Romilly and Hardy were now obliged to exercise even greater caution as R. B. Knowles, a Roman Catholic, found to his cost, when his offer at the end of 1861 to edit an unprinted manuscript of the time of Edward III was declined. Although his work was not publicly acknowledged, he had previously done good service for Hardy in collating the elderly Ellis's *Chronica Johannis de Oxenedes*, but that counted for less than official apprehension of the Protestant Alliance, still lurking in the wings. In March 1863, however, the Alliance was rash enough to imply in its *Monthly Letter* that Turnbull had abstracted certain state papers and concealed his guilt by describing them in his calendar as 'missing'. Through Lemon the office was able to show that the documents mentioned had vanished long before Turnbull came on the scene and that they ought to have been noted as 'wanting' or 'not existing' rather than 'missing'. Some of the documents were enclosures, which had become separated from the letters containing them, and many of them were believed to be still extant although out of place. Romilly's firm assurance that he was satisfied that none of the State Papers had disappeared since he had taken them on charge enabled the government to lay the entire correspondence before Parliament,[12a] effectively silencing the Protestant critics, at least for a time. But Romilly remained wary of them and four years later, when A. S. Larken, a Roman Catholic convert, applied for editorial work, Romilly told the Treasury that, remembering the Turnbull case, he was 'unable to recommend a Roman Catholic however high his qualifications might be to be the Editor of any work published under my directions without bringing the circumstances to the notice of the Lords Commissioners'.[12b]

It was natural that Hardy, who set such great store upon publication, should concentrate upon it so largely in his annual reports as deputy keeper. As early as his second, that for 1862, he reverted to Palgrave's practice of appending lists, calendars, indexes, etc., some of much length. But in reporting for the first time Hardy did not overlook the equally important matter of the desired extension to the central block of the record repository. Besides printing in full Romilly's letter of 6 December 1861 on that subject to the Treasury, he noted trenchantly 'how indispensable it is that these National Muniments and Papers should be removed from their present dangerous risks' to which they were deplorably exposed in several houses in Chancery Lane. He also appended a detailed statement of the research carried out by literary searchers from the time that fees were lifted in 1852 until the end of 1861. The nature of the topics in which readers were interested was extremely varied, and besides general historical research, local and family history, biography and genealogy formed an important part of the whole. There was also a second appendix to the *Report* setting out 'Official Attendance at Record Offices previously to the passing of the Public Record Act' to illustrate how the records were dispersed in 56 repositories, 'many of them very dark, ill-lighted, badly ventilated, and little fitted for the safe custody and preservation of the Public Archives'. Repository or record office was, however, in most cases a misnomer for, apart from those at the Rolls Chapel, Tower of London, Chapter House and the Land Revenue Record Office, the assorted collections of premises were generally no more than departmental annexes to the offices of the courts. For that reason it was hardly apt to describe them as archive establishments despite their housing public records, which, in theory, should have been consultable on demand. The exposure of the grim conditions associated with the former system owed much to Henry Cole who 11 years after his move from the office retained an interest in its activities. During 1861 he was busy preparing

---

12a. *HC Accounts and Papers*, 1863, XLVIII, 321–324.
12b. T 1/6703B/8967/1867: Romilly to Hamilton, 31 May 1867. At the end of 1868 Larken tried again, but was no more fortunate.

for the International Exhibition of 1862, but, when he eventually wrote to Hardy to congratulate him upon his appointment as deputy keeper, he took the opportunity to suggest that as part of the 1862 celebrations the more popular records might be exhibited 'under glass cases and made interesting by full explanatory labels'. But Hardy, like Palgrave, had no enthusiasm for such displays, telling Cole:[13]

> I am sure that the Master of the Rolls would not like to turn the Office into a show place, even for the nonce, but this I can tell you that no person desirous of seeing any of the Records here, as mere matter of curiosity would be refused indeed no one is even denied such a trifling gratification who applies and during the great Exhibition next year, we should of course be doubly anxious to oblige all classes of persons but I do not think it would be proper to advertise such a fact.
>
> Thanks for your congratulation.

Some months later the irrepressible Cole asked if the golden *bulla* attached to the confirmation by Clement VII of the title of 'Defender of the Faith' to Henry VIII, and a few specimens of bookbinding and illumination might be borrowed for a special exhibition of works of art at the South Kensington Museum to be held in the summer, but he was again rebuffed by Hardy, who said that he did not think Romilly would approve.[14] Nevertheless, the office was closed on 1 May 1862, the day appointed for the opening of the International Exhibition, and the workmen were given an extra day's holiday to attend without any of the fuss about the deduction of two hours from their pay which had marred the dispensation granted by Palgrave on the occasion of the Great Exhibition of 1851.

In January 1862 the staff sent an address of condolence to the queen, signed by them all, to convey their sympathy on the death of the prince consort in the previous month, and in November most of them, from Hardy downwards, subscribed a day's pay to help relieve distress in Lancashire and Cheshire, resulting from the cotton famine caused by the American Civil War. The previous branch consciousness had given way to a departmental one, and morale was rising in the expectation of the improved facilities to be provided by the long-awaited extension. Externally, the office's reputation stood to gain from the better provision being made for the small but select body of academics, antiquarians, professional record agents and overseas researchers frequenting the office. The planned improve-

---

13. PRO 2/17, p 420: Hardy to Cole, 10 December 1861.

14. PRO 2/18, p 217: Hardy to Cole, 14 April 1862. In his letter Cole described the *bulla* as the Celini (*sic*) seal, but it is now rather ascribed to Lautizio di Meo: *Guide to Seals in the Public Record Office* (HMSO, 1968), 62–63. In 1872, after a further approach, Romilly agreed that the museum might take a photograph of the seal.

ment bid fair to relieve the cramped conditions of the search rooms, if not their illumination, for lighting in them was non-existent until electricity was installed in 1889. Equally important was the acceptance within Whitehall of the Record Office as part of the machinery of government. The Treasury, making use of its special position, had directed the calendaring of its own records and requested official assistance for Professor Thorold Rogers of Oxford University in connection with his history of prices during the middle ages. In 1862 Rogers was given the help he needed, but when he tried again in 1869 he was met with a polite refusal, which may explain why, when he entered Parliament some years later, he was among the office's critics there.

Ministers and senior officials of departments other than the Treasury were also showing an increasing awareness of the office's practical utility, a notable example being an extensive search made in 1865 for the Privy Council Office for information concerning the number of cattle which died or were slaughtered on account of the cattle plague between 1745 and 1757. Much work was also undertaken for the queen into the early history of Windsor Castle in furtherance of the prince consort's intended investigation, Atkins being closely concerned in the research. A mammoth return was also begun for Parliament, through the Home Office, in 1868 of trust deeds relating to charities enrolled on the Close Rolls under the Charitable Uses Act 1735, and a calendar of them, the work of Kingston and three of the junior clerks, was appended to *The Thirty-second Report of the Deputy Keeper*, occupying no less than 1,062 pages. A further 263 pages of that bulky volume were given over to Russell's and Prendergast's final report to the Treasury on the Carte Papers in the Bodleian Library.

But the office's main contact with departments was through the Committee on Government Documents whose work had so expanded that a second assistant keeper, Redington, was added to its staff in July 1861. Attempts were also being made to settle the dates to which departmental records might be made available to searchers without restriction. By the end of 1862 the Treasury and the War Office had agreed that their records might be opened to 1820, the end of the reign of George III, and the Admiralty and Home Office had decided upon 1760, the end of the reign of George II. The Admiralty's reservations were in respect of the records of the accountant-general of the Navy, and when it later transferred a quantity of letter books, etc. from Whitehall it agreed to open them to 1800. The Colonial Office had also agreed to 1760, except for its North American correspondence, which it was not willing to open beyond 1702, while the Foreign Office was not prepared to open any of its papers later than 1688. In 1864 the Treasury Solicitor's Department refused to grant access to searchers at all except under permit. Permission for controlled access of that kind, which involved official supervision and vetting of notes, could always be sought by searchers wishing to see closed papers, and during 1862 the number of such applications recorded was 11. The office also carried out many searches for departments themselves, and in that same year 4,000 such operations were registered, mainly for the War Office. That work was transferred to the search rooms in 1863, leaving Lascelles and Redington with more time to concentrate upon examining categories of government records in order to determine their disposal with departmental representatives. Particular attention was paid during the 1860s to papers from the Treasury and to the records of the Treasury solicitor and the Audit Office. The inclusion among the Audit Office papers of material from a multitude of departments posed particular problems about public access to them, but it was finally agreed that they might be opened to 1760. Although Redington's duties included the calendaring of Treasury papers, he seems to have felt somewhat sorry for himself because when a report of a review of Admiralty records at Deptford Dockyard issued in April 1869 from the Committee on Government Documents of which he was then chairman, it stated[15]

> that a more disagreeable business, or one more prejudicial to their health
> and their clothes, could hardly have been imposed upon them . . . it has
> been pursued amid clouds of dust and dirt as well as during severe weather,
> and often too by the help of candle and lanterns and has required an amount
> of patience throughout such as gentlemen in the public service are not often
> called to exercise.

Worse still, such activities were seen as subordinate, if not incidental to the work of the department proper. Government records were distinguished from the so-called public records, so that Hardy in the *Thirty-third Report* for 1872, in a paragraph of doubtful accuracy, which must have made Palgrave turn in his grave, could actually say in relation to public access to them about which controversy had arisen:

> While on this subject, it may be remarked, as some misconception prevails
> that all the papers and documents deposited in the Public Record Office are
> public records and come under the Public Records Act, that many of the
> papers and documents belonging to the Treasury, as well as to the offices
> of the Secretaries of State, the Admiralty, and other Government
> Departments are not open to the public because, although preserved in the
> Public Record Office, they do not come within the provisions of the Public
> Records Act.

Although sophistry of that kind illustrated Hardy's preferences, he had no wish to change the role of the Public Record Office as the accepted place of deposit for departmental documents, for which, in any event, there was no other contender. Any ambitions that the British Museum may once have entertained in that connection had long since disappeared, and the official

---

15. PRO 39/1/3, p 411: from the tenth report of the committee appointed to examine etc. the papers of the administrative departments of government.

relationship between the two institutions was good. Proof of that had been demonstrated in 1862 when the museum transferred to the office a series of chancellor's rolls, corresponding to the pipe rolls, which the Record Commission had sent to it in 1833 and 1834. Madden, the office's principal adversary there, got on better with Hardy than with Palgrave and was pleased when he became deputy keeper, thinking he deserved it. Like a number of other British Museum men he was also a Rolls Series editor, being entrusted with the *Historia Minor* of Matthew Paris. Unfortunately for Madden his hope of succeeding Panizzi as principal librarian in 1866 was dashed when the job went to a fellow keeper, John Winter Jones. Madden, desolate and bitter, felt betrayed by Hardy, who had earlier written a testimonial in favour of Stubbs, apparently believing that the museum's trustees were resolved to fill the post with an outsider. Stubbs's failure to get the job seemed providential when the return of a Conservative administration in July 1866 resulted in his appointment to the regius chair of history at Oxford, vacated by Goldwin Smith.[16a] For Madden there was no such consolation. He promptly resigned his keepership of the Department of Manuscripts and was succeeded by Edward (later Sir Edward) Augustus Bond. That change did nothing but good for dealings between the two institutions because Bond, besides being a former record service man and a Rolls Series editor, enjoyed a cordial relationship with Romilly and Hardy. Furthermore, in spite of occasional criticism about inconvenience, neither side was anxious to disturb the situation whereby many state papers existed in private collections in the museum whereas the official State Paper Office archive was in the Public Record Office. Their close collaboration was strikingly displayed in May 1868 when Peter Cunningham, the author and critic, a former clerk in the Audit Office, offered certain accounts of the revels of Shakespearean interest to the museum for 60 guineas. Cunningham claimed to have saved them from destruction on finding them in the damp cellars in Somerset House in 1842. When Bond told Romilly about the offer he immediately declared it improper, and they were thereupon impounded and later sent to the Public Record Office to be reunited with other accounts among the Exchequer and Audit Department's records. Doubts were soon voiced as to their genuineness and for many years they languished under suspicion until cleared by a diligent Shakespearean researcher, Edward Law, with the assistance of the government chemist, and finally absolved by A. E. Stamp, a later deputy keeper, in 1930.[16b]

Hardy's reputation meant that he was increasingly consulted about record

16a. For the background see the article by N. J. Williams in the *Bulletin of the Institute of Historical Research*, XXXIII (1960), 121–125.

16b. A. E. Stamp, *The Disputed Revels Accounts* (Oxford, 1930). For Law's evidence to the Royal Commission on Public Records see *First Report*, I, pt III, 82–83. Another report upon them made by Redington on 25 May 1882 is in PRO 1/47. See also Hubert Hall's undated memorandum in PRO 44/2.

matters generally, but he did not neglect the office's internal organisation. In 1862 he established a Calendaring Department and placed Sharpe in charge. Sharpe was reluctant to move from the Legal Search Room, but before long the fruits of his section's work were to be seen in the calendars, etc., which were regularly appended to Hardy's annual reports. Organisationally, with Secretarial, Search and Copying, Calendaring and Operative Departments, the office establishment was now in line with the pattern that Palgrave once had in mind, save for the additional activity generated from 1859 by the Committee on Government Documents.

Reviewing the department's work in his *Report* for 1863, Hardy took stock of the progress made in bringing into the office the records mentioned in the 1838 act. Accommodation difficulties had, until then, hampered transfers from the various Chancery offices and the fate of the Durham records remained in the balance. A start had, however, been made during the course of that year in securing the first batch of records from the High Court of Admiralty since the passage of the act. The long-outstanding question concerning the deposit of records from the Office of Land Revenue Records and Enrolments had also become active, and, after the exploration of the legal aspects by the law officers,[17a] it was agreed that some of those records might be removed to the Public Record Office. The extent of the transfer was left to the decision of Henry Gay Hewlett, a record agent, who had succeeded Tarver Richard Fearnside as keeper of the land revenue records and enrolments in 1865. Hewlett did not share his predecessor's proprietorial concern for his records and in 1866 transferred many of them and listed others which he thought might be removed at a later date. Hardy believed that the accession of the land revenue documents provided a strong reason to transfer ancient records of a similar description in the Offices of the Duchies of Lancaster and Cornwall. The 1838 act did not mention either office, an omission which Palgrave had unsuccessfully tried to correct at its bill stage. But by 1855, when the Duchy of Lancaster itself wrote to Romilly seeking to deposit its older material, Palgrave was grappling with the problems posed by the State Paper Office merger. He foresaw many difficulties about the duchy's proposal, and told Romilly he intended to set out his misgivings, but he never did so and the application was allowed to lapse. Pressures of current business at that time partly explain why the matter was put on one side, but there was for Palgrave the drawback that the arrangement suggested by the duchy brought with it the strong probability of the transfer to his already far from loyal staff of another old foe, Hardy's brother William, the Lancaster record keeper. The delicacy of that aspect must have weighed heavily with Palgrave, who would not have forgotten the altercation on his own doorstep many years before, when the two Hardys, allegedly,

---

17a. The law officers' opinions are printed in the *First Report of the Royal Commission on Public Records*, I, pt III, 178. See also PRO 1/117.

told him that they would have their revenge and never cease till they had ruined him.[17b] At any rate, the duchy's application was never registered officially, and when it tried again in 1863 it was asked to supply a copy of its original request because none of the earlier papers could then be found.

By that time Palgrave was no longer on the scene, but the office still had a severe accommodation problem, which the Treasury was unenthusiastic about remedying, although it toyed with the idea that the duchy might itself be persuaded to meet the storage costs involved. Nothing came of that notion, but Romilly, like Hardy, remained keen to secure the material and his hand was strengthened in 1866 when the Chetham Society sent a memorial urging the move. The country was still in the heyday of 'Victorian prosperity', and in the following year the Treasury felt sufficiently relaxed to authorise the expenditure of £24,000 during the financial year 1868–1869 to erect and fit up the remaining portion of the eastern block. The building of the so-called Lancaster Tower there, a name that, like that of its twin Domesday or Norman Tower, was soon forgotten, enabled the office to accept the duchy's records. Because they were non-public the queen presented them to the nation and her 'gracious and priceless gift' was fulsomely acknowledged by Hardy in the *Thirtieth Deputy Keeper's Report*, which also included a brief sketch of the history of the duchy. An important consequence of the transaction, not mentioned by Hardy, was that his brother William joined the staff as a supplementary assistant keeper, being placed at the maximum of the first-class scale, partly in recognition of the fact that he was obliged, as a condition of transfer, to give up the private record agency business which he had formerly combined with his post at the duchy. Romilly was far from happy about taking him and would have much preferred to engage two extra clerks instead, but eventually acquiesced because of the Treasury's wish to avoid the payment of compensation.[18]

One of the reasons why Romilly would have liked to strengthen his clerical staff was because he was having to provide not only for the duchy records but also for those of the Palatinate of Durham. The question of their transfer had again become a live issue in June 1867, when he had received a letter from the Reverend Scott Surtees alleging that their state was 'a disgrace to the age in which we live'. Hardy, who had not forgotten the lamentable state of disorder in which he had found them in 1854, was sent to Durham by Romilly once more, where to his dismay he discovered that none of the recommendations he had made earlier had been carried out and that the condition of the records had, if anything, deteriorated. However, in spite of his reporting the probability that but for Surtees's complaint 'many would have been allowed to continue in their present disgusting state of

---

17b. PRO 30/26/109: Palgrave to Allen, 25 April 1832. The quarrel arose from some remarks by Palgrave in favour of directly-employed transcribers, which the Hardys thought injurious to their reputation.

18. The Treasury's papers relating to the negotiations are in T 1/6810B/16046/1868.

decomposition and filth until they had been entirely destroyed',[19] Romilly was agreeable to their remaining at Durham, provided that the county was prepared to find the funds to employ a qualified record keeper to care for them. But the authorities at Durham were no more willing to enter into such an arrangement than their counterparts at Chester had been in 1853, and so a warrant for the removal of the records to London was issued in November 1868. In reporting their accession in his *Report* for that year Hardy also recorded the great service rendered to him by A. T. Watson, one of the office's transcribers, in the removal of the records and their subsequent arrangement. Given sufficient accommodation, Hardy would also have wished to secure the records remaining in the offices of the clerks of assize on account of their historical interest and because there had been disquieting reports about the uncertain custody of those belonging to the Home Circuit. Assize records were not, however, mentioned in the 1838 act any more than were the bishops' transcripts of parish registers, which Hardy would also have liked to accommodate had space been available.

In all these matters could be seen Hardy's concern for the national records and for making them available to the public. He had long favoured the abolition of all fees and set out the case for it in his *Report* for 1863. Three years later he had the satisfaction of reporting Romilly's decision to lift them for legal as well as literary searchers, a move that was timed to coincide with the opening of the new search rooms, which were situated at ground-floor level in the eastern extension of the building. The glass-domed larger room, the Round Room as it came to be known, was reserved for literary searchers, and the other, the Long Room, running parallel with Fetter Lane, for legal inquirers. The office staff was also augmented by the recruitment of a ladies' attendant to superintend the ladies' cloakroom. Romilly, more than anyone, was responsible for the improvements and it was in recognition of his services to literature and in the record field that he had been raised to the peerage in December 1865. The following year a number of the office's readers subscribed towards the cost of having a marble bust made of him, which, on completion by Joseph Durham, was placed in the Literary Search Room in 1867 and may still be seen with portraits etc. of other office notables in the Public Waiting Room at Chancery Lane. Romilly himself thought the bust a beautiful work of art and considered it 'the highest honour bestowed on me and as such I shall ever regard it and so I believe will my children'.[20a]

The building operations at the eastern end were followed by works to complete the centre tower on the south front of the building, including the

---

19. The Durham correspondence is appended to *The Twenty-ninth Annual Report of the Deputy Keeper* (1868), 104–112.

20a. PRO 2/24, p 92: Romilly to W. Hepworth Dixon, 2 January 1867. Currently, the Chancery Lane search rooms provide mainly for the production of legal and State Paper Office records. Their centenary was marked by an article in *The Times* of 18 June 1966 by E. K. Timings 'Where Public Records have been searched for 100 years'.

installation of a water tank there to improve fire precautions. The need for that had been emphasised in 1864 when a fire in a lodge used by the building contractors might have spread to the main building and the Rolls House but for prompt action by Kingston, the police and the fire brigade. Carved out of the stonework of the tower's main cornice were coats of arms of London, Ireland, England, Lord Langdale, Lord Romilly, Wales, Scotland and Westminster; and carved upon its large pinnacles were those of Queen Victoria, the prince of Wales, the prince consort, the princess of Wales, William the Conqueror because of his connection with Domesday Book, and Henry I, King John and Henry VIII to mark the commencement of the Pipe Rolls, the Chancery enrolments and the State Papers respectively. On the exterior, over the portico, were placed statues, carved by Durham, of Matilda, Elizabeth I, Anne and Victoria which resulted in its being known at the time as the Queens' Tower. 'What a fine effect the Office makes with the recent additions', Palgrave's son Francis told Edwards, 'my father would have enjoyed seeing it'.[20b]

Even before the opening of the office's new search rooms and its further development there was a sense in which it had come to be seen as a model of archival rectitude so that when Trevelyan, then financial secretary in India, became involved with the establishment of a record commission there, it was the English experience upon which he drew.[20c] Hardy had wondered whether a record commission might be re-established to oversee the record offices in England (and Wales), Scotland and Ireland, but nothing came of that idea although his own eminence meant that it was to him that the government automatically turned for records advice. When consideration was being given in 1863 to the best way to facilitate the study of Irish history, he was commissioned by the Treasury to report upon the Carte and Carew Papers in the Bodleian and Lambeth Palace libraries. Brewer was appointed to assist him, and in 1865 their joint report was published, leading to a decision by the Treasury to have transcripts made of the more important documents in the Carte Collection and a calendar prepared of the Carew Papers.

Brewer was appointed by the Treasury to make the Carew Calendar jointly with William Bullen, an Irish Protestant scholar. The practicalities of that arrangement initially caused Brewer some concern, but he accepted the position when Romilly made it clear that he was to collate Bullen's work, prepare it for the press and write the preface. Relations between the two men were, however, often prickly. The Treasury also decided to appoint two persons to select the Carte transcripts. Originally it had two Protestants in mind, but after representations from William Monsell, an Irish MP, decided that the Roman Catholic Dr Charles William Russell of Maynooth

20b. PRO 1/31: F. T. Palgrave to Edwards, 17 November 1866.
20c. PRO 2/20, p 414: Trevelyan to Romilly, 27 August 1863.

College should assist the Protestant historian John Patrick Prendergast. Their partnership proved fruitful, but Prendergast's first reaction was extreme for he told Hardy, privately:[21]

> To yoke me to the head of an Army of Priests (and Jesuits, I believe for I
> think Dr. R writes SJ after his name) is no light matter – particularly to
> one much laughed at for giving expression in *Ladies* company (it was quite
> inconsiderate in that respect, but in that respect only) 'Beware of the forepart
> of a woman, the hind part of a mule, but all sides of a priest'. I do not know
> what share the MR has had in the appointment, but a more extraordinary
> one was never, I think, made.

Fortunately, Hardy, who had friends in both camps, managed to quieten Prendergast's fears, and he was, in any case, accustomed to Irish ways, which was just as well because he was not always himself the most tactful of men. After the Carte and Carew investigation he had been sent by the Treasury to Dublin with Brewer for nearly two months in 1864 to inquire into a fierce attack by 'A Critic' upon three volumes of a *Calendar of Patent and Close Rolls . . . in Ireland*, which had been prepared by James Morrin, clerk of enrolments in the Rolls Office there. A year before, in July 1863, Monsell had drawn Parliament's attention to the criticisms, and the Treasury had later come to the conclusion that only a full-scale inquiry could determine if there was any substance in the allegations of plagiarism and incompetence levelled at Morrin.[22] In the event, Hardy's and Brewer's report broadly exonerated Morrin, but the charges did no harm to their author, John (later Sir John) T. Gilbert, librarian of the Royal Irish Academy, who later became a Rolls Series editor and the first secretary of the Public Record Office of Ireland upon its establishment in 1867. For their pains Hardy and Brewer were awarded 100 guineas each by the Treasury, which was well satisfied for the matter to be laid to rest, particularly as the master of the rolls in Ireland, Thomas Barry Cusack Smith, had taken great exception to the manner in which Morrin's work had been assailed.

The Treasury also took the opportunity of Hardy's and Brewer's inquiry into Morrin's work to get them to report upon the records and state papers in Ireland, which were scattered in a number of buildings and not subject to a single authority. To remedy the situation Hardy and Brewer recommended that all records of 12 years' standing should, after weeding, be transferred to a central record office under the keepership of the master of

---

21. PRO 1/29: Prendergast to Hardy, 14 May 1865.
22. The Treasury's papers, including a copy of the critical booklet, are in T 1/6535A. Hardy's and Brewer's lengthy report was later printed and laid before Parliament: *HC Accounts and Papers*, 1865, XLV, 213–236.

the rolls, with the assistance of a deputy keeper.[23] Having had difficulties with the then Irish master of the rolls, Smith, the Treasury was not entirely happy about his place in the scheme of things. However, Smith's death in 1866, and the succession of John Edward Walsh eased the position sufficiently for the Public Record Office to be created by the Public Records (Ireland) Act 1867, and for legal records to be placed under the charge of the master of the rolls there after 20 years and state papers after 50 years. Hardy's and Brewer's proposals for preliminary weeding were not adopted, but the measure broadly followed their recommendations, and was not greatly dissimilar to the English Record Act, although the post of deputy keeper was reserved to the lord lieutenant, with Treasury consent.[24]

The Treasury view was that the English system worked admirably and that there were many reasons in favour of its introduction, suitably adapted, in Ireland. But writing in 1866 to Lord Naas (later earl of Mayo), chief secretary in Ireland, Hamilton had emphasised that the success in England was because 'we have in Lord Romilly a man of a highly cultivated mind, of great historical knowledge and taste, and . . . in Mr. Duffus Hardy, the Deputy Keeper of Records, a man who appreciates and thoroughly understands the value and mode of utilizing public records'.[25] But, Hamilton said, even if it was accepted that the Irish master of the rolls, who already had charge of most of the legal documents, would have to continue in that capacity because the judges would object to anyone else, it would not be easy to find anyone in that office who was prepared to give up as much time to the record branch of his duties as Romilly. For that reason Hamilton thought that the selection of a deputy keeper should be very carefully made and that the advice of Dr James Todd, the distinguished Irish scholar, with whom he had spoken on the subject, would be valuable.

Hamilton also mentioned to Naas that Gilbert had suggested a preliminary inquiry and report by members of the Royal Irish Academy, but Hamilton thought that such proceedings might fetter the government and give the matter too much of an antiquarian taste, particularly because the state papers were more than an object of specialist interest. Taking Hardy as a model, Hamilton thought the new deputy keeper should be not only an antiquarian but a man of general historical knowledge and capable of making available

---

23. T 1/6503A/14612/1864: Hardy and Brewer to Hamilton, 17 October 1864. The same file includes a memorial from the Kilkenny and South East of Ireland Archaeological Society 'praying that the scattered public records of Ireland may be collected into one General Repository in Dublin'. Much of Hardy's and Brewer's survey was reproduced by Ferguson in an appendix to his *First Report*, 1867–1868, as deputy keeper of the records in Ireland.

24. The Treasury's bill papers are in T 1/6757B/20123/1867. For a memorandum on the Irish Record Act and its application to local records, prepared in 1915 by Sir Charles Firth for the Royal Commission on Public Records, see *Third Report*, III, pt II (1919), (Cmd. 368), 59–62.

25. T 168/3, pp 128–133: Hamilton to Naas, [August] 1866.

for public use the documents under his immediate charge. The choice when it came fell upon the 57-year-old Samuel (later Sir Samuel) Ferguson, who lost no time in visiting London to acquaint himself with the way record business was conducted at Chancery Lane. Ferguson believed it was necessary initially to have an assistant deputy keeper to take charge of certification work and a secretary to manage the general correspondence and direction of the office. After 1875 the duties of the secretary were taken over by the assistant deputy keeper, but at the outset the posts were filled by Gilbert and by John James Digges La Touche from the former office of deputy keeper of the rolls. Hardy took much interest in the various Irish developments, and in particular in the battle for the secretaryship that took place between Gilbert, who had his support, and William Hardinge, the keeper of the Landed Estates Record Office at the Custom House. Not surprisingly, in view of Gilbert's success, the much-maligned Morrin chose to withdraw from the Irish record scene, an up-to-date assessment of which was provided for Hardy by Prendergast in a racy letter he sent to him from Dublin at the end of 1867.[26] That year was also marked by Anglo-Irish/American cooperation, when the Library Company of Philadelphia sent to Romilly five volumes of Irish state papers which had been presented to it in 1799, having been removed without permission by some person from Dublin. After copies had been made, Romilly had the originals strongly bound and sent to the Public Record Office in Dublin, suitably inscribed to commemorate the circumstances of their restitution. In acknowledgement of the honourable and disinterested spirit which had prompted the Philadelphia Library Company to make its gift, it was presented by the Treasury, on Romilly's recommendation, with a complete and specially bound set of record publications.

After his visit to Dublin in 1864, Hardy journeyed to Venice in 1865 to investigate the archives and libraries there, and his report was published with Treasury authority in the following year. The Treasury also consulted him specially in June 1866 in connection with the proposed sale of the Paston Letters. Hardy was in no doubt about their value and his belief that they ought to be acquired for the office or the British Museum eventually led to their deposit in the latter and their subsequent editing by Gairdner. In 1867 Hardy, whose special services were to be marked by the award of a £250 gratuity, continued his perambulations by visiting Edinburgh to undertake an inquiry and report for the Treasury, at the suggestion of the lord clerk registrar, Sir William Gibson Craig, upon the Historical Department of the General Register House, the Record and State Paper Office of Scotland.[27a] On that occasion his conclusions, which centred upon the filling of the post of literary searcher and envisaged his and Romilly's association

26. PRO 1/122: Prendergast to Hardy, 5 December 1867.
27a. Hardy's report, dated 14 February 1867, is in PRO 8/2. Treasury papers are in T 1/6724A/15706/1867.

with the scheme for publishing materials for the history of Scotland, proved unpalatable to Craig and resulted in some ill feeling. Generally speaking, however, collaboration between the two offices was good, as was exemplified by the sending of Hood to Edinburgh in November 1865 to undertake the repair of a number of documents. Sanders, still at Southampton, also worked closely with his Scottish colleagues in the making of *Facsimiles of National Manuscripts*. That project had been initiated in 1864 after the reproduction of Domesday was completed. Hardy would much have preferred all such work to have been carried out at Chancery Lane, or at least through normal Stationery Office channels, but Sir Henry James, the director of the Ordnance Survey Department, was a powerful figure and wanted to keep the new photozincographic development under his own control. He was, nevertheless, obliged to give ground to Romilly when a dispute arose in 1865 as to the responsibility for publication, but the reprographic processes were carried out by his staff. The idea of filming national documents of the first rank had come from Gladstone himself, which explained the fair wind that the exercise was to enjoy for the next 20 years. Four volumes of *Facsimiles of National Manuscripts* of England were issued between 1865 and 1869, a similar collection of Scottish manuscripts was issued in three volumes between 1867 and 1873, four volumes of Irish manuscripts between 1874 and 1884, and a series of Anglo-Saxon charters in three parts between 1878 and 1885. Besides assisting in the selection, Sanders provided a short explanation of the documents and translated them where necessary. He was much interested in the technicalities of the reprographic processes, and over the years his reports upon the progress of the work at Southampton were prominently featured in the *Deputy Keeper's Reports*. The series included documents from the reign of William the Conqueror to that of Queen Anne, the earliest being the charter of the City of London in Anglo-Saxon. It included also Magna Carta, the enrolment of earliest writs of summons of the House of Commons, and royal autographs.

The reproduction of Domesday Book at Southampton and the tale of its subsequent rebinding has been fully described,[27b] but it is worth mentioning that the office was not disposed to give the work to anyone on its own staff as it did on the two rebindings in the twentieth century. Cole, as joint secretary of the Department of Science and Art, had been prominent in the discussions with Hardy and Romilly concerning the design of Domesday's cover, and it was upon his recommendation that Robert Riviere was ultimately to supervise the work. The belief that the services of the best possible craftsman should be obtained was understandable, particularly because of the justified criticism of the tightness of the previous binding that Caley had put in hand at the Chapter House in 1819. However, it was apparent that the office lacked confidence in the ability of its own men to undertake such

---

27b. Elizabeth M. Hallam, *Domesday Book through Nine Centuries* (HMSO, 1986).

work, despite the fact that some of them, such as Hood, his son-in-law Beall, the deaf and dumb Charles Foster and Simpson were primarily binders. Although Hood had devised a method of restoring decayed documents by sizing,[28a] document repair was still at a comparatively elementary stage, and a large part of the workmen's time was occupied by mundane tasks such as the flattening, ticketing, sewing, sorting, stamping and numbering of documents. The extent of such activities, which were reported annually in the *Deputy Keeper's Reports*, had much to do with ensuring the security of the records, particularly before production to searchers, which always involved preliminary stamping. Inevitably, better quality work was squeezed out, but there was, in any event, little incentive for men to move on to more highly skilled duties because the entire labour force was lumped in the one workman grade whether employed in the repair workshops or in the repository and search rooms. However, despite the existence of a press list, largely the work of Kentish and Hohler and completed in 1865,[28b] the cumbersome nature of the references to the documents often made their identification on the shelves troublesome and justified the importance attached to the work of production. For example, a requisition for a typical Chancery proceeding would read: Mitford Study Matters, 1735, Michaelmas, Bundle 2061, 24th on the file, Haughton v Wilson. That ticket was, in fact, given out in September 1866 by Kingston as part of a test he set for two of the men. Unhappily, one man took four hours to produce nine out of fourteen documents requested and two of those were wrong, while the other man took three hours without being able to produce a single piece.[29] Fortunately, they were not typical as most repository workmen would have been able to produce all the documents wanted in 30 to 40 minutes. Some of the younger boys, however, had difficulty in producing heavy documents, and it was partly on that account that the grade's starting age was raised from 14 to 16 in October 1866. At the same time, the upper age limit was extended from 25 to 35 to give greater flexibility in recruitment.

The real problem, however, was that, despite the improved promotion opportunities offered by the introduction of the transcriber grade, the four classes of workmen were insufficiently differentiated by the quality of the work performed, so that a number of able men, whether engaged on production or repairs, were trapped in the third and fourth classes at no more than 6d and 5d an hour. Moreover, the pay of the workman class as a whole had barely changed since 1838, and it was revealing that some of the men supplemented their income by working at the Post Office in the evening, being allowed by Hardy to leave the office 15 minutes early for that pur-

---

28a. PRO 2/46, pp 341–343: enclosure to Hardy's letter to the governor-general of India, 28 October 1868.

28b. PRO 13/1–4. It was compiled between 1863 and 1865 and assembled in four volumes, one for each floor of the centre block.

29. PRO 1/31: Kingston to Hardy, 27 September 1866.

pose.[30] The concession must have been welcome to them, but little useful time would have been lost because unlit strong rooms meant that for much of the year, and on cloudy or foggy days, production work, even with a lantern, must often have been extremely difficult, if not impossible, by the early afternoon. The rule allowing searchers to have three documents at a time, promulgated by Hardy in 1866, with the proviso that more might be produced, if needed, at the discretion of the officer-in-charge, came to be seen by searchers of later generations as a restrictive practice. More probably, however, and particularly because of the uncertainty regarding production, it was first introduced to establish equality of treatment for searchers and to keep them supplied, as far as possible, with documents. The peak time for productions was between 12 noon to 2 p.m., and in order to maintain an adequate service during that period Hardy agreed in October 1866 that the workmen's hours should be reduced from 8 a.m. until 4 p.m., with half an hour for lunch, to 9 until 4.30, but with lunch taken on the premises. One result of that decision was the lifting of the former prohibition on cooking within the office and the opening of a refreshment room in the basement, operated initially by workman Kirby and later placed under the management of his daughter. Equipment came from the Office of Works and prices were subject to official control, the first scale of charges being approved by Hardy in April 1867 (Plate 17), including those for alcoholic beverages, such as a pint of ale at 3d, the same as for a cup of tea or coffee, while a pint of porter could be obtained for a mere 2d, which must have cheered the Irishmen on the staff. The supplier of flour to the canteen asked if he might advertise the fact on his cart, but was told that although his service gave general satisfaction publicity was not thought advisable. For all that, the business was on a small scale, and as the room provided measured only 25 feet by 17 feet, and the amount of crockery and cutlery supplied was minimal, no more than six workmen could have been served and seated at one time and a well organised rota system must have operated to regulate attendance.

Such regimentation was not at all resented by the men, whose sturdiness was shown by the way they volunteered, almost without exception, for service as special constables at the beginning of 1868 as a defence force against Fenian outrages. London was in high excitement at the time and as a precaution three extra constables had already been added to the regular police patrol of the Rolls Estate. Additionally, for the first three months of the year the workmen drilled regularly under their drill sergeant, Watson, who was attached to the Queen's Westminster Rifles. When the alarm had died down, Burtt, who had been placed in command, with assistance from Kingston, told Hardy that the men had arrived at a fair state of proficiency in the elementary parts of military drill, and, while he was pleased to say

---

30. PRO 1/27: Roberts to Major General M. F. Willoughby, 11 February 1863.

that there had been no occasion for their services, he was confident that had there been they would have behaved creditably. The relative stability of the manual workforce remained a feature of office life during the 1860s, although towards the end of the decade a change occurred at the upper level when the long-serving Paul retired on pension and Toovey moved up to join Gay as a foreman with Hood as superintendent. Unhappily, within a matter of weeks Toovey was dead and was succeeded by Beall.

The gradual improvements in the workmen's conditions of service after Palgrave's death were due more to Hardy, who was popular with them, than to any collective action on their part. In contrast, the assistant keepers and clerks appear to have concluded by 1867 that they had to take joint action if they were not to be 'seriously affected by the general rise in the prices of the principal necessaries of life', when they petitioned the Treasury in January that year for 'a general increase of pay, coupled with better prospects of promotion, or by any other means that may be thought expedient'.[31] In the past such petitions had generally been signed by all those concerned, but it was clear that the seeds were being sown of a more formal union of administrative officers because a number of members of the senior staff in other departments had also sent in similar memorials, and, significantly, the petition bore the signatures of Sharpe, Burtt, Bond, Turner, Hart and Pike as 'the elected representatives of the assistant keepers and clerks of the Public Record Office'. Romilly did no more than forward it without comment to the Treasury, which treated it with disdain, not feeling 'warranted in acceding to the request of the memorialists'. A year later, however, a minor change for the better took place when the staff's request that their salaries should be paid monthly instead of quarterly was granted by the Treasury.

Treasury control notwithstanding, the staff had the benefit of Hardy's more relaxed regime compared with Palgrave's. Under the latter the incremental progression of Hunt and Knight would scarcely have gone unchecked in the light of their irregularities. Knight, like his one-time master Black, had fallen into the habit of repeated unpunctuality. Just when he seemed to be overcoming his failing, he died at the age of 40 at the end of 1867 and was succeeded by Hart. The nature of Hunt's faults do not appear from the official papers, but twice during the mid-1860s Hardy refrained from certifying his services as fully satisfactory, a censure which Hunt felt acutely despite being allowed his increment. Possibly it had something to do with the fact that according to office tradition, like his father, he was always 'hard up' and sold his leave at a guinea a day.[32] Hardy, despite flashes of temper, was also tolerant of the foibles of Charles Cole, whose editorship of *Memorials of Henry the Fifth*, his sole contribution to the Rolls

31. T 1/6757A/20078/1867: petition of the assistant keepers and clerks to the Treasury, 16 January 1867.

32. Charles Johnson, 'The Public Record Office', in *Studies presented to Sir Hilary Jenkinson*, ed. J. Conway Davies (Oxford, 1957), 187.

Series, had done nothing for his reputation. At the end of 1866 Hardy decided to remove him from the Literary Search Room to the Calendaring Department on the top floor of the new wing. The change unsettled Cole, who was no sooner in his new room than he was asking for a carpet, maintaining that he was sensitive to heat or cold, having suffered from 'rheumatic paralysis'. His plea was rejected because under the regulations of the Office of Works he was entitled only to a rug. Shortly afterwards he reported to Hardy 'that circumstances of the gravest domestic import, which will affect my future career in life, are at present so pressing upon me that I have to ask permission to absent myself until the end of March to settle them'.[33a] Hardy granted Cole's extraordinary request on the understanding that he should forfeit his usual vacation. That would have been a small price to pay to avoid the disgrace that was to follow, but, unhappily for Cole, he failed to sort out the difficulties to which he had referred and on 17 October 1867 was adjudged bankrupt. Bad as that was for his standing in the office, his plight was aggravated when *The Standard* carried a report that he had told the court that he attributed his misfortune to his department's refusal to allow him to go to Paris for a London newspaper as its correspondent at the 1867 Exhibition. An angry Hardy swiftly asked for an explanation from Cole, who denied having made any such statement, claiming he had been misreported. It was a blessing for Cole that new and stricter regulations concerning bankrupt civil servants were not promulgated by the Treasury until December 1868. Yet he was soon in trouble again. In May 1868 Hardy was astonished to receive a confidential letter from Charles (later Sir Charles) Fremantle at 10 Downing Street complaining that Cole had been pestering Disraeli and asking for a stop to be put on the annoyance. An alarmed Hardy responded promptly:[33b]

> I hasten to answer your letter this instant received, and to express my great regret that a member of this Office should conduct himself in such an unbecoming manner towards any gentleman, but especially towards the Premier of this country.
>
> Mr. Cole is at present absent from this Office upon a medical certificate from Dr. Whistler requesting that Mr. Cole 'may rest himself as much as possible and refrain from mental exertion'.
>
> I will take such steps as I hope will save the Premier from any repetition of this annoyance. I feel sure that as soon as I submit this matter to the Master of the Rolls, he will express his displeasure at Mr. Cole's misconduct in the most summary way.

33a. PRO 1/32: C. A. Cole to Hardy, 17 January 1867.
33b. PRO 2/26, p 58: Hardy to Fremantle, 14 May 1868.

At the same time Hardy sent a stern warning to Cole, saying:[33c]

> I have reason to fear that you have been conducting yourself in a disgraceful
> manner towards a Gentleman very high in authority, and I think it my duty
> to inform you that any repetition of the like behaviour will bring about the
> necessity of your removal from this Office.

Cole, writing from his cottage at Kew, replied five days later that he had
been in the country, saying blandly:[33d]

> I am totally at a loss to understand your note of the 14th inst. Will you
> permit me to ask you to be kind enough to explain in what way I have merited
> your 'reason to fear'.

Whereupon Hardy, disconcerted but concluding that the unfortunate
Charles was mad rather than bad, rushed to South Kensington to confer
with his older brother Henry, whose diary for 14 May 1868 records:

> T. D. Hardy came abt. Charles writing to Mr. Disraeli, and to discuss
> putting him into confinement. I entirely agreed and engaged to assist and
> referred him to Vizard.

In the event, Hardy turned for assistance to Seymour Haden, the eminent
medical man, a school friend of Charles Cole from their days at Christ's
Hospital and a close acquaintance of the Cole family. By then Cole's resignation on health grounds was in Hardy's hands. It was lucky for him that
brother Henry's close associations with Hardy had so far shielded him from
the worst consequences of his actions, and it was also fortunate that Haden
was ahead of his time in his recognition of the problems of mental illness.
In reply to Hardy's inquiry, Haden said:[33e]

> Mr Cole's case is this – towards the end of every year he becomes sleepless
> and as this continues, excited – and this excitement increases as the Spring
> advances till it reaches a point which renders him unfit for the steady routine
> of official duty – to this again as his strength fails succeeds a state of
> corresponding depression and enervation which is scarcely more favorable to
> mental occupation than the opposite condition, so that I am not surprised
> that he has found it necessary to relinquish his post in the Record Office. I
> have only to add that, as Mr Cole's case is readily explicable on Psycological
> grounds, he cannot, properly, be held responsible for the irregularities and
> apparent extravagances which grow out of it.

33c. PRO 2/26, p 59: Hardy to C. A. Cole, 14 May 1868.
33d. PRO 2/26, p 70: C. A. Cole to Hardy, 19 May 1868.
33e. PRO 1/33: Haden to Hardy, 24 June 1868.

Hardy immediately replied to Haden, thanking him for his opinion which, he thought, accounted for much that had happened during Cole's official career and enabled an excuse to be made to the Treasury for his behaviour. The result was that, on Romilly's strong recommendation, Cole received a compassionate allowance of £156 2s 2d, just over half of the salary he was then drawing. Cole had been advised to move to another climate, and he later sailed to America where he died in New York at the age of 68 in 1887.[33f]

In dealing with establishment and administrative matters generally, great reliance was placed by Hardy, like Palgrave before him, upon Edwards's services in the Secretariat. It was not surprising, therefore, that in 1866, when Roberts was obliged to retire on medical advice, Edwards was recommended by Romilly to replace him as secretary. As Sharpe and Burtt were both senior to Edwards, the Treasury felt some misgiving about passing them over, but finally decided to consent, relying upon Romilly's assurance that Edwards was the fittest person for the post. S. S. Shelley there questioned whether Romilly should be asked to state the grounds upon which his opinion was formed, pointing to the promotion principles which the Treasury had itself laid down for Romilly's guidance at the time of its previous difficulties with him in August 1861. However, Hamilton did not concur and Hunt agreed that approval might be given, while saying that Shelley was quite right to raise the matter.[34] Burtt, now in charge of the Copying Department, was greatly upset by Romilly's decision. He believed he had been treated unfairly as he had never had the opportunity to undertake work of a secretarial nature, but thought he could soon master it. Foolishly, within months of Edwards's promotion, he became involved in record agency business, leading to a complaint from a party to a law suit in which he was helping the other side and a strong rebuke from Hardy, who ordered him to stop immediately.

Roberts's 'long and meritorious service', as reported to the Treasury by Romilly, led to a superannuation award of £641 13s 4d, an amount somewhat in excess of the normal allowance. Moreover, despite fears about his health, he went on to draw his pension until his death in 1897, outliving Romilly, both Hardys and Edwards. He was then in his ninety-fourth year and *The Times*, in a short notice on 3 February 1897, stated that besides being a member of the Royal Institution he was a friend of Faraday, whose neighbour he was at Hampton Court. In 1865, the year before his retirement, Roberts had had the satisfaction of seeing in print his *Calendarium Genealogicum* for the reigns of Henry III and Edward I, illustrative of the descent of English families, which he had begun to extract from the Chancery inquisitions many years before, while working for the Record Commission. Its

---

33f. *The Times*, 11 March 1887.
34. The Treasury papers are in T 1/6655B/18836/1866.

great value in throwing light upon the early history of the nobility and landed gentry delighted searchers, a number of whom, including William Hardy, W. H. Black and H. G. Hewlett, wanted it continued, petitioning Romilly to that effect in June 1866. However, Roberts's retirement prevented the publication of a further calendar of that kind, but he was later to place at the office's disposal a number of entries for the years 1 and 2 Edward II, and they were appended to the *Thirty-second Report of the Deputy Keeper* for 1870.

From a staffing standpoint the year 1866 was notable because the office lost not only the services of Roberts, but also those of two other long-serving men, Lemon and Lascelles. Lemon had never managed to adjust fully to the 1854 amalgamation and had to endure wounding criticism of his *Calendar of State Papers* compared with those of the external editors. A critic in *The Times*, for 14 May 1859, thought the entries in his calendar meagre, vague and unsatisfactory in the extreme, but the responsibility for that rested more with the State Paper Commission under whose auspices the work, which was published in 1856, was begun, whereas later works in the series were compiled on the fuller basis favoured by Hardy and Romilly. Lemon retired a sick man on an annual pension of £580 at the beginning of 1866 and died a year later. Lascelles, a one-time favourite of Palgrave's, enjoyed a slightly longer retirement before his death in March 1869, but he also gave up work on health grounds, when the sight of his remaining eye began to fail, at the end of 1866. Romilly strongly recommended him for a pension award in excess of the regulated allowance, emphasising his irreparable loss of an eye in 1853 during the course of his official duties. Although Romilly outlined the extent of Lascelles's services for the office and acknowledged their great value, certifying that they had been performed with 'diligence and fidelity', he still felt it necessary to qualify his commendation by adding 'with the exception of some peculiarities of disposition, which have caused him to be reprimanded',[35] probably believing that the terms of the official superannuation proforma required disclosure of the stormy conflict he had had with Lascelles in 1859. Fortunately, the Treasury chose to ignore that unhappy incident and awarded Lascelles a special pension of £320, well in excess of the £232 to which he would ordinarily have been entitled. But, significantly, although Hardy noted Roberts's departure in his *Report* for 1866 and paid tribute to his service, the retirement of Lemon and Lascelles went unremarked.

Between 1863 and 1865 there had been no promotions within the office, but the three departures of senior men in 1866, coupled with the resignation of F. M. Wilson, the former State Paper Office clerk, in November of that year meant a number of important changes. The appointment of Edwards as secretary was predictable, as were the promotions to the first class of

---

35. PRO 2/23, p 409: Romilly to Hamilton, 30 October 1866.

Hans Hamilton, Redington and Gairdner. The worthy Atkins, the former workman, received his reward for good service by being raised to the grade of senior clerk in company with the dependable Tabrum from the Secretariat. Neither promotion was unexpected, but the big surprise was that, at last, Fenwick managed the jump from the basic grade to which he had been confined since 1840. Romilly and Hardy, learning from their failure in 1861, prepared the ground carefully and in submitting Fenwick's name to the Treasury for promotion to senior clerk took care to support the recommendation by a tactfully worded certificate of his ability to perform the duties of the higher grade, subscribed by Roberts, Sharpe and Bond. Charles (later Sir Charles) Rivers Wilson told Hamilton at the Treasury that 'the rule of promotion by merit was not meant, I think, to be construed so as to exclude from promotion for ever an individual who can never manage to be the cleverest of 16, especially in the lower grades'. But such lofty and patronising sentiments formed no part of the acknowledgement by their lordships at the Treasury of the testimony given on Fenwick's behalf, which enabled them to sanction his promotion and to express 'much satisfaction', almost by way of proof of the correctness of their former stand, at 'the exertions which he has made to qualify himself for a higher position'.[36]

At much the same time Romilly was in communication with the Treasury about the continuance of the editing of the series of Chronicles and Memorials. Romilly had thought that the £3,000 granted annually for ten years in 1857 would be sufficient to complete the greater part of the unedited matter worthy of publication. Hitherto, the project had been limited to the editing of material remaining only in manuscript, but Romilly now requested that it should be extended, as Palgrave had urged, to the republication of valuable and rare works no longer in print. In dealing with Romilly's request, the Treasury reviewed the question of record publication generally for the student of history, and the various undertakings it had authorised. It pointed to the preparation of calendars of state papers and to the papers relating to English history at Simancas and Venice, besides other miscellaneous work, such as that on the Carew and Carte Papers, the *Facsimiles of National Manuscripts*, and to Irish and Scottish publications under the direction of the master of the rolls in Ireland and the lord clerk register respectively. The total cost of printing the calendars of state papers and the Chronicles and Memorials amounted to nearly £30,000 to the end of 1865. Of the calendars, 38 volumes had been published and the average sale was 100 copies at 15s each. Of the Chronicles and Memorials, 66 volumes had been published and sales of each averaged 235 copies, originally at 8s 6d and at 10s from 1862. But sales continued to increase steadily and the Treasury

---

36. PRO 1/31: Childers to Romilly, 8 February 1866. The Treasury's own papers are in T 1/6655B/18836/1866.

observed in its minute of 20 April 1866, which was later to be laid before Parliament:[37]

> With reference both to the calendars and chronicles, that it cannot be expected that works of this kind should meet with a prompt sale or find their way into the hands of the general reader. They are rather to be regarded as materials placed in store for the advantage of students of history in all time to come, and their value depends in the main upon the indirect influence exercised by them upon the general history and literature of this country. In that respect few historical works of importance have appeared since the date of these publications which have not been indebted to them either for new facts, the verification of doubts, or more lively and truthful details.
>
> This observation applies not to books intended only for the learned, but for the general information and education of the people. It may be confidently assumed, that henceforth no work can be expected to gain the approbation of the public which ignores the existence of this historical series.

The Treasury remarked especially upon the great services rendered to literature by Hardy's *Descriptive Catalogue of Manuscripts relating to the Early History of Great Britain and Ireland* in the series of Chronicles and Memorials, and did not doubt the expediency of continuing the grant for that series for some time longer and of extending its object as suggested. But, having regard to the amount Parliament was called upon to vote annually for cognate purposes in the three countries, it thought it proper to fix the annual grant at £2,000 until[38a]

> the object contemplated by Lord Romilly has been sufficiently attained. In concluding this Minute my Lords deem it necessary to record the strong sense they entertain of the services rendered to the public by his Lordship, the Master of the Rolls, for 10 years, in conducting the national work which has been entrusted to him. His Lordship's letter to this Board, of January 1857, to which my Lords have referred, sufficiently exhibited his appreciation of the nature and importance of the work; and the judgment, assiduity, and perfect impartiality which he has since displayed, afford the strongest proof of his Lordship's peculiar fitness to conduct it.

Later that year Romilly obtained Treasury authority for the formation of a syllabus of the contents of Rymer's *Foedera*. Brewer's brother, Ebenezer Cobham, started the task, but when he found it took too much of his time resigned the appointment and the editorship was assumed by Hardy, the

---

37. *HC Accounts and Papers*, 1866, LVIII, 89.
38a. *HC Accounts and Papers*, 1866, LVIII, 91.

first volume being published in 1869 and the second in 1873. Romilly was always conscious of the political and financial constraints under which he operated and paid far more regard to them than to criticisms of a purely literary kind, occasionally voiced by reviewers about the choice of texts and their editorial treatment. During 1867, however, there was some press criticism of certain remarks made by Stevenson in his preface to the fourth volume of his *Calendar of State Papers, Foreign Series*, for the reign of Elizabeth I, which were construed as unduly favourable to Philip of Spain and to Rome. As the last thing that Romilly wanted to see was a recurrence of the Turnbull trouble, particularly as the employment of a Roman Catholic on calendaring work had been critically alluded to in Parliament in May 1867, he lost no time in issuing an instruction to his editors, the trusted Brewer excepted, telling them that in future they were to confine any prefatory remarks considered necessary to an explanation of the papers calendared.[38b] Stevenson edited three more volumes of his calendar before resigning at the end of 1869. Earlier that year his wife had died, and he had then decided to enter the Roman Catholic priesthood. The office had previously lost the services through death of Bruce and Bergenroth, and the latter was succeeded at Simancas by Don Pascual de Gayangos. The association with Bergenroth concluded on a sour note with an unfortunate wrangle, arising from the money due to his estate in respect of his work. It was otherwise with Stevenson for whom the break proved no more than an interlude, although it seemed real enough to him at the time. Early in 1870 he gathered together his personal belongings at the office before setting off for St Mary's College, Oscott. He left behind a touching little letter for Hardy, conveying the anguish he felt at their parting:[38c]

My dear old Friend

You will not, I am sure, misunderstand the motive which induces me to spare you and myself the pain of a more formal leave taking. Perhaps I could not have avoided exhibiting how much it distresses me. To leave you, dear old Companion of so many years, is the one pang of today's severance of my connection with this Office. Wherever I am, whatever I am called upon to do or suffer, be assured that you always have your own place in my memory for the past and in my prayers for the future. But I must not write more in this strain.

. . . Now farewell, and may God bless you and yours. It is better for me not to say more.

Yours affectionately,

Jos. Stevenson

38b. PRO 8/29: Romilly's circular to editors of printed calendars, 13 June 1867.
38c. PRO 37/59: Stevenson to Hardy, 12 January 1870.

The loss in one year of three accomplished editors was a blow for the office, but its effect was offset by the fact that it enabled Romilly to put into execution his long-intended wish to have more of the calendaring work undertaken by his own staff. Consequently Stevenson's calendar was passed to Crosby and Bruce's to W. D. Hamilton who had, at last, secured promotion to the senior clerical grade. Furthermore, with the money thus freed from the editorial vote, amounting to nearly £800, Romilly managed to get the Treasury to agree to the expenditure of £350 in obtaining transcripts from the Vatican and other libraries in Rome, £350 to obtain transcripts from Paris, and the remainder for similar work at Vienna and Brussels.[38d] He also hoped he might get Sir John (later Lord) Acton to arrange for the work at Rome, particularly as he had the confidence of the Papal authorities and as early as 1866 had written to him about the possibility of such a project. Dr Russell had later made discreet enquiries for Romilly about the chances of progress but, at that time, without result. At Paris Romilly hoped to obtain the services of Armand Baschet, who had long been engaged upon work of a similar nature, and he proposed to appropriate the sum remaining at his disposal towards the travelling expenses of Gayangos who, he thought, would be agreeable to go to Vienna when he had finished his researches at Simancas.

All these developments were aided by the fact that the new clerks of the 1860s were proving extremely able record scholars and now included among their number talented individuals such as Bird, Selby, Cartwright, Trimmer, Thompson, Sharp and Handcock, Hardy's 'impudent Irishman',[39a] all of whom were soon to make their mark. Additionally, the junior clerical complement was relatively settled, although Jelf, who had joined in 1860, had been forced to retire in 1867 through ill health and Lethbridge had left for India in 1868. Despite the improvement compared with the office's earlier years, Romilly was not entirely happy about the method of recruitment, especially after a case in 1867 and another in 1868 of a candidate who had obtained the highest aggregate score being declared successful in the examination, while others, although unsuccessful, had secured higher marks in French and Latin, the subjects then most needed in the office.[39b] In July 1868 Romilly drew the attention of the Civil Service Commission to the matter and suggested that bookkeeping should be dropped from the exami-

---

38d. T 1/6917A/18901/1869: Romilly to Hamilton, 13 November 1869.

39a. 'G. F. Handcock, editor of the *Calendar of Patent Rolls, Edward I*, . . . was the repository of all the official traditions. He remembered Sir Thomas Hardy's arriving early one morning in the search room and, failing to find the Superintendent, J. J. Bond, losing his temper and calling young Handcock "an impudent Irishman" ': Charles Johnson in *Studies presented to Sir Hilary Jenkinson*, 181.

39b. But perhaps Romilly placed too much faith in examinations because both of the clerks concerned, Cartwright and Thompson, went on to have successful careers, particularly the former who was eventually to become the office secretary and the secretary of the Historical Manuscripts Commission.

nation and replaced by Blackstone's *Commentaries* because he thought that a knowledge of the forms and terms by which lands and other possessions were conveyed was essential if a Record Office clerk was to do his job properly. The commission did not want to behave unfairly towards any candidates who may have been nominated under the old system, but agreed that, after the next examination, the competition would consist of a preliminary examination in 1. Handwriting and Orthography; 2. Arithmetic (including Vulgar and Decimal Fractions); 3. English Composition; 4. Précis; 5. Geography; 6. History of England; 7. Latin (translation); 8. French (translation). Successful candidates would then sit a competitive examination in 1. Latin (translation); 2. French (translation); 3. Blackstone (Books i and ii, 'The Rights of Persons' and 'The Rights of Things'); and would have to satisfy the commission in all the papers.[40]

During that summer of 1868 Brewer went to Hatfield House to inspect the Cecil Papers, the third marquess of Salisbury having proved more forthcoming in allowing access to them than his father whom he had succeeded in April of that year. Brewer's visit had been arranged through Romilly, who was struck by the wealth of material remaining unexplored yet vital to supplement the State Papers from which they had become detached. It was not surprising, therefore, that Romilly's mind turned once more to the need to seek out the private papers relating to public affairs existing in the great family houses and the muniments of colleges, corporations, ecclesiastical bodies and similar institutions. In 1859 Romilly had poured cold water on George Harris's proposal for a commission to enquire into the whereabouts and contents of private collections, but indicated a willingness to carry out, through the Record Office, such parts of the plan as the government might think desirable. The Home Office had never responded to that offer and Romilly did not pursue it until the beginning of 1869, when he wrote to the Treasury, forwarding the sketch of a plan of action which would have formed the basis of his proposals had he been invited to submit them to the Home Office.[41] Although it has been suggested that Romilly made no effort to resurrect the matter until he knew that his building extensions were assured, it is by no means clear that he was quite so calculating. More plausibly, it seems that his interest was re-awakened by Brewer's preliminary survey of the Cecil Papers and his own contacts about access to them with Salisbury, whose support for a commission was evidenced by the fact that, as Lord Robert Cecil MP, he had been one of the signatories to Harris's memorial in 1859. Since that time Romilly's attention had been drawn on more than one occasion to the riches to be unearthed in private collections, such as the Paston Letters, and he had never entirely lost sight of the matter. But

---

40. PRO 1/33: Walrond to Romilly, 11 and 14 July 1868. Handcock and Purser were the first clerks appointed under the new arrangements. Purser did not stay long, resigning in 1871 to take up an appointment as an inspector of schools in Ireland.

41. T 1/6939A/21162/1869: Romilly to Hamilton, 21 January 1869.

whatever the explanation for his renewed approach, the 'wild plan', as it had been dubbed by the Home Office in 1859, was no longer seen as such by the government, although the Treasury suspected that its cost was being underestimated by Romilly and there was a suggestion that the project might be managed more appropriately by the British Museum. However, Romilly had Hamilton's ear and within a remarkably short time the wheels were set in motion to establish a commission which was formally constituted in April 1869 with Romilly as its chairman. Hardy had much to do with the mechanics of the operation and had hoped that the post of honorary secretary might be filled by Bruce. His proposal was, however, declined by Bruce, who died later that year, and the work was taken over by Wilford George Brett, Romilly's chief clerk and elder brother of William, a future master of the rolls.

The commission's links with the Public Record Office were strong and its distinguished membership included Hardy and two of his editors, Russell and Dasent. Office facilities were provided at Rolls House and its English Inspectorate comprised A. J. Horwood, Hardy's son-in-law, and Riley, both of whom were also editors. Another editor, Gilbert of the Irish Public Record Office, was appointed inspector for Ireland and John Stuart of the General Register House was given responsibility for Scotland, while Stevenson was deputed to inspect certain Roman Catholic collections at the request of their owners. From the outset Romilly had greatly underestimated the magnitude of the problem. He had originally hoped that gentlemen connected with the Record Office or the Manuscripts Department of the British Museum might be willing to give up their vacation to work for the commission, but that proved altogether too sanguine, the payment to the inspectors of two guineas a day and travelling expenses hardly being generous. Romilly told the Treasury that the commission should be tried for five years and cease if it failed to fulfil expectations. Perhaps that was no more than a tactical ploy because the office's practical support for the commission and its objects was real enough and had endured for no less than 90 years when the commission, fortified by a new royal warrant, attained a greater degree of independence and moved to its own offices in Quality Court.

The year 1869 was noteworthy not only because it saw the establishment of the Historical Manuscripts Commission, but also because of Romilly's success in obtaining a knighthood for Hardy. The story behind the grant of a particular honour rarely emerges, but the survival of G. A. Hamilton's private letter book reveals how much Hardy owed his distinction to the persistence of Romilly. Writing to him on 28 January 1869, Hamilton said:[42]

> I was about to write to you on the subject of your letter when it reached me
> this morning. Mr. Gladstone has been in communication with me regarding

---

42. T 168/4, pp 58–59.

yours to him of 22 inst. I need scarcely say that if your Lordship's expression of opinion respecting the merits of Mr. Hardy required anything to be added to it, which I am sure it does not, I shall be most ready to supply it. The only question which presents itself to my mind (and it was upon it I was about to write to you) is whether it was not intended that the Civil Division of the Bath as established in 1859 should supersede as regards meritorious civil servants the ancient mode of acknowledging such services by the distinction of Knight Bachelor. The amended statutes of the Bath ordain that there shall be three classes and that each class shall contain two sub-divisions whereof the one shall be Military and the other Civil, and subsequently that no person shall be nominated to the Civil Division who shall not by personal service 'or by the performance of public duties have merited our Royal favour'. The CB or Civil Division of the 3rd class is limited to 200 and a badge etc. is provided so that the CB is a personal mark of Royal favour in the case of civilians conferred by reason of the performance of public duties, and in the List I find the names of Mr. Booth, formerly Board of Trade, Captain Galton, Mr. H. Cole, Mr. Merivale, and Mr. Romaine. On the other hand, in the list of Knights Bachelor during the last two years, with the exception of Mr. Pennell, formerly in the Admiralty, and Mr. Mallett, I do not find the names of any in the ordinary permanent Civil Service. The Knights are usually either legal or Irish made by Lord Lieutenant, or Mayors or meritorious individuals such as Sir C. Bright, or Sir S. Waterlow not in the Civil Service. Sir F. Sandford was created a Knight after the Exhibition of 1862.

Before speaking to Mr. Gladstone I should be very glad to know from your Lordship confidentially whether you think the honour of CB could sufficiently meet the case. With the exception of the prefix, and the extension of the title to the Knight's lady, the CB seems rather the more appropriate and honourable distinction, because it was created for the purpose and the rewarding Civil Servants now by the dignity of Knights Bachelor seems rather to depreciate the CB.

I should also like to enquire whether *in point of literature* Mr. D. Hardy can be considered as pretty much on an equality with Sir F. Palgrave.

But in spite of Hamilton's obvious reservations, Romilly was not to be lightly diverted, and must have continued to press the matter because three months later Hamilton wrote to him again:[43]

I took an opportunity since I saw you of speaking again to Mr. Gladstone as to your Lordship's suggestion that the honour of Knighthood should be

---

43. T 168/4, p 86: Hamilton to Romilly, 5 May 1869.

conferred upon Mr. Duffus Hardy. He did not seem to make any objection, on the contrary, he seemed to think it might be done but repeated what he had said on the former occasion that he thought it would be better to wait for a while. He added that the honour of Knighthood conferred upon Sir M. Costa was certainly the act of the Queen. In our conversation I mentioned that Mr. H's predecessor had been made a Knight whereupon he asked whether Mr. H stood amongst literary men at all in the position of Mr. Palgrave. Of course I felt myself hardly competent to give an opinion, but if your Lordship should be disposed to say anything on that subject I should be glad to have your views.

Suitable assurance by Romilly must have outweighed official caution because Hardy was knighted by the queen at Windsor Castle on 9 July 1869. Once again, the Public Record Office, whose officers sent Hardy an address of congratulations at the end of July, had at its head a peer and a knight. In contrast with the Langdale period, however, relations between Romilly and his deputy keepers had never been other than harmonious. But the confidence reposed by Romilly in him, coupled with the ending of the branch organisation, meant that Hardy felt no need to seek the advice of his senior colleagues in the way that Palgrave had done before him. Edwards and, to a lesser extent, Kingston were close to him, but essentially as good executives. He also communicated regularly with Bond as superintendent of the search rooms, but in so far as he sought counsel on policy it tended to be with Brewer, who was not on the regular staff. Indeed, Hardy's very pre-eminence meant that an ominous gap had opened up between him and his assistant keepers, placing a question mark against the possibility of one of them being chosen to succeed him.

Chapter IX

Thomas Duffus Hardy, 1870–1878

The present arrangements for the preservation of the records of Government Departments are governed by an Act of 1838 which we believe was not meant to apply to them, an Act of 1877 which makes the selection of records for preservation about as complicated as it can be, and an agreement of 1845–6, which removes from those responsible for the ultimate preservation of the records a proper oversight of them.

(*Report of the Committee on Departmental Records* (1954), (Cmd. 9163), para 55)

By 1870 Romilly and Hardy were feeling their age and had lost much of their former zest. Returning from Normandy in the summer of that year, Hardy, whose annual leave allowance had been increased from 42 days to 48 in 1866, complained that he felt no better for his holiday, but hoped that Romilly, who was away at the time, would return rejuvenated. In addition to general debility, Hardy had been troubled for many years by vertigo and had to be careful about stooping, so much so that a high desk was provided for him as a precaution. The office's firm friend at the Treasury, Hamilton, had retired and it was anxious to establish an equally good relationship with his successor as permanent secretary, Ralph (later Lord) Lingen. Early in 1870 Hardy, commenting upon a letter concerning the office's publications, told the Treasury that the government never expected to make a profit, the outlay being seen as a contribution to historical literature in the same way as contributions to the advancement of other sciences. Comparing the two types of publications issued, Hardy said:[1]

> A Chronicle may be said to be perfect in itself, but it must be remembered it is only the view of an individual author. We have in our days a Hume, Macaulay, Mackintosh, Lingard and a Froude, as we formerly had a Beda, Malmesbury, Hoveden and Matthew Paris; each writing on the same subject, and from the same materials, and we know how differently those materials are used by each – each gives his individual opinion of events and transactions from the State Papers of the period.

> The Calendars (certainly the more important of the two) on the other hand are a species of historical literature peculiar to this country – exclusively of English birth and growth – for no other nation as yet has attempted anything of the kind though both France and Germany are now commencing works of the same description and on the same plan.

---

1. PRO 1/35: Hardy to Welby, 7 March 1870.

Hardy thought that price alone did not much affect sales and that, if the idea was to popularise the various record publications, the best way was to present them to the larger free libraries, by which he meant those having 3,000 or more readers. Nevertheless, his suggestion was brushed aside by the Treasury, when it reviewed the question of distribution in 1873. But Hardy's emphasis upon calendaring work was tactically wise although his own preference was for the Rolls Series. During the 1870s he received honorary law degrees from Oxford and Edinburgh universities, both awards reflecting the links which the series had created between the office and the academic world. Hardy's scholarly contacts counted for a great deal with him, as did his work for the Historical Manuscripts Commission of which he was the leading member.

Hardy was too bound up with record work ever to tire of the day-to-day routine of office administration, but must have felt dismay at the continuing pressure on accommodation. Romilly's forecast to the Treasury in 1866 that the eastern wing would provide enough space for at least a century already seemed hopelessly over-optimistic, and one of Pennethorne's last acts before formal retirement in June 1870 was to pass over to Hardy his plans for an extension to the west, fronting Chancery Lane.[2] His first drawings had envisaged the demolition of the Rolls House and the Rolls Chapel, but Romilly took exception to the destruction of the latter and so Pennethorne revised his scheme to provide for its incorporation within the proposed development. A further worry for the office was the government's intention to establish the principle of unrestricted open competition for Civil Service appointments, and so complete the reforms begun in 1855 as a result of Northcote's and Trevelyan's report. The proposed alterations found little favour with Romilly, who thought that the nomination system provided a better guarantee of the character and suitability of candidates if their sponsors were known to be trustworthy. He also predicted that entrants under the proposed system would not stay in the Public Record Office for long, but use their positions as mere stepping-stones to appointments elsewhere.[3a] As it happened, that very argument was about to be used by the Irish record authorities against the system then in force, because one of their clerks, Michael Moloney, had just left them for the better pay and prospects on offer in the Public Record Office in London.

Moloney's opportunity had arisen because of the unexpected death in February 1870 of F. C. Thomas, the first clerk to be recruited through the Civil Service Commission examination way back in 1859. Academically Thomas was not as accomplished as those who followed him, and Moloney himself, like most of the clerks who entered the office during the 1860s, was a graduate. But what Thomas lacked in brilliance he made up for in other

---

2. PRO 1/35: Pennethorne to Hardy, 23 June 1870. The plans are in MPI 69.
3a. PRO 2/29, pp 1–4: Romilly to Law, 29 January 1870.

ways although the handicap of a speech impediment made it improbable that he would rise to the same heights as his father. His death at the age of 30 was a blow for the office, but an even greater one for his mother: she had no pension and her claim some three years earlier for a special payment in respect of her husband's *Historical Notes* had been turned down by Romilly, who was unwilling to forward it to the Treasury. Moloney and another clerk, Henry St James Stephen, entered the office in 1870 through the limited examination scheme, taking the special subjects agreed in 1868, because it was recognised that it would be unfair to penalise candidates who may have been nominated before the system came up for review. It was, nevertheless, clear that the Treasury was unwilling to accept Romilly's special pleading except for minor grade posts which it agreed could continue to be filled by nomination. The upper age limit for workmen was, however, reduced from 35 to 20, except for ex-servicemen who could be admitted under special regulations. The transcriber grade was reserved for promotion from the workmen class and the entry age for charwomen was fixed between 25 and 40.

As regards the clerks, it was agreed that they should be taken from candidates successful in class I of the open examination for senior appointment in the Civil Service. Romilly was resolutely opposed to accepting candidates from the lower class II examination or introducing 'writers' into the office, arguing that the record clerks required special knowledge and training in order to make office copies of the ancient documents upon which they were all engaged to a greater or smaller extent. In so far as an intermediate grade was needed, he thought it was adequately provided by the existing class of transcribers. Romilly also strongly resisted any idea of restructuring which might result in a reduction in staff numbers, pointing to the increased workload resulting from the inflow of departmental documents and the burden of having to make lengthy returns for Parliament, such as those concerning record publications and charitable trusts. The Treasury was not unsympathetic to Romilly's plea to keep up his complement and took his point about the relative lack of attraction of a record clerkship to a class I candidate, who could obtain a post offering a starting salary in excess of £200 in many departments whereas the best the Public Record Office could offer was £100 with uncertain prospects thereafter. Accordingly, in April 1871 it commissioned Alexander Finlaison of the National Debt Office to examine the difficulty and to recommend how it might be overcome. He proposed that record clerks should enter the office at £200, but that there should be compensating savings elsewhere.[3b] Romilly thought the £200 starting salary could be justified, but that the proposal was unfair to the existing clerks since it involved a substantial worsening of the salary scale for the

---

3b. T 1/7142A/19613/1871. Hardy's letter of 25 September 1871 stating Romilly's objections to Finlaison's report was printed in 1875 as an annexure to the Second Report of the Civil Service Inquiry Commission: *H C Reports of Commissions etc.*, 1875, XXIII, Appendix E, 99.

senior clerical grade to which they had every expectation of rising in due course. It was, therefore, decided to stick with the class I method, drawbacks notwithstanding, and to leave the pay of the record clerks unaltered. To ensure that candidates were suitable, however, Romilly wanted them further tested in geography, précis and Blackstone's *Commentaries*. The Civil Service Commission refused his request, although it agreed in December 1871 to examine them additionally in Latin and French translation which Romilly had also urged.

The first two clerks recruited in that way were R. A. Roberts and H. G. Overend, who entered the office in March 1872. They were followed in 1873 by R. F. Isaacson and G. J. Morris. All four eventually became assistant keepers and Roberts went on to hold the secretaryship from 1912 to 1916. Another candidate was E. S. Vernon, who fell at the Latin hurdle, but, having subsequently qualified himself in that respect, finally decided to decline the appointment when he found he would have to start at £100 a year. Consequently, when it became necessary to fill two record clerkships in 1874, the Treasury and Civil Service Commission decided it would, after all, be wise to hold a special competition similar to that in force before 1870, and so Blackstone's *Commentaries* were given a further lease of life alongside the more general subjects. E. G. Atkinson, a later assistant keeper, and H. E. Lawrance, who retired because of ill health in 1891, were the candidates declared successful in that special competition, but as will be seen later, when the Civil Service Inquiry Commission of 1874 to 1875 (the Playfair Commission) failed to recommend a separate scheme of recruitment, as the office and its staff wished, clerks were once again taken from the general class I examination.

As well as losing F. C. Thomas, the office experienced many changes to its clerical complement during the early 1870s. The long-serving Temple retired on health grounds in 1871 at the age of 56 on an annual pension of £100. The transition from the State Paper Office had always been too much for him and he was never able to master Latin or French. His general unhappiness may have accounted for the drink problem to which he succumbed in his later years. On the other hand, Fenwick held down his senior clerical post until his death in 1872, performing rather better than Hohler whose promotion to that grade did not work out well and who died in 1873. The senior clerical grade was further affected by the death in 1875 of Tabrum, who besides underpinning Edwards in the Secretariat had also held the post of assistant secretary to the Historical Manuscripts Commission from 1872. His death was a loss not just to the office but to Islington and Finsbury whom he represented on the London School Board and to the poor boys of the North London Shoe-black Brigade of which he had been the honorary secretary for 19 years. An active Nonconformist, he also contributed regularly to the *Islington Gazette*.

During the same period a further loosening occurred of the links with the former record service with the deaths of Charles Devon in 1871, W. H. Black in 1872 and C. P. Cooper in 1873. The office had already taken the decision to print Black's volume of *Docquets of Letters Patent, Charles I* as it stood and abandoned hopes of progress of his 'Iter Britanniarum: The Portion of the Antonine Itinerary of the Roman Empire relating to Great Britain' which he had been commissioned to edit in the Rolls Series. Black had been a lonely figure for many years, and his congregation at Mill Yard, which in 1853 Palgrave said had numbered about forty, had almost ceased to exist. An observer in 1870 wrote:[4a]

A more curious spot in all London is not than Mill Yard Meeting-house.
The day I was there, after a service of nearly two hours, it was established
by the learned minister, who is an F.S.A., and calls himself elder of the
congregation (he must often stand a good chance of being junior as well), that
the title of the Book of Proverbs was only to be applied to the first part, that
it consisted of divers distinct sections, and that generally the book was
found in the Bible after the Psalms. Evidently the preacher is a learned
painstaking student of the Dryasdust School – full of crotchets; but the
biggest crotchet of all is that he should go on preaching year after year in
Mill Yard.

But Hardy, despite his many clashes with Black, was to remember him rather more kindly, inserting a footnote to his own preface to the *Syllabus of Rymer's Foedera* expressing deep regret about his death, saying:[4b]

He was a man that could be ill spared from the world of letters, especially
that branch of it on which he was a recognised authority. His mind was richly
stored with archaic learning and palaeographical knowledge, which he was
always alike ready to impart to the youthful student and to give to the world
at large.

As it happened, that was not quite the end of the office's connection with Black because in the summer of 1873 it was discovered that among his books, which were coming up for sale by Sotheby's, were a number of an official character which Edwards succeeded in recovering for the record service from Black's solicitors.

Of the younger men, Rhodes had left in 1872 on appointment as deputy keeper of the Land Revenue Record Office, a post he held until his suicide in 1895. Ewald was promoted senior clerk in Fenwick's place and succeeded in getting his book, *Our Public Records*, published by Pickering in 1873. Two years later *The Young Pretender* also appeared from his pen, but did nothing for his career when it was found that he had written it partly in official time. Ewald might have escaped censure but for being reported by

---

4a. J. Ewing Ritchie, *Religious Life of London* (London, 1870), 166.
4b. II (1873), xxv.

a somewhat difficult habitué of the search rooms, James Phillippe, a geneal-ogist, who styled himself Field Marshal Plantagenet Harrison. Much greater fame was to be achieved in the field of record publication by C. T. Martin, Hohler's senior clerical successor, with his famous *Record Interpreter*, the value of which shows no sign of lessening. Martin, a scholar by temperament, was the son of Dr Samuel Martin, the eminent Nonconformist divine. He often invited younger colleagues to share his boat on the river on Sundays, and it was his jest that he subscribed to the Lord's Day Observance Society to reduce the crowds on the water. Despite a slight stutter Martin was a fluent talker, and he was unique in bringing his bulldog with him to the office.[4c] Another senior clerk, Crosby, who had been promoted when the long-serving Kentish died unexpectedly in 1874, was making his mark by continuing Stevenson's Foreign Calendar. An even younger man, Cart-wright, was coming into prominence because of his administrative skills. In 1875 he became assistant secretary of the Historical Manuscripts Commission in succession to Tabrum, whose place as senior clerk was taken by the capable Pike. Selby was proving his worth in the search rooms where Bond, although nominally superintendent, was to be told by Jessel, Romilly's successor, in 1876 that an officer of his rank should not attend upon the public and was to occupy his time in calendaring.

The office also had a new superintendent of the workmen in Watson, who was promoted from the transcriber class when Hood died suddenly in 1871. Watson, a versatile man, was to compile an index to a list of emigrants to America, but was lucky not to become Plantagenet Harrison's second victim when accused in 1874 of taking documents out of the office for that purpose, a charge that he managed to rebut. Hood's death was said to have been caused by the strain of the many moves of records into the new north-eastern wing. His death created a serious gap in the Repair Department, although the long-serving first-class workman, Joseph Blainey, who finally retired in 1876 after 43 years' service, enjoyed a deserved reputation there as a talented repairer of ancient records. Hood, primarily a binder, had also, as already mentioned, made a particular contribution on the repair side with his introduction of a valuable 'sizing' process, and recognition of his services was shown when Mrs Hood, on Hardy's strong recommendation, was awarded £100 from the Royal Bounty Fund, one of the purposes of which was to make payments to needy widows of deceased servants of the crown. Romilly's and Hardy's influence also secured for her an annuity of £20 from the National Benevolent Institution. Shortly after Hood's death there was another untoward event when J. T. Lea, a first-class workman, whose service went back to 1841, was arrested for debt. Under the Treasury's more stringent rules things could have gone very ill for him had friends not relieved him from his distress, which had

---

4c. PRO 8/55, pp 154–155: J. V. Lyle to R. H. Ellis, 15 February 1951.

arisen from heavy charges levied upon him by the parish authorities for the maintenance of his daughter who was confined in a mental asylum. Initially he was suspended, but Hardy had no hesitation in reinstating him on learning the facts, and he remained in post until his retirement on health grounds in 1884. Three years after Hood's death an even longer-serving officer, Henry Gay, died after 50 years' service. His place as senior foreman was taken by Thomas Beall, Hood's son-in-law, who was in turn succeeded as junior foreman by Thomas Steward. Gay's widow, Sarah, like Mrs Hood, also benefited from the Royal Bounty Fund although she was not treated quite so generously, receiving only £50.

When the new regulations for appointment were under review in 1870 consideration was also given to the method of filling the post of deputy keeper, Romilly being anxious that his statutory right of nomination, subject to crown approval, should be confirmed. In the course of the exchanges about it Hardy must have realised how lucky he had been to succeed Palgrave, whose determination to remain in post, far from keeping him out, had that been the purpose, actually worked to his advantage. In 1855 Romilly had made no secret to the Treasury of his intention to seek an outsider in the event of a vacancy, but there was no copy of the letter he wrote to it alluding to that matter in the office's own records. Consequently, when the Treasury referred to the 1855 reorganisation, Hardy asked for, and was supplied with, a copy of the letter that Romilly had written at that time. Its contents must have been made plain to Hardy just how close he had once been to disaster, particularly as he had never come to terms with the way he believed he had been unfairly deprived of the deputy keepership in 1838. At any rate, he was now determined to secure a change for the future if at all possible and towards the end of 1872, when he knew that Romilly was soon to resign, he drafted a confidential memorandum for Charles Rivers Wilson at the Treasury advocating the separation of the office of keeper of the records from that of the master of the rolls. Romilly was unenthusiastic, although making it clear that he believed that Hardy should be appointed keeper if a change were made. Wilson told Hardy that the chancellor of the Exchequer was sympathetic and Gladstone was also well disposed to an alteration, but it was evident that the absence of Romilly's whole-hearted endorsement was seen as an insuperable obstacle. In a long submission to the Treasury Hardy argued that the appointment of the master of the rolls as keeper in 1838 had been due entirely to the circumstances at that time. Historically the master of the rolls had never been responsible for the records of the courts of common law. Moreover, even the custody of the Chancery records had for many centuries been vested in their respective keepers at the Tower and the Rolls. Neither would it always be the case that the office of master of the rolls would be filled by persons who took such a keen interest in records, and were so uniquely qualified to deal with them, as Langdale and Romilly. Separately Hardy sent the Treasury the draft of a short bill to effect the change and also set out what he thought should be the qualifications and duties of a keeper general of the public records (Appendix XI).[5]

Hardy's proposals were not helped by the need for new legislation to effect a change, and any early hope of that was dashed when the Gladstone administration suffered defeat in the elections of 1874. Hardy's chance of success might have been improved had a new act to deal with the question of the disposal of records thought valueless then been under consideration, but legislation for that was not thought necessary at the time. Romilly and Hardy had never doubted the right of departments to destroy their own documents if they wished and looked upon the Committee on Government Documents as a convenient body to ensure that the public interest was consulted before destruction took place. Romilly had written to the common law courts in April 1866 urging them to rid themselves of documents not thought worth preserving permanently and schedules had been drawn up for that purpose. It had been thought by Hardy that if records had previously been sent to the office from classes scheduled for disposal they, too, might be destroyed, but objection to that course was taken by Bond, who pointed out that some of them had already been produced to the public. At Romilly's instance the clerk of the Petty Bag was also engaged upon the sorting and weeding of Chancery masters' documents prior to their transfer from the vaults of the commissioners of patents for inventions in Southampton Buildings, where the space they occupied was urgently required. The bulk of those papers were not public records at all but documents such as deeds, abstracts of title etc., which had been left in the Court of Chancery by suitors and originally placed in the custody of the clerk of records and writs of that court under the Court of Chancery Act 1860.

Although more progress might have been made, Romilly took it greatly amiss when he received a long letter from Hart in November 1870 which argued that the administration of the office would benefit by the elimination of valueless material preserved there, such as duplicates, unused pages of bound volumes, etc. Besides offering his services as a reviewer for that purpose, Hart wrote another letter seeking further editorial employment. Six months earlier he had repeated to Romilly his one-time suggestion of a collection of materials relating to ancient charters, but had received no encouragement. When his new approaches met with a further rebuff he decided to write to the Treasury, a move which drew from an infuriated Romilly a vigorous defence of office policy and, as an added reason for not employing Hart, an allegation about the unsatisfactory nature of some work that he had undertaken many years before on records of the Treasury solicitor. But the Treasury, always looking for economies, was not prepared

---

5. Papers about the proposed alteration are in PRO 1/133. The envelope in which they are contained is endorsed, apparently in Lyte's hand, 'Important: Correspondence etc. of Sir T. D. Hardy concerning the proposal to separate the office of Keeper of the Public Records from that of the Master of the Rolls, 1872–3'.

to ignore the matter entirely, and when Hart wrote again in February 1871 directly to the chancellor of the Exchequer, Lingen decided it was time to look into the problem himself and to visit the office which he had not done until then. Needless to say, Hardy prepared to receive him with care and Lingen left fully satisfied that the office was tackling the question appropriately. He also took away with him a memorandum from Hardy on the existing practice, which concluded 'there are reasons too (which need not be mentioned here) which would render the employment of Mr Hart as destroyer of the ancient records of the realm entirely out of the question', to which a pencilled note was added, apparently in the Treasury, 'cf: disturbance some years ago about Mr. Turnbull's appointment. Mr. Hart is in like position'.[6a] A year later, when the office was under attack in the press, Hart was among those who leapt to its defence, but it is doubtful whether it felt any sense of shame, still less that Hart would have written as he did if he had known of the way he had been blackened. Although Hart returned to the record agency activities he had undertaken before his engagement by Palgrave, working from Lincoln's Inn Chambers in Chancery Lane and describing himself as 'late of the Public Record Office', it was only a combination of persistent canvassing on his part and the passage of time which accounted for his eventual re-engagement by William Hardy as a Rolls Series editor in 1882.

By that time both Romilly and Hardy, neither of whom ever really forgave Hart for his attack upon their authority, were dead. Nevertheless, they had supported his application in 1873 for admission to the roll of attorneys practising in the Queen's Bench, and Hardy later expressed a willingness to try to get him employment on the revised edition of Hasted's *Kent*. In 1875, after Hart's various attempts to secure reinstatement had failed to bear fruit, he confessed to Hardy, somewhat reproachfully, that he wondered whether his conversion to Catholicism had caused a prejudice against him, although with Stevenson's case in mind he thought that hardly possible. Hardy professed great pain at the implied accusation, defending his record on the Catholic question and taking the line that he could easily find work for Hart if the government would provide the money. He also indicated that he would assist Hart if he knew of any Roman Catholic owners of papers who might recommend him to report upon their collections.

Nothing very positive emerged, which must have left the luckless Hart sorely tried, particularly as he had had the misfortune to break his arm in a carriage accident and had suffered losses as a result of fraud at the London and Westminster Bank. He could certainly have been forgiven for feeling aggrieved, especially when he contrasted his treatment with that of his fellow convert, Stevenson, whose work on the Vatican Archives since 1872 had just received further easement as a result of the interposition with the

---

6a. T 1/7184B/7676/1872: annex to Lingen's memorandum of 17 February 1871.

authorities there of Cardinal Manning and the Foreign Office. Both Hart and Stevenson had resigned their posts quite voluntarily in 1869, yet in March 1872 Stevenson secured an annuity of £100 on the Civil List in recognition of his record services. The ever cautious Romilly had qualms about taking a leading part in promoting Stevenson's cause, but it is inconceivable that without his testimony as to the value of his work and Hardy's unwavering support Stevenson's memorial to Gladstone for a pension could have succeeded. Moreover, a little earlier it had been agreed that Stevenson, by then the Reverend Joseph Stevenson of St Mary's College, Oscott, should be engaged to make transcripts of the documents and papers relating to British history preserved in the Vatican and elsewhere in Rome. Stevenson almost ruined his chances by quibbling about the £350 a year offered, which related purely to the making of transcripts and did not provide the security of a fixed salary. Fortunately for him, he realised just in time that he could expect no better, especially when even Hardy's patience began to run out. The Vatican project had long been dear to Romilly's heart, and as early as 1865 Dr Russell had been making enquiries for him about the possibility of gaining access to the Papal Archives. In 1866 Sir John Acton began to interest himself in the matter and in 1869 Romilly engaged him to superintend the work he had in mind. In the event, Acton was unable to proceed, but thought that Stevenson, who had by then been ordained in the Roman Catholic priesthood, was the ideal man for the task. Aware of the religious pitfalls, however, and because the work was to start with documents of the reign of Henry VIII, Romilly took care to append to the *Thirty-fourth Report* for the year 1872 a full statement about Stevenson's engagement, which he had drafted with help from Russell. In it he emphasised that Stevenson's 'mission is entirely unconnected with controversies of doctrine' and printed his instructions in both English and Italian. Romilly's caution was soon justified when Dr John Waddington, a Dissenting minister, visited Rome in November 1872, and afterwards tried to wreck the venture by suggesting to Gladstone that no confidence could be placed by the public in any report that Stevenson might make.[6b] But the government was not disposed to interfere with Romilly's choice and so Stevenson's membership of the select band of editors working abroad was confirmed, the others being Rawdon Brown at Venice, Gayangos at Madrid, Vienna and Brussels, and Baschet at Paris, where life was returning to normal after the disturbances occasioned by the setting-up of the 'Commune' in 1871 and its subsequent suppression.

The work of the office's continental editors has since provided historians with a rich crop of material, but it seems odd that, despite the preoccupation of the age with ecclesiastical affairs, Hardy spent so much time between 1871 and 1873 in elucidating the finer points of the Athanasian Creed, a copy of which was discovered by Rawdon Brown in St Mark's Library at

---

6b. T 1/7279A/1300/1873: Waddington to Gladstone, 13 January 1873.

Venice. The significance of the document, a facsimile of which was appended to the *Thirty-third Report*, lay in its confirmation of the English text in the Book of Common Prayer. A committee of bishops was set up to examine the matter, and Hardy, Romilly and even the Foreign Office were subsequently concerned in obtaining from the University of Utrecht a photographic copy of the Apostles' Creed in a document preserved there which had once been in the Cotton Collection. Hardy's report upon that manuscript, in which he assigned its date to the close of the sixth century, was, in turn, to provoke controversy, but although the Royal Commission on Public Records 1910 to 1919 was to note his involvement in the affair as the most curious result of his interest in external documents, it doubtless provided a welcome diversion from the more mundane but all too real problems continuing to press at home.

The year 1872 opened on a sour note for Hardy because of an acrimonious correspondence that had arisen with an old foe of the office, and of Bond in particular, Henry Grove, a member of the Tithe Redemption Trust. In that capacity Grove was searching land tax records on behalf of the Reverend Cuthbert Carr, rector of Witton Gilbert and Kimblesworth in Durham, but had been denied access to a Treasury index he wished to see. Almost certainly the index would not have helped Grove, but because it had been marked up to indicate papers that had recently been weeded it was not thought advisable to continue to make it available to the public. The resulting furore persuaded Hardy to state in the *Thirty-third Report* the distinction he drew between public records and departmental documents, to which reference has already been made in the preceding chapter and which was based on the absolute right of departments to regulate access to their records as they felt fit. Carr and Grove were given an opportunity to counterattack when a report of the mutilation within the office of certain Treasury documents appeared in the press. That matter had been reported to Hardy in January 1872 by Redington, who believed that the guilty person had torn off a portion of the papers concerned to conceal his carelessness in spilling ink over them. The evidence pointed to Hohler, the flamboyant volunteer, as the culprit, but because he professed ignorance Romilly decided to examine him before the assembled assistant keepers. A Chancery shorthand writer was appointed to take down the proceedings and Hohler was told that he might bring a friend, but would not be allowed to have an advocate to conduct his defence. Rather than face such an awesome ordeal, a penitent Hohler, already in execution for debt, admitted that under the stress of domestic misfortune he must have been responsible, and Romilly, after some heart-searching and in the light of a plea for clemency from Mrs Hohler, decided to abandon the hearing, but to suspend his increment until he had received satisfactory reports on his work and conduct for two years in succession. Hohler's death in March 1873 meant that he was never put fully to the test, but because he had been involved in numerous unhappy incidents down the years Romilly's decision to treat him relatively leniently led to a strong protest from Burtt. Romilly took no notice of Burtt's objection, apart from commenting: 'a kind, considerate letter by a person who never inter-feres except to do a kind' action – to be preserved'.[7] But Burtt was not willing to let matters rest, and Romilly and Hardy had no doubt of his responsibility for a paragraph in *The Athenaeum* of 10 February 1872 which read:

We regret to hear of a painful scandal in the Records Office. Some of the documents have been mutilated, yet the offender has hitherto been allowed to pass unpunished. Lord Romilly may have been influenced by reasons of which we know nothing, but some explanation is desirable as the destruction of public documents is a matter that concerns the nation.

That report was, in turn, reproduced in the *Daily News*, which on 12 February printed a letter signed 'AB' which attacked the office in such strong terms that Hardy thought it actionable and tried unsuccessfully to get the paper to disclose its correspondent's identity. He considered Grove to be responsible. The writer, who called for a parliamentary inquiry, alleged that the office was in a sad state and that many important documents were missing. Complaint was also made of the long delay in producing records caused by the hold-up in impressing unstamped documents and of the unfairness of paying £25,000 annually to the record officials who, in spite of their large salaries, 'were never to be seen by the public at the office. Each officer appears to have his private room and there is only one of the superiors visible to the public'. Over the next few weeks a number of letters appeared in the press on the same subject, including some from record agents and regular users, such as Hart, praising its administration. On the other hand, *The Globe* of 16 February carried a letter from another anony-mous correspondent, DCE, which broadened the attack to contrast the salaries of the senior officers with the 'inadequate' pay of the workmen whose complement should, it considered, be strengthened in order to speed up the production and stamping processes. It also stated that the superior staff were not overworked because the average attendance of the public, excluding record agents, did not exceed a dozen a day. Two days later, however, the *Sunday Times* retorted that every sane person knew that the expenditure on the record service did not go to pay officers to attend on the public, but included the amount paid for 'the magnificent series of volumes on historical subjects, edited by the best archaeological scholars in England. It is amazing how little knowledge of facts is necessary to constitute a grumbler'. That paragraph must have given some comfort to Romilly and Hardy as well as an editorial in *The Globe* of 14 February which thought

7. PRO 1/37: Burtt to Romilly, 5 February 1872. Despite his military connections, Hohler's health had always been indifferent, and as he had a history of epilepsy his death was no surprise. With Hardy's support Mrs Hohler was granted £60 from the Royal Bounty Fund.

257

that both at the British Museum and at the Public Record Office students 'experienced uniform courtesy and intelligent assistance'. To attack the officers of either institution for attempting to protect their holdings from felonious members of the public was, it considered, unfair, arguing that it reflected 'a deplorable state of public honesty that the people cannot safely be trusted with their own treasures'.

But at that moment what concerned Romilly and Hardy rather more than public trustworthiness was that Burtt, the most senior assistant keeper after Sharpe, could no longer be relied upon to act discreetly where office business was concerned. Neither did he attempt to conceal his responsibility for the original report in *The Athenaeum* or for a critical paragraph in *The Guardian* of 20 March, referring to the slur upon all the officials of the department being 'felt heavily'.[8a] Left to himself Hardy would have taken severe action against Burtt, whose gossiping to journalists had given the office's critics a golden opportunity to air their grievances. Romilly's first reaction was that nothing should be done to extricate him from the situation in which he had placed himself, but he eventually decided to take no note officially of Burtt's behaviour. Three days before *The Athenaeum* report he had told the Treasury about the damage to its documents and explained why he had decided upon a lesser step than dismissal of Hohler, whom he did not actually name, but whose removal would, he said, have resulted in 'utter ruin to him and his family'. Subsequently an arranged question was asked in the Commons on 21 March 1872 about the reported mutilation of documents in the Record Office, which enabled the secretary to the Treasury to say that he did not think he could do better than read out Romilly's letter. Over the next few months, however, Lord John Manners MP, prompted by Grove and Carr, asked a number of questions about office business, desisting only after Hardy had written to him privately in an effort to reassure him. One of the main complaints of the critics was the delay in productions, allegedly because only one man was employed to stamp documents, but that took no account of work going on behind the scenes and Hardy was able to refute the charge by pointing to the fact that eight men were engaged upon stamping and numbering and a further fourteen undertook production duties from 103 record rooms spread over four floors. No attempt was made to answer the point concerning the low pay of the workmen. That might have been impossible to ignore had the workmen themselves been restless, but the nomination system had ensured the domination of the force by a limited number of families, such as the Watsons and Bradleys, who felt a strong sense of loyalty both to the office and to Hardy personally. Associated with that was a fearsome degree of pressure upon those who failed to conform, which was

---

8a. For the various press cuttings see PRO 8/14, pp 200–202.

signally evident in April 1874 when Hardy wrote the following memorandum:[8b]

The Workmen having heard that Memorials by the Second and Third Classes of Officers had been presented to the Lords of the Treasury for increase of their pay, considered that they had equal claims to have their wages also increased; and taking advantage of a slight absence from indisposition of the Superintendent of the Workmen, got up a petition to the Deputy Keeper requesting him to take such steps as he deemed requisite for the increase of their wages.

Nine of the Workmen refused to sign this Petition, and others were afraid to refuse to sign. This Petition was sent to the Deputy Keeper and he refused to take any steps in the matter except through the Superintendent especially as he had heard that the Petition was not unanimous. Ten of the Workmen, however, who had signed the Petition addressed a letter to the Superintendent regretting having done so, and requesting to have their signatures withdrawn; notwithstanding these circumstances the Petition has been forwarded to the Master of the Rolls; each Workman has been asked whether he sent that Petition to the Master of the Rolls, or was, directly or indirectly, a party to its transmission to His Honour. Each man, however, denies having sent it, or being a party to its being sent.

- [Annexed] -

9th April 1874

To Mr A. T. Watson

Dear Sir

A petition has been drawn up and signed by some of the men in the office, asking for their wages to be increased, and as we the undersigned, regret having signed it, therefore we shall be much obliged if you will kindly erase our names from the petition when it is brought to you for presentation to Sir Thomas Duffus Hardy.

We are, etc.

J. Blainey	F. Bradley
Edward Jennings	J. Simpson
John Watson	H. F. Le Dieu
R. H. Bradley	W. Swain
Charles Foster	H. Jennings

8b. PRO 1/39: Workmen's Memorial, 22 April 1874.

- [*Annexed*] -

Statement (sent anonymously to the Master of the Rolls).

On the 22nd instant a petition from the Workmen of the Public Record Office, was sent to your Honor with a Statement and Schedule annexed.

At 10.30 a.m. Mr Albert Thomas Watson, the Superintendent, called upon each Workman to know, if he had sent the petition to your Honor, stating that he came from your Honor with that message, each man answered No, being afraid of the Affirmative, on account of being, as it is termed in the Office a marked man, to substantiate which, shortly afterwards Mr A. T. Watson stated that in placing the petition before your Honor would no doubt necessitate the discharge of several of the Workmen in consequence of which this statement is only made through fear of losing our Bread.

Memorandum.   The Master of the Rolls (through Mr Jenkins) returned the memorial to the Workmen. 23 April 1874.

Against that miserable episode it has to be said that normally the atmosphere in which the workforce operated was relatively relaxed, possibly too much so if a circular issued by Hardy in July 1873 was anything to go by. In it he said that his attention had been drawn to the habit of several workmen of going to sleep during office hours, while others acted as scouts to prevent them being found out. It is impossible to believe that the behaviour described by Hardy could ever have occurred at Carlton Ride under Cole's strict regime, and Palgrave would certainly have dealt with the matter in a summary fashion had anything of the kind come to his notice. Hardy, however, merely contented himself with a warning that anyone discovered would be subject to suspension. The hierarchical organisation of the office, coupled with the rambling nature of the building and the absence of lighting in much of it, did nothing to help efficient working. When not engaged upon taking out or replacing documents, the production staff were expected to stamp, number, flatten and pack records, but that was often easier said than done because, although there were gas lights at intervals in the corridors, sufficient it was jokingly said to play cards by, there was no lighting in the small slip-rooms in which the men were based on each floor or in the strong rooms where the records were kept. Work was, therefore, at a standstill by early afternoon, when darkness set in during the winter or on cloudy or foggy days, the 'peasouper' being a notorious feature of London life. The reason for the sparing use of gas remained the fear of fire, although gas lighting had been successfully introduced in the repair workshop in the central or Queens' Tower[8c] and in certain other parts of the building such

---

8c. The name 'Queens' soon fell into disuse, although the statues of Matilda, Elizabeth, Anne and Victoria still remain on the tower's exterior over the portico.

as the coal cellars, boiler room, police lobby and lavatory. However, the public reading rooms had no means of lighting, neither had the rooms occupied by the assistant keepers and clerks. In the latter, candles and oil lamps were used during the winter, but, quite apart from the fire risk, there was the possibility of damage to the records from grease and oil. For that reason Hardy forbade the use of candles in 1876 except in cases of necessity, and then only with special authority. Twenty-one years before, he was one of the assistant keepers who had told Palgrave that they did not want any of the rooms in the new building to be lighted since portable lamps would do, and so his view had not much changed.

At that time searchers' conditions were even more primitive, but since the building of the Round Room and Long Room there had been some attempt to make life more tolerable for them, as in the provision of a small room close to the main entrance grandly termed the 'luncheon room'. Almost opposite was the workmen's kitchen, which had been moved from the basement and from which, until the mid-1870s, light refreshments were supplied. The management of the refreshment business originally lay with Miss Kirby, but she had left in March 1875 and her successor, Frederick Allen, purveyor of luncheons as he was known, continued only until July 1876 when Hardy introduced new regulations forbidding the cooking or preparation of food within the office.[9a] In practice no great hardship was caused to the staff because the enterprise had not been well supported and thereafter food for the workmen was brought into the office between twelve and two o'clock from neighbouring eating houses. However, it was not surprising that the number of searchers beginning to become restless was increasing and the press criticisms of the office in 1872 were an early indication of gathering discontent. Its leading spirit was Grove, and at the end of 1872 Hardy attempted to placate him by giving him permission to search unbound assemblies of land tax records without insisting that every individual sheet should first be stamped. In July 1873, in deference to a complaint made by Grove and a lady searcher that the clock in the search room was invariably 15 minutes fast, he issued an instruction that it should show the correct time in future, although the reason for its being set that way was to warn searchers when it struck four o'clock of the approach of closing time.

Possibly Hardy might not have been quite so conciliatory but for the earlier agitation, which, in a rather different way, may also have been responsible for the engagement of Henry Savage Sweetman, an Irish barrister and regular user of the search rooms, to edit a calendar of instruments and entries relating to Ireland to the reign of Henry VII. For many years Sweetman had been seeking such an assignment and his eventual success may well have owed something to the staunch backing he had given to the

---

9a. PRO 8/29, p 643: Hardy's circular concerning refreshments for workmen, 10 July 1876.

office during its trouble with Grove and his friends. At any rate, his work did not command unqualified approval and Lyte was to tell the Royal Commission on Public Records in 1911 that it was not good. For the later period of Irish history Russell and Prendergast continued to operate. They had completed their work on the Carte Papers and were now editing a *Calendar of State Papers relating to Ireland of the reign of James I*, covering all papers wherever deposited in the United Kingdom. Meanwhile, Brewer and Bullen were approaching the final stages of their *Calendar of Carew Manuscripts in Lambeth Library*, a project which was completed in 1873.

The value of Brewer's continuing work on the Henry VIII calendar had been recognised in 1871 when his salary was increased from £350 to £400. Mrs Green, who had completed her work on the state papers of Elizabeth I and James I, had moved on to those of the Interregnum, the *Calendar of State Papers, Domestic Series, of the reign of Charles I*, commenced by Bruce, having been completed by W. D. Hamilton. Mrs Green's task was complicated because the records of the Interregnum were not in good order. She wondered whether certain bound volumes, such as the Royalist Composition Papers, should be broken to create a better arrangement, but Hardy ruled decisively against such a course on grounds of both cost and archival rectitude. Nevertheless, the nature of the job meant that to pay Mrs Green solely on the basis of work sent to the printer was no longer appropriate, and so it was agreed that from April 1873 she should be paid at the rate of £200 a year and £5 5s a printed sheet.

The appendixes to Hardy's *Reports* continued to publicise the work carried out by the office's own editorial section, particularly calendars and lists of the Durham records and of those received from the Duchy of Lancaster. A lengthy index to parliamentary petitions to the king in council, prepared by Atkins, appeared in 1873. Extensive reports from Sanders also continued to be printed annually, detailing his superintendence of the making of *Facsimiles of the National Manuscripts* at the Ordnance Survey Office, Southampton. Likewise, reports were printed between 1872 and 1874 from Sainsbury on a rich collection of papers presented to the office in 1871 by the earl of Shaftesbury through the Historical Manuscripts Commission. Among the papers were the first set of the constitutions for the government of Carolina framed by John Locke. Hardy's great interest in the work of the Historical Manuscripts Commission meant that other gifts and deposits were finding their way into the office from the same source and that members of the staff were giving assistance, with his blessing, to the commission. An early deposit was 'The Golden Grove Book', in four volumes, which had been placed in the commission's care by the earl of Cawdor in 1870 and which related to Welsh heraldry and genealogy. Three years later it was at the centre of a minor storm when some ink marks were found upon it, the reader who had been inspecting it being forbidden to use ink while in the search room. It was later decided that as a temporary measure that book might be seen only under supervision in the office Library on the ground floor of the Norman or Domesday Tower at the back of the Round Room. The rebound Domesday Book was also kept there, under glass in a specially constructed case. The Library itself, which had started life in the Rolls House before being transferred to the top floor of the new central block, was moved to its new home in 1871 on the completion of the eastern wing, although shortage of space meant that it was not possible to accommodate all of its holdings there.

Besides its work on particular classes and collections, the office was also continuing to calendar Treasury papers from 1697 under Redington's direction. In 1872 the Home Office asked for a similar calendar to be prepared of its papers from 1760 to 1829, a task that was assigned to Redington and Atkins. While activity by the office's own staff continued on a broad front, it can be seen in retrospect as largely in response to particular needs and situations rather than a concerted and systematic attempt to list its holdings. A trenchant critic of the office in that respect was John Pym Yeatman, whose attack upon official failings was, as will be seen later, to lead him into fierce conflict with Hardy. On the other hand, at the very time Yeatman was berating Hardy, Frederick James Furnivall, the less than diligent editor of the *Chronicle of Robert Manning of Brunne* in the Rolls Series was to tell him:[9b] 'Your Office is, thanks to you, the most delightfully free from red-tapism in the whole world, I do believe'. Hardy must have found that reassuring because he had been very undecided whether to continue in post when Romilly departed in March 1873. He was particularly concerned that Stanhope, with whom he had clashed sharply in 1867 about access to certain state papers, might succeed Romilly as chairman of the Historical Manuscripts Commission. Hardy believed that it was essential for the master of the rolls to hold that office if the confidence of manuscript owners was to be assured, and his confidential approaches to the home secretary were successful in ensuring that Jessel was placed at the head of the new commission when it was issued on 7 December 1875. Stanhope was among those reappointed, but any difficulty he might have caused evaporated when he died soon afterwards.

Romilly had been much moved by an address of thanks which the staff had sent to him when he retired. In responding, he singled out particularly his deputy keeper, saying 'to yourself, my dear Hardy, who has so long been associated with me, I need scarcely say what I feel. It resembles rather the feeling of a brother than any other I can describe'.[9c] Since he had entered upon his duties in 1851 great changes had taken place during Romilly's keepership, and when Hardy came to acknowledge his services officially in the *Thirty-fifth Report* he laid particular emphasis upon his abolition of fees and upon his decision to launch a records publication programme. But the combination of judicial and record activities had taken their toll and Romilly

9b. PRO 1/39: Furnivall to Hardy, 7 August 1874.
9c. PRO 1/38: Romilly to Hardy, 27 March 1873.

did not enjoy his retirement for long, dying in December 1874 after a short illness.

When Langdale resigned as master of the rolls in 1851 Romilly succeeded him without a break, but more than four months were to pass before the appointment of Sir George Jessel, the solicitor general, was announced. The attorney general, Sir John (later Lord) Coleridge, had been Gladstone's original choice, but after some hesitation he had declined and so the vacancy was offered to Jessel, his fellow law officer, who, having had the distinction of being the first Jew to hold office as a minister of the crown now became the first member of his religion to sit on the High Court bench. Like Romilly, Jessel was a Liberal MP, having first been elected for Dover in 1868, but because the Judicature Act, soon to come into force, expressly forbade a judge from sitting in the Commons he decided to resign his seat, although technically, but not necessarily wisely, he might have stayed.[10a]

Hardy did not enjoy the same intimacy with Jessel as with Romilly, but any apprehensions that he may have had about working with someone of the same race as Palgrave were quickly dispelled. Almost as soon as Jessel was in post Hardy represented to him the pressing need for a further extension to the repository, and Jessel lost no time in urging the Treasury to give directions accordingly. Jessel was also very concerned to ensure the safety of the records from fire and it was at his instigation that a full survey was undertaken by the Office of Works into the construction of the building and its security, which concluded with the publication of a printed paper on the matter by Hardy in July 1876.[10b] A further consequence of that investigation was that from the beginning of 1876 the entire responsibility for protecting the building from fire and patrolling the premises on the Rolls Estate passed to the Metropolitan Police, one sergeant and ten policemen being attached to the office for that purpose. The need for vigilance was soon to be shown when a fierce fire broke out at the premises of the Scottish Corporation in Crane Court, Fleet Street, in November 1877, and there was a fear that it might spread to houses at the Fetter Lane end of the repository. Fortunately the fire brigade managed to bring the blaze under control in the early hours, although within the repository and its surrounds the police were on full alert and had taken a number of precautionary measures under the direction of Kingston, still permanently resident in Chancery Lane.

The main reason for the pressure on space in the repository was renewed demands for further accommodation from government departments, particularly the Admiralty regarding Greenwich Hospital documents and the War

---

10a. Jessel proved an outstanding judge. An excellent account of his distinguished career was given to the Jewish Historical Society of England by Israel Finestein in 1955: *The Jewish Historical Society of England Transactions*, XVIII, 243–283.

10b. PRO 8/29, pp 645–654: 'An Account of the Construction of the Public Record Office, and the Means adopted for its security from Fire; drawn up at the desire of the Right Honourable, Sir George Jessel, Master of the Rolls'. Printed (1876).

Office concerning records at the Tower. Requests for assistance had also been received from the Royal Mint and the National Debt Office, but it was not possible to accept their material although investigations were carried out into their holdings. In the case of the Mint the delay proved lengthy and it was not until the second half of the next century that their records finally came to the office. The cost of the new block which was planned to be built at the south-east end of the repository to run along Fetter Lane was estimated at £100,000, a figure which greatly alarmed the Treasury. Writing privately to Hardy on 16 November 1874 W. H. Smith, the bookseller and by then financial secretary to the Treasury, said:[11]

> I could not off hand commit the Government to so large an expenditure; but you must forgive me for enquiring whether the purpose and intention of a Record Office is served by the preservation of all these documents.
>
> Pardon my ignorance if I am wrong, but my first impression on reading the report was, are we not accumulating such a mass of paper and ink and print as to render it absolutely impossible for the future student of the Records of these times to make any use of the materials he will find. Will he not be completely overwhelmed with the masses of perfectly valueless matter which he will find.
>
> Should not these documents be in a sense 'edited' before they are put away; and would not your existing space prove to be sufficient and your store infinitely more valuable if some such scheme was practicable.

Such reservations had long been held at the Treasury Chambers. As far back as 1858, before the setting up of the Committee on Government Documents, P. G. Julyan there had written: 'two or three sensible men (not too strongly imbued with that reverential and indiscriminate love of old paper which so largely prevails in the bureaucratic classes of old countries) drawn from the branches of the Service most interested and acting cordially together would in all probability do away with the immediate necessity of adding another wing to the Repository'.[12] Five years later Hugh Powell Cotton, assistant superintendent of the Treasury registry, noted a 'want of courage' on the part of the Record Office to destroy documents because its business was to preserve them 'and I can answer for it that they have well performed in this respect'.[13] Hardy himself was quite prepared to see the question of disposal tackled firmly, but was hampered because Jessel considered that without parliamentary consent the office ought not to involve itself in the business of destruction, the legality of which he doubted. Consequently Redington had been told to discontinue his work on the

---

11. PRO 1/39. Treasury papers are in T 1/7401A/17520/1874.
12. T 1/6161B/20397/1858: Julyan to Trevelyan, 21 December 1858.
13. T 1/6459B/13252/1863: Cotton's report, 29 August 1863.

Committee on Government Documents and made a closing report in May 1874. Moreover, the clerk of the Petty Bag, while continuing his review of Chancery masters' documents, had been forbidden to destroy any of them because Jessel was much opposed to decisions about destruction being taken by a single individual, however competent. Contrariwise, government departments were destroying as much as they wished since Jessel, while doubting whether they had a right to do so, considered he had no power to interfere unless their records were brought into his legal custody by a warrant countersigned by the lord chancellor, a procedure that had never been followed for their material. The anomalous position of departmental records, whereby Treasury Board papers actually in the office continued to be weeded by Cotton without hindrance, coupled with the pressure for additional accommodation, meant that some way out had to be found and Hardy, in replying to W. H. Smith's unofficial enquiry, alluded to Jessel's proposal, nearly a year earlier, for the appointment of a commission to review Chancery masters' documents.

The accommodation problem had worsened since then because of the transfer, under countersigned warrant, of over 15 tons of records from the Palatinate of Lancaster. Hardy had been intimately concerned with that operation, and, apart from spending over a fortnight in Lancaster and Preston, had taken the opportunity of the *Thirty-fifth Report* to provide a brief sketch of the history of the palatinate and to emphasise that its records were to be distinguished from those of the duchy. The preparation of the records for transfer had been undertaken by Watson, assisted by two of the transcribers, Woolby and Bradley, all of whom had spent over three months at Lancaster and Preston for that purpose. The total cost of travelling, subsistence and the removal itself amounted to nearly £325, the loading at Lancaster and unloading at Euston, before cartage to Chancery Lane, being accompanied by the plentiful supply of beer to the office's workmen and to the London and North Western Railway porters involved in the movement of the documents.[14]

To add to his preoccupations, and as something of a diversion from the problems of accommodation and disposal, Hardy was also involved in marshalling information about the work and staffing of the office for the Civil Service Inquiry Commission under the chairmanship of Lyon Playfair. Hardy's belief was that the office had no need for clerks drawn from the second division, because there was little or no routine work to be done, and his clerks had to be trained to perform work of a superior character altogether peculiar to the office. Statements were also forwarded to the commission by Bond as representative of the assistant keepers, by Turner on behalf of the senior clerks and by Pike for the juniors. On 12 March 1875 the commission

---

14. PRO 1/38: expenses in removal of the records of the Duchy of Lancaster from Lancaster and Preston, 12 December 1873; PRO 1/39: expenses in removal of the records of the Duchy of Lancaster from Preston, 2 February 1874.

examined Bond, Turner and Kingston jointly, and later that day Pike.[15a] The common thread running throughout their evidence was the special knowledge and duties required of the clerks and assistant keepers, which made it highly desirable that the Public Record Office should be sufficiently attractive to hold them. The intellectual content of their work was stressed, Pike emphasising that all the junior clerks were most decidedly 'men of education' and that many of them had either been called to the Bar or had entered an Inn of Court with that intention in view. Voice was also given to dissatisfaction with the scale of pay, which had led to a memorial being sent to the Treasury in March 1874, but without positive result.[15b]

Before considering the records staff's case the commission had already issued its *First Report* in which it recommended the division of Civil Service work into two tiers, the higher division of which would be comparatively small and drawn from the class I open competition. Such entrants should, it thought, be placed on a scale of £100 to £400 with the possibility of receiving up to £200 additionally as 'duty pay'. Hardy thought the commission's proposals unsuitable for the office, and the clerks believed that once through their apprenticeship their special attainments should automatically attract 'duty pay', although Kingston conceded that on the formation of the office there were two or three clerks who, while doing well enough in their class, were unfitted for higher-grade duties. The Playfair scale would have suited the more junior of the clerks, but those at or near the £200 maximum could lose since the increase they might soon expect on promotion to the senior clerical grade outweighed the benefits of gradual progression to £400. Pike told the commission of his own misgivings in that respect, but he was fortunate enough to be promoted soon afterwards to fill the vacancy caused by Tabrum's death. It was also clear that the clerks and the assistant keepers did not share Hardy's somewhat romanticised view of the transcribers, who he maintained possessed 'a knowledge of the ancient handwritings in which the records are written, of Latin, Norman-French etc., and in abstracting ancient documents, in short, a knowledge not inferior to that of the junior clerks'.[16] Bond said that he had employed them on one occasion to make some copies, but the work had not been done very well, and he did not think they could expect to be promoted to an official position in the body of the establishment. Similarly Pike insisted that an ordinary commercial education was not good enough for a record clerk, and, although he admitted to have had no personal contact with the transcribers, he understood that they assisted the editors of the calendars of state papers and that they dealt mostly with documents which were in English.

15a. For the minutes of evidence and for the papers submitted to the commission by the department and its staff see the appendix to its *Second Report (H C Reports of Commissioners etc.*, 1875, XXIII).

15b. T 1/7379A/11038/1874.

16. PRO 2/33, pp 16–17: Hardy to Murray, 1 July 1872.

The employment of outside editors was a particular irritant to the clerks, who represented to the commission, through Pike, their belief that all calendaring should be left to the permanent staff, whose educational qualifications were sufficient guarantee that it would be well done. The clerks also emphasised the importance of the work they undertook in making searches for the heads of government departments as an added reason for an improvement in their status. However, in making its *Second Report* the commission did not think the Public Record Office should be treated differently from any other government department, particularly as a special knowledge of languages could be made a condition of appointment. But the office remained lukewarm about moving in the direction pointed by Playfair. Indeed, in seeking to fill a clerical vacancy from the class I competition in April 1876, Hardy told Lingen that he thought it unwise to entrust the making of office copies to 'men clerks or boy clerks imperfectly educated'.[17a] But the Treasury's next move was to write direct to Jessel to enquire:

> Whether your Honour is satisfied that the class of Transcribers might not
> be increased and some of the copying now manually performed by Clerks
> of the Superior Class be delegated to them.

> The new Lower Division offers the means of introducing respectable youths
> who would gain experience in deciphering and might in time become
> competent to deal with at least the more simple and intelligible documents,
> under the supervision of Clerks of a higher Order.

The transcribers could have known nothing of the Treasury's suggestion or the still more surprising response from Jessel, who indicated that, having consulted Hardy, he had no objection, but in that case thought it necessary to regrade them as clerks of the lower division, and, possibly, to reduce their number from eight to six in order to save expense. In view of the disparagement of the transcribers before the Civil Service Inquiry Commission a year earlier the change proposed in their fortunes was extraordinary, but they had subsequently taken great exception to the remarks made about them to Playfair and, when Alfred Lowson, the senior transcriber, made representations to Jessel, Bond was obliged to admit that the case he had quoted was an isolated one and had occurred many years before. Better still for the transcribers, Jessel felt it necessary to place all the facts before the Treasury, which, on Hardy's recommendation, agreed in July 1875 to raise their maximum from £1 12s to £2 a week, clearly no more than they deserved.

In its letter suggesting the extended use of transcribers within the office the Treasury also queried the possibility of merging the clerical and senior

---

17a. T 1/7563/20213/1876: Hardy to Lingen, 4 April 1876.

clerical grades, on a scale running from £100 to £400 in accordance with the Playfair recommendations. Jessel replied that it might be done by retiring some officers if sufficient inducement were offered to them. The Treasury was not, however, prepared to go beyond the normal provisions of the Superannuation Acts or to approve the regrading of the transcribers without knowing if it would result in a reduction, even prospectively, in the number of clerks borne on the higher division, and thought it desirable that any reorganisation should embrace the entire office. Replying on 19 June, Jessel said that he saw no advantage in a comprehensive scheme, maintaining that the existing arrangements appeared to work very well. Realising that further argument was pointless, since it was apparent that Jessel had no intention of doing anything which might disturb the vested interests of the assistant keepers and clerks, the Treasury, somewhat tamely in view of its earlier stand, agreed to allow the office to fill its vacant junior clerkship by open competition under class I, as it had first wanted. The result was that J. R. V. Marchant entered the service on 7 August, but soon becoming dissatisfied with his pay and prospects resigned in January 1878 to take up a teaching appointment. Ultimately he entered the law and went on to become a county court judge. So much for the abortive exchanges about the reorganisation of the office, or rather part of it, since no one considered any alteration at that time in the lowly place of the 48 workmen, numerically the largest group within the office. Nevertheless, there were signs of unrest in that quarter, perhaps precipitated by the tightening-up of the regulations concerning lunch-time breaks in July 1876. At any rate, on the 22nd of that month Watson presented a request on the men's behalf that they might work longer each day to increase their earnings, as they understood the Treasury was unwilling to improve their basic rates of pay. Whether through indifference or because he knew the likely reaction, Jessel did no more than direct Hardy to send the petition to the Treasury for its information without remark, thereby relieving their lordships of the need to do more than acknowledge its receipt.

Of even greater moment to the office than its staffing problems was the critical question of accommodation, which resulted in a decision that the Copying Room on the first floor overlooking Fetter Lane should be converted into a record room for the rolls of Chancery from the reign of King John. That was effected in 1877 and explains why the room continued to be known as the Rolls Room when it became a search room in 1961. Consideration was also being given to the appropriate way to reduce the bulk of the office's holdings in line with the suggestions made to Hardy by W. H. Smith in November 1874. Following up that letter, Jessel had emphasised to the Treasury:[17b]

17b. T 1/7480B/18300/1875: Jessel to Law, 21 January 1875.

That unless some measures be taken to limit the indiscriminate admission of documents belonging to the Courts of Law and Government Offices into the Public Record Office, and also to get rid of the useless documents already there, it will soon be overcrowded with vast quantities of rubbish and serviceable matter will be smothered by worthless hoards of papers, the accumulation of many years.

After explaining the need for a committee to tackle the problem, Jessel went on:

It should have power to deal not only with department-papers, but also with the great masses of rubbish called legal documents, which have been sent from the Law Courts and legal offices. It should, I think, consist of three persons, being men of practical and general knowledge, and of legal and historical acquirements, and they should have power to examine the documents to be sent in future to the Public Record Office in order to ascertain whether they are worthy of being preserved. They should also consider what documents, (legal as well as civil) at present in the Public Record Office might safely be removed therefrom without detriment to the public service, to individual rights, or to historical investigations. But before the recommendations of the Committee for destroying documents and papers be carried into execution such recommendations ought to be submitted for approval to the Court or Office to which they belong and from which they had been removed, and if such destruction be objected to, the Treasury should decide on the validity of any objections that may be made.

Besides its new-found concern to regulate departmental reviewing activities the office was also anxious about the rules governing public access. Hardy, in particular, felt that existing practice was too lax and it was mainly at his urging, after a report from Atkins, that the Home Office withdrew from the office certain early-nineteenth-century material, including law officers' opinions and papers relating to the movements of French naval and military forces and to Irish affairs. At much the same time the War Office, hitherto willing to open its papers to 1820, decided that, in view of the transfer of more sensitive material from the Tower, access would be discretionary in future. But Foreign Office papers remained open until 1760, the date to which, not before time, access had been advanced from 1688 in 1872. Colonial Office papers were also unrestricted to 1760, the previous embargo on North American correspondence after 1702 having been lifted in 1872. Additionally, Foreign Office papers to 1802 might be seen under permit. On the other hand, the Treasury, in spite of its proclaimed desire to thin the records to make them more accessible, was moving in the other direction. Under Trevelyan its policy, as befitted Macaulay's brother-in-law, was liberal, and even after his departure it agreed in 1862 to throw open its papers to 1820. But the Carr/Grove case had set alarm bells ringing and towards the end of 1874 Cotton wrote an astonishing, but perhaps not unexpected, letter to Hardy:[18]

> As I have always conceived it to be the intention of my lords that the Record Office authorities should possess the power of exercising a wholesome control over these documents, with regard to the public inspection thereof: I was surprized to learn that a person, claiming the right, had been allowed to overhaul several years' Papers indiscriminately, and had taken notes without let or hindrance; and that in fact he is doing it at the present time.
>
> This I do not believe was ever their Lordships' intention when they graciously allowed their Records to be opened to the Public up to the year 1820; but I am humbly of opinion that the permission was meant to be restricted to such legitimate objects as the Record Office could recognize – such as Historical, Literary, Biographical, and so forth.
>
> Knowing the peculiar nature of these Records – how many there are relating to claims of all sorts and kinds, and to property, escheated to the crown, and a thousand important matters – I feel that you will forgive me expressing an opinion somewhat strongly, that granting unlimited access to these Documents would be to furnish persons with information with which they could have no possible concern, and I verily believe it would entail no end of trouble and expense.
>
> It is only within this week that I have come across some Papers in one of what are called the 'Bundles', relative to flogging some of the Black girls at Berbice, but modesty forbids my entering into details. I merely allude to this, because if it got wind out of doors that such things are to be found in the Treasury Papers only for the seeking, it might excite much idle curiosity and lead to an unpleasant run upon the searches.

Hardy lost no time in passing Cotton's letter on to the Treasury, but his own letter suggests that it was not really the stirring of the stranger recesses of the Victorian mind which he feared but the continued activities of the irascible Grove. Claiming that he had always done his best to restrain individual curiosity, even despite the threat of legal proceedings, Hardy wrote:[19]

> To give you some notion of the extent to which this privilege of inspecting the Treasury Records has been carried I may state that in the Quarter ending 30 Sept last, no less than 46,360 Treasury Board Papers were stamped for

---

18. PRO 1/39: Cotton to Hardy, 16 December 1874.
19. T 1/7418A/19572/1874: Hardy to Lingen, 18 December 1874.

the use of one individual; for it is necessary that every Document should be stamped before it is produced to a searcher. I will forward to you in a few days a detailed account of the number of Documents to the end of the year 1874 which have been inspected by this individual alone, without payment of any Fee.

The same dangerous use of the Treasury Records will continue unless some decided check be imposed by their Lordships, for the permission having been granted by the Treasury and published in the Deputy Keeper's Annual Reports laid before Parliament, can only be altered by the Treasury, and such alterations must be laid before Parliament.

If I might be allowed to make a suggestion it would be that no Treasury Board Paper should be open to public inspection from the commencement of the reign of George III downwards, without the *special* permission of the Treasury.

As for protecting the records from the gaze of the ungodly, such a course had not previously occurred to Hardy or anyone else and to be effective would have required a mind-boggling degree of censorship, since material which might appeal to the prurient could just as readily be found before the reign of George III as after. But the problem of troublesome searchers was nothing new, and as far back as 1853 Hunter was registering unease about certain Americans 'entertaining it is well known extravagant notions of obstructed rights to property and even hereditary honours in England',[20] and the assistant keepers customarily tended to be contemptuous of readers of insufficiently serious intent. Paradoxically, Hardy, while no populist of the Cole school, had previously been more inclined to accommodate readers than most of his colleagues, and much of his early reputation rested upon his kindness and helpfulness to searchers despite their foibles. More than anyone he had been responsible for extending the principle of free access to legal searches, the very area most likely to attract the attention of deluded fortune-seekers and the like. But now, with advancing years, uncertain health and signs of unrest among searchers and at the lower levels of the office, Hardy's former tolerance was under increasing strain.

Prominent among Hardy's critics was John Pym Yeatman, a long-time user of records and a barrister of the Middle Temple. Disappointed at the Bar, not having had the preferment to which he thought himself entitled, Yeatman had set himself up as a fierce opponent of the theories of the

---

20. PRO 35/1: Returns or Reports of the Assistant Keepers (Hunter to Palgrave, 7 January 1853). Hunter's misgivings were more about record agents who acted for such persons and might masquerade as literary searchers in order to avoid fees, a supposition that Palgrave was disinclined to take seriously. Hart was one of the persons who fell under Hunter's critical eye, the other being H. G. Somerby, an American.

Oxford school of historians, such as Freeman and Stubbs. In 1874 in his *Early English History* he attacked them, criticised the system whereby public money was distributed 'amongst a party of clergymen and ladies who amuse themselves at the Record Office', and questioned whether the newly appointed master of the rolls knew of the jobbery which, he alleged, was perpetrated there.[21]

Despite his strictures, Yeatman would willingly have joined the ranks of the office's external editors had he been given the chance, and his bitterness knew no bounds when an offer he made early in 1875 to continue the transcription of Curia Regis rolls, begun by Palgrave under the Record Commission, was turned down by Hardy.

That rejection led to an intemperate letter to Jessel roundly condemning the publication policies followed by Romilly and Hardy, and, more seriously, asserting that in a return to Parliament in 1872 about office expenditure and staffing Hardy had deliberately concealed the additional payments that he and his brother had received for editorial work. Having investigated the charges and found them untrue, Jessel was in no doubt that Hardy should receive the government's full protection, and a threat by the Treasury solicitor to take libel action against Yeatman was withdrawn only after he had made a written apology, although, unknown to him, the law officers had concluded that the government should stand aside and the Treasury had decided to take their advice. In any case, Yeatman's retraction was no more than tactical and in September 1875 he repeated his allegations in a full-length pamphlet in which he attempted to expose what he saw as the mismanagement of the office.[22] In it he spared neither Hardy nor the lately-deceased Romilly, whom he described as weak and vain and 'dupe of cleverer men about him', a harsh verdict which runs counter to the evidence of the official correspondence. But Yeatman's real villain was Hardy, whose conduct he cruelly likened to that of Caley who, he said, had continued to draw his salary as secretary of the Record Commission when no longer able to perform the duties owing to his great age.

As for the office's defenders, Yeatman wrote that Oxford 'fastens on to the sugar cask of the Record Office like wasps and flies', while various clerical gentlemen 'hang like vampires upon the establishment'. He compared the 'comfort and convenience' of the British Museum with the miserable conditions at the Public Record Office, whose malaise he attributed to 'hereditary corruption'. But unlike Nicolas, in his onslaught upon the Record Commission some 45 years before, Yeatman could not look for inside support. Moreover, although he drew a parallel between the underpaid tran-

---

21. J. P. Yeatman, *An Introduction to the Study of Early English History* (London, 1874). Yeatman presented a copy to the office Library.

22. J. P. Yeatman, *An Exposure of the Mismanagement of the Public Record Office* (London, 1875). There is a copy of this pamphlet in T 1/7462B/14780/1875, which also contains Treasury papers about Yeatman's charges against Hardy.

scribers of the 1870s and those of the 1830s, their respective duties were very dissimilar. Nevertheless, Yeatman pointedly singled out from that former talented band the Hardys and Cole, who had 'risen to the chief posts in the Office. Yes, and to their shame they allow these iniquities to continue'. It was not surprising that the assistant keepers and clerks, enjoying, as they did, a position of dominance within the office, had no time for Yeatman, even Burtt being hostile to him. In mounting his attack, therefore, Yeatman had to rely upon such sources as parliamentary returns and Hardy's own *Reports*. In combing them he managed to identify, as any latter-day Public Accounts Committee would have done, the 'incredible' sum of £27,000 spent needlessly on wire doors for the repository presses, which might just as well have been used 'to cage the monkeys at the Zoological Gardens'. Palgrave, whose responsibility that was, escaped being named for the miscalculation, although in proof of the contention that the Record Office had always been a 'nest of corruption' he was censured for the vast sums he had drawn many years earlier for work said to have been carried out by his underpaid subordinates.

Yeatman also drew extensively upon the printed evidence given by the junior clerks to the Civil Service Inquiry Commission in which they had attacked the system of employing outside editors to calendar state papers, since the assistance enjoyed by Brewer and others from the full-time members of the staff seemed to involve an element of double payment by the Exchequer for the same work. Yeatman had also got wind of the trouble that the office had experienced with its workmen in the spring of 1874, which must have been common gossip at the time, and, besides his strong condemnation of Hardy's 'intimidation', contrasted the 'enormous salaries' of the officers with those of the work people, 'who are only kept from getting up a strike under terror of instant dismissal'. Commenting on the Latin inscription, thought to have come from Brewer's pen, on Romilly's bust in the Round Room, Yeatman said that instead of reading 'He opened the fount of learning' it should have been the purse strings of the nation. The root of the trouble, argued Yeatman, was Romilly's sponsorship of the 'Materials for the History of England', a project filched from Stevenson with whom, despite attacking the payments made to him, Yeatman believed it should have been left as many of the works were still in print and the 'only persons to have benefited by this waste are the Stubbs's and Brewers who have undertaken to edit them'. But, interspersed with the exaggerations and personal vituperation, Yeatman made some good points about the inadequacy of many of the office's calendars and indexes, the long wait for documents and access difficulties. Less fairly, he attacked the office for the destruction of documents that had already taken place which, he thought, was probably unlawful. On that issue, if on no other, Jessel would not have dissented, but Hardy could see no redeeming features in Yeatman's diatribe and, although the office's own records contain no reference to his pamphlet, a short note (Plate 18) drafted by Hardy after its publication has survived in a bundle of miscellaneous papers and reveals the extent of his anger at the way he thought, not without justification, he had been traduced:[23]

A libelous and malignant pamphlet entitled 'An Exposure of the Mismanagement of the Public Record Office by Pym Yeatman' has just been published, and as some time must elapse until the matter can be brought before the proper judicial tribunal, I think it incumbent to declare at once that every one of the allegations in the pamphlet against myself are scandalous and mendacious. I would, however, state that I commenced a criminal information against the writer of the pamphlet in question for charging me with making false Returns to Parliament, but as he wrote to my legal advisers and begged to withdraw his accusation, and to make me a suitable apology I abandoned my action out of pure charity to the libeller. As he has, however, repeated his libellous charge in the pamphlet no other course is open to me.

Despite his brave words, Hardy had little stomach for an expensive and long-drawn-out clash in the courts, particularly as his position with Jessel and the Treasury was quite secure, and Yeatman's attack was seen officially as no more than the ravings of a demented and disappointed man, which were best ignored. Robbed of a contest on that front, Yeatman then turned to another by joining with Grove and Carr who were continuing to wage their campaign for access to land tax material and were now attacking Hewlett, the keeper of the Land Revenue Record Office, as well as Hardy and Jessel. To remove any ambiguity about the conditions governing public access to the documents, Jessel issued a new set of rules in May 1875. However, his insistence that the inspection of departmental records was subject to the leave of the head of the department concerned eventually resulted in Yeatman applying, on Carr's behalf, to the Divisional Court at Westminster on 31 July 1876 for a *mandamus* to allow the inspection of the records to which access had been refused. Yeatman's claim that the master of the rolls was *ultra vires* in making his rule was not upheld by the judges, Lord Coleridge, the chief justice of Common Pleas, stating:[24]

That the Court did not disclaim their jurisdiction to make such an order, supposing a case made for their exercise of the jurisdiction; but in this case they were of opinion that no case was made for its exercise. The meaning of

---

23. PRO 37/72: note in Hardy's hand [September 1875]. Hardy's reference to his charitable forbearance should not be taken too seriously: he had earlier had no compunction in confidentially drawing the Treasury's attention to a report arising from proceedings in the Divorce Court involving Yeatman. Yeatman's petition for the dissolution of his marriage was dismissed when he was found to have deserted his German wife whom he had married at Gretna Green: J 77/68/Y 182.

24. *The Times*, 2 August 1876. Papers concerning Grove's allegations about the abstraction of land tax records from the Land Revenue Record Office are in LRRO 36/37 and LRRO 36/38.

the Act is clear – there is to be such access of the public to the records 'as is consistent with their safety and the policy of the realm'; and, with that view, searches are to be subject to such rules as the Master of the Rolls may lay down, and he has made rules, one of which in certain cases requires the leave of the head of the department; and it is admitted that such leave has not been obtained. So far therefore, from there being any case made out for the exercise of our jurisdiction, it is very clearly shown that there is no case for its exercise, and the application must be refused.

Although the lord chief baron and Mr Justice Archibald both concurred, Yeatman was undeterred and two days later appealed *ex parte* Carr to the Court of Appeal where his application was heard before Lords Justices James, Mellish and Baggallay at Lincoln's Inn. The object, Yeatman said, was not to gratify mere curiosity but to obtain evidence in regard to tithes in the county of Durham, a matter of great importance to the clergy there. The court dismissed the appeal, saying there was 'no general right in all the Queen's subjects to inspect the documents in the Record Office. Some particular right must be shown. The appellant was in the position of a mere stranger, and the public time could not be wasted in hearing such an application'.[25] Similar impatience with Yeatman was soon to be felt in the Home Office to which he had made some wild accusations about the improper sale of public records at Sotheby's in 1869. They turned out to be baseless as the documents concerned came from solicitors acting for the family of the duke of Leeds. He had also discovered certain Record Commission documents in the British Museum, but any hope he had of blaming Hardy disappeared when it was found that they had been acquired from Charles Devon in Madden's time. Nevertheless, Hardy felt keenly the attacks upon his probity, and only the expense of legal action and the knowledge that his reputation remained officially unharmed reconciled him to the observance of no more than contempt for his assailant.[26] The court's ruling on the right of the public to inspect documents meant that, unless the master of the rolls chose to exercise his 'charge and superintendence' over departmental records, under the 1852 order in council, by taking them into his actual legal custody by countersigned warrant, which he clearly had no wish or intention of doing, heads of departments were at liberty to restrict access to their records as they pleased. The situation stemmed directly from the 1838 act, although the consequences could hardly have been foreseen by its framers. Because Parliament was responsible, only Parliament could provide the remedy, but the campaign by Yeatman and his friends commanded no support outside their own tiny circle. Had it been otherwise a

---

25. *The Times*, 3 August 1876.
26. The Home Office file does not appear to have survived, but there are copies of the correspondence, including Hardy's letters rebutting Yeatman's charges, in PRO 2/41, pp 353–358 and PRO 2/42, pp 11–12, 21.

golden opportunity existed to make an advance because, even while their case was before the courts, a new bill concerning public records was in the Commons where it had received a formal second reading in July 1876.

Its purpose was confined to the long-outstanding question of the destruction of 'valueless' documents. To assist members W. H. Smith circulated an explanatory statement on 1 August 1876, which Hardy had prepared for him, with Jessel's approval, the previous November, to which was annexed lists of records which it was suggested might be pulped. In his memorandum Hardy referred to the 'large masses' of legal and governmental documents in the office which were wholly useless for legal, historical, military, statistical, economic or official purposes and of no possible interest to anyone:[27a]

> It may be safely asserted that if such papers and documents had been
> preserved from the Norman Conquest to the present time, a building of 10
> times the dimensions of the present Repository would be insufficient for
> them, and really valuable materials for history in all its branches would be
> swamped and crushed by their surroundings of useless rubbish.

On 4 December 1875 Hardy had followed up by sending to Smith the draft of a bill, approved by Jessel, 'to authorise the removal from the Public Record Office of useless writings and to make provision as to the Chancery Documents removed from or now deposited in the Offices of the late Masters in Chancery'.[27b] The bill provided for the appointment from time to time by the Treasury of a committee to report upon the matter and for any proposed scheme of destruction to be laid before Parliament where it might be wholly or partially vetoed. By the quaintly-termed 'writings' was meant:

> Papers or parchments either written or printed or partly written and partly
> printed and whether bound in Books or unbound which by virtue of the
> Public Records Act 1838 are or shall for the time being be deposited or
> intended to be deposited in the Public Record Office whether in pursuance
> of any warrant under sections three or four of the Public Records Act 1838
> or deposited there by or with the consent of any Public Department.

As regards Chancery masters' documents, the bill placed them under the control of the master of the rolls as though they were public records, subject to rules as to their inspection, and empowered him to deliver up any of value to their rightful owners when ascertained. Not surprisingly, the amateurish drafting was not to the liking of parliamentary counsel, who prepared a

---

27a. *HC Accounts and Papers*, 1876, LX, 597. Printed in *First Report of the Royal Commission on Public Records*, 1912, I, pt 11, 34–35.

27b. T 1/7480B/18300/1875. Later Treasury papers about the bill are in T 1/7548B/18292/1876 and T 1/7598A/10115/1877. Parliamentary bill papers are in *HL Public Bills*, 1877, V, 415–433, and the Hewlett papers in LRRO 67/308.

fresh version to much the same intent early in 1876, but with the added proviso that before any disposal schedule was laid before Parliament notice should be given in the *London Gazette* and it should be available for inspection at the Public Record Office for six months to enable objections and representations from the public to be considered. That provision was later dropped, as was any reference to a Treasury-appointed committee, the Exchequer being anxious to avoid a commitment to unnecessary expense. Instead, it was left to the master of the rolls to draw up rules to regulate the disposal procedure, subject to Treasury approval and the further consent of the court or department concerned. Such rules were to be laid before Parliament for 60 days before taking effect. The act was also to be cited as the Public Record Office Act, perhaps to prevent its scope being widened and to avoid problems of definition which might have occurred had it been styled the Public Records Act. The new measure's preamble referred to 'divers records and papers (in this Act referred to as documents)', which led to the 1954 Grigg Committee pointing out that the first act, also now officially described as the Public Record Office Act 1838, defined public records as 'all Rolls, Records, Writs, Books, Proceedings, Decrees, Bills, Warrants, Accounts, Papers and Documents' and to wonder, impishly, 'whether the destruction of (for example) Writs that has taken place since 1877 is within the law', a matter on which it was happy not to have to express an opinion.

The bill was not introduced into the Commons until July 1876, too late in the session to complete its stages. It might have been otherwise but for the unease about it felt by certain members, particularly Ralph Assheton, Conservative MP for Clitheroe. The result was a decision by the government to try again later in the Lords in the hope that it might enjoy an easier passage there. Accordingly, the lord chancellor presented it to that House in February 1877, where, at the suggestion of certain lords who had held the offices of lord lieutenant and custos rotulorum, a clause was added to bring quarter sessions records within its ambit. Lord Houghton, who as Richard Monckton Milnes MP had been associated with Buller in pressing for a new repository in the 1840s, wanted any documents scheduled for destruction to be offered to the Society of Antiquaries for preservation or disposal as it might think fit, but failed to carry his amendment. However, the Lords agreed to strengthen parliamentary scrutiny over the destruction of records under the master of the rolls's rules by inserting a requirement for proposals to be laid before both Houses for not less than four weeks to enable their expediency to be judged.

With its alterations the bill was referred on 13 March to a select committee, which was appointed on 22 March and which took evidence from Hardy and Jessel on 19 and 26 April.[28] Jessel took great care to explain the distinction he

---

28. *HL Reports Committees*, 1877, VII, 399–444. For excerpts from the minutes of evidence see *First Report of the Royal Commission on Public Records*, 1912, I, pt II, 35–37.

drew between legal and departmental records, but his, and Hardy's, portrayal of the mass of rubbish with which the office was weighed down contrasted sharply with their assurance that any destruction would be subject to the closest oversight by the learned committee that they had in mind. According to Hardy, it was intended that the committee should examine not just every class of document, but every paper within it. Jessel thought the presumption should always be in favour of keeping records and that it was 'the duty of the Keeper of the Rolls to preserve them, not destroy them'. They both made it clear that it was not their intention to destroy any document earlier than 1715, and a prohibitory clause was inserted in the Commons at a later stage. It was evident, however, that, although they wished to thin their legal holdings, their main aim, since the government was unwilling to build another wing, was to prevent departments from dumping records upon them – shovelling them over as a member of the committee put it. It was also hoped to safeguard the public interest by supervising the destruction by departments of their documents, although Jessel disclaimed any intention of settling with them the papers which should be sent to the office, while saying it could be done by the adoption of the kind of machinery in use in the Historical Manuscripts Commission. Jessel was also at pains to clarify the position about the right of searchers to examine the records which, he said, applied only to those held under countersigned warrant. Departmental records were held in accordance with the original letter of understanding with Langdale, and it was, in Jessel's opinion, quite impossible to allow unrestricted access to them since many were of a confidential nature which ought not to be communicated to the public.

Having also heard evidence from Archibald Murray, clerk of the Petty Bag, concerning his operations on Chancery masters' documents, the committee allowed the bill's main provisions to go through unaltered, but it decided to accede to petitions which had been received from the justices of the peace of Cumberland, Kent, Northumberland and Warwickshire by striking out the clauses concerning county records. In doing so the committee also took account of evidence given to it against the proposed inclusion of such documents by the clerks of the peace for Surrey and Middlesex and the answers given by certain other clerks to a circular it had addressed to them on the matter. Houghton, who had managed to get onto the committee, questioned Hardy and Jessel about the possibility of adding an outside antiquary to the proposed review body, but he did not press the issue when Jessel said that he was not opposed to such a person attending as an observer, without a vote. Questions were also asked about the possibility of selling unwanted documents instead of destroying them but were not pursued, perhaps because it was evident that the committee was itself divided as to the propriety of such action, particularly in the light of past scandals. At various times the committee's questioning indicated concern that historical research might be handicapped because valuable material in government offices might not be made available, or might not even find its way into the office. But Jessel and Hardy made no secret of their acceptance of departmental paramountcy in that respect, and the former made it clear that the only restriction he wanted on ministerial authority was over the destruction of documents. Despite Jessel's and Hardy's evident caution H. G. Hewlett was highly critical of the lists of documents suggested for destruction which had accompanied Hardy's memorandum of November 1875, and at his urging the government added a clause to the bill when it returned to the Lords in May which provided that the approval of the commissioners of woods, forests and land revenues should be obtained before any rules were made by the master of the rolls concerning the disposal of Land Revenue Record Office documents. On further consideration, however, the government decided to drop that requirement, accepting Hardy's contention that it was unnecessary because the disposal rules were already subject to the consent of the heads of departments concerned.

The Lords having no further amendments to make, the bill passed to the Commons in June 1877 where it encountered but slight opposition, mainly from Assheton, and some queries from Beresford-Hope, who had been briefed by the Hewletts, H. G. and his cousin W. O. They thought that many documents useful for establishing the rights of the crown might be at risk and may also have seen dangers to the family record-agency business in the proposed measure. William Hewlett also expressed his misgivings to the president of the Society of Antiquaries, who forwarded his letter to Jessel. But apart from having to endure some carping from that quarter, and a resolution of protest from the chapter of the College of Heralds, the government had no difficulty in piloting the bill through the Commons, merely inserting a clause to prevent the destruction of any document of earlier date than 1715, and indicating more precisely the manner in which schedules concerning disposals were to be prepared for submission to Parliament. It received the royal assent on 14 August 1877, by an odd coincidence 39 years to the day after the young Victoria had assented to the original act. As with that earlier statute, it was some time before the new measure came fully into force, although Jessel lost no time in promulgating special regulations concerning the inspection by the public of Chancery masters' documents, which the act brought under his 'charge and superintendence', while safeguarding the possibility of their return to their lawful owners.[29] The act's preamble rehearsed the expediency of preventing 'the Public Record Office from being encumbered with documents of not sufficient public value to justify their preservation', and Hardy was confident that, with the conversion of the large Copying Room to a record room, the accommodation problem had been solved for the next 25 years. But that belief failed to take account of the worsening condition of the rickety old

---

29. The rules were subsequently reproduced in *The Thirty-ninth Report of the Deputy Keeper* (1878), 3–4.

houses used to store records in Rolls Yard and Chancery Lane, which was to lead to their demolition in 1891–1892 and eventual replacement by a new block facing Chancery Lane.

Hardy believed that the 1877 act would ease the office's storage difficulties, but he was less happy about Parliament's action during that year in requiring a return to be made of warrants which had been issued for the transfer of records and in seeking another concerning record publications. In both cases he suspected that the office's critics were after ammunition for a further onslaught. But as demands upon the office's resources both returns were dwarfed by the order of the House of Commons in March 1877 for the names of members of Parliament 'from so remote a period as it can be obtained', to complement a return, ordered in 1876 and already in hand, for like information from 1696. The story of that mammoth undertaking has been splendidly recounted elsewhere[30] and need not be repeated here, but among the many clerks who participated in the enterprise may be particularly mentioned Kingston, Trimmer, Sharp and Lawrance. New names were coming into prominence because the original band of clerks continued to dwindle, notably with the death of Burtt in December 1876 and the retirement on health grounds in January 1877 of Sharpe after 56 years' service. From a narrow office standpoint Sharpe's contribution was the more distinctive and Hardy, who as a young man had worked alongside him at the Tower, paid tribute in the *Thirty-eighth Report* to the length and value of his services, particularly as regards his calendars of close and patent rolls. On the other hand, the departure of Burtt, who had been disaffected ever since being passed over for the secretaryship by Edwards in 1866, was noted without special remark. But outside the office Burtt was remembered rather more favourably as he had enjoyed a considerable reputation in the antiquarian world and for many years had been honorary secretary to the Royal Archaeological Institute besides undertaking valuable work on the Westminster Abbey muniments. Some of his Palgravian prejudices were to be taken up by his able pupil, Pike, thus ensuring that old feuds were to go rumbling on. To take Burtt's place Sanders, the last of the assistant keepers of the old second class, was promoted to the first class, but allowed to remain at the Ordnance Survey Office, Southampton, where he was currently superintending the photocopying of Anglo-Saxon charters, while the senior clerical vacancy was taken by Bird. Sharpe's resignation led to the promotion of Turner to the assistant keeper grade and of Cartwright to be senior clerk. Additionally, two newcomers entered the office from the class I Civil Service examination. One of them, E. T. Gurdon, stayed for just over a year and is best remembered as an England rugby international and as a leading member of the Rugby Union – hardly the man, it might

---

30. E. L. C. Mullins, 'The Making of the "Return of Members" ', *Bulletin of the Institute of Historical Research*, LVIII (1985), 189–209.

be thought, for what Palgrave called the record avocation, although Gurdon gave as his reason for resignation the poor pay and prospects of the office's clerks. By contrast, the other 1877 entrant, J. W. King, had a frail constitution and it was his poor health which obliged him to resign in 1885. Early in 1878 an unforeseen vacancy had occurred in the senior clerical grade with the death of Atkins, the former workman, at the age of 52. Atkins, who was replaced by Selby, had fully justified Palgrave's faith in him, and had his health held up there is little doubt that he would have become an assistant keeper. His widow was left to bring up seven children on her own without any pension. Hardy and Jessel managed to get £100 for her from the Royal Bounty Fund, poor recompense in the circumstances although Mrs Atkins was more than grateful for small mercies.

Of equal, if not greater, importance than the changes among the permanent staff was the appointment of Brewer to the crown living of Toppesfield in Essex at the end of 1876. However, besides keeping his post at the Chapel, Brewer continued his editorial links, superintending part-time the calendaring work of Gairdner and Martin. For the latter duties he was paid £200 a year, leading one journal to comment waspishly 'Rolls well Buttered'.[31] But Jessel was not anxious to upset the prickly Brewer, who had taken amiss his decision in February 1876 to limit editors' prefaces to 50 pages. That ruling drew a protest from the Society of Antiquaries, who thought it represented a censure on Brewer, and reflected upon his introduction to the fourth volume of *Letters and Papers of Henry VIII*, which had provoked some controversy owing to his strong criticisms of aspects of the Reformation and of the king and Anne Boleyn.

Another change of importance was at Rome where Stevenson was succeeded at the beginning of 1877 by W. H. Bliss of the Bodleian Library. Like Stevenson, Bliss was a Roman Catholic convert and former Anglican clergyman, but that counted for little with the Vatican bureaucrats and it was some time before they fully recognised him. His eventual acceptance at the Papal Court owed much to the patient diplomacy behind the scenes of Cardinal Manning, who was convinced of the importance of the work and had already done much to smooth Stevenson's path. On 22 February 1878 the office might also have lost its keeper when a shot was fired at him outside the Rolls Court by the Reverend H. J. Dodwell, an aggrieved litigant, which was to result in an Old Bailey trial and Dodwell's confinement in Broadmoor. Responding to a message from the staff, congratulating him upon his escape, Jessel said: 'I shall always feel it to be an honorable distinction to be at the head of so well regulated an Office as the Public Record Office, and I

---

31. *Whitehall Review*, 13 January 1877. The main burden of the article, which may have come from Yeatman's pen, was the scandal produced by a loophole in the act against pluralities which enabled Brewer to hold two livings concurrently. The writer was in error in saying that Brewer was reader at the Rolls Chapel because he actually held the more senior office of preacher there.

fully appreciate the kindness which prompted so early and spontaneous an expression of goodwill on the part of the officers and workmen of the establishment'.[32]

It was fortunate for the office that Jessel was spared. His removal at that stage would have been a great blow because it was obvious that the Treasury had given no more than perfunctory attention to the implications of the new Record Act. Writing privately to Hardy at the beginning of February 1878, Lingen confessed:[33]

The Act of last session seems to have put rather an inconvenient spoke in our wheel, and to extend even to documents not yet removed, but only about to be so.

I had contemplated henceforth weeding our papers *here, before* we sent them, de anno in annum to you.

But it seems doubtful whether this will be lawful.

I certainly did not calculate on a debate in Parlt. over the destruction of every cart load of rubbish, which, for years past, has been proceeding so usefully and peacefully.

A worried Hardy defensively, but hardly accurately, laid the blame upon 'Mr. Hewlett of the Land Revenue Office, and a man of the name of Grove, well known to the Treasury'. Both would have been flattered by the influence Hardy attributed to them, but Jessel knew exactly what had been intended and in a memorandum of 23 February 1878 his views were fully set out by his chief secretary, George T. Jenkins. Agreeing that, until rules were made under the 1877 act, the destruction of departmental documents not removed into the custody of the master of the rolls under a countersigned warrant remained as 'lawful' or 'unlawful' as previously, it stated:[34]

But, bearing in mind that all such documents are, by the original Act, under his charge and superintendence, with power for him to make orders for their 'preservation', etc. only, and that the Act of 1877 authorizes the destruction of documents by the Master of the Rolls, subject to the consent

---

32. PRO 1/43: Jessel to Hardy, 26 February 1878. There is a report of the trial in *The Times*, 16 March 1878. An attempt was made at the turn of the century to secure Dodwell's release, but it was not successful.

33. PRO 1/43: Lingen to Hardy, 1 February 1878. Cotton had retired from his weeding work at the Public Record Office and Lingen was looking for someone to replace him.

34. T 1/7700A/18813/1878: memorandum of 23 February 1878 accompanying Hardy's letter to Lingen of 26 February 1878.

of the Treasury and of the heads of the Departments, and does not authorize their destruction by any other person, or in any other manner, it is clear that the Department ought not to destroy any document of a 'public nature' (within the definition contained in the original Act) after the passing of the Act of 1877, unless in the mode prescribed by that Act, viz., under rules made by the Master of the Rolls in pursuance of the Act. Although such documents may not be in the custody of the Master of the Rolls under a countersigned warrant, they are all documents 'which can be removed to the Record Office'.

It could not be supposed that Jessel's interpretation was any more welcome at the Treasury than his draft rules, which Hardy forwarded to Lingen on 12 March 1878 and which centred upon the formation and duties of a permanent committee of three inspecting officers who were to meet daily. Two members were to be nominated by the master of the rolls, one of whom was to be an officer of the Public Record Office and the other a barrister. The third was to be appointed by the Treasury, and departments were entitled to appoint an additional member whenever their own records were under review. The Treasury thought the proposals too elaborate and did not take kindly to Jessel's proposal that, as the appointment of a barrister was somewhat experimental, he might be offered a salary of at least £800 a year. Neither did it care for the suggestion that the record officer should receive an addition to his normal salary because the task was more onerous and responsible than his usual work and not so agreeable. Feeling that it had been manoeuvred into a false position, the Treasury was disinclined to come to an early decision, which much vexed Jessel, and his hopes of securing a speedy settlement began to recede as it gradually became evident that Hardy was unlikely to achieve his ambition of continuing in post until the following year and so complete 60 years' continuous record service.

There were already some tell-tale signs of Hardy's decline, although as recently as the previous autumn he had journeyed north with a transcriber to superintend the transfer to London of a collection of documents belonging to the Duchy of Lancaster relating to the manor of Halton. By early May 1878 Hardy had come to realise that his health would prevent him from continuing much longer, but he managed to struggle into the office until 29 May, his last day of attendance. His retirement was now seen as inevitable, as may be judged from an entry in Kingston's diary:[35]

---

35. Regrettably, Kingston's diary, at one time in PRO 8/144, fell to the Public Record Office's own weeders after the Second World War, but a few entries from it survive among the notes made by J. R. Crompton, an assistant keeper, in connection with an earlier abortive history which was planned in the years immediately preceding the celebration of the first centenary of the office in 1938. The references to the diary will be found in PRO 8/47 among Crompton's papers in 'Sources and General, Part 2'.

June 4: Mr. Jenkins, the Master's Secretary, had a long conversation (in private) with me touching the Department and the choice of a successor in the event of Sir Thomas's retiring. I recommended Mr. Wm. Hardy in the warmest way. Mr. Jenkins made notes as to the Assistant Keepers generally.

Eleven days later Hardy was dead and on 17 June, which was a Monday, Kingston recorded:

Occupied a great part of the day in getting an address of condolence to Lady Hardy, which I had prepared, signed throughout the Department. It was done with an unanimity and good feeling by everyone which delighted me.

Of the many obituaries quite the most fulsome was that in *The Athenaeum* of 22 June, which was probably written by Hardy's old friend Jeaffreson, who had been among those at his graveside two days earlier at Willesden Lane Cemetery. In it was stated:

It is not generally known that Lord Langdale had actually promised Hardy that he should be the first Deputy-Keeper under the Public Records Act, before he was subjected to the strongest ministerial pressure to give the place to Sir Francis Palgrave. Whilst much was justly said of Mr. Palgrave's unquestionable fitness for the office, it was urged that his appointment was required by financial considerations, as it would be necessary to compensate him for the appointment taken from him by the Records Act, if he were not provided with a post of equal or greater value. In his embarrassment Lord Langdale revealed the state of the case to his *protégé*, who, it is needless to say, declared that he would endure any mortification rather than be the occasion of further discomfort to his patron. Hardy had therefore to wait twenty-three years before he attained the office which his death has now rendered vacant for a second time; and when he at length succeeded to it, he was indebted to Lord Langdale's successor at the Rolls for his promotion to the long-wished-for post.

Subsequently, that story was repeated by Hardy's nephew, William John Hardy, when writing his uncle's entry for the *Dictionary of National Biography*, and it received further embellishment in Jeaffreson's *Recollections* in 1894, by which time few were around to challenge it even had they been disposed to do so. Jeaffreson's racy tale of the fisticuffs at the Tower in 1832, with Palgrave getting the worst of it, also rapidly became office lore, but it was much to Hardy's credit that shortly after that clash he had candidly confessed that it was 'a circumstance, however, which I have never ceased to deplore, on many accounts'.[36] However, none of those echoes from the past should overshadow his own gifts and remarkable career. It was a grievous misfortune for him to have to endure the attacks by Yeatman upon his integrity and to find himself at odds with his Land Revenue Office colleague, Henry Gay Hewlett. But it was Hewlett, writing in *The Academy* on 22 June 1878, who struck the most authentic note about him. After recounting the highlights of Hardy's record services and his great activity and enterprise, he concluded:

> The unfailing readiness which Sir Thomas showed to communicate the vast stores of his knowledge to all scholars who solicited his aid, and his urbane courtesy of manner, made him a general favourite. As the chief of a large public department, he had a difficult part to play, for which his studious habits to some extent disqualified him, and he was perhaps unduly sensitive to the petty annoyances which any obscure person, if sufficiently noisy and pertinacious, has the power of inflicting upon a man of highly-wrought nervous temperament. As a colleague, he was genial and sympathetic, especially to the younger members of his staff. His strong affections occasionally led him astray, and an impulsive temper betrayed him into hasty acts and words which sometimes provoked animosity, but he was always ready to make an *amende* or to accept overtures of reconciliation, and his essentially generous and kindly nature could not be misapprehended by those who knew him well.

Whether Hardy would have appreciated the frankness of his old friend is an open question.

---

36. T. D. Hardy, *A Letter to His Majesty's Commissioners for Public Records in answer to certain passages in Mr. Palgrave's 'Reply to the Statement of the Secretary to the Commission in respect to the Parliamentary Writs'*, (London, 1832), 37. Although the relationship between Hardy and Palgrave never recovered from their early bruising encounters, Hardy's later contacts with his old rival's family were always perfectly proper. As late as 28 February 1876 there is a friendly letter to him in PRO 1/122 from Reginald Palgrave asking if he might borrow W. D. Christie's *Life of Shaftesbury* from the office.

Chapter X

William Hardy, Third Deputy Keeper, 1878–1886

The Master of the Rolls, with a view to a general improvement of the actual position and future prospects of the members of this establishment, in exercise of the statutory authority vested in him by the Record Act, 1 and 2 Vict. c.94, nominated me, then an Assistant Keeper, to the important trust of the Deputy Keepership, which the death of Sir Thomas Hardy had left vacant.

(William Hardy, 9 June 1879: *The Fortieth Report of the Deputy Keeper* (1879), iii-iv)

His [William Hardy's] Reports are meagre and uninteresting and throw very little light on the personal history of the staff or the organisation of the Office.

(*First Report of the Royal Commission on Public Records*, 1912, I, pt II, 108)

Unlike the situation after Palgrave's death, there was no obvious successor to Hardy. Of the men on the original establishment at the time of consolidation in 1840 only Edwards and Redington remained. Edwards, an excellent organiser, had served both deputy keepers well, but his failing health was reducing his effectiveness. His archival experience was also limited and he had never been fitted for a directorial role, being essentially an executive. Redington had done good work on the Committee on Government Documents, but he was somewhat isolated from his colleagues and his knowledge of the ancient records was mainly confined to those of the Exchequer. John Bond, the next in line, had a sound repository background from his days at Carlton Ride, and during the 1860s had acquitted himself well as superintendent of the search rooms. He had to his credit also the publication in 1866 of a *Handy Book of Rules and Tables for verifying dates of Historical Events and of Public Events and of Public and Private Documents*. He was an odd character, however, and, although the world regarded him as Sir Henry Cole's brother-in-law, he had convinced himself that he was really the natural son of the duke of Sussex.[1] Foremost of the remainder was the genial William

---

1. PRO 1/676. In a note on this file, dated 18 September 1945, Jenkinson says that when he first joined the office in 1906 there were still a number of stories current about Bond. Another member of the staff, R. L. Atkinson, records that it was an office legend that Bond believed himself related in some way to Queen Victoria, and the forgetmenot at the end of his *Book of Dates* was supposed to allude to that connection. Atkinson told Jenkinson that he 'generally understood (as may be the case) that it merely indicated that our predecessor was subject to delusions'. See also Maunde Thompson's letter of 12 September 1920 to Stamp in PRO 1/85.

Hardy who was almost 71 years old. Besides being chief examiner of office copies, Hardy had the advantage of a good reputation in the antiquarian world, having previously been engaged in many peerage cases in the House of Lords as well as in other actions where like expertise was required. Those outside activities helped to strengthen his claim to the deputy keepership, although it could be argued that they had been undertaken at the expense of his former position of keeper of the Duchy of Lancaster records. According to the duchy's historian, Sir Robert Somerville, he did comparatively little work of note while there, having been allowed to carry on a lucrative business as a record agent.[2a]

None of the other assistant keepers was a serious contender. Sanders's lameness was an increasing handicap and he was far too settled at Southampton to be moved, especially as his pay there was supplemented by a generous allowance of 16s a day. Gairdner, Turner and H.C. Hamilton had worked only on the editorial side of the office and had never displayed any interest in duties elsewhere. Hamilton, in particular, maintained a low profile and many years later Maunde Thompson of the British Museum was to recall his habit of carrying 'a lawyer's blue bag, stuffed with a monstrous lunch which he munched the whole day through – six mortal hours'.[2b] At the next level Kingston, besides being a fair record scholar, was highly practical and had responsibility for the day-to-day running of the repository as well as being permanently on the site as caretaker, as he was still officially known. But as a senior clerk he could hardly expect to jump over his assistant keeper colleagues any more than could the gifted young graduates now occupying the lower rungs of the office ladder, even if Jessel decided upon an internal appointment. Kingston, who may have had his eye upon the next vacancy but one, had no doubt that the choice should fall upon William Hardy, and it says much for his standing at the time that Jessel's chief secretary should consult him on the matter. Meanwhile, Jessel was making his own soundings, as appears from a letter written a few years later by Acton to Mary Gladstone about an award of a Civil List pension to S. R. Gardiner, the historian and director of the Camden Society, who he said:[3]

Ought to be at the Record Office instead of the present Hardy. It is in
Jessel's gift, and he asked my advice, specially excluding clergymen and
thereby losing the two best men, Brewer and Stubbs. I suggested Freeman,
Gardiner and Bond. Freeman sent me word that he would not take it. Jessel
told me he would appoint Bond – who is now the very good and estimable,
but gloomy successor of Panizzi: – but that he had been told that Bond was

---

2a. Robert Somerville, 'The Duchy of Lancaster Records', *RHS Transactions*, Fourth Series, XXIX (1947), 13–14.

2b. PRO 1/85: Maunde Thompson to Stamp, 12 September 1920.

3. Herbert Paul, *Letters of Lord Acton to Mary, daughter of the Right Hon. W. E. Gladstone* (London, 1909), 149–150.

a Catholic. He said that a Jew was not strong enough to appoint a Catholic Keeper of the Archives. Bond is a Broad Churchman, and the report arose only from my recommendation. Gardiner, therefore, remained; but it was resolved, under I know not what pressure, to keep the thing in the Hardy family.

Pike, for one, did not believe that the qualifications required for the deputy keepership were widely understood, and when he gave evidence to the Royal Commission in 1911 he cited Acton's letter, saying:[4]

> From the advice which Lord Acton gave, it is quite clear that he had not considered the words of the Public Record Office Act, 1838, by which it is required that the office shall be filled only by 'a fit person duly qualified by his knowledge of records'. One of the persons whom he recommended was neither a lawyer nor in any sense an expert in records. It was E. A. Freeman, who had written a History of the Norman Conquest – a work dealing largely with a period for which there are no public records at all, and giving references not to original MSS but to printed books. Freeman, however, most honourably declined the offer. It is probable that there are many who, like the late Lord Acton, do not know what is the nature of the Public Records as a whole, and what are the qualifications required for dealing with the most ancient of them, and those which are of the greatest importance.

Acton's reference to Brewer, then elderly and querulous and to die within the year, was strange, as was his mention of Stubbs for whom the post could hardly have been any more attractive than it was for Freeman. It seems barely credible that Jessel should have thought of either of them seriously, and his objection to clergymen may have been intended jocularly as only a few months had passed since a cleric had taken a pistol to him. Rawson Gardiner clearly had some claim and Edward Bond of the British Museum even more so. As it happened, Bond was more than compensated later that year when promoted to the principal librarianship at the museum at a salary of £1,200, which was £200 more than the deputy keeper maximum. Whether or not Jessel seriously contemplated appointing an outsider is unknown. Certainly the staff could have had no idea of what was in his mind, so that when Acton's letters were first published in 1904 the passage about the discussions in 1878 must have surprised those whose memories went back that far.

On the face of it, the selection was entirely straightforward because Sir Thomas died on Saturday, 15 June, and on the Monday following Kingston wrote in his diary:

> June 17. With Wm. Hardy a great deal about the Deputy Keepership. The

---

4. *First Report of the Royal Commission on Public Records*, 1912, I, pt III, 169.

MR saw him and promised him the post subject to the consent of Government.
Mr. Jenkins came in later and expressed much pleasure at the news.

Next day Jessel wrote to Disraeli to ask for crown approval. But protocol
required that he should have written to the home secretary and there was
therefore a slight delay in obtaining the necessary consent, which was finally
given on 4 July. Meanwhile, Jessel had been shocked to find that Lady
Hardy, who was only 54, had been left penniless. Avoiding any moral
judgment, he lost no time in making her plight known to the premier, and
his efforts, and those of other influential friends, eventually resulted in the
award to her of a Civil List pension of £100 a year.[5]

Apart from the 1877 act little of moment had occurred during Sir
Thomas's last ten years, and brother William's appointment to succeed him
and the consequential promotion of Kingston to assistant keeper hardly
portended a new dawn. Despite the success of the photographic process at
Southampton in the reproduction of Domesday and other national manuscripts, the office displayed no interest in its further development, such as
the provision of photocopies for the public. Part of the explanation was that
copying work gave the clerks valuable training in reading ancient documents,
and its importance in official thinking was illustrated by the printing in the
Deputy Keeper's Fortieth Report for 1878 of the comprehensive instructions
issued for the guidance of the staff when making office copies. Neither was
the office's senior management disposed to branch out in other ways, an
excellent example being the arrival in September 1880 of an elementary
school party wishing to see Domesday which resulted in a virtual call to the
barricades. Kingston's senior clerk, Trimmer, described the visit for his
master:[6a]

To pass on to other affairs I may amuse you by telling you I had a
schoolmistress and 14 young ladies (from Board School) to see Domesday
etc. the other day. They applied in the usual way to see the book and I
showed it accordingly. Bond was more than amused at the affair as he tells
me that Sir H. Cole is advocating the exhibition of historical muniments for
purposes of education and is writing a book on the subject in which he
recommends Board Schools to send children to see Domesday among other
things. He thinks my case was the first of many and mentioned it to the D.K.

---

5. J 113/4, p 78: Jessel to Beaconsfield, 28 June 1878. Treasury papers are in
T 1/16186. Hardy had a modest insurance policy on his life but made it over to his
stepdaughter, Isa, shortly before his death, no doubt realising that if Lady Hardy was
the beneficiary it could affect adversely the amount of any pension the government might
award her.

6a. PRO 1/131: Trimmer to Kingston, 8 September [1880]. Trimmer's main purpose
in writing was to tell Kingston, then on leave, of the sudden death in the search room
of John Sell, a workman and father of one of the transcribers.

Mr. Hardy is quite opposed to encouraging the idea and intends to institute some new regulations about the showing this book. He will show them to you (or talk to you about them) on your return before putting them into effect.

I was under the impression that Domesday Book ranked like any ordinary Patent or Close Roll and that if we refused to show it in a *private* room the public could demand to see it in the Search room.

The Deputy Keeper sent for me and he, Mr. Edwards and Bond had a chat on the subject without arriving at any very definite conclusion, except that I am to refuse to show it to large parties of the ordinary public, in fact to use my discretion in showing it, and not look upon the office of showman as part of the duty of your room.

While the office had little desire to display its wares, it would have liked to provide a home for wills, parish registers, records of assize and similar documents, but was unable to do so because of its continuing shortage of accommodation. Owing to the steady stream of accruals from courts and departments, a crisis would already have arrived but for the gradual removal of legal departments from the Rolls Estate to the new Law Courts being built in the Strand. Considerable help came from that source in 1881, when the ugly building on the south of the repository, officially known as Judges' Chambers, but in legal parlance the Bear Garden, was vacated and taken over for use as offices. Outside London there were also stirrings of unease, but a bill which was submitted to Jessel in May 1879 by Earl Spencer, custos rotulorum of Northampton, to provide for the deposit of inclosure awards and assize records in the counties was not thought to provide the answer.

Certainly at Chancery Lane relief was much needed because the 1877 act had still not been brought into operation despite the fact that Jessel's draft rules had been with the Treasury since March 1878. The main stumbling block remained his wish to appoint a barrister at £800 a year to the Inspecting Officers' Committee he had in mind, and it was not until August 1880, and only after an appeal to Gladstone who had not long returned to the premiership at the general election, that he obtained the necessary Treasury authority. It had been Jessel's intention to engage an outsider, recommended to him by Judge Lush, the author of the standard book on common law practice; but a protest from five of the clerks, all themselves barristers, persuaded him that it might be wiser to choose someone from within the office. The Treasury welcomed his change of mind because it had been worried that the Inspecting Officers' Committee might develop into a separate department and involve additional expense. The looser the arrangements between the Record Office and departments, and the less formal the structure of the Inspecting Officers' Committee, the better the Treasury liked it. It had no difficulty in approving Jessel's choice of the deputy keeper, Redington and Pike, a barrister, as the first inspecting officers, especially as no increase in staff complement was envisaged. Also Redington was well known and trusted at the Treasury because of his work on the former Government Documents Committee and editorship of the *Calendar of Treasury Papers*. In the normal way, Crosby, the most senior of the barrister clerks, might have been nominated, but he had been stricken by paralysis and had to resign from the office altogether shortly before his death in 1881. Although the deputy keeper had told Jessel that he was prepared to perform his further duties without extra reward, the Treasury was sufficiently relieved at not having to find £800 for an outside barrister that it agreed he should have a once and for all payment of £300 for his pains. It also agreed that the committee might start work in April 1881 and that Redington and Pike should each receive supplements to their pay of £150 and £100 respectively as recommended by Jessel.

In January 1882 Jessel signed rules governing the disposal of 'valueless' records under the 1877 act by the various courts and government departments, and they were subsequently approved by the lord chancellor and the Treasury. The rules specified that the inspecting officers were to be drawn from the Public Record Office and appointed by the Treasury upon the recommendation of the master of the rolls. They were to be not less than three in number, one of whom was to be the deputy keeper for the time being, one an assistant keeper and one (whatever his rank in the office) a barrister of not less than seven years' standing. Additionally, when departmental documents were under review, the head of the department concerned was to nominate an officer 'specially conversant with the records of his department' to act with the inspecting officers, who were required to present to the master of the rolls at least one schedule of documents for disposal every year, 'to exercise all possible diligence with the object of relieving the Public Record Office from the encumbrance of useless matter' and 'to take every precaution against the inclusion in the schedules of documents which can reasonably be considered of legal, historical, genealogical, or antiquarian use or interest, or which give any important information not to be obtained elsewhere'.

The rules further provided that the inspecting officers might start their duties 'by the inspection of the documents of Her Majesty's Superior Courts of Common Law', a task upon which they had, in fact, been engaged since the previous April. They were therefore able to submit to Parliament their first schedule in March 1882 in respect of documents on the Plea Side of the Court of Queen's Bench. Accompanying it was a commendably full explanation of the types of records scheduled for destruction and an account of the processes of the court, which had been prepared by Pike and which was reminiscent of Palgrave's earlier exercise in 1840. The schedule met no obstacle in Parliament, but Yeatman, an out-and-out preservationist, was so provoked by what he saw as the mischievous consequences of the 1877 act that he immediately denounced it in the preface to the reissue of his pamphlet attacking the mismanagement of the office. Sir Thomas Duffus Hardy being dead, Yeatman's main target was now Jessel, but he might just as well have saved himself the expense of printing because he could not count upon any popular support and official policy was still to ignore him.[6b]

Meanwhile, the Treasury had told departments in April 1880 about the serious accumulation of papers in the Public Record Office, explaining the recent changes in the law as regards departmental records.[7a] It emphasised that no destruction was to take place until a system was arranged under the 1877 act, and wanted to receive information from departments about how that might be done. It suggested that papers might be kept within departments for a set term, after which classes earmarked for destruction could be sent for pulping under disposal schedules approved by the Treasury and the master of the rolls. In theory, once the rules signed by the master of the rolls in January 1881 came into effect the way was clear for action because they covered both legal and departmental records. However, they were designed mainly for the courts, and while the Treasury had no objection to their further application to departmental records already in the Public Record Office, it was as strongly opposed to their adoption for records remaining in departments as it had been to Jessel's draft rules of March 1878, which had caused so much fuss. The difficulty, as the Treasury saw it, was that departmental weeding activities would be hampered by such rules because, before a schedule could even be drawn up, the records had to be examined by the inspecting officers. But Jessel had come a long way since 1878 and, having co-operated with Lingen in drafting the Treasury circular of 1880 to departments, had no objection to the principle of 'weeding at home', as the Treasury called it. He readily agreed, therefore, to make additional rules for the records of the Treasury itself in August 1882, and drew up a further set for adoption by departments collectively. In commending them in a circular sent to departments in November 1882, the Treasury made it clear that when a schedule was prepared under such rules it was first to be sent to the master of the rolls for approval, who would pass it to the inspecting officers to settle with the appropriate departmental representative.[7b] By early 1883, 26 heads of departments had subscribed to Jessel's additional rules, some, perhaps, in the knowledge that Treasury authority for any extra accommodation that they might want would not be granted unless they did so. Unlike the Treasury's rules, which had specified that no documents would be reviewed until 25 years old, the general ones laid down no set term before departmental weeding might begin. Seven more departments signed in 1886, and by 1889, when the rules were revised to

---

6b. John Pym Yeatman, *An Exposure of the Mismanagement of the Public Record Office*, 2nd edn (Boston, 1882).

7a. T 1/14745. This box contains the Treasury's files of correspondence with departments. The War Office's problem with its papers was particularly acute and it set up a departmental committee, whose proceedings will also be found in the box.

7b. Printed in *First Report of the Royal Commission on Public Records*, I, pt II, 37.

spell out the role of the inspecting officers more precisely, over twenty departmental schedules had been issued, leaving, if nothing else, some kind of indication of what had been destroyed.[8]

In 1876 the Treasury had caved in, quite uncharacteristically, when the office turned its back on the recommendations of Playfair's Civil Service Inquiry Commission. But it had never reconciled itself to that situation, and persuaded Jessel that when the staffing arrangements under the 1877 act were settled an inquiry should be carried out into the organisation of the office. Jessel was quite happy about that proposal because he believed that the office was in a fair state of efficiency and had nothing to fear from an investigation. Nevertheless, he was becoming worried because in 1878 and 1879 he had lost four of his sixteen clerks, three of them with relatively short service, owing to their dissatisfaction with their pay and prospects. In December 1880 a petition was submitted to him, signed by Haydon on behalf of the senior clerks and by Thompson on behalf of the juniors, arguing that their pay should be brought into line with class I clerks in other government offices. In passing it on to the Treasury, Jessel suggested that it might now be appropriate to have the inquiry which had long been mooted. He also pointed out that the amount of money spent annually on the employment of outside editors had been falling steadily and that three of the calendars of state papers were now being edited by the staff at no extra cost to the Exchequer. A few years earlier Jessel had conducted an inquiry jointly with Lingen into the staffing of the Patent Office for which he was also responsible, and the Treasury now proposed that they should again combine to examine the organisation of the Public Record Office. In doing so, the Treasury thought it advisable to warn Jessel that it did not enter upon the inquiry in any way committed to raising the total cost of expenditure on the service, but it would be glad if some encouragement could be given to staff with special qualifications by a readjustment of salaries and a division of the work to reduce the number of higher-grade posts and to regulate admittance to the various parts of the service by different examinations. Thinking his own direct involvement unnecessary, Jessel decided to leave negotiations to the deputy keeper who, besides providing the Treasury with a full account of the work and staffing of the office, indicated that he was prepared to move in the direction pointed by allowing seven higher-grade posts to remain unfilled as vacancies occurred until the number of assistant keepers had fallen from seven to six, the senior clerks from twelve to ten and the junior clerks from sixteen to twelve, and to make no promotions from class to class until those numbers were reached. On the other hand, he proposed that the number of transcribers should be increased

---

8. Reproduced in *Statutes, Rules and Schedules governing the disposal of Public Records by destruction or otherwise, 1877–1913* (HMSO, London, 1914).

from eight to twelve and that salary scales should be greatly improved as follows:

Secretary	£600 × 25 − £800	(£600 × 25 − £700)
Assistant keepers	£520 × 20 − £700	(£400 × 20 − £600)
Senior clerks	£315 × 15 − £500	(£250 × 15 − £400)
Junior clerks	£150 × 10 − £300, first two years at £100	(£100 × 10 − £200)
Transcribers	£80 × 5 − £200	(24s to 40s a week)

In drawing up his proposals Hardy received much practical assistance from Cartwright and took into account the views of the assistant keepers, particularly Redington, Turner and Gairdner. Kingston also contributed to the review, but, while advocating better pay scales, was reluctant to concede any reduction in office staffing because of the increase in calendaring duties, formerly performed by editors, and the growth in the work undertaken for government departments.[9a] In June 1881 Hardy followed up with a scheme of reorganisation for the workmen, from whom he had received a memorial for increased pay, including a request for a change in their title to attendants. A year earlier the grade's recruiting arrangements had been altered because experience had shown that, although some men could pass the Civil Service Commission examination, they could not perform the heavier work of the repository, such as producing large documents. For that reason a class of workman on trial had been introduced, the members of which were engaged for six months to test their all-round suitability before they were nominated for establishment. Work in the dark and chilly repository was far from popular and not helped by the physical condition of the records, many of which were inadequately packed and labelled. In making proposals for the new organisation of the workmen, the deputy keeper's aim was to strengthen the supervision of repository work in order to improve the state of the records and to facilitate their production and return. His proposals involved a reduction in the number of classes of workmen from four to three and an increase in their maximum pay from 32s to 40s a week. Correspondingly, he proposed that the superintendent's wages should be increased from 48s to 56s a week and those of the two foremen from 36s to 48s. He also wanted to pay an extra 4s a week to four workmen as 'Foremen of the Floors'. Finally, he wished to recruit a responsible man as hall porter at 36s a week to control admittance to the search rooms where there had been complaints about the presence of 'unsavoury and unclean persons' whose purpose was more to seek a refuge than to consult the records.

With such sweeping proposals affecting all grades, it was not surprising that Lingen, who had made it his business to visit the various branches of

9a. PRO 1/140.

the office, should need time to consider them properly. When his report eventually arrived early in 1882, it was an odd commentary upon the way the office was being run that it should be Kingston, rather than Edwards, who wrote:[9b]

> I went to Mr. Hardy a little after 3 o'clock who told me that the Master of the Rolls had received yesterday an answer from the Treasury to his letter on behalf of the Office – The Treasury accepts the Scheme in part and in such a manner as to largely benefit the whole Department. The details will be communicated in a few days – I told Haydon, (with Rodney), Bond, Selby, Bird, Trimmer, Pike, Black, W. D. Hamilton, Reddington [sic], Roberts.

> I asked them not to go to Mr. Hardy for details until he had communicated the new arrangement to the Department himself.

In the normal course of events communications affecting the staff would have formed part of the secretary's responsibilities, but Edwards had been away sick for many months in 1880 and some of his duties had drifted to others, including Kingston. Furthermore, with the arrival of William Hardy, a far less determined deputy keeper than either of his predecessors, something of a policy vacuum had been created at the head of the office which Kingston had been only too ready to fill. That state of things did not escape Lingen's notice and led him to propose that when Edwards's post fell vacant it should not be filled until consideration had been given to splitting its duties between the deputy keeper, the resident assistant keeper and a less highly paid clerk in charge of accounts. Lingen agreed that while Edwards remained he might continue as second-in-command to the deputy keeper, but ruled that the gap between his pay and that of the assistant keepers, which marked his precedence, should be restricted to £50. Apart from that, Lingen broadly endorsed the rest of the office's proposals. The deputy keeper was delighted that he should have done so, although he thought that he had misunderstood the nature of the secretary's duties. But believing that no reply on that score was necessary at that stage he remained silent, an omission which, when it came to the Treasury's notice after his death, earned a strong reproach from its new permanent secretary, Welby, who thought that in fairness to Lingen any misapprehension ought to have been cleared up at the time. However that may be, it was plain that the office had every reason to feel satisfied because on the central issue of the special status which it had always claimed for itself Lingen had conceded its arguments in a key passage:[10a]

9b. PRO 1/131: Kingston's memorandum, 26 January 1882.
10a. PRO 1/47: Lingen to Jessel, 23 January 1882. Treasury papers are in T 1/12885 and T 1/12993.

The duties of the Department in part turn upon the mechanical details of the custody and search of documents, and in part are of a more strictly literary character, under the name of 'calendaring', which consists in collecting the documents deposited of some particular period, and concisely exhibiting the contents of the most material of them in volumes for publication, so as to guide students to the originals, whenever they wish to consult them, and, in the meantime, to furnish them with information of the most authentic kind in a shape which makes it at once available. It need not be said that such work requires sound historical and antiquarian knowledge, and also familiarity with old handwriting and style, and this often in more than one language . . .

. . . Of the seven Assistant Keepers 1, of the twelve senior clerks 3, of the sixteen Junior Clerks 1, and of the eight Transcribers 4, appear to be occupied wholly with duties which are not literary. Several other members of the establishment in each grade appear to be partially occupied in certifying or making Office Copies, which, however, is not ordinary copying, but affords to the Juniors the means of learning to decypher.

At this point, a serious question arises, whether the literary and administrative work have any necessary connexion, and whether they might not advantageously be separated. On looking, however, to the detail of the establishment, it will be seen that this distinction is already, to a large extent, observed; for, of the ninety four persons who compose the establishment (excluding the House Keeper and domestics), forty eight belong to the class of Workmen or attendants, and forty six to the clerical class, including, as shown above, nine who appear to be wholly occupied with administrative duties.

It is, however, evident that, on the whole, the Record Office approaches in its character much more nearly to a Library or Museum than to an ordinary Executive Department of the State. The records are in constant requisition for administrative, legal and literary purposes and the persons who have to direct the storing of them and to make them accessible to the various classes of inquirers, must be sufficiently well educated to be able to gain a considerable acquaintance with the nature of their contents, and this for the discharge of other duties about the Record Office than those which consist in actual calendaring. The analogy of the British Museum has been, and may fairly be, appealed to, provided the comparison be not pushed too far.

Nevertheless, Lingen thought that before the number of transcribers was increased careful consideration should be given to the recruitment of writers for ordinary copying where it could be distinguished from what he described as 'antiquarian work'. He also wondered whether the next clerical vacancy should be filled from the class I examination or whether a special examination should be held as in the case of indexing and abridging clerks in the Patent

Office. He said that the Treasury would be guided in their decision by Jessel's own opinion, and confirmed that since the work of the assistant keepers, senior clerks and junior clerks seemed to be so well defined it had not been thought advisable to introduce the uniform Playfair scale of £100 to £400 with duty pay, which it would not have been difficult to have done.

The effect of the various changes was to improve markedly the pay of the existing staff, although a heavy price was to be exacted in years to come with fewer opportunities for promotion as the number of higher posts fell. Immediately, however, the only person left out of the general largesse was Hardy himself. At the outset of the investigation it had been suggested by Redington and Turner that he should receive £1,200 and a residence.[10b] That proposal was never made officially, but he was subsequently allowed by the Treasury to move to his maximum in recognition of his services under the 1877 act. Another Hardy, the deputy keeper's 22-year-old second son, William John, was also a beneficiary under the same act, having been appointed by Jessel in 1879 as clerk in charge of Chancery masters' documents at a salary of £100 a year. His duties were not onerous and in 1881, when the inspecting officers met formally for the first time, his father instructed him to sit with them as their secretary. Initially, his post was borne on the Chancery vote, but it was later transferred to that of the Record Office and counted against the department's junior clerical complement. Several attempts were made to have him upgraded accordingly, but they foundered because the Civil Service Commission insisted that he should first pass the class I examination, which proved too much for him, although he was well able to cope with the full range of a clerk's duties within the office, including the ability to read the older documents. To supplement his pay he was allowed by the master of the rolls to undertake a certain amount of record agency work, but in 1885 he decided to resign. Perhaps that was just as well because by then the Treasury was displaying a distinctly unfriendly interest in his private activities. Subsequently, he joined the Historical Manuscripts Commission as an inspector, and also became editor of the *Calendar of State Papers, Domestic, William III*, besides earning a notable reputation as an antiquarian. He was succeeded as the clerk in charge of Chancery masters' documents by Cumberland Henry Woodruff, who held that post until its abolition in 1904. The Treasury would have liked to dispose of it when W. J. Hardy left, but yielded in the face of strong resistance from the master of the rolls.

Independently of the office reorganisation, the somewhat specialised duties of Selby and Bird in the search rooms, where they were now known as the superintendents of the Literary and Legal Search Rooms respectively, were recognised in 1882, Selby being awarded an additional £50 a year. His reputation stood high in the antiquarian world and he was soon to play a

---

10b. PRO 1/140: Redington and Turner to W. Hardy, 10 January 1881.

leading part in founding the Pipe Roll Society. Bird was favoured with the grant of accommodation in an unfurnished house, 6 Rolls Yard, conditional upon his acceptance of further responsibilities as assistant resident officer. Neither man was to be envied in the unlit and draughty search rooms. Rain still occasionally came into the Round (Literary) Room through the dome, and there was a new nuisance in the Long (Legal) Room where increased traffic through Fetter Lane was creating a noise problem for searchers. In 1880 a number of searchers, led by Grove and Yeatman, had petitioned Jessel for artificial lighting, but had received short shrift because of his fear of the risk of fire from the extension of gas lighting. Some two years later a small gas 'sunlight' was installed in the dome of the Round Room, but merely to check a down draught after complaints had been received from a number of readers, including a Mr Henry Maxwell Lyte of whom more was soon to be heard. Apart from the environmental drawbacks of the search rooms, Selby and Bird were in the front line of the war still being waged against the office by its old foe, Grove, hardly a month passing without charges being made against them personally or complaints being submitted of official maladministration. Grove's criticisms were all the harder to bear because, according to Selby, he was unable to read the older documents. It was also his practice – and not only his – to try to drum up business for himself by advising parties likely to be interested when he came across material which they might wish to have copied. On one occasion he actually wrote to the Palace about some original letters of the late duke of Kent which he had found.

Jessel had been sitting exclusively in the Court of Appeal in Lincoln's Inn since the autumn of 1881 on ceasing to be attached to the High Court of Justice as a result of the Supreme Court of Judicature Act of that year. The Rolls Court, in which he had sat at first instance, was still being used for legal sittings, but under Judge Chitty of the Chancery Division. In 1882 both Jessel and Chitty moved to the new Law Courts in the Strand. Inevitably, when Jessel left the Rolls Estate his contacts with the office were lessened, and that marked the point at which the authority of the master of the rolls as its head began to decline. Not long after Chitty's departure from the Rolls House the little court there was converted into a Library and the room facing west at the back of the Round Room, where the principal works of reference had been kept, as well as notable documents such as Domesday, became the Government Search Room for students with permits to see documents not generally open to the public. The royal arms and the canopy over the judge's seat remained in the new Library, but the picture of the redoubtable Sir William Grant, a former master of the rolls, which had formerly hung there, was sent to the National Portrait Gallery.

Elsewhere in the Rolls House, Edwards, who was still in poor health, had at last succeeded in getting the Office of Works to provide gas lighting in his first-floor room at the rear of the building. Normally the most patient of men, he had complained that on a dark or foggy day he could barely recognise anyone entering his room. In the office generally, Moloney had left on health grounds in 1879, and Crosby's place as senior clerk had been taken by Thompson. Five new faces in the clerical ranks were Salisbury, Hall, Rodney, Brodie and J. G. Black, two of whom, Hall and Rodney, were soon to make their mark. The early 1880s also saw King's retirement on health grounds and the resignation of the learned barrister, St James Stephen. On the editorial side the death of Dr Russell in 1880 had led to the abandonment of the Irish Calendar for the reign of James I because his co-editor, the staunchly Protestant Prendergast, notwithstanding his first misgivings about their joint venture, was unwilling to continue on his own. Shortly afterwards Sweetman's health broke down and his calendar of early Irish documents was abandoned apart from the fifth volume for the years 1302 to 1307, which was completed by Handcock and published in 1886. In 1883 the death occurred of Rawdon Brown and his editorship of the Venetian Calendar was taken over by Cavendish Bentinck. A new editor, the Reverend W. D. Macray, was breaking fresh ground by searching for British material in the libraries of Denmark and Sweden, where Bliss, taking a break from Rome, had been at work in the State Archives at Stockholm. Baschet continued at Paris until 1885 and Gayangos remained on the strength, disgruntled about his remuneration and making but slow progress with his Spanish Calendar. Without Sir Thomas Duffus Hardy the Rolls Series was in the doldrums and the tale of its laggard editors has been told so often before, and so splendidly by Professor Knowles in his presidential address of 1960 to the Royal Historical Society, that it need not be recounted here apart from noting that it was customary for the Treasury in the early 1880s to deduct a sum of up to £1,000 from the office's annual estimates for non-completion of publications.

The deputy keeper was sitting on a Stationery Office committee concerning the disposal of unsold stocks of record publications, and a Foreign Office committee about the international exchange of state documents. Links were being established between the office and the Canadian Archives which were to expand as the years went by. That development would not have surprised Palgrave, who would have been in his element given the same opportunity. Even before becoming deputy keeper he had no doubt about the significance of the country's records for English-speaking people world-wide, and, commenting on the rolls of the medieval royal court, wrote:[11]

> But the interest of these legal records is not local, or peculiarly appertaining
> unto this our country. They are the property not merely of England, but
> of the English people, wheresoever settled or dispersed. We have here the
> germ and foundation of the laws obtaining in those States, which, rising
> beyond the ocean, seem appointed to preserve the language and institutions

---

11. *Rotuli Curiae Regis* (Record Commission, 1835), I, iv, and quoted by the archivist of the Dominion of Canada in a report on Canadian Archives appended to the *Deputy Keeper's Forty-third Report* for 1881.

of England beneath other skies, when the empire of the parent Commonwealth shall have passed away like a dream.

More mundane, but no less important, was the serious blow to the office Bindery at the beginning of 1882 when Beall, who had come into money, resigned. He was succeeded as senior foreman by Steward. Steward's place as junior foreman was taken by William Bradley, whose services went back to Langdale's day and who was the most senior of the five Bradleys still on the staff. The office could ill afford to lose Beall because three years earlier it had also lost the services of one of its most experienced binders, the deaf and dumb Foster, who had finally retired at the age of 87 after 33 years' service. Simpson, who was also a skilled binder, remained in post, but the priority so far as the deployment of the 50-strong workforce was concerned remained the production of documents, still gravely handicapped by the archaic requisitioning system under which a reader had to enter lengthy details of any record he wanted. Until the root cause of the difficulty was remedied, which lay in the inadequacy of the office's lists and the absence of a uniform and readily understood system of call-numbers, little progress could be expected. The same was true on the binding side, with the difference that the trouble there lay primarily in the labour supply. Some years earlier, in 1873, the Stationery Office had been approached to see if it was possible to borrow some of its men for six months but, not unexpectedly, that had received a very stony response. The reality was that the only limit to the amount of binding and repair work that could be done was the size of the labour resources made available for it. From the formation of the office somewhat meaningless figures of output were included in the *Deputy Keeper's Reports*, but apart from indicating, very roughly, that the number of documents receiving attention annually remained fairly constant, it is difficult to establish a clear pattern since detailed registers of repairs survive only from 1882, and then in rather rudimentary form.[12a] In 1892, however, when application was made to the Treasury for the purchase of three iron presses and a paper-cutting machine it was stated that about ten workmen were constantly employed on repairing and binding records.[12b] The year 1882 saw another break with the office's early days with the death of Sir Henry Cole, soon after completing his *Fifty Years of Public Service* in which he had given much space to the efforts of the campaigners for record reform in the 1830s and the drive to persuade the government to build a new record office. William Hardy had been on the periphery of those

---

12a. In PRO 12.

12b. PRO 2/64, p 332: Lyte to Treasury, 21 March 1892. In July of that year the Treasury approved the expenditure from savings of £83 for binding of 166 volumes of Royalist Composition Papers, the work being executed on the premises by contractors. A foreman and seven repairers were said to be on the directly-employed staff at that time, two of whom sometimes did binding.

events, but when Cole called upon him at the Rolls House in November 1880 he found that his old friend seemed to have forgotten those times and was more interested in describing the latest aberrations of Cole's luckless relative, John Bond.[13] As it happened, Bond did not survive Cole for long, dying at the end of 1883. Bond's increasing mental instability meant that his non-replacement as an assistant keeper, under the arrangements agreed with the Treasury, was not as serious as it might otherwise have been. A more significant loss for the office had occurred in March of that year with the death of Jessel, who had been in poor health for some time. Although he had not concerned himself with the day-to-day administration of the office to the same extent as his predecessors, the 1877 act was very much his creation. Inside the office he enjoyed a good reputation, and, when an address of condolence was sent by the staff to Lady Jessel, the part he had played in the 1882 reorganisation was warmly acknowledged. It also mentioned that he was the first master of the rolls to pay an annual visit from room to room in the department. However, some of those still on the establishment would have recalled the rather similar annual visitations by Langdale to the principals in their branches, which Palgrave found so tiresome. It was an oddity of his position that as a Jew Jessel should have the patronage of the Rolls Chapel, but he had no difficulty in discharging his ecclesiastical responsibilities, and Martin was to tell the story of how Jessel, on first being shown round the office in 1873, asked to see the Chapel, and, admiring it, said: 'As you do us the honour of worshipping a member of our nation here, I shall come in some Sunday morning and see how you do it'.[14]

Jessel's successor as master of the rolls was one of his fellow appeal justices, Sir William Baliol Brett (later Lord Esher), a one-time Conservative MP and former solicitor general. A strong, but not profound, judge, Brett did his best to keep in touch with office activities, but the growing burden of his judicial duties made that difficult although a room was set aside for him in the Rolls House for record business. Shortly after his appointment a small change for the better occurred when the deputy keeper decided to increase the leave allowance of the superintendent (Watson) and of the senior transcriber (Lowson) to 18 days. Additionally the foremen's allowance was increased to 12 days, while the inspectors and foremen of the floors were each granted 10 days and the hall porter 8 days. Missed out from the improvement were the workmen whose allowance stayed at 6 days.

At the end of 1883 the deputy keeper was knighted. It was difficult to see why, because there had been no new initiatives since he had taken over and,

---

13. Cole Diary, 3 November 1880. Record matters were much on Cole's mind at that time. Two months earlier he had presented some volumes to the office Library. One of them, containing papers he had assembled about the proceedings of the 1836 Select Committee, is now in PRO 36/58.

14. *The Jewish Historical Society of England Transactions*, Session 1893–94, 24.

for practical purposes, Kingston was the power behind the throne. It was, therefore, a heavy blow for Sir William when Kingston died suddenly in April 1885. The assistant keeper vacancy thus created was taken by Haydon, who nevertheless continued to calendar the Patent Rolls and took over examining and certification duties in connection with office copies, he being by common consent one of the best palaeographers in the country. Kingston's work in the Government Search Room passed to Sainsbury, who was later to be given an extra £50 but only after a struggle with the Treasury. Bird, soon to change his name by deed-poll to Scargill-Bird, became caretaker, while Cartwright, a man of increasing importance within the office, became additional resident officer and moved into the house in Rolls Yard formerly occupied by the Kingston family. The work at Southampton ended in August 1885 with Sanders's retirement, and the assistant keeper vacancy thus created was supplied by Hunt, who was able enough at record work but lacked managerial skills.

Without Kingston, the deputy keeper, who was himself ailing, was in obvious difficulty and by October 1885 it was plain that his retirement was merely a matter of time. It was a serious reflection upon the office's organisation that it was now proceeding aimlessly. If a sense of direction was to be restored it had to come from outside. The man most likely to do that was, in Esher's opinion, the 37-year-old Henry Maxwell Lyte, a familiar figure in the search rooms. An inspector of the Historical Manuscripts Commission, Lyte was already well known for his *History of Eton College* and he was near to completing the early *History of Oxford University*. Nevertheless, he was taken aback when asked by Hardy whether he would be prepared to accept the deputy keepership if it were offered to him. Quite when he indicated that he was willing is by no means clear, but by early 1886 it was an open secret that he was soon to succeed Hardy, who resigned formally on 27 January 1886.

Much criticism has since been levelled at Sir William Hardy for his alleged mismanagement. Certainly he had neither Palgrave's vision nor his brother's energy, although it is fair to say that the latter, by remaining in post too long, became increasingly reluctant to tackle fundamental defects in policy and practice, so that at the time of his death the department was already running down. Office discipline was also slack and Sir William's tolerance of his son's private activities while on the staff could have done nothing but harm. Yet the transcribers and the workmen owed much to him, and he managed to persuade the Treasury of the hybrid nature of the office's activities, which made it unique in Civil Service terms and demanded special consideration. Referring to Hardy's retirement Lyte wrote in his first report as deputy keeper, the forty-eighth in the series, that 'Your Majesty has lost in him a servant of great experience and erudition, distinguished by his uniform kindness and courtesy towards all with whom he was brought into contact'. However, the rather cruel parody that the office:

In good Sir William's golden days . . .
Did nothing in particular
And did it very well[15]

probably sums up his seven-year stewardship not unfairly.

---

15. 'Sir Henry Churchill Maxwell-Lyte: 1848–1940': *Proceedings of the British Academy*, XXVI, 8.

Chapter XI
Lyte at Rolls House, 1886–1895

*Certain recognised indulgences might be gently discouraged pro communi
salute: e.g. such as are believed to give rise to (surely) needless scandal
at the expense of the Service; namely, prolonged conversation (which
wastes at a moderate computation ⅓ of the time of half the Office),
habitual reading of the newspapers; letter writing; amateur cookery; and
all other attempts to convert the Office into a private club.*

(Hubert Hall to Lyte, [January 1887]: PRO 1/140)

*The present Deputy Keeper, Sir Henry Maxwell Lyte, on his accession
to office in 1886, found that the plain intentions of Parliament had not
been carried into effect, and made a complete change of policy. Since that
time the work of arranging the records and making them accessible has
been steadily pursued with a success universally acknowledged among
scholars, and the benefit conferred on the public has been altogether out
of proportion to the limited means at the disposal of the Master of the
Rolls. During the last twenty-five years the Public Record Office has made
immense progress towards becoming what the national collection of
archives ought to be, and the credit of this achievement is due in a great
measure to the administrative ability and personal work of Sir Henry
Maxwell Lyte.*

(*First Report of the Royal Commission on Public Records*, I, pt I, 2 (1912) (Cd. 6361))

It was not surprising that Lyte's appointment as deputy keeper, reflecting
as it did upon the existing staff's competence, was greeted in the office with
dismay. The assistant keepers, all of whom had joined the record service
before he was born, were, for once, united, even if only in resentment. Yet
none of them had a strong claim, death having removed Kingston, who
might have come into the reckoning. It was plain that more purposeful
direction was urgently needed, although the office, as it neared its half
century, had become invested with its own peculiar mystique, buttressed
by the esteem in which it was held by the learned institutions and the
emerging breed of professional historians. In particular, the work of the
middle and younger generation of record scholars, such as Martin, Pike,
Selby and Hall, was strengthening and extending the foundations for the
study of English medieval history begun by Palgrave and T. D. Hardy.

Realistically, however, it had never been remotely likely that any of them
at that time, whatever their talents, would break through the rigidities of
the grading structure to head the office. As for the assistant keepers, all
were elderly and, Redington excepted, lacking in administrative experience

although sound enough records men. From that standpoint Gairdner and Haydon were probably the most distinguished with Turner not far behind. Gairdner was preoccupied with *Letters and Papers, Henry VIII* while Haydon was superior and temperamental. Although he had been promoted to the assistant keeper grade when Kingston died, it was significant that the latter's duties in the Government Search Room, which had brought him into close contact with departments, were then passed to Sainsbury, one of the senior clerks. Redington, and perhaps one or two of the others, could have managed a going concern, but none was capable of providing the new dynamic required. Furthermore, Esher believed that it would only rarely happen that a serving officer would be chosen as deputy keeper because the duties required 'professional and other peculiar qualifications not ordinarily to be acquired in the public service'. Although Esher had got on well enough with Sir William Hardy, it was plain that he thought social background and connections were as crucial as the statutory 'knowledge of records' required by the 1838 act. In particular, he had in mind the need for the deputy keeper to deal with 'literary persons of high distinction and rank'.[1a] It was not difficult, therefore, to see why his nominee should be Lyte, Eton and Christ Church, a man of letters, with sound work for the Historical Manuscripts Commission behind him. Lyte was also related through his mother to the Churchills as well as being the grandson of Henry Francis Lyte, the famous hymnist whose well known works included 'Abide with me' and 'Praise my soul the King of heaven'. Apart from such considerations, perhaps Lyte's greatest asset was his first-hand experience of the search rooms, which had made him aware of the difficulties there and the need for improvement. He was also quite outside the personal antipathies and jealousies which continued to linger on in the office, rooted in past rivalries and the sectionalism of the former branch organisation.

Nevertheless, to most of the staff Lyte came as a complete stranger, and an unwelcome one at that. Taking office could not have been easy for him, and even before his appointment was officially announced Yeatman tried to embroil him in a dispute in which he was engaged with Selby. But Lyte was not the man to be browbeaten by Yeatman or anyone else although he always treated correspondents, critical or otherwise, with politeness. In his eyes a senior officer should no more read a newspaper at his desk or conduct private business during working hours than a workman behave in an unseemly manner, as illustrated by a special order he issued in July 1886 forbidding them to spit in any part of the building. By that time he was firmly in charge and his authority was underlined, rather than undermined,

---

1a. T 1/8269A/19268/1886. Esher's views were made known to the Treasury by G. B. Rashleigh, his private secretary, in February and March 1886, when the question of Lyte's superannuation was raised and it was agreed that he should be allowed to reckon '7 added years'.

by the fact that he was himself rarely to be seen in the office until midday.[1b] That emphasised the distinction he drew between the leader and the led and reflected his confidence in his ability to mobilise effectively the talent and experience available to him. Of far greater concern was his discovery that much material in the office remained unchecked and unlisted. The glaring inadequacies of the office accommodation also troubled him, as did the state of the Rolls Series, certain works having been grievously neglected by their editors for years.

One such case was F. J. Furnivall's *Chronicles of Robert Manning of Brunne*, with which he had been toying since 1865 when its publication was sanctioned. The Hardys had been no match for his evasions, but when he attempted to deal flippantly with Lyte by referring to the diversions caused by his sculling and social activities he met with a frosty reception and a warning that he was endangering the Civil List pension which Gladstone had awarded him in 1884 for literary services. Despite Furnivall's continued facetiousness, Lyte succeeded in bringing him to heel and his work appeared in 1887 as did that of W. A. Wright, whose *Metrical Chronicle of Robert of Gloucester* had first been authorised in 1868. A delay had also arisen in the completion of the *Cartularium Monasterii de Rameseia* owing to differences between Hart and his fellow editor, the Reverend Ponsonby Lyons. Hart's chequered association with the office ended abruptly with his sudden death in 1888, but his preface to the third and final volume had come in for much criticism from Lyons on the grounds that it contained, among other things, an unjustified attack upon T. D. Hardy and Freeman. On reading it for himself, Lyte agreed that it should be revised, but Lyons remained dilatory, which led to the preface being abandoned and the indexing placed elsewhere. A fire at the printers delayed the work still further and it was not until 1894 that it finally appeared. An even more difficult case was that of Sir George Dasent's *Icelandic Sagas*, which had first been approved for publication in 1859, but which had been brought to a halt by an acrimonious dispute between Dasent and his editorial associate, Gubrand Vigfusson, reader in Icelandic at Oxford. Vigfusson's two volumes of the original texts were brought out in 1887, but Dasent's translations failed to appear until 1894. Despite Dasent's standing as first Civil Service commissioner and as a member of the Historical Manuscripts Commission, Lyte was not to be fobbed off, even threatening to report the matter to the Public Accounts Committee. By degrees Lyte managed to bring all his editors into line, but while he was determined to complete all the works authorised before his appointment, he did not object to Esher's decision in 1886 not to commission any more volumes for the time being or attempt to counter the Treasury's evident wish to discontinue the series. Shortly afterwards, however, two

---

1b. PRO 8/55, pp 154–155: Lyle to Ellis, 15 February 1951. 'The late Sir Henry Lyte seldom made his appearance before 12 noon, a sign of independence, which we, less fortunate, respectfully admired'.

further works were sanctioned, the first in 1888 being Gilbert's *St Thomas the Martyr, Dublin: Register of the Abbey* after the government, sensitive to the charge of ignoring Irish material, had yielded to academic and political pressure and made £300 available for an Irish work, notwithstanding a rebuttal by Lyte of the allegations of neglect made by the critics. The second, in 1889, was *Memoranda de Parliamento*, which stood four square on its merits, being founded on one of the earliest of the ancient rolls of Parliament and edited by F. W. Maitland, whose appointment could hardly be faulted in view of the distinguished place he already occupied among students of the constitutional and legal history of the middle ages. At the behest of the Council Office the Treasury also put in hand the publication of the Privy Council registers from Henry VIII in continuation of the series begun by Nicolas for the Record Commission, the editorship being given to J. R. Dasent.

Lyte made no secret of the fact that he intended to concentrate his publishing resources on improving finding-aids to the records already in the office and to issue them separately rather than in the form of appendixes to the annual reports of the deputy keeper. As he pointed out on more than one occasion, without such elementary lists the office itself did not always know what material existed for full-scale literary calendars. Lyte was also acutely sensitive to the accusations of jobbery levelled by Yeatman and others against the management of the Rolls Series, and he was determined to avoid any undertakings which might bring the office into disrepute. Although one of Grove's friends, the Reverend E. Henville, was threatening to call for a public inquiry into the Record Office in 1889, searchers generally had much to thank Lyte for because in that year, in which he received a CB, he succeeded after a long battle with the Office of Works in getting electric lighting installed in the three search rooms. His plan to produce a series of Lists and Indexes was also designed to help search-room workers, as was his decision to replace Thomas's *Handbook* by a new *Guide*, a work he gave to Scargill-Bird and which appeared in 1891. On the other hand, his success in persuading Esher to issue new rules, which forbade the use of ink by searchers and introduced a fee for the inspection of legal documents of later date than 1760, led to a storm of protest. Esher had, in fact, been hesitant about charging fees, but had eventually yielded to Lyte, who was, in turn, responding to Treasury pressure, while resisting the views of those there, such as Welby, who would have liked him to have gone even further. Lyte was also the driving force behind the supplementary rules, issued a year earlier, limiting the public's right of access to superseded or obsolete lists or indexes by making their production subject to his special order. Similarly, his consent had first to be obtained by searchers before they could see documents under arrangement or of exceptional value or interest, such as the Gunpowder Plot papers. Besides reducing the wear and tear on valuable documents and minimising disruption of the office's editorial work, the purpose of the supplementary rules was to deal with the annoyance caused by Grove, who was constantly seeking material mentioned in earlier

308

Record Commission or deputy keeper's reports but which had since been re-arranged. Had more care been taken at the time to record just what had been done and to key up former references, much trouble might have been avoided. The importance of doing so was not always recognised at the time and could only rarely be put right later. All the supplementary provisions were embodied in the new rules and regulations of April 1887, which were subsequently laid before Parliament in accordance with the 1838 act.

Shortly afterwards Esher received a memorial of protest, bearing 64 signatures, including those of several authors and editors of historical and topographical works and the secretaries of the William Salt Archaeological Society and the London and Middlesex Archaeological Society. The petitioners asked for the rules to be abrogated or modified because they pressed heavily on 'Antiquaries, Historians, Genealogists, Barristers, Solicitors, Clergymen, Record Agents, Copyists and the Public generally'. As regards the use of ink it was argued:[2]

> that no satisfactory substitute for ink exists; that all pencil-writings are
> objectionable in themselves; are subject to early deterioration and
> obliteration; and entail the necessity of immediately re-writing in ink the
> matter obtained; a very severe task when the whole of the six hours of the
> day during which the Record Office is open have been employed in writing
> the matter in pencil.

> Probably your Lordship is aware that soon after Sir Francis Palgrave died,
> Sir Thomas Duffus Hardy, who succeeded him as Deputy Keeper,
> suggested to Lord Romilly the use of ink, which his Lordship permitted and
> which has been in use for more than twenty years.

Some two months later Esher received a counter-memorial, which was certainly no surprise to him because efforts had been made with semi-official blessing to seek support for the new arrangements. Among its 78 signatories were the principal officers of the British Museum and College of Arms, as well as many librarians of university colleges and directors of learned societies and similar institutions. It was said later that many of these worthies had never set foot in the search rooms, but the prohibition upon ink was compelling because of the danger to the records from spillage on the desk as much as from ink spilt directly on them.

The case for the introduction of fees as set out by Lyte in the *Forty-ninth Report of the Deputy Keeper* was that the influx of more modern legal records had led to a change in the character of the work of the Long Room, which in 1885 and 1886 was uncommonly crowded by 'solicitors engaged in ordinary professional business' and by others, whom Palgrave would cer-

---

2. *The Forty-ninth Report of the Deputy Keeper* (1888), vii.

tainly have recognised as 'persons who imagined themselves to be entitled to unclaimed funds in Chancery'. Nevertheless, the inspection fee of 1s for a legal document of later date than 1760 and of 2s 6d for a search relating to a particular suit, action or matter was later modified in favour of barristers consulting records for their own instruction or to use by way of citation or authority before the court. A slight reduction was also made for certain kinds of copies wanted by solicitors, but it was the ban on ink which most upset the regular users, one of whose number, T. C. Noble, felt sufficiently aggrieved to tell the master of the rolls:[3]

> It only remains for me to express regret that it should have fallen to my lot to be compelled to complain of the office about which I have the honour of knowing so much, and the history of which I shall have the privilege some time hence of chronicling. And I should have wished to have been spared the historian's duty of recording that your Lordship ever considered it applicable to the preservation of the Records to make the rule (under the circumstances complained of) which you see has occasioned so much personal loss and inconvenience.

Of Noble's projected history no trace can be found, and it may be doubted whether it would have been particularly informative, since it was highly unlikely that the records of the period would have been made available to him. The best that could be done was probably something on the lines of Ewald's *Our Public Records* of 1873, which was to be followed in 1888, not long after Noble's letter, by *Records and Record Searching*, a guide written by Walter Rye, the Norwich antiquarian.

What cannot be doubted is the debt that the searchers of that time, and even more those that followed, owed to Lyte's clear vision of what was needed for the classification and arrangement of the records. From the outset he took such work under his personal direction and, reviewing his first year in his *Report* for 1886, he explained:[4]

> The accumulation of documents in the General Repository of Records has been so rapid, that, despite all that has been done by the officers of this Department since its establishment in the early part of Your Majesty's reign, there still remains a great number of volumes, bundles, packages, and boxes whose contents have not been ascertained. Very many of them are not enumerated in any list, or officially stamped. An earnest attempt is being made to reduce them to some order, and to render them eventually accessible to the public. Certain miscellaneous documents of the Chancery Division have been dealt with first, as being in special need of arrangement. One hundred

---

3. PRO 2/58, p 487: Noble to Esher, 20 February 1888. Noble was warden of the yeomanry of the Ironmongers' Company for whom he wrote a brief history in 1889.
4. *The Forty-eighth Report of the Deputy Keeper* (1887), xi.

and forty large sacks which had not been examined since they were brought from the Tower of London, and twenty-seven large sacks found above the vaulting of the Rolls Chapel, have been emptied, and their contents have been distributed into classes according to their nature. As a result, large additions will be made to the series of Chancery Proceedings, Ministers' Accounts, Royal Letters, Ancient Deeds, Court Rolls, Petitions, and to other series. Inasmuch, however, as most of these medieval documents require to be flattened, repaired, stamped and numbered, some time must necessarily elapse before they can be made available for consultation in the Search Rooms.

Lyte also understood the need for the office to spread its wings if it was to command greater public respect, and his recognition of the possible benefits to be obtained from a more outgoing posture was to be seen in the reception of a party from the Library Association of the United Kingdom in September 1886 and the encouragement he gave in that year to the celebrations to commemorate the 800th anniversary of Domesday. Lyte was a member of the organising committee which drew up a programme of events held between 25 and 29 October 1886, starting with an exhibition of documents at the Public Record Office. At 3.30 on the first afternoon the assembled visitors, more than three hundred strong, were addressed from the Round Room gallery by Hubert Hall on the official custody of Domesday Book. In August of the following year the office also arranged an Anglo-Jewish Historical Exhibition. Lyte would have liked to have done more by way of displays but was hampered by lack of space. However, it was a measure of his concern that within three months of his appointment he was querying the arrangements for the custody of documents of exceptional importance and in receipt of a report from Scargill-Bird stating that, apart from Domesday, such documents as the Golden Bull of Pope Clement VII confirming the title of 'Fidei Defensor' on Henry VIII, early charters, Gunpowder Plot papers and similar records were kept in a yellow tin box in his private room.[5a] The office's accommodation problems were to be further aggravated in 1886 when space had to be found in two of the houses in Rolls Yard for records left in the Stone Tower, which was wanted in connection with restoration works then going on at Westminster Hall.

So at last, nearly fifty years after the 1838 act, the records were gathered on one site. Movement between the main repository and the houses in Rolls Yard was difficult, however, because there was no throughway for carts and barrows except by Chancery Lane, Fleet Street and Fetter Lane, three sides of the square. Pedestrians could get to the office's main entrance from the west by entering Rolls Yard through an arch in the centre of the range of houses in Chancery Lane, crossing to the Chapel and walking along an

---

5a. PRO 8/32: Scargill-Bird's memorandum, 16 April 1886.

adjacent passage which ran between the houses known as 1–2 Rolls Yard, formerly used as the Rolls Chapel Office. These undistinguished houses had been built on the south of the Chapel in the late eighteenth century for the use of the clerk of the records there and of the secretaries of the master of the rolls. Lyte had no compunction in urging their demolition so that a roadway might be constructed to link the various parts of the office. The existing passageway was also thought to be a possible source of danger because the Fenians were still active and it would have been easy to conceal explosives in it. As early as April 1886 Lyte was pressing the Office of Works for action, but over three years passed before the improvement he wanted was effected. Good communications ranked high in importance with him, and it was at this time that a documents lift was installed at the eastern end of the main building next to the Round Room; a letter-copying press, useful for duplicating circulars, also made its appearance in the Secretariat; and telephone links were established between the Rolls House, the Officers' Chambers and the repository. It was not until the late 1890s, however, that the department was connected to the main government exchange.

Traditionally, the office had set its face against the employment of writers for straightforward copying work, fearing dilution of the clerical grade. But Lyte had no such inhibitions and, besides increasing the number of transcribers from eight to ten, obtained Treasury authority to spend up to £100 a year for the employment of copyists from the Civil Service Commission to work on modern legal documents. As the starting pay of the transcribers was only 30s Lyte thought it right that any workman who might be promoted should be allowed to retain the pay he was receiving, if higher; but he was unable to persuade the Treasury, which insisted that a successful workman had to start at the minimum of the transcriber scale, and even made the extraordinary suggestion that the existing rates of pay seemed to indicate that the workmen were being overpaid, a proposition which was firmly rejected by Lyte. In fact, the matter was somewhat academic because it was unlikely that any of the older men, while skilled enough in their grade, would be suitable for the very different duties required of the transcribers, one of whom, Woolby, Palgrave's former servant, was at that very time undertaking work on some sixteenth- and seventeenth-century feodaries surveys of the Court of Wards which had been left unfinished by Kingston. Scargill-Bird was exercising a general superintendence over that work, but the need for recruits to possess similar talents was reflected in the notice issued by Lyte to the workmen about the examination to fill the two places. The competition was held in the Round Room on a Saturday afternoon in April 1887, candidates being required to show their proficiency:[5b]

(1) By copying parts of English records of the 16th and 17th centuries.

5b. PRO 2/57, p 396: Lyte's Notice to the Workmen concerning the examination for transcribers, 9 March 1887.

(2) By answering, on paper, questions as to the Latin names of the days of the week, the Latin names of the four legal Terms, the Latin names of the numerals from 'primus' to 'centesimus', and the order of succession of the Kings of England from Richard II to William IV.

(3) By reading at sight the names of the English counties as ordinarily contracted and other proper names.

Candidates were also advised that:

Mr Redington, who will conduct the examination will, in apportioning marks for the copies, pay regard to their accuracy and neatness, no less than to the amount transcribed within the allotted time. Some marks will also be given for length of service in the office, so that in the event of equality, or approximate equality, seniors will be preferred to juniors. The salary of the successful candidates will begin at 30/- a week, whatever may have been their previous salary as workmen.

Details of the results have not survived but the two young men appointed, George Pilbeam and Albert Gregory, went on to have highly successful careers on the clerical side of the office. There was little doubt that, although they had left school at an early age, their general intelligence and the further knowledge they had acquired within the department made them at least the equal of second division clerks elsewhere in the Civil Service, and the office valued them. Generally, however, the workmen were having a hard time because their intimate contact with the records meant that Lyte demanded that their characters should be above suspicion. Always an autocrat, Lyte found irksome the protection that established status gave to those whose services he did not regard as fully satisfactory, but for the grade as a whole it was fortunate that such a shield existed.[6a] Watson was still their superintendent, but Steward and W. Bradley had gone, their places as foremen being taken by Watson's son John and J. G. Simpson, the binder. Misdemeanours were generally dealt with by stoppage of pay or downgrading, and in 1888 regulations were issued for the enforcement of discipline, especially as regards unpunctuality, idleness and insubordination. The last was particularly likely to attract censure, and six months later the workmen were advised, through Watson, that promotions were entirely at the discretion of the deputy keeper whose decisions were supreme and that[6b]

6a. There is an undated draft of Lyte's in PRO 1/174, which indicates that he wanted power to dismiss on 'general grounds', after there had been a number of cases of petty pilfering which could not be proved against any individual. He passed it to Cartwright for 'careful consideration', but it seems that he was dissuaded from sending it to the Treasury.

6b. PRO 2/59, pp 510–511: Cartwright to superintendent of workmen, 14 November 1888.

If after this notification any workmen shall set up a claim to any particular place or publicly complain of non-promotion such conduct will be regarded as insubordinate and consequently liable to punishment.

Any man the worse for drink was certainly in for serious trouble, and special regulations were issued in 1889 forbidding gambling by workmen, such as betting, tossing for money, getting up sweepstakes on races, etc. The office staff were also noticing the effect of the new regime because Lyte reverted to Palgrave's old practice of requiring progress reports on editorial work and the completion of monthly attendance sheets. Perhaps a little unfairly, and possibly more to encourage the others, one of the younger clerks, J. G. Black, found his work under particular scrutiny. The opportunity to tighten up had been presented to Lyte at the end of 1886 when an enquiry was received from the Royal Commission on Civil Establishments (Ridley Commission) about office organisation and how greater economy and efficiency might be achieved. Evidently feeling the need to carry the staff with him as far as possible, Lyte invited their comments, but may well have been surprised at the frankness and variety of their replies. On one point, however, they were practically all agreed, namely the desirability of a fixed age of retirement at 65 or after a specified number of years of service. Rodney also argued for some reduction in staffing, submitting a plan to abolish the posts of secretary and clerk in charge of Chancery masters' documents and reduce the number of assistant keepers to four, each of whom would superintend various parts of the office. Selby and Handcock also advocated some form of divisional organisation, but the staff as a whole were opposed to any cuts at the higher levels of the office, and when it leaked out that such proposals had been made all of them, apart from Rodney, Pike and Hunt, signed a memorial calling for the retention of the secretaryship and the six assistant keeper posts.

Besides widespread complaints about the slowness of promotion and the inadequacy of the pay, which Salisbury thought compelled men to take outside work, there was much criticism about what was recognised as the unsatisfactory state of the office. Cartwright went so far as to say that three or four of the existing staff were not capable of performing the duties required, while Rodney emphasised the need for a stricter discipline and deplored the carrying out of other occupations such as 'Editor, Journalist, Preacher, Tutor, Barrister, Ironmonger, Greengrocer, etc.'. Among the measures Rodney advocated was the introduction of a time book, a move supported by Haydon, and a check on the reception of unofficial visitors. Hall made plain his support for any steps taken to combat the leisurely ways into which the office had fallen. He also favoured the engagement of more junior clerks, and more effective use of transcribers or lower division clerks. Martin thought that the introduction of female clerks would be a definite economy, because not only would the lower salary still draw good candidates but the existence of a marriage bar would ensure that few of them would reach their maximum. There was nothing new about his idea, which had already been put into limited effect in the Post Office, and Lyte did not follow it up. More positively, Martin thought that office copies might be authenticated at a lower level, a view supported by a number of others, including Gairdner and Pike. Pike, looking to his own position, also argued for the appointment of a barrister both for the work of the Inspecting Officers' Committee and for the office generally. Redington maintained that the assistant keepers ought to be consulted more than in recent years and quoted the practice in Palgrave's time. Ewald, who was never slow to take to the warpath and might have suspected that some of the criticism was directed at him, attacked the amount of time wasted by idle chatter among the junior clerks, which, he said, had always been excessive, while arguing that too much stress ought not to be laid on 'mere punctuality', an innuendo which may not have been lost upon Lyte. Promotion should, Ewald thought, be by seniority and he believed that the office should argue its case on its merits and not quail at the very mention of the Treasury or threat of attack from the public as 'has been its custom since the days of Sir Francis Palgrave'. Morris favoured job interchangeability, but Selby thought it would be 'a source of danger' to have new hands in the Search Department until they had a knowledge of the various classes of records as it was undesirable to make official ignorance public. Selby also wanted the post of superintendent of the search rooms upgraded. There was, too, some feeling that no more work on chronicles should be given to serving officers because of the temptation for them to undertake it in official hours.

Haydon, himself an editor, shared that view, but his main concern was the need for the clerks to possess the necessary intellectual qualifications, and he praised the existing method of open competition which he thought had brought in a set of juniors to the office more uniformly well prepared than any of the previous systems. He very much favoured a good general education and not a merely commercial one:[7]

Any noodle fresh from 'High School' with his flowing commercial hand and without his aspirates, or with a superabundance of them, with his mean ideas and low views of life can 'tot up', and even do sums in what he is pleased to call his 'mind'. But he would not be quite up to the work – even the easiest work of the PRO. And further, an appeal to the 'open market' for gentlemen who are absolutely precluded from 'striking' is simply 'fudge' – because the market, to begin with, is not 'open' . . .

I myself was appointed under the system of patronage, which occasionally led to the grossest abuses. I knew a case in which the sons of a man who had relieved a powerful nobleman of the burden of one of his mistresses (by

---

7. PRO 1/140: Haydon to Lyte, 3 January 1887. The comments of the other assistant keepers and clerks are also on this file.

marrying her) were appointed to clerkships in a Public Office of which his lordship was the chief and pushed on over all sorts of official heads and shoulders.

Naturally enough, the last thing that Lyte wanted was to let the Ridley Commission know the weaknesses revealed by his enquiry. He concentrated instead upon the growth in the work of the office despite the gradual decrease in the number of higher posts as a result of the 1882 reorganisation, and he took the opportunity to indicate that the changes at that time had not applied to the deputy keeper whose salary had remained the same since 1855 although his duties and responsibilities had greatly increased. He also represented to the commission the case made to him by Sharp about the way the reorganisation had borne heavily upon the junior clerks then in post, placing them at a disadvantage compared with new entrants to the grade. But apart from conveying the staff's views concerning compulsory retirement, his main point was that economy, in the sense of cutting the staff or their salaries, could not be carried further without seriously damaging the working of the service. Although Lyte offered to attend the commission in person if it wished him to do so, and Pike also offered to give evidence, no further communication was received from it. In fact, the benefit of its inquiry so far as the office was concerned was the insight it gave Lyte about the thinking of the staff, and the evident impatience of the younger men for the clearing out of what they regarded as 'dead wood'.

As it happened, within little more than a year three vacancies occurred in the office's senior ranks. Edwards and H. C. Hamilton retired on health and age grounds and Haydon, whose sight had been troubling him for some time, committed suicide. Edwards's place as secretary was taken by Cartwright, and Sainsbury and Martin were promoted to the assistant keeper grade, the latter jumping over W. D. Hamilton and Ewald. Consequentially, Sharp, Handcock and Overend were promoted to be senior clerks. Cartwright's appointment was not unexpected because he had long borne the brunt of the work in the Secretariat owing to Edwards's failing health. Moreover, through his work for the Historical Manuscripts Commission, first as assistant secretary and then as secretary, he was one of the few members of the staff to have had dealings with Lyte in his pre-deputy keeper days. However, not everyone in the office welcomed Cartwright's appointment, and both Pike and Scargill-Bird, who were senior to him, submitted letters of protest to Lyte. Furthermore, there was much argument with the Treasury before his appointment was ultimately confirmed on a lower pay scale of £500 × 20 − £600. In practice, that meant that Cartwright was paid as though he was an assistant keeper because he already received a further £100 for his work for the Historical Manuscripts Commission.

As previously seen, the Treasury felt it had been tricked by Hardy about the future of the secretary's post, but Lyte, while strongly defending his predecessor on that score, did not think that discussion of the rights or wrongs of the past was particularly helpful. He thought it appropriate, however, to point out that he disapproved of Hardy's policy in the management of the Rolls Series and in very many internal affairs, especially in encouraging a premature reduction of the staff, which to his mind had greatly impaired the efficiency of the department. He emphasised that his own burden was particularly heavy because he was running the office practically on his own, rarely seeing Esher, except by appointment, and then, perhaps, only every other month. For all these reasons Lyte argued that it was imperative that he should have someone to assist him on matters of administration and discipline, a view that the Treasury at length grudgingly conceded, although still making its point by its insistence upon a reduction in the secretary's pay. In Lyte's eyes, however, the secretary must have retained his special status in relation to his own because, just as he had been presented to the queen shortly after his appointment, he arranged with the Home Office for the like presentation of Cartwright. The only difference was that whereas Lyte was allowed to wear the Civil Service uniform of the third class at the levee, Cartwright was authorised to wear only that of the fifth class, a distinction nevertheless accorded to no other officer of the department. Ceremonial propriety and official dignity meant much to Lyte, as did official smartness which was symbolised by his decision to have the hall porter decked out in an official uniform. The pay of that post had been cut by over 10s when the original incumbent had died in 1887 and so the additional expense of the clothing was more than covered, although that did not prevent the auditors, in the fashion of the time, querying the outlay, initially £4 17s 3d. Nothing escaped their scrutiny and it would not have been surprising had they asked to see the cat for whom meat was regularly bought from 1875, and probably even earlier, at an annual cost in the region of £1 10s.

It was a paradox of the age that while great schemes of reform could be instituted in areas such as education, agriculture, law, local government and many other spheres, for which funds could be found, the Treasury was still prepared to battle endlessly when it came to minor detail. Since it invariably conducted such exchanges at the highest level, the explanation seems to lie less in the realities of national finance than in the psychological assertion of its control. Frequently, it seemed imperfectly informed on the underlying policy issues, as when Lyte's request in 1888 for an additional clerk prompted it to ask for how long the work of destroying valueless documents under the 1877 act was expected to continue. It was, of course, quite unrealistic to suppose that, once started, the regulation of the disposal process could be abandoned, and Esher had no difficulty in stating that no accurate date could be given, but it would certainly not be less than five or six years. Lyte's real worry was that the act was not working as well as it should because the role of the inspecting officers was insufficiently defined, and consequently there was a tendency for some departments to act almost as a law unto themselves once they had submitted a list of documents they wished to destroy to the master of the rolls. In 1889 an opportunity to remedy that defect came when it became necessary to draw up new rules because it was wished to present a quantity of parchment duplicates of Pipe Office declared accounts, among the records of the Court of Exchequer, to the Bodleian Library instead of destroying them. Commending the new rules to the Treasury, Lyte said that the main change was that it enabled the master of the rolls to direct the transfer of unwanted material 'to the curators, trustees or other governors of a library in Great Britain or Ireland'. But he made no mention of the equally important new clause which provided that departmental officers were to submit destruction schedules to the inspecting officers in the first instance instead of directly to the master of the rolls. As a result of that change Lyte also intended to ensure that specimens of documents which departments wished to destroy should be submitted for inspection. In view of the protracted dispute between Lingen and Jessel some ten years earlier about the role of the inspecting officers, it was surprising that the Treasury failed to appreciate the significance of what was being suggested. As it was not obvious that money and men might be involved and the master of the rolls and the lord chancellor had given their approval to the proposals, the Treasury gave its consent in the belief that 'it is more their affair than ours',[8a] a very proper sentiment but one which made a nonsense of all the wrangling that had taken place before.

Lyte was rapidly learning that, while deliberate subterfuge was self-defeating, too much frankness could be dangerous, and he had not forgotten his mistake in disclosing to the Treasury his predecessor's private notes criticising Lingen's views on the secretary's post. Similarly, when Treasury probings in 1889 seemed to threaten the mission at Rome, to the intense alarm of Bliss who had made his home there, Lyte counselled him to be cautious and was unwilling to forward to the Treasury a memorial Bliss had prepared on the matter. Lyte was anxious to secure the future of the work, but thought it needed to be reorganised so that Bliss's transcripts could be made more accessible to students. He was mindful of the concern of historians about the material and had received weighty representations from Gardiner. His skilful diplomacy succeeded in persuading the Treasury to sanction the continuation of the mission and laid the ground for the later *Calendar of Papal Letters*. To ensure that the new scheme got off to a good start Lyte visited Rome in October 1890 to superintend its introduction. The Treasury approved of his journey there, but, as Welby chaffed him, in a physical not a religious sense. Lyte also took a keen interest in the work at Venice where Cavendish Bentinck had been succeeded by Horatio Brown. At Simancas, too, some change had been introduced, Gayangos's work being supplemented by that of Major Martin Hume. In 1893 Hume, a life-long Protestant, was surprised to find the *Church Intelligencer* and other evangelical papers jubilant about his Spanish Calendar for its exposure of the wickedness of the 'romanists', which, they wrote, was the more remarkable because

---

8a. T 1/8404B/8776/1889: Bergne to Welby, [3] May 1889.

Major Hume, being a Catholic, was 'untainted with the suspicion of prot-estantism'.[8b] Hume took it all quite calmly, confident that religious consider-ations had played no part in his editorial work, but Lyte must have been relieved to know that, inaccurate although the articles were, they hardly foreshadowed another Turnbull case.

Besides his personal oversight of the office's publications, Lyte kept a close watch on departmental finances. Thanks to Cartwright's prudent man-agement he was able to turn prospective surpluses to good account by getting Treasury consent to use them in a variety of ways rather than surrender them to the Exchequer at the end of the financial year. Until the Treasury decided to trim the vote by making a cut for anticipated savings, he was able to engage outside bookbinders for a limited amount of rebinding work in 1892 and again in 1894. Similarly, in 1890 and 1891, he secured two Welsh plea rolls for £7 7s, the Gondomar Manuscripts relating to the Sim-ancas Archives for £105 and 12 volumes of extracts from the De Banco and Coram Rege Rolls for £240. Those volumes were the work of the sometimes troublesome searcher, the self-styled General Plantagenet Harrison, and were offered to the department after his death by his daughter. The same year saw, for the first time, a systematic attempt to provide for reprography by the construction of a temporary structure on the estate for use as a studio by approved applicants wishing to photocopy documents. It was also intended for the use of persons or firms commissioned specially by the office for the execution of photographic work, such as the provision at the request of the Colonial Office of certain photographs of original documents for display by the governor of Jamaica at an exhibition on the island, and the supply of photocopies of the Gascon Rolls for the French government.

Despite his successes Lyte was far from happy about his position as working head of the department, believing himself to be undervalued. Shor-tly after appointment he had been taken aback when he found that Redington was receiving £850 a year against his own £800. That anomaly arose because Redington's pay on the maximum of the assistant keeper scale was sup-plemented by an allowance of £150 for his duties as an inspecting officer. After Lyte's efforts to secure a similar addition for himself failed, he tried to have the deputy keepership removed from membership of the Inspecting Officers' Committee when new rules were drafted in 1889, but found Esher adamantly opposed.[9] At the beginning of 1890 he was actually rebuked by the Treasury for submitting a proposal for an increase in his own pay through Cartwright, a subordinate officer, instead of the master of the rolls. At the end of that year, when he was on his maximum, his pay was increased to £1,100 from 1 January 1891, but only on a personal basis.

8b. PRO 1/155: Hume to Lyte, 16 May 1893.

9. PRO 17/3: Rashleigh to Lyte, 11 April 1889. 'His Lordship is unwilling to entrust such important duties as those of the Inspecting Officers under the Public Record Office Act 1877 to any Committee which does not include the Deputy Keeper of the Records'.

In tackling the office's problems, Lyte looked as much, if not more, to the second tier, the senior clerks, as to the assistant keepers. It was, therefore, a heavy blow for him when Walford Selby, the officer-in-charge of the Search Department, died in 1889. Extra-officially, Selby was the leading light of the Pipe Roll Society, which had been founded in 1883 for the publication of the Great Rolls of the Exchequer. In his *Report* for 1889, Lyte expressed his sense of the very great loss suffered by the department by Selby's death, 'one of the ablest officers who have been connected with it since its establishment'. Selby's decease followed an attack of typhoid fever in November 1888, which, it was suggested, had been caused by the insanitary conditions of the office. Investigations were subsequently carried out into that possibility, but Lyte was fully satisfied that the blame lay elsewhere. The vacancy thus created was filled by the promotion of R. A. Roberts, who had to his credit the *Calendar of Home Office Papers* for 1770 to 1772, and Anthony Story-Maskelyne was brought in from the Diplomatic Service to fill the vacant junior clerkship. Maskelyne was not the first clerk to enter the office by sideways transfer: a year earlier Arthur Hughes and Charles George Crump had been transferred from the Post Office, where there was a promotion blockage, and placed under Turner for training. Crump had originally joined the Indian Civil Service, but had to retire through illness. He may at first have thought that his third department was equally as fated for him as the other two because quite early on he had the misfortune to spill some ink on two court rolls and, besides being officially reprimanded, was told he was lucky not to have the same penalties imposed upon him as on Hohler some twenty years before. Fortunately, he soon recovered from his early mishap and was to play an important part in the office's development, a future deputy keeper, Jenkinson, being among his pupils. A further consequence of Selby's death was that his editorship of *The Red Book of the Exchequer* in the Rolls Series, which had been sanctioned in 1885, was passed to Hubert Hall and John Horace Round, who was rapidly making his name as a medieval historian and as a Domesday scholar in particular. Round, an unrelenting critic of Freeman, was a controversial figure and withdrew from the undertaking in 1890, ostensibly on health grounds, but possibly on account of differences with Hall because he was later engaged by Lyte to make a *Calendar of Documents preserved in France, illustrative of the History of Great Britain and Ireland, 918–1206*, which was published in 1899. At any rate, when Hall's work appeared in 1897 it became the subject of bitter controversy between the two men, causing much discomfort to their mutual friends.

In the department generally, the Ridley Commission's recommendations led to the introduction of attendance books in October 1889 and, after a fierce struggle with the Treasury, a seven-hour day in 1892. Although that change, embodied in new regulations issued by Esher in 1895, enabled the search rooms to remain open for an extra half hour daily until 4.30 p.m., Lyte thought that the longer hours were harmful to those engaged constantly on record work. Hardly consistently, he also argued that they were unfair to the younger clerks because they limited the amount of time that a number of them gave to calendaring and indexing for the Historical Manuscripts Commission out of office hours. For officers earning less than £500 a year but in post before 1890 some compensation was payable for the longer day, varying between £20 and £30 a year for the clerks and from 3s to 3s 6d a week for the transcribers. Nevertheless, the men from the Post Office, Hughes and Crump, were particularly upset about the new arrangements, but it was typical of the time that in registering their protest they expressed the hope 'that our present action will not be thought to be in any way a violation of official propriety'.[10] The workmen were already working more than seven hours daily, but the change for the office staff meant that their times had also to be adjusted. At first it seemed that the twenty or so workmen who worked regularly in the evening at the Post Office as auxiliaries would be badly hit, but that problem was overcome when they were allowed to start and leave earlier each day than their workmates. That arrangement was relatively short-lived because in 1894 changes in Post Office practice meant that evening work there for many of the Record Office workmen came to an end. As will be seen, the workmen grade was reorganised at much the same time, and one of the incidental consequences was a most unpopular decision by Lyte to require the men to work their full conditioned hours of eight a day despite his blithely disregarding official requirements himself.

At the Treasury's insistence, and against Lyte's objections, the introduction of the longer seven-hour day for the office staff was accompanied by a cut of two in the number of clerks. But the change of most consequence for the clerks resulted from the Ridley recommendation about compulsory retirement at 65, which led to the departure during 1891 of four assistant keepers, Redington, Turner, Hunt and Sainsbury, and one senior clerk, W. D. Hamilton. The death of Ewald and the retirement on health grounds of Lawrance meant the loss in the same year of no less than seven officers, and the severance of the last links with the Record Commission with the retirement of Redington, whose long connection with the record service was singled out by Lyte for particular appreciation in the *Fifty-third Report*. Lyte also took the opportunity to praise Turner's great palaeographical skill and Hunt's industry, as well as stating that Sainsbury and Hamilton would continue in the department's employ in editorial capacities, in connection with the *Calendar of State Papers, Colonial* and *Domestic, Charles I* respectively. Lawrance's high promise and work on the *Return of Members of Parliament*, which had finally been completed in 1891, was also mentioned, but, significantly, no special reference was made to Ewald apart from a note of his death. Nevertheless, but for his decease in June 1891 it seemed probable that Ewald would have succeeded Sainsbury in the Government

---

10. PRO 1/57: Crump and Hughes to Lyte, 18 October 1892.

Search Room although, much to his indignation, his junior colleagues, Pike and Scargill-Bird, had been promoted over his head when the first two assistant keeper vacancies arose in March of that year. Subsequently, Trimmer and Thompson were advanced to the assistant keeper grade and Isaacson, Morris, Atkinson, Salisbury, Brodie and Hall became senior clerks. During 1892 Isaacson and Morris were also appointed to the Inspecting Officers' Committee with a special allowance of £25 a year each, an addition which the Treasury thought barely justified and would have liked to end. Of the assistant keepers in post when Lyte took office in 1886 only Gairdner now remained, but he, too, retired in 1893 being replaced by Sharp, who was, in turn, succeeded in the senior clerical grade by Rodney. In his *Report* for that year Lyte made special mention of Gairdner's important work upon documents of the reign of Henry VIII, which, with Brodie's assistance, he was continuing to edit although no longer on the permanent staff. The effect of the various changes could not have been other than profound, and there was a further refinement in that the occasional employment of copyists from the Civil Service Commission had been superseded by the introduction in 1891 of two boy clerks, the forerunners of the clerical officers of the twentieth century. The Treasury would also have liked to introduce less highly paid 'abstractors' or 'assistants' at £80 to £150 a year as vacancies occurred in the transcriber grade, but Lyte managed to fend off such an alteration when the death occurred in 1893 of the one-time rebel, G. W. Thompson, and when Woolby retired shortly afterwards. Two of the workmen, Theodore Craib and Benjamin Poulter, were promoted in their place and were later to be regraded as supplementary clerks, the approximate equivalent of latter-day executive officers.

In addition to the three clerks transferred from other departments between 1888 and 1890 six newcomers later entered the office through the examination process. Four of them, Fowler, Lyle, Giuseppi and Waine, sat a special open competition in 1891 and two, Pedder and Drake, were assigned from the class I examination in 1892. Within less than a year of their commencement, however, the three last named obtained transfers to other departments, a practice that was subsequently to be tightly regulated. Lyte wanted to recruit men of high intellectual attainment who could be trained for record work after entry, and was convinced that the reason for the wastage was the attraction of the better pay scales on offer to class I men in other offices. The Treasury thought that the difficulty lay in recruitment through the class I competition in which candidates could choose the papers they wished to sit from a wide range of subjects; and that although potential Record Office clerks were further tested in Latin and French, a quite different method of recruitment should be attempted based upon an examination confined to subjects of direct relevance to Record Office work in order to attract candidates of an archival bent. It was also beginning to lose patience with Lyte with whom its relations were unprecedentedly bad as a result of the difficulties with him concerning his salary and the introduction of longer working hours. Towards the end of 1892, Bergne, a somewhat pugnacious principal clerk at the Treasury, thought the time ripe to launch a counter attack, commenting sharply upon a request from Lyte for an improvement in the salary scales of Record Office clerks:[11]

> As Mr. Maxwell Lyte neither gives, [n]or appears to wish to give, us any help, he cannot much complain if we do not take more trouble to help him.

> As however, I think we are of one mind as to removing [the] Record Office from Scheme I examination, the first step towards that would be to remove it from Schedule A of the O[rder] in Council of 4th June 1870.

> This we can do ourselves as all appointments in the Record Office are made by the Treasury under Sect. 6 of the Act I & 2 Vict c.94. (The Master of the Rolls may remove persons so appointed, but must report his reasons for so doing to the Treasury).

> A simple Notice in the Gazette is all that is necessary, &, as soon as the vacancies now announced for competition have been filled, I think it had better be inserted. This done we could, under the same Act & section, & after communicating with the C.S.C. prescribe any Scheme of examination we choose.

> It is greatly to be regretted that Mr. Lyte cannot try to meet our wishes a little, but I think we have had nearly enough of his obstinacy & *non-possumus*.

> We were obliged to *order* the adoption of the 7 hours because further discussion was useless; & I see that the time has about come to take this question of examination & admission into the Office into our own hands, as we are empowered by statute to do & put Mr. Lyte on one side.

> It is not impossible that he might resign; if he did it would greatly simplify the task of getting the Record Office in order.

With Welby's consent a letter to that intent went off to the master of the rolls in January 1893, but, evidently not wishing to be caught in the crossfire, Esher suggested a reference of the matter to the Consultative Committee established in 1890 expressly to deal with disputes between the Treasury and departments arising from the implementation of the Ridley recommendations. Lyte had previously urged such a reference, but, commenting upon Esher's letter, Bergne somewhat disingenuously, wrote:[12a]

---

11. T 1/8705B/19313/1892: Bergne to Mowatt, 21 December 1892. In the following year Mowatt was knighted and succeeded Welby as permanent secretary.

12a. T 1/8789C/18580/1893: Bergne to Mowatt and Welby, 2 February 1893.

The Master of the Rolls has, I infer, taken this question of the Record Office Establishment out of the hands of Mr. Maxwell Lyte: at any rate this is a reasonable & businesslike Letter which we may well meet as far as possible.

Lord Esher admits that simply to level up Salaries would be a 'crude remedy'; he disclaims any wish to increase the cost of the Dept; & does not reject the proposal to 'Lower the Standard of Examination', though he does not like it (as to this I must observe that removal from Schedule A need not have this effect necessarily).

But he asks for a report by the Consultative Committee before we proceed to gazette out of Sch A (as we have declared our intention of doing); so under present circs I can't say that this is unreasonable.

But, as in any case the Consultative Committee is not a body likely to work very fast, I would stipulate that if we agree to the reference, we shall not be asked to permit any more transfers from the Record Office until the decision of the Committee is arrived at.

There are 2 new clerks just about to be appointed to the Record Office & I would not allow them to go elsewhere, at least for some time.

Soon after Bergne's letter, A. E. Stamp, a future deputy keeper, and Charles Johnson joined the office as junior clerks through the normal class I examination. A little later a further vacancy arose and was filled by the transfer at his own request of Horace Headlam, a class I clerk, from the Legacy Duty Office of the Inland Revenue. All three men found record work congenial and there was never any danger of their departure. Meanwhile, the struggle between Lyte and the Treasury remained unresolved and, so far as outsiders were concerned, unseen, since the deputy keeper in his *Report* for 1892 merely stated:

The attention of the Lords Commissioners of Your Majesty's Treasury has been called to the inconvenience arising from such transfers [i.e. of clerks to other departments] and to other matters connected with the organisation of this Department.

One of those other matters crying out for settlement was the problem of the office's workmen. As far back as February 1890 they had submitted a petition to be put on a par with attendants in the British Museum and in November of that year they sent in a further memorial seeking reconsideration of their title and pay. They did not belong to a trade union and it was indicative of the primitive state of the industrial scene that the membership of a committee which they had formed to represent them was adjusted in

1894, possibly after official pressure.[12b] Superintendent Watson was also far from content, because the dramatic improvement of the pay of the transcribers in 1882 meant that had he not been promoted from that grade in 1871 he would, as it turned out, eventually have been some £50 a year better off than he was as head of the workforce. His humour was not helped when he suffered serious injuries in 1893 on falling through the gap after the careless removal of an iron grating from the upper floor of one of the strong rooms. He was not the first, or the last, member of the staff to be injured in that way, but in advance of the first Workmen's Compensation Act of 1897 the Treasury refused to make any payment to him except for medical expenses. However, in 1894 the continued pressure for a review of his pay and that of the workmen generally resulted in the reference of the entire matter by the Treasury to Sir Charles Fremantle, deputy master of the Mint, and Henry (later Sir Henry) Primrose, secretary of the Office of Works, for investigation and report. The department itself warmly welcomed the review because it had come to realise that many of its difficulties arose from the lumping together of the men in a single grade. As early as 1887, when Lyte invited comments upon ways of improving efficiency, Rodney had urged the division of the grade into those carrying out skilled and responsible work, and those acting as messengers or engaged in portering. Fremantle and Primrose were not slow to take the same point, and in a key passage in their report to the Treasury in May 1894[13] observed that a man with no particular aptitude for better class work might continue as a cleaner or coal porter throughout his career, yet still rise to the class I maximum of the workmen's scale. They noted that Lyte had engaged some men on the understanding that they had no claim to rise beyond the third class, and they were concerned that the existing method of recruitment provided no guarantee of securing men for the higher ranges of the workmen's duties, commenting:

> It is indeed remarkable that with a scale of pay so little tempting as compared with the wages that can now be earned by artisans, with no special facilities for selecting capable men, and with a literary test of candidates of a most elementary kind, the present system should have resulted in providing the Record Department with a subordinate staff so capable, as the one it now has, of performing the various, and in many cases highly skilled, duties that devolve upon the Workmen.

At that time 16 workmen were engaged in the production and replacement

---

12b. PRO 1/174: Watson to Lyte, 7 March 1894. 'I may here mention that the men having some doubts as to their Committee being competent in all respects to appear before the Committee of Inquiry have elected another one, which now consists of R. Robins, J. Pratt, H. Weatherley, A. Byerley and G. Scoins'.

13. T 1/8393A/18204/1894: Fremantle's and Primrose's Report to the Treasury, 2 May 1894.

of records, 8 on repair and binding work, 8 on messengerial and doorkeeping duties, 5 as labourers and 11 on stamping, arranging and clerical duties, such as the extraction of information from official records for government departments. Instead of a workman grade of three classes, undifferentiated save as regards pay, Fremantle and Primrose proposed that there should be 36 established attendants and repairers, split into two classes, who would be recruited through the Civil Service Commission as hitherto. The skilled character of the repairers' work was self evident, but the claim of the attendants, while less obvious, lay in their position of trust as virtual custodians of the records and in their knowledge of the location and contents of the various record classes. Additionally, a complement was recommended of 14 messengers, doorkeepers and porters, all of whom would be unestablished, although recruited as far as possible from pensioners of the Army, Navy or Police Force. The Victorian liking for display was shown by the suggestion that the search-room attendants, messengers and doorkeepers should all be supplied with a simple but distinctive uniform, and protective clothing should be issued to those men producing records. At the supervisory level it was proposed to replace the senior and junior foreman and the foremen and inspectors of floors by the appointment of three foremen and three sub-foremen. It was also recommended that work of a clerical nature should be performed in future by boy clerks. In classifying the staff under the new arrangements the office's aim was to improve the position of as many men as possible. Certain posts had deliberately been left unfilled on becoming vacant in order to give greater room for manoeuvre, but despite the office's efforts some men received no benefit. Watson was particularly upset as his pay was left unchanged, although in recognition of his special services he was awarded a gratuity of £100. Whatever the merits of the payment to him there was no doubt that he was a versatile man, and his skill as a repairer was shown by the fact that in October 1892 the office had sent him to York to give advice to the corporation when its records were damaged by floods. He was also competent on the editorial side and had to his credit work for the Middlesex County Record Society.

Under the Fremantle/Primrose recommendations there was an immediate increase of 2s a week in the pay of the men regraded as attendants and repairers. The pay scale of those in the first class was also extended at the maximum by 5s to 45s, and of those in the second class by 3s to 37s. On the other hand, the maximum of the new unestablished class of messengers and porters was set at 24s, which was 2s a week less than that of the former third class. The estimates for 1895–1896 also included the sum of £75 for the supply of uniforms and protective clothing. The good effect of the various changes was, however, partly offset when, as previously mentioned, Lyte decided to require the men to work their full conditioned hours of eight a day. The reason was that in order to provide properly for the longer opening hours of the search rooms until 4.30 p.m. more time was needed at each end of the day to keep business under control. As Lyte knew that the Treasury would not sanction an increase in staff, he ruled that all the men had to attend from 9.15 a.m. to 5.15 p.m., although half of them were still allowed to leave at two o'clock on Saturdays and the remaining half at four. As some compensation Lyte managed to secure from the Treasury an extra 1s a week for those who had not received any benefit from the reorganisation. Despite that small improvement the rumblings of discontent continued and were brought to an end officially only when Lyte declined to receive any further memorials from the grade on the matter and issued printed regulations governing its employment in April 1895.[14a]

Industrial troubles provided an unwelcome diversion for Lyte from the more constructive aspects of office life. His general aim had always been to further the progress of historical science, and in his presidential address to the Historical Section of the Royal Archaeological Society in 1893 he had advocated the establishment of an institution such as the French Ecole des Chartes.[14b] It was natural, therefore, that, when Sir George Duckett, the archaeologist, wrote to Lord Salisbury at the Foreign Office in January 1894 to urge the attachment to the Public Record Office of a school of palaeography, Lyte gave a warm welcome to his proposal. However, the Treasury made it quite plain that it was not prepared to entertain any such idea, Welby telling Sir John Hibbert, the financial secretary, that Lyte was difficult enough to deal with and that he did not think much of a case had been made out 'for another step by government in undertaking work which is not government work'.[14c] At much the same time, Lyte's long-running feud with the Treasury about the recruitment and pay of the office's clerks was coming to a head. The independent members of the Consultative Committee to which the matter had been referred were Sir Robert Meade, permanent under-secretary of the Colonial Office, William J. Courthope of the Civil Service Commission and Alfred (later Viscount) Milner, chairman of the Board of Inland Revenue. Welby was also on the committee, as was Lyte, who had the satisfaction of carrying the day on the main issue, the committee agreeing with him in its report in April 1894 that the Record Office's clerks should continue to be recruited from the class I competition. As regards salaries the committee recommended that the distinction between senior and junior clerks should be abolished and that they should be placed on a common scale of £150 × 15 − £300, rising, after an interval of five years and subject to a certificate of efficiency from the deputy keeper, by £20 annually to £500. The committee also recommended that on entry to the department clerks should be told that transfers elsewhere would be allowed only 'when they are distinctly for the advantage of the public service'. It saw no need for the post of secretary, maintaining that all important questions of

---

14a. PRO 1/174: Regulations for the subordinate establishment of Attendants and Repairers, Messengers and Doorkeepers, and Porters, 9 April 1895. For Treasury papers concerning the men's hours see T 1/8917A/3229/1895.

14b. *The Archaeological Journal*, L (1893), 353–363.

14c. T 1/8810/4548/1894: Welby to Hibbert, 27 March 1894.

discipline should be settled by the deputy keeper alone, minor questions being left to the officers in charge of the several departments. But Lyte, who had previously asked for the secretary's salary to be raised to £700, refused to give ground and insisted upon submitting a minority report, which gave the Treasury, otherwise rebuffed, the opportunity to save some face by commending to Esher's attention the observations of 'four officers of the highest rank and experience in the Civil Service' and expressing[14d]

> much regret that the Deputy Keeper of the Records has not been able to concur in the suggestions, and they must request that upon the occurrence of a vacancy in the Office of Secretary, no steps may be taken to fill it until this Board has had an opportunity of considering the future arrangements. In the consideration of this question My Lords will of course give due weight to the views which Mr Maxwell Lyte has placed on record in his separate addition to the Report.

While Lyte failed to get his way on the secretaryship, his victory on the more important issue of the clerks was warmly welcomed by them, all 20 subscribing to a letter thanking him for his efforts on their behalf. There was no doubt that the office was operating more efficiently than for many years, a fact of which the Treasury, on the evidence of Bergne's comments about Lyte, seemed perversely unaware. Lyte's firmness had clearly ruffled a few Treasury feathers, but his achievement in bringing the publications programme under better control ought not to have been overlooked by his financial controllers, any more than his success in coping with an increased workload with fewer staff. Every year saw some growth in the office's holdings, and there had been a considerable increase in the work done for government departments, particularly the War Office and the Admiralty. By the standards of later generations the number of searchers was small, but the twenty to thirty persons frequenting the search rooms daily in the 1870s had grown by the 1890s to forty to fifty. Similarly, the 23,000 applications for documents in 1872 had risen by 1892 to 43,000. The gradual increase in record awareness was also reflected in the foundation in 1888 of the British Record Society with the purpose of preparing and printing calendars and indexes to wills, Chancery proceedings, inquisitions post mortem and similar documents. Royal interest was shown by an official visit to the office by the prince of Wales in March 1893. The setting up of county and county borough councils under the Local Government Act 1888 also created the possibility of a co-ordinated approach to the problem of housing local records and making them available. But a bill drawn up by W. P. W. Phillimore in 1889 'For the Preservation of Public and Private Records', which provided for the establishment of a central record board, under the

---

14d. T 1/8806B/3656/1894: Treasury minute of 12 May 1894.

master of the rolls, to administer what would have been a national archives service, through government and local authority agencies, received no encouragement from Lyte while Esher was entirely against it.[15a] Undeterred, Phillimore drew up two draft bills for the establishment of local record offices under the general superintendence of the Local Government Board in 1891 and in 1899, but to no avail.[15b]

Lyte's reluctance to become directly involved with the fate of local records was understandable because he was already hard pushed to fulfil his statutory obligations under the 1838 act. Moreover, whatever the exact status of the departmental records, the reality was that departments were constantly making demands on the Public Record Office to make searches for information from deposited material and to accommodate further accessions. The Departmental or Government Search Room where this work was carried out also catered for private persons with permits to see records not generally open to the public. The number of such searchers at any one time could rarely have exceeded three or four, but during the 1890s productions for them still amounted to some 7,000 to 10,000 annually, mainly of records of the Colonial Office, Foreign Office and Admiralty. When Sainsbury retired in 1891 as head of that room, his place was taken by Hubert Hall, who rapidly became known for his knowledge of the records of departments. Stamp, who started his official career with Hall, recalled in a paper read to the Royal Historical Society in 1928 that[16a]

> In 1893 there was not a typed list or a typewriter in the Office. Indeed, I think I am not speaking a word more than the truth in saying that the only way for a stranger to find out anything in the records of either of these departments [War Office and Admiralty] was to explain what he wanted and trust to the staff to produce it.

> For officers of the department there was a back room in which sat an ancient attendant surrounded by MS. War Office lists in all stages of decay and illegibility. Tradition said that he knew his way among them, but few dared to approach him, and those who did were as a rule only rewarded with a supercilious stare over ancient *pince-nez* and the answer that the question propounded was a difficult one and required mature consideration. So far as my own experience went, it seldom received it.

There was no common access date for departmental records, and in 1886,

---

15a. J 113/8: Rashleigh to B. G. Lake, 14 January 1890. There is a draft of the bill between pages 61–64 of this volume. For Public Record Office correspondence see PRO 2/61, pp 77–78, 193–195.

15b. For copies of the bills see PRO 1/720.

16a. A. E. Stamp, 'The Public Record Office and the Historical Student – A Retrospect', *Transactions of the Royal Historical Society*, Fourth Series, XI (1928), 21.

when Lyte became deputy keeper, the dates to which documents could be seen without permit were:

Admiralty	31.12.1799
Audit Office	25.10.1760
Board of Trade	29.1.1820
Colonial Office	25.10.1760
Foreign Office	25.10.1760
Home Office	31.12.1772
Treasury	31.12.1799
War Office	20.6.1837

At the best, therefore, a searcher might see a nearly fifty-year-old document, but in most cases unrestricted access was given only to documents much older than that. In November 1888 the subject of greater public access was touched upon in Parliament in the Committee on Supply with no evident result.[16b] However, in 1891 Lord Salisbury decided that Foreign Office records ought to be made more readily available, and agreed to open them to the public to 1830 with a permit and to 1802 generally, apart from French correspondence which remained subject to a permit owing to the continuing dispute with France about the Newfoundland fisheries. Similar rules were later adopted by the Colonial Office, but, some difficulties having arisen on such papers as those concerning the Wyoming massacre, it was decided in June 1892 to modify the concession by requiring that searchers wishing to see Foreign or Colonial Office records of later date than 1760 had first to state, in writing, the object of their search. Foreigners were also required to apply through their embassy. At about the same time the Treasury was discussing with Lyte the question of fees when it seemed that, under the cover of a permit, a searcher was exploiting its records for his own financial purposes. Under Esher's revised rules of 1887 searches in legal records from 1760 were already subject to fees, and so the Treasury decided that an inspection fee of 1s should be levied for each document produced from its records of later date than 1759, and a charge of 3s 6d a day for a general search relating to a specified person or matter. It also mooted the possibility of fees being charged similarly by other departments, but did not follow it through when it became clear that Lyte thought that such a move would create more trouble than it was worth. The yield at the time from inspection fees was, in any case, no more than £250 or thereabouts a year, but Lyte's main objection was that, unlike Treasury searches, most of the searches in the records of other departments were of a literary kind. Indeed, even after

---

16b. *Hansard*, third series, CCCXXX, 579–591.

fees were introduced for searches among the Treasury's closed records it was not unusual for them to be waived when the object was for a historical purpose. In that sense, the Treasury may be said to have moved on since Welby's day because he had never been convinced of the case for free access to the records at all and in 1889 wrote:

> I cannot see what justification there is for expensive staff being kept for the benefit of private individuals, often foreigners, who amuse themselves or seek their bread in literary pursuits. The government does not give outdoor relief on this principle to bankers or stockbrokers or other trades, or even to the working classes, and the Record Office itself has imposed fees on lawyers seeking information in pursuit of their trade. A moderate fee is fair. It is not necessary to raise the question just now, but it would properly be raised if opportunity offered, such as increased charge of establishment.

But he evidently decided not to press the point when Lyte told him bluntly:[16c]

> I am not going to write a dissertation on the duties of an enlightened government towards literature and art, or as to the consequent conditions on which libraries, archives, museums and picture galleries should be open to the public. But if at any future time a proposal should be made to levy a tax on the researches conducted here by such men as the Bishop of Oxford, Gardiner and Lecky, we shall probably urge the analogy of the British Museum, where a staff far more expensive than ours is maintained for the benefit of private individuals and where a large sum is also spent yearly on the purchase of books and manuscripts for them.

Three years later, when Lyte was in correspondence with Welby's eventual successor, Mowatt, about charging fees for the Treasury's own records, the legislative background came under review and Lyte candidly admitted that it was not at all easy to give a 'perfectly consistent and accurate explanation' of the Public Record Office Acts. Nevertheless, he said, the order in council of 1852 had been interpreted to mean that records brought under the 'charge and superintendence' of the master of the rolls might then be taken into his custody by a countersigned warrant if so desired. The records of the Palatinate of Lancaster had, in fact, been brought into the office in that manner in 1873, but Lyte pointed out:[17a]

> It might perhaps be argued that the twentieth section of the [1838] Act defining the word 'Records' to mean all documents, etc. 'of a public nature

---

16c. PRO 1/170: Welby to Lyte, 29 April 1889 and Lyte to Welby, 6 May 1889.
17a. T 1/8674A/14812/1892: Lyte to the secretary to the Treasury, 14 April 1892. Printed in the *First Report of the Royal Commission on Public Records*, I, pt II, 118.

belonging to Her Majesty' limits the jurisdiction of the Master of the Rolls to the records which should be open to public inspection. Such an argument, however, would give to the word 'public' a different meaning to that which it bears in other statutes, and it appears more probable that the Master of the Rolls has the 'charge and superintendence' of all documents, etc. belonging to Her Majesty which relate to public affairs. It should, moreover, be observed that the Public Record Office Act 1877 (40 & 41 Vict. c. 55) seems clearly to recognise some jurisdiction on his part not only over documents actually removed to the Public Record Office from other Departments without a countersigned warrant, but also over documents elsewhere which can be removed thereto.

Whatever, however, may be the statutory powers of the Master of the Rolls with regard to documents which have not been brought into his 'custody' by the issue of a countersigned warrant, the uniform practice of this Office has been to regard documents transferred to it without such a warrant, as belonging still to the Department by which the transfer has been made. They are received here without any more formality than an interchange of the necessary official letters, and the head of the Department depositing them lays down, subject only to the normal arrangements and the convenience of this Office, the conditions under which they may be inspected. They may be removed hence either singly or otherwise by order of the same authority. Within the last few weeks, the Lord President of the Council has caused the records of his Department, which have been here for many years, to be re-transferred to Whitehall in consequence of the inability of the reduced staff of this Office to arrange them and prepare lists of them.

Departments could recall their own records at any time, but could not obtain those of others without special permission, as the War Office's Intelligence Division discovered in 1895 when it tried to requisition a Colonial Office map. There was, however, no provision for the regular transfer to the Public Record Office of departmental documents at one time advocated by Palgrave. Even when a department wished to deposit material, acceptance was dependent partly upon the availability of space and partly upon some assurance that the office would not be unduly burdened with a large increase in the number of searches for official purposes. While the intention of the 1877 act was to regulate the inflow of documents it also provided some safeguard against indiscriminate disposal. In 1891 the inspecting officers' intervention saved many of the muster rolls and crew lists of merchant seamen which might otherwise have been destroyed by the General Register and Record Office of Shipping and Seamen. In the same year they joined with the registrar general in resisting the suggestion of the Local Government Board and the Office of Works that the census returns of 1851 and 1861, then in the Clock Tower of the Houses of Parliament, need not be preserved. On the other hand, lack of space was partly responsible for sealing the fate of the marked-up electoral poll books, 1843 to 1870, from the Lord

Chancellor's Office. Worse still, owing to an administrative oversight the specimens which it was intended to select to illustrate the method of voting before the introduction of the ballot were not preserved. The disposal of port books under a schedule of 1896 was also the subject of much critical comment at a later date.

The question of public access to the departmental material sent to the office for permanent preservation placed a heavy responsibility upon the Government Search Room officers, and on more than one occasion they found themselves in an embarrassing position when operating the varying regulations. In 1889, for example, the Home Office raised the question of certain papers which had been irregularly published in W. J. Fitzpatrick's *Correspondence of Daniel O'Connell*, evidently from closed material in the Public Record Office.[17b] The Home Office was particularly sensitive about such matters and for many years had embargoed volume IV of the calendar prepared by R. A. Roberts of its papers for the reign of George III for the years 1773 to 1775. In a confidential letter to the master of the rolls in 1885 Sir William Harcourt, the Liberal home secretary, pronounced himself as 'a good Whig of the Rockingham period' with no desire 'to foul the nest of my predecessors even a hundred years ago'. Four years later he wrote again to Esher confidentially, saying:[18]

You will see that serious doubts were expressed by Sir T. Hardy in Nov. 74 as to the publication of the Irish Union papers, and that Cross, after consultation with Ld. Beaconsfield, declined to allow their publication, and they were accordingly returned to the H.O. It appears by the minute of Cross of 1879 that all the Irish papers were treated as in the custody of the Master of the Rolls to be kept by him as Baillee for the Home Office.

The same principles of Public Policy in my opinion apply to the secret history of the American War and to the Irish papers at the end of the last century. As my consent is asked to the publication of these papers I must withhold it. There is no distinction between the Calendar and full publication as any person may have access to the originals of the documents when calendared.

Harcourt took the line that there were some matters that ought never to be revealed, but there was no widespread public demand for greater access and most searchers wishing to see closed material could obtain a permit to do so, although their notes and any copies they made from the records were subject to censorship. There were a few historians, Oscar Browning for one, who urged the official publication of eighteenth- and early nineteenth-century material, but the main interest remained in the middle ages and in

---

17b. PRO 1/54: E. Leigh Pemberton to Cartwright, 23 January 1889. Home Office papers are in HO 45/9595/94519.
18. PRO 1/163: Harcourt to Esher, 25 January 1885 and 4 March 1889.

the records of the sixteenth and seventeenth centuries, particularly those concerning the Reformation and the fall of the Stuarts. Apart from Pike's *Year Books, Edward III*, Hall's *Red Book of the Exchequer* and a few volumes authorised many years earlier, the Rolls Series was gradually being run down. By Treasury decision the *Recueil des Croniques et Anchiennes Istories ... par Jehan de Waurin* and Martin's continuation of Hardy's *Descriptive Catalogue of Materials relating to the Early History of Great Britain and Ireland* had been abandoned.[19] The editorial vote had sunk from £5,957 in 1875–1876 to £3,550 in 1895–1896, but that was partly compensated by Lyte's policy of employing his own staff as far as possible to calendar and list documents of the medieval period with particular emphasis upon the Chancery enrolments. Pride of place was given to a new series, the *Calendar of Patent Rolls*, under Lyte's personal supervision, in which Handcock, Black, Morris and Isaacson were all involved. Lyte was also closely associated with the *Descriptive Catalogue of Ancient Deeds*, much of the work for which devolved upon Handcock, Salisbury, Woodruff and Thompson. W. H. Stevenson, the Oxford historian, was, however, brought in to edit the *Calendar of Close Rolls* and Round was commissioned to calendar early documents in France concerning Great Britain and Ireland founded upon a series of transcripts made for the former Record Commission. The aim of the calendars remained to give sufficiently full abstracts to obviate the need to consult the originals for most purposes. To complement them a new series of Lists and Indexes, designed mainly for the use of those who wished to work in the search rooms, was initiated, and the first volume, *Index of Ancient Petitions of the Chancery and the Exchequer*, largely the work of Rodney, with some assistance from Crump, appeared in 1892.

The great series of *Calendar of State Papers, Domestic* continued to trundle on, and by the 1890s over 125 volumes had appeared. No fewer than one third of them had been edited by Mrs Everett Green, who besides completing the Elizabethan period begun by Lemon had produced all the volumes relating to the Commonwealth and the Interregnum and the first ten of the reign of Charles II. She continued to work right up to her death in November 1895. Gardiner, with his detailed knowledge of the Puritan revolution, thought that she 'could be depended on in 99 cases out of 100, but I fancy she was in too great a hurry to enquire thoroughly into papers requiring prolonged attention'.[20] For that the system of payment, partially based upon piece work, may reasonably take some of the blame, but, overall, her work may fairly be said to have stood the test of time. It is to Palgrave's credit that he was prepared to give a woman the opportunity to enter the editorial field, although he was himself elderly by then, and it was to Romilly to

---

19. Martin's material is preserved among the Public Record Office archives as PRO 37/75–79.

20. PRO 1/64: Gardiner to Lyte, 5 December 1899.

whom she turned for editorial guidance in the all-important early years when the pattern for the state paper calendars was being set.

Mrs Green's death removed a notable personality from the ranks of the editors of the State Papers, which now included F. H. Blackburne Daniell, who was calendaring the domestic papers of the reign of Charles II from 1671, and W. J. Hardy, who was dealing with those of the reign of William and Mary from 1689. The calendar for the papers of Charles I, which had been continued in retirement by W. D. Hamilton, was abruptly interrupted in 1894 when he died by his own hand and was later entrusted to Mrs S. C. Lomas, a niece and assistant of Mrs Green. Death also robbed the office of the editorial services of Sainsbury in 1895, and the Hon. J. W. Fortescue succeeded him as editor of the *Calendar of State Papers, Colonial. Letters and Papers, Foreign and Domestic, Henry VIII*, continued to make progress under the direction of Gairdner, assisted by Brodie. The *Calendar of State Papers, Ireland*, for long the preserve of H. C. Hamilton, the late assistant keeper and sandwich muncher, was being continued officially by Atkinson. Additionally, a list of volumes of state papers relating to Great Britain and Ireland and the Channel Islands, prepared by Roberts, was issued in 1894 as the third in the new series of Lists and Indexes, the second having been published a year earlier on the Declared Accounts from the Pipe Office and the Audit Office. In the same year, efforts were made by a number of historians, including Gardiner, Tout and Firth, to get the *Calendar of State Papers, Foreign* resumed. Lyte was very much in favour, but the Treasury refused to sanction the undertaking until 1896 when the editorship was given to A. J. Butler. Under the original proposal it had been envisaged that the work would be undertaken by W. A. Shaw, but he was more than satisfied when entrusted instead with the *Calendar of Treasury Books and Papers* from 1729, which had been hanging fire ever since Redington completed the editing of the papers to that date in 1889.

Although Lyte had been particularly concerned from the outset of his deputy keepership with publication questions and matters affecting the staff, never a year passed without efforts on his part to improve working conditions and to increase office accommodation. The development of the site as a whole remained the long-term aim, which was why Esher had no hesitation in turning down a request from the Metropolitan Public Gardens Association in 1888 to allow the public to have access to the open space adjoining the office. In addition to securing the demolition of 1–2 Rolls Yard, in 1889 Lyte succeeded in having the business of the discharge or foreclosure of mortgages, which had been customarily transacted at the Rolls Chapel, transferred to the Chancery Registrars' Office in the Royal Courts of Justice. The change resulted in a reduction in the fees received by the office for attendances, a price well worth paying since an officer of the department was no longer required to be present to perform duties quite unconnected with the Record Acts.

Lyte followed up in December 1889 by drawing the Treasury's attention to the continued highly unsatisfactory condition of the range of houses on the Chancery Lane frontage. Originally they were known by the Chancery Lane address, but when they were taken over by the office they became part of Rolls Yard. The front doors of those containing records were blocked up and the back doors became the official entrances under the survey of the police patrol. Lyte suggested that the time had come to pull down numbers 13 to 20 on the northern portion and to build the first half of a new block fronting Chancery Lane, which would eventually be linked with the main repository over the site of the Rolls House, leaving the Rolls Chapel unaffected. However, the Office of Works saw many objections to the retention of the Rolls Chapel as a separate building and Mowatt at the Treasury was sufficiently concerned to visit the site in February 1890 with John Taylor, Pennethorne's successor. Reporting to Welby and William Jackson (later Lord Allerton), the financial secretary,[21] Mowatt confirmed the 'ruinous' condition of the Chancery Lane houses, and their liability to fire since they were incapable of supporting the weight of fire-proof standard cases. Consequently he did not think the government ought to carry any longer the risk and discredit of using them for the national records, particularly as for much of the year inspection of the documents stored in them was possible only by candle or lamplight, which was in itself a fire hazard. Neither did Mowatt think that there was more than limited relief to be obtained from a more active weeding policy, which, in any case, was likely to run counter to public opinion. He concluded, therefore, that the only practicable plan was the extension of Pennethorne's original building even if it meant the destruction of the Rolls Chapel, 'a building wholly without architectural beauty or interesting associations' and from which the heraldic glass could be introduced into the window of the new building and the three monuments of interest transferred to the Temple Church. Perhaps rather more prudently Bergne had previously suggested that if the fabric of the Chapel could be worked into the new building it might serve as a sort of Valhalla of past masters of the rolls.

From the standpoint of churchgoers there was little to be said in favour of the Chapel: its average congregation was no more than five, and there were three large, poorly attended churches nearby, St Bride's, St Dunstan in the West and St Clement Danes, besides the Temple Church and Lincoln's Inn Chapel. Its removal would also result in a saving of the yearly sum of £225 charged to the Consolidated Fund under the Rolls Estate Act 1837 and payable to the preacher for distribution as directed by the master of the rolls. Even Welby, never an enthusiast for public works, accepted the case for a new building, but observed:[22]

---

21. T 1/8538B/18751/1890: Mowatt to Welby and Jackson, 12 February 1890. Despite Mowatt's assertions about the Chapel lacking interesting associations, there is an unsigned comment among the papers that Butler's sermons were preached there.
22. T 1/8538B/18751/1890: Welby's note, 13 February 1890.

The men of whom the Weeding Committee are composed are naturally somewhat timid, since as far as I know them, they are not of sufficient standing to take a bold line. I think a stronger Committee might now be appointed to lay down some lines for extensive weeding.

Welby's reservations about the inspecting officers were not followed up in any way, and the new building project got ministerial clearance in March 1890, when the chancellor of the Exchequer, George (later Viscount) Goschen agreed that the matter might be taken in hand, while advising caution in dealing with the Chapel and the monuments. Esher was, therefore, asked by the Treasury to get the Office of Works to discuss with the deputy keeper how the obstacles to the development of the site might be removed without sacrificing any part of the Chapel which possessed features of architectural or historical interest.

In April 1890 Cartwright told the Treasury that Esher entirely agreed that Pennethorne's designs should be adhered to as closely as possible when the central block came to be extended. He was also of the opinion that the interior of the Rolls Chapel ought to be retained and the monuments which had been set up there, some of which were of high artistic value, should be left undisturbed. Esher was also willing to cede his patronage of the Chapel and to discontinue services there provided the preacher and the reader were compensated. The first steps to that end were subsequently taken under the Public Accounts and Charges Act 1891, whereby the annual sum of £225 at the disposal of the master of the rolls in respect of the Chapel was to cease on the next vacancy for a preacher.

As far as the new buildings were concerned, the Office of Works believed that the best plan was to develop the entire Chancery Lane frontage in one operation and then to link it with the old block over the site of the Rolls House and the Rolls Chapel. Lyte would have preferred that the first section should be built in two stages because he was reluctant to give up the two houses used as official residences, 6 and 12 Rolls Yard, which were occupied by Scargill-Bird and Cartwright. Ultimately, Treasury backing for Works was decisive, particularly as it doubted the need for one resident officer, let alone two, and demolition of the entire row of houses was commenced just before Christmas 1891. Taylor proposed that many of the records stored in them should be placed in a temporary structure at the Fetter Lane end of the site, but that plan was dropped when it was found that the vacant ground would probably be wanted as a masons' yard for the pending building operations. It was then suggested that the records should be transferred temporarily to Greenwich Hospital, but Esher and Lyte made it clear that they would prefer somewhere nearer, and ultimately the bulk of the records, amounting to 124 van-loads, were moved to the late Barge Dock at Somerset House during the course of 1891. Of the remainder, some were transferred to the central repository and others were stored temporarily in the basement of Officers' Chambers and in the roof of the Rolls Chapel, Esher being adamantly opposed to any idea of the reappearance of document presses in its interior.

The Treasury had hoped to do away with the resident officer posts altogether on the demolition of the Chancery Lane houses, but met with strong resistance from Lyte and Esher. It was, however, quite unwilling to build a house on the estate and the most it was prepared to sanction was an allowance of £150 a year towards the cost of accommodation nearby.[23] Scargill-Bird, the senior caretaker, was offered the appointment, but withdrew when unable to find a suitable dwelling nearer to the office than Bloomsbury Square, which Esher thought too far away. For a short time Cartwright undertook the responsibility, but in December 1891 he was replaced by Hubert Hall, who took up permanent residence in his chambers close by in Staple Inn. Somewhat earlier in the same year a proposal was made that when the new building was constructed a post office might be accommodated within it, a suggestion which Esher, in the absence of any provision for the residential accommodation he would have preferred, had no hesitation in turning down.

Towards the end of 1892 the foundations were laid for the new block which was estimated to cost £79,650, and during 1893 work was begun on the superstructure by the building contractors, Messrs Foster and Dicksee. Meanwhile, Spencer Holland, whose grandfather, Lord Gifford, a former master of the rolls, had been buried in the Rolls Chapel in 1824, was expressing alarm to Lyte about a press report that the Chapel was to be converted into a museum for selected documents. Replying in July 1892, Lyte assured him that nothing had been decided, but that if it became a museum it would almost revert to the previous state of affairs when the Chapel was the storehouse for the records of Chancery and the documents were kept not only in the presses put up for the purpose but also under the seats and elsewhere. A month later, anxious to forestall unwelcome developments, the secretary of the Society for the Protection of Ancient Buildings wrote to the Office of Works to ask whether, in view of the great historical value of the Chapel, said to be of the time of Edward I, there would be 'a sufficient space outside to admit of the exterior being properly seen'.[24a] Basing its reply upon a minute prepared by Taylor, the Office of Works stated clearly that it was not intended to leave space round the Chapel's exterior, but that its structure would be embodied in the new building so as to preserve the interior where of ancient date, and the monuments it contained. The society took the assurance of the Office of Works to mean that the Chapel was to remain unchanged, an assumption which was hardly justified by the answer it had been given, although, when it

---

23. PRO 1/56: Mowatt to Esher, 28 August 1891. Treasury papers are in T 1/8620D/18599/1891.

24a. WORK 12/67/2: Thackeray Turner to the secretary of HM Office of Works, 29 August 1892.

wrote again to the Office of Works in September 1892 to express its pleasure about the official intention to preserve the Rolls Chapel 'in its integrity', no attempt was made to disabuse it of the impression it had formed.[24b]

During 1892 the clearance of the houses numbered 3 to 20 Rolls Yard proceeded apace, and the official referees, who had occupied several rooms in numbers 3 and 4, moved to the new Law Courts building in the Strand. Construction then began in earnest, and the new block was finally completed in the autumn of 1895. Its general character was similar to the Gothic style of Pennethorne's earlier portions, but, as the original stonework was already showing signs of decay, Portland oolite was substituted for Church Anstone sandstone and Babbacombe limestone for Kentish rag. It ran for 225 feet along Chancery Lane, with a depth of 44 feet at the northern end and 65 feet at the southern end. It was 84-feet high and had four ranges of windows, with a central tower over the gateway and octagonal turrets at the north-western, south-western and south-eastern angles. There were also two statues in niches over the gateway on the eastern side, as planned by Hardy and Pennethorne as far back as 1869. One was of Henry III, who founded the House of Converts on the site for Jews who became Christians, and the other was of Edward III, who united the office of keeper of the House of Converts with that of keeper of the rolls of Chancery. Above the gateway on the first floor was a small exhibition room for the temporary display of documents of special beauty and interest, the ultimate intention being to establish a purpose-built museum in the further block, which was to be built to complete Pennethorne's grand design.

The rooms at the southern end of the new building were taken over by Lyte, Cartwright and the other staff from the Rolls House in October 1895. An exception was William Hayes, the long-serving housekeeper, whose services were no longer required. He was retired on a pension of £80 1s 4d. Working conditions in the new offices were infinitely better than those at the other end of the estate. The unfortunate users of the Government Search Room had to put up with the unpleasant smell of horses' manure from the nearby premises of the London Parcels Delivery Company, and the boisterous language of the boys employed there. The Round Room was reasonably insulated from outside disturbance, but readers in the Long Room had to work against a background of incessant noise from the traffic in Fetter Lane. There was also the general pollution caused by the thick black smoke from the several printers' chimneys in Fetter Lane. In contrast, all the rooms in the new block had good natural lighting, supplemented by electricity, a great boon for those working on ancient manuscripts. The one annoyance reported was the noise of footsteps on the wood block floors owing to the absence of carpets, but that sound was nothing compared with the chorus

---

24b. WORK 12/67/2: Thackeray Turner to the secretary of HM Office of Works, 16 September 1892.

of disapproval, soon to disturb Lyte's peace, as a result of the decision of the Office of Works to pull down the Rolls Chapel.

Chapter XII

Lyte's Middle Years (1895–1911) and the Origins of the Royal Commission on Public Records

I thought for some time that I was under sentence of excommunication by the Society of Antiquaries, on account of the demolition of the Rolls Chapel, but they have lately elected me a member of the Council for the year 1896–97.

(Lyte to R. B. Brett, 11 May 1896: WORK 12/67/2)

The demolition of the Rolls House and the Rolls Chapel was not begun until December 1895, but the fate of both had long been sealed. Divine service had not been held in the Chapel since the autumn, and arrangements had been made to pay compensation to those affected by its closure, the principal beneficiary being the Reverend W. R. Milroy, the preacher, who also held the living of Carisbrooke in the Isle of Wight. The demolition of the Rolls House, which had been built in the neo-classical Palladian style by Colin Campbell between 1717 and 1724, was accomplished without fuss, but no sooner was the work of dismantling the Rolls Chapel started than extensive protests broke out. The alarm was first given by the *Westminster Gazette* on 17 December, which stated that a solemn undertaking had been given, although it did not say by whom, that the Rolls Chapel would not be touched but would be incorporated within the expanded Public Record Office as a museum. Among a number of letters which were to follow in *The Times* was one in its edition of 30 December from a furious Lord Archibald Campbell, deploring 'the desecration and destruction going on in Chancery Lane' and asking:

Have we no one strong enough to stay the execution, no one intelligent
enough to perceive that we are in honour bound to preserve the chapels of
the land – historic chapels – the destruction of which no money can replace.

As it happened, it was none other than Esher's son, Reginald Brett, by then secretary of the Office of Works, who had to explain the limits of the pledge that had been given. On New Year's Day 1896 *The Times* carried his reply in which he maintained that, while it was the intention to adhere to it as far as practicable and to preserve all that was of historic interest 'the main walls of the building, composed of rubble, were found to be in such a state of decay as to render the removal of portions of them an absolute necessity'.

Backing for Brett came the next day in an article in *London* and was followed by one in *The Architect* of 3 January 1896, but *The Builder* of 4 January would have none of it, writing about the 'wrecking' of both the Rolls House and the Chapel. By now the Society for the Protection of Ancient Buildings was also on the warpath and on 10 January, having persuaded the Office of Works to stay the demolition of the south wall, sent its representatives to the site to discuss with Taylor what it thought ought to be done. As agreement could not be reached it was left that it would make written representations to Akers-Douglas, the first commissioner, but even before it had done so it wrote to *The Times* arguing for the preservation of the remaining walls, an action which drew forth a stern rebuke from the Office of Works, which, nevertheless, indicated its willingness to wait a few days longer for any statement which the society might still wish to make. Accordingly, it wrote to the Office of Works again on 17 January to urge that piers be built against the walls so that the new structure might be carried on arches over them. While admitting the poorness of the mortar in the fabric of the Chapel, it did not accept that its condition justified demolition since it was no worse than the mortar in other medieval buildings. The office's old foe, Grove, also joined the fray in a letter to *The Times*, arguing the illegality of what had been done, a case which was easily refuted. Of far more embarrassment was a hostile resolution from the Society of Antiquaries, which led to Akers-Douglas receiving a deputation from it early in February and giving an undertaking that in future any similar proposal would first be submitted to outside professional advice. On the main question, however, the first commissioner gave his full support to Taylor's opinion that the Chapel's external walls and its wooden roof had to go, and the Society for the Protection of Ancient Buildings was advised to that effect on 7 February. Although the criticism of 'high-handed officialdom and vandalism' continued for a little longer in the press and elsewhere, Lyte, who had publicly defended the Office of Works, besides writing a letter to *The Times* in January under the pseudonym 'One who knows', was seeking to mend his fences with the Society of Antiquaries, and by the spring had done so with such good effect that he was even elected to its council. Still greater distinction came in 1897, Jubilee Year, when Lyte and Taylor were knighted by the queen at an investiture of the Order of the Bath.

A year earlier, in making the *Fifty-seventh Report*, Lyte had appended a full-length account of the history of the Rolls Chapel, complete with drawings and plans. In compiling it he received help from Hall and Story-Maskelyne, and their assistance was duly acknowledged as well as that of Alfred Higgins of the Society of Antiquaries and W. Dyer, the clerk of the works. Many particulars concerning the Chapel's early history as the House of Converts were drawn from a paper prepared by W. J. Hardy and printed in *Middlesex and Hertfordshire Notes and Queries* in the same year. From retirement Redington, who did not regard the Chapel as of great architectural merit, told Lyte that he would not have thought that so many interesting details about the building would have been found on record, and he doubted whether they ever would have been but for its demolition. Construction work on the new building was started in February 1896 and the dismal 'Officers' Chambers', from whose steps Mrs Green used to feed the pigeons, came down in February 1899. But nearly twelve more months were to pass before the resulting wilderness was laid out as a garden. In 1901 a small lodge was built at the Fetter Lane entrance for the use of the police, and the improvements at that end of the site were completed when the temporary palings there were replaced by iron railings in 1903. For working purposes, most of the new block was taken into occupation in the spring of 1899, and in 1902 the large room covering the site of the Rolls Chapel, with the burials enclosed in a special vault below it, was opened to the public as a Museum. Besides containing selected documents and objects from the records, it also featured, as promised, items of historical or artistic value from the former building. Foremost was a large monument to Dr John Yong, master of the rolls from 1508 until his death in 1516. By general consent it is of exceptional interest and beauty, and is almost certainly the work of Pietro Torrigiani, the celebrated sixteenth-century sculptor. During his time as deputy keeper, Palgrave was particularly conscious of its merit and did all he could to ensure that it was properly preserved. Two other monuments, mainly of alabaster, were also re-erected. One was to Richard Alington of Lincoln's Inn who died in 1561, and the other to Edward, Lord Bruce of Kinloss, master of the rolls, who died in 1611. Additionally, three memorial tablets were re-affixed to the walls and some of the stained glass was placed in the new windows on the south side. In the course of demolition part of the thirteenth-century chancel arch was discovered and was re-assembled on an outer wall. The Rolls House made little appeal to Victorian eyes, and practically nothing survives from it. However, the marble statue of George I in ancient Roman costume, which had previously occupied a niche over the judicial bench in the Rolls Court, was placed in a corner near the Museum entrance. On its pedestal was a leaden tablet inscribed 'G.R. 1717', taken from the foundation stone of the Rolls House. The bell of the Chapel was also placed on display in the corridor.[1]

Elsewhere, the office continued much as formerly, although in 1900 the gallery running along the west side of the Long Room had been removed, and so searchers no longer felt compelled to watch the acrobatic struggles of the attendants when fetching the heavy indexes which were kept there. The development of the site also ended the use of the open ground for tent-pitching practice by the 2nd London Rifles, which had occasionally been permitted in former years. In fact, after a small strip of land at the south-west corner of the site had been acquired from Serjeant's Inn in 1901,

---

1. A full account of the monuments and windows will be found in the Introduction to the 1974 edition of the *Museum Catalogue*. Much of the information in this and the previous chapter about the development of the site has been derived from notes kindly made available to me by Mr R. H. Ellis.

Lyte, who already had more extensions in mind, wanted the government to purchase the site of Clifford's Inn to the south when it came on the market in 1903. It was, however, purchased by William Willett of Sloane Square for £100,000 since the Treasury was unwilling to find the money. No further action occurred until 1912, when Lyte, backed by the Royal Commission on Public Records, succeeded in persuading the Office of Works to acquire the Clifford's Inn garden and a few houses to the east of it against future needs. Inside the building little changed during the early years of the century apart from the opening of the new Government Search Room in 1901 on the south side of the building overlooking the lawn. There were also some rather ineffectual alterations in 1902 to the heating and ventilation in the Round Room where the descent of the printers' blacks through the dome continued to be bothersome. Additionally, the corridors in the older part of the building were improved by the substitution of glass pavement lights for iron gratings in 1904 and the laying of mosaic flooring in place of tiles during 1905 and 1906.

When the Rolls Chapel ructions were at their height Charles Johnson was in Rome, where he had been sent by Lyte to help Bliss whose work had come under fire from a number of Irish parliamentarians. Lyte accepted that there was some justification for the criticisms, but he believed that the difficulties arose from placing the entire responsibility for collation upon one person. Johnson was peculiarly qualified to assist owing to the special knowledge he had of papal bulls and because he had been indexing Bliss's *Calendar of Papal Registers: Petitions to the Pope*, out of office hours. Lyte did not intend Johnson to stay at Rome permanently and after some months there he was replaced as Bliss's coadjutor by J. A. Twemlow from Christ Church, Oxford, who possessed the advantage of having had two years' training at the Ecole des Chartes. As a further sop to the Irish critics Lyte also obtained Treasury approval to engage Robert P. Mahaffy a Cambridge graduate of high promise, to edit a *Calendar of State Papers relating to Ireland* from the beginning of the reign of Charles I in 1625 until 1670 after which date the Irish material was included in the *Calendar of State Papers, Domestic*, then being undertaken by Blackburne Daniell and W. J. Hardy, and the *Calendar of Home Office Papers*. Both Lyte and the Stationery Office had long wanted to publish the fourth volume of the latter series, covering the period 1773 to 1775, which R. A. Roberts had edited many years earlier and which had been suppressed by Harcourt. In 1899 the Home Office decided that the embargo might be lifted, although Lyte did not mention its issue in his *Report* for that year, possibly because the question of freer access to Home Office and other departmental papers was once again exciting some interest and he did not wish to draw attention to the papers now made public until the general policy was resolved. Codification did not, in fact, come until 1903, but in 1899 the main agitation came from the Irish Nationalist MPs, who were incensed at the way they believed they were discriminated against in securing access to state papers in Dublin in contrast to opponents of Home Rule, such as the historian Lecky.[2] Some parliamentary probing had also been inspired by H. W. Wilson, a writer and original member of the Navy League, who was engaged on a history of England between 1793 and 1815 and had been refused access to Home Office material.

At much the same time Sir George Sitwell and other searchers were complaining about the retention by the Land Revenue Record Office of 'vast numbers' of ancient manuscripts. Thanks to Lyte their transfer to the Public Record Office was finally secured in 1900. Initially the move was firmly resisted by the Office of Woods and Forests. In 1887 the Land Revenue Record Office had moved from Spring Gardens to 6 Whitehall, but when it was obliged to vacate its premises there, the site being needed for the new War Office building, and its records were moved to insecure and otherwise unsuitable accommodation in St Stephen's House on the Victoria Embankment, second thoughts prevailed and the release of much of the older material was agreed. Earlier, the idea of moving the entire Land Revenue Record Office to the Chancery Lane site had been mooted, but Lyte did not wish to share accommodation with another concern and Brett at the Office of Works feared it would delay for several years the planned demolition of Judges' Chambers. On the Land Revenue side negotiations were conducted by Maurice Hewlett, the lawyer, novelist and poet, who had done much legal work for the Duchy of Lancaster before succeeding his father as keeper in 1896. Among those considered for the post at that time was Hall, who was also then engaged with the Webbs in the planning of the London School of Economics where he was to be appointed a part-time lecturer in palaeography, diplomatic and economic sources. Lyte told the Treasury that he would be very sorry to lose Hall, but the office was in the gift of the first lord and in the event Balfour decided that the Hewlett connection should be retained.[3a] However, in March 1901 Hewlett resigned his appointment on grounds of ill health and because he wished to have more time to write. Two years later the Office of Woods acquired from him for £200 the Hewlett record agency papers which were subsequently deposited in the Public Record Office with other papers of the Land Revenue Record Office. Shortly before Hewlett's appointment in 1896 a proposal that land revenue work might be undertaken by the Land Registry had been rejected, but the commissioners of woods took the opportunity of his departure to suggest to the Treasury that the office's record agency work should be hived off and its enrolment functions passed to the Public Record Office or that its records should be taken under their own wing. The reason given was that the amount of work had fallen off and that the salary of £700 payable to the keeper was no longer justified. However, the Board of Trade had misgivings because it thought that the

---

2. *Hansard*, Fourth Series, LXIII, 1159–1178, 30 June 1899.

3a. T 1/9092B/17074/1896. A copy of Lyte's letter to Mallet at the Treasury about Hall was at one time in PRO 8 but no longer survives, and the original has not been traced. Slingsby's note in OBS 1343 refers.

government would be placed in an invidious position unless it enjoyed the exclusive services of one officer in all cases affecting crown title.

At an interdepartmental committee set up by the Treasury to consider the question the board's representative dissented from the other members, urging not only the continuation of the post of keeper of the land revenue records and enrolments but the addition to his duties of responsibility for compiling a manorial index and register or history of titles and dealings with foreshores. The committee set out the various possibilities in its report to the Treasury in December 1901, but it was not until a year later, and only after making further inquiries, that the Treasury decided to entrust to a professional record agent, paid by fees, the work of establishing the crown's title in legal cases and to appoint Lyte, who had represented the Public Record Office on the committee, keeper of the land revenue records and enrolments.[3b] In consideration of Lyte's additional responsibilities his personal salary was increased from £1,100 to £1,400. It was a peculiar circumstance that Mowatt, who recommended the increase to the chancellor of the Exchequer with some reluctance, was under the doubly-mistaken impression that Lyte, who was born in 1848, was already 60 and due to retire at 65. Although it had at one time been thought that legislation would be needed, the various changes were, in the event, authorised administratively by the Treasury. Two clerks and a boy copyist employed as a typist were also transferred from the Land Revenue Record Office and steps were taken to simplify the enrolment of crown leases and deeds and conveyances of crown lands. The records were removed to the Chancery Lane repository in April 1903, and the words 'Land Revenue Office' were painted on the door of the former Government Search Room, which was set aside for its business. The senior of the two clerks transferred, W. J. Green, had undertaken the keeper's duties between the time of Hewlett's resignation and Lyte's appointment, and he was placed on a scale of £350 rising to £500. However, enrolment work proved light and he was not replaced when he retired prematurely in 1906. On the other hand his junior colleague, P. J. McKenna, was initially graded as an abstractor before being appointed a supplementary clerk in 1904.

One of Lyte's first moves as keeper of the land revenue records and enrolments was to arrange for the destruction under schedule of a large number of drafts and duplicates of accounts and similar material, which had been cluttering up the Land Revenue Record Office. Some of them dated from the late seventeenth century and could not have been dealt with under the 1877 act had it not been amended by the Public Record Office Act 1898. That measure carried back from 1715 to 1660 the date from which documents might be destroyed, and also changed from 60 days to nine weeks

3b. Treasury papers, including the report of the committee, are in T 1/9916B/20479/1902. Public Record Office papers are in PRO 1/117 and those about the purchase of the Hewlett Papers in T 1/9925A/848/1903.

the period for which rules under the original act were required to be laid before Parliament, mainly because the Lords did not ordinarily sit more than four days in a week. In advocating it, Lyte stressed the need for the office to rid itself of pre–1715 material, such as duplicates, abstracts and the like, which were said to have no further value as the information they contained could be found in a more convenient form in original documents which were to be preserved. The bill was introduced in the Lords in February 1898 and emerged from there without debate or amendment. Apart from some reservations about the fate of Irish and Scottish records expressed in the Commons at its second reading in April, it excited little interest and became law on 1 July 1898. Another statute of the decade which concerned the office was the Copyhold Act 1894. Under its provisions court rolls and other manorial records could be placed in the custody of the Board of Agriculture or the master of the rolls after enfranchisement of the lands of the lordship to which they related. Since it was purely permissive little changed until enfranchisement became automatic under the Law of Property Act 1922 and the master of the rolls was enabled to cause the records to be deposited in a suitable local repository.

When Lyte first raised the possibility of an amendment to the 1877 act Esher was still master of the rolls, but in November 1897 he was succeeded by Sir Nathaniel (later Lord) Lindley. Although relations between them had always been perfectly correct, Lyte often found Esher difficult and welcomed the change, especially as he got on remarkably well with Lindley. Their official association lasted only until 1900, when Lindley became a lord of appeal in ordinary, but Lyte thought him to be the most effective of the nine masters of the rolls with whom he worked during his 40 years as deputy keeper.[3c] Part of the explanation might have been that Lyte himself was more relaxed than he had been at an earlier stage of his career, when he was attempting to get the office into shape while fighting a running battle with the Treasury. The turning-point came in 1897 when he joined the select band of Whitehall knights. Two years later he was admitted to the company of the 'great and the good' when Balfour, on Mowatt's recommendation, appointed him a member of the Committee on Local Records. The information collected by that body about the various classes of local records was valuable, but although it favoured the setting-up of local record offices and their inspection by officers appointed by the Public Record Office, it stopped short of recommending legislation other than that of a permissive and enabling character.[4a] Subsequently, Lord Salisbury presented a Local

---

3c. PRO 8/47 (Sources and General Bundle, Pt 2): J. R. Crompton's notes of interview with Lyte, c.1936–1937. In 1900 Lindley was succeeded by Sir Richard Webster (later Lord Alverstone) who gave way after barely six months to Sir Archibald Levin Smith. A year later Smith resigned and died shortly afterwards, being replaced by Sir Richard Henn Collins.

4a. *Report of the Committee on Local Records* (1902) (Cd. 1335).

Records Bill in the Lords in 1904, to provide for the better custody of local records, but it got no further than its first reading. In 1914 Lyte was to tell the Royal Commission on Public Records that he was more inclined to an element of compulsion than some of his colleagues, but that he did not wish the report to be other than unanimous. Nevertheless, he was well disposed towards the activities of local archaeological and record societies, particularly in his own county, Somerset, and welcomed the formation of bodies such as the Navy Records Society established in 1893 for the purpose of printing rare or unpublished works of naval interest. In 1899 he was also instrumental in obtaining a disguised subsidy of £100 from the Treasury payable to the British Record Society in respect of its transcription, arrangement and publication of indexes of the six clerks' books of Chancery proceedings between 1649 and 1714.[4b] Recognition of his high standing in the learned community came in 1902 when he was made a fellow of the newly established British Academy.

The various honours conferred upon Lyte meant that he held a commanding position in the still narrow record world, although complaints were voiced by users from time to time about search-room facilities, and as late as December 1899 Pym Yeatman was expressing concern about the 'vexatious rules' of the master of the rolls. But the office was no longer plagued with the rancorous kind of criticism that had bedevilled T. D. Hardy's final years. Lyte did not take too seriously the occasional outbursts in Parliament by the Irish and Welsh members about the alleged neglect of the records of their countries, and firmly resisted a suggestion made in the Committee of Supply in June 1900 that a Welshman should be recruited to the staff, especially as he maintained that he already had such a person in R. A. Roberts. Lyte also enjoyed a reasonable relationship with his colleagues in the British Museum, as was demonstrated in 1894 when they made no difficulties about releasing a quantity of writs which had been sent to them in error by the dean and chapter of Westminster. Unlike the museum, however, Lyte did not possess any funds to acquire material and so had little prospect of recovering valuable records which had strayed from official custody, which was why some royal Wardrobe books from the time of Edward I from the Phillipps Library found their way to the museum on coming up for sale, an attempt by Lyte to claim them from the Phillipps Trustees as public property in March 1895 having been brusquely rejected. In 1897 Lyte did succeed in recovering four ancient rolls of Chancery found by two members of the Selden Society among the manuscripts at Lord Ailesbury's seat at Savernake. It was believed that these rolls had at one time been in the possession of one of Ailesbury's ancestors, Lord Bruce of Kinloss, the master of the rolls whose monument was in the Museum. The Treasury sanctioned the payment of £200 for the rolls, but that was not

---

4b. T 1/9327B/19439/1898.

officially regarded as a purchase so much as an honorarium to Ailesbury for restoring the documents. Of equal concern to Lyte was the retention by departments of older material which might have been transferred and so made available to searchers. Not having any direct powers to compel transfers he realised he could only move with caution, but by the turn of the century he had persuaded both the War Office and the Board of Trade to release certain older records. In the War Office's case the position was remedied only after a reference to the Treasury by Lyte. He lost patience with the Army authorities, who had practically come to regard the office as an out-registry for live material, which·was frequently recalled for official purposes.[4c]

Apart from occasional skirmishes of that kind with departments, and the outcry about the demolition of the Rolls Chapel, the final decade of the nineteenth century was one of relative tranquillity for the office, once its post-Ridley organisation had been settled. After Johnson, Stamp and Headlam joined the staff in 1893, the higher establishment remained unchanged until 1898 when J. B. W. Chapman, who had previously been employed by the Board of Customs in arranging and listing its early records, was transferred to the office, although not admitted formally to the permanent staff until 1900 when Pike resigned on grounds of age and ill health. In the *Deputy Keeper's Report* for that year Lyte paid tribute to Pike's marked ability and indicated that he would continue to edit the *Year Books of the reign of Edward III* in the Rolls Series. For his part Pike had always laid great stress upon the importance of legal knowledge in the training of the staff and had to his credit the *History of Crime in England* published between 1873 and 1876. But Lyte's arrival meant that Pike's ambitions were thwarted and some of his disappointment was shown in his relative detachment from, and lack of influence upon, the younger men. Half a century later Lyle, looking back on his service in the old Rolls House, recalled:[5]

> My most vivid memory was of a portly bearded AK named Pike (an authority
> on early 'Year Books') who was reported to keep a supply of bottled beer
> in his room and when I used to read office copies to him, a duty then
> performed by junior clerks, he would sometimes retire behind a screen,
> ostensibly to consult a legal text book, but his visits I thought at the time,
> were not unconnected with the aforesaid bottled beer!

Handcock, an altogether more genial personality, was promoted to the vacant assistant keeper post, but Pike's place on the Inspecting Officers' Committee was taken by Scargill-Bird, the superintendent of the search rooms, because of his wide knowledge of the contents of the office. Unlike

---

4c. Treasury papers are in T 1/9192C/16539/1897 and T 1/9209A/18503/1897.
5. PRO 8/55: Lyle to Ellis, 15 February 1951.

Pike, Scargill-Bird was not a barrister, and so Roberts was added to the committee as its legal member. Lyte wanted Scargill-Bird to be given an additional allowance of £100 and Roberts to have £50, but the Treasury was not prepared to sanction more than £100, which Lyte then divided between them. As with the clerks there was very little movement among the support grades during the 1890s, although following the outbreak of the Second Boer War in 1899 a few of the porter-messenger reservists were recalled to the colours. The major change was in May 1900 when Watson retired after 46 years' service and was succeeded by Swain, who had served diligently since joining the office from St Dunstan's School in 1860. Swain's duty pay of 8s a week as superintendent was increased to 10s in 1904, and he remained in post until 1907 when he was followed by J. R. Pratt, who had entered the office in 1874 and had long been a debonair and popular figure in the Round Room.

Watson's retirement marked a clear break with the old order: there had always been a gulf between the higher and lower establishments, but he was the last of the generation of workmen to have been on terms of respectful familiarity with the senior staff and had been a particular favourite of Sir Thomas Hardy and Kingston, besides undertaking outside editorial work on Middlesex records which had brought him into close contact with W. J. Hardy and the garrulous Jeaffreson. Lyte was altogether more aloof than the Hardys, and Cartwright, Scargill-Bird and, until his retirement, Pike, who all exercised much authority over the men, were martinets, who kept a 'Red Book' in which infringements of discipline and good order were entered and penalties recorded. It was also made clear in the regulations issued by Lyte in 1895 concerning the conditions of service of the members of the 'subordinate establishment' that each foreman, under the superintendent, was responsible for his men's behaviour no less than for the efficient performance of their duties; and he was at once to report any neglect of duty, breach of discipline or damage to a record or be held responsible equally with the offender unless 'able very clearly to acquit himself from blame'.

A further factor was that since Craib's and Poulter's promotions to the transcriber class in 1893 there had been no more upgradings of that kind. The type of recruit who might at one time have joined the office as a workman and moved to the clerical side had been, in effect, superseded by the boy clerks recruited from the Civil Service Commission. Their services had come to be greatly valued by the office as the copying and indexing work upon which they were much employed was invariably well done and cost the Exchequer very little. However, under the regulations of the time boy clerks had to be discharged when 20 years of age, and as there was no recognised avenue of promotion for them in the office they usually sat examinations before then in the hope of securing appointments elsewhere in the Civil Service. Their need to study in their off-duty hours explains, perhaps, why they had little interest in enrolling in the Cadet Corps, under the aegis of the Boy Clerks' Friendly Society, when the proposal was made to them, through Lyte, in 1903. Nevertheless, their entry into the department undoubtedly contributed towards its more efficient performance, although it tended to sharpen the divisions between the office staff and the manual workers. That the support grades were expected to know their place was shown in 1897 when the attendants were sternly admonished by Cartwright for a 'gross breach of discipline' and an 'act of larceny' after official stationery was used to communicate their names to *Kelly's London Directory* for insertion in the section dealing with the office in which the names of the transcribers and the superintendent customarily appeared beneath those of the higher grades. The bid – it may have been more of a wheeze – failed because the publishers referred the list back to the office as it had been sent to them anonymously, apparently by one or more of the attendants. What was, perhaps, more surprising about the staffing at that time was that the office remained a largely male preserve, although there were many female record agents to be seen in the search rooms, including Miss Ethel Stokes of the British Record Society. Moreover, the United States Government Despatch Agency and the Canadian record authorities were employing a number of lady copyists, who attended the office to work on American Loyalists' and other papers. Mrs Sophie Lomas had succeeded her aunt, Mrs Green, on the editorial side of the department, but with the exception of the part-time cleaners and the ladies' attendant she was the only female on the strength. By the turn of the century, however, the office had made some concession to modernity when it was connected to the government telephone exchange, albeit ex-directory. A typewriter had by that time made its appearance in the Secretariat where it was used for outgoing correspondence, but lists were usually sent to the Civil Service Commission for typing. It was not until the end of 1902 that the manuscript series of letter books, dating from Thomas's engagement in 1838, were discontinued. Facilities for photography continued to be provided, but there was no suggestion that the department should itself become directly involved although Lyte was a keen photographer.

Repair operations continued steadily and it was a sign of the growing expertise that had been developed within the office that it had no difficulty in giving advice to the agent general of the Cape of Good Hope in 1897 about the best means of protection for books against insects. From 1904 the removal of dust and dirt from documents in the repository was assisted by the introduction of vacuum cleaners. A new area of activity had opened up when the Museum was established and the repairers prepared documents for display. Interest was also being taken in outside scientific developments of possible archival benefit. In November 1902 Crump was in communication with the government chemist about the chances of restoring the writing on certain parchments which had been blackened in the past by the indiscriminate use of so-called ink revivers. There was an irony in his interest in the matter in view of his early mishap in the use of ink for which he had been sharply rebuked. Crump, who had a knowledge of chemistry, was a man of many parts and was among those who had contributed to Sir Robert Harry

Inglis Palgrave's *Dictionary of Political Economy*. Like Hall, he was also anxious to widen the office's outside contacts. It was through Hall, the original choice for the job, that Crump became one of a team of three which undertook work after office hours on the new Oxford edition of the *Dialogus de Scaccario*. That imaginary dialogue about the workings of the country's financial system in the early middle ages had been compiled in the twelfth century by Richard Fitzneale or Fitznigel, otherwise Richard of Ely, from his own knowledge of the Exchequer as Henry II's treasurer and had first been printed in Madox's *History and Antiquities of the Exchequer* in 1711. Its reissue by the learned Record Office trio, the other members being Hughes and Johnson, strengthened still further the department's links with the academic world.

To the members of the history schools in the universities at home and abroad publication was of the essence, and it was Lyte's enduring achievement to fill many of the gaps that had been felt by them hitherto in the office's contents. Between 1890 and 1899 no fewer than 72 calendars appeared. Twelve were of the medieval patent rolls, most of the work being undertaken within the office by Handcock, Isaacson, Morris, Black and Fowler. Ten volumes were also issued in the new series of Lists and Indexes, notably a *List of State Papers* prepared by Roberts, a *List of Sheriffs for England and Wales from the earliest times to 1831*, compiled by Hughes, who was already considered one of the best readers of manuscripts within the office, a *List of Foreign Accounts enrolled on the Great Rolls of the Exchequer*, the work of Crump, and a *List and Index of Court Rolls* prepared by Sharp. Twenty-two volumes were also published in the Rolls Series, which was, nevertheless, rapidly running down with the single exception of Pike's *Year Books*. Despite a recommendation by the Royal Commission on Public Records of 1910 that the series should be continued the *Year Books* were to mark its demise.

Much work was also being done by Martin and Thompson on the Ancient Correspondence of the Chancery and the Exchequer and on Ancient Deeds respectively, while Story-Maskelyne, a skilled genealogist, was making good progress in arranging and indexing inquisitions post mortem. Under Scargill-Bird's direction Rodney and Giuseppi were active in dealing with unsorted documents and the re-arrangement and relabelling of a multiplicity of classes, particularly those most wanted by searchers. Another development came in 1897 when A. B. Hinds, an Oxford graduate with two years' experience at the Ecole des Chartes, who had been assisting Stevenson in his work on the *Calendar of Close Rolls*, was given the entire responsibility for the third volume in that series for the reign of Edward III, dealing with the years 1333 to 1337. Lyte himself kept a close watch on all publication work and took personal responsibility for the compilation of the *Museum Catalogue*. The all-round and purposeful progress had not passed unnoticed at the Treasury, which had itself shared in the general advance through the issue of two volumes of the *Calendar of Treasury Books*, the newly-appointed editor, Shaw, having done his best in the second volume to meet the wish

352

of the waspish Bergne for greater compression. But Bergne was soon to take over the superintendence of the Registry of County Court Judgments, and was succeeded by E. S. Spring-Rice, who was more sympathetic towards the office's needs.

It could be argued that much of Lyte's success was because there had been very few staff changes during the 1890s. But it has to be remembered that it was largely owing to him that the Consultative Committee of 1894 decided to recommend the integration of the office's senior and junior clerical grades. It was that decision, more than any other, which persuaded the younger men in the office to make their careers in the record field, once they had a reasonable certainty of at least rising to £500 and some prospect of promotion to the assistant keeper grade thereafter. Early in the new century, however, the deaths occurred in quick succession of J. M. Thompson, after a few hours' illness, in December 1902, and Lyte's trusted lieutenant, Cartwright, in January 1903. Much of Thompson's official career had been spent in the Round Room and he was succeeded by another search room stalwart, Overend, a fellow of the Society of Antiquaries, whose main experience had been in the Long Room and who had done much useful work for the Huguenot Society. Cyril T. Flower, an Oxford graduate, entered the office as a clerk through the class I examination. As Lyte expected that the Treasury was likely to make difficulties about a replacement for Cartwright, he suggested to it that the bulk of the secretary's duties should pass to Scargill-Bird, who should then receive a further £100 on top of his assistant keeper pay. Lyte produced figures to show that if an additional assistant keeper post was also authorised and a junior clerk recruited there would still be a saving of the order of £2,000 over the next ten years compared with the salaries paid formerly. The Treasury did not entirely accept Lyte's calculations and turned down flat his further suggestion that the allowances to the two senior inspecting officers should also be raised. On the understanding, however, that the independent post of secretary was to be suppressed Scargill-Bird's appointment was agreed, and Roberts, the senior of the clerks, was promoted to the assistant keeper grade, while 30-year-old Sidney Ratcliff was transferred from the Irish Record Office to fill the clerical vacancy. Subsequently, Roberts was also appointed to succeed Cartwright as secretary of the Historical Manuscripts Commission, but the £100 he was given for that duty came out of the commission's vote. Although Cartwright had been contemplating retirement, his sudden death created something of a crisis in the Secretariat because Alfred Lowson, the senior transcriber there, was also about to retire. Consequently Lyte decided that Stamp, who had not long returned to the office after an extended period of sick leave as a result of lung trouble, should be deputed to assist Scargill-Bird, with particular responsibility for the accounting side of the work.

Lyte was disinclined to fill Lowson's place by promoting a workman, but obtained authority for the engagement of W. H. Bennett, a 23-year-old class II clerk with previous service in the Census Office and the Treasury. His recruitment was seen as in the nature of an experiment, but owing to a sharp reduction in the department's land revenue enrolment work he was declared redundant and transferred to the Inland Revenue at the beginning of 1904. By then Lyte had realised that something had to be done to provide sufficiently for the long-term future of the minor administrative and less specialised editorial work of the office, especially as the transcribers no longer thought their title appropriate and were seeking an improved scale of pay. The upshot was that in June 1904 the Treasury agreed that all of them, together with McKenna, the abstractor, should be regraded as supplementary clerks on an improved scale, rising to £250; and that vacancies among them should normally be filled from the boy clerks in the office, subject to their being able to satisfy the Civil Service Commission that they possessed the necessary ability. The Treasury also approved additional allowances of £15 a year to two of the supplementary clerks as draughtsmen in respect of the copying of maps, plans and drawings. The attendants and repairers, seeing that their former avenue of advancement had been decisively blocked, began to press for some improvement in their own conditions, and achieved a small measure of success in 1905 when the number of first-class posts was increased by two. In general, however, their position had hardly changed since the Fremantle/Primrose report of 1894, although their lunch break had been extended from 30 to 45 minutes in May 1899.

The clerks, too, had long had a grievance about their pay scale on account of the five-year wait for their increment at the £300 point. The quickening of recruitment to the class from 1903 added to the pressure for a change because the younger men were able to cite the better scales on offer elsewhere, and Lyte was anxious to avoid any return to the kind of losses of junior staff experienced in the past. The result was that the Treasury agreed to concede the case of the clerks and from 1904 they were allowed to proceed to their maximum of £500 by annual increments without a break. It had long been evident that the staffing calm of the second half of the 1890s could not continue indefinitely, but after the deaths of Cartwright and Thompson the retirement of Trimmer and Hughes in 1904 on account of ill health came as a rude shock. Both were to die soon afterwards and Lyte took the occasion of his *Sixty-sixth Report* to pay tribute to their services. Hughes's son, Richard, went on to achieve fame as a writer, particularly for his novel *A High Wind in Jamaica*. Lyte's *Report* mentioned another change caused by the death of C. H. Woodruff, keeper of the Chancery masters' documents since 1885. Woodruff had also undertaken much indexing work in connection with the office's publications, but his distinctive post was now abolished. A further misfortune occurred in 1905 with the death of G. H. Overend. The various vacancies thus created were filled by the promotions of Isaacson and Morris to the assistant keeper grade and the appointment of A. E. Bland and M. C. B. Dawes as junior clerks. Hall joined the Inspecting Officers' Committee in place of Morris. For that duty Hall was allowed a further £25 a year, which must have been of little comfort to him when a year later Haydon's one-time pupil, Rodney, latterly Scargill-Bird's right-hand man

354

in the Repository, was promoted assistant keeper over his and three other heads, in succession to Martin who retired and whose great loss to the department was singled out for special mention by Lyte in his *Sixty-eighth Report*. A little earlier the clerkship vacant as a result of Morris's promotion had been filled by C. H. Jenkinson from Pembroke College, Cambridge. He was taken under Crump's wing and was soon to make his presence felt. The vacancy caused by Rodney's promotion was filled by the appointment of J. J. O'Reilly.

The first decade of the new century also saw a number of editorial changes. In 1905 Horatio Brown resigned and was succeeded at Venice by Hinds whose work on the Close Rolls passed to W. H. Bird, an inspector for the Historical Manuscripts Commission. For a short while Lyte's son, Arthur, had done some work on that series, but he had resigned on appointment as a junior examiner at the Board of Education. In 1906 calendaring work on the Colonial Papers was taken over by Cecil Headlam, an Oxford graduate, in succession to Fortescue who had been appointed librarian at Windsor Castle. Bliss's death in 1909 led to the appointment at Rome of J. M. Rigg, another Historical Manuscripts Commission inspector and a son of the most eminent Wesleyan minister of the day. In the following year A. J. Butler died and was succeeded as editor of the *Calendar of State Papers, Foreign* by Mrs Lomas. Butler had once served in the Education Department where he professed to have learned how to stick postage stamps on the ceiling. In the volume of studies presented to Sir Hilary Jenkinson in 1957, Charles Johnson tells the tale, which Butler told against himself, of how he was in Martin's room and carelessly compared someone whom he disliked to 'a dissenting preacher', whereupon Martin pointed to his own father's portrait hanging over the fireplace and asked 'Anything like that?' In 1910 Hume also died and he was replaced at Simancas by Royall Tyler, an expert on Spanish studies. Crump, who had been dangerously ill, spent time at Rome in 1908 and 1909, Lyte taking the opportunity of the need to examine certain registers of the Avignon popes to send him there during the winter months for that purpose and to aid the recovery of his health.

One event of the period to which Lyte gave no publicity was a report, received through the War Office shortly before Cartwright's death in January 1903, about a large quantity of military and naval records in the possession of a second-hand book dealer in New York. Police inquiries were immediately put in hand on the assumption that the papers must have been stolen. In fact, the documents, chiefly duplicate ships' logs and Audit Office copies of Army payrolls, proved to have been scheduled for destruction, but contrary to instructions had not been mutilated before being sold as waste paper. Both Lyte and Pigott, controller of the Stationery Office, were highly apprehensive about a possible outcry, particularly as the War Office's informant was concerned lest the transaction be seen in the United States as further proof that the old country's finances had been reduced to such a parlous state that it had to sell the national records. However, once assured that steps had been taken by the Stationery Office to prevent any repetition, the

Treasury saw no reason for alarm and refused to sanction a request from Pigott, still fearing a scandal, to negotiate the repurchase of the material. In the absence of a Black, Burtt or Yeatman, there, as luck would have it, the matter rested until the Royal Commission on Public Records unearthed it eight years later and reproduced the correspondence in its *First Report.*[6] Needless to say, the commission expressed disquiet about the Stationery Office's precautions for the destruction of 'valueless' documents and cited the mishap in support of its own strong criticism of the manner in which the 1877 act was being administered. Because the act of 1877, as amended by that of 1898, was restricted to documents of later date than 1660, the inspecting officers had no reason to fear criticism from medievalists, whose presence had long dominated the Round Room. But as searchers' interests began to shift to the records of later centuries, it was evident that the inspecting officers could expect their work to be subject to greater scrutiny. In that respect the parliamentarians had been remarkably mute, the laying of schedules before them having proved little more than a formality.

There had been an important extension of policy by the office in 1908 when an additional rule was made by the master of the rolls enabling certain Colonial Office documents, such as those of the New Zealand Company and duplicates of correspondence with colonial governments, to be presented to the colonies concerned instead of being destroyed. Meanwhile, in the Government Search Room the ever-alert Hall was making every effort to ensure that problems concerning the use of departmental records were dealt with as they arose. To be fair, the days when departments considered it a piece of impudence for anyone to ask for leave to consult papers were already past. Indeed it was in an effort to simplify matters that Lyte, in consultation with the departments affected, had issued new regulations for searchers in 1903, setting out the varying dates to which their records were freely open in the search rooms and the rules to be observed by readers who were given a permit to see records of later date.[7a] Between 1878 and 1907 the number of permits issued was 1,348, and it was estimated that more than a fifth of them went to readers from abroad. During 1907 the total number of new permits issued was 79. Such readers had to give up their notes for examination, and they had to be written in English or French. The names of secret service agents were forbidden to be copied, as were law officers' reports. Neither was it permissible to copy or quote departmental minutes or memoranda or any 'document manifestly of a confidential nature'. In 1889, for example, objection had been taken to a paper of 1809 reflecting on the competence of the president of the United States, the notorious profligacy of the vice-president and the intemperate language of the secretary of state. Another specimen of the kind of letter to fall foul of the censors

---

6. *First Report of the Royal Commission on Public Records*, I, pt II (1912), 51–53.
7a. I, pt II, 64–65.

was one of 1811 to which exception was taken 80 years later on the grounds that it reflected on the character of a New South Wales author who had been a convict.

Of the most popular records, Foreign Office classes were generally open to 1780 and those of the Colonial Office to 1802. The Foreign Office decided in 1902 that subject to the usual oversight, its papers to 1850 might be seen under permit, but the Colonial Office did not specify a cut-off date to material for which a permit was required. In all cases, Newfoundland documents later than 1759 were normally excepted owing to continuing disputes, originally with the French and then with the United States, about the fisheries there. The Colonial Office also embargoed records dealing with British Guiana and later the Falkland Islands, Malta and Gibraltar. The Foreign Office reserved papers relating to the frontiers of Holland because of the presence among them of reports from secret agents between 1790 to 1792, when Holland was overrun by the French revolutionary armies. A ban, maintained until 1910, was placed by the Colonial Office upon North American despatches concerning the military clash at Bushy Run during Pontiac's War in 1763 and the Wyoming massacre during the War of Independence in 1778. The reason was the reports of barbarities, such as scalping, shown to have been committed by British forces and Indians in their service in the aftermath of the battles.

At the turn of the century the Home Office, whose papers remained restricted to 1779, obtained authority from a reluctant Treasury for limited expenditure in order to review documents in the Record Office to 1815 to see if some of them might be released. Hopes of progress were dashed in 1904, when an application to see closed Irish papers resulted in ministers, Balfour included, confirming the existing restrictions because of the fear of reviving controversy concerning the Act of Union. The following year, however, a fresh situation was created with the election of a new government and the appointment of James (later Viscount) Bryce as chief secretary in Ireland. Besides having been associated with the foundation of the *English Historical Review*, Bryce had also served on the Committee on Local Records, taking over the chairmanship in 1901 on the death of Dr Creighton, the bishop of London. With that background it would have been remarkable had his views on the needs of historical researchers not differed markedly from those which had been expressed some years earlier by his fellow Liberal, Harcourt. It was not surprising, therefore, that it was his hand which the Home Office thought it detected in a letter it received from the Irish Office in 1906, in which the suggestion was made that the records at Dublin should be opened to 1847 instead of 1790. In the climate of the time that was a bold proposal, but to be fair to the Home Office it was itself beginning to take a more liberal posture, its main reservation being about the release of records which might reveal the names of spies or the opening of collections, such as the Bouillon Correspondence, which might damage the *entente cordiale*. At any rate, in the summer of 1907 H. J. Gladstone, the home secretary, obtained Campbell-Bannerman's approval to set up an

Interdepartmental Committee to consider what relaxations might be permitted.[7b] Subsequent consultations resulted in the establishment of such a body in April 1908, under the chairmanship of Sir Herbert (later Lord) Cozens-Hardy, who had been appointed master of the rolls a year before in succession to Sir Richard Henn (later Lord) Collins.

When the committee was first suggested, Lyte had hoped that Hall might join him on it because of his special knowledge of departmental records. But Gladstone did not want too large a committee, and since it was intended that it should confine itself to matters of high policy it was decided that no more than one senior official should be appointed from each of the seven departments primarily concerned, namely the Admiralty, Colonial Office, Foreign Office, Home Office, Irish Office, Public Record Office and War Office. However, it was Hall who drafted a long memorandum for the committee, setting out the existing practice and making certain recommendations. It was not one of Hall's better efforts, perhaps because he seemed as much concerned to stress the difficulties of administering the Government Search Room under the existing regulations as to provide clear guidelines for the future. But he could not have thought too badly of it himself because when he became secretary of the Royal Commission on Public Records, in 1910, he was to reproduce it as one of the many appendixes to that body's *First Report*.[8] Nevertheless, if the committee was looking for enlightenment it would hardly have found it from Hall's bewildering and overlong statement of conclusions. While rightly saying that the date chosen for closure was crucial, because if that was sufficiently remote the question of the subjects to be restricted was academic, he implied that the entire exercise was fatuous by saying that the balance of learned opinion thought that the consultation of original documents of the nineteenth century was unnecessary. Furthermore, not only were there few applications to see post-1830 material, but in many cases permit-holders did not trouble to find out if the information they wanted had previously been printed. Historical scholars often alleged foreign practice was more generous, but Hall thought that doubtful. Only in England could a student be sure of finding all the documents relating to a given period, but question marks hovered over the closure of some of them and there was a need for greater consistency in access policy. For example, said Hall:

> The Home Office imposes a strict censorship upon all official reports of conflicts between the troops and the populace during the notorious riots of the first half of the 19th century. At the same time, any reader who can sign his name is at liberty to publish an autograph letter of the Prince Consort, stating that Queen Victoria was opposed to the substitution of pistols for

---

7b. HO 45/10166/B26102 and HO 45/13290.
8. I, pt II, 56–62. Hall's draft is in PRO 1/73. Lyte's papers are in PRO 39/3.

carbines in the case of the Household Cavalry on the ground that the latter weapon would be more effective against a London mob.

Probably there are few of the subjects now prohibited by the Secretaries of State's Departments that could not be supplied wholly or in part from other official sources. Quite recently, when an American scholar had been at the pains to obtain a permit through his Embassy to copy Foreign Office despatches relating to the critical question of the Oregon Boundary in 1844, he found that he had the choice of deriving his text from the closed Foreign Office archives or from a duplicate in the War Office archives which were open to public inspection.

It might, he said, be suggested that the issue of historical publications since the existing restrictions were first drafted some fifty years earlier had left very few political or personal secrets to be revealed, but recent political events had brought new dangers to the state. International judgments about old colonial boundaries and the practice of neutrality had shown the vital importance to the national interest of certain types of documents, such as maps, treaties and law officers' reports, for supplementing or controverting case law. Nevertheless, Hall still concluded that 1837, the year in which Queen Victoria came to the throne, was a suitable terminal date for general opening, and one acceptable to the Home Office, Colonial Office, Royal Household and Admiralty.

Although no mention was made by the committee of Hall's submission in its report, which it made in November 1908,[9] it agreed with him that the records of all government departments should be opened to 1837, saying that it was satisfied that no possible harm would result to the public service or to private individuals from such a relaxation. In reaching its conclusion, which was unanimous, the committee examined the reports of the review which the Home Office had conducted a few years earlier when it was considering the possibility of releasing its records to 1815. The committee also looked into the question of opening classes of records hitherto reserved by the other departments represented, and took into account, on the basis of information supplied by the Foreign Office, the practice abroad, which was found to be generally less liberal. The committee saw no reason to exempt law officers' opinions and departmental minutes and memoranda from the general rule, or, if seen under permit, to place an absolute prohibition upon the making of copies of them. Shortly before the report was signed, however, one of its members, Eyre Crowe, finding himself disowned by the Foreign Office on the question of giving access to law officers' reports before 1837, felt obliged to ask his masters[10]

---

9. The committee's report is printed in full in the *First Report of the Royal Commission on Public Records*, I, pt II, 62–64.

10. Correspondence is in FO 370/16 and FO 370/23.

whether we should not do wiser to withdraw from the Committee, whose
whole *raison d'être* was to devise means for making our public records more
readily accessible. An alternative would be that I do sign the report, as
representing my own views, and that the Secretary of State should decline to
accept its recommendations. There are obvious objections to either course.

Sir Charles (later Lord) Hardinge, the permanent secretary, thought it
desirable that Crowe should sign the report, and so it was decided to adopt
a suggestion from Sir William Davidson, the legal adviser, that before
volumes of Foreign Office general correspondence from 1781 to 1837 were
made generally available the law officers' opinions should be extracted from
them. It was a revealing aspect of the discussions on the matter, and the
limited circle in which they were resolved, that Davidson recorded during
the course of his exchanges with Crowe that he had met the master of the
rolls at a dinner party at Lyte's house during the summer and did not
understand him to favour the unrestricted publication of law officers' opinions. If the master of the rolls was correctly reported, it is by no means
clear how he squared his views with his position as chairman of the committee. Suffice to say that Davidson was in no doubt of the need to maintain
confidentiality, particularly when papers revealed divisions between the law
officers or changes of opinion. Although no early danger from disclosure
was involved, he made much of the wobbling that had taken place on the
part of the various law officers concerned with the Kowshing incident in
1894, when a British vessel was sunk by the Japanese with the loss of 1,500
Chinese troops. It was uncertain if a state of war between the two countries
existed at that time. The question then arose of liability in international law
for compensation to the shipowners, a matter which was settled with a claim
on the Chinese government, but only after an earlier draft charging the
Japanese government with responsibility had been cancelled when the lord
chancellor overruled the law officers. Davidson also foresaw difficulties if
publicity was given to the differing opinions of the law officers on the long-
standing controversy on the subject of 'continuous voyage', involving the
right of a belligerent to intercept contraband on a neutral vessel sailing
between neutral ports but ultimately bound for an enemy destination. Davidson's forthright views notwithstanding, Crowe had hoped that Sir Edward
Grey, the foreign secretary, might support his stand, but he was disappointed
because Grey endorsed the majority view that publication might 'very seriously embarrass the conduct of diplomatic negotiations with foreign governments, involving issues of great moment to this country'.

With Treasury authority the removal of the law officers' opinions went
on well into 1910. Although that exercise was not advertised, the public had
reason to be grateful to the Interdepartmental Committee because it made
it clear that permits to see records of later date than 1837 should normally
be granted to 'all *prima facie* competent and responsible persons engaged in
historical or biographical research, and that they should not be confined
to writers of established reputation or to individuals personally known to

Ministers'. The committee also thought that, contrary to the course favoured by Hall who was anxious to maintain conformity, it would not be right to withdraw the facilities already enjoyed by the public of inspecting certain Admiralty and War Office documents beyond 1837.

As part and parcel of the new arrangements, and because the 'open door' policy concerning admittance to the search rooms was no longer thought appropriate, the master of the rolls issued revised regulations concerning the public use of the records in 1909. Under the new rules searchers wishing to consult the records for literary or historical purposes were required to give satisfactory evidence of their respectability and good faith by applying for a student's ticket on a set form, or, in the case of foreigners, by means of a letter of introduction from their embassy or legation. By the end of the year, 733 such tickets had been issued. The opportunity was also taken to change from 1760 to 1800 the date after which fees were charged for the inspection of legal records, although the deputy keeper's power to remit them under the previous regulations of 1887 was dropped. Taking its lead from the general liberalisation, the Treasury also decided that it would no longer levy fees for the inspection of its records, which, in accordance with the Interdepartmental Committee report, it agreed to open, with certain exceptions, to 1837.

Overall, the committee's proposals resulted in the release to searchers of much valuable material, particularly as Grey agreed that Foreign Office records might be inspected under permit to 1860 instead of 1850 as formerly, so releasing material relating to the Crimean War. But the advance had to be set against the committee's affirmation of departmental freedom, subject to the consent of the master of the rolls, 'to withhold for any time any records, including more especially Law Officers' opinions, which cannot be made public without possible prejudice to the public service'. Those words resulted from the reservations that Crowe had been instructed to press, and were coupled with a statement that the public need be informed only 'that the opening of the records down to 1837 may be subject to certain temporary exceptions'. In practice, the master of the rolls delegated the entire operation of the new system to the Public Record Office, which did no more than ask departments which classes they wished to exempt, assuring them that no publicity would be given, except in response to a direct application to see the records concerned. Undoubtedly, however, the committee's proposals led to an appreciable move towards greater openness, and its recommendation that departments should be approached by the master of the rolls at ten-yearly intervals to see if the general access date might be advanced a decade represented another step forward.

For over ten years, ever since the battle about the Rolls Chapel, Lyte had enjoyed a comparatively quiet life. The old conflicts between the Hardy men and the Palgravians were little more than a memory, and the resentment provoked by his arrival in the office from outside had quite faded away. He had, too, the added advantage of a gifted band of men on the staff, and, not being afraid to delegate, he was able to employ their talents to their own and the office's benefit. Nevertheless, there were rumblings of discontent to be detected on the part of the attendants and repairers, and as Lyte approached his sixtieth birthday in 1908 there were signs that his Welsh critics were remobilising their forces for a fresh attack. Until then, Lyte had treated them, like the Irish, with some disdain, but the renewed complaints of a number of Welsh scholars, mainly members of the Honourable Society of Cymmrodorion, about the alleged neglect of their national records, persuaded him to refer to the Inspecting Officers' Committee the contents of some sacks and bundles of Welsh records that had remained in the office unsorted for over sixty years. The outcome was that the records concerned were scheduled and presented to the National Library of Wales at Aberystwyth in October 1909. But the Welshmen were not appeased, and in the very month that the unwanted records were returned to the principality a cutting from an unidentified newspaper was given to Roberts by the superintendent presaging trouble to come. Under the heading 'Wales and the Record Office' it read:

> The Welsh members are being galvanised afresh into action. A deputation consisting of Sir Alfred Thomas, Mr William Jones and Mr Llewelyn Williams have just waited on Mr Hobhouse as representing the Treasury to urge the special appointment of a Welsh expert on the staff of the Public Record Office. At the Public Record Office there are a large number of documents which relate to Wales alone, and it is felt that the services of a competent Welsh expert should be secured in order to elucidate and arrange this mass of documents as to make it of value to Welsh historians and archivists. In spite of the undisguised hostility of Sir Maxwell Lyte, the present Deputy Keeper, to the proposal there is every reason to believe that it will be carried into effect. The mere shadow of Mr Lloyd George's influence is omnipotent at the Treasury, and it is sufficient to say that he is in full sympathy with this and with every other proposal that concerns the national prestige of Wales.

In January 1910 the Welsh campaigners were given a boost when an article on 'The National Archives' appeared in the influential *Quarterly Review*,[11] then under the editorship of George (later Sir George) Walter Prothero, who was also co-editor of the *Cambridge Modern History*. Among other things, the article, while paying tribute to the great improvements in the administration of the Public Record Office under Lyte, singled out the inconvenience of the extent to which the Welsh records had been absorbed in English series. But the main complaint was that historical scholars were not involved in any way in the work of scheduling documents for disposal under the 1877 act or consulted about record publications. It was also

---

11. 212, no. 422 (January 1910), 32–52.

argued that important series of records were being retained in departmental archives, the powers of the master of the rolls to take them into his custody under the order in council of 1852 being little more than a dead letter. The article, besides complaining about restrictions on access to the records, contrasted the lack of preparation for those entering record employment in Britain with the training given to continental archivists in their schools of charters. It was unsigned, but 15 years later any doubts about its authorship were dispelled when sections of it were incorporated by Hall, who had by then retired, in his *British Archives and the Sources for the History of the World War*, which carried an acknowledgment of his indebtedness to the *Quarterly Review* and other publications for allowing him to use material from contributions he had previously made to them. On the whole it was a powerful and reasoned critique, even with its lofty condemnation of the state archivist, who 'gains his position in the same examination that qualifies the pupils of a crammer to write official *précis* or to cast accounts of revenue', possibly a reference to clerks in departmental record sections. Lyte, knowing Prothero's and Hall's common interest in the work and activities of the Royal Historical Society, must have suspected, even if he could not be certain, who wrote the article, but that would hardly have made it more palatable to him, particularly because its appearance in such a distinguished journal meant that it could not easily be shrugged off.

Indeed, inspired by it, Llewelyn-Williams, the Liberal MP for Carmarthen and a governor of the National Library of Wales, who had been on the deputation arguing for the appointment of a Welsh record expert in the previous autumn, tabled a motion in the Commons in April 1910, seeking a return to Parliament of information concerning practically every facet of the office's activities. Much of the information requested, such as the enumeration of the various classes of records not yet transferred, the classes missing or destroyed without statutory authority, and details of records in need of repair, would have been almost impossible to ascertain or could have been compiled only with great difficulty. On Lyte's advice Charles Hobhouse, financial secretary to the Treasury, replied courteously in the House to that effect, while M. F. Headlam from his private office wrote to Llewelyn-Williams stating the willingness of the Public Record Office to supply him with as much information as possible on application being made to it direct. Apologising for proffering the services of the office so freely, Headlam told Scargill-Bird: 'But as I believe that the object of the motion was not information but politics perhaps you will not be troubled'.[12] Headlam's suspicion that Llewelyn-Williams's real aim was to get special treatment for Wales was well founded because, taking advantage of the spring recess, he introduced a motion on the adjournment on 28 April 1910, to which Lloyd George himself made a short reply, indicating the government's

---

12. PRO 1/75: Headlam to Scargill-Bird, 20 April 1910.

sympathy with the idea of some kind of inquiry into the public records. Only the day before Llewelyn-Williams had written to Lloyd George, repeating many of the arguments in the *Quarterly Review* article, and calling for the appointment of a Royal Commission.[13]

Given Lloyd George's willingness to accommodate his countrymen, the establishment of a Royal Commission was merely a matter of time. Rosebery, a key figure in the Lords because of the controversy then raging about the Parliament Act, was the first to be thought of to head the commission, but in the event the post of chairman was offered in July 1910 to Sir Frederick Pollock, the eminent jurist and associate of Maitland. Three of the eight members subsequently appointed were Welshmen, Llewelyn-Williams not only being rewarded for his pertinacity, but being joined on the commission by Sir Henry Vincent Evans, another governor of the National Library of Wales, and Dr Henry Owen, its treasurer. Pollock had very much hoped that Prothero might be appointed, but he was obdurate that he was unable to find the time, and so Montague Rhodes James, the provost of King's College, Cambridge, was appointed instead. Professor Charles Firth, the regius professor of modern history at Oxford, was an obvious choice, and the other places were filled by Sir Sidney Lee, editor of the *Dictionary of National Biography*, Henry Tedder, the antiquary and secretary and librarian of the Athenaeum, and Sir Frederic Kenyon, director and principal librarian of the British Museum. Irrespective of his *Quarterly Review* article, Hall must have been well known to the Liberal establishment through his friendship with the Webbs and with Beveridge. His *Studies in English Official Documents*, published in 1908, must also have acquainted a different audience with his work, and, coupled with his special knowledge of the departmental records, meant that his appointment as secretary of the Royal Commission was no surprise. When the master of the rolls was first asked for his views about the government's intention to have an inquiry, he said he thought it desirable and that no objection could be raised by the record authorities. Lyte was less forthcoming, but let it be known that he was prepared to release Hall, believing 'his zeal and knowledge would prove useful to the Commission', but saying, significantly:[14]

> From the tone of your letter I gather that the Chancellor of the Exchequer and Sir Frederick Pollock do not think that the position of a member of the permanent staff of this Department would be in any way incompatible with that of Secretary to an independent inquiry into its administration. So far as I am concerned Mr Hall would be a 'persona grata'.

From that time onwards the activities of the commission, which was

---

13. Appendix XII.
14. T 172/35: Lyte to Clark, 23 August 1910.

formally constituted by Churchill as home secretary in October 1910, are minutely detailed in the three voluminous reports which it issued between 1912 and 1919. In many minor instances its recommendations were anticipated by internal reforms or tacitly adopted at a later date, but little or no notice was taken of its main findings, which would have involved a major change in the government of the Public Record Office itself by the introduction of a board of management, the establishment of a record office in Wales, and radical changes in the recruitment and training of record staff.

For Hall the inquiry was a personal tragedy because it brought him into conflict with Lyte and effectively prevented the further development of his career within the office. No one could have laboured with greater dedication – at the height of the commission's activities he was working from seven in the morning until eleven at night – but he probably knew too much about the office for his own good, and as a serving officer he was in an invidious position when, as will be seen in the case of the port books, the inevitable skeleton was found in the cupboard. For Lyte, who had no time for what he saw as the Welsh pretensions, Hall was almost in breach of trust in aiding and abetting them. To add to Hall's embarrassment, Fortescue, the Windsor librarian and military historian, who had long thought that the departmental records ought to have been linked with the British Museum, not only criticised the office management when he appeared before the commission in June 1911, but made a savage attack upon Lyte in a confidential memorandum which he put in subsequently.[15] According to him there was no *esprit de corps* in the Public Record Office, and the atmosphere was too often one of 'weariness, slackness and apathy'. The higher-grade officials, he said, had brains and good-will, but did not know how to command men. He blamed Lyte, who did not give the personal supervision necessary, unlike Sir Edward Bradford, who had restored the spirit of the Metropolitan Police by riding every day through one of his districts and speaking face to face with every man upon promotion.

Against that, the office was not short of defenders. Round did not deign to appear before the commission, but did not disguise his contempt for it, while Reginald Lane Poole, editor of the *English Historical Review*, made plain his approval of the way the department was managed in a written submission. Lyte himself put up a spirited performance when questioned for two days in February 1911, and Scargill-Bird, Roberts, Rodney, Salisbury, Headlam, Bland, Jenkinson and Pratt emerged unscathed. Lyte had specially asked the commission to examine Bland and Jenkinson as representatives of the younger clerks on the staff, and the attendance of the others had been with his approval. The supplementary clerks and the attendants and repairers had also wished to present evidence orally, but Lyte had refused to allow that although he subsequently passed to the commission statements

---

15. PRO 44/3: Fortescue's memorandum, 3 July 1911.

which they had drawn up with a view to an improvement in their position in the office. Earlier still, the attendants and repairers must have been in touch with Llewelyn-Williams, for in the summer of 1910 he had tabled a question in the House seeking the abolition of the distinction between the two classes into which they were divided, but the Treasury was unwilling to make any change. Emerging from retirement, Gairdner, Martin and Pike also gave evidence. The 83-year-old Gairdner, whose experience went back to the 1840s, quite stole the show with a masterly account of the office as it was and the progress that had been made. Lyte must have been rather more pleased with his contribution than with that from Pike, who took the opportunity to criticise his method of publishing the Close Rolls, comparing him unfavourably with Palgrave in that respect. Neither would Lyte have much appreciated the reservations expressed by Martin about the method of recruiting clerks, which, he maintained, did not always ensure that their Latin was up to the high standard required. Eight departmental officials, including the controller of the Stationery Office, were also examined, and evidence was taken from 42 other witnesses, drawn mainly from the universities, learned societies and Welsh interests as well as from overseas archivists, record agents and regular users of the search rooms. Rider Haggard, the author, did not quite fit into any of those categories, but attended because he wanted the office's publications to be sold more cheaply for the benefit of students and in order to make them more widely known. He was also concerned because many were no longer in print.

Major E. Poynton, the author of many antiquarian and genealogical papers and the holder of the first student's ticket to be issued in 1909, graphically described the inadequacies of the lighting and ventilation in the search rooms:[16]

> I do not like the light in the Round Room. The sun is very dangerous through the skylight when it is hot, and it is extremely cold in winter, and there are great draughts in the room. The hot air I think also is very unpleasant, and, for people who are at all of any age and affected by bronchial attacks or anything of that kind, it is most dangerous. In fact, I have friends who tell me that it is impossible to come to the Record Office; they are afraid to enter it. Then, if I may pass to the Legal Search Room, the fitting of the glass in the windows appears to me totally unsuited to give light; the ventilation by large openings in the window is also, I think, injurious. The Parcel Office, which is established at the back of the Record Office, leads to an enormous traffic over the asphalte in Fetter Lane. The other evening there were no less, I should think, than 50 two-horse waggons, besides motor cars and other vans drawn up near it; there is a great deal of refuse from the horses, and that is blown into the Search Rooms, at least

---

16. *First Report of the Royal Commission on Public Records*, I, pt III, 93.

into the Legal Room which I am speaking of. Then those rooms which look on to Fetter Lane have large openings in the windows, and when they are open the awful smoke from the factories is most dirty and prejudicial, not only to the documents but to those who are reading. It comes in dropping large blacks on to your paper. The other evening it had quite penetrated into the Literary Search Room, the Round Room, I suppose through the ventilators. I would like to add that there is a great amount of dust raised by this constant traffic up and down Fetter Lane, and that penetrates also; so that if you sit in the Legal Room for some hours and the window is open, you are perfectly covered with dirt when you go home afterwards. On the other hand, if the fresh air is excluded it is very injurious with those partially decaying documents to sit over them, I think, because the hot air dries them very rapidly. A document will come down which is fairly moist, a big Plea Roll, and you have to turn it with great care; but in the course of two or three days you will find that, by being out in the Search Room, it becomes practically dry and prepared almost to curl up; so that the whole time one is examining those big rolls there must be a great escape of dust and other matters from the rolls.

Not all the witnesses found the search rooms so uncongenial as Poynton, but there were a number of complaints about the delays in obtaining documents and the lack of works of reference, as well as fears that the accommodation would soon be inadequate. The question of greater access to Foreign and Colonial Office records was of some concern to such as H. A. L. Fisher, a fellow of New College, Oxford, later president of the Board of Education, and H. W. V. Temperley, the future co-editor of *British Documents on the Origins of the First World War*. Reference was made on more than one occasion by the non-official witnesses to the poor physical condition of certain records and the need for greater protection for seals. Some misgivings were also expressed about the office's editorial and publication work and the inconvenience of the censorship of notes when records were seen under permit. But although several witnesses thought that a more formal training for archivists, as on the continent, would be beneficial, the impression conveyed by much of the evidence was that, except on the vexed question of the Welsh and Chester records and some allegations about misguided destruction of material under the 1877 act, no great matters of principle were involved and that the office's problem related as much to lack of resources as to mismanagement or defects of policy. However, beneath the surface turbulent currents were swirling around and were soon to disturb the calm.

Chapter XIII

Lyte's 40-Year Reign: The Last Stage, 1912–1926

The First Report of the Commission was followed by a lively passage of arms which, to some people, will doubtless form a pleasant interlude in the study of archivistic literature.

(From Hubert Hall's *British Archives and the Sources for the History of the World War* (Oxford, 1925), 242)

Besides examining witnesses orally and considering a small amount of written evidence, the Royal Commission on Public Records arranged for a number of its members to visit archive establishments in France, Belgium and the Netherlands as well as those of departments, some of which, such as Admiralty dockyards, were in the provinces. An inspection was also made of the record offices at Chester and Ruthin, and a vast quantity of information was assembled by Hall and Professor Firth about the early history of the office and its later development. Most of the material gathered by them was subsequently reproduced in a series of appendixes to the commission's *First Report*. Given the comparatively short time at the disposal of the two men and the ill-arranged state of such records as were available to them for research, it was an extraordinary achievement, which was to establish their work as an authority of the first rank for the history of public records administration from the time of the Public Record Office Act of 1838. Because of the commission's wide terms of reference it was not surprising that it felt some concern when it heard early in 1911 that the master of the rolls had set up a small committee, with Rodney representing the Public Record Office, to advise him about the method of filing Chancery documents. The reason for the inquiry was the inconvenience experienced by searchers from the way documents relating to a particular action were scattered among a variety of classes according to the type of record. What the Public Record Office wanted was the introduction of a dossier system under which all the documentation for a case was brought together. The courts, however, were opposed to a break with the old system, and well over fifty years were to pass before they accepted the need for a change, which had by then the added blessing of the Denning Committee on Legal Records of 1966.[1]

The Royal Commission was not bothered so much about the detail of the master of the rolls's investigation as by the lack of recognition of its own interest in all matters affecting the work of the office. Its fears were height-

---

1. LCO 2/336 and PRO 1/76. Rodney's evidence to the Royal Commission on Public Records about this exercise will be found in its *Second Report*, II, pt III, 61a–63b. See also *Report of the Committee on Legal Records, 1966* (Cmnd. 3084).

ened when it also found out that the office had issued warrants at the end of 1910 to the clerks of assize of the several circuits to transfer their older records into the custody of the master of the rolls. The commission saw such a step as likely to prejudice any recommendation that it might make concerning the deposit of records locally, and to forestall future similar moves by the office it considered issuing an interim report. In the event it did no more than write to the office secretary in July 1911 asking to be told when further operations of that kind were contemplated. It came as something of a shock to the commission, therefore, when it learned some months later that a quantity of material was being brought into the office from Durham and Lancashire. It felt especially aggrieved because the possibility of returning Welsh, Cheshire, Durham and Lancashire records to their own regions was one of the matters which had been proposed to it in July 1911 by, among others, the distinguished medievalist T. F. Tout in the course of his evidence. But Lyte was adamant that the commission could not expect to arrest the normal working of the office, particularly as the records involved were in continuation of classes already transferred or had been purposely left behind for current business at the time of the original transaction. His attitude did nothing to help the relations between the two bodies, which were already strained as a result of investigations which the commission had been making into the fate of port books and coast bonds. From evidence given to it by Rodney in March 1911 it got to know that some such records were being held by the office in bulk, but were thought by him to be valueless. That opinion was not shared by N. S. B. Gras of Harvard University, who was carrying out research into the English grain trade from the twelfth to the late seventeenth century, and it was mainly owing to his representations, and those of the librarian of the Board of Customs and Excise, that the office agreed to allow certain commissioners to make a personal inspection of the port books and coast bonds it was still holding. When Pollock and some of his fellow commissioners visited Chancery Lane for that purpose at the end of July 1911 they were astonished to find that the records concerned were stacked on the floor of the western turrets in the roof of the repository, buried under heavy slates, and exposed to vermin and the elements. Shortly before their visit Scargill-Bird had written to Hall to tell him that as a result of schedules issued by the inspecting officers in 1896 and 1899 the post-1660 coast bonds and the port books of the Port of London after 1697 had been condemned, although the books from the ports other than London, the outports, were specifically excluded.[2] He also said that the second schedule, which had been drawn up after the 1898 act to provide for the destruction of documents before 1714, had still to be acted upon. However, Scargill-Bird was mistaken because both schedules had been executed many years previously. Consequently the records seen by the

---

2. PRO 1/76: Scargill-Bird to Hall, 20 July 1911.

commissioners, although they did not know it at the time, were pre-1660 coast bonds, outport books and pre-1697 books of the Port of London.

The port books seen by the commissioners were lucky to have survived at all because they had suffered many vicissitudes since the end of the eighteenth century, when as a result of a parliamentary inquiry the practice of depositing them with the king's remembrancer of the Exchequer as a check upon the activities of the revenue officers was discontinued. In theory, since much the same information should have been held by the customs officers themselves, their indefinite preservation was difficult to justify, but when the question of their disposal was considered by the Record Commission in 1833 C. P. Cooper, its secretary, wisely counselled caution because of the huge loss of customs documents when Custom House was destroyed by fire in 1814. In 1842 Cole reported to Palgrave that there were about two hundred and fifty sacks of coast bonds and seven sacks of port books at Carlton Ride. Cole entertained no doubt about the destruction of the coast bonds, but he thought that although the port books were never consulted they should not be destroyed, at least until it was seen whether they formed a link with the series of customs accounts then being arranged by Hunter. Palgrave agreed, saying:[3a]

> As far as I can judge all the earlier Port Books would certainly require to be preserved. As concerning the later ones I can give no opinion, yet I am not prepared to say that the circumstance of their never having been consulted in the recollection of the Queen's Remembrancer would be a sufficient reason for their destruction.

All the more remarkable, therefore, that a year later, in his *Fourth Report*, Palgrave should misstate Cole's views by agreeing with him that, because the coast bonds and port books had never been known to be searched and were considered useless by the Exchequer officers, they might be destroyed. Many record scholars have since expressed surprise at Palgrave's lapse from grace, and even as late as 1854 he was saying that they were of 'very little if of any use' and that he understood 'it might be thought desirable to destroy them'.[3b] Nevertheless, he took no action to rid himself of either class, and both were later moved to the Stone Tower, Westminster, before their eventual transfer to the new repository at Chancery Lane. When it came to review these records between 1896 and 1899 the Inspecting Officers' Committee had no difficulty in scheduling the later coast bonds for destruction. Similarly, it authorised the disposal of the London port books from 1697 to 1799 because they were incomplete and because many were decayed or illegible. Also it had ascertained that the information they contained was

---

3a. PRO 2/90, pp 100–101: Palgrave to Cole, 27 January 1842.
3b. PRO 2/4, p 282: Palgrave to Hunter, 9 December 1854.

to be found in a more convenient form in the customs ledgers of imports and exports. The same was not thought to be true of those from the outports and for that reason they were specifically reserved for further examination and consideration. Possibly because Pike, the inspecting officer most concerned, retired shortly afterwards, the intended investigation was forgotten and by 1911, when the commissioners visited the roof, the status of the surviving documents had become something of a mystery, not least to Rodney, the assistant keeper in charge of the Repository. However, as a result of the commission's probings they were immediately moved to more appropriate accommodation and editorial work was begun upon them as a matter of urgency. By the end of 1911 many of them were available to readers and as the news of their existence spread they became a happy hunting-ground for economic historians.

Had the case of these documents been an isolated one the commission might have been content with its success in getting them listed and made accessible; but there were also large masses of files of the common law courts, dating from the thirteenth century to the nineteenth, in a similar unsatisfactory condition. In fact, the bulk of them were to remain sacked and unsorted until after their banishment to the Hayes repository from the Chancery Lane tower in 1964, when a search room on the roof was planned, a project which was later abandoned. Until his death C. A. F. Meekings, the distinguished post-Second-World-War assistant keeper, did much useful work upon them at Hayes, and both before and since their return to the Chancery Lane tower in 1986 the task of bringing them to order has been in the hands of David Crook. Besides its concern about these files, the Royal Commission was also alarmed about a large quantity of Chancery masters' documents, which remained unarranged, and a long-neglected collection of more than a hundred large bundles of supplementary state papers. In addition it was highly critical of the past activities of the Inspecting Officers' Committee and thought it was essential that at least one of its members should have a special knowledge of departmental records and be well acquainted with historical literature. While it may have been thought that Hall's membership of the committee disposed of any immediate difficulty in that respect, it was perfectly understandable that when the commission came to make its *First Report* at the end of September 1912 it should make much of the defects it found, but in its zeal for reform it so far forgot itself as to claim that as a result of its 'discovery' the port books and coast bonds 'have had a narrow escape from destruction at the hands of the Committee of Inspecting Officers'.[4]

Needless to say, Lyte, who had been a party to the original decisions concerning those documents, was indignant about the way he believed the commission had libelled the office. He was also angry about the manner

---

4. *First Report*, I, pt I, 9 and 18.

in which it had assailed the office's treatment of the Welsh records: it complained that they were badly arranged and that no separate series of publications had been devoted to them. Neither was he in any way appeased by the tribute paid to him personally by the commission in its recognition of the 'immense progress' made under his administration towards making the national collection of archives what it ought to be. Lyte was concerned that the commission's report would come to be seen as an authoritative statement of conditions in 1912, and so he thought it necessary that it should amend or withdraw those passages which were factually incorrect. Not surprisingly, the commission was not prepared to do anything of the kind although Hall frankly admitted responsibility for having misled it about the port books, blaming, somewhat disingenuously, the garbled information which had been supplied to him by the office at the time. Despite his mistake, Hall had had the full backing of Pollock, who was convinced that, whatever the niceties, but for the commission's intervention, the port books would have been left to rot in the turrets. However, there seems little doubt that Hall was perfectly sincere when he told the commission, in commenting upon Lyte's observations, that he hoped his own remarks would in no way appear 'disrespectful to a chief whose age and attainments entitle him to the profound respect' with which he had always regarded him.[5] How far that respect was then reciprocated must be a matter of conjecture, but it is possible that Lyte's decision to soldier on when he became 65 in 1913 was not unconnected with his unwillingness to open the way for the possibility of Hall's further advancement. However that may be, there was no doubt that Lyte, and for that matter the master of the rolls, were looking to their defences. One of their first moves, evidently in response to the commission's proposal for a board of historical scholars to direct the office's publications, was to take steps at the end of 1912 to establish an advisory committee of historians to assist in the formulation of policy. Wisely, Cozens-Hardy did not attempt to exclude sworn critics, several being among those who accepted his invitation to join the committee, the initial membership of which comprised Lyte, C. H. Firth, regius professor of modern history at Oxford, P. Vinogradoff, professor of jurisprudence at Oxford, R. Lane Poole, keeper of Oxford University Archives, H. W. V. Temperley, fellow of Peterhouse, Cambridge, A. F. Pollard, professor of English history at London, and T. F. Tout, professor of medieval and ecclesiastical history at Manchester. Crump, Stamp, and Johnson were also appointed, the last-named as secretary. All three were disciples of Hall, and so it was clear that every effort was being made to contain the voices of dissent. Hall may have had only one other ally within the office, possibly Jenkinson, because in commenting upon a paper written

5. PRO 44/3: Hall's memorandum, 22 January 1913.

by Crump on record classification Hall had told Johnson in the previous year:[6]

> Firth is primed and will be able to testify that there are 4 just men in our city. I wish with all my heart that we could have had some better evidence but I hope to make the art[icle] on Records loom large somewhere or other.

Certainly Hall needed all the friends he could muster and must have hoped that they would not now desert him, because, besides upsetting Lyte, the dismissive remarks made by the commission about the master of the rolls having ceased to control the office and being only 'nominal custodian of the public records' could scarcely have gone down well with Cozens-Hardy. In fact, whatever his personal feelings, Cozens-Hardy was not opposed to the Royal Commission's proposal for a board of commissioners to govern the office, drawn in equal proportions from the judiciary, the public offices and the world of historical studies, provided that he was not only a member but also ex-officio chairman. Nevertheless, when Lyte, possibly with tongue in cheek, reproached the Royal Commission for understating the role of the master of the rolls, it may be assumed that he did so with Cozens-Hardy's blessing. The main burden of Lyte's critical observations at that time, however, was to counter the unfair manner in which he considered the office had been castigated for its treatment of the port books and the Welsh records. But the fact that he also introduced the subject of the master of the rolls presented the commission with the opportunity both to turn down his request to amend its report and to put him in his place by pointing out:[7]

> In the special circumstances of this Commission any representation or inquiry addressed by the Master of the Rolls to the Commissioners would have their most respectful attention; but my Commissioners feel that the only person with whom they could now properly discuss the office and position of the Master of the Rolls in relation to the Public Record Office is the Master of the Rolls himself.

> The Deputy Keeper's criticism seems to assume, in sundry places, that the Commissioners have relied wholly on oral or written testimony. In fact

---

6. PRO 9/15: Hall to Johnson, 3 May 1911. Jenkinson who was close to Crump could not, of course, have made up the quartet if Hall included himself, but it is also possible that Stamp was no longer counted among the righteous by Hall. The article mentioned was written by Crump and appeared in the eleventh edition of the *Encyclopaedia Britannica* (New York, 1910–1911), XXII, under the heading 'Record'.

7. PRO 1/78: Hall to Roberts, 27 February 1913. The correspondence was later published in *The Times* of 21 May 1913, having been sent to it by Pollock when Lyte's counterblast appeared in his *Annual Report*.

several of the statements to which he takes exception are made from the personal knowledge and inspection of members of the Commission, who have no reason to doubt the witness of their own eyes.

In justice to other persons whose statements, and the Commissioners' inferences from them, which the Deputy Keeper disputes my Commissioners feel bound to say, generally, that they fail to find in his Memorandum anything amounting to proof of material errors or outside the range of ordinary controversial difference.

Unabashed, Lyte played his trump card, his *Annual Report*, the seventy-fourth in the series, using it shamelessly to take the commissioners to task for the errors into which 'they as a body or a minority of them' had fallen, 'of course unwittingly'. It would be tedious to set out in detail his onslaught, which the commission thought in doubtful taste, but on the work of the inspecting officers he made the very valid point that while the commissioners had prominently instanced the single case – it concerned some Admiralty records – where the views of a department in favour of preservation had prevailed, they were silent about the numerous cases in which records had been saved from destruction by the committee. Confident that there was nothing to hide, Lyte also responded to a suggestion from the commission that the disposal schedules should be published by arranging for them to be reprinted in a single volume, which appeared in 1914. However, at the home secretary's suggestion Lyte's sarcastic reference in the report as originally printed to 'the nine gentlemen whom your Majesty was graciously pleased to appoint' was toned down to read simply 'the nine Commissioners'. Similarly, the words 'For reasons which it is unnecessary to enquire' were deleted from the section dealing with Wales, so that it began, hardly less effectively: 'The Welsh Records have received from the commissioners an amount of attention somewhat disproportionate to their number or importance'.

The effect of the jousting between the two sides was to blunt the force of the commission's main proposals, particularly as there was no disposition on the part of either the Home Office or the Treasury to lend support. Neither department wished to become entangled in the argument, and it was soon apparent that, except for minor improvements and adjustments capable of introduction administratively and acceptable to Lyte and Cozens-Hardy, no early or radical changes were in prospect. The commission had certainly not won the first round but it had by no means given up the struggle, and it must have hoped that its exposure of the absurdity of the 1852 order in council, whereby the master of the rolls had it in his power to disrupt the Civil Service at a stroke, had prepared the ground for the reshaping of the 1838 act. Despite its admission that 'in this, as in many other cases, the work of English public servants is more intelligent than their official rules', many of the changes the commission envisaged, such as the removal of the master of the rolls as head of the office, could not be accomplished without legislation. It was a weakness of its report that it did not spell out the statutory implications of its major proposals and that they tended to be obscured by the many recommendations it also made which were of secondary importance, such as making the use of book rests by searchers obligatory. It was not, therefore, surprising that its proposals failed to make any dramatic impact. Even its suggestion that the restrictions on the production of departmental records should be loosened failed to strike a chord with a wider public. In a sense, of course, its reference to the records being generally open to 'such a late date as 1837', which already made them at least 75 years old, was hardly in advance of its time. Yet its wish to see departmental records transferred at regular intervals except for those which were 'really confidential' was wholly praiseworthy. Moreover, while making plain its intention to defer to a further report its consideration of departmental and other archives not yet transferred to the Public Record Office, it did not conceal its belief that it was wrong that papers already there which were never confidential, or had ceased to be so, should be treated as though there was some mystery about them. In a statement to cheer latter-day campaigners for freedom of information it also affirmed its conviction[8a]

> that no useful purpose can be served by the suppression of historical facts
> or the concealment of documentary evidence except in the case of matters so
> recent as to be still confidential.

Meanwhile the Welshmen, undeterred by Lyte, and in the knowledge that the commission was backing their case for a record office for Wales, had drafted a Public Records (Wales) Bill and a number of Welsh municipalities had drawn up addresses or prepared brochures in which claims were laid for the proposed record office to be established in their own localities. The bill was introduced in 1913 and again in 1914 but failed to make progress because, although it had attracted support from both sides of the House, the Cheshire members were opposed to it and managed to talk it out. With the outbreak of the First World War it was quite forgotten, the one concession to Welsh sentiment being the issue of a volume in that year in the series of Lists and Indexes dealing with the records of the Principality of Wales and the Honour of Peveril, as well as those of the Palatinates of Chester, Durham and Lancaster. In 1925 a Welsh MP, Haydn Jones, asked the Treasury when it was proposed to carry out the Royal Commission's recommendations, but he did not succeed in getting any action.[8b] Suggestions for change continued to be made from time to time, notably by the Welsh Reconstruction Advisory Council in 1943. But nothing altered until the Public Records Act 1958 when a number of Welsh record offices were among

---

8a. *First Report*, I, pt I, 38. Home Office papers are in HO 45/10997/198563.

8b. T 161/250/S26870. The later proposals of the Welsh Reconstruction Advisory Council are in PRO 1/602.

those appointed places of deposit for public records created locally and of predominantly local interest, such as those of magistrates' courts and hospitals. Even more important, the bulk of the records brought up from the principality to Chancery Lane by Charles Roberts in the 1850s were transferred to the National Library of Wales at Aberystwyth in 1962 under another clause of the same act.

Not all the Royal Commission's proposals took so long to mature. Its call for more resources for repair work resulted in some increase in the Treasury grant. There had been a gradual expansion in that side of the office's activities over the years so that by 1912 the number of men engaged upon conservation duties had risen to 19 as against 12 at the turn of the century. Salisbury, who was promoted to the assistant keeper grade when Handcock retired in 1911, was also given special responsibility for the Repair Department, which had not previously enjoyed regular supervision at a senior level. Its distinctive existence and the growing systematization of its work were seen in the appearance of short papers in 1912 and 1914 written by Albert Byerley, the chief repairer and binder, concerning the method of repairing documents, the first of which was prepared for the information of the Cape Archives Commission.[9] Greater attention was also being given to the protection of seals, and in 1913, in conjunction with the government chemist, R. C. Fowler, who had a scientific background, was given responsibility for an investigation into their chemical composition with a view to their better preservation in future. Editorially, seals had previously been neglected, but in 1912 Sir William St John Hope of the Society of Antiquaries was invited to make a catalogue of them – a task which he started the following year and continued until his death in 1919, when Fowler, by then an assistant keeper, succeeded him, combining the work with his duties as officer-in-charge of the Repository. The Royal Commission had been of the opinion that the pay of the office's lower grades compared unfavourably with that of similar staff in other departments, and its recommendation for an improvement, which was backed by Lyte, resulted in the introduction in 1913 of new pay scales, taking the first-class men from a maximum of 45s a week to 50s and the second-class men from 37s to 40s. Pratt's pay as superintendent was also raised by some £20 a year to £165 and Byerley went from 52s to 60s a week, but only after strong representations from the office in response to the Treasury's initial refusal to increase the pay of either of them. The men were a closely-knit band and their activities extended to the social side, taking them as far away as the Ship Hotel, Southend-on-Sea, for their annual dinners. On the evidence of the toasts in 1913, neither the master of the rolls nor the deputy keeper had to fear for their loyalty (Plate 23).

---

9. PRO 1/77: enclosure to Roberts's letter of 15 February 1912; and PRO 1/79: Byerley's memorandum of 23 July 1914.

Two more of the Royal Commission's recommendations were adopted in 1914: the resident officer's allowance was increased from £150 to £200; and the allowances to the members of the Inspecting Officers' Committee were increased from a total of £150 to £250 but distributed differently. Whereas previously the two assistant keepers received £50 each and the two clerks £25, in future the barrister member was to have £100 and each of the other three £50. Both as resident officer and as one of the inspecting officers Hall, who was already receiving an extra £250 as duty pay for his services as secretary to the Royal Commission, benefited from the changes. Outside the office he also drew a salary of 100 guineas as literary director of the Royal Historical Society, a post he had held since 1891, but the possibility of accommodation being provided for him on the Chancery Lane site remained as remote as ever despite the commission's recommendation to that effect. Neither did anything emerge from its backing for an improvement in the pay of the supplementary clerks, and it was only after they had taken their case to the Conciliation and Arbitration Board for Government Employees in 1917 that it was agreed that up to four of them might proceed to a maximum of £300. The increase was, in fact, restricted to George Pilbeam and Albert Gregory, the two senior men. At the same time the superintendent withdrew a claim he had made to the board, when the Treasury agreed to increase his salary to £180 a year to maintain his differential with the men beneath him who had received a war bonus.

Inevitably, the outbreak of war in 1914 created many problems for the office, aggravated by the fact that a number of staff changes had occurred in 1912, when Scargill-Bird retired as secretary and was succeeded by Roberts, whose place as secretary of the Historical Manuscripts Commission was taken by Stamp. The same year also saw the retirement of Sharp and Isaacson. Lyte recommended both for appointment as companions of the Imperial Service Order, but membership was limited and only Sharp received the distinction. He was the first member of the office to do so, although when the order was instituted in 1902 Lyte had contemplated naming one of the assistant keepers, having first confirmed that Lowson, then approaching retirement, was ineligible, the transcriber class to which he belonged not being considered sufficiently senior to qualify.[10] The unnamed assistant keeper – it may well have been Martin, who had by then lost some of his gaiety – declined the honour, perhaps because it hardly stood comparison, in that class-conscious age, with the CB awarded to Gairdner in 1900 in recognition of his work on *Letters and Papers, Foreign and Domestic, Henry VIII*. Sharp, who had done much good service in connection with the *Return of Members of Parliament*, had no compunction about acceptance and went on to draw his pension until 1951, when he died aged 103. Scargill-Bird's and Isaacson's retirement led to Johnson and Flower joining

---

10. PRO 1/175: Hewby to Lyte, 15 August 1902.

the Inspecting Officers' Committee, the latter becoming its legal member in 1919 when Roberts finally retired. The three assistant keeper vacancies were filled by the promotion of E. G. Atkinson, Brodie and Hall. Brodie was soon to assume sole editorial responsibility for *Letters and Papers*, because Gairdner resigned on account of eye trouble in July 1912 and died shortly afterwards. In 1914 another assistant keeper vacancy occurred with the retirement of Morris, whose editorial and other services were set out by Lyte in the *Seventy-sixth Report* and who was succeeded by J. G. Black. The foreman, H. W. Weatherley, also retired in 1914 after more than forty-five years' service and had the distinction of being the first member of the office's manual staff to be awarded the Imperial Service Medal, although a number of others were honoured similarly thereafter. Of the six clerks who entered the office during this period only R. L. Atkinson was to serve for any length of time. O. C. Chapman came in from the Post Office but never settled down and, after spells on loan to other departments during and after the war, moved to the Colonial Office in 1923. In 1926 he was offered back, but to the disgust of the Colonial Office, which thought it had been misled, the office declined to take him. J. G. Phillimore was transferred from the Inland Revenue in 1912, having been sponsored by Lord Aberdare, but the war left him an invalid and he was pensioned in 1919. Neither E. Elgey nor T. Ameer Ali stayed for more than a few months. W. R. Cunningham was on active service throughout the war and left in 1925 on appointment as librarian of Glasgow University. R. L. Atkinson, on the other hand, returned from the front with the Military Cross in 1919[11] and went on to play a prominent part in the life of the office and of the Historical Manuscripts Commission of which he was appointed secretary in 1938.

One higher-grade clerk, one supplementary clerk and five attendants lost their lives while on military service. In 1922 an alabaster tablet was placed in the Museum on the north wall to commemorate them.[12a] Among those who fell was Alfred Bland, who was killed in action on 1 July 1916, the opening day of the Battle of the Somme, and Leonard Benstead, an attendant, who was awarded the Military Medal in 1918 for gallantry as a stretcher bearer. Bland was one of the most promising of the office's younger clerks, and apart from work on the Fine Rolls had been a lecturer for the Workers' Educational Association. He also edited with R. H. Tawney and P. A. Brown *English Economic History: Select Documents* which was published in 1914. The editorial work of the office was badly hit by the war, particularly that of the editors whose work took them abroad. It was also obvious that as long as it lasted there would be no special events, such as the Shakespearian

---

11. PRO 8/55, p 194. According to *The Times* of 19 July 1917 he assumed command of his company in the Royal West Surrey Regiment when his commander was killed, reorganised it and with great bravery led it to its final objective which he successfully consolidated.

12a. Papers of the War Memorial Committee are in PRO 39/6.

Exhibition which had been held in April 1913, but the horrors of aerial warfare had still to be fully appreciated. In a letter to the Office of Works soon after the outbreak of war Roberts wrote:[12b]

> The building as no doubt you are aware, is believed to be practically fireproof and the fire-extinguishing appliances are supposed to be as perfect as possible. Nevertheless, a dropped bomb might do great and irreparable damage. The roof is partly of slate and partly of iron. It has been suggested that it should be protected either by strong wire netting or by bags of sand. The latter plan would seem to promise the greater effectiveness.

For a time the Museum continued to function normally, but not long after the air raids began in the summer of 1915 it was closed and the glass removed to a place of safety. Elsewhere in the office, accommodation had been found for the Military Branch of the Historical Section of the Committee of Imperial Defence and for the corresponding branches of the Canadian and Australian forces, including the provision of a photographic studio in the basement for filming regimental diaries and other documents. An Army Spectacles Depot also operated from a hut erected in the garden of Clifford's Inn. Although the fear of intensified air raids led to Domesday Book, the Chancery enrolments and other valuable records being evacuated to Bodmin Prison in February and March 1918, the building remained relatively unscathed. Apart from a little shrapnel damage, the most serious incident was in October 1917 when a shell fragment came through the glass roof of the Round Room. Shortly after the removal to Bodmin a further batch of records, including palatinate documents and material from the Colonial Office and the Foreign Office, was placed in the Post Office underground railway at Newgate Street, which had originally been intended to provide shelter for Domesday but which was not ready in time. Pratt had supervised the bulk of the removals to Bodmin, but Domesday Book was taken down in person by Crump and handed over to Story-Maskelyne who had been put in charge, following his promotion to the assistant keeper grade in 1917 when E. G. Atkinson retired. In all, some thirty van-loads were moved out,[13a] but that was only a small percentage of the whole. It was an odd feature that while the removal of the more precious records was thought essential, the lower corridors of the building continued to be open to the public as a refuge during air raids. Hall was on the spot throughout as resident officer in nearby Lincoln's Inn, and his first incident report was typical of others that followed:[13b]

> I was on duty here at 10.30 p.m. when an alarm was received by telephone.

12b. PRO 1/79: Roberts to Office of Works, 22 October 1914.
13a. Schedules of evacuated documents are in PRO 1/83.
13b. PRO 1/80: Hall to Roberts, 9 September 1915.

Mr Rodney (for Special Constabulary) was informed by messenger, as arranged. I kept observation with the Police Sergeant till 10.50 p.m. when the anti-aircraft guns all round us opened fire and the search lights showed a large Zeppelin advancing slowly from S.E. to N.W. and after dropping bombs in the City she turned W. coming directly over this Office with a furious fire directed on her from the guns. I heard a large piece of shell (presumably) strike one of the roofs. I went on to the Repository roof with the Sergeant but saw nothing. The Zeppelin was then receding towards the N.W. rising all the time. The fumes from the guns were very noticeable but did not penetrate into the Repository.

I remained on duty till 1 a.m. when all was quiet and no fires observed anywhere near the Office.

Throughout the war years the department continued to cope with a large number of searches in the census records of 1841 and 1851, which had been deposited in the office in May 1912. Palgrave's vigilance had first saved them from destruction, but their eventual arrival in the repository was mainly so that enquiries from pensions officers and the Local Government Board, arising from claims under the Old Age Pensions Act of 1908, might be dealt with, because many applicants were unable to supply evidence of age. Consequently the census returns were treated as legal documents and their production was subject to fees. Not long after their arrival the office had been obliged to engage four extra boy clerks, and since by 1917 no man eligible for military service remained on the strength, the work was a considerable drain on clerical resources. Most of those absent from the office were in the forces,[14a] but some had been seconded to other departments. One of those in that category was Fowler whose work in the Casualty Section of the War Office was to be recognised in 1918 by the award of the OBE.

The office also had to deal with an increased demand from the Home Office for denization documents wanted for proceedings against aliens, as well as from persons of foreign extraction claiming to be English. There were also searches for the War Office to check the services of re-enlisted soldiers who might be entitled to proficiency pay. In one important respect, however, the office was fortunate because even before the war broke out the Repository organisation was operating at a higher state of efficiency than had ever been the case before. Most of the credit for that was due to Harley Rodney, who had been responsible for that side of the work since his promotion, out of turn, to the assistant keeper grade in 1906, a move which had provoked a strong protest at that time from E. G. Atkinson, the most senior of those passed over. For departmental records, short call-numbers

---

14a. The armed services record of the staff will be found at the back of PRO 1/84.

had largely been substituted for the earlier cumbersome references, so that instead of writing 'Foreign Office Embassy Archives, Prussia and Germany, 1819', a searcher now wrote 'FO 244/10'. A few of the legal classes had been dealt with similarly, but it was not until 1929 that the entire system was made uniform. Unfortunately old references were not always sufficiently keyed up so that many years later Buckland could refer disparagingly to the 'rash (or Rodney) school'.[14b] The Royal Commission had also criticised shortcomings in that respect, particularly in relation to the great sortation of material at the time of the move into the new building which had resulted in the history of individual documents often being irretrievably lost. On the other hand the production work of the office had been transformed by the improvements effected, without which it would have been quite unable to meet subsequent jumps in demand. A further innovation was the introduction of a Summary of Records, giving concise details and location of the many classes held. As a result of a Royal Commission recommendation cardboard boxes and cartons were also being introduced for the storage of unbound documents previously wrapped in brown paper and tied with string. It was recognised that boxes were easier to handle and kept out dust, but there was some fear that they were less effectual against damp.

Giving evidence to the Royal Commission in 1911, Rodney described his relationship to the search rooms as 'those of the cook to the waiter in the restaurant'. His practicality and large store of common sense made him the obvious successor as secretary in 1916 to Roberts, whose deputy he had been since 1912. Rodney's appointment to the secretaryship resulted in an assistant keeper vacancy which was filled by Crump. Rodney could have served until 1923 when he was 65, but in 1918, quite out of the blue, he decided to retire, telling the 70-year-old Lyte, pointedly, that he wished to have leisure in his old age. A little earlier Story-Maskelyne, who had been writing to him constantly about his personal accommodation difficulties at Bodmin and his worries about the presence of mildew on the records there, was in correspondence with Lyte, who was inclined to take his complaints about the 'risky experiment' at the prison rather more seriously than Rodney. But Story-Maskelyne could be wearing and it may be wondered if Lyte's intervention may have upset Rodney sufficiently to decide that the office might just as well do without him. Whether or not that was the case, the result was that Rodney went to live, and play chess, at Hastings while Stamp, who had been assisting on the administrative and accounting side of the office for some time, stepped into his shoes as secretary. The assistant keeper vacancy created by Rodney's retirement eventually went to Fowler, Stamp's reward being £100 a year extra on top of his clerical pay and the

---

14b. PRO 1/94: Buckland to Flower, [30] April 1927. Buckland was reporting on the Petrie Papers.

£100 a year he was already getting as secretary of the Historical Manuscripts Commission.

The year 1918 also saw the retirement on health grounds of Cozens-Hardy as master of the rolls. The health of his successor, Sir Charles Swinfen-Eady (later Lord Swinfen), was also soon to fail, and he was replaced in 1919 by Lord Sterndale. But for the war, and these changes at the head of the office, Lyte's continuance as deputy keeper might well have been called in question, especially as he was becoming increasingly detached from day-to-day business. As it was, and since there was no doubt about his wish to remain and there was no strong contender for his post, he was allowed to indulge his antiquarian tastes with the help of his staff in a new edition of *The Book of Fees*, otherwise known as the 'Testa de Nevill', which contained copies entered about 1307 of a number of returns and lists preserved in the Exchequer.

In the same year that Sterndale became master of the rolls the third and final report of the Royal Commission on Public Records, dealing with local records of a public nature, was published. The commission's second report, which concerned records in departmental archives, had appeared in 1914, but very few of its recommendations had been carried out. Its main conclusion was that departmental record sections should be manned by trained staff and reorganised as branch repositories under the supervision of the Public Record Office. Such a policy flew in the face of all that had been attempted before in bringing the records together on one site, and it was difficult to see how it could in any way further the interests of searchers. But the commission argued that the policy of concentration had practically broken down and that the Public Record Office could not be enlarged on its Chancery Lane site indefinitely. The commission's exhaustive enquiries, fully detailed in its voluminous report, also indicated that the extent of departmental holdings was very much greater than previously supposed and much was of great value for historical purposes. In other countries the national record office was supplemented by departmental and district record offices, and it thought that a similar policy should now be followed in Britain, at least, so far as departmental records were concerned, until they could be treated as merely materials for history. What the commission did not say was that Britain was unique in having a highly centralised governmental system and did not have the state and provincial administrations invariably found in other countries. The inter-relationship of the various cogs in the Whitehall machinery of government meant that the union of their preservable records was of immense value to searchers, and the abandonment of that concept could hardly be expected to appeal to them. It was surprising that Hall, of all people, did not recognise that fact because when it came to knowledge about the records of departments few would have quarrelled with the tribute paid to him by the royal commissioners in their *Second Report*: in recording their debt to him, they said that in their judgment 'no living person is his rival in comprehensive acquaintance with the archives of this country both within and without the Public Record Office'.[15] At that time, however, the feelings of admiration were not entirely reciprocated, and in an unsigned article on 'The National Records' in *The Edinburgh Review* of October 1914 Hall described the proposals of the commission for housing the archives as 'slightly confused and somewhat ineffective' while reserving his main scorn for the imperfections of the Public Record Office compared with the scientific administration of continental repositories.

Hall's differences with the commissioners arose from their willingness to see some expansion at the Chancery Lane repository as well as in departments. Some additional land had been acquired in Clifford's Inn by the Office of Works in 1912, and in 1913 Fowler had drawn up plans for extending the Public Record Office southwards at its Fetter Lane end to provide accommodation for 70 literary and 40 legal searchers. Fowler's scheme also envisaged the conversion of the 45-seat Round Room to a departmental search room and racking up the Long Room for record storage. Lyte was strongly in favour and the commission endorsed the idea. Alternatively, Lyte suggested a suburban repository or a branch record office in the Whitehall area for records not yet open to public inspection. Hall, on the other hand, preferred to concentrate exclusively upon the fitting and equipping of departmental archives. He was even more anxious for local records to be deposited locally, as had first been proposed by the Committee on Local Records of 1902, of which Lyte had been a member. Lyte's evidence to the commission on the matter in November 1914 proved that he still remained of that mind. He also took the opportunity of his re-appearance before the commission to bring it up to date about strayed public records, having recently succeeded in recovering a fourteenth-century register of the Black Prince and some assize records. In both cases the documents were handed over voluntarily and honoraria were paid, but the office's position had been greatly strengthened in that in July 1914 the law officers had advised that, on the assumption that the crown had never owned the documents as personal private property, they could not be alienated and the master of the rolls was entitled to issue a warrant for their recovery.[16a] The day before Lyte appeared before the commission it received evidence from Sidney Webb, the leading authority on local government, who favoured as much centralisation as possible.

The commission was prevented by the Treasury from proceeding with the publication of its findings until the end of hostilities, and as a result of the delay, coupled with the enormous growth in governmental activity as a result of the war, it decided to look again at its earlier proposals for the retention by departments of their archives. Some shift in thinking was already to be seen in a further unsigned article written by Hall on 'The

---

15. *Second Report* (Cd. 7544), II, pt I, 4.
16a. PRO 1/79: enclosure to Muir Mackenzie's letter of 30 July 1914 to Rodney.

Archives of the War' which was published in *The Quarterly Review* in April 1917. By then there had been a proposal for a National (later Imperial) War Museum in which, it was suggested, the war records might be housed. Lyte's first reaction was ambivalent, but on fuller reflection he considered the idea flawed, and his doubts were strengthened when his one-time critic, Fortescue, the military historian and Windsor Castle librarian, told him that he thought the scheme 'sheer imbecility' because he believed that it was impossible 'to separate the doings of any section of the nation (such as an army in the field) from those of the nation at large'.[16b] Sir Martin Conway, the future director-general of the museum, felt badly let down by Lyte, but did his best to save the records project by seeking the commission's support. However, Firth, for one, had reservations, and the consensus of opinion was that to place records spanning a limited period of years in a separate repository would be a great inconvenience both to historians and to departments and would cut across the archival principle of preserving the continuity of any body of administrative records. Nevertheless, the changed situation created by the war resulted in the commission proposing, in what was to be its final report, that instead of its original recommendation for departmental record offices a brand new office of the Public Record Office should be built next to the museum to take all departmental records after the reign of Queen Victoria.

Although the report was signed in April 1918 it was not published until the following year. Its main emphasis was upon the local records, such as those of clerks of the peace, town clerks and ecclesiastical authorities, which, it thought, should be brought under the control and superintendence of the master of the rolls. However, nothing concrete emerged from its recommendations and so far as its *volte-face* on departmental records was concerned it soon became clear that the possibility of a new purpose-built branch record office was no more than a pipe-dream. Moreover, when Hall, reluctant to admit failure, allowed himself to be drawn into tentative discussions with the Office of Works about the possibility of utilising the basement of the proposed War Museum for record storage, he found himself disowned by Firth, who felt it necessary to write to the War Records Disposal Committee, then sitting at the Public Record Office, to make it clear that the commission could not support any such suggestion. By then the hapless Hall must have realised that any hope he may at one time have entertained of helping to usher in a new record order was no longer feasible. His gloom had already been made apparent in a memorandum he had sent to Stamp in March 1919 in which he candidly confessed that 'my own [position], unfortunately does not seem to be a very pleasant one'.[17] Two years later he chose to resign

---

16b. PRO 1/82: Fortescue to Lyte, 6 September 1917. A précis of correspondence etc. relating to the Imperial War Museum proposal will be found in the Royal Commission's *Third Report* (Cmd. 368), III, pt II, 125–129.

17. PRO 1/84: Hall to secretary, 14 March 1919.

rather than to continue a year longer as he could have done under the retirement rules. The Treasury seized the opportunity to attempt to abolish the resident officer post, but met with strong resistance from Sterndale, and eventually Hall was succeeded in that position by Story-Maskelyne. Hall had the consolation of being awarded the honorary degree of doctor of letters by Cambridge University in 1920 and in 1925 his *British Archives and the Sources for the History of the World War* appeared. In 1931 and 1932 he visited the United States to advise the Huntington Library on the arrangement of its collection of British family manuscripts. It says a great deal for him that he did not allow his disappointments to turn to bitterness and that he welcomed the fact that others, such as Jenkinson, whose classical *Manual of Archive Administration* was to be published in 1922, were expounding the science of archives of which he had been a tireless advocate. As early as October 1914, writing in *The Edinburgh Review*, he seemed to sense that the efforts of the Royal Commission, in which he had placed his hopes, were, after all, unlikely to disturb the entrenched powers and privileges of the office, fortified as it was by an act still seen as sacrosanct. It is not surprising, he wrote[18]

that the mere existence of a Public Record Office should have been regarded as a subject for national congratulation, and its administration as above criticism. Again, the Record Office, like other institutions, serves as a sort of club for many of its regular readers. Even to the initiated a record is still to some extent a privileged revelation which must be accepted thankfully and without question. It has been remarked that the devout reader usually resents criticism of the existing administration of learned institutions, partly from a feeling of scholarly fellowship with the officials, and partly from obvious motives of self-interest.

This sense of loyalty on the part of the public, coupled with the *esprit de corps* of the department itself, must make the task of inquiry one of peculiar difficulty. In the first place, the evidence taken by the Commission will be conflicting. Then, as we have seen, the investigations of the Commissioners will be limited by the facilities and information which must be obtained from official sources. Moreover, as soon as it is known that an inquiry is on foot, every effort will be made to anticipate the recommendations of the Commission by internal reforms, the credit for which will eventually be regarded as due to the department itself. Therefore, unless the inquiry is conducted with knowledge, tact, and resolution, the actual result may be quite inconclusive, and the recommendations of the Commission will be of little permanent value.

Hall died in 1944 on his eighty-seventh birthday from shock after his

---

18. *The Edinburgh Review* (1914), 220, 378–379.

house at Walderslade, near Chatham, had been severely damaged by a flying bomb, but the three reports of which he was the architect remain as a fitting memorial to his work and have provided, and will continue to provide, for countless record officers and users a beacon illuminating the state of the national records down to the First World War.

Even had the Royal Commission's recommendations been fully accepted, and not all of them deserved to be, their implementation would have been a matter of peculiar difficulty because the period between the two world wars was mostly one of economic stringency and retrenchment symbolised by the abandonment in 1922 of the printing of the *Reports of the Deputy Keeper* and their submission in typescript for the next 27 years. In the same year the custodial arrangements were altered, also as an economy measure, and the night-time patrolling inside the building passed from the Metropolitan Police to nightwatchmen employed by the Office of Works. During the day, however, there was a policeman at each gate, and two more patrolled the courtyard and surrounds during the hours of darkness, a fitting accompaniment, some might have thought, to a building once said to combine the general effect of 'the workhouse, the jail and the Manchester mill'.[19] In such an atmosphere it was fanciful to suppose that money would easily be found for new building work, and although Sterndale set up a committee consisting of Lyte, Stamp, Fowler and representatives of the Treasury and the Office of Works, with Johnson as secretary, to consider post-war accommodation needs, it was clear that its chances of success were slim.[20] Nevertheless, as a result of its recommendations some additional land was acquired from the owners of Clifford's Inn in 1923 to straighten the southern boundary of the office and to allow the site eventually to be developed more economically and safe from risk of fire.[21a] An alternative proposal for a repository in the London suburbs was rejected, the Treasury view being that its provision would encourage departments to keep more material than necessary. However, to meet immediate needs the disused county gaol at Cambridge was taken over for record storage in April 1920 and Craib, the librarian, was placed in charge. He was accompanied by Pratt, who was coming up for retirement and who was given free quarters and a small weekly allowance in return for his assistance. Craib and Pratt had to share bathroom and other facilities, which would never have been sanctioned had Pratt not been regarded as of the 'superior working-class type'. After his death in 1923 the arrangement was ended and a local man was engaged as a temporary clerk instead. By then W. S. Wright was in charge, having

---

19. *Saturday Review*, 17 November 1855, p 49, as quoted in G. C. Tyack's PhD thesis, 'The Public Record Office to 1870: Sir James Pennethorne, Architect and Urban Planner' (London University, 1987).

20. The committee's minutes and papers are in PRO 39/5. Treasury papers are in T 161/166/S15399 and T 161/166/S15399/01.

21a. WORK 12/250.

been sent to Cambridge on Craib's recall to Chancery Lane in 1922 when Gregory retired on health grounds. Craib had entered the office as a workman and Wright as a boy clerk, and so both had come a long way; it was a measure of the office's confidence in them that it was prepared to allow them to operate independently. Between 1920 and 1923 the superintendent's post passed in quick succession to W. H. Powell, A. W. Byerley and H. Pellatt. Byerley's place as chief binder and repairer went initially to Pellatt and then to Archibald Fewster in 1923. On Fewster's death in 1925 he was succeeded by B. Pilbeam, the other Pilbeam, George, his uncle, having done even better, by rising from the workmen's ranks to head the office's clerical establishment as a staff officer on a salary of £400 to £500 a year. By 1926 there were three higher clerical officers and eleven clerical officers under him. The number of first-class attendants and repairers was 18 on a scale of 47s 6d. × 2s 6d to 55s. Three of them, the chief binder and repairer and two foremen, received 6s extra a week, and three more 2s extra as sub-foremen. Beneath them were 27 men of the second class receiving 25s at the minimum and rising by 2s increments to 45s. A few HMSO binders, accompanied occasionally by women sewers, were brought in from time to time as a trade-off for the office undertaking the binding of its own library books. Lyte and Stamp were anxious that the men should have a better scale than the normal Civil Service paper keeper or library attendant. Although the examination which they had to pass on entry was of an elementary character, they were expected to have the ability to decipher the older documents sufficiently to distinguish between one class and another. Moreover, the excellence of the repairers' work was widely recognised, and repairs were regularly undertaken privately for outside institutions and individual owners with official cognizance. The highest post to which most of the attendants and repairers could aspire was that of superintendent, but, exceptionally, they could be promoted to the clerical grade. As the normal method of entrance for clerical officers, when examinations were resumed after the war, required them to be educated to matriculation standard, it was only with reluctance that their representative on the Whitley Council accepted the principle of an occasional promotion of that kind. One of the first to benefit was R. E. White, who had at one time been on Lyte's household staff.

All these arrangements, including those for the 22 porter-messengers and the introduction of increased leave allowances for the support grades, resulted from the post-war reorganisation of the office, which also saw the establishment of a Departmental Whitley Council in 1919 with Fowler as first Staff Side chairman. Perhaps the most important feature of the revised structure was the integration of the boy clerks and the supplementary clerks into the newly-formed general service clerical class. Like their transcriber predecessors, some of them worked on seventeenth- and eighteenth-century documents, while others were employed on accounting, repository, registry and library work. All those duties, as well as the making of office copies of documents in English, were carried out under the supervision of the assistant keepers. Indeed, the reversion in 1920 of the higher-grade clerks and the assistant keepers to their former titles of assistant keeper II and assistant keeper I was not only to prevent confusion with the new-style clerks, but also to devolve the certification of modern office copies on less senior officers. The class I men, ten in number, were placed on a scale of £600 × 25 to £900, with an efficiency bar at £750. A further post of assistant keeper and secretary, who was to represent the deputy keeper in his absence, was authorised at the same salary. The pay of the fourteen assistant keepers II was fixed at £200 × 20 to £500, and allowances of £200 and £100 were also payable to the resident officer and the legal inspecting officer respectively. Alongside Stamp as secretary the top ten assistant keepers at the time of reorganisation were Salisbury, Brodie, Hall, Black, Crump, Story-Maskelyne, Fowler, Lyle, Giuseppi and Johnson. By 1926 the first six had retired, Brodie with the ISO, and Headlam, J. B. W. Chapman, Flower, Ratcliff, Dawes and Jenkinson had been promoted. Besides underpinning Stamp on the secretarial side, Flower continued as legal inspecting officer, and Dawes took Story-Maskelyne's place as resident officer in 1926. For just over six months in 1923 and 1924 Ratcliff was on loan to the newly-established Public Record Office of Northern Ireland.[21b]

Of all the assistant keepers Jenkinson was, perhaps the most active at the time, constantly striving for higher standards of archival care and never slow to bring defects to the notice of his seniors. It hardly made him popular and may explain why, when he followed in Hall's footsteps on appointment as a part-time reader in diplomatic and English archives at King's College in 1925, Lyte did not attempt to interfere but made it clear he did not encourage his officers to undertake regular work outside. Jenkinson was harshly critical when documents were accepted from departments in less than ideal condition because, having taken over responsibility for repair work from Salisbury, he felt that everything should be done to avoid adding to the enormous stock of documents already awaiting attention. In the Repair Department itself he had arranged for a survey of the physical condition of documents throughout the office and he had drawn up a set of rules to assist the staff. He had systematically re-arranged the works of reference in the Round Room so that they were no longer haphazard but as far as possible followed the classification of the records to which they referred. Believing fervently in the integrity of the records, he insisted that all old labels and marks should be incorporated in rebound volumes, that evidence of original make-up, such as filing strings and sewings, should always be carefully preserved, and that an accurate account should be kept of work done. He also experimented in seal repairs and the making of moulds and casts, and brought in mercury-vapour lamps to assist the reading of faded documents. At times

---

21b. For papers concerning Ratcliff's mission see PRO 1/184.

searchers could find him trying, as when he refused to separate uncut pages of a newspaper, but there could be no doubt that it was his influence which was responsible for a general improvement in working methods. It was a pleasing feature of the period that individual talents were beginning to blossom and that the assistant keepers were being made more responsible for their own work. Charles Johnson, for example, was making an annual report upon the work of the Library and Atkinson similarly for the Museum. In 1924 photocopies of certain documents were displayed at the British Empire Exhibition at Wembley. In that year the number of visitors attending the Museum annually was, for the first time, approaching 10,000, of whom some 1,500 came in parties out of hours. A few showcases were reserved for special exhibitions, 1924 being noteworthy for one mounted for American barristers at the request of Sir Ernest Pollock (later Lord Hanworth), who had been appointed master of the rolls when Sterndale died a year earlier. Pollock's tenure of the office was notable for the extension of his powers as keeper of the records to manorial records when he was given the 'charge and superintendence' of them under the Law of Property (Amendment) Act 1924. An immediate consequence was a small increase in the office's clerical staff to compile registers of particulars of the court rolls and other documents concerned, and the appointment of Fowler as secretary of a Manorial Committee. Pollock took a strong personal interest in that work, which involved much contact with stewards of manors, solicitors and others, and gave a decided impetus to the study of local history and local records as a result of manorial material being made accessible to students in approved places of deposit.

Throughout the 1920s the publication work of the office was gradually recovering from the blow dealt to it by the war. Hinds had resumed at Venice and Twemlow, whose wings had to be clipped from time to time, was doing occasional work at Rome although the work on material dealing with the relations between Elizabeth I and the Vatican came to an end with Rigg's death in 1925. At Paris Leon Bogaert was carrying on the transcription work at one time undertaken by Baschet. Mrs Lomas and Dr Shaw also remained on the editorial staff, which had been joined by Francis Bickley who took the editorship of the *Calendar of State Papers, Domestic* after F. H. B. Daniell's death in 1921. Although the Consultative Committee on Publication was still in being it hardly ever met, the odd difficulty being dealt with by correspondence with individual members. Progress continued to be made inside the office on existing series and from 1921 direct responsibility was assumed for the publication of *Acts of the Privy Council of England*, initially undertaken from retirement by E. G. Atkinson, who was succeeded later by Lyle. A beginning was also made on texts of the early Curia Regis rolls. But from the point of view of the general user of the records the most important publication of the period was the issue in two volumes in 1923 and 1924 of a new *Guide to the Manuscripts preserved in the Public Record Office*, the work of Montague Giuseppi, then in charge of the Search Department. Unlike much of Scargill-Bird's work, which it superseded, it was not subject based but described the records throughout in their groups and classes, leaving it to the index to bring together the subject matter of their contents. The first volume was devoted to the legal records, the second to state papers and the departmental records. It proved a great success, and both volumes were still sufficiently useful some forty years later to form the basis of the new printed guide published in 1963. Some recognition of Giuseppi's contribution to a better understanding of the office's holdings came in 1925 when he became the third member of the department to be appointed to a companionship of the Imperial Service Order.

Notwithstanding the criticisms levelled at the Stationery Office by the Royal Commission about the printing and binding of record publications, it retained its responsibility for that service despite complaints by Lyte from time to time of printing delays and the employment of unsuitable firms. Moreover, the price of calendars had been more than doubled and but for Lyte would have been increased even more. The Royal Commission had also been critical of the limitations imposed upon the free distribution of record publications to institutions, particularly newly-founded universities. As a result of its criticisms a departmental committee had been set up in 1913 with Johnson as secretary which recommended a wider and more rational distribution. However, the outbreak of war led to the matter being placed in cold storage, and when it was again considered in the 1920s the Treasury decided that, although a limited exchange scheme might be operated, free issues should not normally be made; it was also arranged that up to fifty back copies might be supplied to a university, public library or similar body if it placed an order to purchase record works for the next 15 years.

The Treasury was also responsible for an increase in 1921 in fees charged for the production of legal documents after 1800, from 1s 0d to 1s 6d for a single document and from 2s 6d to 4s 0d for not more than ten in the same action, suit or matter. The new regulations, which replaced those of 1909, made provision for the first time for the certification of photographic copies. The actual photographic work was contracted out to a private firm, Monger and Marchant, which had been established in 1895 and which had offices in Bream's Buildings, off Chancery Lane. For that purpose a room had been made available to it in May 1920 and the Canadian government's photostat machine was taken over on hire. The firm undertook to pay for the electricity used and to make copy prints at 1s 8d a sheet and 1s a half sheet. Six months later, however, an increase in the price of paper resulted in the introduction of a two-tier tariff of 2s 6d a sheet and 1s 6d a half sheet for official copies and 3s 0d and 1s 9d for copies made for the public. As regards the search rooms, some attempt had been made to increase opening hours, notably by the Royal Historical Society and London University, but no changes were made. On the whole searchers seemed reasonably content, and casual enquirers could often get as much satisfaction by writing as by attending in person. Writing to the superintendent of records at the India Office in December 1925, Stamp explained:[22]

> We have a printed form which says that this department does not undertake searches for the public; but we administer the rule rather easily.
>
> If any one asks if a certain document is in the office we try to say yes or no, even if the search involves some trouble, especially if the enquirer wants a certified copy.
>
> If the demand is for information about a person or subject and we can give an answer without more than a few minutes searching, or if we think that we can get the information ourselves with less trouble to ourselves than would be involved by having the enquirer in the search room (e.g. services in army or navy) we make a search; especially for the more illiterate enquirers. Otherwise we offer to supply the names of capable record agents.

The invigilation and superintendence of the search rooms at that time was undertaken exclusively by assistant keepers. Then, as now, a member of the public must have felt somewhat bewildered on his or her first entrance. The search room assistants, who manned the first line of defence, were well able to deal with the less involved queries because their knowledge of the whereabouts of lists and indexes was considerable. They also had some familiarity with the course of a Chancery action and were able to trace the services of officers and men in the Army and Navy. Among the frequenters of the office the medievalists remained much in evidence, the launch at the turn of the century of the Victoria County History, to which some of the assistant keepers were contributors, having given a further stimulus to work on the older records. After the war, usage had also been affected by the foundation in 1921 of the Institute of Historical Research, the University of London's centre for the postgraduate study of history, and the appearance in the same year of an Anglo-American conference of historians, which was eventually to become an annual event. It was natural that the assistant keepers, with their traditional links with older bodies, such as the Camden Society, which had been amalgamated with the Royal Historical Society in 1897, the Selden Society, the Pipe Roll Society and the Canterbury and York Society, should consider that their main function was to support the learned community. Among that community had now to be numbered a gradually increasing section whose interest lay in the more recent records, which remained, generally speaking, open to 1837. However, in 1919 Balfour authorised the opening of the Foreign Office's records to 1860, mainly because Queen Victoria's letters had just been published to that date. Over-

---

22. PRO 1/91: Stamp to Mitchell, 12 December 1925.

all, there was no great pressure for the further lifting of restrictions, but the advent of a minority Labour government in 1924 led Harold Laski to place before Ramsay MacDonald a memorandum prepared by Professor Charles (later Sir Charles) K. Webster of the University College of Wales, Aberystwyth, criticising the existing policy and suggesting that a 40-year closure period would meet all objections. The Foreign Office was willing to go a long way towards meeting Webster by opening its records down to 1878. That was because it knew that another batch of the queen's letters was soon to be published to 1876 or 1878, and because that period, which coincided with the origins of German colonial policy and Anglo-German friction, formed a suitable break point. In May 1924 Stephen Gaselee, the cultivated librarian and keeper of papers at the Foreign Office, wrote to Laski to that effect. Gaselee also made it clear that a fixed term of years for closure, which would result in the date being moved forward year by year, was unacceptable because a decision to release papers at any given moment depended upon the special features of the period and also on 'the part played by the men (or their sons) who may be living and possibly occupying eminent public positions'.[23a] At the same time Gaselee wrote to the deputy keeper to ask him to consult departments generally as it was thought desirable that any changes should be adopted by them all.

It was hardly surprising, therefore, that the Foreign Office, which was doing its best for researchers, should be greatly angered a month later when Webster, who must by then have known what was intended, wrote a critical article for *The Nation and The Athenaeum* of 21 June 1924 on government secrecy and the habit of intercepting diplomatic despatches, entitled 'The Labour Government and Secret Diplomacy'. The Foreign Office was particularly annoyed because Webster alleged, inaccurately, that its papers were closed to 1837, which gave rise to a parliamentary question from V. H. Finney, the Liberal member for Hexham, but gave Ponsonby, the undersecretary, the opportunity to tell the House that the prime minister had under consideration a substantial advance and that consultation was taking place with the dominions. However, the Zinoviev letter and the subsequent general election put paid to any chance of Labour bringing the intended reform into effect, the credit for which went to Austen Chamberlain, Ramsay MacDonald's Conservative successor as foreign secretary. In the event Chamberlain went one better, giving his approval to the further decision of the Foreign Office to throw open the law officers' opinions as well as its general correspondence. That decision must have been especially poignant for Eyre Crowe, now permanent secretary, who had been outgunned in 1908 on that very matter by his masters, when representing the Foreign Office on the Interdepartmental Committee then dealing with the question of public access to governmental records. But Davidson, his main adversary at that

23a. FO 370/203, f 181: Gaselee to Laski, 6 May 1924.

time, had departed and Sir Cecil Hurst, now legal adviser of the Foreign Office, was a man of quite different stamp and not at all perturbed by the thought that the opinions occasionally revealed differences between the lawyers. Accepting that there were few subjects of difficulty on which learned men did not at times differ, Hurst wrote:[23b]

The period of which the archives are now to be thrown open to the public covers years which, from the international law point of view were very important, particularly the international law which affects this country, viz that relating to belligerent seizures of neutral property afloat because it covers the years of the American Civil War. The opinions given by the eminent lawyers who advised the Government of the day on these questions are peculiarly instructive and helpful in arriving at a just appreciation of the action of the Government at the time. What makes international law is the practice of governments, and to know in any particular case not merely what the Government did but why it did it, i.e. the particular circumstances in the case on which its view was based, is what makes the precedent valuable as a guide for the future. Unless the papers which constitute these precedents are open to the public this source of knowledge is lost. It is really scarcely an exaggeration to say that international law is to a great extent being made now on the American continent because the United States Government is so much more ready and willing to publish its proceedings than any other Government that it is usually the practice of the United States which alone is known to the writers on international law.

By 1926 most departmental papers could be seen down to 1878, although the War Office insisted upon sticking to a 50-year rule and the Treasury, wary of the increased demand which greater access might generate, was not willing to open its records beyond 1850. Some time also elapsed before the Colonial Office was prepared to agree to restrictions being lifted on material concerning Gibraltar and the Falklands. However, closed documents could still be seen under permit, the most notable example being at Cambridge, where a small search room had been opened and where Temperley and Gooch were examining papers dealing with the events leading up to the outbreak of the Great War, about which they had been commissioned to write officially.

The gradual shift in emphasis towards the use of more modern records was reflected in the work of the inspecting officers, who dealt with over sixty schedules between 1919 and 1925, half of them concerning departments, or

---

23b. FO 370/203, ff 210–211: Hurst to Gaselee, 5 December 1924. For a more complete account of Foreign Office views see K. A. Hamilton's 'The Pursuit of "Enlightened Patriotism". The British Foreign Office and Historical Research during the Great War and its aftermath', *The Bulletin of the Institute of Historical Research*, LXVI, 316–344, October 1988.

branches of departments, which had sprung up during the war. The inspecting officers' aim was to preserve all documents dealing with matters of principle or precedent or containing material of historical, technical or legal importance. On the other hand, routine papers dealing with the application of principles to individual cases were generally scheduled, although it was the practice to keep specimens. Such records were numerous in the great executive and military offices, such as the War Office and Air Ministry and the Ministries of Food, Munitions and Pensions. The Board of Trade, which had been soundly rebuked by the master of the rolls in 1917 for an earlier unauthorised destruction of pre-1890 passenger lists, also had a great mass of particular instance papers, as they came to be known, from the many wartime emergency departments placed under its control. On more than one occasion Hall referred critically to what he alleged was the want of method and knowledge on the part of the early inspecting officers. But his main scorn was reserved, not entirely fairly, for Lascelles, Redington and their opposite numbers in departments because of their work on the original Government Documents Committee. However, the more serious gaps in the nineteenth-century material, notably in the records of the Home Office and the Board of Trade, can hardly be laid at their door. It must also be remembered that until after the First World War there was a constant seepage of important material, owing to ministers and officials looking upon their records as their own private property and taking them away when they left office. In fact, the Treasury's complaint had always been that the inspecting officers were too timid and it was in an attempt to reassure the sceptics there that Stamp wrote to it in 1923 to say that Lyte had pointed out to him[24]

> that we cannot tell what rubbish may be stored in government offices until they try to send some of it to us: then we insist on a schedule . . . we have just taken out for destruction some thousands of 19th century muster books, and I think it was only objections on the part of the Admiralty that prevented our being more drastic. We did destroy a set of duplicate pay books some 20 years ago and the late Sir J. K. Laughton went for us at intervals on account of it, till he died.

By that time Hall had left and a more robust line could be detected on the part of the Inspecting Officers' Committee, consisting of Lyte, Stamp, Fowler, Flower, Giuseppi and Johnson. Additionally, letters were sent to a number of departments in March 1923 suggesting the destruction of certain series then being preserved in the office.

At the heart of the matter was the problem of accommodation. It was obvious that no extension at Chancery Lane was likely in the forseeable

---

24. T 161/166/S15399/01: Stamp to Ravenshear, 11 January 1923.

future despite the purchase of more land. Minor relief had been obtained by fitting-up four rooms in the basement for records, but to the disgust of the master of the rolls economy had dictated the use of wooden shelving, which had provoked him to tell Lyte what a shabby lot he thought they were at the Treasury.[25] The make-do-and-mend approach was also evident in the half-hearted attempts by the Office of Works to prevent the roof of the Round Room from leaking, which led to a string of complaints from Jenkinson, but to little avail (Plate 28). However, the office had some success in the years 1924–1925 in the fitting-up of a map room on the B or first floor, and the installation in the well of the staircase at the eastern end of the building of a lift, designed mainly to carry an attendant and a barrowload of documents from floor to floor. At the other end of the office one of the men's lavatories had to be specially adapted for the use of the first female member of the senior staff, Mary (later Dame Mary) Smieton, who came in as an assistant keeper in 1925 from the Civil Service administrative examination along with J. R. Crompton. They were the first young graduates recruited since the war straight from university. Six other assistant keepers had joined the office since the armistice, but they had been taken from the reconstruction competitions for older candidates who had been prevented from entering the Civil Service straight from college owing to the war. Of those obtained in that way the prize catch was one of Tout's pupils, Vivian Galbraith, although he later left for the academic world, eventually becoming regius professor of modern history at Oxford. Another entrant with a high reputation was C. S. B. Buckland, who was specially recruited as a modernist. Roberts's place as the office Welshman was taken by D. L. Evans, who was to have the double distinction of becoming deputy keeper and then the first full-time keeper under the 1958 act. The three other mature recruits, P. V. Davies, A. C. Wood and K. H. Ledward, failed to reach the same heights although Davies, who married Stamp's daughter, eventually took Flower's place as barrister member of the Inspecting Officers' Committee and was to be much involved in its work. Jenkinson apart, the assistant keepers were a dutiful band and generally easy to manage. There were fewer feuds than in earlier times, although Dame Mary Smieton recalled that Fowler and Chapman, who once shared a room, were not on speaking terms. There was a large bookcase between them, and having entered their office to introduce herself to one of them, she then found it necessary to retire and knock again to repeat the performance with the other.[26]

Unlike the industrial world, the department was comparatively unaffected by the General Strike of 1926. Under orders from Whitehall a register of volunteers for emergency duties was compiled. Except for those on leave all members of the assistant keeper and most of the clerical grades signed up.

---

25. PRO 1/88: Sterndale to Lyte, 12 January 1923.
26. Interview with Dame Mary Smieton, 10 September 1987.

Mary Smieton recalled cycling into work from Wimbledon, while Wood walked all the way from Chiswick. Two of the younger clerical officers, Russell Farmer and George Santer, went into service, the one as a motor car driver at Dunmow, assisting the county authorities, and the other at East Ham Public Baths. Four of the messengers enrolled in the special constabulary. No official record exists of the attitude of the support grades more generally, but a drawing in a Search Department scrap book suggests that some may have supported the stoppage.[27] However, the importance of 1926 for the office lay not in the General Strike but in the completion by Lyte of 40 years' service, an event which produced a message of congratulations to him from the staff. For many years much of his time had been occupied with work on *Historical Notes on the Use of the Great Seal of England*, and it was only when it was on the point of publication in the autumn of the same year that he decided to retire at the age of 78. During Lyte's twilight years the day-to-day running of the office had devolved upon Stamp, who had managed it with a quiet efficiency, and so it seemed both just and natural that he should succeed to the deputy keepership at the end of October 1926. But he was not in the normal run of assistant keepers and his promotion to the top job over the heads of men with longer service and wider record experience, such as Fowler and Giuseppi, left some resentment.

Like Lyte, therefore, Stamp by no means had the whole-hearted support of his senior colleagues on taking up his appointment. But he was better placed than his illustrious predecessor in that he was taking over a going concern even if it had still to emerge fully from the Edwardian era. For instance, it had never shown any enthusiasm for Hall's wartime campaign for the greater employment of women as archivists, and it must be doubtful whether left to itself it would have appointed a woman to an assistant keeper post. As it was, it did not even have one female typist at the time and saw nothing wrong in giving typing work to its clerical officers, whose talents were far from fully exploited. Since the Royal Commission's probings some changes for the better had taken place, but, Jenkinson excepted, no influential voice was calling for improvements. The Treasury straitjacket remained very much in place, and although under Stamp the office was in the hands of a competent, down-to-earth administrator, his past record suggested that he would wish merely to loosen the bonds, not try to break free.

---

27. PRO 8/63, f 81. Among a collection of notes and cartoons, mainly written and drawn by Jenkinson during his time in charge of the Round Room, under the caption, 'The great Record Office strike: Picketing scene in Chancery Lane' it depicts a somewhat bemused Chapman, listening to the arguments of a burly picket.

Chapter XIV

Stamp and Flower: The Quiet Deputy Keepers, 1926–1947

I have no objection to students of archive administration seeing them [the Public Record Office's domestic records], *but I think we ought to be assured that they are serious students. The old correspondence is full of personalities which I should not care to put at the disposal of any irresponsible writer, who might, for instance, like to publish a comic history of the office.*

(A. E. Stamp to M. S. Giuseppi, 1 June 1933: PRO 1/102)

I thank you for listening so patiently to what may have seemed rather shallow, trivial and commonplace. If you have found it so you will of your charity please to remember that I am only a Civil Servant who has never posed as an historian.

(A. E. Stamp's concluding remarks in an address to the Royal Historical Society in March 1928 on 'The Public Record Office and the Historical Student': *RHS Transactions*, Fourth Series, XI, 17–37)

I am, like you, one of the few people who can get enjoyment out of indexing.

(C. Flower to E. A. Fry, 18 September 1933: PRO 1/102 (Miscellaneous file))

While Alfred Stamp, with his drooping moustache, did not have the commanding presence of Lyte, his strength lay in a natural administrative ability, combined with editorial competence, the latter talent being exemplified in his work on the publication of the close rolls of Henry III from 1227. He was nominated deputy keeper by the master of the rolls, but his appointment as keeper of land revenue records and enrolments was made by the Treasury, which after some hesitation agreed that he might retain Lyte's salary of £1,400 in respect of both posts. As a result of Stamp's appointment Ratcliff succeeded him as secretary of the Historical Manuscripts Commission and O'Reilly was promoted to the AK I grade. However, Stamp did not sever his connection with the commission altogether, taking Lyte's place as 'acting commissioner'. The unpopularity surrounding Stamp's promotion lingered on and D. B. Wardle told the author that it was still there when he first joined the office in 1929. Rightly or wrongly, there was a belief that the appointment had something to do with family influence at the Treasury.

Stamp was not enamoured of the age of Whitleyism which he thought had been inflicted upon the office. He was not a man for new initiatives, but he was able to adapt more readily to the post-war world than many of his contemporaries, who continued to hanker for the old order. His death in 1938 robbed him of any chance of a knighthood although he was appointed CB in 1931. If he had a quirk it was about the telephone which he disliked intensely, finding conversation on it difficult. Once he was obliged to apologise to Hankey, the Cabinet Office secretary, for failing to recognise him when he rang about the deposit of the 1918 Doullens Agreement. There were similar episodes with senior Treasury officials in which he might have been spared embarrassment had he enjoyed the services of a personal secretary to take his calls in the first place. His record interests were not entirely medieval, and his early training with Hall had brought home to him the growing importance of the modern records. In particular, he kept a watchful eye on the provincial repository at Cambridge, having an unofficial contact in Temperley, his cousin, who was frequently in the search room there in connection with his work with Gooch on the origins of the First World War. Yet the office that Stamp headed could hardly be regarded as modern, even for a short while reverting to its all-male status in 1928, when Mary Smieton managed to get a transfer to the Ministry of Labour as an assistant principal. She had not entered the office by choice but at the direction of the Civil Service Commission, and was glad to leave, taking the first steps in a dazzling career in which she was to rise to the deputy secretaryship of her new ministry before moving higher still to the permanent secretaryship of the Ministry of Education in 1959. Brief as her spell in the office was, it led to a life-long friendship with a junior colleague and later keeper, Harold Cottam Johnson, and with his wife, Esmé. In retirement Dame Mary, as she had by then become, was to renew her acquaintance with the record world through her membership of the Advisory Council on Public Records from 1965 to 1973. By that time the position of the very many women in the office had changed beyond recognition. Certainly it would have been unthinkable for any of them to have been forbidden, as she was, to wear dungarees when working upon grimy documents because it was thought likely to undermine discipline among the support grades.

The office, and in particular Flower, Stamp's successor as secretary, remained rank-conscious and there was a clear divide between the assistant keepers and the rest of the staff, even the clerical grades, but in their case it began to assume less importance when most of them were absorbed into the executive grade after the Second World War. In the inter-war years their talents were, generally speaking, imperfectly utilised, but all of them, irrespective of their main job, nevertheless had some editorial work given to them under assistant keeper supervision. Some of them also supplemented their income by indexing calendars in their own time, for which they were paid on a piece-work basis. More than once the three men at the top of the CO seniority list, White, Farmer and Santer, whose way ahead was blocked by the relative youth of the three HCOs and the one staff officer above them, were recommended for promotion when openings occurred in other departments. However, their restricted experience must have counted against them because they never had any success. Farmer, probably the most able of the three, was thought by the office to be sufficiently compensated by his official residence at the then country repository at Canterbury, which was why he was excluded when an unsuccessful bid was made to the Treasury in 1933 to have White and Santer upgraded to the junior executive grade. A year later, when certain executive posts in the Customs were advertised, Farmer was put forward along with the others, although he could hardly have been helped by the naivety of Stamp's comments about them, one instance of which was his remark that Santer was 'a really beautiful typist on occasion'.[1a] Perhaps it was fortunate that in that very year the clerical officers were to be relieved of much of their typing work when Miss L. Henwood was engaged. In asking the Civil Service Commission for a candidate, the office said that while shorthand was not wanted she should have a good general education, including, if possible, an elementary knowledge of Latin. So far as the younger COs were concerned, the office recognised their intelligence and promise, despite its tendency to patronise them at times. They had entered the office straight from grammar school, through the highly-competitive examination of the pre-war years, and it was therefore not surprising that their careers were ultimately to blossom. Three of them, Monger, Mabbs and Penfold, were to reach the assistant keeper grade, Mabbs going on to the keepership itself, a remarkable performance by any standard. The first such entrant, H. A. Johnston, who joined the office in 1928, retired in 1971 as an inspecting officer, and J. A. Gavin, who began in 1936, rose to the position of establishment officer. Stamp and Flower would have been amazed, yet it was to their, and to Jenkinson's, credit that the barriers first began to come down in 1937 when Safford, the Repository HCO, having been 'severely tested in Latin and French', was appointed an AK II and W. L. White, the understudy to Fox, the staff officer in the Secretariat, was promoted to be an HCO. No such startling advance as Safford's, the one-time boy clerk, had been seen since Atkins's promotion from the workmen grade in 1852, and it marked the beginning of a slow process which was eventually to loosen the rigidities of the office's grading structure. Those rigidities were in evidence not only between the assistant keepers and the clerical grades, but also between the clerical and manual grades. Yet the latter's superintendent remained a powerful man, dealing with the pay sheet of the entire weekly-paid staff and being closely concerned, through his membership of the Official Side of the Departmental Whitley Council, with all questions affecting their promotion and local conditions of service. In 1931 the holder of that post, H. I. Pellatt, retired after 47 years in the office and was succeeded by E. H. Balls. There was a real sense in which the attendants and repairers under their superintendent were regarded almost as NCOs, with the porter-messengers, now much engaged upon cleaning and removal duties within the repository, making up the strength as privates. The well-known critic of the Civil Service 'caste'

1a. PRO 1/104: Stamp to the secretary, Custom House, 26 July 1934.

system, the redoubtable W. J. Brown MP, general secretary of the Civil Service Clerical Association, would have found ample evidence of its existence in the Public Record Office of the 1920s and 1930s, with the assistant keepers in their internal correspondence addressing each other, by official injunction, as 'esq. etc., etc.'

Yet it would be wrong to think that between the wars the office was an unhappy one or rife with discontent. Indeed, a special effort was made in 1928 to foster a good spirit by the issue of a kind of newsletter, quaintly termed 'Office Memoranda', which appeared irregularly over the next 13 years.[1b] In so far as tensions existed, they revealed themselves as much within as between grades, and could be explained to a large extent by the smallness of the office, where people's private backgrounds were more intimately known than they would have been in a larger organisation. Among the assistant keepers it was partly a question of social station, but even more a sharp difference of outlook between those who saw themselves as administrative civil servants just doing another job and those who thought the assistant keepers were nothing if not professional archivists. Stamp fell supremely into the first category, while Jenkinson was the leading exponent of the other school of thought. D. B. Wardle recalls Evans saying that he would like to see a cartoon, on the lines of H. M. Bateman, of a stern-faced Jenkinson telling Stamp 'you, too, are an Archivist'.

Unlike the assistant keepers, where there was sometimes an undercurrent of unease between the older public school men and the newer entrants from grammar school, the clerical officers were more of a muchness socially although most of those who came in from the forces after the war were markedly less adaptable than those recruited subsequently straight from school by a testing examination. But between all of them there was much rivalry. In 1927 that reached a pitch when the single staff officer post at the pinnacle of their establishment fell vacant on the retirement of George Pilbeam after 50 years' meritorious service in the office. His successor, Benjamin Poulter, had also started as a workman, but his health was not good and as he was due to retire early in 1929 it was obvious that he was no more than a stop-gap. Consequently most of Pilbeam's establishment and sub-accounting duties passed to the 32-year-old Oliver Fox, who was promoted to the higher clerical grade at the same time. It was therefore fairly clear that Fox was being groomed for the succession despite being junior to Wright and Matthews, the other HCOs. On grounds of general ability and experience Fox, who had joined the office as a boy clerk in 1910, and who had served in the Admiralty, and then in the Army, during the war, had a good claim. For many years he had worked for Rodney on census searches and then for Fowler in the Repository. However, his obvious ambition did not help his standing with his clerical colleagues, particularly

---

1b. PRO 45/12: Public Record Office Memoranda I-XIII, 1928 to 1941.

as he had represented them on the Whitley Council between 1921 and 1924 and was now seen very much as a poacher turned gamekeeper. On his moving to the Secretariat both Stamp and Flower came to value his accounting skills. Fox also made it his business to master establishment practice, and from then onwards was inclined to see himself as the Treasury's watchdog. When the newly-formed Attendants' and Repairers' Association took the office to the Industrial Court in 1927 with a claim for greatly increased pay, it was Fox who went with Stamp, Flower and the Treasury representative to the hearing on behalf of the Official Side. Fox's presence was not surprising because he had done much of the devilling for the office's statement of case and his hand could be seen in the section concerning the men's starting pay in which it was stated:[2]

> The pay claimed is larger on entrance than that at which members of the clerical staff usually begin and continues so for eight years.
>
> The examination of candidates for these posts is of a simple character and can be passed by men who have been educated at an elementary school; the clerical class have to pass an examination of a much more difficult type. The Clerical Class have to deal with the contents of 17th and 18th century documents and, under supervision, are in charge of the library, the storage of records, the office accounts and the like. It is therefore undesirable from the point of view of internal discipline that the two scales should approximate, still more that the Subordinate Staff should have the better scale of the two at any point.

But the office's main contention was that the simplification of the means of reference to the records had removed much of the difficulty concerning their production, and that, while it was essential that those attendants who worked in the search rooms should have good manners, their work presented no undue trouble once they had acquainted themselves with the position of the lists and indexes. There were nine such men at that time with a further twelve working on the floors on the production and replacement of records. There were also 22 repairers whose work was admitted to be technical, but it was argued that their skills were acquired in the course of their employment. It was stated, somewhat disparagingly, that they had to deal with torn or improperly packed documents, sometimes merely by repacking or flattening them, sometimes by mounting them in files or (in extreme cases) by the use of sheets of gauze. Two of them were also engaged in repairing and making casts of seals. While no direct comparison was possible with other classes of workers, it was admitted that the trade union rate for outside binders was 80s a week, but it was argued that that figure was more than

---

2. T 162/706/3086/2: Official Side statement to the Industrial Court, September 1927.

offset by the absence of security of tenure, pension provision and shorter working hours. It was perhaps a weakness on the men's part that both of their representatives at the hearing, Cyril Eades and Herbert Walton, were themselves attendants who, like the outside official who accompanied them, had no detailed knowledge of the repair processes. The probable explanation was that the attendants were the more outspoken of the two groups, because, unlike the repairers who very often undertook private work with the office's blessing, they had few opportunities to supplement their income. At any rate, the court decided against the men on the main claim, but ruled that the two classes into which they were split should be merged and that they should be placed on a common scale, rising to the existing 55s maximum of the class I grade, and with a small increase at the minimum compared with the former class II starting pay; it also agreed that there should be a slight improvement in the incremental progression of the superintendent. In the circumstances of the time the outcome was moderately encouraging for the men, and much of the credit for it went to their chairman, Eades, who, although quite junior, was soon to be appointed foreman of the floor attendants. Walton, who worked in the Government Search Room, did not progress so rapidly, but he was eventually promoted to the clerical ranks and at the close of his career had risen to the higher executive grade and had charge of the Ashridge branch repository.

Needless to say, Fox's known role hardly endeared him to the attendants and repairers and he was greatly disliked by the younger assistant keepers, who resented the influence he was able to exercise upon the head of the office on establishment matters. Wright, who had served as a naval lieutenant paymaster during the war, would have been much more acceptable to them, but the office did not want to move him back to London. Indeed, Stamp thought that Wright's growing responsibilities at Cambridge justified making him an assistant keeper. But the Treasury was not persuaded, although it did eventually agree that Wright might have an additional £25 a year. The other HCO, Edward Matthews, was a man of uncertain temperament, who had come into the office from the Port of London Authority in 1913 on the nomination of the master of the rolls. His arrival as a supplementary clerk over the heads of the boy clerks already in the office, including Fox, was naturally very unwelcome to them. But now the tables were about to be turned and the long-standing rivalry between Matthews and Fox became even more pronounced. Nevertheless, when Fox was promoted staff officer in August 1928 after Poulter's premature retirement through ill health, the office moved Matthews from the Repository to the Census and Copying Department and tried, unsuccessfully, to obtain an additional allowance for him for draughtsman's duties. Matthews's place in Repository was taken by Safford, who had volunteered for the Army immediately war was declared and who had served throughout, although initially under age. He had done much good service in the Library under Charles Johnson and he entered the Repository at a critical time because work was soon to go ahead there on the preparation of a new Summary, short titles for groups and class numeration having been made absolute. The unexpected death of Fowler in 1929 also brought him directly to the notice of Jenkinson, who moved sideways from the Search Department to fill the gap, Fowler's place on the Inspecting Officers' Committee being taken by Dawes. Jenkinson's move presaged many changes in the Repository. He had long felt its organisation needed tighter regulation, and he had clashed in the past with Fowler, who thought that some of Jenkinson's suggestions, such as the issue of rules for handling documents, were too involved for practical use.

Jenkinson's place in the Round Room was taken by Crompton and the AK I vacancy was filled by the promotion of Atkinson, whose work, nevertheless, remained centred on the Museum. Small special exhibitions and the reception of school and other parties were already a regular feature there and postcards of selected records were on sale to visitors, the one of Domesday Book proving by far the most popular. That innovation had an unexpected consequence. The original set of cards included one of the 'Scrap of Paper' treaty of 1839, guaranteeing the neutrality of Belgium, but it had to be hastily withdrawn in 1928 in the alleged interest of Anglo-German relations, following representations from the Foreign Office which had received protests about the card from two MPs. The Foreign Office, more than most, took an interest in record matters, but it was at the direct initiative of Austen Chamberlain himself,[3] the foreign secretary, that a proposal to open the records to 1885 was made to Stamp in April 1929. Sensing complications, because the Foreign Office thought it desirable that other departments should be asked to fall into line, Stamp tried to sidestep trouble by suggesting that the Foreign Office should let it be known that a permit would be issued to any searcher who wished to inspect its records to that date, which Chamberlain thought marked the 'beginning of a bi-partisan approach to foreign affairs'. The Foreign Office was not so easily deflected and consequently Stamp was obliged to write to departments to seek their reaction with what proved to be a mixed result. The Interdepartmental Committee of 1908 had recommended a common general access date, but departments were unwilling to surrender their autonomy lightly. The Home Office, under Sir John Anderson, its permanent secretary, deprecated any extension beyond 1878 because, it argued, its papers, unlike those of the Foreign Office, dealt with domestic matters 'in many cases of a personal or even a scandalous nature, and if generally accessible might easily be used for other than purely historical purposes'.[4] It had in mind papers relating to the Fenian outrages of 1884 and the agitation over the Criminal Law Amendment Act 1885 concerning the 'age of consent' and W. T. Stead's imprisonment under it. Looking ahead to the next batch of papers, the Home Office was profoundly uneasy about the public having access to material about the

---

3. FO 370/320, f 287: Chamberlain to Lindsay, 11 April 1929.
4. HO 45/13290: Anderson to Flower, 13 June 1929.

Trafalgar Square riots or notorious criminal cases, such as that of Mrs Florence Maybrick, who was found guilty of poisoning her husband, the Oscar Wilde prosecution and the extradition from the Argentine Republic for fraud of Jabez Balfour, the former MP, in 1895. However, most of the other departments eventually agreed to fall into line, particularly as Henderson, Chamberlain's Labour successor, had no wish to alter his predecessor's policy. By 1930 most records were open until 1885, although the Treasury, and its subsidiaries, refused to go beyond 1850 on the grounds that the matter had last been settled in 1924 and no general review was due until 1934. A little earlier the War Office had abandoned its 50-year rule which the office had found difficult to administer and it, too, gave its consent to 1885, with certain exceptions, principally court-martial records, which it refused to open beyond 1858. The Admiralty, which had previously agreed to open its law officers' opinions, went one better, not only consenting to 1885 but also lifting its previous ban on papers relating to Greenwich Hospital. Similarly, the Dominions Office consented to the extension, having first cleared the matter with dominion governments. The Colonial Office also agreed to 1885 although at first it was hesitant about opening papers which might embarrass officials still living, a fear which the Foreign Office thought misplaced. When the matter first came before him, the colonial secretary (Sidney Webb, by then Lord Passfield) indicated that he had no objection to that point of view being sent on to the Foreign Office, saying:[5a]

> But it must be borne in mind that this objection seems to have no exceptional relation to Colonial or Dominions Office records any more than to those of other Departments. If uniformity is pressed for I am not disposed to *stand out* for secrecy.

More reasonably, the Paymaster General's Office was unwilling to open registers which might reveal details about pensioners, but there seemed less excuse for the absolute prohibition by the Office of Works on access except by special application or the reluctance of the Public Record Office itself to open its domestic records.

Hanworth was well disposed towards the Foreign Office's initiative. Stamp was less keen because of the continued pressure on accommodation, a reservation shared even more strongly by Jenkinson who made no attempt to disguise his misgivings from the Colonial Office during the course of discussions he was having with it about the transfer of more of its records. The Home Office also presented a problem because it had still transferred records only to 1871 and Stamp was not anxious to take more although its records were theoretically open to 1878. Fortunately for the office there was no great public agitation for change, the number of searchers seeking a permit to see

---

5a. CO 623/1053/60943/1929: Passfield's minute of 18 June 1929.

16 *The central block, Chancery Lane repository*

CHARGES FOR REFRESHMENTS.

	s	d
Soups—Gravy, Vermicelli, &c.	0	6
„ Thick Soups	0	8
Mutton Broth, with Chop	0	8
Mutton Chop, weighing ⅓ of a lb.	0	6
Rump Steak, weighing ¼ lb.	0	8
Joints of Meat, (hot or cold, per plate), weighing 6 oz.	0	7
Hashed Mutton	0	7
Potatoes or other Vegetables	0	1
Salad, plain	0	2
Ditto, dressed	0	3
Plate of Sandwiches of Beef or Ham	0	6
Half ditto ditto	0	3
Fish and Oysters at the Market Prices.		
Pot of Tea or Coffee, with Sugar and Milk	0	6
A Breakfast Cup of Tea or Coffee, with Sugar and Milk	0	3
Fresh Eggs	0	2
A Roll, Biscuit, Bun, or Slice of Bread	0	1
Cheese	0	1½
Butter	0	1
Porter, per pint	0	2
Draught Stout	0	4
Ale, Bass' or Allsop's, per pint	0	4
Other Ales, per pint	0	3
Bass' or Allsop's Pale Ale, imperial pints	0	6
Ditto, ditto reputed ditto	0	4
Guinness' Stout, imperial pints	0	6
Ditto reputed ditto	0	4
Lemonade	0	4
Soda Water	0	3
Ginger Beer	0	2

Approved,

T. DUFFUS HARDY.

17 When the office opened a refreshment room in 1867 it had high hopes for its success, but it proved unable to compete with neighbouring eating houses. (PRO 8/29, p 511)

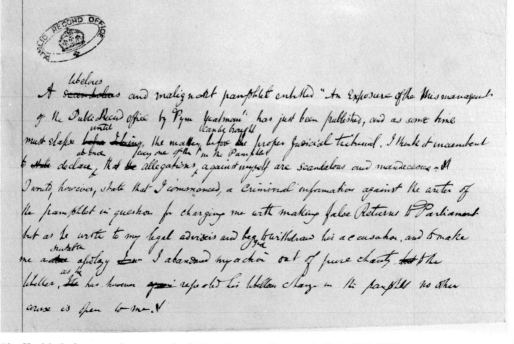

18 Hardy's draft memorandum announcing his intention to sue Yeatman for libel. (PRO 37/72)

19 *Rolls Yard and House.* (PRO 50/59, no 7)

20 *Rolls Yard gate looking out to Chancery Lane.* (PRO 50/59, no 3)

21 *The Rolls House shortly before its demolition.* (PRO 8/61, p 4)

22 *Rodney (centre right) examines the work of the boy clerks engaged on making extracts from the census returns. Poulter, who had risen from the workmen's ranks to that of supplementary clerk, is standing next to him with Fox a later establishment officer, o his right. The photograph was taken shortly before the First World War.* (PRO 8/23)

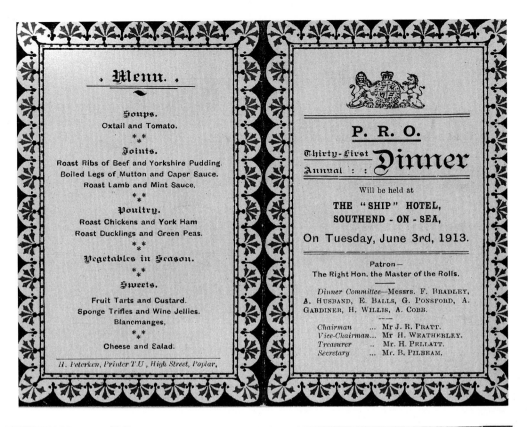

. Menu. .

Soups.
Oxtail and Tomato.

Joints.
Roast Ribs of Beef and Yorkshire Pudding.
Boiled Legs of Mutton and Caper Sauce.
Roast Lamb and Mint Sauce.

Poultry.
Roast Chickens and York Ham
Roast Ducklings and Green Peas.

Vegetables in Season.

Sweets.
Fruit Tarts and Custard.
Sponge Trifles and Wine Jellies.
Blancmanges,

Cheese and Salad.

H. Peterken, Printer T.U , High Street, Poplar,

P. R. O.

Thirty-First
Annual : : **Dinner**

Will be held at

**THE "SHIP" HOTEL,
SOUTHEND - ON - SEA,**

On Tuesday, June 3rd, 1913.

Patron—
The Right Hon. the Master of the Rolls.

Dinner Committee—Messrs. F. BRADLEY,
A. HUSBAND, E. BALLS, G. PONSFORD, A.
GARDINER, H. WILLIS, A. COBB.

Chairman ... Mr J. R. PRATT.
Vice-Chairman... Mr H. WEATHERLEY.
Treasurer .. Mr. H. PELLATT.
Secretary ... Mr. B. PILBEAM.

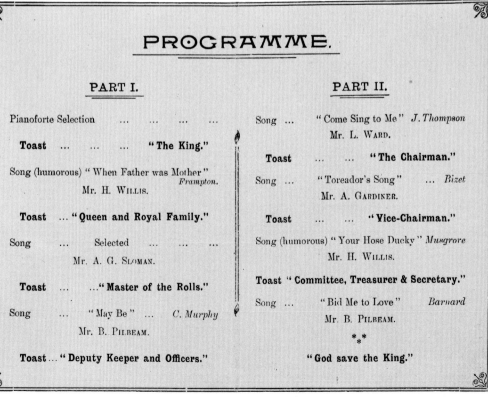

PROGRAMME.

PART I.

Pianoforte Selection ... ...

Toast ... ... **"The King."**

Song (humorous) " When Father was Mother "
Frampton.
Mr. H. WILLIS.

Toast ... **"Queen and Royal Family."**

Song ... Selected ... ...
Mr. A. G. SLOMAN.

Toast ... ..."**Master of the Rolls.**"

Song ... " May Be " ... *C. Murphy*
Mr. B. PILBEAM.

Toast ... **" Deputy Keeper and Officers."**

PART II.

Song ... " Come Sing to Me " *J. Thompson*
Mr. L. WARD.

Toast ... ... **"The Chairman."**

Song ... " Toreador's Song " ... *Bizet*
Mr. A. GARDINER.

Toast ... ... **" Vice-Chairman."**

Song (humorous) " Your Hose Ducky " *Musgrove*
Mr. H. WILLIS.

Toast " Committee, Treasurer & Secretary."

Song ... " Bid Me to Love " *Barnard*
Mr. B. PILBEAM.

" God save the King."

23   *When the assistant keepers dined out it was in a fashionable West End restaurant. But for the support grades – a loyal band to judge from the toasts – it was a trip to the coast.* (PRO 8/80)

24   *A E Stamp,*
deputy keeper 1926–1938

25   *Sir Cyril Flower,*
deputy keeper 1938–1947

26   *Sir Hilary Jenkinson,*
deputy keeper 1947–1954

27   *Sir David Evans,*
deputy keeper 1954–1958;
keeper 1959–1960

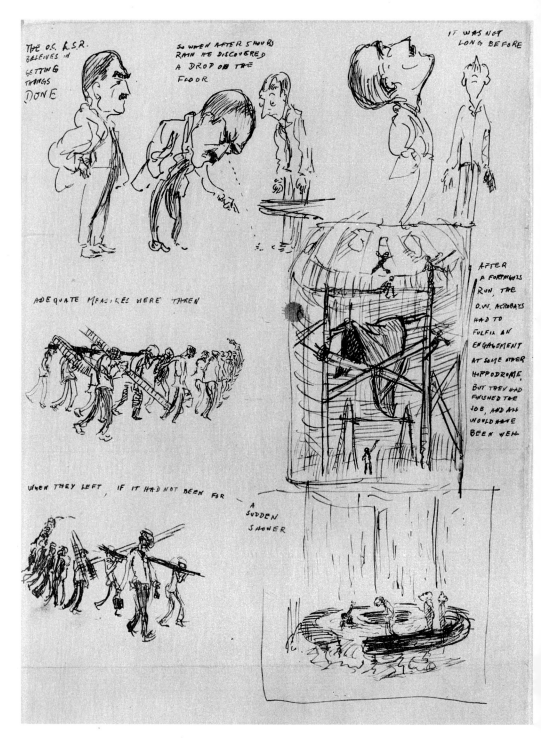

28 *Jenkinson's tussles with other departments were legendary. These sketches from his pen depict one of his many battles with the Office of Works in the 1920s when he was the officer-in-charge of the Round Room. (PRO 8/63, f 93)*

29 *A picture of the office during the blitz, taken from the south side of Fleet Street at 2 am, 30 December 1940.* (PRO 50/59, no 113)

30 *Fire-fighting practice on the roof of the Chancery Lane repository during the Second World War.* (PRO 50/59, no 92)

31   *Harold Johnson kneeling in the midst of evacuated records at Shepton Mallet prison, c. 1945. (PRO 18/7)*

32   *Leonard Hector (far right) and staff with evacuated records in the Banqueting Hall at Haddon during the Second World War. (PRO 18/5)*

33 *The Rolls Room as it appeared before its conversion to a search room.* (PRO 50/59, no 76)

34 *A 1953 photograph showing racking at Hayes intermediate repository before the huge influx of documents from departments.* (PRO 55/1)

35 *Conservation staff working in the huts on the North Terrace at Chancery Lane (from post-Second-World-War leaflet advertising vacancies)*

36 *Entrance to Hayes ('Limbo') repository*

37 *A view of some of the huts used to accommodate records at Ashridge repository*

closed material averaging no more than twenty annually. Hope of any extension at Chancery Lane had been abandoned long since and there was some doubt over the future of the repository at Cambridge. However, when the County Council decided in 1929 to exercise its option to acquire the site, the Prison Commission was able to offer alternative premises at the former House of Correction at Canterbury, which was preferred to a similar building at St Albans. The upshot was that at Jenkinson's insistence the accommodation there was reserved exclusively for departmental records not yet open to public inspection. Wright was placed in charge and the move – a triangular affair since Chancery Lane was also involved – was to provide a useful rehearsal, not realised at the time, for the large-scale evacuation of records at the outbreak of war in 1939. Some experience had, of course, been gained at the time of the Zeppelin raids during the First World War, but those involved had since left and the new generation had not previously been engaged in bulk movements of that order. At Canterbury itself Wright was fortunate to have assigned to him as a clerical officer Russell Farmer, whose initiative and drive had not always been appreciated in the sombre surrounds at Chancery Lane, where his one-time habit of riding in on a motor bike had gained him the reputation as something of a maverick. The office had also hoped that it might operate a van service between Canterbury and London, but that was ruled out on grounds of cost. Consequently when records were wanted by departments they were either sent by registered post or despatched by passenger train and then collected at the terminus parcels office by messengers. Additionally, room was found in the repository for older records from the District Probate Registry, an arrangement which resulted in Wright and Farmer obtaining a small annual allowance from that department for dealing with public enquiries about them.

Although Stamp reacted to rather than initiated events, his scope for expansion was slight because of the Treasury's constant emphasis upon economy. Indeed, in 1927, when the Treasury wished to cut the office still further, Stamp felt obliged to tell it that he thought the limits of squeezing had been reached. He had the utmost difficulty in obtaining an increase in the Library purchase grant from £150 to £200 a year, a claim that was eventually conceded in 1928. He also had a struggle to get sanction for a slight increase in the amount of money which might be earned by his external editors, of whom Hinds, Shaw, Bickley, W. H. B. Bird, Twemlow and Cecil Headlam remained on the books. Mrs Lomas had retired, and the eighth volume of state papers of the reign of William III which had been hanging fire ever since the death of W. J. Hardy in 1919 was finally completed by Miss Ethel Stokes of the British Record Society and published in 1927. In that same year the transcripts from Paris were interrupted with the accidental death of Leon Bogaert and later resumed by his daughter. The Spanish Calendar had remained in suspense ever since the Spanish archives in Brussels had fallen into the hands of the Germans during the war. The final volumes were not published until after the Second World War, but much of the editorial work had been undertaken earlier by Garrett Mattingley.

Stamp had been long enough at the centre of events to have no illusions about the Treasury's attitude towards increased expenditure. But that in no way softened the blow when it refused to allow the printing of his first *Annual Report*, which he thought might have been treated exceptionally because it contained a full tribute to Lyte's services over the previous 40 years. It was therefore fortunate for the office that, despite Treasury constraints, it enjoyed, for the most part, the advantage of a stable workforce. Among the clerical and support grades the personnel remained practically unchanged from year to year, except for the occasional retirements. The situation regarding the assistant keepers was rather different: first Mary Smieton in 1928, and then Stephen Wilson in 1929, had obtained transfers out after very little service, having found record work insufficiently congenial. Privately, Flower was inclined to regard them as misfits, later observing sourly that they had asked to be transferred 'to other Offices where they can better satisfy their urge to benefit humanity and perhaps themselves in the process'.[5b] Paradoxically, Wilson after a highly successful administrative career, not unlike Mary Smieton's, was to return to head the office in 1960 as its keeper. However, J. H. Collingridge, H. C. Johnson and H. N. Blakiston, who had all entered similarly through the general Civil Service examination, seemed likely to settle down, as did F. H. Slingsby who had come in from the Treasury for which he had not proved well suited. But the office had suffered a severe blow when Vivian Galbraith resigned in 1928 on obtaining an appointment as university reader in diplomatic at Oxford. Later, as regius professor, Galbraith was to recall his assistant keepership as a 'stick in the mud job', while doubting if he would ever find any nicer mud to stick in.[5c] Be that as it may the office's troubles were compounded at the beginning of 1929 by the unexpected death of the learned Fowler, whose antiquarian activities extended well beyond the office and who was a particular authority on Essex topography. Eve Potter, a graduate of London University, took Galbraith's place. She was the last to be recruited through the administrative class examination because in an effort to prevent future wastage a new method of appointment by competitive interview was introduced by the Civil Service Commission in the summer of 1929 after consultation with the office. D. B. Wardle of University College, Oxford, was the first assistant keeper to be selected in that way.

The underlying reason for the alteration was that the typical candidate for the Home, Indian and Colonial Civil Service did not find a career in the Public Record Office particularly appealing, being more interested in modern economic subjects than in Latin and history. On the other hand, there were

---

5b. PRO 1/97: Flower to Lee, 19 June 1930.

5c. Information supplied by Kenneth Timings. Galbraith's remark was made to Ronald Latham, like Timings, a later head of Search Department.

graduates whose university performance was as good as that of administrative recruits, but who did not care for the work of an ordinary government office, being attracted instead to a museum or similar career. Inevitably, the new system of recruitment marked a significant change in the position of the assistant keepers because they were no longer formally tied to the general administrative structure although still seen as closely allied to it. They had for some time been unhappy about the pay and prospects of the AK IIs and in 1928 their branch of the First Division Association, as part of a general campaign on behalf of assistant principals, had written to Stamp, who forwarded their complaint to the Treasury, but without any obvious effect. Their new isolation hardly augured well for any early improvement, especially as the Treasury had recently rejected out of hand a plea from Flower for an increase in pay as secretary with which had been coupled the suggestion by Stamp that if that was conceded his own pay as deputy keeper could not remain unchanged. Stamp could not have been expected to appreciate the Treasury's attitude in that instance, but he shared with it a distrust of proposals, then before it, concerning a projected 'History of Parliament'. The architect of the scheme was Colonel Josiah (later Lord) Wedgwood, but the enormous strain which the nineteenth-century *Official Return* of MPs had placed upon the office had already become part of its folklore and Stamp was determined to avoid any repetition. Nevertheless, he became a member of the committee which was set up under Wedgwood's chairmanship to superintend the undertaking, and Dawes was appointed joint secretary.

On a personal plane Stamp's relations with the Treasury were quite cordial and he was privy to its manoeuvrings to contain the parliamentary history project, including its vain attempt to keep William Page, editor of the Victoria County History, off the organising committee by telling him that it would involve much of his time.[5d] Essentially, Stamp was a man of peace and his dealings with other departments were generally good, but in 1928 he fell out with Lieutenant-Colonel Scorgie, deputy-controller of the Stationery Office, over remarks he had made to the Royal Commission on Museums and Galleries about the discreditable state of decay of many late-nineteenth-century calendars due to the poor quality of the mechanical wood-pulp paper on which they were printed. Stamp went on to say that the office had made it too hot for the Stationery Office for it ever to happen again, which drew an angry response from Scorgie who demanded a correction, saying:[6]

I have no wish to minimise the importance we attach to representations, hot or cold, from the Public Record Office but those of us in authority in this

---

5d. PRO 1/96: Stocks to Wedgwood, 5 March 1929.
6. PRO 1/95: Scorgie to Stamp, 25 September 1928.

Office today can hardly believe that it was prophetic fear of your choler in 1928 which moved our predecessors to do right in 1892.

More worrying for Stamp was the decline in the output of calendars and historical publications which had been approximately halved since the war. Furthermore, while the burdens imposed upon the office by the Law of Property Act in respect of manorial documents, and the growth of public interest in the records generally had increased, the higher staff had been reduced from a figure of 27 in 1914 to 23. There was also an urgent need for more repair work, and great concern was felt about the physical environment within the repository where mildew was appearing in certain rooms and was under investigation by the Imperial College of Science. Stamp's various public and private submissions to the Royal Commission were not without effect because in its final report,[7] the D'Abernon Report as it was known, the commission urged the government to find an additional £3,000 to £4,000 a year to meet the office's more pressing needs. On past form that might not have much impressed the Treasury, but the commission's more general complaint that economies on museum and associated services had been pushed beyond the limits of prudent administration had put it on the defensive, and besides making a guarded promise to make greater provision for record purposes in 1931 it also authorised a last-minute increase of £1,000 in the office estimates for 1930. While Stamp welcomed the improvement he had come to believe that the Public Record Office Acts were out of date and, although he did not press the point with the Royal Commission, he doubted whether the difficulties could really be remedied without a fresh act.[8] The easing of the purse strings in 1930 enabled the office to bring in an additional CO, a repairer and two porter-messengers. In 1931 five more porter-messengers were recruited, three less than the office wanted but still sufficient to make an impression upon the cleaning and shifting of records in the repository in order to maintain the regular decorating of strong rooms which Jenkinson thought essential. Charles Drew and Leonard Hector, two young Oxford graduates, had also entered in 1930 as assistant keepers, having been selected from a short-list of 14 drawn from 155 applicants. One post was new, but the other arose from the retirement of Charles Johnson whose reputation as a scholar was, as Stamp wrote in his *Annual Report*, acknowledged wherever medieval institutions were studied. Johnson's AK I post was filled by the promotion of Buckland, whose great knowledge of the nineteenth century was proving invaluable in dealing with the many accessions for that period being received from the Foreign Office and with family deposits such as the Granville Papers. Johnson's place on the Inspect-

---

7. *Final Report of the Royal Commission on Museums and Galleries*, II (Cmd. 3463) (1930), 36–38.

8. PRO 1/96: Stamp's memorandum for the Royal Commission on Museums and Galleries, 18 November 1929.

ing Officers' Committee was taken by Flower's assistant, and Stamp's son-in-law, P. V. Davies.

The slight easing of the restraints upon the office also allowed Stamp to try the experiment of offering temporary employment to a small number of young scholars, anxious to equip themselves to follow an academic career as teachers of history by acquiring, through the medium of editorial work, a knowledge of archives and original sources. One of the first to be engaged in that way was R. B. Wernham, who was later to rise to the professorial ranks at Oxford, besides maintaining his connection with the office through his editorship of the *Calendar of State Papers, Foreign* and other record publications. Stamp's idea was to have two or three such temporary assistants on the staff at any one time at a nominal salary of £200 a year, but the scheme had to be modified in 1932 when cutbacks became necessary after the national financial crisis of 1931 and it petered out altogether in 1934. The following year, however, one appointment was sanctioned and H. E. Bell of St John's College, Cambridge, was engaged for two years. Although Charles Johnson left the strength in 1930, he kept up his contacts with the office through his work on the *Medieval Latin Dictionary*, the committee for which enjoyed accommodation and other facilities at Chancery Lane. There was a real break with the past in the same year with the news of the death of Rodney whose reputation was in process of restoration now that the younger men were seeing for themselves the practical difficulties of dealing with unsorted records in bulk. At any rate, Flower felt sufficiently concerned about the debt the office owed to his memory to send an appreciative obituary notice to *The Times*. Rodney's contemporary Hall was, however, still active through the Royal Historical Society, and he had also been helping Beveridge in his work on *Prices and Wages in England from the Twelfth to the Nineteenth Century* by examining the Winchester pipe rolls. Echoes of the past were also to be found in an article he had written for *The Quarterly Review* in 1928, in which he drew particular attention to the wealth of documentary material for research among the relatively untapped Chancery masters' documents.[9] The revision in that year by the master of the rolls and the Treasury of the regulations for the inspection of those records may not have been unconnected with Hall's interest in them. No great surge in their use resulted, however, although among the few applications to inspect them was one from R. H. Tawney on behalf of one of his students at London University, which remains of interest now if only because of its reference to the shock resignation of Oswald Mosley from the Labour government on the issue of unemployment.[10]

That was, of course, the burning question of the day, and undoubtedly the security of tenure which establishment gave to those fortunate enough

9. H. Hall, 'New Materials for History', *The Quarterly Review*, CCLI, 79–85.
10. PRO 1/97: Tawney to Sankey, 21 May 1930. By mistake it was wrongly addressed to the lord chancellor.

to be on the permanent staff of the office went far to explain the infrequent changes in its personnel. In a minor way the Americans were also helping to keep up the office's numbers because in 1928 a small room had been fitted up as a studio for making photostatic copies of documents for the Library of Congress in order to throw light upon the history of the United States. That arrangement, which allowed for the reimbursement of the office's expenses in producing the records, was placed under the supervision of Ledward. In the repository generally Jenkinson was omnipotent, and Stamp and Flower were the unfortunate recipients of his complaints whenever the working arrangements involving other sections of the office or government departments fell short of the high standard of excellence he considered necessary. Inevitably his relations with outside departments, particularly the Office of Works and the Stationery Office, were frequently stormy. In retrospect, it can be seen that Jenkinson's *amour propre*, which led him to secure the involvement of the top officials in other offices, was often counter-productive as many of the matters in dispute might better have been dealt with at a lower level. But Jenkinson was rarely willing to delegate, even D. L. Evans, his lieutenant, being unkindly known as 'the conjuror's assistant'. Nevertheless, under his strong hand great improvements were achieved in the general level of efficiency and cleanliness in the repository, which set a laudable standard for his successors to follow. To his credit stood new rules concerning the method of stamping documents and strictly regulating the internal transfer of documents from one class to another. He also introduced an improved Register of Accessions and Withdrawals, the 'Transfer Register'. It was due to him that the search rooms were closed for a week in 1930 for stocktaking, which became thereafter an annual event. In a move reminiscent of Palgrave he converted one of the strong rooms into a Safe Room, which was brought into service in 1933, to provide additional security for documents and objects of special value, or of a kind which it would be unwise to keep on open shelves in a normal strong room. He also managed to have steel racking substituted for the wooden racking installed in four rooms as an economy measure in 1923. Hygrometers and psychrometers for the measurement of the relative humidity were also taken on hire from the Meteorological Office in an effort to deal with the problem of mildew. At his determination a sceptical Office of Works was finally prevailed upon to return to the use of distemper, instead of oil-bound paint, when decorating strong rooms. But not all Jenkinson's theories proved well founded, and the suspicion that the paint was in some way responsible for the mildew was no more correct than his earlier misgivings about the paste used for repairing documents. Even the installation in 1932 of an artificial system of ventilation by the use of fans and ducts proved less effective than hoped in dealing with the nuisance. In so far as the problem has become less acute since his time it probably owes more to the increased light and better passage of air as a result of the redevelopment of the former *Daily Mirror* and other sites on the worst-affected north side of the building in the 1960s than any other factor.

Jenkinson's overriding concern between the wars was the poor condition in which records too often arrived at the office from departments. In an effort to deal with the problem, and after representations to the Treasury, regulations governing transfers were issued by the master of the rolls in August 1929, but in some cases defects could not be put right easily because of the poor quality of the original materials. In March 1930 Jenkinson submitted a long memorandum to Stamp on the matter, urging remedial action and mentioning the interest being taken in the subject generally by the Commission Internationale de Cooperation Intellectuelle and the Library Association. Three months later the master of the rolls wrote to the prime minister to point out the need to regulate the quality of paper supplied to government departments and the manner in which files should be made up to minimise the difficulties which might otherwise be caused in storing records selected for permanent preservation. It was natural that when the papers were referred to the Treasury it should seek the views of Deputy-Controller Scorgie of the Stationery Office, who had little patience with the Record Office desiderata, observing sarcastically:[11]

> Of course if departments kept them [the records] properly 'filed and cased' according to methods of which the Record Office would approve, and they could only be looked at through a vita-glass screen after the applicant had filled up a special application form and had a turkish bath, they would last longer and give the Record Office less trouble. I have known Hilary Jenkinson for close on 25 years. He is an expert on diplomatic and the repair of documents and a very learned man, but so far as I know he has no experience of the conditions under which the documents are first written and used during their real life. A man may be a good post mortem analyst and a very bad physician.

Despite Scorgie's belief that the Record Office's idea of good and bad papers was that the former were no sooner created than dead and the latter were the active ones which became dog-eared, he thought it might be fun – *de gustibus* as the Treasury observed – to have a departmental conference: 'it will at least bring the Record Office up against real life'. A sub-committee, with Stamp as chairman and Wardle as secretary, was subsequently set up to report to the Treasury Establishment Officers' Committee.[12] It was a difficult job for Wardle because Stamp was not a good chairman any more than was Jenkinson a good committee man. To worsen matters Jenkinson was too assertive for Stamp's liking, which hardly helped the fashioning of a common Record Office line. Neither was the sub-committee's work assisted

---

11. T 162/151/E 24256: Scorgie to Crombie, 5 August 1930.
12. The committee's correspondence and papers will be found in PRO 39/7/1. A copy of its report is in PRO 39/7/2. I am much indebted to my former colleague, Bernard Wardle, for information concerning its proceedings.

when Jenkinson queried the nomination of the departmental representatives as being of insufficient standing. Its composition was then revised, but the changes could have made very little difference to its findings. Jenkinson made his presence felt whenever technical matters came up for discussion, but by no means had it all his own way, and a number of his pet ideas and proposals were cut out or amended by the other members, without hindrance from Stamp. He was also unable to prevent the insertion in the committee's report of a paragraph concerning a more robust approach to weeding by departments. Banham, the Treasury representative, was subsequently to minute:[13]

> The fundamental necessity seems to me to be to bring about a change of heart as to the hoarding of Government pp. The paragraph as to more ruthless weeding, of which I am the author, was carried through the Committee with some difficulty since it was scarcely within the terms of reference, but I think it has the strong personal support of Mr. Stamp. I feel sure that we must revise our ideas as to the proportion of matter which should be entrusted to the P.R.O. for preservation for all time.

Although Stamp was ready to meet the Treasury more than half way on that issue, he gave his support to the rest of the committee's recommendations. Its key proposal, in which the hand of Jenkinson could still be seen, involved departmental papers being secured before transfer by a form of binding, which was already in general use in the office's Repair Department, known as 'guarding and filing'. It was also proposed that paper and stationery supplies should be graded by the Stationery Office according to the likely permanence of the papers for which they were intended. But most departments thought that proposal unworkable, while the Treasury believed that 'posterity-consciousness was a vice of the worst kind'. Certainly fault could hardly be found with its view of the absurdity of asking civil servants to consider whether their memoranda should be preserved indefinitely before committing them to the appropriate grade of paper. It was to Jenkinson's credit that he was not prepared to tolerate the indiscriminate dumping of documents on the office by departments, but matters were not helped by his reluctance to compromise. To strike the right balance in which the best did not become the enemy of the good was not easy, but the practical outcome of the various discussions was that the bulk of departmental files came to be tidied and boxed before transfer to the office, while the Foreign Office and Colonial Office, which had customarily bound their papers, continued as formerly. However, the Foreign Office practice had more than once led to tussles with the inspecting officers because it was felt that too many ephemeral papers were being included in its bound volumes.

---

13. T 162/334/E 27704: Banham memorandum, 17 August 1932.

412

By 1935, when the make-up question had been under discussion for nearly five years, the Treasury was anxious to lay it to rest, but as the master of the rolls and the prime minister had referred the issue to it in the first place it knew the matter could not just be swept under the carpet. As luck would have it, the work of the Public Record Office was coming up for parliamentary scrutiny that year, which enabled the Treasury to bring out the cost of maintaining the country's records, then running at £69,000 annually. That led the Select Committee on Estimates to report:[14]

> As regards the more ancient records, there is presumably little practicable alternative but to continue broadly on the present lines, but the immense increase in recent times in the functions and activities of Government Departments has created, or will shortly create, a new and important problem. While it is conceivable that some current documents may acquire an equal interest for scholars [at] some future date, if the surviving mass is not too great, your Committee do not think it justifiable to incur expenditure in preserving Departmental files and papers after their utility for current or future business has disappeared.
>
> Your Committee trust that the possibility of reducing the number of papers selected for permanent preservation will be seriously considered.

In examining the department's work the Select Committee had taken evidence from Stamp and made an inspection of the office, but their questioning did not suggest undue concern about weeding. Neither was any enquiry made about the work of the Inspecting Officers' Committee, although the unspoken assumption was clearly that too much was being kept and that the Public Record Office was to blame. But the system under which the inspecting officers operated was wholly negative, their role being confined to authorising the destruction of papers when departments wished to be rid of them. Indeed, it could be argued that, at times, the inspecting officers were too ready to accommodate departmental wishes. In 1932, for example, over half a million files of the former Court for the Relief of Insolvent Debtors were consigned to oblivion when the space they occupied in the basement of the Stratford Labour Exchange had to be vacated urgently. Very little trace of that melancholy jurisdiction, Dickens's 'Temple to the Genius of Seediness', now remains and it is difficult to believe that mature consideration was given to that decision. Other examples could be quoted which would show the inspecting officers in a rather better light. However, Craig, the Treasury representative, attended the Select Committee throughout and there seems little doubt that the critical paragraph was inserted at his prompting, especially as the preparation of a circular to departments

---

14. *H C Reports, Committees, 1934–35*, VI, xi.

about the treatment of their records was held up until it had reported. The Treasury thought that Stamp might object when the draft of that circular was sent to him for comment because its tone was very different from that of the 1930–1932 committee over which he had presided. But Stamp recognised that the office had been outflanked and did not bother to send a reply, particularly as Jenkinson had grudgingly come to accept that the 'guarding and filing' of papers which he favoured, and which he had persuaded the committee to recommend as a standard, could not be generally applied because the vast number of records involved made it far too costly. Jenkinson remained contemptuous of departmental registries, however, and believed that the circular ought to have stressed the need for their improvement so that records might be properly managed from the outset. In fact, the Treasury circular dwelt almost exclusively upon the necessity for a policy of more drastic destruction of official papers, as recommended by the Select Committee, which departments were asked to undertake by reviewing their disposal schedules in conjunction with the Public Record Office. Reference was also made to the 1932 proposal about the need for more weeding. In justification the Treasury argued that, owing to the growth of twentieth-century government activities, the bulk of papers was so great as to hinder their examination and discourage research if too many were kept, quite apart from the expense involved. On the question of the form and make-up of preservable papers the Treasury said that the responsibility lay with departments, who, before despatching them to the Public Record Office, should remove metal paper-fasteners and rubber bands and then straighten the records and place them in boxes of an approved type obtainable from the Stationery Office. Finally, departments were asked to consider with the Stationery Office if materials used for the documents likely to be kept permanently were satisfactory and if further economies could be achieved in downgrading the class of paper used for ephemeral purposes.[15] But the Treasury made no attempt to follow its exhortation through apart from issuing a circular in July 1938 urging a reduction in the periods fixed in destruction schedules for the retention of accounts and vouchers, which varied considerably between departments.

Although the role of the Public Record Office in the preparation of records for transfer was not even mentioned in the 1935 Treasury circular, the truth was that it was under no obligation to accept documents from departments which were in a bad condition. Accordingly, it was able to insist upon certain minimum requirements. But it was not helped by its lack of a minister, and because it was remote from the mainstream it frequently betrayed an unawareness of the changing nature of the Civil Service. Yet the relentless growth in government bureaucracy meant that the problem of records could not be wished away by departments themselves and, to that

---

15. T 162/396/E 32180: Treasury circular 30/35 of 22 October 1935.

extent, they were obliged to seek the office's help from time to time. In 1932 the Cabinet Office, which had never wanted to be brought under the 1877 act, was concerned to learn that many of its papers were finding their way onto departmental files. Its attention had first been drawn to the matter by the Dominions Office, which pointed out that many Cabinet papers would then inevitably finish up in the Record Office and eventually be made available to searchers. The question was thought of such importance that a special conference of the interested parties, including the Public Record Office, was convened by the Treasury in May 1933. Hankey, the Cabinet secretary, did not think disclosure much mattered after 50 years, but in a memorandum circulated beforehand by Sir Rupert Howorth, his deputy, it was stated that 'it may well be that the character of Cabinet memoranda and similar documents would alter if it came to be generally recognised that at some future date these documents would be open to public inspection'. Stamp, who represented the office at the discussions, thought that that would speak ill of the writer. He believed the real danger was that it might impair a man's usefulness in the public service, particularly in the foreign and colonial spheres, if his confidential advice became publicly identified with him while he was still available for service.[16] The outcome was an agreement that Cabinet minutes were to be removed from departmental files but a record of the conclusion might remain; Cabinet papers dealing with defence were also to be removed. On the assurance that at least one set of secret papers would be maintained by the Cabinet Office itself, and because few departments placed such papers on their files, Stamp acquiesced. He did so reluctantly, and because he was convinced that public opinion was moving in the direction of greater openness he told the Treasury:[17]

I still think that the proposals of the committee will mean an unnecessary disturbance of official procedure, because they will be obsolete before the time comes for them to have effect.

Moreover, I do not believe that any government of the future will find independent experts like Temperley and Gooch to set out a case without letting them see for themselves the relevant cabinet papers.

No immediate leap forward was to be expected. A year earlier the Foreign Office had indicated that an extension of the 'open' period beyond 1885 was not likely for some time. Neither did it seem that the regular users of the search rooms were much concerned about the restrictions on access. In so far as complaints were voiced they tended to relate to working conditions in the search rooms, such as the inadequacy of the heating in the Long

16. PRO 1/103: Stamp's pencilled comments on Howorth's memorandum of 18 March 1933, circulated by the Treasury on 3 April 1933.
17. PRO 1/105: Stamp to Craig, 30 January 1934. For the Cabinet file see CAB 104/2.

Room. Much concern was also expressed when the Fetter Lane gate was closed as an economy measure for most of the day in 1935. Attendances which varied between 80 and 100 a day were on something of a plateau and the number of searchers holding permits to see closed records rarely exceeded 20 during the course of the year. A good proportion of readers were Americans or other foreigners. The number of productions in the Round Room was averaging 55,000–60,000 annually, with 25,000–35,000 in the Long Room and 4,000–5,000 in the Government Search Room.

The office welcomed the levelling off in the rate of growth. It had never been publicity conscious, and had no wish to make its services better known. Queen Mary's visit in 1933 passed quite unnoticed outside, not even being mentioned in the *Deputy Keeper's Report*. That was nothing new because a visit she had made some twenty-five years earlier as princess of Wales went similarly unrecorded, even although office lore has it that the future Edward VIII amused himself on that occasion by prancing up and down the pair of high steps in the deputy keeper's room. However, the discovery of some Shelley letters in 1930 found its way into the press and short articles invariably appeared when special exhibitions were mounted in the Museum, as at the time of the Jubilee in 1935 or on popular subjects such as the mutiny on the *Bounty*. But the office remained practically unknown to all but those engaged in serious research or to the comparatively few who needed to visit it for legal purposes. No one officer was responsible for public relations which was, perhaps, just as well when in 1938 the king, disliking the appearance of his signature on a Museum postcard, asked for its withdrawal. Much to the office's embarrassment the news of his request was leaked to the press and, despite a rigorous inquiry by Jenkinson, the source was never traced.

Strangely, there was a moment in the mid 1930s when Stamp feared a recurrence of old controversies, because a letter was received from the United Protestant Council, then in fierce dispute with the Catholic Evidence Guild, urging the publication of letters relating to alleged Vatican plots during the sixteenth and seventeenth centuries. Privately, Stamp believed that if the Protestants became aware of the background to the Roman Calendar it would be unfortunate for the office because the last editor, Rigg, whose religious views were supposed to have disappeared at the time of his appointment, was later said to have gone over to Rome. At any rate, having taken his second volume down to 1582, Rigg had reported that subsequent years were not worth calendaring. Soon afterwards his memory began to fail and he eventually died in 1925. Lyte, trusting to Rigg's report, and perhaps being unwilling to fish in troubled waters, decided to stop the calendar. Had it gone on all might have been well, but Stamp felt that to resume it at the request of the Evangelical Alliance, even in defence of the government of Elizabeth I, was quite another matter. Not that Stamp, whom the Protestants thought well disposed towards them – they were concerned that his eventual successor might not be so favourable – held a brief for the Catholics because in a memorandum for the information of the master of the rolls he pointed out:[18a]

> Curiously enough this is the third time at least that this Office has got into trouble by appointing editors who were Roman Catholics or became Roman Catholics during the period of their engagement.

Nevertheless, although Hanworth was to authorise publication, the calendar came to grief when Hinds, who had been given the job, resigned the editorship in 1936 owing to dissatisfaction about the method of payment. Paradoxically, when the former editorial assistant, H. E. Bell, a Protestant, took on the task in 1938 it was a Roman Catholic master of the rolls, Sir Wilfrid (later Lord) Greene, who approved his appointment and sanctioned the calendar's resumption. With the Catholic O'Reilly following his co-religionist Giuseppi as head of the Search Department, the Protestants had suspected the worst when Greene became master of the rolls after the resignation of Lord Wright, who had succeeded Hanworth briefly between 1935 and 1937.[18b] However, it was Mussolini's declaration of war in 1940 which was to stop the enterprise. Progress on other publications was limited by shortage of funds. In 1934 death claimed two of the longest-serving editors, W. H. Bird and Cecil Headlam. The latter's *Calendar of State Papers, Colonial* was taken over by Dr A. P. Newton of King's College London then nearing retirement from the Rhodes professorship of colonial history. Meanwhile, the *Calendar of State Papers, Domestic, William III* was being brought to a conclusion by Edward Bateson.

In the office itself Horace Headlam retired from his superintendence of the Government Search Room in 1933. He was not a man to seek the limelight and is best remembered for his work in the office garden where he transformed the uninteresting grass plots and ivy beds into lawns and herbaceous borders. Lyle and Giuseppi followed him into retirement in 1934 and Chapman, as much in love with the world of nature as the world of records, in 1936. Eve Potter, who had earned a high reputation during her stay, resigned on marriage in 1934 and was succeeded by Ronald Latham, who had been first reserve at the previous year's open competition for assistant keeperships. The successful candidates on that occasion had been Roger Ellis and Ralph Pugh, whose careers, as it happened, were to develop outside the office, although still in the historical field. The AK I vacancies as a result of the various retirements led to the promotion of Ledward, Wood, Evans and Crompton. Ratcliff took Giuseppi's place on the Inspecting Officers' Committee. On the clerical side stagnation persisted but Pilbeam's retirement as chief repairer in 1934 resulted in the promotion of J.

18a. PRO 1/107: Stamp's memorandum of January 1935 on Miscellaneous file.
18b. See 1937 Protestant Truth Society booklet *Papal Plots against the British Empire during and after the Great War* on Miscellaneous file in PRO 1/113.

Gilkes. A new post of chief binder was created in 1936, the special skills of T. Hassell being recognised by his appointment.

Throughout this time Stamp, whose health had never been robust, was under much stress and he was not helped when knocked down by a car in 1934. Flower and Jenkinson were rarely of the same mind and Stamp often found himself involved in their disputes, which centred upon Jenkinson's belief that if economies were necessary they should be in the area of publication and not on measures to conserve the records. Jenkinson generally got his way in the end, although when the assistant keeper pay scales were consolidated in 1936 Flower was given primacy over the other AK Is by being named principal assistant keeper and secretary and given an advantage of £200 a year, while Davies moved up to the AK I grade. Stamp's attempt to improve his own position was dismissed with scorn by the Treasury, which did not think the job of deputy keeper was of sufficient importance to justify any increase in his pay. The assistant keepers' branch of the First Division Association – the 'Soviet' as it had been christened by Lyte, and was still known – was dismayed by the reorganisation, particularly as the AK Is were uncoupled from the corresponding administrative grade of principal at a slightly lower maximum. The branch argued for the creation of three new posts of principal assistant keeper as some compensation but the most the Treasury was prepared to agree was that two of the AK Is might be allowed £100 a year extra in respect of special responsibilities. One of those, very properly, was Jenkinson and the other O'Reilly. A further important consequence was that the number of AK I and AK II posts was equalised at 11 each, which meant some improvement in the promotion prospects of the junior grade although two assistant keeper posts were sacrificed in the process.

Stamp's battles with the Treasury over the assistant keepers' and his own pay, and its evident determination to hold the office in check, may have given rise to the sourness with which he greeted a claim by the attendants and repairers for a substantial improvement in their scales. His first reaction was to tell the Treasury that it seemed 'preposterous' to him, but then, pointedly, 'but various things have worried me lately into a disposition to think everything preposterous'.[19a] Fortunately for the men their position was soon to be strengthened when the rather similar grade of search officers in the General Register Office succeeded in obtaining a favourable award at arbitration. But matters dragged on for more than two years before a settlement was reached through the Whitley machinery. At one stage the office, and Jenkinson in particular, had toyed with the idea of regrading those employed upon production duties as paper keepers. In 1938, however, it was finally agreed that half of the men might proceed to a maximum of 85s as against a previous maximum of 79s a week. A foreman post was also

19a. T 162/706/3086/3: Stamp to Wardley, 28 December 1935.

418

authorised in the search rooms and a sub-foreman post in the Repair Department. In all, there were nine supervisory posts, with allowances ranging from 3s 6d to 8s a week extra. The superintendent's maximum was also increased from £277 to £300 a year. Although the various increases fell significantly short of what had been claimed, the grade as a whole was well pleased with the outcome. While their pay was modest, a steady job meant a great deal and the cordial relations which then existed between the office and its manual staff was to pay a handsome dividend when extra duties were thrown upon them as a result of the wartime evacuation of the records. An illustration of the good spirit had, in fact, been provided as early as 1936 when repairer Mason invented a labour-saving machine for rubbing down parchment, for which the office obtained an award of £15 from the Treasury for him. The Repair Department also continued to enjoy a high reputation in the record world generally. In 1936 a demonstration of its work was given for members of the British Records Association and during 1937 two trainee repairers were attached to it from the Henry E. Huntington Library in California and from Ceylon respectively. The American student was later to publish a detailed account of the work of the Repair Department in the first number of *The American Archivist*.[19b] Meanwhile, Jenkinson was maintaining his international contacts, being the country's representative at the World Congress of Universal Documentation in 1937. The development of microphotography was much in the minds of delegates there, and inside the office thought was beginning to be given about how it might be exploited. Monger and Marchant were continuing to provide a limited photocopying service, but there were criticisms of their work from time to time, and it was already clear that, in the event of expansion, the staff would be directly employed, initially from the ranks of the attendants and repairers.

A continuing constraint upon the department was lack of accommodation. In 1934, when Clifford's Inn was being developed for residential flats, it had been proposed to take over two of the old houses there, but that had to be abandoned when they were found to be structurally unsuitable. A year earlier Jenkinson had wanted a new block on the North Terrace for the repairers and for the possibility of an official photographic unit, but the Office of Works was unable to find the money. In 1937 the opportunity to acquire the lease of St Dunstan's House at the Fetter Lane end of the site was also lost. Every year, however, records flowed in, making ever greater demands upon space and upon editorial and other resources. A small relief resulted from the outward transfer to the Royal Archives in 1935 at the king's request of certain documents relating to the conduct of Caroline, princess of Wales. There was some doubt about whether all the papers concerned were really Home Office records, and it was with that depart-

---

19b. L. Herman Smith 'Manuscript Repair in European Archives', *The American Archivist*, I, 1–14.

ment's consent that two out of three bundles were returned. Nothing was said publicly at the time, and, although there was a half-hearted attempt by the Palace in 1951 to secure the third bundle as well, the application was not pressed when the office objected.[20a] Another withdrawal occurred in 1937 when a small number of ancient records brought to London from Scotland during the reign of Edward I were returned there under the Public Records (Scotland) Act 1937. Atkinson, still in charge of the Museum, which now opened daily at one o'clock instead of two o'clock, carried the documents in person across the border for a handing-over ceremony in the General Register House, Edinburgh. The Scottish would have liked more, but the office was adamantly opposed to the removal of documents of the English administration relating to Scotland from existing series, and it was only after protracted negotiations that a further batch was released in 1948. A similar firm line had been taken with dominions governments whenever the return of original documents was requested, although every facility was given to them for the supply of photocopies. In a number of cases duplicates and similar unwanted records had been presented to them under schedule, and further rules permitting presentation of documents to libraries in the dominions as an alternative to destruction were introduced in 1936. By contrast, the British Museum found itself in hot water with Stamp when it thoughtlessly accessioned some Audit Office documents sent to it irregularly by the lord chamberlain. Comparing museum practice with that of the office, Stamp said: 'your people on the other hand swallow all, whether public records or not. Do you not think that a little reciprocity would improve the feeling of affection between our two departments?'[20b]

Two months later an even stronger rebuke went to the newly-established Tithe Redemption Commission which conjured up an amusing picture of Stamp struggling to keep pace with Lord Wright, the master of the rolls, while telling him of the commission's iniquities. They arose from its failure to consult the office, about a clause in the Tithe Act 1936 which placed the diocesan and parish copies of instruments of apportionment under the 'charge and superintendence' of the master of the rolls. That matter was eventually regularised by rules issued by Wright's successor in 1946, the delay having been caused by the war. However, the effect of Stamp's broadside upon the commission may well be imagined from the following extract:[21]

He [the Master of the Rolls] is an extremely busy man with an enormous

---

20a. H. M. Hyde MP raised the matter in Parliament on 2 February 1956, but without positive response (*Hansard* 548, 1081–1082). There is a cutting of a critical leading article from the *Evening Standard*, written shortly afterwards, in PRO 8/61, p 190. For office papers see PRO 1/107, PRO 1/1216, PRO 1/1614.

20b. PRO 1/110: Stamp to Forsdyke, 14 January 1937 on British Museum file.

21. PRO 1/111: Stamp to Richardson, 13 March 1937 on Miscellaneous file.

amount of judicial business on his hands in addition to administrative work
which he is not able to delegate to assistants.

I had a few minutes conversation with him some time ago as we were walking
in the same direction in the street and found him still very indignant, as
indeed I am myself, that the promoters of the Tithe Act should have copied
into it the record clause from Lord Birkenhead's Act without consulting
him or anyone who would be responsible for the working of this clause in
the new Act or with experience in the working of the old one . . . I believe
he thinks that there is nothing for him to do at the present juncture, but no
doubt, if you make any suggestion which does not conflict with his own
opinion something may come of it.

'What an admirable letter', said Wright, 'I agree with every word of it'.
But Stamp generally preferred the rapier to the blunderbuss and did not
often give vent to his feelings. Inside the office he invariably tried to calm
passions, especially when Jenkinson was in one of his explosive moods.
That was not always easy because on most matters Stamp's own views
corresponded with those of Jenkinson's official superior and rival, Flower.
Even Flower could be gently chided as when he wrote to Stamp, then on
holiday at Seaton, about some strayed eighteenth-century tellers' bills and
was reminded by Stamp in a postscript to his reply that 'the late lamented
George Pilbeam had a habit of sending an envelope with letters requiring
an answer. An excellent habit'.[22] The status of records which had been
removed from official custody continued to trouble the office throughout the
1930s because no two cases were identical and the law was uncertain. Where
a person's public spirit was not susceptible to appeal a mixture of bluff and
threat was sometimes effective, but no cases went to court. One of the most
useful repossessions was that of a quantity of assize records from the former
Norfolk circuit.

The defect lay in the inadequacy of the 1838 act, but most of the assistant
keepers were more concerned about the fact that in 1938 the Public Record
Office would be 100 years old. In June 1935 a branch meeting of the
First Division Association decided that a small sub-committee should be
appointed to prepare a scheme to mark the occasion by a special publication.
The result was a decision to prepare an Office History, the work being
entrusted mainly to J. R. Crompton, then in charge of the Round Room
and soon to be promoted to the AK I grade when Chapman retired in 1936.
Crompton was popular with staff and searchers alike, but by the standards
of the time his family background was undistinguished and in the early
stages of his career he seemed to have thought that a disadvantage. He had

---

22. PRO 1/109: Stamp to Flower, 4 June 1936 on Miscellaneous file. Pilbeam died
in 1935.

been helped through university by Lord Edmund Fitzmaurice who was acquainted with his father, the headmaster of the County Secondary School at Bradford-on-Avon. Crompton's natural ability was undoubted, but it was soon clear that the amount of research needed to do justice to the planned volume was much greater than had originally been thought. Writing to Atkinson and Crompton in August 1935 Flower, evidently thinking it was intended to give some of the work out to individual assistant keepers, said he considered it logical to separate selection of records for preservation and destruction from their care when selected. He also made it clear that he would not approve of Jenkinson, who was on the Editorial Committee, writing an account of the work of the inspecting officers. In the event Crompton kept the work to himself, believing it necessary in the first instance to concentrate upon the early history of the public records. He also undertook some preliminary research into the Record Commission and the Public Record Office itself and travelled to Somerset to interview Lyte. The intended scope of his investigation was such that it seemed highly improbable that the various strands could be brought together in time for publication in 1938, the centenary year. But the matter was never put to the test because on 17 June 1937 Crompton failed to return from lunch and the office was plunged into shock when it was discovered that he had taken his own life by throwing himself under a train on the underground railway. It was thought by some that he may have been affected by the earlier death of his mother, but among certain of the younger assistant keepers it was believed privately that the tragedy had its roots in a friendship of an unorthodox kind which had put his forthcoming marriage in jeopardy and placed him under an intolerable strain. Whatever the explanation, a discreet silence was maintained by them and so the possibility of the sad event giving rise to scandal was avoided. Inside the office more generally, as in the outside world, the unhappy business remained shrouded in mystery and was soon forgotten, marked only by a short obituary notice from the pen of Charles Johnson in *The Times* of 24 June. Office sensitivity about the death may partly account for its reaction to a light-hearted column by A. L. Rowse in *The Spectator* of 12 November 1937 concerning search-room users – 'we all know we are slightly mad' – which led to the master of the rolls promising to have a word with him. What was certain was that the department had lost an officer of rare talent, and one seen by many as a future deputy keeper. It was also clear from Crompton's own copious and neatly assembled notes,[23] especially on the earlier fortunes of the ancient records in the Treasury of the Exchequer and elsewhere, that had he managed to fashion his undertaking to his own grand design it would have emerged as a work of high literary, as well as historical, merit.

Crompton's place as an AK I was taken by J. H. Collingridge, but no

23. See PRO 8/47.

one was given specific responsibility for the History although a scheme for a readable book of about two hundred and fifty pages was proposed by Noel Blakiston. His plan would have placed an emphasis upon personalities throughout, while dealing with the following themes:

(1) The Public Record Office's functions.

(2) Its origins based upon Crompton's work.

(3) How the Public Record Office started: the Record Commission and the 1838 act.

(4) The history of the Public Record Office, 1850 to 1938.

(5) The building.

(6) The history of research – eleventh to twentieth century.

(7) Destruction, preservation, repairs.

(8) Comparison of English and foreign archive administration.

(9) The Public Record Office and the future.

When his proposal was considered by an Office History Committee in October 1937 an alternative plan, based upon a scheme suggested by H. C. Johnson, was preferred. Under his proposal an historical introduction written by the deputy keeper was to be followed by chapters dealing with the 1838 act and the building of the office on the Chancery Lane site. Subsequent chapters were to concentrate upon specific aspects of the department's work for which the various sections were to be responsible. An editorial board was to exercise overall control, and the final editorial work was to be given to a senior officer. Even that proved too ambitious for early completion, although Roger Ellis managed to prepare a draft chapter on the building of the office which was to form the basis of an article which appeared many years later in a volume of *Essays in Memory of Sir Hilary Jenkinson*, published in 1962. If other work was done for the project it has not survived, but in any event, with Stamp's illness and death compounding the difficulties, it was soon plain that nothing worthwhile was going to be produced in the time available. Therefore the office decided to hold a special Reception and Exhibition of Work instead, along lines suggested to it by the Association of Assistant Keepers in November 1937. Greene gave his whole-hearted blessing and for once the Treasury proved no obstacle, the chancellor of the Exchequer, Sir John Simon, approving the estimated expenditure on hospitality of £250 and sanctioning the provision by the Stationery Office and the Office of Works of the necessary support services.

Almost a year later, on 26 October 1938, more than one thousand guests thronged the office, which was adorned with floral decorations and bay trees, for what proved a glittering occasion. In addition to the duke and duchess of Kent, there were present members of the diplomatic corps, British and overseas archivists and historians, judges, and representatives of the Civil

Service, the universities and learned societies, to say nothing of Cardinal Hinsley, archbishop of Westminster, resplendent in his flowing red robes. Former members of the staff and other persons with personal or family connections with the department also attended. In the Round Room light music was provided by the band of the Welsh Guards, which must have given Lyte a chuckle in view of his past battles with their compatriots. At various strategic points within the building special exhibitions were mounted of treaties, seals, maps, bindings and repairs. Three of the 140 normally tightly-secured strong rooms were opened for inspection by the visitors, and the Long Room was laid out with plans and prints illustrating the growth of the office on the Rolls Estate. Supplementing them were portraits of masters of the rolls, deputy keepers of the records and architects and others who had been involved in the planning and building of the repository. Next door to the Long Room there was an exhibition of various finding-aids to the records including the Summary, Giuseppi's *Guide*, specimen lists and some old manuscript indexes to the Close Rolls. The special importance attached to diplomatic documents was illustrated by the earliest known inventory of the records prepared at the direction of Bishop Stapeldon, treasurer (1320–1322), and the Compendium of records in the Treasury at Westminster compiled in 1610 by Arthur Agarde, a famous antiquary whose list of perils for archivists to guard against, 'Fier, Water, Rates and Mice, Misplacinge', is still often recalled. Besides refreshments, all guests were given a carefully edited printed programme, explaining lucidly the activities of the Repair and other departments whose work was on display. At the last moment, on the day of the reception itself, a number of Australian documents were also placed on view because of the previous evening's announcement of the duke of Kent's appointment as governor-general designate of the Commonwealth of Australia. Jenkinson was the vital force behind the entire proceedings and it was his imaginative direction which ensured success. On the night he revelled in the part of *major domo*, a distinction he had earned even if the message it seemed to convey was that he, not Greene and Flower, by then deputy keeper, was the real master.[24]

At the year's end the Historical Association marked the centenary by publishing in *History*, its quarterly journal, an article by Wernham surveying briefly what the 1838 act had meant for historians and the efforts made by the office to implement it. Wernham, who was by then back in academic life at Oxford, concentrated particularly upon publication policy, and especially upon the reforms introduced by Lyte. He also outlined the progress made in preserving the records and making them available to searchers. For its part the association lamented the deaths of Stamp and Crompton, which had made it impossible to produce an Official History in time for the centenary, but hoped that the work would appear later.

---

24. For material concerning the reception see PRO 1/116.

Had Stamp lived, the centenary celebration might fittingly have rung down the curtain on his career. Unfortunately he had never recovered from an operation at the end of 1937 and his death occurred at the beginning of March 1938. Flower's appointment to succeed him was generally expected within the office except by Jenkinson who had convinced himself that his pioneering archival work as a writer and practising exponent could not be overlooked. With Hanworth he had also been closely involved in the formation of the British Records Association in 1932, and from its inception had been its joint secretary, the other being Dr Irene Churchill, whose interest in archives had begun during the First World War when she had been one of the honorary secretaries of a committee started by Hall to further the employment of women archivists. Jenkinson had also been active with Giuseppi in the work of the Surrey Record Society. When ill health forced Hanworth to give up work in 1935 Wright became master of the rolls on the understanding that he would not carry the burden for long, and Greene took his place in 1937. Consequently Greene had little time to judge the leading contenders for himself, but Stamp had long let it be known that Flower should succeed him. Moreover, while Jenkinson could rightly claim to be supreme as an archivist, his administrative experience was limited. He was also a difficult man to deal with and during 1937 had embroiled the office in a bruising battle with the Foreign Office concerning its binding practice, which had provoked Gaselee, its librarian, to complain to Flower about the waste of time caused by Jenkinson's constant criticisms and to suggest that the question might be given a rest for a few years. 'Perhaps mark your file: "Bring up 1st January 1943" '.[25] That the issue had become completely fouled by personalities was evident after the war when normal transfers were resumed and the Foreign Office went over to the 'guarding and filing' system without demur.

It was bad enough that Jenkinson was at odds all too often with other departments, but worse still that Stamp and Flower found themselves dragged into his quarrels and assailed by him whenever they displayed any inclination to compromise. Somewhat nearer home, Flower had been much irritated when Jenkinson defied his request for a short list of records which might be evacuated immediately in the event of war. In collaboration with O'Reilly, and after many months' work, Jenkinson produced instead a huge schedule of classes which might remain at Chancery Lane, amounting to about half the contents of the office. But there was method in Jenkinson's apparent madness because in his infuriating way he was trying to impress upon Flower, who could not bring himself to believe war likely, the scale of the problem facing the office: if half the records might stay the other half must go. In fact, something like half of the office's contents left London during the war years, but since it was clearly impractical to move them at

---

25. PRO 1/110: Gaselee to Flower, 18 May 1937 on Foreign Office file.

5

one fell swoop Flower could hardly be faulted for seeking a priority list, particularly as an onslaught from the air was generally expected to follow, if not coincide with, any declaration of war. There was the further consideration that expansion at Chancery Lane was again under discussion, including the provision in any new building of special protection in a deep bomb-proof shelter for those records with the highest claim to be preserved. At any rate, Flower must have felt sufficiently confident of his own stand in relation to Jenkinson to reveal his rival's behaviour to Greene in January 1938. Ostensibly, Flower's report concerned the state of the office's readiness in the event of an emergency, but as Greene must have been assessing the two men's merits at the time Jenkinson's claim could hardly have been helped.

Within the space of two months both men were among the mourners at Stamp's funeral. Greene was also there and gave a clear pointer to his intentions when he was heard to ask Flower to let him have a brief for a tribute to the late deputy keeper for *The Times*. Formal confirmation of Flower's appointment followed early in April, but news of it did not become generally known for some weeks, the delay leading Lyte, who it was said had never once invited Jenkinson to take a seat in his presence, to ask Flower anxiously what was afoot because no announcements had appeared in the press. It must have been a bitter blow for Jenkinson, but it would have been even worse had Dawes, the senior assistant keeper, taken the post of secretary offered to him by Flower. When he declined Flower had little option but to offer it to Jenkinson, whose acceptance was immediate and who joined the Inspecting Officers' Committee at the same time. A minor consequence of his elevation to the secretaryship was that he managed to alter his entry in the *Imperial Calendar* from C. H. to Hilary. Much to Jenkinson's annoyance, Flower had always refused to make any amendment on the grounds that Hilary sounded too epicene. But Jenkinson's reputation in Whitehall was already such that it was difficult to believe that there was ever any danger of mistaken gender.

A little earlier J. H. Collingridge had joined the Inspecting Officers' Committee as a result of Ratcliff's retirement in January 1938. Flower remained on the committee, but *ex officio* as deputy keeper, and handed over his duties as legal inspecting officer to P. V. Davies. The AK I vacancies created by the changes were filled by the promotion of H. C. Johnson and F. H. Slingsby, while R. L. Atkinson took Ratcliff's place as secretary of the Historical Manuscripts Commission, and R. W. N. Gilling and T. H. Brooke entered the office as AK IIs through an open competition. Meanwhile, apart from the promotion of Safford to assistant keeper in 1937, the outlook for the clerical grade remained bleak although Wright had been restyled custodian at Canterbury and given a nominal £4 increase of salary. Efforts to improve Fox's position had not succeeded, but as some consolation he was awarded the MBE at the beginning of 1939. Although Flower continued to press the Treasury for an improvement, neither he nor Jenkinson had any enthusiasm for enlarging the clerical grade's area of activity if that meant interfering with tasks which the assistant keepers had traditionally undertaken. Yet it was plain that in many instances assistant keepers were performing duties of a clerical, even sub-clerical nature, such as entering up the correspondence registers in the Secretariat and the production registers in the Search Department. An entirely new factor was that the younger assistant keepers were a different breed from their older colleagues and saw little sense in performing routine tasks of that kind except, possibly, for a short time by way of acquainting themselves with the work. Towards the end of 1937 three of them, Blakiston, Drew and Pugh, went so far as to complain about their misemployment on such duties and their protest was to lead to a small expansion in the clerical complement to undertake it instead. Pugh felt particularly strongly on the subject of departmental organ-isation and incurred Jenkinson's wrath when he set down some of his ideas during the early months of the war.[26] At that time Pugh had temporarily taken charge at Canterbury where Wright had fallen ill and Farmer had been called up despite the office's protests and attempt to have him released. In the light of his experiences there Pugh thought that because the branch held closed records only clerical grading was entirely appropriate and that the post of custodian ought to be upgraded to that of staff officer, but when Wright, resentful at what he saw as headquarters indifference to his staffing difficulties, returned to duty his attitude did nothing to further his cause. Worse still, he was to earn a written reprimand from Flower for letting the office down by failing to produce documents for a searcher who had journe-yed from London specially to see them and whose visit had been notified in advance. Fortunately for Wright, operations at Canterbury were soon to run down and a large portion of the records there were removed when France was overrun in the summer of 1940 and a German invasion of England seemed likely. Finally, between October 1941 and January 1942 the rest of the records were transferred out, the building being given up to the Admir-alty as a place of detention for naval offenders.

By that time the records generally were already well scattered around the country. Following his earlier brush with Flower in 1937 Jenkinson had constructed seven categories of what he called *evacuanda*, the first being major series which had not been published and the last consisting of speci-men records from classes not evacuated. Contingency planning for evacuat-ing public records had been the subject of confidential discussions with the Office of Works since 1933 and in 1934 two country houses in Bedfordshire were provisionally allocated for their reception. When inspection of the properties proved them to be too small they were reluctantly discarded and the possibility of storage in underground railway tunnels was considered but

---

26. PRO 1/358: Pugh's report upon the Canterbury repository, [February] 1940. 'No, no, no', said Jenkinson, 'this theory that it is below the dignity of an AK to know, by practical experiment, the inwardness of technical processes of all kinds is most dangerous.'

eventually abandoned because those offered were found to be too wet. D. B. Wardle hit upon the novel idea of placing records in a railway train in a remote siding, so that the collection might be moved elsewhere if danger threatened, but that suggestion proved impracticable. By the time of the Sudeten crisis in 1938 the office had been offered the use of the women's wing of a disused prison at Shepton Mallet by the Prison Commission. It was an odd coincidence that Lyte was living at Dinder Hall in the next parish, and he was to take a keen interest in the various developments at Shepton Mallet. Consequently it was entirely appropriate that when he died in October 1940 Harold Johnson, the assistant keeper in charge of the repository there, should represent the office at his funeral. In addition to the accommodation offered by the Prison Commission at Shepton Mallet the Ministry of Health placed at the office's disposal a recently-built casual ward of a workhouse at Market Harborough. In the autumn of 1938 arrangements had been made for loaded lorries to leave for both destinations when news came through of Neville Chamberlain's mission to meet Hitler at Munich and his subsequent ill-fated announcement of 'peace in our time'.

A year later there was no last-minute reprieve and Leonard Hector, soon to move to Haddon Hall, initially took charge at Shepton Mallet to which 300 tons of records, including Domesday Book, were to be transferred, a move which began in August 1939, when it was evident that war was imminent. Harold Johnson took over from Hector within a matter of weeks and quarters were provided subsequently for an attendant, R. Collie, and his family. Similar arrangements were made at Market Harborough, which was placed under the charge of P. V. Davies who was accommodated in a house about a mile away. Some 140 tons were stored there and a further 375 and 200 tons respectively at Belvoir Castle and Haddon Hall, which were placed at the office's disposal by the duke of Rutland. With Treasury approval the duke was appointed an honorary assistant keeper, a rank he held until his death in April 1940. For Jenkinson and Flower, as for their predecessors, the theory behind his appointment, that records should never leave official custody, was held almost metaphysically, and was as much an article of faith as transubstantiation was for the medieval churchmen. A similar honorary appointment was made in 1941 of Dr A. Guillaume, principal of the Oxford Diocesan Training College at Culham, which was taken over in that year for 450 tons of records. Its allocation had been the subject of a sharp tussle with other claimants, particularly the Air Ministry which had wanted it for RAF personnel, but the office was saved when it was found that the college could not be fitted up for the airmen in time. Some art treasures had been moved from London museums and galleries to underground caves, but the office was at first reserved about that method of storage when it was suggested to it by the Ministry of Works. Gatliff of the Treasury thought he saw in the rejection the hand of Jenkinson, 'who seems to me nearly as empty of sound judgment as he is full of words', and wondered whether it might be worth mentioning the matter to Flower, 'a much more temperate person'.[27] However, in 1943 the office gave serious consideration to removing records in the event of further emergency to Winsford salt mine in Cheshire. At that time fears were felt about the safety of records at Culham because an aerodrome had been sited nearby, but in the event the request for space in the mine was withdrawn when Evans reported that its brine-sprinkler system made it unsuitable as a record repository.

Initially, Wood took charge at Culham, but he was later replaced by Charles Johnson, who agreed to come out of retirement. In addition to Culham the earl of Onslow's mansion at Clandon Park was taken over in 1941. Some 300 tons of records were housed there under the elegant and accomplished Blakiston and his wife (Georgiana Russell) who moved into residence there. Clandon could have proved an unfortunate choice because when the flying-bomb offensive started the path of the missiles took them directly overhead. Luckily no disaster occurred before the launching sites were overrun after the invasion of France in 1944. In 1942 the list of wartime repositories had been completed with the provision of accommodation for 250 tons of documents at Grittleton House, near Badminton. Ledward was put in charge there and at much the same time Wood took over from Dawes at Belvoir. Meanwhile, Wright was posted to Market Harborough after a short attachment to the Admiralty when the Canterbury branch was closed.

All the documents evacuated were packed in cardboard containers, which were secured with steel banding, and despatched by road transport. The staff, from the assistant keepers downwards, were pressed into the work of packing and Johnston, the Repository CO, recalled the diminutive Slingsby, in shirt sleeves and braces, getting the back of his trousers accidentally hitched to the banding apparatus, provoking an amused Latham to observe that while 'Strength through Joy' was all right for the Nazis 'Rupture through Rapture' would never do for the PRO. In the early part of each day up to three lorries were loaded and a member of the staff sat by the driver's side to ensure that the doctrine of official custody remained inviolate. At least that was the theory, although it may be suspected that breaches occasionally occurred as when Domesday, arriving at Shepton Mallet early, was said to have been left in the van while the driver and escort went off for a cup of tea. Everywhere the containers, about 88,000 in all, were stacked in their temporary homes in bulk. In case of need, however, individual items could still be easily located and produced by reference to the duplicate despatch tickets which listed the contents of each container, everyone of which bore an easily identified and distinctive number or letter. For the most part the assistant keepers in the country repositories were engaged upon a variety of editorial tasks, while the attendants undertook production duties and performed much repair, binding and packing work. The same was true of those attendants who remained in London. In fact, the skilled

---

27. T 162/642/E 38789: Gatliff to Usher, 21 July 1941.

character of their repair work in dealing with damaged paper and parchment resulted in the issue of a Treasury circular to all government departments in December 1941, drawing attention to the services which they could provide in the event of important documents being damaged by enemy action. Far better, thought the Treasury, that the office should be occupied in that way than in 'meditating on ancient history'.[28a] Actually the office's activities in that respect extended way beyond the sphere of public departments, and much advice was given to parish incumbents, solicitors, city companies and others about the treatment of war-damaged documents. Work was also carried out privately for such persons and institutions by members of the Repair staff in their own time. But the benefits were not all one way because the experience gained in dealing with charred and scorched paper and shrunken parchment, to say nothing of documents that had lain in water for some time, was of great value.

When evacuation had been completed the records remaining at Chancery Lane were concentrated in the less dangerous lower floors of the repository. The search rooms were closed on the outbreak of war, although legal records could still be seen in an emergency on a court order. However, in December 1939 a single room was opened with limited facilities for research. Luckily demand was light and throughout the war years it was rare for more than ten searchers to attend on any day. Under Safford, who had been appointed chief ARP officer in April 1938, the staff received training in the various branches of air-raid precautions and attended classes afterwards. When war broke out practically all the available staff volunteered for duty in manning and protecting the building. At first they were organised in three shifts from 8 a.m. to 3 p.m., 3 p.m. to 10 p.m. and 10 p.m. to 8 a.m. The drawback was that general office business was much dislocated because only one-third of the staff was present at any given time. After a few weeks, therefore, the scheme was modified by a combination of 24-hour and short-duty stints, which enabled work to be carried on with some semblance of normality. The office being constantly staffed, the resident officer post no longer had to be filled. That removed a difficulty which had been experienced since the beginning of 1939 in replacing Dawes, who had decided to give up his responsibilities for those duties. The Treasury thought that if the job was necessary it could be performed quite adequately by someone of the superintendent's rank, but the office insisted that it must have an assistant keeper, although as none of them was prepared to accept the post permanently on the same terms as Dawes the necessary attendance had to be provided on a roster basis. When the war ended that system was re-introduced with the difference that sleeping accommodation was made available in the building itself. The Treasury continued doubtful, but the arrangement lasted until 1

28a. T 162/646/E 44676: Gatliff to Thompson, 22 December 1941.

December 1977 when the entire responsibility for night-time cover passed to the custody guards.

The provision of men for the protection of the building at Chancery Lane became increasingly difficult as the war progressed because staff had to be found for the country repositories, and by 1941 about a quarter of the 120-strong staff had been called up for the forces or lent to other departments. Testing time had arrived in earnest in the last five months of 1940 when 418 alerts were sounded lasting for 1,169 hours. Bombs first fell near the office on 7 September and subsequently premises adjacent to it were at various times in flames. In 1941 the Temple and most of Fetter Lane were a scene of utter devastation, but miraculously the office itself sustained only minor damage. Addressing members of the Royal Historical Society in April 1942, Flower said:[28b]

> There were several occasions on which the office itself had its incidents. From 9 September onwards the watchers on the roof saw destruction on all sides and had, from time to time, to avoid showers of debris and shrapnel. In the early hours of 19 September a heavy high explosive bomb and the south-east turret caused mutual disintegration; part of the roof and a number of windows were shattered; and the empty museum and the clock over the entrance, which nevertheless continued its proper function, were hit by fragments. A few days later, while half a dozen fires were burning within 200 yards of the office, four incendiaries fell on the roof and two on the north terrace; but all were either extinguished or burnt themselves out without doing worse damage than some broken slates. Since then only casual incendiaries have fallen within the premises; twice floods of flames rolled up to the very walls of the building and illumined it. Even though they once numbered 23, the incendiaries were put out without difficulty; and the flames did not even scorch our stones. On several nights it was possible to read a newspaper in the glare of neighbouring fires.
>
> The damage done to the records has been trivial – less, in fact, than has in the past been done by a burst water pipe, mildew or energetic rodents. One or two Chancery Proceedings were injured, but not destroyed, by fragments of shell on 19 September some fifty yards from the point of impact and explosion. On one of the journeys to the west some packages became very wet because in the course of a heavy shower of rain the fastening at the back of a lorry became loose; they were returned to headquarters next day and, after receiving expert treatment, appeared to be little the worse for their wetting. And that, so far as is known, is all.

In the renewed Luftwaffe attack in the early months of 1944, nearby

---

28b. C. T. Flower, 'Manuscripts and the War', *RHS Transactions*, Fourth Series, XXV, 21. The turret was restored in the late 1950s.

buildings were damaged by fire, and in July slight damage was caused to the repository when a flying bomb fell sixty yards away. In some ways a more serious blow had occurred the year before when Safford died from a heart attack. Under his guidance the members of the various shifts defending the office had been brought to a high state of efficiency as fire fighters, first aiders, telephonists and decontaminators. The same year also saw the death of Dr Shaw, the long-time editor of the *Calendar of Treasury Books*, followed in 1944 by that of Buckland from pneumonia. His memoranda on the office files, and particularly those relating to Foreign Office accessions, provide a lasting testimony to the extensive knowledge he possessed of nineteenth-century diplomatic and can hardly be missed owing to the neatness and distinctiveness of his handwriting which was exceptionally tiny although always legible. But for the war Buckland's area of operation might have been expanded because early in 1939 the Foreign Office was proposing that the open date might be moved forward from 1885 to 1901. In once again taking the initiative the Foreign Office action stood in sharp contrast to that in Nazi Germany which had taken a step in the opposite direction in 1937 by introducing more restrictive rules, a move deprecated by Flower. In the United States, however, greater openness was the vogue, the view being taken there that the more that legitimate historical research could be encouraged the greater the likelihood of the government securing the support and trust of the thinking public. There was little sign that English departments, other than the Foreign Office, were giving the matter much thought, although in so far as difficulties might have arisen about any change in access policy it was clear that the major problem would have been for the office to find room at Chancery Lane for hitherto closed material which would need to be transferred from Canterbury or departments. In Jenkinson's opinion any change could well take three years to implement, although it may be suspected that in taking that line he was intending to use any alteration of policy as a lever to secure more accommodation. In fact, a minor change had already taken place in 1938 when Greene issued new rules extending to 1843 the date to which legal documents might be seen without the payment of fees.

The onset of war put paid to any further moves in the direction of more openness and also gradually increased the work of the inspecting officers, the salvation officers as Flower called them, who had now to regulate, assist, control and check departmental salvage drives besides being kept busy with the abnormal accumulations resulting from the war. In 1940 a circular letter was sent out to 45 departments inviting them to make new schedules shortening the prescribed periods of retention for unwanted documents. But the statutory procedure proved altogether too cumbersome and in 1941, after liaison with the Paper Shortage Committee which had been established with the object of saving paper in government offices, a new regulation was introduced under the Emergency Powers (Defence) Acts 1939 and 1940 enabling periods of retention to be reduced by simple agreement without any of the formalities attached to the making of schedules under the 1877 act. An even more momentous change in the office's practices stemmed from negotiations which had first started in 1939 between Jenkinson and Eugene B. Power of University Microfilms, Ann Arbor, Michigan, concerning the microfilming of important manuscript material in British collections for the Library of Congress. Among other things the discussions involved Jenkinson in a trans-Atlantic telephone conversation, certainly the first secretary of the office to conduct business at that distance in that way. Under the arrangement the office was supplied with a Graflex camera from Kodak in 1941 and a large Microfile camera was subsequently shipped from America. Later still a microfilm reader was sent over to enable the film to be checked before despatch, a prudent precaution because even with careful operators it was rare to find a whole roll of exposed film which corresponded perfectly with the original. The scheme was highly advantageous to the office. Not only was it agreed that the Microfile camera should be handed over to the office free of charge at its conclusion but the Americans also met the costs of the staff employed upon the work. Furthermore, the making of a copy gave the office some insurance against the risk of the original document's destruction, besides providing valuable experience in the new technique. A rather similar agreement was also in operation with the British Museum, which led to some disquiet being expressed to the Board of Trade by the Institute of British Photographers and by Monger and Marchant, who suspected that University Microfilms, the technical agency for the various schemes, was intending to exploit its foothold for its commercial clients in the United States and so deprive British firms of business. In fact, those fears proved groundless and Monger and Marchant, who had moved out of the office when the search rooms were closed in September 1939, were, in any case, no longer greatly interested in the kind of record work they had done before the war. The firm's move to Bishop's Court in Chancery Lane, where it went into association with another, Studio Brigg, was to result in its undertaking a considerable amount of work for other government departments and, although it had been understood that it would handle occasional orders for making copies for searchers if required, it came as no surprise when in 1944 Studio Brigg, which had by then taken over the predominant interest in the business, wrote to terminate the arrangement.

By that time the office was, if anything, relieved to be free of what might have been an awkward commitment because its own photographic activities were expanding all the time. The original arrangement with University Microfilms had led to the Graflex camera being sent down to Shepton Mallet to be operated by Collie, who had been instructed in its use. Wardle, who was interested in photography, supervised operations generally and some training was given to the various office operators by the Air Ministry. The Library of Congress work was concentrated upon the filming of the Colonial Office's America and West Indies class, and some work was also undertaken for government departments. A further most important development came in 1942 when Flower, not without reluctance, but under the pressure of events, obtained the approval of the master of the rolls to make office copies by using the photostat machines which had been installed originally for the use of the Library of Congress and the Canadian government. Provision for the authentication of such copies had been made as far back as 1921, but in practice the office stuck to the old method even when the demand was mainly for copies of legal documents of comparatively recent date. Because the clerical staff, which normally supplied that need, had been reduced to less than a half by enlistment and evacuation, the office had little alternative, particularly as it concluded that it would not be possible to employ additional typists and make typescript copies. The scarcity of typists of sufficient calibre was one objection, but an even stronger one was the possibility that typescript copies might be altered after certification without much chance of detection.

O'Reilly insisted that the certified and sealed photostats should fulfil the legal requirements, and only gave his consent when Wardle hit upon a format in which the document being copied was presented in positive form (black on white) and the legal headpiece and tailpiece in negative (white on black). Despite the fact that the new rule restricted the work to modern documents in English there was no doubting the revolutionary nature of the change because of the importance which the department had traditionally placed upon the making of office copies by hand. Inevitably, the decision led to the supply of uncertified copies to the public as well and the expansion of microfilming as a regular service.

When the American microfilming scheme was concluded at the end of 1945 it was followed by a vast programme of filming for the Australian government, a project which, but for the war, might have started in 1939 although the mechanics of its operation might then have been very different. As it was, the various developments automatically resulted in the operatives concerned being given the departmental style of photographer, within the attendant and repairer class, when a reorganisation agreement was settled in January 1947 with the Civil Service Union to which most of the support grades belonged. The main effect of that reorganisation was to equate the superintendent with the general Civil Service office keeper grade and to introduce a new class of unestablished attendants from which established posts would normally be filled. The office had wanted to link its attendants and repairers with the service-wide paper keeper class, thinking that that would be to their advantage, but it found the Treasury unwilling to concede. On the other hand, the Treasury was quite helpful as regards the development of photographic work, although anxious to ensure that costs were fully recovered. The relations between the two departments were not, however, good, and the office had not forgotten how the Treasury had jumped at the opportunity presented by the war to stress how difficult it was going to be to find money or retain staff for record services beyond the minimum necessary to keep documents reasonably safe. By way of defence, Jenkinson had suggested that certain duties, such as intelligence or censorship, might be taken over by the office *en bloc* as a branch of a larger department. That suggestion was not taken up, but the assistant keepers were given certain war diary analysis work when the War Office Historical Section moved into several rooms at Chancery Lane in 1940, reminiscent of the similar move during the First World War by the Records Sections of the Committee of Imperial Defence and the Australian and Canadian forces. The assistant keepers had been getting restless at their lack of involvement in war work and earlier that year seven of the class II men had written to the deputy keeper asking for posting to other departments. For a time Buckland served in the Home Office and the offices of the War Cabinet, and Pugh and Latham were to spend most of the war years in the Dominions Office and the Petroleum Departments respectively where they were to achieve principal grading. Gilling went to the Air Ministry and transferred to the Ministry of Civil Aviation after the war on completion of service in the RAF. Ellis took a commission in the Royal Northumberland Fusiliers and Brooke also joined the Army. Wardle, having been in the thick of the evacuation planning and the development of photocopying, had a short spell in the Dominions Office in 1943 before joining the Air Force a year later.

Despite the calls of the conflict, post-war reconstruction was never far from the minds of Flower and Jenkinson or the assistant keepers. But from February 1944 Jenkinson was removed from the centre of affairs when seconded for special duties in connection with the protection of continental archives. In that capacity Jenkinson worked with the War Office adviser on monuments and fine arts and later with the appropriate sections of the occupying authorities for Italy, Germany and Austria. Many years later H. E. Bell, the pre-war editor, and Ellis and Brooke, who had been specially released from their Army units for similar work, were to set down vividly what they clearly regarded as their memorable encounters with the great man – 'Uncle Hilary' as they dubbed him – in Italy.[28c] Subsequently, Ellis returned to the office and was promoted to AK I, but Brooke transferred to the Tate Gallery and then to the Ministry of Town and Country Planning before becoming secretary of the Royal Academy in 1952, a post he held until his resignation in 1968. He then developed his interest in gardening and by the time of his death in 1988 had become an acknowledged world expert in the cultivation of roses. The Copying Department HCO, E. C. Matthews, was also lent to the Control Commission for Germany to take charge of the British Element's Archive Section and was never to return, probably because Fox, increasingly influential in establishment matters, did not want him back. For a time Matthews was assisted by one of the office's pre-war clerical officers, Flight-Lieutenant Johnston, who had previously been distinguishing himself as a flying instructor. Meanwhile, Russell Farmer, by then Major Farmer, had been promoted higher clerical officer

---

28c. H. E. Bell, 'Archivist Itinerant: Jenkinson in Wartime Italy', in *Essays in Memory of Sir Hilary Jenkinson*, ed. A. E. J. Hollaender (Chichester, 1962), 167–177; R. H. Ellis, 'Recollections of Sir Hilary Jenkinson', *Journal of the Society of Archivists*, IV, 261–275; T. Humphrey Brooke, 'An Archivist Liberating Rome', The Petty Bag: A Miscellany of News from the Public Record Office, no. 6 (March 1976).

in absentia and given a year's deferment from demobilisation to take charge of the Archive Section of the British Element of the Allied Commission for Austria. On the civilian side George Santer, the Library's pre-war clerical officer, Stamp's 'beautiful typist', had been lent to the Board of Trade at the beginning of the war where he had rapidly risen to staff officer rank and decided that that was where his future lay. On retirement in the 1960s his Public Record Office experience was brought back into play when he was persuaded to take charge of the Royal Mint's Record Section, still at that time at Tower Hill, ahead of its transfer to Llantrisant in South Wales.

Towards the end of 1944 Pugh, sensing that the war would soon end and believing that the country was ready for radical change, sent Flower a number of proposals for the reorganisation of the office when peace came. Pugh's views were shared by Latham and concentrated upon the development of the office as a centre for historical research. Flower was not unsympathetic. He had not long given up the directorship of the Institute of Historical Research in London University, which he had held from 1939 in an unpaid capacity until passing over the burden to Galbraith, who took the post on a full-time basis with professorial rank. Always reserved about Jenkinson's involvement in the technicalities of the care and custody of the records as against their editorial exploitation, Flower probably viewed Pugh's ideas as a useful counter-weight, and besides discussing them with him arranged for them to be circulated to the assistant keepers for comment. But Pugh's suggestion that the office should be a powerful centre for historical studies, 'a nest of singing birds', provoked a sceptical Davies to wonder how long it would be before the Treasury cat made short work of the canaries.[28d] Flower himself and most of the assistant keepers were more inclined to agree with Harold Johnson that the office's job was to help students to find what they needed and to explain its significance as a record, but to leave its historical or legal interpretation to them. No doubt Jenkinson would normally have had much to say, but he was too occupied with Control Commission business at the time to make more than a marginal contribution to the debate. In any case, the Treasury continued to look upon the higher echelons of the office with a jaundiced eye and when the assistant keeper scales were revised at the end of the war reiterated its belief that the duties and responsibilities were not comparable with those of a principal or an assistant secretary in a major department. Nevertheless, in response to continuous pressure from Greene and Jenkinson it had carried out a thorough review of the position, including an on-the-spot inspection of the posts concerned in 1946. The result was a higher establishment of one principal assistant keeper, four assistant keepers directing sections, and sixteen assistant keepers divided into two classes but without a fixed numerical pro-

---

28d. PRO 1/616: Pugh's memorandum of 14 October 1944 and Davies's letter to Drew of 15 November 1944.

portion. It was also agreed to increase the deputy keeper's pay to £1,750. The four director posts were filled by D. L. Evans taking repository, repairs and photography, P. V. Davies becoming responsible for the work of the Inspecting Officers' Committee, J. H. Collingridge taking charge of exhibitions, publicity and the Museum, which was re-opened in September 1946, and H. N. Blakiston heading the Search Department.

Jenkinson, in particular, was concerned that no place had been found for Harold Johnson, who was senior to Blakiston, but it was only after many months that a fifth director post was approved and Johnson was given responsibility for editorial work and training. Whether personalities or the delay in the recruitment of new assistant keepers accounted for Johnson having to wait, or whether the fact that Blakiston, being the only man with recent Search Department experience, tipped the scales in his favour does not come out from the office's records. Johnson, unlike Blakiston, was no Etonian but a Yorkshire grammar school man; his father was a distinguished north-country Labour alderman, who had at one time been Arthur Greenwood's agent. Johnson himself took no active part in politics although Collie, who admired him greatly and who was with him at Shepton Mallet at the time, remembered the delight there when news came through of the Labour landslide in 1945.[29] Johnson was as much, if not more, concerned about the promotion of Collingridge, who had entered the office by the same examination in 1926, as he was about that of Blakiston. By general consent Collingridge, although perfectly able, was not Johnson's equal as a scholar but, like Flower, he was a barrister and he was thought to have the edge on Johnson on the administrative side. Johnson was by no means appeased when told by Flower that 'scholarship was its own reward'. It was fortunate for him, therefore, that his abilities were recognised by Jenkinson, whose resolve to fit him in at a senior level eventually succeeded. On seniority grounds three other AK Is, Wood, Ledward and Slingsby, might have had reason to complain, but none of them was cut out for an administrative role and their non-preferment was not unexpected. To alleviate the office's staffing difficulties at that time O'Reilly, who reached retirement age in 1945, had agreed to continue in a disestablished capacity as an AK II until newcomers could be engaged. Dawes, who succeeded him in charge of the Search Department chose to take his leisure on retiring in 1946 and so let in Blakiston. All these movements at the top of the office resulted in Hector, Ellis, Pugh and Latham joining the AK I ranks to which Wardle and Drew had been promoted a little earlier. In 1947 recruitment was resumed and C. A. F. Meekings, A. H. K. Slater, E. K. Timings, K. G. Davies, J. R. Ede and J. Fagg joined the department as AK IIs, Cambridge University Appointments Board being responsible for finding five of the six. On the day on which applications closed Davies journeyed up specially from Cam-

---

29. Information supplied to the author by R. Collie in September 1953.

bridge to deliver his papers that evening to a surprised Collingridge, then on duty as resident officer. A stickler for the rules might have excluded Meekings, a pre-war habitué of the search rooms whose application was delayed. But before demobilisation Meekings had been seconded from his regimental duties to the position of archives officer to the British Element of the Control Commission for Germany. In that capacity, and through work for the Surrey Record Society, he was well known to Jenkinson, who was determined that no technicality should stand in the way of his appearance before the selection board. It was not surprising, therefore, that having reached the interview stage Meekings, with his record of experience, should eventually head the list of those declared successful in the competition. His contemporaries were in no doubt that in him the office had appointed a future deputy keeper, but fate did not prove so kind.

Changes were also afoot as regards the clerical grades, particularly as the Treasury had issued a circular to all departments early in 1947 about the extended use of the executive class. Fox, who had held the post of staff officer since 1928, was regraded senior executive officer and formally recognised as deputy establishment officer. White, Farmer and later Johnston were appointed higher executive officers. It was clear that other pre-war clericals such as Flight-Lieutenant Monger, who had been a specialist navigator with Coastal Command, Lieutenant Gavin, back from war service in India, Lieutenant Penfold, who had been in command of a mine layer, and Sergeant-Instructor Mabbs, who had been a lecturer in advanced wireless and radar before teaching Latin, French, applied mathematics and civics under the RAF Educational and Vocational Training Scheme, were not going to accept tamely routine clerical jobs, having more than proved their worth in the services. In fact, the office was highly alarmed at the thought that it might lose them, and realised that it had to offer them strong incentives if they were to stay and hold out better prospects for the class as a whole if new recruits were to be secured. Given a fair wind from the Treasury, the office was even prepared to consider arranging for promising young clerical officers to take either a university course to give them the knowledge of French and Latin to qualify for possible promotion to assistant keeper or a specialised course in archive work. Nothing came of those particular notions, and although the office welcomed the possibility of introducing executive grading it was by no means clear in the early post-war years that it would succeed in its wish to retain its younger clerical men, certain of whom, such as Mabbs, had already passed the reconstruction executive class examinations held by the Civil Service Commission and had the option of moving elsewhere. Nevertheless, new areas of opportunity were opening up which offered them hope for the future, and almost without exception the individuals concerned had grown to like record work and felt a strong sense of loyalty to the office, which made them reluctant to transfer to another department. Some of the more experienced also supplemented their pay by indexing work in their own time, which, in Monger's case, had enabled him to buy and run a car before the war.

Expansion was predictable in photographic ordering, and establishment and accounting work. Moreover, the issue by the master of the rolls in 1946 of rules concerning the custody of tithe documents had resulted in the transfer to the office of an additional clerical officer, Barbara Eames, from the Tithe Redemption Commission and that activity, too, could expand. But it was quite clear that the most promising development for the pre-war clerical staff was going to be on the Repository side. In the first instance, the evacuated records had to be brought back and accommodation had to be found for those which had previously been stored at Canterbury which was no longer available. To overcome that difficulty a deep wartime shelter at nearby Furnival Street, a few hundred yards from the office, had been allotted to the department for use as a repository on a four-year lease. By June 1946 the evacuated records, which had begun to flow back in September 1945, had all returned without the loss of one of the half a million involved. The master plan was Jenkinson's but Evans, who had been closely involved throughout, with particular assistance from White and Wardle, was to receive the OBE. A cynic might have wondered whether it had all been necessary because Chancery Lane had emerged practically unscathed and the wartime repositories had experienced more than one scare when bombs had been jettisoned in their vicinity. On the other hand, the relief from day-to-day concerns had led to the performance of much useful editorial and conservation work and an opportunity to rethink the future. That was particularly the case in respect of the enormous problem of records still in departments but no longer in current use for which accommodation had to be found urgently and for which it was evident that executive staff would be needed. Nominally, all those records came under the charge and super-intendence of the master of the rolls, and it was that consideration which had led to the issue of a circular to all government offices in July 1941 inviting information about where their archives were to be found. From their replies it was calculated that their records were spread over nearly four hundred places of which about one hundred and fifty were in London or the suburbs. Greene had been greatly concerned for their safety from the outset of war and also about the mass of irreplaceable manuscripts and records in non-government hands. The wartime salvage campaign presented a particular threat to those local and private archives and had led to a strong campaign by the British Records Association to ensure that documents of value were not wantonly destroyed. In the words of the indefatigable Joan Wake of the association's Record Preservation Section: 'If English history does not matter, all this destruction does not matter in the least, and the sooner we boil down Domesday Book to make glue for aeroplanes and use the famous "scrap of paper" to make wads for cartridges the better'.[30]

---

30. As reported in *The Times*, 13 November 1940. For an account of the association's preservation work see Oliver D. Harris's 'The Drudgery of Stamping', *Archives*, XIX, 3–17.

Hilary Jenkinson, as joint secretary of the BRA, was in the thick of that campaign, but he was also painfully aware of the inadequacies of the existing arrangements for the protection of the departmental records. The office had not, for example, been consulted at all about the storage by the War Office of a vast mass of extremely valuable First World War records in a disused factory at Walworth, which was to be destroyed in an air raid. A like calamity had occurred from the establishment of a similar store by the Ministry of Works at Elstree Film Studio for records from various departments, again without any intimation to the Public Record Office. In 1943, when post-war reconstruction was in the air, Jenkinson was responsible for the establishment by the master of the rolls of an interdepartmental committee of representatives of the Treasury, the Ministry of Works and the Public Record Office to make recommendations concerning the return of records from the wartime repositories, the provision of increased accommodation for the public records and future policy concerning records in departments no longer wanted for current work.[31] All three questions were closely related, the general conclusions being that Chancery Lane should be extended when conditions permitted after the war, and that a suburban repository should be provided for departmental documents which were not wanted for more than occasional reference but a considerable proportion of which might ultimately be thought worth keeping permanently. In this intermediate stage departments would continue to handle and be responsible for their own deposits, but the overall control of the repository would be in the charge of the Public Record Office, which would be responsible for the allocation of space and proper conditions of storage. In February 1944 departments were advised of the proposed scheme, which came to be known as 'Limbo', and asked to state their likely requirements. Accordingly, when the war ended the Public Record Office had a fair idea of the size of the problem with which it was faced, but it was not until 1946 that a start could be made with providing the necessary facilities when, in addition to the former deep shelter at Furnival Street, similar shelters were taken over at Goodge Street and Belsize Park. By a strange coincidence, the latter was but a short distance from the spot at Hampstead Green where Palgrave lived and where the Royal Free Hospital now stands. In the nature of things, much of the work involved in the implementation of the scheme was executive in character and on return from Austria Russell Farmer, with the assistance of Mabbs and Gavin, was given the responsibility for its execution, under the general direction of Roger Ellis. Originally Wright had been earmarked for a leading role in the service, operating from Furnival Street, but that plan had to be abandoned when he was compelled to retire in 1946 on health grounds.

It had at one time seemed likely that the demands upon storage would

---

31. PRO 1/541.

be much affected by the nationalisation measures of the post-war Labour government. In 1946 the records of the National Coal Board had been declared public under the Coal Industry Nationalisation Act of that year, mainly because of strong representations from Greene. In 1939 the law officers had ruled that the records of the Electricity Commission, which had been established in 1919, were also public, but it was largely a regulatory body and subject to the Ministry of Transport. On the other hand, the pre-war London Passenger Transport Board's records had not been brought within the scope of the 1838 act any more than those of Imperial Airways in 1939 or the Bank of England and the newly-established air corporations in 1946. When the question was considered in connection with the bill to socialise the railway, canal and road haulage undertakings, S. S. Wilson, the one-time assistant keeper, who by an odd coincidence had charge of the legislation, feared that to bring his erstwhile colleagues into the picture would create nothing but a headache for the new British Transport Commission because 'every railway ticket returned to a ticket collector, every timesheet for every employee, every indent for a few screws for a motor-lorry, every waiter's check in a hotel, etc., etc., would become public records'.[32] He was quite prepared for the more important records, such as board minutes, to be brought under the control of the Public Record Office, but Greene, Flower, Jenkinson and Davies were agreed it must be all or nothing. Wilson then wondered if it might be possible to defer declaring the records public until a day appointed by the minister to enable destruction schedules to be drawn up first so that existing disposal practices might not be interrupted. That course was not favoured inside his ministry and ultimately the matter was referred for a decision to the Cabinet Committee on Socialised Industries. In the ensuing discussions Flower and Jenkinson created a deplorable impression upon Herbert Morrison, the lord president, by unwisely lecturing him on archive theory.[33] It was no way to win friends and influence people, and it was not surprising that they failed to get the support of the Official Cabinet Committee which they attended, along with Davies, on 28 January 1947. The government took rather more notice of Greene whose influence in the Lords was feared. Nevertheless, Morrison, who had always wanted the nationalised bodies to have as much freedom as possible from Whitehall and to be in no way regarded as government departments, eventually got Greene to accept, albeit reluctantly, the exclusion from the Public Record Office Acts of the bodies nationalised from 1947 onwards, on the assurance that the office's expertise and technical assistance would be welcome to the corporations concerned if given semi-officially. Paradoxically, the passage of time and

---

32. PRO 1/767: Wilson to Jenkinson, 18 October 1946.
33. S. S. Wilson's private letter to the author, 4 June 1984. For an official account of the dispute see Sir Norman Chester, *The Nationalisation of British Industry* (London, 1975), 927–930.

financial pressures led to the British Railways Board being only too glad in 1972 to pass over responsibility to the Public Record Office for its historical records, then housed at Porchester Road, Paddington, although it was not until 1984 that they were officially declared public by an order in council under the 1958 act.

As a result of the government's decision not to place the records of the nationalised bodies under the master of the rolls but to encourage informal liaison, there was an inevitable extension of the department's existing extra-official activities, which were already heavy. In particular, to all intents and purposes the services of Atkinson had been entirely lost, so heavy were the calls upon his time as secretary to the Historical Manuscripts Commission which continued to operate from the office. Its work had been greatly expanded when a National Register of Archives was created under its authority in 1945 to collect information about the existence and location of local and private archives. That body, which was directed by Lieutenant-Colonel G. E. G. Malet, sprang from the proposals for the care of British records after the war, formulated largely by Jenkinson through the British Records Association and referred by Greene to a special 'Master of the Rolls Archive Committee' in 1943. Even before Dr G. H. Fowler became chairman of the Bedfordshire County Records Committee in 1913 and set to work on creating an informed opinion concerning the need for care of county muniments the office had maintained close, but unofficial, contacts with the local authorities about their record problems. Flower and Jenkinson maintained and extended that tradition, an achievement which was the more remarkable as the office's own burdens began to increase after the war. But something had to give and one casualty of the intensified activity was the Office History which it had been hoped might be revived. Momentarily, in 1946, it seemed that progress might be made and before being overborne by the pressures of the Limbo scheme Ellis had produced some thoughts for Flower, who cautioned, perceptively, against too neat a rationalisation of the office's development which he suspected 'to have been on the whole, a haphazard attempt to meet individual difficulties as they arose'.[34]

Through his wartime directorship of the Institute of Historical Research Flower was no stranger to historical studies and in 1941 at R. A. Butler's invitation he had become a member of an Advisory Historical Committee to the Cabinet Committee for the control of Official Histories of the Second World War and later succeeded Butler as chairman of the editorial board of the Official Medical History in that series. But he did not have a high opinion of all of his colleagues and when the Office History was under discussion before the war disapproved of the idea of appending a list of the

---

34. PRO 1/774: Flower to Ellis, 22 July 1946.

assistant keepers because there were 'too many "wash-outs" '.[35] Flower, whose advice has not been followed in this work (see Appendix XV), lacked Jenkinson's flair, yet he was both an accomplished scholar and a sound administrator. While he did not possess the light touch that so often make Stamp's letters a joy to read, his legal training enabled him to master the essentials of complex issues swiftly and he was able to set down in writing the nub of a case in an expert manner. He played a notable role in the work of the old-style inspecting officers, but he would have been less at ease had he needed to liaise with departmental record staffs of all grades as required of later inspecting officers. H. A. Johnston recalled with distaste an extremely embarrassing Whitley Council meeting at which Flower seemed to take unfair advantage of an inarticulate messenger. Nevertheless, Flower greatly admired the contribution made by the support grades to the effectiveness of the ARP squads during the war, and after the centenary celebrations he made a point of writing to the superintendent to say how proud he was of all the men. He had little sense of fun, unless the occasion be counted when he found Slingsby asleep in the Library and shook him from his slumbers by dropping a huge tome from the gallery to land with a resounding thud on the table at which the miscreant was snoozing. But the stern face which sent Slingsby scurrying suggests the intervention was not meant playfully. In 1939 the honour of CB was conferred upon Flower and he was knighted in 1946. By then he was making no attempt to disguise the fact that he was getting a little tired of being pushed from behind by Jenkinson. Under Civil Service regulations Jenkinson would have been obliged to retire when 65 in November 1947, whereas Flower as deputy keeper was above the normal rules and could, in theory, continue indefinitely, or at least long enough to put paid to Jenkinson's pretensions. But the war had taken its toll of Flower's health and, although Greene declined to accept his resignation in 1946, he did so, reluctantly, a year later. Consequently Flower retired on 31 March 1947, his sixty-eighth birthday, after 45 years' service in the office. However, he continued to transcribe the Curia Regis Rolls, the editorial work for which he is best remembered, until his death in 1961. Inevitably, his departure let Jenkinson into the kingdom which he had long thought his by right, and which few would have wished to deny him. Some heads must have shaken at the Treasury and Greene, perhaps like Langdale contemplating the appointment of Palgrave, could have been forgiven for wondering, uneasily, what turbulence was looming on the horizon. What could not be doubted

---

35. PRO 8/48: Flower's pencilled comment on scheme for centenary volume, accompanying his minute of 29 August 1935 to Atkinson and Crompton. Flower believed strongly that an assistant keeper needed to be both a good scholar and a competent administrator. He claimed to have seen many who were profound scholars, but could not look after a search room, while others who were efficient administrators could not be trusted to make a calendar or list without continual checking and supervision: T 214/167: Flower to Greene, 10 July 1946.

was that Jenkinson, unlike Stamp and Flower, was resolved to be no quiet deputy keeper.

Chapter XV

Jenkinson and Evans: The Last Old-Style Deputy Keepers, 1947–1958

The good Archivist is perhaps the most selfless devotee of Truth the modern world produces. That form of devotion has not been common in late years . . . without the deliberate perversion of Truth, the elevation of Untruth to the position of a Science if not a Faith . . . without these the European War as we have known it could not have been launched. I am not so foolish as to claim for the work I have endeavoured to describe to you the quality of a panacea from the evils from which we are all suffering: but the men and women who take it up may, I think, tell themselves that at least in their Profession the world has found one answer to the Propagandist.

(From *The English Archivist: A New Profession*, being an inaugural lecture for a new course in Archive Administration delivered at University College, London, 14 October 1947 by Hilary Jenkinson)

It [the Grigg Report] *is going to disturb what might otherwise have been the even tenor of the rest of my official career, but I bear you no grudge. It is as a matter of fact a very good Report; lucid and easy to read; and I congratulate you on a first class piece of work.*

Handwritten PS. *If I hadn't been writing officially, I should have described it as a damned good report.*

(D. L. Evans to K. H. Clucas, 3 June 1954: T 222/615)

Ever since Jenkinson took control of establishment and secretarial matters as the principal assistant keeper in 1938, he had been skirmishing on and off with the Treasury, which must have feared that even worse trouble lay in store when he was appointed deputy keeper in April 1947. Barely two months before, Jenkinson had seized the opportunity presented by a Treasury circular about establishment training in small departments to launch an attack upon what he saw as its mismanagement. In an interview with Lionel Thompson, the assistant secretary responsible, he argued forcibly that Treasury policy was utterly mistaken in its application to small departments because it was designed for large ones. He was shocked that young Treasury officers should be taught that their services were of more value than those of their contemporaries in 'cultural' departments. That made it almost impossible for them to deal sympathetically with promotion and salary questions in non-administrative bodies. He deplored the view he thought commonly held in the Treasury that the staff in departments such as the Public

Record Office were narrow specialists. A records man had to be more, not less adaptable than his counterpart in a large department, and he pointed with pride to the activities of the office's clerical officers during and since the war. He condemned the Treasury policy of perpetuating departmental classes which, he thought, led to justifiable suspicion that an attempt was being made to treat them less well than their nearest comparable 'Treasury' grade, and he gave the example of the office's long negotiations with the Treasury to bring its attendants and repairers into line with the class of established paper keepers.

Surprisingly, Thompson found it valuable to be acquainted with Jenkinson's views, with which he had a certain sympathy, but when he later received a note from Jenkinson as a record of their conversation, its tone and content did nothing for the office's cause. In it Jenkinson spelt out bluntly his belief that nothing short of making heads of small departments responsible for the detailed allocation of their annual grant would satisfy him because [1]

> the considerations affecting such issues were numerous and of a technical
> character with which the Treasury Official could not be familiar: whereas the
> Heads of Small Departments were few and were generally persons eminent
> in their profession; so that it should be feasible, even for a harassed Treasury
> Official, to satisfy himself by means of reference books and a few personal
> contacts that they were competent and honest.

No doubt Jenkinson felt better for getting his resentments off his chest. It is difficult to believe that he seriously thought that the Treasury would concede his demand for autonomy. Inside the office he remained supreme and was held in awe, if not dread, even by his director colleagues. His position of pre-eminence was further emphasised when he was knighted in 1949. By that time he was extending his international connections, being one of the first vice-presidents of the International Council on Archives which had been established a year before under the auspices of Unesco. He went to Jamaica in 1950 to advise the colonial government about its archives, and was later responsible for taking into the office's custody a large block of neglected material from Antigua, having been instrumental in scotching an earlier proposal that it might be sent to the Bodleian. It was a measure of his personal magnetism that despite his autocratic ways those who knew him best liked him most. Right from the start of his deputy keepership his intention to stamp his personal authority upon the office was made plain with the issue of a seven-page circular setting out the form to be followed in the writing of letters and memoranda, including his predilection for

---

1. PRO 1/803: Jenkinson's memorandum of his interview at the Treasury, 24 February 1947. The Treasury file is T 162/1027/E 50446.

capitals for reasons of 'Courtesy and Respect' and to pick out particular words for the 'Reader's Convenience'.[2] Should anyone be interested in PRO diplomatic a thousand years from now they will have no difficulty in dating any strayed office manuscript of the Jenkinson period. His inauguration, shortly after his appointment, of a Consultative Committee on Publication, on a rather broader basis than the one formed in Lyte's day, was clearly designed to provide useful backing if his editorial plans ran into difficulty with the Treasury. Invitations were sent to the vice-chancellors of all universities in Great Britain and Northern Ireland to nominate a representative, and, besides the director of the Institute of Historical Research, its membership also included representatives of the British Academy and the London School of Economics. Apart from its defensive possibilities its practical utility was to be shown in its endorsement of Wernham's new *List and Analysis of State Papers, Foreign* in continuation of the former calendar. Details of the new work, which Wernham continues to edit to this day, were given by him in a paper appended to Jenkinson's *Report* for 1951. The Consultative Committee also supported the cessation of work upon series drawn from foreign archives except that it agreed to an arrangement with the Irish Manuscripts Commission for the resumption of the publication of the *Papal Registers*, which had made no progress since Twemlow's death. The Reverend Urban Flanagan OP was given responsibility for that work, and a somewhat similar agreement was entered into with the French government for the preparation of an edition of the Gascon Rolls under the direction of Professor Renouard of Bordeaux. Dr Pierre Chaplais was also appointed to edit the Treaty Rolls, the chief of the series of Chancery enrolments still unpublished.

Despite Jenkinson's paramountcy it was noticeable that inside the office itself the staff were no longer so docile as formerly. At the behest of the younger assistant keepers the Treasury had even been taken to the Civil Service Arbitration Tribunal in 1950 by the Association of First Division Civil Servants, which they had rejoined after a lapse of some years. The result was slightly better starting pay for AK IIs and £50 more at the AK I maximum. That, in turn, led to Jenkinson's own pay being raised to £2,125, but only after pressure by the master of the rolls, who believed that even at that level the post was underpaid in comparison with university professors and the directors of large museums. Neither did Jenkinson think it in any way right that he, with responsibility for the whole of the national archives, should be paid less than the general Civil Service under-secretaries. The younger pre-war clerical men, with their excellent service records behind them, had been absorbed into the executive structure, and were more outspoken than had once been the case. A minority among the assistant

---

2. PRO 1/824: Departmental Rules for the Form of Letters and Memoranda, 21 April 1947.

keepers might refer disparagingly to Farmer's 'window dressing' and to Monger as 'our village Hampden', but the sensible majority, despite the threat to their own grade, recognised that the pre-war position was no longer tenable. Moreover, young and energetic executive recruits were coming into the office by way of the Civil Service examination and they were underpinned by a number of post-war clerical entrants, many of whom were later to rise to responsible positions in middle management, and in some cases beyond. For Jenkinson, who believed that to understand the modern records fully it was necessary to have a proper appreciation of the medieval classes from which they had sprung, Latin was still the *sine qua non* for an assistant keepership. Consequently, while he valued the contribution the clerical and executive officers might make, there was a limit to the ground he was prepared to concede in order to accommodate them.

Jenkinson also had to contend with a weakening of the old family tradition among the support grades, which had previously kept them so loyal and provided a reliable source of recruitment. For that reason the office was finding it increasingly difficult to fill its complements adequately at the lower levels. In a letter drafted by Drew for Jenkinson in 1951 the Treasury was told that in recruiting porter-messengers 'we are forced to consider applicants whose appearance, intelligence and physique suggests the ultimate scrapings of the labour market'.[3] The days of the humble petition were over and it was commonplace for Fox, who undertook most of the work connected with industrial relations, to find himself in discussion with full-time officials of the Civil Service Union to which most of the manual staff belonged. Fox also played a major part in the 1951 reorganisation of the attendant and repairer grade, which not before time was split into three distinct groups of craftsmen, photographers and repository or search-room assistants. The department regretted the grade's demise because of the flexibility it gave it in the deployment of its resources, but the division was logical, particularly as since 1948 the craftsmen had been housed outside the main building in new, but hideously ugly, pre-fabricated huts on the North Terrace. A mess room, providing tea, coffee and light snacks, was also situated in the same area, under the management of a staff committee, the main administrative burden being borne for many years by N. H. Smith, one of the craftsmen and a later foreman. The office itself was no more able to support anything grander than it had been in Hardy's day, and at lunch time it was customary for many of the staff to use the nearby Land Registry or Patent Office canteens. The link with the Land Registry building in Lincoln's Inn Fields, later to house census and other records as an out-station, went back to 1914 when the office had been advised of the opening of a Refreshment Club there. But things had radically changed since that time, when the warning had been given that there was room for only one or two more very junior

---

3. PRO 1/1306: Jenkinson to Stephen, 30 November 1951.

men, such as boy clerks, but that the more senior staff could dine in the smaller half of the room reserved for them on the payment of 6d table money.

Not long after the move to the North Terrace the retirement occurred of J. Gilkes, the highly-skilled chief repairer, who had spent the war years at Belvoir. His departure opened the way for the creation of a new post of superintendent of binding and repairs, which was filled by T. E. Hassell. Changes were also taking place in the rapidly expanding Photographic Section. By 1952, when a principal photographer, T. J. Morgan, who had previously served in the National Maritime Museum, was brought in to supervise its technical operations, it constituted nearly ten per cent of the office's authorised establishment of 177. Wardle, who had attended evening classes to acquaint himself with the art of photography, was glad that the section was at last under proper professional control. It was odd, he thought, that Jenkinson, usually so insistent upon appropriate qualifications, allowed attendants and repairers to continue to deal with the business as it expanded into the public domain and as additional processes, such as the making of 'still' photographs, were introduced. But Jenkinson's main concern was the care of the records, which led him to believe that, given training, the work was best left to men whose primary skill lay in handling documents.

In addition to its work for the public, the Photographic Section's duties had been boosted by an arrangement made in 1950 for the regular production of film copies for the Canadian National Archives, similar to that already in force for the Australian Commonwealth National Library and the Mitchell Library, Sydney. Close liaison was maintained with the Canadians, through the medium of their London staff who continued to have the use of a room within the office, an arrangement that did not end until 1959. In 1948 H. A. Paice had replaced the long-serving Balls as superintendent, but apart from controlling the porter-messengers he rarely intervened elsewhere. Certainly he would have been unwelcome in either the Repair or Photographic Sections, while Cyril Eades, the Repository foreman, who ruled his men with a rod of iron, was quite capable of managing them on his own.

Charles Drew as establishment officer and Fox as his deputy carried the brunt of the work concerning staff and organisational matters, but both kept in close touch with Jenkinson, who was jealous of his ultimate control as head of the department and unwilling to delegate it to others even on comparatively unimportant topics. Fortunately, both men got on well with him, and Drew was widely thought to be his chosen successor for the deputy keepership. Drew had worked closely with Jenkinson since 1938 and so it was not altogether surprising that when Jenkinson succeeded Flower in 1947 his first move was to promote Drew, although not the senior man, to be a director. Less expected was his decision to give him the title of secretary and establishment officer. Those duties had previously been undertaken by Jenkinson himself as principal assistant keeper, the number two post in the office hierarchy. It was plain that Jenkinson did not think that D. L. Evans, the genial Welshman who had been his pre-war Repository lieutenant and whom he now chose to be his deputy, would be any match for the hard men of the Treasury. Consequently that job was shorn of its secretarial and establishment content and Evans merely carried with him to the higher situation his existing responsibilities for the direction of Repository and technical services. In itself, that might not have bothered Evans, but he was dismayed to find that Jenkinson also decided to retain oversight of the Limbo scheme. If Evans could derive any consolation from the move, apart from the financial one, it was that he thereafter was able to become much involved in lecturing on the newly-established archive diploma course at London University with the full blessing of Jenkinson, who had been foremost in getting it started. Along with Drew he also joined the Inspecting Officers' Committee, a position he much enjoyed and in which he made a distinctive contribution.

Because of wartime accumulations of records the work of the inspecting officers had become increasingly heavy and in 1950 more schedules were made than in any single year since the 1877 act came into operation. The task of 'weeding' had become much more complex because modern filing methods resulted in important papers being often mingled with those of a purely routine nature. To help departments Jenkinson drew up and circulated two memoranda, the first based upon a wartime leaflet, prepared by the British Records Association in close consultation with the office, entitled *Modern Records: What may we destroy?* and the second addressed specifically to departments entitled *Elimination of Official Documents not considered worthy of Permanent Preservation*. To cater for wider research requirements the inspecting officers were also keeping in touch with the newly-formed Inter-departmental Committee on Social and Economic Research. The hard-working but somewhat abrasive P. V. Davies, the barrister member, who carried the main responsibility for the work of the Inspecting Officers' Committee, was nevertheless known to be reserved about the 'long-haired men and short-haired women' he thought likely to emerge from that quarter. Since 1949 another inspecting officer, Collingridge, having passed his responsibilities for the care of the Museum to Jeffery Ede, had been responsible for records liaison with government departments and with the various organisations governing the nationalised industries. He was also to be the office's contact with such bodies as the Joint Consultative Committee on Captured Enemy Documents, the British Film Institute and the British Institute of Recorded Sound. Also in 1949 Greene, who remained greatly disappointed that the publicly-owned corporations had mainly escaped his statutory 'charge and superintendence', resigned and was succeeded as master of the rolls by Sir (Francis) Raymond (later Lord) Evershed. But before leaving, Greene had shown his special interest in the fate of the records of the nationalised industries by calling a conference of the authorities concerned in April 1949, at which they were recommended to adopt certain broad principles for the care of their records, and assured by Jenkinson of the office's strong desire to liaise with and be of assistance to them. Greene had also remained concerned about the fate of local and private archives and bequeathed to

Evershed a small committee under the title 'The Master of the Rolls' Archive Committee (1949)' to formulate legislative proposals, and a newly-appointed assistant keeper, Ernest Denham, was named as its secretary.

Meanwhile, in the search rooms official searches had been increased as a result of the British Nationality Act 1948, which had led to numerous inquiries on behalf of persons resident in India and Pakistan seeking to obtain United Kingdom citizenship. The Round Room had been reopened in May 1947, and students working under permits were moved from the former Government Search Room to the Long Room alongside fee-paying legal searchers, who were soon to be relieved of stamp duty on copies of, and extracts from, legal records as a result of the Finance Act 1949. The Government Search Room, facing the lawn, was re-christened the South Room and reserved for readers working on large documents or those which needed to be produced under special conditions. Ledward, the old Harrovian, was in charge there, but spent much of his time in calendaring medieval Chancery rolls. The newer and developing administrative side of the office had little appeal for him, his real interest being in royal genealogies. Pugh in the Long Room was busily engaged in the arrangement and listing of modern records and in the preparation of the Colonial Office and Commonwealth Relations Office sections to a proposed new *Guide to the Public Records*. With Drew's support he had played an active and successful role in promoting an extension in public access, beginning with the opening in July 1948 of the records of the Foreign Office and the Colonial Office down to 1902. Certain other departments were to follow suit, including the Ministry of Works whose records had previously been available only under permit but which now agreed to open without restriction those that had been transferred. It was the first time that the office had itself encouraged departments to take a liberal line, although it might have done so sooner had there not been difficulty in finding space for the extra records which had to be accommodated. In the case of the War Office, which had indicated as early as 1946 a willingness to open many of its records to 1902, there had also been an initial difficulty because it wanted the office to exercise a degree of censorship which was found unacceptable. Pugh's services were, however, to be lost to the department in November 1949, when he resigned to assume the editorship of the Victoria History of the Counties of England. A little earlier K. G. Davies, one of the 1947 assistant keeper intake, had also resigned to take up a post at the London School of Economics, although he was to be engaged subsequently as editor of the *Calendar of State Papers, Colonial* in succession to Dr Newton. At the time of writing he was continuing with that task.

Another move in the direction of improvement for the public came in 1952 when the office was responsible for getting the Home Office and the Treasury to agree to the abolition of fees for the inspection of census returns. It was vainly hoped that the change would lead to a fall in census searches because local libraries would be more likely to order microfilm copies relating to their own districts. Extensive filming of the returns did, indeed, follow, but more often than not the effect was to generate further demand upon the office rather than reduce it. Of equal importance to searchers was a new arrangement in 1950 to keep the Round Room open until 5.30 p.m. from Mondays to Fridays, the resident officer taking duty for the final hour, with one attendant remaining to handle documents. In 1956 it was, however, found more convenient to advance by half an hour the hours of opening and closing of the search rooms, which then ran from 9.30 a.m. to 5.00 p.m. Record agents, university dons, fortune seekers and lawyers and their clerks still provided clearly-defined elements among users. As in the nineteenth century there were a few eccentrics, including one or two whose purpose seemed to be to pass away the time of day rather than pursue any clearly-defined study. Research students were increasingly in evidence as were members of the general public seeking their ancestors, but it was not until well into the 1950s that the reading rooms became uncomfortably crowded. Exact comparisons with pre-war conditions were not possible because of differences in the method of counting, but productions were up by approximately one third. In 1957 ten more seats were provided in the Long Room, bringing the total seating capacity of the three search rooms to 100. Yet by 1958 there was a clear indication of the crisis to come in the next decade when on a single day 150 searchers passed through the rooms, compared with the previous maximum of 130. As attendances and productions began their rapid rise it was clear that the days had long since gone when the assistant keepers in the search rooms could provide whatever information was needed about the use of the records by reference to the manuscript registers of productions. But old habits died hard and it was not until Stephen Wilson became keeper in 1960 that the gathering of statistics was put on a scientific basis.

To the extent that the office's existence became better known in the post-war years Jenkinson, who was always anxious to obtain as much publicity as possible, could rightly claim the credit. For over twenty-five years the annual *Report of the Deputy Keeper* had appeared only in typescript, but in making his first report for 1947 Jenkinson managed to get the Stationery Office to print and publish it once more. His argument was that in no other way was it possible for archivists at home and abroad to be kept in touch with the office's activities. Even so no account was given in that first production of the discussions that had been resumed in 1946 with Dr William Angus, keeper of the registers and records of Scotland, and representatives of the Scottish Records Advisory Council about the release of a further batch of documents to Edinburgh. The silence was understandable because relations between the two camps had become prickly particularly since Jenkinson had taken over from Flower. Jenkinson admitted that the Scots had a case on grounds of sentiment, but he was opposed to it from the standpoint of archival propriety, and would have preferred to meet the convenience of Scottish students by the supply of microfilm or other copies. Realising that Jenkinson and Angus were never going to agree, Greene decided that he must determine the Scottish claims by himself in the light of the arguments advanced by each side and in accordance with his power to effect transfers under the Public Records (Scotland) Act 1937. For his pains he was warned by Jenkinson at one stage that 'he was presenting these gentlemen with power to raid the Record Office'.[4] Nevertheless, by a definitive direction and declaration Greene disposed of the matter in July 1948 by agreeing to the transmission, with a few minor exceptions, of the medieval documents claimed by the Scots and a small number of others not claimed but of similar provenance. He also agreed to the transfer of a series of warrant books for instruments under the Scottish Great and Privy Seals covering the years 1670 to 1709. Apart from the last two of these books, which were duplicates of others retained, none of the post-Union records for which the Scots asked was released. A much abbreviated account of the negotiations and detailed schedules of the documents affected were set out by Jenkinson in his *Report* for 1948. Jenkinson also made it clear that the documents would not be transmitted until photographic copies had been made for the office, and emphasised that although they would no longer be in the charge and super-intendence of the master of the rolls he retained the right to secure their temporary return if they were wanted for departmental business. Reporting in the following year the transfer of the first batch of the records concerned, Jenkinson must have derived much pleasure from detailing at the same time the acquisition by 'the Official Repository of the Nation's accumulation of Treaties and Treaty Documents' of a nearly perfect second copy of the signed and sealed articles agreed in 1604 between the English and Scottish Parliaments for a treaty of union between the two countries. Until its dis-covery only one of the three copies known to be made, the Scottish copy, was thought to survive and that, in contrast to the one acquired, was much damaged and lacking the seals and signatures of the 39 English and 28 Scottish commissioners. The price paid, £450, was not revealed by Jenkinson although he acknowledged that the purchase had been made possible by a generous grant from the Pilgrim Trust.

In the same *Report*, the 111th in the series, Jenkinson also announced the publication of *Part 1 (Introductory)* of a new *Guide to the Public Records*, intended to introduce the department and its work to the general public. Jenkinson, who edited it, must have been delighted that its first print of 2,000 copies was soon so far exhausted as to necessitate a second edition. That did not enjoy the same demand, but for many years it served as a primer inside the office for new recruits to the executive and assistant keeper ranks, updating as it did the account given by the Royal Commission on Public Records nearly forty years earlier of the evolution of the department. In the absence of an Official History, a project which had been abandoned for the time being, it was an estimable enough work. Playfair at the Treasury

---

4. PRO 1/814: draft notes of discussion on 20 November 1947 before the master of the rolls on the Scottish claims.

thought it admirably written, but with its abundant use of capitals and numerous footnotes it was not to everyone's taste. Neither was it suitable for distribution to all grades within the office. That need required the issue of a more general Staff Handbook, which although long planned did not appear until 1960. Ellis had prepared a short work for that purpose in lieu of a full-length History, but it was put on one side by Jenkinson, who decided to write something himself as a preliminary to his own grand design.[5a] Had the office possessed the resources, the occasion for a rather more substantial publication than either had presented itself in 1951 when the 100th anniversary of the laying by Romilly of the first stone of the new building fell to be commemorated. But wartime austerity had still not entirely disappeared and economic circumstances allowed no more than a modest sherry party on centenary day, 24 May, for guests from the courts of justice and public departments for which an exhibition of illuminated royal portraits from the King's Bench plea rolls was mounted. A pamphlet written by Jenkinson describing the exhibition, based upon research by Dr Erna Auerbach, was later reproduced as an appendix to the *Hundred and Thirteenth Report*. On the day of the reception *The Times* also carried an article from him on the 'Preservation and Housing of Public Records: A Century of Expedients' in which, like Hall many years before, he observed with sadness that 'England had lagged somewhat behind the Continent'. His description of Cole as secretary to the Record Commission was well wide of the mark and Devon, for whom Cole was ever 'a discharged clerk', must surely have twitched in his grave.

Despite the stricture on earlier practice Jenkinson was more often a worshipper of the past, and homages to it, through the medium of record displays, presented him with a relief from the stresses of office. In 1948 a Special Exhibition Room was fitted out and Queen Mary visited it for the first exhibition which was of famous treaties. To make the existence of the office and its contents better known to the élite Jenkinson also invited permanent heads of departments, members of the diplomatic corps, and officers of the British Museum for private views. When a special exhibition of naval records was mounted in 1950 it was decided to extend it into 1951 in connection with the Festival of Britain. Unfortunately the office found itself at odds with the Festival's Design Research Unit, which had its eye on Cook's and Flinders's journals and Bligh's log for display in the sea section of the 'Dome of Discovery' on the South Bank. The office had always been against the removal of documents from official custody and Jenkinson, ultra-conservative in such matters, also thought that the traditional arguments against exposing documents to loss or damage in transit had additional force when the records concerned were important and unique.[5b] However,

---

5a. There is a copy of Ellis's work in PRO 1/1039; it was found among Jenkinson's papers after his retirement. For the 1960 Staff Handbook see PRO 54/34.

5b. PRO 1/1189: Jenkinson's memorandum, 10 February 1951.

departments had always been at liberty to recall their own records, and the lords commissioners of the Admiralty were prevailed upon, as Collingridge suspected they might be, to overtrump Jenkinson by requisitioning them for the Festival organisers. Needless to say, Jenkinson was not best pleased, and although some softening of the office line in regard to loans was eventually to take place it was only after his departure.

For Jenkinson an altogether happier episode had occurred in his first year as deputy keeper when he travelled to the Isle of Wight to present an address, signed by the master of the rolls and all members of the staff, to J. E. Ernest Sharp, the former assistant keeper, on 11 August 1947, his 100th birthday. Sharp had retired in 1912 after nearly 44 years' service, but his death in 1950 meant that he failed to achieve the aim of every civil servant, very rarely realised, to draw his pension for as long as he had worked for it. Only a few of those on the staff, including Jenkinson and Fox, still remembered Sharp, but the office itself had not changed all that much since his day. Entering it on appointment in May 1947, Kenneth Timings, a later officer-in-charge of the Search Department, recalled his first impression as one 'of drabness, of dust and dirt, and a sense of disillusionment in many of my senior colleagues'.[6] With other new assistant keepers he was initially attached for training to Harold Johnson, whom he remembered almost lying on his back to focus the light on to the faded words of a vast parchment heavily stained with gall, and remarking severely 'gall is no substitute for intelligence'. Such quality was certainly not lacking in Johnson for we have Timings's testimony, and that of many others, that in the art of deciphering even the most obscure texts he was never defeated. Jenkinson, whose brainchild the new Editorial and Training Division was, had much enthusiasm for its work and was delighted at the way it was developing. During their first three months the probationer assistant keepers received instruction from Johnson in the reading of the handwriting and forms of the public records of all dates. Archive administration, the history of the Public Record Office and its predecessors, the nature and arrangement of its contents and the development of the courts and departments in which they originated also formed part of their tuition. Similarly, they were encouraged to read widely and make good use of the office Library. For the remainder of their probationary service it was intended to attach the trainees to each of the various sections for a long enough period to become acquainted with their work. In practice, the needs of the office itself meant the curtailment in many instances of that part of their programme, and before long the new recruits, with the exception of Slater, who was soon to transfer to the Ministry of Civil Aviation, found themselves with specific duties. The year 1947 was exceptional in seeing the entry of six new assistant keepers,

---

6. E. K. Timings, 'A La Recherché du Temps Perdu: 30 years on', The Petty Bag: a Miscellany of News from the Public Record Office, no. 3 (July 1975).

something that has never happened again. Consequently, the training of subsequent entrants gradually became less formal.

The years 1948 to 1951 saw the arrival through the open competition of E. W. Denham, Miss D. H. Gifford, N. J. Williams and R. A. Brown; and A. W. Mabbs was promoted, exceptionally, from the executive grade in 1950, having satisfied Johnson and Hector of his ability to deal with the older records as well as those of a more recent date. With the exception of Brown, who was to become professor of medieval history at King's College London and to earn a high reputation as an authority on castles, all of that second crop were to play a prominent part at a senior level in subsequent decades. Mabbs became keeper in 1978, with Denham as his deputy, and Neville Williams resigned to become secretary to the British Academy in 1973, having held successively the posts of records administration officer and deputy keeper from 1967. Williams had to his credit a number of successful historical works, mainly of the Tudor period, but died tragically young at the age of 52 in 1977. Miss Gifford retired as a principal assistant keeper in 1982 and is particularly remembered for her work on Domesday and her liaison with outside bodies, such as the British Standards Institution, on reprographic and related matters. Over the seven years from 1951 the rate of entry of assistant keepers fell still further, and of the seven recruits during that time, three, R. L. Storey, Miss S. B. Challenger (later Mrs Storey) and J. R. Rea had careers of comparatively short duration. Storey and Rea, like Davies and Fagg from the first post-war batch and Brown from the second, both resigned for academic appointments. Mrs Storey resigned on marriage, but for some time afterwards was employed editorially, indexing the *Calendar of Liberate Rolls*. The remaining four, R. F. Hunnisett, L. Bell, Miss P. M. Barnes and N. E. Evans were all to make their mark, although Bell left in 1977 on appointment as secretary of the board of the British Library and Miss Barnes became head of the Library and Records Department of the Foreign and Commonwealth Office in 1985.

In the immediate post-war period it had been hoped to give systematic training to the clerical/executive grades, and particularly to those who showed promise. But the rapid expansion of the office's accounting, listing and photographic work meant that it was not possible to provide instruction for them to the same degree as for the assistant keepers. Nevertheless, most of them began by spending a short time in the Editorial and Training Section in the charge of Monger, who was given a special allowance for the purpose and who also superintended the clerical and executive work relating to manorial and tithe documents, besides liaising with the Stationery Office on printing matters and preparing statements of progress for the Consultative Committee on Publication. In practice, the EOs and COs sent for training were either assigned to another part of the office soon after arrival or found themselves engaged full-time upon the arrangement and listing of new accessions. Monger himself was highly dissatisfied about his personal situation and it was a relief to him when he was lent to the Ministry of Education in October 1951 to supervise the arrangement and weeding of its files with the acting rank of higher executive officer. His allowance post than passed to Gavin, who was himself lent to the Office of the Commissioners of Crown Lands as an HEO when Monger returned in 1953. In both cases their absence was offset by the posting to the office of an executive officer from the borrowing department in exchange. On return, Monger was allowed to keep his higher rank in a personal capacity, but when Gavin came back in 1954 he was obliged to revert to his former position. Two years later, however, he was promoted once more to take charge of the intermediate ('limbo') repository at Bourne Avenue, Hayes, Middlesex. Originally, it had been hoped to obtain a large building on a site at Feltham for that purpose, but at the last moment it was taken by the Ministry of Supply, and the office had to make do with a former Royal Ordnance Factory at Hayes instead, which it did with the best grace it could. Until Gavin's appointment executive management of the site rested with Farmer, whose base remained at Chancery Lane. Day-to-day business was handled by a CO and a porter-messenger took up permanent residence in a wartime Tarran hut.

In addition to Hayes the office had subsidiary repositories of the same type at Yeading, between Hayes and Northolt, and at Leake Street, near Waterloo Station. A fourth at Grosvenor Road, Pimlico, was closed in 1953 and the Ministry of Transport records it contained were sent to Hayes. Of the three in operation at the time of Gavin's appointment in 1956, Hayes was by far the largest, accommodating no less than 512,500 foot-run of documents, as against 65,000 feet at Yeading and 16,000 at Leake Street. The ultimate aim being to concentrate the records on one site, those at Leake Street were transferred to Hayes in 1958 and those at Yeading in 1964. Although the intermediate repositories and the allocation of space within them were under the general control and management of the office, departmental staffs, who were normally accommodated on site, continued to be responsible for the weeding and preparation for transfer of their own records, subject to the guidance of the inspecting officers. In the early days documents wanted from Hayes by central London ministries were sent by Ministry of Works vans, supplemented by vehicles from the Admiralty and other departments as required, but in 1956 arrangements were made for all such work to be undertaken by the Interdepartmental Despatch Service (IDS) vans, then under Post Office control.

Hayes came to the fore as the pivot of the Limbo scheme after 1948, when the government decided that because of the worsening international situation and the need for precautionary measures the deep shelters in which the records were then being stored were needed for civil defence purposes. Hayes itself was acquired in 1950 and by 1952 the deep shelters at Furnival Street, Belsize Park, Camden Town, Clapham Common, Clapham North, Goodge Street and Stockwell had all been cleared. Furnival Street presented a particular problem because it was housing permanently preservable material, such as that housed at Canterbury before the war, which could not be accommodated at Chancery Lane. The Ministry of Works had therefore suggested that Hayes should be used not only for 'limbo' documents, but also as a branch repository, a suggestion which the office strongly resisted. Quite apart from the differing storage requirements at an intermediate, as opposed to a branch repository, the office wanted the latter to be well outside the danger zone in case an emergency should occur and to have sufficient space and proper facilities in that event to accommodate important material from Chancery Lane, which might need to be evacuated in a hurry. Nevertheless, for a time Furnival Street material was kept at Hayes and Jenkinson's insistence upon an assistant keeper's superintendence led to Denham, who lived on that side of London, being detailed to visit the site at least once a week. Additionally, the resident officer was driven down in a government car every Sunday to make a tour of inspection. Those arrangements ended when a new branch repository was provided in 1951 at Ashridge Park, near Berkhamsted, Hertfordshire, in buildings erected as a hospital during the war and subsequently used as a temporary teachers' training college. Earlier the office had had its eye on a property at Saunderton, near Thame, but the asking price was an obstacle and the proposal fell through. In all these matters the Ministry of Works eventually did the office proud. Jenkinson's persistence and the fact that Evershed, besides lobbying Cripps, chancellor of the Exchequer, and Morrison, lord president, managed to use his influence to good effect with Stokes, the minister of works, accounted for most of the success. The excellent relations established by Farmer with his opposite numbers in the various works departments must also have been a positive factor, offsetting to some extent Jenkinson's tendency to give voice to his frustrations about the vast amount of time spent in the examination of the various abortive schemes and in lengthy negotiations in which he, Evans, Ellis, Wardle and White were all involved.

On the establishment of Ashridge Jenkinson placed J. R. Ede, a future keeper of public records, in charge, with an executive officer, R. A. Anslow, as his assistant. Jenkinson, backed by Evershed, thought it essential for an assistant keeper to be appointed to the post because of the nature and importance of many of the records intended to be stored there. The Treasury was not fully convinced, but gave way on the assurance that research facilities for the public were to be provided. Although that was done, Ashridge proved too far off the beaten track for searchers to go there in the numbers that Jenkinson had hoped. However, a van brought documents to London daily and ancillary repair and photographic services were set up on the site, where the staff, from Ede down, lived. By 1958 the repository was fully equipped and could accommodate 154,000 foot-run of records, although only 82,000 feet were occupied. The following year Ede was brought back to Chancery Lane to assume direction of a new Modern Records Department, and command at Ashridge was subsequently to pass to the executive grade. In 1951, however, the office's decision concerning Ashridge was to bring executive dissatisfaction to a head and to lead to a claim for the further extension of that class within the office.[7] Gavin, the secretary of the local branch of the Society of Civil Servants, was responsible for drawing it up, and although much annoyance was felt about Ashridge it admitted 'some of these proposals may appear to be extreme and even revolutionary but this, it is felt, is largely due to the distribution of duties consequent on the grades of staff available in the Department before the introduction of the Executive Class'.

In brief, the society wanted Fox's post to be upgraded to chief executive officer and Farmer's and White's posts to senior executive officer and five more higher executive posts to be conceded, mainly by removing non-editorial work from the assistant keepers. The office was prepared to meet the society part of the way, but only on the basis of the executive's existing duties. Besides obtaining Treasury approval for the upgrading of Farmer and White, it argued the case, but without the same success, for something extra for Fox and the upgrading to higher executive officer of two of the five posts claimed. Behind the scenes Fox was maintaining that the changes might make it easier for the assistant keepers, then relieved of lesser duties, to secure an increase in pay, a contention that Jenkinson thought 'insidious but fallacious'. Jenkinson feared the bad effect of the proposals upon the assistant keepers because he believed that the need was for 'more editorial work (output) – not a more editorial type of AK'. To that end two young graduates, F. J. W. Harding and D. McN. Lockie, had been employed for a short while as temporary editorial assistants along the lines of Stamp's pre-war scheme, but the incentives offered were insufficient and the arrangement came to an end in 1951. A year earlier the Consultative Committee on Publication, prompted by Jenkinson, had passed a resolution noting the increase in non-editorial duties owing to the large accruals of modern records and the office's increased responsibilities. It strongly urged that steps should be taken to restore the old balance by increasing the assistant keeper staff, both in the interests of historical studies and those of the department itself. The solution of hiving off non-editorial work to the executive grades had no appeal for Jenkinson, and at a meeting with David Stephen of the Treasury in February 1951 he had made it clear that he considered control of such duties as the shifting, packing and cleaning of records, the cleaning and painting of the building, the making of records available to the staff and public, and fire and damp precautions was a necessary part of an assistant keeper's duties. Some months later, after Evershed had written to Sir Edward Bridges, the head of the Civil Service, implying that the Treasury

---

7. PRO 1/1276: Johnston to Drew, 28 June 1951, enclosing a claim for the extended use of the executive class in the Public Record Office. Observations of the PRO branch of the Association of First Division Civil Servants are contained in a letter from Timings to Drew, dated 7 August 1951, on PRO 1/1314.

was being dilatory in providing additional assistant keeper posts, Stephen wrote:[8]

> Why on earth Sir Hilary Jenkinson did not approach me first instead of putting up the Master of the Rolls to write to Sir Edward Bridges is beyond my comprehension but that, I am told, is typical of his way of doing business . . . He is the kind of autocrat who has not the least idea of what is going on in his own Department, which, as a result, is a pretty fair administrative muddle.

Stephen thought it a waste of time to argue with Jenkinson because when he spoke about freeing assistant keepers from administrative duties he was referring to what was really executive work. For that reason Bridges did no more than make the right noises for Evershed's benefit, but in October 1951 the office was to receive a severe jolt when a new Conservative government was elected and, being faced with a serious balance of payments crisis, decided to make a substantial cut in the Civil Service based upon the numbers in post on 1 October 1951. By mischance the office's actual complement on that date was only 159 as against an authorised establishment of 177, mainly owing to difficulties of recruitment among the support grades. When the Treasury circular conveying the government's decision was received the staff had risen to 164, but the Treasury still insisted upon a reduction to 154 despite an appeal by Evershed to Butler, the chancellor of the Exchequer. Jenkinson was furious, and in May 1952, evidently wishing to cause the government maximum embarrassment, decided to close the Museum and the South Room. Little more than a month later H. Montgomery Hyde, the writer, at that time an Ulster Unionist MP, in a motion on the adjournment on the night of 25 June 1952 drew attention to the difficulties being experienced by museums and galleries, owing to the cuts in their staff. Both Hyde and Woodrow Wyatt (later Lord Wyatt), then a Labour MP, who followed him referred to the Public Record Office's problems. John Boyd-Carpenter, financial secretary to the Treasury, stung in particular by the tone of Wyatt's speech, counter-attacked strongly, maintaining that the office had suffered a cut of no more than five, and even then its complement of 154 compared favourably with its pre-war strength of 127, adding that those figures 'spoke for themselves'. For Jenkinson that was like a red rag to a bull, and Evershed was equally indignant, assuring him that if Boyd-Carpenter had been accurately reported [9]

> my fury will be very seriously aroused and I should be strongly inclined to write a letter to *The Times*, which might leave Sir Edward Bridges, like the Spanish galleon in the poem, 'ill content'.

---

8. T 218/84: Stephen to Mrs Abbot, 14 July 1951.
9. PRO 1/1321: Evershed to Jenkinson, 27 June 1952.

460

However, second thoughts prevailed and, having consulted George (later Sir George) Coldstream, the clerk in crown of Chancery and soon to be permanent secretary to the lord chancellor, Evershed decided instead to take up an offer of a discussion with Boyd-Carpenter. The result was that on 14 July, when Boyd-Carpenter wound up a heated debate forced by the opposition on the museum cuts, he made a somewhat half-hearted and hardly accurate attempt to correct the record by acknowledging the increased burden placed upon some of the institutions in recent years, admitting[10]

> The extreme example is undoubtedly the Public Record Office, which has
> to cope with the vast increase in paper which seems to flow from modern
> methods of government, and which has also taken over, in its dump at
> Hayes, which I think has the attractive name of 'Limbo', categories of
> documents which, previous to the war, were not thought to be in the Public
> Record Office phase of life at all.

Although Evershed affected to believe that the Treasury's officials, rather than its ministers, were to blame, relations on both sides remained uneasy, especially when it became known to the politicians that Wyatt had been to see Jenkinson before the debate. Evershed returned to the charge when Butler said in response to a supplementary question in the House on 21 October that he had not been altogether happy at the spirit in which cuts in the general museum field had been accepted. Butler's own reaction was defiant and he told Bridges:[11]

> I purposely said what I did and had reason for it. The M. Rolls is v.
> sentimental. As far as I'm concerned he can say what he likes. I am sorry the
> cap fits Sir H.J.

In fact, it was the Tate Gallery that Butler had in mind, and when told that Evershed and the staff of the Public Record Office had taken it as an insult fired directly at them he minuted 'Hooray', leaving it to Bridges, with his customary skill, to smooth the ruffled feathers. Despite the Treasury's belief that Jenkinson was using the closure of the Museum as a form of blackmail it had to tread warily because, as Boyd-Carpenter pointed out, 1953 was Coronation Year and there could then be a renewed agitation to have the Museum re-opened. The Treasury was also anxious to mend its fences with Evershed and there was the further consideration that, despite Jenkinson's scepticism, its Organisation and Methods Division was engaged upon a review of the office's activities in order that its staff requirements might be re-assessed. It soon became apparent, however, that there was

---

10. *Hansard*, 14 July 1952, col. 1883.
11. T 218/85: Butler's comment on Bridges's minute to Armstrong, 6 November 1952.

never going to be an agreement with Jenkinson, who remained utterly uncompromising, on the staffing needs of the office, notwithstanding a warning from Evershed that 'we must on no account give the impression that we refuse to listen to any sort of suggestion from anybody'.[12a] Nevertheless, after tortuous negotiations the staffing level for 1953–1954 was fixed at 164, the Treasury conceding that acceptance would not prejudice consideration of the estimate for 1954–1955 upon which Jenkinson reserved his position. Although he agreed to place certain documents on display to the public in a Special Exhibition Room until the permanent Museum was re-opened, that in no way altered the belief of the Treasury that nothing was likely to be achieved in the way of remodelling the Public Record Office until Jenkinson was removed. Writing to Bridges on 13 April 1953, Sir Thomas Padmore, one of the second secretaries, queried whether the time had come when Jenkinson, 'having reached the fairly ripe age of 70', should disappear into retirement because, Padmore said, he was far from popular in the Public Record Office and his relations with the rest of the public service were by no means good.[12b] The difficulty was that the appointment was held 'at pleasure', which meant that any approach to Evershed, who had the right to terminate his services, needed to be handled delicately. Not wanting to start any gossip, Padmore had refrained from making enquiries about a possible successor, but he thought it virtually essential that such a key post, because of its technical content, should be filled from within the office and he told Bridges on 16 April that 'there is a Deputy named Evans, who is thought to be quite competent, and there are no less than five assistant keepers (first class) among whom there are thought to be several worthy of advancement'. Padmore was further confirmed in his belief that Jenkinson's time was up when the deputy keeper took the opportunity presented by the appointment of a Government Organisation Committee, sitting under the chairmanship of Sir David Milne, to submit a long memorandum challenging the credentials of the Organisation and Methods Division to advise the Public Record Office on anything other than elementary office procedure, and questioning the seemliness of comparatively junior organisation and methods officers criticising responsible and senior departmental officials of much experience and special knowledge. Bridges, too, had long shared Padmore's disquiet about Jenkinson and sympathised with O and M in 'battling with this obstinate but able old mountain of prejudice. I have faith that the mountain, at any rate, is not irremoveable'.[13a]

Bridges's faith was by no means ill founded because he was pinning his hopes on a solution coming from the work of the Committee on Departmental Records, which under the chairmanship of Sir James Grigg had been

---

12a. PRO 1/1321: Evershed to Jenkinson, 11 July 1952.

12b. T 214/471: Padmore to Bridges, 13 April 1953.

13a. T 222/720: Bridges's comment of 12 June 1953 on Simpson's minute to Padmore of 11 June 1953.

appointed jointly by Butler and Evershed a year earlier, just before the manpower squabble with Boyd-Carpenter. Indeed, that squabble may itself have assumed the proportions it did because Jenkinson was still smarting from his exclusion from the committee whose terms of reference were

> To review the arrangements for the preservation of records of Government Departments (other than records of Scottish Departments and records transmissible to the Keeper of Records of Scotland) in the light of the rate at which they are accumulating and of the purposes which they are intended to serve, and to make recommendations as to the changes, if any, in law and practice which are required.

Naturally Jenkinson and Collingridge were consulted by the committee from time to time, but Jenkinson's conviction that where records were concerned his was the last word did nothing for his standing with Grigg or with the members of the committee. His condescension towards them was all too evident from an informal discussion which he had with them in December 1952 which he began by saying:[13b]

> I assume that the problem is to be treated seriously – that we are not to discuss the question whether we need, after all, keep archives at all.

It was hardly the right note upon which to start, although it may have inspired the since oft-repeated Grigg dictum 'that the making of adequate arrangements for the preservation of its records is an inescapable duty of a civilised state'. Nevertheless, the committee was to feel obliged to qualify its injunction, Jenkinson's obstinate adherence to the old order notwithstanding, by going on to say:[14a]

> Not only is this an obligation which in England and Wales is not at present being adequately performed, but we consider that a good deal of the money that is being spent on the existing arrangements is being wasted. We believe that this state of affairs cannot be remedied within the framework of the existing law.

By April 1953 Grigg had become convinced that nothing but obstruction could be expected from Jenkinson, and so he was quite prepared to help Bridges to deal with the problem of what he called 'The Old Man of Chancery Lane' once the main lines of the committee's report had been settled.[14b] The committee's origins went back to March 1949 when Ellis, quite unofficially, had told an old Treasury friend, T. D. Kingdom, about

---

13b. PRO 1/1334: Jenkinson's notes for a meeting of the Grigg Committee, 12 December 1952.
14a. *Committee on Departmental Records Report* (HMSO, 1954) (Cmd. 9163), 6.
14b. T 214/471: Grigg to Bridges, 28 May 1953.

the Limbo scheme and the need for Treasury help to obtain the co-operation of departments. Although Kingdom alerted the Organisation and Methods Division, the matter might well have rested there had not Norman Brook (later Lord Normanbrook) written soon afterwards to Bridges to complain about the destruction by the Ministry of Health of early plans for the evacuation of school children, which had come to his notice in connection with Titmuss's *Problems of Social Policy* in the series of Official Histories of the Second World War.[14c] Those papers had been taken over by the Ministry of Health from the Home Office ARP Department and emphasised the risk, thought Brook, of important material being lost when transferred from one department to another or when functions such as those concerning wartime reconstruction were wound up. That concern had long been felt by the official historians,[14d] and, although they had an informal liaison with the inspecting officers, Professor W. K. Hancock, the chief civil historian, was worried about what he saw as Public Record Office complacency and was convinced that the scheduling system was out-of-date.

The Treasury's attention had already been drawn to the problem of record-keeping in the United States, revealed by the Hoover Commission on the Organisation of the Executive Branch of Government, and wondered how far its recommendations might be applied to Britain. The result was that after consultation with a somewhat unco-operative Jenkinson it was decided that the Organisation and Methods Division should carry out a study into departmental arrangements for weeding and preparation of material for transfer to the Public Record Office, particularly as the Ministry of Works was expressing alarm at the spiralling cost of the Limbo scheme about which the Treasury felt it had not been kept fully informed.[15] The Treasury was also conscious of the wider record problem, and, apart from the fact that Brook was continuing to urge a full and independent investigation to take account of the needs of future historians, it had received a suggestion for an inquiry into the modernisation of the public records law from J. A. R. Pimlott of the Lord President's Office, who had heard from a 'knowledgeable friend' of the inconvenience and inefficiency of the 'obsolete requirements relating to the Public Record Office'.[16] The Treasury decided that although the scheduling system might not be quite so wooden as sometimes suggested it must still press ahead with its own survey. By October 1951 that had been completed and revealed that at least 250,000 feet of documents in departments could be destroyed immediately if weeding arrears could be cleared.

14c. T 222/537: Brook to Bridges, 14 April 1949.

14d. It is clear from CAB 103/305 that the problem had been worrying the official historians for some time. As early as 1944 the question of improving record keeping was under discussion with the Treasury.

15. T 222/537: rough notes of meeting between the Treasury and the Public Record Office, 27 April 1950.

16. T 222/537: Pimlott to Simpson, 8 March 1950.

It also found that permanently preservable records destined for the Public Record Office would more than double its existing holdings. Commenting upon the findings, Jenkinson said that a conference at which the Public Record Office might take part would be welcome, but by then the Treasury was fully persuaded that something more ambitious was required. Consequently, on 20 December 1951, Bridges told Jenkinson that it seemed to him that consideration ought to be given to an inquiry into the fundamentals of the record system and that the office would be consulted about the form which it might take. As luck would have it, on that very day Churchill was voicing to Bridges, who had been his wartime Cabinet secretary, his misgivings about the large sum of money being spent in the coming year by the Ministry of Works on filing cabinets. The opportunity being too good to miss, Bridges told the prime minister what the Treasury had in mind and got his blessing there and then for a high level inquiry as a matter of urgency.

Armed with Bridges's directive, Edward (later Sir Edward) Playfair was soon at work to set the wheels in motion, but, having had a trying session with Jenkinson ('a real cough drop'), Evans, Collingridge and Drew on 18 January 1952, he felt obliged to return to Bridges at the end of that month to tell him:[17]

> It is not a difficult thing to set up this Committee, but I am bound to say that Sir Hilary's personality is a complication. He has many talents, and it seems to me a good deal of charm, but he talks incessantly and is perfectly convinced that he knows all the answers, whereas over much of the field (all that concerns the daily working of an office) he is as innocent as a child.

For all that, Playfair did not think it was going to be easy to exclude Jenkinson, whose idea was that both he and Collingridge should be members of the proposed committee and that when he was too busy to go Evans should attend in his stead. He was emphatic that there was no source, other than the Public Record Office, from which suitable spokesmen could be found from the newly-formed archival profession. To try to get round the problem Bridges decided to ask the chancellor of the Exchequer to see Evershed privately, despite Jenkinson's known contention that the master of the rolls would insist upon his appointment. It was not until 4 April that a meeting between the two men was arranged, the only other person present being Bridges, who had some qualms because he feared that Evershed disliked him. As it happened, Butler must have been at his most persuasive because he managed to get Evershed to agree to Jenkinson being kept off the proposed committee. Neither did Evershed press his earlier suggestion

---

17. T 222/538: Playfair to Bridges, 30 January 1952. In a less restrained minute on the same file to Johnston on the 22nd about Jenkinson's alleged failings, Playfair, no doubt humorously, said he hoped that when the time came for it to be sent to the Public Record Office 'this note will be regarded as one to be weeded'.

that Evans might be a member, it being felt simplest to say that Churchill himself had decided that no serving civil servant should be appointed, which coming from Number 10 was 'a pronunciamento of the best possible vintage'.[18] There was general agreement that the inquiry should not extend to Scotland and that Grigg, if willing, would make an excellent chairman. It was also agreed that Jenkinson and the head of the Organisation and Methods Division, as well as any other Treasury official, should be available for consultation throughout the committee's inquiry. With those points settled, no difficulty was experienced subsequently about the composition of the committee, although a recommendation from Hancock in favour of Pugh as an historian was vetoed by Evershed, no doubt to avoid offending Jenkinson further. A much earlier suggestion involving another former assistant keeper, Galbraith, had fallen by the wayside because he was not thought to be a good committee man.

The office itself, prompted by Evans, proposed Professor J. G. Edwards, the director of the Institute of Historical Research, as an historian and strongly recommended H. R. Creswick, the Cambridge University and formerly Bodley's librarian, to represent the library world, while Evershed favoured Denys Buckley, junior counsel to the Treasury for the Chancery Division, as a lawyer. All three were accepted without ado. The words 'England and Wales' were struck out of the terms of reference because Evershed and Jenkinson feared that, although Edwards was Welsh, he might not be thought sufficiently so to placate nationalist feeling, which on record matters, as in the case of the Royal Commission of 1910, was liable to break out from time to time. That left three places, one of which went to another Welshman, Professor H. J. (later Sir John) Habakkuk, an Oxford economic historian with wartime experience in the Board of Trade. Grigg himself managed to secure S. P. (later Sir Paul) Chambers, an ICI director and former member of the Board of Inland Revenue, and Hancock nominated Mrs M. M. Gowing, a member of his team, who had a strong interest in the project and whose knowledge of departmental archives was to prove of much value to the inquiry. Had Evershed objected to her appointment the Treasury was prepared to yield because it appreciated that there was an element of special pleading in its argument that as an official historian engaged for a specific project Mrs Gowing was neither a civil servant nor a representative of a departmental view.

To put the record straight Churchill was told about the committee's formation and the decision to exclude from it the 'creators and hoarders of files'. Churchill welcomed the action taken and was glad that Grigg had been invited to act as chairman. Grigg himself was flattered to be asked to deal with all the papers that the 'thinkers' were pouring out, no less, he observed,

---

18. T 222/538: Bridges's note for the record, 4 April 1952. Bridges's own papers were not available when this chapter was written, his file concerning Public Record Office staffing (T 273/120) being retained by the Treasury.

under a Conservative than a Labour government. Undoubtedly the formation of the committee without Jenkinson was a shattering blow to him. He
regarded himself as the world authority and believed that everything would
be simple, as he had told Playfair earlier, if only his favoured methods were
adopted at once. But as they revolved around a system based upon the
segregation of ephemera at the outset and the wholesale registration of the
rest, the Treasury was unimpressed, doubting whether it had been feasible
even when advocated by Jenkinson in his *Manual of Archive Administration*
in 1922 and thinking it pure fantasy in 1952. Nevertheless, when Kenneth
(later Sir Kenneth) Clucas, who had been taken from his post as a labour
attaché in Cairo to assume the secretaryship of the committee, came to study
the *Manual* for himself he found much to admire in it, telling Grigg in
September 1952 how interesting he had found Jenkinson's arguments. Yet
Clucas, while liking Jenkinson's thesis that neither the archivist nor the
historian should play any part in the selection of documents for permanent
preservation, marvelled that Jenkinson should still find nothing wrong with
the existing scheduling system in which the inspecting officers (archivists)
played the decisive role in collaboration, in difficult cases, with the historians. That card was to be used later against Jenkinson with devastating
effect. Clucas took issue also with Jenkinson's definition of archives as
'Documents drawn up for the purposes of, or used during the conduct of
Affairs of any kind, of which they themselves formed a part, and subsequently preserved by the persons responsible for the transactions in question, or their successors, in their own custody for their own reference'. On
that definition, said Clucas, once a document ceased to be of use administratively it ceased to be an archive, which was absurd. On the other hand,
he thought it was easy to see why Jenkinson argued as he did and the
element of truth in what he said because medieval and later documents were
kept not because they were thought of historical importance but because it
was the administrative practice to retain them. Accordingly, in its report
the committee itself, while accepting Jenkinson's definition of archives,
inserted the rider that the words 'for their own reference' should be omitted.
The all-important point was also made that the term 'public records' – 'the
Archives of the Central Government', according to Jenkinson, and accepted
by the committee – bore a very different meaning in 1954 from the one it
did in the early nineteenth century or even as late as 1871, when Sir Thomas
Hardy could say that the records of government departments were not
'public records' at all because they were not 'public', by which he meant in
the older sense of being open for all to see as 'the people's evidences'.

Although Clucas found himself closer to Jenkinson than he thought he
would, especially in his emphasis upon the quality of 'impartiality' of the
archives, he took him to task for his advocacy of the registry as part of the
machinery of archival control, arguing:[19]

---

19. T 222/540: Clucas to Grigg, 23 September 1952.

Any additional registers, record of phone conversations etc., not necessary for administrative purposes, would be *ipso facto* kept, not for administrative use, but for posterity, The 'memorial' idea is a myth, and to suggest that an administration should create such a memorial for administrative purposes is really a piece of crooked thinking on Jenkinson's part so as to fit in his practical requirements with his general theory.

Clucas went on to tell Grigg of his own preliminary ideas which related preservation to long-term administrative usefulness and were to be developed and eventually emerge in a committee recommendation of a system of first and second reviews of records, normally at 5 and 25 years, at the second of which consideration would be given to their historical importance. A little earlier the Organisation and Methods Division had prepared a memorandum in which it had recommended that in dealing with records an attempt should be made to distinguish between those which were needed administratively and those which might be of value to the historian. The committee believed that any document not needed administratively at first review should be discarded on the assumption that if it was no longer wanted for departmental purposes after so short a period it was unlikely to be historically important, a theory which accorded with Grigg's own instincts and experience of administration. At second review, however, account would be taken of historical value. In so far as differences arose in the committee they were mainly about how the reviews were to be carried out by departments and whether the Public Record Office or the Treasury should be given executive powers over them. Grigg himself was quite clear in his own mind that it would be constitutionally improper for one department to be given control over another and that if differences arose they should be settled departmentally or, failing that, at Cabinet level. So strongly did he feel on that issue that at one stage he was talking of resignation. Fortunately his view finally prevailed and was one of the reasons for the committee's further recommendation that the headship of the Public Record Office should pass from the master of the rolls to a minister of the crown.

In deference to the historians, and to Edwards in particular, the committee originally thought that the Public Record Office's inspecting officers, who would be charged with the oversight of the reviewing arrangements, should be assistant keepers because they were the persons best qualified to exercise the historical criteria on account of their intimate knowledge of the interests of researchers. But that proposal ran counter to Jenkinson's one-time view that archivists, like historians, should not be concerned in the selection of records for preservation, an argument which the committee, tongue in cheek, intended to deploy in criticising the involvement of the assistant keepers in the scheduling system introduced as a result of the 1877 act. There was the further point that, as the disposal of the bulk of departmental papers was to be decided on administrative grounds, the oversight to be exercised by the inspecting officers turned largely upon the mechanics of the reviewing system and keeping departments up to scratch. Accordingly, when the

468

committee finally came to make its report it did not specify the source from which the inspecting officers would be recruited apart from saying that it might be from departments themselves and the Public Record Office. Significantly, however, it also said that in the exercise of the historical criteria the inspecting officers should, where necessary, take into consultation the archivists (assistant keepers) in the Public Record Office. On the other hand, the statement in the final draft that the experience required for the inspecting officer posts was administrative and managerial was dropped, presumably because of Edwards's continued misgivings. Grigg himself also had some reservations because he feared that if the historians were critical it would encourage the government to do nothing about the committee's report.

The shift in the committee's thinking brought it more or less into line with that of the Treasury, which, unofficially, was aware of what was happening and had at one time been concerned that Grigg might be unable to restrain some members of the committee from recommending a large increase in the number of assistant keepers. But probably the most important factor in the committee's changed stance arose from the report it received from Chambers and Habakkuk, who had visited the United States on its behalf in October 1953 to look into arrangements there. Their main purpose was to investigate the possibility of microfilming as a means of saving space, but they also examined American record practices generally. Both men were much impressed by the detailed scheduling system in force across the Atlantic, but accepted that differences in the record systems of the two countries made its adoption in Britain impractical. They concluded, all the same, that if papers could be subject to an intensive initial investigation at first review it might be possible to destroy as much as ninety per cent at that stage, avoiding the need for the proposed second review. There should, however, be a reappraisal of material transferred to the Public Record Office after a suitable lapse of time. While agreeing that it should be the duty of the Public Record Office to keep the papers in its charge under continuous review, the committee was not prepared to abandon its proposal for a second review at 25 years. Nevertheless, it was seen as a weakness of the British system that, unlike the American, it did not have a Records Management Division operating alongside the National Archives, or a corps of record managers, seen by Chambers as a cross between O and M officers and archivists. That defect led the committee to recommend that each department should have its own record officer, under the director of establishments, and that there should be a new breed of inspecting officers to liaise with them, the archivists being available for consultation at one remove. Only in that way, thought the committee, especially Chambers, Habakkuk and Mrs Gowing, would there be the necessary drive to get rid of documents by destruction or by transfer to the Public Record Office.

Jenkinson was not opposed to a system involving two reviews, having pointed out to the committee at an early stage in its deliberations that the institution of a second review of papers provisionally selected for permanent preservation had been a characteristic of some recent schedules. The stumbling block for him was any suggestion to amend or replace the 1877 act, which he regarded as sacrosanct. On the other hand, most departments had indicated to the committee as early as the spring of 1953 that they had no objection to its proposals. The Admiralty was almost alone in having some reservations, its attitude much annoying Grigg because its reviewing arrears were greater than those of any other department. It was not surprising, therefore, that when the committee's report appeared in 1954 the Admiralty, although not named, was censured for still having in its possession unreviewed documents from the eighteenth century lying on the floor at Hayes, possibly the same ones seen by the Royal Commission in 1910 when they were in its attics. Grigg was determined that not only the Admiralty but also the deputy keeper should be 'roasted' in the report, which dealt still more savagely with the imperfections of the scheduling system. Typical of the scorn it poured on the imprecision of the terms used in the schedules was its reference to one of recent date which required reviewers to identify papers from particular categories of records (e.g. Insecticides and Fungicides) on the basis of vague descriptions such as 'miscellaneous matters', 'general papers', 'minor matters', and 'papers of ephemeral importance'. Neither did the committee make any bones about the antiquated nature of the law concerning public records, stressing the need for change, *pace* Jenkinson, because[20]

> The present arrangements for the preservation of the records of Government
> Departments are governed by an Act of 1838 which we believe was not
> meant to apply to them, an Act of 1877 which makes the selection of records
> for preservation about as complicated as it can be, and an agreement of 1845–6
> which removes from those responsible for the ultimate preservation of the
> records a proper oversight of them.

If that was true in 1954 it had been equally true in 1910, but whereas Grigg grasped the nettle the Royal Commission had failed to do so. The difference was that the Royal Commission was set up primarily to appease the Welsh and had no departmental backing or clear idea of what it wanted. The Grigg Committee, on the other hand, was appointed because of Cabinet Office concern about the fate of historically valuable papers under the old nineteenth-century system and because the Treasury had taken fright at the rate at which departmental records were accumulating. The Treasury also saw the inquiry as a golden opportunity to bring about changes in the way the Public Record Office was being run. To meet the major concerns of both the Cabinet Office and the Treasury was no mean achievement given their differing objectives. To deal with Jenkinson was less difficult because his wilful refusal to give proper consideration to the Organisation and

---

20. Grigg *Report*, para 55.

Methods Division proposals made it inevitable that the committee should recommend that the Treasury should conduct an early inquiry into the organisation and staffing of the Public Record Office and bring it into the normal machinery of government. The committee recommended that it should be represented by a minister and should have a new official head with the title 'keeper of the records'. Serving under him would be a deputy keeper, who as the senior archivist would be in charge of the records once they were transferred to the office for permanent preservation, and a records administration officer, who would be charged with the oversight of records before their transfer to the Public Record Office and be assisted by the new-style inspecting officers. The committee attached the greatest importance to the appointment of a capable official to that post, but on Edwards's representations dropped the recommendation that the appointment should come from outside the Public Record Office, leaving that question open, while recommending that his rank should not be inferior to that of the new deputy keeper. The report also made it plain that the new post of keeper of the records would be an administrative one, but the relevant paragraph had been drafted with care to meet the wishes of Edwards, who was anxious to safeguard the interests of his fellow Welshman Evans. It stated that the appointment might come from within the office if the person concerned had the necessary administrative ability. Left unsaid was the opinion of the committee as a whole that that was unlikely to be the case.

The advantages enjoyed by the Grigg Committee over the Royal Commission might not have counted for quite so much had Clucas not been attached to and stationed at the Treasury, which enabled him to clear the committee's lines with it informally at crucial points. At the outset Jenkinson could have had a joint secretaryship for the Public Record Office, but he maintained that he could not spare anyone, which according to Playfair was because he suspected that acceptance might be used as an argument against his own membership of the committee. That was to prove one of Jenkinson's many miscalculations, although he may also have had at the back of his mind the unhappy precedent of Hall's secretaryship of the Royal Commission. Of course, Jenkinson was well aware of the Treasury influence and it was surely a Freudian slip on his part that allowed a reference to be made at one point in his *Report* for 1953 to the 'Treasury Committee considering, under the Chairmanship of Sir James Grigg, the problem of modern Departmental Records in the light of the rate at which they are accumulating'. It was obvious that the Grigg Committee, with the backing of both the Treasury and the Cabinet Office, was powerfully placed, but its proposals derived their real authority from the logic of the arguments it advanced and because of its extensive consultation with government departments. The views of the British Film Institute, the Royal Society and the Society of Genealogists had also been obtained, and information had been gathered about practice in a number of other countries from their missions in London. As regards microfilming, Chambers and Habakkuk did not find that American experience supported the use of film as a solution to the storage problem. That it was not an economical proposition in normal circumstances was confirmed by further inquiries nearer home, although the committee recommended that the Public Record Office should keep technical developments in the field under constant review. Most important of all, the committee proposed that to ensure the steady flow of preservable records to the Public Record Office, yet to prevent it being swamped with valueless material, the Public Record Office Acts 1838 to 1898 should be repealed and replaced by an act to facilitate the new reviewing system, which had been designed to ensure that the method of selecting records for preservation was administratively practicable. Recognising the close connection of the office of master of the rolls with the department since its formation, it further recommended, at Buckley's suggestion, that the holder should be *ex officio* chairman of a newly-formed Advisory Council to advise the minister on those aspects of the department's work affecting the interests of its users. The committee also recommended that photographs and sound recordings thought worth keeping should be deposited in the office, but that government films should be kept by the British Film Institute in the National Film Library as the office's agent. Realising that its terms of reference did not cover certain records, such as those of the courts of law, the committee said that arrangements for their preservation would also need to be considered when the new legislation was being drafted.

The general tenor of the Grigg Committee's report was, of course, highly unpalatable to Jenkinson. In a critique of its conclusions just before his retirement in April 1954, he argued that it had not considered sufficiently the possibility of developing existing resources and suggested that all ends might be met if the deputy keeper was allowed to lay before Parliament, after consultation with the master of the rolls, a reasoned statement of his requirements in his annual report. The duty of its presentation could then be placed upon an independent minister without the need for new legislation, which he thought would lead to complications, particularly as regards the legal records. At the same time he hastened to add that he did not even want to hint at the possibility of two record offices 'which some ignorant people would probably [think that they would] like'.[21] If that sounded unrepentantly defiant it was probably because he could have been in no doubt that a number of the committee's barbs, although disguised and not apparent to the casual reader, were directed at him personally. In that category, for example, fell the questioning by the committee of the factual basis for the doctrine of unbroken official custody, Galbraith being quoted not only to refute it – 'for centuries the national archives were mainly left to rot in damp cellars or attics' – but to criticise the principle as having in practice done more harm than good.

---

21. PRO 1/1445: Jenkinson's memorandum on 'General Policy Questions raised by the Grigg Committee's Report', 7 April 1954.

To add insult to injury, where Jenkinson's own views corresponded with those of the committee it used them with great skill to reinforce its own recommendations. It was of little consolation to Jenkinson that in so doing it was acting defensively rather than maliciously. The committee's draft report was not circulated until the beginning of 1954, but he had been painfully conscious for some time previously of the direction in which it was moving. By the late summer of 1953 it was noted at the Treasury that 'PRO gossip has it that the DK has all but retired from the hurly-burly of administration and is devoting his time to writing brochures on Seals and Domesday Book'.[22a] Treasury intelligence was good and was to be confirmed in the publication soon afterwards by the Stationery Office of an illustrated *Guide to Seals in the Public Record Office* and an account of the results of the investigation undertaken during the rebinding of Domesday Book, entitled *Domesday Rebound*, for which much valuable and detailed research into its assembly was undertaken by Dr D. H. Gifford. T. E. Hassell, who executed the binding work, was to die later that year, but although he was a fine craftsman his operations on the volume did not escape criticism, which was why, as Dr Hallam has related in *Domesday Book through Nine Centuries*, a comprehensive rebinding was undertaken of both Great and Little Domesday in advance of the Ninth-Centenary Exhibition of Domesday Book held at the office in 1986. Jenkinson had enjoyed a long association with Hassell, who had been awarded the British Empire Medal in 1952, and greatly lamented his loss, paying particular tribute to his services in the *Hundred and Fifteenth Report of the Deputy Keeper of the Records* for 1953. Jenkinson recorded in that same report the death of another former close colleague, M. S. Giuseppi, whose daughter had joined the office's editorial ranks in 1951, and who went on to compile a list and index to proceedings in the Court of Requests.

Neither death, while grieved by Jenkinson, compared with the misfortune he had suffered the previous year when Charles Drew, his secretary and establishment officer, had died unexpectedly in September 1952. Drew, a cultured and diplomatic man, who translated French plays and was an active and devout Anglican, enjoyed Jenkinson's confidence more than any other member of the staff and, had he lived, might have helped him to chart his way through the choppy waters that lay ahead. Thus bereft, Jenkinson entrusted establishment affairs to Evans. He had no real interest in them, so that yet more of those duties devolved upon Fox. Evans nevertheless relinquished his duties in connection with the repository, repairs and photography, and by deputising for Jenkinson on general administration allowed his master to indulge his editorial propensities in a fashion that had been denied to him for many years. The post of secretary was then taken by Hector, who also joined the Inspecting Officers' Committee but retained

---

22a. T 222/720: Jordan to Jefferies, 12 August 1953.

his position as virtual editor-in-chief of the office's publications, being the recognised authority on such matters as typography and lay-out. He was also an accomplished palaeographer and his book on *The Handwriting of English Documents*, published in 1958, continues to have a deserved success. The changes were completed by the promotion of Wardle to a director's post to take sole charge of the Repository and Photographic Sections, and responsibility for the Repair Department was given to Ellis. He also took over the Seal Catalogue, a work to which he was later to return as an editor on retirement from his post as secretary to the Historical Manuscripts Commission.

In April 1953 Grigg had decided that because of Jenkinson's reluctance to entertain change outside the existing record framework he should not be consulted about the draft of the committee's report until it got to its final and more or less definitive stage, which was not reached until February 1954. By the time that the draft was received at the office it was generally known that Jenkinson's retirement was fixed for the end of March or early April. Indeed, not long before Christmas 1953 Jenkinson had told the Consultative Committee on Publication that it was probably the last meeting over which he would preside. Possibly because he knew he would soon no longer be personally involved Jenkinson's comments were less bitter than Clucas and Grigg had anticipated, but there was some feeling within the Treasury that he might be holding his fire and that he could well cause more trouble from the safety of retirement by sniping from the public gallery and writing to *The Times*. To some extent the memorandum he sent to Evershed just before his retirement tended to support that theory, but immediately Jenkinson was more concerned to place on record the fact that the reason why the master of the rolls had never exercised his full powers under the act was because the office had never been in a position to accommodate large transfers. On the question of the vagueness of the descriptions of documents in the destruction schedules he blamed departments rather than the office. Neither did he accept the committee's conclusion that the Limbo scheme as operated had merely led to the postponement of reviewing work. He also entered a mild protest about the implication that the office had not planned ahead and put in a plea for accounting records which the committee was not disposed to rate highly. At that late stage, however, any fundamental change was out of the question, and in any case, having studied Jenkinson's memorandum, the committee thought that his complaint that its report was less than fair to the Public Record Office was groundless. Nevertheless, Clucas was directed to make any amendments that appeared desirable in the light of Jenkinson's comments to ensure that the feelings of individuals were not unnecessarily hurt and that the committee was not itself open to criticism on matters of fact. Clucas had, as it happened, taken great care to be accurate, and in his researches into the early history of the Public Record Office had discovered to his surprise that Jenkinson was not always reliable in his statements about that period. While he had no intention of tweaking the lion's tail, he could not resist documenting for Collingridge after Jenkinson's departure some minor blemishes in his *Guide to the Public Records*, the most odd of which was the erroneous statement that the Select Committee of 1836 had proposed that the public records should be placed under the authority of the master of the rolls when its actual recommendation was for a reconstituted commission.[22b] Anyone who has researched the ill-documented events connected with the Public Record Office's origins can only sympathise with Jenkinson's slip.

Jenkinson's real venom was not for the Grigg Committee but for its begetter, the Treasury. His opportunity to hit back came with the much-delayed *Hundred and Fourteenth Report* for 1952 in which he lambasted the Treasury for recommending to the office changes in methods which, he said, were nearly all impracticable, having been tried out, considered and rejected or superseded many years before. In like vein he said that he had always been doubtful about how far its officials, having no archival experience or training, could be in a position to advise the office on technical matters, and he regretted that their investigations had resulted in the expenditure of a large amount of staff time which he would gladly have seen employed elsewhere. Fondly thinking Grigg might like to see his comments, Jenkinson sent him a copy, only for it to be passed straight to Clucas with a note that he could not possibly read it. But the organisation and methods men at the Treasury had read it and were incensed at what they considered a 'vile' and improper attack upon them. However, R. W. B. (later Sir Richard) Clarke said that Playfair had once told him never to be indignant about anybody's conduct in the art world and his own inclination was to have a frank word with Jenkinson's successor. Bridges thought it was the funniest thing he had seen for years and was admirably timed as showing the ludicrousness of the present situation.[22c] In fact, behind the scenes discussions had been taking place on high about who might succeed Jenkinson, the worry being that any PRO man, once in occupation, might stake out a claim for the new post of keeper envisaged under the arrangements proposed by Grigg. In a confidential memorandum Johnston at the Treasury said:[23a]

> The present Deputy Keeper is a person of strong personality who has fixed views on many subjects, large and small. The process of administration under the Deputy Keeper consists to a large extent of endeavouring to guess what his view on any issue is likely to be. Nor is it profitable to entertain independent views. It is said (with what truth I do not know) that work is chopped up among the staff and changed from time to time in a way that makes it difficult for any one subordinate to exercise any real responsibility.

22b. T 222/615: Clucas to Collingridge, 23 April 1954.

22c. The comments of the Treasury men are at the back of T 222/606.

23a. T 222/800: Johnston's memorandum 'The Public Record Office, present organisation', 11 March 1954.

It is not easy to foresee how members of the subordinate staff are likely to behave once Sir Hilary Jenkinson has gone. None of them seem to be forceful characters or to have very marked ability – they might not have survived if they had been so.

On tradition, said Johnston, Evans, the next in line, should succeed but, although it was generally thought that he would run the office competently and be successful in handling the staff, he was 60 and somewhat lacking in energy. It was thought that Jenkinson himself favoured Hector, who had to a considerable degree the gift of divining his views on any issue and who was probably abler than Evans and might have made a better deputy keeper. Of the other senior men Collingridge was thought to have been quite good in dealing with departmental records within the limitations of the existing system, and the O and M investigators thought well of Johnson. However, Grigg and some of his committee felt strongly that both the proposed new posts of keeper of the records and records administration officer should be filled from outside the department, a view held also at that time by Evershed. The problem, Johnston thought, could be met either by the more obvious way of choosing a candidate from within the office as a caretaker deputy keeper or by bringing in an outsider who would take the keeper post in due course. In the latter event Johnston considered Collingridge should then be appointed records administration officer for the sake of office morale. Nevertheless, Johnston saw some advantages in appointing Evans as deputy keeper for one or two years before retirement, particularly if it could be coupled with a general investigation into the PRO. Shortly afterwards a meeting took place between Evershed and Bridges, when it became clear that Evershed was resolved upon Evans's appointment, although he undertook to warn him that he would not necessarily continue to be head of the office if the Grigg Committee's proposals led to changes in the department's organisation. Jenkinson no longer had any *locus* in the matter and if he believed he could manipulate his one-time apprentice from behind the scenes he was soon to be disappointed. In fact, by the time of his formal leave-taking ceremony at the office he seemed to have decided it was a case of *après moi le déluge*. Most of those present recall it as an embarrassing and somewhat undignified occasion with a few words of no great consequence from Evans and still fewer from Jenkinson, who indicated a readiness to sign any off-prints of his, which were present in abundance for the edification of any members of the staff who cared to take copies away.

Much of Jenkinson's final *Report*, the 115th in the series, covering the year 1953 and signed on 7 April 1954, three days before his retirement, took the form of a review of the seven years during which he had held office. It read remarkably like an apologetic for his cautionary approach to any variation in traditional practices. Alluding to the treatment of decaying paper, he wrote of 'a problem of terrifying magnitude and perhaps the greatest technical difficulty confronting the modern Archivist'. Noting the introduction of the lamination method of repair and the use of acetate foil, as in

America, Jenkinson hoped that the Repair Department might develop into an experimental centre. He drew attention to the course for a diploma in archive science at London University, with which several members of the staff were connected as lecturers, and to the links which had been forged between the senior craftsmen and the London School of Printing and Graphic Art in connection with courses in document repair. Referring to the introduction into the office of the executive class, he indicated some modification of his earlier thinking, accepting 'a greater differentiation of some of the higher types of work as between ancient and modern Records becoming possible or even necessary with the increasing bulk of the latter'. Coming from him that was a remarkable *volte-face* because less than eighteen months earlier, in the *Hundred and Thirteenth Report* for 1951, he had written:

> It has always been held, and is generally agreed, that ability to deal with later Records in this Country, where administrative development has been so continuous from medieval to modern times, should be based on a technique gained by close familiarity with classes of all dates – a familiarity which must include not merely the handling but the reading and comprehension with equal readiness of medieval, Tudor and Stuart Records. Such a familiarity has been gained by Assistant Keepers in the past only through long periods of work of an 'editorial' kind – it cannot in fact be gained in any other way – and I view with apprehension the possibility of a lowering of past standards.

How far his views had really changed is debatable for a year later, in 1955, in his presidential address to the Society of Archivists, he was referring to the danger of the 'tendency (no one who has had experience of dealing with Finance Divisions over questions of Staff can doubt it) to employ for the administration of Modern Archives, if that is made a separate affair, persons of a lower educational grade, or, at least, persons not qualified by special training to act as Archivists'.[23b]

In his final *Report* he regretted the fact that he had not been able to carry his projected *Guide* further than the *Introductory* section, but said that he hoped it might be possible for him to retain some editorial connection with its publication after retirement. In that he was to be bitterly disappointed because Evans and Johnson, in the light of critical comments from O and M and with the full backing of the Consultative Committee on Publication, were eventually to decide that although such a *Guide* was desirable as a long-term project the immediate need was a revised edition of Giuseppi to be published within two and half years. In the event the updating of that work proved more exacting than originally thought and it did not appear until 1963. But Jenkinson's rather grander vision was not forgotten and the new

---

23b. H. Jenkinson, 'The Future of Archives in England', *Journal of the Society of Archivists*, I, 60.

Guide, which began to take shape from the late 1970s, owes much to his original conception. It was inevitable that Jenkinson, who, when he heard at second-hand what was afoot, submitted a special paper to the Consultative Committee on the matter, should take the decision badly. Only those close to him could have known how hurt and offended he was by the action of his former colleagues who he thought had deliberately kept him in the dark about what was planned, which he saw as a breach of ordinary courtesy and of scholarly propriety, let alone friendship, which he had not deserved.[23c] Thereafter, such few contacts as he had at the office were at arm's length, but he remained on good terms with Evershed and Ellis and continued to sit on the Historical Manuscripts Commission, besides playing his part as a presidential figure in the archive movement which owed him so much. In his first *Report* as deputy keeper, Evans placed on record Jenkinson's many services to the office from the time of his entry in 1906, and after Jenkinson's death in 1961, a year in which the deaths of Flower and Charles Johnson were also mourned, S. S. Wilson recalled him, aptly, in the *Third Annual Report of the Keeper of Public Records* as 'a scholar and teacher and as a tireless organiser and propagandist for the preservation on scientific principles of all archival material'.

That Jenkinson had his faults is undeniable but neither can it be doubted that he put the Public Record Office on the map, although an unwise assertion of his own supremacy was to identify it to the Treasury as recalcitrant territory and to have dire effects for him. The excellence of the physical arrangement of the records on the shelves owes a great deal to the disciplines he imposed, creating order out of disorder and establishing clear guidelines for repository practice. He introduced the same high standards into the working of the Conservation Department. It was a great mortification to him that the Lincoln copy of Magna Carta was to suffer some damage from fading while in the office for repair in 1951, but generally speaking the record of achievement was immense. He was never the man to accept second best and it was typical that in 1931 he locked away some certified copies of court rolls etc. sent from the commissioners of crown lands when Stamp and Flower refused to agree to return them as being unsuitable for deposit because they consisted of loose papers and included some documents in purple typescript.[24a] When they were found among Jenkinson's remains the office had no scruples about accessioning them and wondered how Jenkinson would have reacted had one of his own subordinates been equally defiant. His most notable success was the foundation he laid for the development of the archival profession. A pen-portrait written anonymously by Harold Johnson in the volume of *Studies Presented to Sir Hilary Jenkinson*, edited by Dr James Conway Davies, his senior pupil, and published in 1957, brings out

---

23c. Jenkinson's personal papers on the matter are in PRO 30/75/36.
24a. PRO 1/98: Jenkinson to Flower, 23 December 1931 on Crown Lands file.

the extent of his contribution to historical knowledge and to the archive service. A congratulatory volume of essays planned by the Society of Archivists for his eightieth birthday was interrupted by his unexpected death in 1961 and appeared a year later under the editorship of Dr Albert E. J. Hollaender. Palgrave's early years excepted, Jenkinson was quite the most expansionist of the deputy keepers. It was tragic that his career in the office ended in the way it did, but while there is much that can be criticised about his administration much can also be forgiven in the record of a man whose reverence for the evidential quality of archives is testified so eloquently by his statement of the archivist's creed printed at the head of this chapter.

His retirement coincided with the drawing together by the Grigg Committee of the final strands of its report. As a matter of prudence its conclusions had been sent for comment to historians such as Hancock and Ashworth and had received their broad approbation. Edwards had also passed certain sections of it to Pugh who had one or two reservations, mainly about its proposal that 'no attempt should be made to keep records for genealogical or biographical purposes'. Pugh pointed out that a considerable proportion of searchers consulted the records for biographical information. He also maintained that, whereas the future interests of historians and antiquaries could not be foreseen, it could confidently be predicted that mankind's interest in its ancestors would remain a fundamental characteristic. However, the Society of Genealogists had informed the committee that, in general, their main source of information was the General Register Office, although service records which gave dates of birth and parentage before compulsory registration of births began in 1837 and those of a later date relating to men in Scottish and Irish regiments would be of interest to genealogists. Jenkinson had also pointed out earlier that servicemen's records were often the starting point for searches on all kinds of matters. The result was that the committee agreed to a slight modification in its original proposal which was redrafted to read: 'This means that no attempt should be made to keep in the Public Record Office records which would not otherwise be preserved, solely because they contain information which might be useful for genealogical or biographical purposes'. While the committee's investigations left little doubt that the Public Record Office was in need of radical reorganisation, the committee looked to it, when remodelled, as the vehicle for change. Significantly, Pugh had observed of the committee's proposals about the future administration of the Public Record Office that none was wiser than that which recommended that 'the Treasury should conduct an early enquiry into the organisation and staffing of the Public Record Department' because[24b] 'it has long been clear to me that both are sadly inefficient, and the exposure of this Report bears this out'.

24b. T 222/614: Pugh's memorandum of 8 February 1954, enclosed with Edwards's letter to Clucas, 23 February 1954. Another memorandum from Pugh to Edwards, 18 February 1954, will be found in T 222/615.

The committee bluntly rejected any notion that the policy of housing the public records in one central group of repositories should be abandoned and a policy of decentralisation substituted for it, such as placing particular classes of records in universities or other academic institutions. Neither was it impressed by a proposal that some, if not all, departments should keep their own records permanently, any more than it was by a last-minute suggestion from Pugh that the committee's findings ought to be related to those thought likely to emerge from the Master of the Rolls' Archive Committee, then formulating legislative proposals for the safeguarding of local and private archives, under the chairmanship of Professor T. F. T. Plucknett. Pugh envisaged the creation of a National Archives Council covering the entire record field, an arrangement which, in his opinion, would remove the need for a minister or judge to be superimposed upon the keeper of public records and be in accord with the board of administration proposed by the Royal Commission of 1910.

The committee was not to be diverted by proposals of that kind, realising that it would be fatal to stray from its remit. It was concerned not only that it should confine its recommendations to departmental papers but that it should carry departments with it, particularly on the question of public access to their records. It attached especial importance to ensuring that the quality of 'unselfconsciousness' of officials should not be impaired. For that reason it concluded that there should be a 50-year closure period, but that after the new system of reviewing had been in operation for five years the question of whether certain classes of records should be opened sooner should be re-examined. That decision was in line with that proposed for Cabinet papers for which informal discussions had resulted in Brook agreeing to a like period. On the committee itself Habakkuk and Edwards were somewhat concerned lest the wish of historians of diplomacy to have access to records after 40 years led to damaging criticism of the report. That view was supported by the Foreign Office, which led Clucas to think that it was staffed by exhibitionists.

Subsequently, some misgivings were also voiced by Temperley's one-time associate, G. P. Gooch, and by A. J. P. Taylor, but there was no general outcry. Had the committee been tempted to have second thoughts, any fears would have been dispelled by a forthright letter from the eminent official historian, Sir Llewellyn Woodward, written from Princeton in March 1954, in which he stated:[24c]

> I have read the report with great interest and admiration for the enormous
> amount of work you have put into it. As far as my narrow experience goes
> I agree with you on the tests, methods and general criteria for the preservation
> of material. The future historian will have *enough* material – some things he

---

24c. T 222/615: Woodward to Grigg, 31 March 1954.

may find missing – but he can make up on the swings what he loses on the roundabouts, and the overall total is as much as he can want or cope with – indeed his *real* problem will be and indeed already is – coping with it.

I was most interested in the section on microfilming – what you say is surprising but convincing. There is also, of course, no doubt that [it] is very much more difficult to work with microfilms than with documents. I think 50 years is a fair 'timelag' from the point of view of opening material to scholars, though I have some doubts about it in the case of Cabinet minutes – especially the more detailed annexes to those minutes. I am not sure whether these should be kept at all except for administrative purposes. Of course the historian would like them, but I don't feel altogether certain that the fact that they *will* be open even after 50 years may not have a bad effect on the freedom of Cabinet discussion. However, you are much more qualified than I am to judge a psychological question of this kind. For ordinary departmental papers 50 years is long enough.

One thing that has struck me in relation to Foreign Office papers, and I think this would apply even more to the papers of the Cabinet Office, is that a high proportion of the number of applicants to read 'closed' papers are not genuine scholars, but persons wanting to get at the material in order to attack HM Government and British policy generally. This category of student includes Egyptians, Arabs, Indians, Germans, a good many Americans, and some of our own fellow-countrymen.* These people will, of course, queue up for the opening date of CID and Cabinet papers unless there is a change of fashion in the Levant, the Middle and Far East, and among United States research students, and silly attacks on British 'imperialism' or 'colonialism' as it is now called, no longer has a market value. However, I suppose we must put up with this.

    *Africans will join in the hunt as soon as we have taught enough of them the elements of historical research!!

Inside the Public Record Office, both Wardle and Ellis had reservations about the complications attached to a rolling opening date in which every year a further batch of records were to be made available, the 'creeping barrage' system as Ellis called it. Pugh, with his search-room experience, had similar doubts, particularly concerning the amendment of lists, but the committee was not disposed to make too much of such problems, which it thought, quite correctly as it turned out, could be overcome with a little ingenuity. Grigg, impatient of argument and easily dispirited, had had his doubts at one time about persisting, but all was now coming right, largely owing to Clucas's diplomacy and powers of persuasion. Indeed, practically the only paragraph in the committee's report not written by Clucas himself was its final one in which Grigg acknowledged, on its behalf, its warmest thanks to its secretary whose 'initiative, patience, resource and tact have been unfailing. He has met every call that we have made upon him, and it is in no small degree due to him that we have found it possible to produce a unanimous report'. The Treasury was relieved and pleased at the drift of the report, with its implication that some of the work then done by assistant keepers should pass to executive staff, and it even authorised Clucas to celebrate with a farewell dinner for the committee, allowing him £25 for the purpose. The Treasury was also relieved that the committee had heeded its advice to leave open the question of who should be minister by saying no more than that the choice would seem to be between the chancellor of the Exchequer, the lord president of the Council and the home secretary. Bridges initially thought that if the report foundered it would be on the question of the headship of the office and the proposed displacement of the master of the rolls, but until he studied its arguments fully he had not appreciated the involved series of events which had led to the choice of Langdale in 1838. The committee itself favoured the lord president, but Evershed, while accepting the broad thrust of the report, was highly apprehensive of the effect of the changes if the legal records were placed under a political minister. He was also concerned, not only for himself but also for subsequent holders of his office, if its lead of £1,000 over the other judges was threatened, a point upon which the Treasury was happy to reassure him. However, it was due to Evershed that ministerial responsibility for the Public Record Office was eventually assigned to the lord chancellor. Knowing Evershed to be touchy, and wishing to accommodate Buckley, the committee had gone out of its way to take issue with the Royal Commission of 1910 which had wished to sever the office's links with the master of the rolls on the grounds that he had ceased to control it and was merely the nominal custodian. In contrast, the Grigg Committee drew attention to Greene's comments in 1947 that, although the master of the rolls may at one time have been a mere figurehead, that was no longer the case, so much so that he even wondered whether the time had come when he should be relieved of his responsibilities as keeper of the records in view of his heavy duties as a judge.

Evershed realised all too well the force of that argument, but he also felt a personal responsibility for the office and did not want it thought that he was leaving it in the lurch. Evans was fully aware of Evershed's anxiety on that score, but he was not himself looking for a fight with the Treasury and genuinely wished for improved relations with it. As a gesture of goodwill the correspondence registers in the Secretariat were abandoned, as had earlier been recommended by the Treasury and a new filing system was introduced in 1956. Evans, with the full support of Johnson, who had been appointed principal assistant keeper and establishment officer, also made it plain to the Treasury that they were willing to examine with an open mind any proposals recommended by the Organisation and Methods Division remaining unsettled from the Jenkinson era as well as any new problems likely to arise as a result of the Grigg Report. One matter which remained to be resolved was the question of the grading of the establishment officer post. Almost Jenkinson's last act had been to put in a plea to the Treasury for Fox to be upgraded to chief executive officer although he was unwilling to alter his title of deputy establishment officer. Neither Evans nor Johnson was keen upon any early change, partly because during the crucial negotiations ahead they wanted to keep control in their own hands and partly because Fox was in many ways a difficult personality. He was far from popular and in some eyes his only redeeming feature was that on Mondays it was his custom to bring in the remains of his Sunday joint to feed Tom, the office cat. Even that stopped in the mid-1950s when Tom died and was not replaced. Less well known was the fact that Fox had, on occasions, given tangible help to members of the support grades who had fallen on hard times. But officially he was a stickler for the rules and looked upon himself as the Treasury's watchdog. All the more surprising, therefore, that in a memorandum he wrote in 1956 he chose to cast aspersions on the conduct of O and M's investigation into the Establishment and Accounts Division. The Treasury's response was so indignant that Johnson, who had allowed the memorandum to slip through, sent his apologies and withdrew the offending passages on the office's behalf. That blunder notwithstanding, it was plain that for many years Fox had been carrying the main burden of the office's establishment work. Accordingly, in April 1957, when the main outlines of the future organisation of the department had been settled, Johnson withdrew from the field entirely and Fox was promoted to the rank of chief executive officer and named establishment officer.

That change represented a notable advance for the executive grades, but the real breakthrough for them had come a year earlier when it had been finally agreed that the new inspecting officer posts should be graded at senior executive officer level. Four such posts were authorised of which two were filled from within the office and two by competitive interview, open to departmental staff generally. Farmer, a public-spirited man, who combined his official duties with service on the Herne Bay Urban District Council as an independent member, was an obvious choice, but as he was already an SEO his appointment was not a promotion. Because of Farmer's special experience Collingridge later tried to obtain chief executive officer grading for him, but Fox, once again top dog among the executives, had no enthusiasm for the proposal which was turned down after a Treasury staff inspection. For a short while after retirement in 1962 Farmer took charge at Ashridge in a disestablished capacity, but in 1963 he left to advise the Iranian government on the organisation of its archives, under the UN technical assistance programme, an appointment he held until his death in 1970. The other internal promotion went to Monger, whose place as HEO in Editorial and Training was taken by Penfold, who was later to rise to the assistant keeper ranks and become the office's expert on maps. Monger's spell with the Ministry of Education gave him the edge over Johnston, who was slightly senior to him and who was to join the team in 1961 when K. F. Huggons, after a successful stint, decided to return to the Ministry of Works, his parent department. F. T. Williams, however, from the Treasury decided to stay and during the final part of his career was to hold the establishment officer post for which his earlier experience made him well fitted.

In the early stages of its negotiations with the Treasury about the inspecting officers the department maintained that they should be assistant keepers, although it was prepared to stretch a point in Farmer's case by promoting him to that grade. However, the local branch of the Society of Civil Servants, reading between the lines of the Grigg Report, enlisted the support of its headquarters for its claim to the posts. Unknown to the branch, it was in a strong position because O and M had already decided that executive grading was appropriate. Evershed gave his full support to Evans's defence of the old order, thinking that the assistant keepers, as a result of their specialised training, had the right kind of 'nose' for the job. But the extent to which he was out of touch with reality was his assumption that, in the early stages, the job of an inspecting officer would not be one requiring full-time attention. As it happened, the younger assistant keepers were not disposed to argue for the posts and their attitude must have been of crucial importance in the eventual acceptance by the office of executive grading, subject to the attachment of an assistant keeper to the Records Administration Division to give historical guidance. Once that course had been agreed it was to the credit of Evans, Johnson and Collingridge that they did all in their power to ease the new men into their posts and sustained them vigorously thereafter. The good will was mutual and the Christmas sherry party which the inspecting officers threw for their colleagues in the Search Department, Repository and other sections who had helped them during the course of the previous 12 months rapidly became the social event of the office year, breaking down many of the former grade barriers. It was also customary for invitations to be sent to the departmental record officers of the larger departments, and that helped to widen the office's horizons.

The first assistant keeper to be attached to the Records Administration Division was Ernest Denham, who continued to look after the secretarial side of the outgoing Inspecting Officers' Committee which had residual functions to perform pending the repeal of the 1877 act. The division also carried responsibility for Hayes where Gavin was in charge. The assistant keepers were the more ready to accept the new arrangements because they had in Mabbs, the secretary of their branch of the First Division Association, a man who understood the qualities which his former colleagues in the executive grade could bring to their task. A further consideration was that the assistant keepers had the consolation of seeing Collingridge appointed to head the division as records administration officer. He had narrowly succeeded at the selection board held under Coldstream's chairmanship at the end of 1955. Evans, who sat on the board, was convinced that Collingridge's appointment was essential and his advocacy, coupled with a good performance by Collingridge himself, just carried the day against strong opposition. By that time Collingridge had begun to modify his views about how the inspecting officers should be graded, having recognized that since organising ability and knowledge of registry systems were the qualifications principally needed there could be no objection to the choice of officers of the executive grade, at least in the early stages. But Grigg, whose opinion of Collingridge was coloured by having seen him primarily as a Jenkinson acolyte, was dismayed at the news, which, coupled with the selection of the lord chancellor as the responsible minister, led him to conclude, far too pessimistically, that his report was 'already in ruins'.[25a]

Elsewhere in the office movement among personnel was a feature of the period. Women were already beginning to play a prominent role, and they had, for the first time if the Stationery Office women be excepted, made their appearance in the Repair Department with excellent results. Women were also soon to be recruited in increasing numbers for the rapidly expanding Photographic Department, now equipped with a machine for the continuous and automatic processing of microfilms, which had been constructed by Mason, the one-time repairer, with the help of Morgan. Wardle, as director, took a leading role in all these developments. To the extent that the aim was to recover the direct and indirect costs of production from the charges made for photocopies the Treasury put no difficulties in the way of the engagement by the office of the extra staff required. It had been the office's fear that the increased charges it was obliged to levy would lead to a decline in orders, but there was little slackening in demand. Four women typists were also busily at work, three of them sharing an office and the other, Catherine Wetton, a shorthand-typist, acting as personal secretary to the deputy keeper. That last arrangement had been begun, not before time, under Jenkinson, and resulted in part of his grand room on the first floor, overlooking the lawn on the south-west of the building, being partitioned off for his secretary. From the staffing point of view one of the most difficult of the office's problems was the recruitment of repository or search-room assistants, but it was not until the 1960s that women began to be engaged for that work and they then rapidly proved their worth. White, in particular, had reservations because of the heavy nature of some of the work, such as the production of plea rolls many of which could weigh as much as thirty pounds. But the women were to prove more than capable of undertaking the full range of duties of the grade, and the misgivings once entertained about the dangers that might arise to office morals from women's presence in the numerous and scattered strong rooms proved illusory.

Similarly, the introduction of female messengers was to prove wholly beneficial. It released men for the portering work involved in the cleaning and internal movement of records, which was a daily feature of Repository life, the aim being to redecorate up to ten strong rooms a year. Eades, the long-serving foreman of the floors, had retired at the end of 1953 and been succeeded by A. E. Wade. A year later Paice retired as superintendent and was succeeded by S. J. Rich, who had served under age during the First

25a. PRO 54/29: Grigg to Evershed, 12 November 1955.

World War and who had been commissioned in the Second. In 1955 the foreman of repairs, Palmer, who had once been on Lyte's household staff, retired and his place was taken by R. H. Lane, who besides instructing in document repair at the London School of Printing was also Staff Side secretary. The Swain family's connection was also ended in that year with the retirement of Duncan from his post of master craftsman in which he had specialised in the repair and moulding of seals. The older families were dying out, although Arthur Sloman, whose father had served for many years before him, had been installed as Rich's deputy and Alec Hassell, brother of Tom, was foreman of binding. Binding work was proving a problem for the office because since 1951 the arrangement whereby binders were specially brought in from the Stationery Office to deal with arrears of binding and rebinding had been ended. Although new forms of make-up had replaced traditional binding work, a certain amount remained which was to lead to much dispute with the Civil Service Union in the years ahead about how it should be remunerated.

On the editorial side of the department a notable break with the past occurred in 1956 with the death of Hinds at the age of 85. A year earlier C. J. B. Gaskoin, who since 1949 had been engaged on a catalogue and index of High Court of Admiralty prize papers of the eighteenth century, also died. Bickley had withdrawn from active service and his *Calendar of State Papers, Domestic, James II* was being brought to completion from within the office under the editorship of Kenneth Timings. Other editors working during the 1950s, apart from several former members of the staff and others mentioned earlier, included Miss M. H. Mills, who was engaged on a list of sheriffs' accounts, and H. E. Bell, who was dealing with records of the Court of Wards and Liveries. J. Conway Davies worked upon records of the Augmentations and the Palatinate of Durham, and was to be much involved at a later date with records of the Prerogative Court of Canterbury upon whose history he was especially knowledgeable. In 1956 a short illustrated catalogue of the contents of the Museum was published compiled by Miss Gifford. The same year saw the re-opening of the main Museum, which over the previous two years had been refloored and fitted with new show-cases. Its monuments and windows had been restored by the Ancient Monuments Inspectorate of the Ministry of Works, making it altogether more attractive for visitors. In the process of that work particular attention had been given to the tomb of Dr John Yong because of the need to arrest the decay of the stone of the sarcophagus. But for the Museum's closure those improvements might have been indefinitely deferred so that some good came out of Jenkinson's response to the Treasury manpower cuts after all. A further relief provided by the vacation of the Museum was that in 1954 it allowed the office to store and process there a massive transfer of embassy and consular archives sent back from China at the time of the Korean War, an operation which could not have been undertaken so conveniently anywhere else. The second half of the 1950s was also to see the mounting of a number of special exhibitions, including one to celebrate the 350th anniversary of the first permanent colony in North America at Jamestown, Virginia, and another to mark the centenary of the inauguration of British Columbia as a crown colony. During 1957 records relating to the Jews in England were shown in connection with the tercentenary of the resettlement of the Jews in the British Isles. In December the same Special Exhibition Room was lent to the British Records Association for an exhibition of records preserved through its initiative as part of the celebrations to commemorate its twenty-fifth anniversary. Finally, in December 1958, a special exhibition of Chancery records was opened to illustrate the development of the office of master of the rolls, especially as keeper of the records of Chancery, and his connection with the Public Record Office.

At the higher level of the office Wood and Davies had retired in 1953, Atkinson in 1954 and Ledward in 1955. Of that original crop of World War One men, Evans excepted, only Slingsby now remained. He was always an eccentric and the replacement of coal fires by central heating in the staff rooms in 1956 meant that on rainy days he could no longer toss on to his fire the sodden pieces of cardboard which he cut out from cornflake packets to plug the holes in his shoes; and because he now had a radiator it was no longer necessary for him to drop his wet socks from the top of the staircase, on the second floor, to the basement below, to be dried on the stove in the porter's kitchen for ceremonial return in the afternoon along with his pot of tea. Slingsby's particular expertise lay in his knowledge of the financial reforms of the late seventeenth century, which made him the automatic successor to the redoubtable Dr Shaw as editor of the *Calendar of Treasury Books*. During the morning he rattled along at a rare pace, but in the afternoon either his long train journey from Worthing, which he left at the crack of dawn, or the glass or two of wine he drank at lunch time began to tell and he often nodded off. When challenged, he maintained that to be asleep half the time was a great deal better than to be half asleep all the time like some of his colleagues. But it was a great trial for the junior staff who were called in to read over to him the rolls of declared accounts against his galley proofs. One method employed to keep him awake was to turn the checking into a musical duet, a mixed-up combination of Gregorian plain chant, the singing of multiplication tables and a recital of the litanies. Dotty as the methodology was, it in no way reduced output because the rhythmic intonations gave the reader more time to pick out the Roman figures in the roll, for example, ccclxxxix:vii:ii against £389:7:2 in the printed proof. Any reference to Adam de Cardonnel, collector of customs at Southampton, was invariably the occasion for a particularly energetic response from Slingsby, who swore that the man haunted him at night. As he had written several pamphlets on witchcraft, when not potholing or climbing, no one thought to contradict him. But his zany behaviour was to have one beneficial effect because it was eventually decided to get an adding machine, the first in the office and later a great boon in the accounting and costing work of the burgeoning Photographic Section. But initially the machine was used to add up the figures in the proofs received by Slingsby from the printers. As there were endless columns of them, there was a strong presumption, discounting compensating errors, that if the total in the machine agreed with that in the original roll, the galley from which it had been computed could be passed for press. That machine was a help to Slingsby in other ways because, despite his leaky shoes, he was no pauper and it greatly eased his chores when the time came to tot up for tax purposes his own and his wife's large accumulation of dividend warrants. By general consent Slingsby was a strange case. His academic career at New College, Oxford, had been outstanding and during the war he had been awarded the Military Cross; but he had not fitted in at the Treasury where he had started his career after demobilisation, and there were those who thought that some of his stranger antics could be ascribed to his wartime experiences. Nevertheless, when the office was reorganised in 1957 one of the three allowance posts given to assistant keepers went to him, evidently in recognition of his editorial talent and understanding of the financial intricacies of Exchequer accounting. The others went to Meekings, the outstanding medieval scholar, who had taken over the Library from Wood, and to Latham, a later head of the Search Department, whose name will always be linked with the Medieval Latin Dictionary, for which he toiled extra-officially under the aegis of the British Academy, and whose material continued to be housed in the office.

At the same time that Johnson gave up the establishment officer post Hector relinquished that of secretary and took up enlarged responsibilities as director of publications. Thereafter, the secretarial work was distributed between Johnson and the heads of sections, and the distinctive post of secretary was appended to Johnson's title which became principal assistant keeper and secretary. The Johnson/Evans partnership might have been shaky because there had once been some tension between them, the Welshman suspecting the Yorkshireman of being out to upstage him. But once Evans was in the top job they got on well enough, and it was to Johnson, rather than to Collingridge, the other member of the troika at the head of the office, that Evans generally turned for advice on policy. Another change of some significance was that when Atkinson died in 1957 the job of secretary of the Historical Manuscripts Commission was taken by Ellis, whose director's post, to which he had been promoted in 1954, was allowed to lapse. At the time of his death Atkinson was no longer on the office's strength, having retired in 1954, but he had immediately been re-employed by the commission. The commission's work had expanded so greatly that its secretaryship could no longer be combined with an assistant keepership, and so Ellis was transferred to it full-time on loan. His former job as officer-in-charge of the Repair Department was then absorbed by Wardle as director of repository and technical services. The loss of a director's post was a severe blow to the assistant keepers, but a recovery was staged in 1959 when Ede was brought back from Ashridge to take charge of a newly-formed Modern Records Section to deal with the expansion of editorial work as a result of the 1958 act. Ede's post at Ashridge was then regraded as HEO in accordance with O and M's recommendations, which the assistant keepers must have thought a small price to pay, particularly as none of them was yearning for the rural life. The higher Civil Service positions were out of the reach of the staff of such a small department as the Public Record Office, but they could not complain of being ignored in the Honours List. Evans was knighted in 1959 and Johnson, Collingridge, Blakiston, Wardle and Hector all held the OBE. Of that number Blakiston was, perhaps, the best known outside the office, both as a writer of short stories and for his knowledge of nineteenth-century Italy.[25b] Among the executives Fox, Farmer and White held the MBE, and Fox was awarded the OBE shortly before his retirement in 1960, when he was succeeded by White who was later to receive the additional honour of the ISO.

If such awards were seen as sweeteners they were hardly necessary because staff relations generally were relatively peaceful throughout the 1950s. Even Whitleyism continued to operate tranquilly despite the Staff Side's assertion of a new-found independence in 1954 by revising its constitution, which had previously provided that its chairman should be an assistant keeper. The exact genesis of that particular provision can only be suspected, but at any rate it had been settled at a full meeting of the Departmental Whitley Council, under Jenkinson's chairmanship, in 1948. However, the resultant replacement of Atkinson as Staff Side chairman by White was indicative more of the growing influence of the executive grade in the department's affairs than the harbinger of a 'red dawn'. In 1956 the idea of a return to pre-war hours was finally abandoned. There was some heart-searching, particularly by the assistant keepers, but for most the change was more than offset by the introduction of a five-day week. In the same year the Suez debacle temporarily led to some friction amongst the staff, cutting across political loyalties, but passions abated when the hostilities proved short-lived.

The underlying reason for the relative contentment within the office was the belief that, once the Grigg Report had propelled it to the centre of the stage in relation to the enormous problem of dealing with departmental records, some expansion was inevitable. In fact, its pace was to prove too slow for a number of the younger executives who entered the office during the period. Their departure to more rewarding opportunities, inside and outside the Civil Service, was to leave a gap in the office's middle management in the years ahead, but immediately the prospects of the pre-war and early post-war entrants were a great deal more enticing than had once seemed likely. So far as the assistant keepers were concerned the office was waging a resolute rearguard action on their behalf, ensuring that if ground had to

---

25b. Blakiston died in 1984. His many activities included work on the archives of Eton College where he had been a king's scholar and editing Cyril Connolly's letters to him when they were young men under the title *A Romantic Friendship*. Writing Blakiston's obituary, Roger Ellis described him as 'the most widely-known archivist of his generation in England' (*Journal of the Society of Archivists*, VII, 560–562).

be yielded to the executives it would be recovered elsewhere. Similarly, the support grades could see greater opportunities in the offing. There was the further assurance that in July 1955, in answer to a parliamentary question, the recently re-elected Conservative government announced its intention to introduce changes in the arrangements for preserving the records of government departments in England and Wales along the lines recommended by the Grigg Committee. It was, however, stated that some of the recommendations, including that on the period after which various classes of records could be made available for public inspection, would require further examination. One of the matters mentioned at the Cabinet itself was the likely effect on relations with South Africa if papers concerning the South African War were opened; a further consideration was the traditional belief by Cabinet ministers that their discussions would remain confidential. At a later stage anxiety was to be expressed rather more about the release of sensitive papers of a personal nature, which might offend the susceptibilities of the public if opened. But, in general, the principle of a 50-year closure period was agreed, and such difficulties as were foreseen were met by giving power to the lord chancellor, the minister named responsible for the public records, to prescribe a longer or shorter period for particular records on the application of the authority primarily concerned. Jenkinson's fear that a division might be made between the legal and the departmental records – he really meant between the ancient and modern – was never contemplated.

The government committed itself to follow the Grigg recommendation that the ancient link between the master of the rolls and the records from which his title had sprung should not be severed. Accordingly, he was named *ex-officio* chairman of the Advisory Council on Public Records, the rest of whose members were to be appointed by the lord chancellor. He also retained responsibility for the records of the Chancery of England, encompassing most of those relating to the executive government of the country to the end of the sixteenth century, all of which were already in the office. In practice, therefore, his charge rested with such records as the continuing series of patent rolls, coronation rolls and warrants under the Great Seal. At one time there had been difficulties with the Central Criminal Court about its records, but in 1952 the law officers had thought them to be public and they were to be caught by the new act. Equally, the legal obstacles which had prevented the deposit in the office of probate records because of the powers of the president of the Probate Division of the High Court to determine where they should be deposited were to be overcome. The long-outstanding difficulty remained of Chancery masters' documents, many of which were held by the courts but which could not be seen by searchers even when known to be of considerable historical interest. That point was one of those which had been made to the Grigg Committee by Pugh, particularly in relation to the papers of Lieutenant-Colonel Gideon Gorrequer which contained a wealth of material concerning Napoleon's captivity on St Helena. Accordingly, the act was to provide that where private documents had remained in court custody for more than fifty years without being claimed they might be transferred to the Public Record Office, subject to the approval of the master of the rolls. Another large block of records which had escaped the Public Record Office net was that of the India Office. Their status as public records was not questioned, but the specialist nature of many of them led to the Public Record Office making clear its readiness to consent to the appointment of the India Office Library of the Commonwealth Relations Office as a place of deposit for its own material. Quite apart from space considerations Evans and his colleagues were well aware of the claim by the governments of India and Pakistan for the transfer of those records to them and were not anxious to be pushed into the front line and take the main fire arising from any dispute of that kind. The insertion in the act of a clause enabling the lord chancellor to appoint places outside the Public Record Office for the deposit of public records was, however, mainly intended for the appointment of county and borough record offices as the appropriate repositories for records of predominantly local interest, such as those of quarter sessions and hospitals. Some thought was also given to the anomalous position of the National Coal Board's records compared with those of other nationalised industries, but the board's wish for its records to remain public was to be conceded. Its isolation was lessened by another decision to bring under the act the records of the newly-created United Kingdom Atomic Energy Authority. To provide for organisations created in the future the lord chancellor was given power by order in council to declare further categories of records to be public. That provision was to be used in 1984 to secure the historical records of the British Railways Board, which had been under the office's umbrella since 1972, first at Porchester Road, Paddington, and then at Kew, despite the wrangling about their status at the time of nationalisation in 1947.

The bulk of the work connected with the preparation of the bill for parliamentary counsel rested with H. Boggis-Rolfe and J. Cartwright Sharp of the Lord Chancellor's Department, who received much assistance on technical points from Collingridge, with Denham doing the devilling. Although the first and second review of records recommended by Grigg is often wrongly referred to as 'the statutory review', the new act made no attempt to define the precise procedure to be followed. Instead it provided for suitable arrangements to be made administratively by laying upon those responsible for public records the duty of selecting and preserving them under the guidance of the keeper of public records, who was to be responsible for the co-ordination and supervision of such action, including the all-important provision that records selected for permanent preservation should be transferred not later than thirty years after their creation to the Public Record Office or to an approved place of deposit. Indeed, well in advance of the act becoming law, Collingridge and his inspecting officers were busily engaged in working over with departments existing accumulations of papers and planning the introduction of the new reviewing procedures. In most cases departmental record officers had already been appointed as recommended by the Grigg Committee, and in order to meet the needs of the transitional period the office was hard at work on the preparation of a provisional *Guide for Departmental Record Officers* which was eventually issued early in 1958. When the government first took the decision to adopt the Grigg recommendations the Treasury had thought that a high-powered committee might be formed to supervise the preliminary arrangements. It was, therefore, a tribute to the effectiveness of the way that the newly-formed Records Administration Division was tackling its task that the Treasury and the Lord Chancellor's Department should decide that no further oversight was needed.

The office's main regret was that the new legislation should sever its formal connection with the master of the rolls. There was no chance of altering that, although the decision attracted some criticism in record circles, typical of which was a letter to *The Times* from Charles Johnson on 12 July 1955 deploring the proposed break and testifying, from personal knowledge as a one-time inspecting officer, to the services of Lord Cozens-Hardy and Lord Swinfen, names not normally associated with the office of keeper of the records. On a rather different tack, Evans, like Palgrave when considering the 1838 act, saw the planned legislation as an opportunity to recover for the nation those of its records that had passed improperly out of its custody. He felt deeply about that issue because in 1956 it came to his notice that a fourteenth-century account book of the clerk of the king's works at Westminster, which had been purchased in 1829 by Sir Thomas Phillipps from Craven Ord, antiquary and collector and an officer in the King's Remembrancer's Office, was being offered for sale by a firm of bookdealers. The matter was of especial interest to the office because through Collingridge's membership of the Steering Committee on the official *History of the King's Works* it was known that the editor of that work, H. M. Colvin, wanted to consult the document as part of his research and there was a fear that it might go abroad. As it was being offered at what Evans considered the exorbitant price of £5,000 the question was referred to the law officers whose opinion left no hope of recovery through the courts. Evans was, therefore, pitchforked into awkward negotiation with the sellers, yet by persistence managed to knock them down to £3,500. At that figure the Pilgrim Trust agreed to find £1,800 and the Treasury, which Evans thought behaved handsomely, accepted responsibility for the rest. Although the office pressed very hard for a recovery clause in the proposed act, it was decided that it would be too controversial because it raised difficult questions about compensation and personal property rights. While the act was to give the keeper power to acquire records, the notion of buying back public property was distasteful to the office, and in any case the Treasury controlled the purse strings.

Once the main heads of the bill had been settled departmentally and cleared by the Cabinet Legislation Committee, it went to the full Cabinet in November 1957 where it was agreed to introduce it in the House of Lords. No final decision was taken about giving the public access to Cabinet records, but that was not an immediate issue because records of its proceedings did not begin to be regularly recorded until 1916, which meant that even if opened after 50 years they would not become available until 1967. As it happened, it was to prove academic because that year was to see another act, this time under a Labour government, reducing the normal access period to 30 years, which jettisoned one of the considerations upon which the Grigg Committee had made its recommendation for a 50-year period, namely the need to keep papers of officials closed within their lifetime so as not to impair the quality of 'unselfconsciousness'. In 1957, however, Johnston at the Treasury, who was superintending legislative progress, was less concerned about the outcome of individual clauses than with the fate of the bill itself. It was, therefore, a relief to him to know it was to be taken by the upper House where their lordships would, in his opinion, be far better employed in dealing with it than debating – it was in the aftermath of Suez – 'absurd motions (e.g. on refugees from Egypt)'.[26] On 28 November the bill was formally introduced and on 16 December it received its second reading. Opening the debate, Lord Kilmuir, the lord chancellor, said it was an important bill not only from the point of view of historians and research workers but also for good administration and economy. The magnitude of the problem was illustrated by the fact that at Chancery Lane and Ashridge the Public Record Office had 46½ miles of shelves full of records. It was estimated that there were already in the pipe-line a further 120 miles of records in government departments which might ultimately be transferred. The rest of his speech, amounting to just over twenty minutes, was devoted to explaining the various clauses of the act and the recommendation of the Grigg Committee upon which they were largely based. In doing so he acknowledged the debt the country owed to successive masters of the rolls, particularly Evershed, and welcomed the fact that despite the headship of the office passing to a minister of the crown the master of the rolls would continue to be linked to the office through his responsibility for the ancient records of Chancery and as *ex-officio* chairman of the Advisory Council, besides retaining his chairmanship of the Historical Manuscripts Commission.

In a short speech on behalf of the Labour opposition, Viscount Alexander of Hillsborough gave general support to the measure, admitting that the slight reservations he had once had about the change in the office's headship had been partly allayed by the lord chancellor's explanation. He was sorry that relative costs seemed to place a bar for the present on the extended use of microfilm and could not resist a brief allusion to the mystery surrounding the Zinoviev letter of 1924. The longest speech, taking just over half an hour, came from Evershed who had previously taken the precaution of warning the Treasury that he intended to use the occasion to make some criticism of the restrictions it had placed on economy grounds upon office

---

26. T 216/352: Johnston's minute of 21 October 1957.

staffing and the consequent bad effect upon record publication policy. But his attack was really quite mild and his main purpose was to record his consent to the alterations proposed. In particular, he emphasised that times had changed since 1396 when King Richard II had ordered that 'one strong horse, not aged', should be sent to the Chancellery to convey the rolls and records to John de Scarle, then master of the rolls. He approved fully of the choice of the lord chancellor as the responsible minister and hoped that the vexed question of records that had strayed from official custody might be committed at an early stage for consideration by the Advisory Council. He stressed the responsibility he felt to the 'loyal and skilful servants of the Record Office', saying that he would feel he had failed in his duty if their claims in the new organisation were liable in any way to be discounted or displaced. He quoted with approval Hancock's reference a year earlier to the historian taking all the glory, but that he would have been altogether hopeless without the work already done for him by the archivist. In conclusion, he hoped that future masters of the rolls would continue to render the country the kind of special service in connection with records that the title of the office and its history had associated with their predecessors.

Evershed was followed by the earl of Harrowby, who in a maiden speech spoke feelingly on the bill as one who had made use of the office. While praising its performance he objected to giving it powers to acquire records, other than public records, because he did not think it had the resources to cope with private collections. Although he was too polite to say so, his concern arose from the ill condition in which he had found the Colchester Papers which had been deposited in the office some time previously. For papers of that kind, which included those of Charles Abbot whose name will always be associated with the original Record Commission, Harrowby's remedy was for greater concentration upon binding, foliating and indexing. He was also apprehensive on the question of destruction and thought unwanted material might be offered to learned bodies. He wanted universities to be defined as suitable for appointment as places of deposit, and urged some superintendence of the records of nationalised industries. He regretted not having more time to study the provisions of the bill. There were only two more speeches, one from Lord Saltoun, who shared Harrowby's misgivings about destruction, and the other from Lord Silkin, who wound up for the opposition. Saltoun expressed some reservations about the control of records, which he thought ought to be independent of Parliament to avoid the possibility of political manipulation, a point upon which Alexander had also entered a caution. Silkin, looking at the attendance in the House, did not think anybody would imagine that such an important matter in the life of the country was under discussion. The bill not being party political, he took leave to differ from Alexander by giving his full support to the principle of ministerial control, while wondering whether the lord chancellor was really the right minister for the job. He hoped the matter might be reconsidered and given to one of the three ministers suggested by the Grigg Committee or even to the minister of education. It was a sound enough speech, but spoilt because he chose to complain about the office being shut in the mornings, having been misled by the notice at its entrance referring to the Museum hours of 1 p.m. to 4 p.m. That allowed Evershed to state that the search rooms were, in fact, open from 9.30 a.m. to 5.00 p.m. daily and gave the lord chancellor the opportunity, in his winding-up speech, to point out that during 1957 there were no fewer than 100,000 searches. Kilmuir's speech, which took little more than a quarter of an hour, also dealt courteously with the various points raised and included congratulations to Harrowby for his contribution with the suggestion that they might have a discussion before the committee stage. If that discussion took place it must have been satisfactory to Harrowby because he did not return to the charge when the bill went into committee on 30 January 1958. It left there the same day practically unscathed, apart from some minor amendments, including a government proposal to add the Coal Industry Social Welfare Organisation to the list of 'fringe' establishments whose records were declared to be public records. By a mistake probate records in the Isle of Man had been included in the original bill and that provision was dropped, but to enable non-public records, such as those of the Duchy of Lancaster, to be accepted a short sub-section was inserted. A proposal by Lord Clitheroe that the keeper of public records should be vice-chairman of the Advisory Council was not pressed when Kilmuir, Silkin and Evershed made plain their opposition. On the other hand, Kilmuir responded more kindly to Clitheroe's suggestion that, in authorising any destruction of public records in the Public Record Office or other place of deposit under the act, restraint should be exercised in adopting the alternative course of disposing of them in some other way, the point being taken that if they were not worth keeping in their essential context it seemed doubtful whether they were worth keeping at all. On 11 February the bill, as amended, was reported to the House and two more amendments were moved by the lord chancellor. One was no more than a matter of tidying-up, but the other remedied a defect in the original bill which would have prevented the deposit of records of quarter sessions and magistrates' and coroners' courts in the National Library of Wales. Thus amended, the bill was read for the third time on 13 February and having been agreed without further debate was sent to the Commons.

There it languished until 26 March when it was read a second time after a short debate, opened by Sir Harry Hylton-Foster, the solicitor general, who spoke along much the same lines as Kilmuir in the Lords; but in referring to the future role of the master of the rolls he brought out the fact that he would retain his statutory superintendence over manorial documents and instruments of apportionment under the Tithe Acts. From the Labour benches the main contributions came from Eric Fletcher (later Lord Fletcher) and Joseph Sparks, both of whom were known in the office search rooms. Fletcher, himself something of a medieval scholar, thought that few could fail to feel a thrill on visiting the office and mentioned Maitland's ecstasy on his dazzling discoveries there, which revealed, in his own words 'the most glorious store of material for legal history that has ever been gathered in one place'. But while giving the bill a general welcome he queried the choice of the lord chancellor as the responsible minister and deplored past Treasury parsimony, which he thought had created part of the problem the Grigg Committee had set out to solve. From the opposition front bench J. Chuter Ede voiced some doubts about the responsibilities of the local authorities, a point upon which a government supporter, Edward (later Sir Edward) Du Cann, also wanted some clarification as regards his own county, Somerset. The Ulster Unionist, Montgomery Hyde, another user of the office, in a wide-ranging speech thought it would be very sad and unfortunate if the post of keeper of the records were to be used to provide for a misfit elsewhere.

Between May and June the bill was discussed at three sittings of Standing Committee E before returning for its third reading on 4 July. In committee the Labour members had tried unsuccessfully to substitute the lord president for the lord chancellor as head of the office or even to leave the master of the rolls in that post or to delegate certain duties to him. Part of their case was that if a minister had to be chosen it was better that he should be more closely concerned with departmental records and more accountable to the House of Commons. They were similarly defeated when they divided the committee on amendments seeking to write into the bill the need to take into account historical and non-administrative criteria when selecting records for preservation, and for a statutory requirement upon the keeper to provide adequate accommodation for the inspection of the records by the public. That last point was again pressed by Sparks at the third reading, but was finally withdrawn after Hylton-Foster had given his assurance that the government was seized of the problem and would take account of what had been said about the inadequacy of the search-room accommodation at Chancery Lane to which Hyde had also drawn his attention. A number of minor amendments agreed in committee were accepted by the House without demur, but Emrys Hughes, with the support of a group of fellow Labour MPs, tried to reduce the closed period for public access from 50 to 40 years, mainly because of the continuing controversy about the existence and authenticity of the diaries of Sir Roger Casement which were said to have been circulated at the time of his trial and execution for treason in 1916. On being put to the vote, the amendment was defeated by 38 votes to 22, the low attendance being explained by the fact that the debate was on a Friday afternoon. The bill was then returned to the Lords where the various amendments were agreed to *en bloc* on 21 July. Two days later it received the royal assent, bearing the short title the Public Records Act 1958, with the further proviso that it should take effect from 1 January 1959.

In making the 120th and last *Report* of the deputy keepers of the records, Evans acknowledged the great services of successive masters of the rolls as keepers, singling out Langdale and Evershed for especial praise. Noting that early *Reports* often included extensive lists and calendars of records, he drew attention to the recent production of a large number of office lists in microfilm form, a project which had been sponsored by the Committee of Cultural

Experts of the Council of Europe. The growing links with overseas archivists was also mentioned, a development which a year earlier had seen the visit of Blakiston to Malaya to advise and report upon the establishment there of a central record office. Evans also mentioned the preparations being taken for implementing the new act, including the review of regulations for the public use of the records and of fees and charges. Preliminary enquiries were being made similarly of departments concerning any exceptions to the provision that their records should be available for public inspection 50 years after the date of their creation. Discussions were taking place at the same time with the Stationery Office about the protection of crown copyright in public records and in photographic copies made of them. Besides summarising the work of the various sections of the office, including the substantial progress being made by the Records Administration Division, Evans recorded the return to the lord mayor of London of a notable exemplar of the inspeximus and confirmation by letters patent of Edward I of the Magna Carta of 1225, dated 28 March 1300. That document had for long been preserved among records of the Exchequer, but it had been established that it was none other than the one reported as missing from the City of London's muniment room in 1869. It was thought probable that it had at one time been entrusted to T. D. Hardy for transcription and had been incorporated in the public records in error. Its restoration was, perhaps, more than offset by the presentation to the queen in the previous year from across the Atlantic of the headquarters records of Sir Guy Carleton, commander-in-chief in America 1782–1783. That gift from 'Colonial Williamsburg', received by her majesty from President Eisenhower in Washington, was presented by her to the master of the rolls for preservation with the public records. It comprised more than twenty thousand documents, bound in 107 volumes.

Although reference was made in the debate on the Public Records Bill to the office's accommodation difficulties, nothing was said by Evans on that in his final *Report*. There was merely a brief reference to the installation of a lift in the 'H' Block at the Chancery Lane end of the building in which the staff offices were mainly housed. Yet the office had not been entirely inactive and in May 1958 Wardle had drawn up proposals for an extension at Chancery Lane and the provision of an expandable repository outside London. Some three years earlier a new storage room for maps and plans had been brought into use. The possibility of acquiring the former *Daily Mirror* building to the north of the site had also been tentatively considered but not pursued. Neither was the Grigg Committee's suggestion that the Hayes and Ashridge sites might be expanded thought desirable. The need for more accommodation was undeniable, but it was evident that Evans saw his main task as mending fences with the Treasury and smoothing the way for the introduction of the new procedures soon to come into force under the provisions of the 1958 act. For its part the Treasury, while suspecting it may have been outsmarted by the wily Welshman, had always seen the new legislation as providing the opportunity to put a top administrator into the office. The removal of a chicken bone from Evans's lung had done wonders for his health, which had been troublesome for many years and he had done rather better than generally anticipated as deputy keeper. The Lord Chancellor's Department, therefore, thought it quite the best arrangement to appoint him keeper for a short while before retirement. In the wings, however, Brook, the head of the Civil Service, had already pencilled in the name Stephen Wilson, then with the Iron and Steel Holding and Realisation Agency, to take over the reins on Evans's departure. For Wilson that was to provide a stern challenge and to result in the office being dragged, not before time, fully into the twentieth century. But that is another story and one best told as part of the process of modernisation which was to lead to the purpose-built repository at Kew, with its computerised requisitioning system, and beyond.

Chapter XVI
Conclusion

From the 1830s onwards there was some – it came to seem scandalously little – editing and translating of Anglo-Saxon materials most notably by Thorpe and Kemble. There was the important though scrappy work of Sir Francis Palgrave. There was even some effort, negligently carried out, towards properly arranging and housing the national archives.

(J. W. Burrow, *A Liberal Descent* (Cambridge, 1981), 119)

The above is a stern judgment, although fair in view of the slow progress in bringing the records to order and the lack of resources made available to the service from the Exchequer, but it would be wrong to blame Langdale, Palgrave, Hardy and Cole, the men principally associated with the first Record Act, for negligence or lack of effort. The fact that Palgrave did not get on with the others was a disadvantage, but all four laboured tirelessly for the centralisation of the records in a specially-built repository. Langdale, 'The Father of the Records', is remembered as the principal figure behind the drive for a new building, and Hardy came to enjoy a reputation, by no means undeserved, as a record scholar and administrator. Yet in practical terms an equal, if not greater, contribution to the establishment of the Public Record Office was made by Palgrave and Cole. In the first instance it was Cole's lobbying and friendship with Charles Buller MP that was to lay the foundations for the 1838 act, which at the time he saw primarily as a measure of law reform to help poorer litigants. It was also Cole's determination that was to achieve so much in the way of the preliminary sortation and arrangement of the records. When Cole left for the 1851 Exhibition it was Palgrave who continued to press and scheme for the new building and saw it through to fruition. Palgrave never viewed the public records narrowly, and vigorously campaigned for the office's brief to be extended beyond the legal records to those of the departments of state. While he may have had his doubts about the centralisation of the records in one building – at least until he was sure of the deputy keepership – he interpreted the term 'public record' in the widest possible sense and the bill which he drafted in 1837 was more comprehensive in that respect than the one enacted in 1838. Ten years later, when the Treasury decided to merge the Public Record Office and the State Paper Office, Palgrave thought it would be likely to prove the greatest boon ever conceded by any government to historical literature. When the provisions of the 1838 act were extended to the records of government departments by the order in council of 1852 Palgrave saw the move as heralding the time when the Public Record Office might become 'the strong box of the Empire'.

Yet after his death Palgrave was soon forgotten except by the small band who remained loyal to his memory and who continued intermittently to feud with the more numerous Hardy men almost to the turn of the century. The younger better-educated clerks who entered the office from the 1860s knew Palgrave, if at all, only when in decline, and it was natural that they should look up to Hardy and accept the story of how he had been deprived of his inheritance in 1838. The result was that the contribution made by Palgrave to the development of the record service was depreciated and that made by Hardy was exaggerated. Indeed, there is a sense in which after the new building was begun in 1851 and the order in council was obtained in 1852 the office did little more than mark time and made no effort to translate into reality Palgrave's one-time vision of the Public Record Office as 'the Treasury not only of your Majesty's Legal Records, but of the Archives in the most extended use of the term'. A mere glance at the office's manpower figures between 1838 and 1958 (Appendix XIII) reveals how slow was the pace of expansion. By comparison the progress in the early years seems quite good, despite Palgrave's complaint in 1849 that record business was 'a matter about which no one cares except ourselves'. Nevertheless, many saw the 1838 act as a notable piece of reform and as early as 1844 Nicolas, whose attacks upon the Record Commission had first given rise to the agitation for change, had told Palgrave how gratified he was by the state of the record system which he thought nearly perfect. That was altogether too complacent an assessment, although compared with previous conditions, with high fees and the irregular attendance of the supposed custodians, there had been a remarkable improvement.

Under Langdale's successor, Romilly, literary fees were abolished, a cause long dear to Palgrave's heart, and the great series of *Calendars of State Papers* were launched. By that time Palgrave's health was beginning to falter, and T. D. Hardy was to move to the forefront, eventually taking over the deputy keepership in 1861 after the death of his old rival. The Rolls Series was Hardy's particular pet, an enterprise which he saw as the completion of the *Monumenta Historica Britannica* begun by Petrie, the former keeper at the Tower, to whom he owed so much and whom he revered. But Hardy could not have carried the undertaking through had he not enjoyed the whole-hearted support of Romilly, whose advocacy of its merits persuaded the Treasury to find the funds. Because the bulk of the editorial work was performed by external editors, it cannot be assumed that had the series not been begun the savings would have been diverted to other record purposes. What was certain was that as its consequence an academic tradition was to be firmly established within the office and links were to be forged with the universities. It thereby acquired its peculiar mystique as a part-governmental, part-scholarly institution. Hardy seemed at one time to be hoping that, with luck, he might emerge as keeper of the records of the entire United Kingdom, but that was not to be. It is now possible to understand in greater detail the intricacies of the Hardy years and to see for the first time the darker side of the picture, which was to be portrayed in an extreme form by the onslaught upon alleged office maladministration by Yeatman and others. While overstated, there was sufficient force in the arguments of the critics to make inevitable the choice of Lyte as deputy keeper in 1886

500

to rescue the office from the slackness into which it had slumped under William, the younger of the Hardy brothers, a kindly man but an ineffectual administrator. But it would be wrong to place the entire blame upon him because Sir Thomas, by staying in post too long and by taking far too much upon himself, had failed to provide sufficiently for a reserve of administrative talent which could be tapped when need arose. Kingston alone came closest to taking up the challenge, but his death robbed the office of a possible future deputy keeper, and in any case the feuding between individuals, stemming from the parochialism of the former branches and old quarrels, pointed to the need for a new broom.

In office mythology Lyte has always been a towering figure, and there can be no doubting his achievement in concentrating his resources upon the publication of the Chancery enrolments. He also managed to stem the wastage from the office of its younger clerks by obtaining for them in 1894 a greatly improved pay scale, with the abolition of the former distinction between junior and senior clerks. Lyte also pressed ahead with the completion of the building and successfully weathered the storm caused by the decision to pull down the Rolls Chapel. More than anyone else he was responsible for the foundation of the Museum. But by the time of its establishment he was no longer looking for fresh fields to conquer, and his very position of eminence meant that few sought to question his authority. The Welsh alone had no such inhibitions and were largely instrumental in the appointment of the Royal Commission on Public Records in 1910. Hall and some of the younger men were uneasily aware that the office was not operating as it ought, and misgivings were beginning to be felt about the work of the inspecting officers under the 1877 act. But the commission had no departmental backing and by drawing attention to the neglect of the port books further alienated Lyte who had never reconciled himself to its appointment. On many minor matters the commission's often sensible proposals were either anticipated or adopted, but its major recommendation for the replacement of the master of the rolls by a board of administration was quietly pigeon-holed. In essence, the commission did no more than repeat the proposal of the 1836 Select Committee on the Record Commission, and although paying tribute to his services it was clearly Lyte it had in its sights.

Some have argued that the act of 1838 stood up to the test of the Royal Commission, but it would be truer to say that, having highlighted its imperfections, the commission failed to produce any practical proposals to put in its place. Hall, its secretary, had many admirable qualities, but clarity of thought was not one of them, and Maitland, who thought him the most unselfish of men, was surely right when he referred to 'poor Hall' having 'a curious fluffy mind'.[1] The commandeering of disused prison accommodation

---

1. Maitland to Lane Poole, 7 September 1898: *The Letters of Frederic William Maitland*, ed. C. H. S. Fifoot (Selden Society, 1965), 225.

after the First World War, first at Cambridge and then at Canterbury, was the official response to the problems posed by the accumulations of records in departments. The office's preferred solution was expansion on the Chancery Lane site, but much of the inter-war period was clouded by economic depression and the money for new building could not be found. In retrospect, perhaps that was no bad thing because the Chancery Lane repository, with its 140 cell-like, fireproof strong rooms, spread over four floors, and with its search rooms at one end of the building, was ill designed to cope with the massive increase in productions which gathered pace from the 1960s. Neither Lyte's successor, Stamp, nor Flower was of the stuff of which reformers were made. Nevertheless, Stamp was conscious of the need for a new act if the problem of departmental records was to be tackled, and he displayed a creditable toughness in seeking to protect the interests of searchers when the question of dealing with Cabinet papers came up for discussion in the 1930s. Most of Flower's term as deputy keeper coincided with the Second World War, when activities were reduced to a minimum and about half of the office's contents were dispersed throughout the country. But the Chancery Lane building, under constant threat of aerial bombardment, was manned day and night, and Flower was at its head throughout the blitz of 1940 to 1941 and the doodlebug and rocket attacks in 1944. For much of the war he also took responsibility for the direction of the Institute of Historical Research. When peace came in 1945 he was a tired man and quite ready to hand over two years later to Jenkinson, who had never disguised his impatience to step into his shoes. As an archivist Jenkinson was supreme, but his record as deputy keeper was spoilt by his constant battling with the Treasury and his unwillingness to accept the changing requirements of the post-war world. Despite his brave front, it cannot be doubted that his departure in 1954 owed much to his recognition that whoever was to head the new department envisaged by the Grigg Committee it was not to be him. It was his zeal that had put the office on the map, but the effect, so far as the Treasury was concerned, was to identify it as hostile territory.

It has been said that the Grigg Committee's report somewhat dented Public Record Office morale, but that was true only of the assistant keepers, and by no means all of them. The executive and clerical grades welcomed it unreservedly, and the same was true of the support grades. Jenkinson's belief that in order to deal with modern records it was necessary to have a mastery of those of the middle ages as well was no longer tenable and today seems quite ridiculous. Obviously, Latin and French and palaeographic skills remain essential to deal with the older records, but equally an understanding of the complexities of twentieth-century public administration and a lively appreciation of contemporary history are the vital requirements necessary to cope with questions of policy affecting the selection, classification and disposal of modern records. Since 1958 the growth in machine-readable records, and the exploitation of computer techniques in records management and in making the office's contents accessible to the public, also demand qualifications of a kind wholly different from those required when, apart from editorial work, so much revolved around the examination by the assistant keepers of hand-made copies of the older records. The office was slow to come to terms with the changing environment in which it was operating. Had it responded more flexibly, an outside enquiry, such as that of the Grigg Committee, might not have been necessary. In part, an inadequate understanding by the office of its own development gave to its origins a mystical quality which they never possessed. It is a strange paradox that the very institution responsible for the national memory should have drawn so imperfectly upon its own. Yet it suited the defenders of the *status quo*, such as Jenkinson, to stand by the 1838 act, and until Grigg no effective challenge was mounted to the unspoken assumption that the formal and informal arrangements of the nineteenth century remained adequate and had been carefully designed. Nevertheless, the Royal Commission of 1910 did point out the absurdities of the order in council of 1852 under the act's provisions, and these pages have set out the manoeuvrings which led to the State Paper Office being swallowed up by the Public Record Office despite Foreign Office and Home Office disquiet. Indeed, the notion, which came to be accepted, that as soon as the Public Record Office came into existence departments were clambering to send documents to it is quite fanciful. Even in the much quoted case of the Admiralty records in 1841 the initiative came from the Public Record Office when the documents were discovered lying in a neglected state at Deptford. The key to the subsequent organisation was when Palgrave persuaded the Treasury to send its records to the Public Record Office rather than the State Paper Office. Trevelyan at the Treasury was a great centraliser and consequently sympathetic to the concept of a single authority, but had the State Paper Office resisted more successfully it might have been the pivot of future developments rather than the Public Record Office.

During the Hardy regimes the departmental records were not highly prized, and only when Hall took over the Government Search Room were efforts begun to get them into better order. Between the wars Buckland was the office's only recognised modernist. Collingridge was to become the expert in the late 1940s, while continuing to spend some of his time in calendaring sixteenth-century patent rolls. Just as in the war years some government agencies in the United States began to operate record centres for their non-current papers, the office, through Jenkinson, launched its Limbo scheme to the same intent. But the system whereby departments were at liberty to transfer or not to transfer their records as they pleased made a mockery of a coherent programme of records management, particularly as no regular arrangements existed for the processing of selected material. In the absence of fresh thinking on the office's part the appointment of the Grigg Committee came not a moment too soon. Its exposure of the nonsensical nature of much of the 1877 scheduling system was timely, and its proposals for a two-stage reviewing procedure thoroughly practical. The principle of administrative usefulness as the main test at first review with historical criteria being taken into account at the second is easily understood and still seems compelling. In so far as it has been criticised, notably by the Committee on Public Records in 1981, it has been its implementation rather than its philosophy which has been attacked. Only when the records of the late 1950s, when the scheme started, begin to come on stream in sufficient quantities will it be possible to judge the adequacy of the new selection processes. It may well be that too much, rather than too little, will be found to have survived. Should that prove the case, the 1958 act enables disposal of transferred material to take place. It must be remembered that all selection involves some distortion and the written record is only one facet of the original event. A mumbled 'yes' heard on a tape recording, accompanied by a guilty expression when seen on a video, means infinitely more than the same response as part of a trial transcript. No doubt that is an extreme example, but it would be wrong to regard the written record as more than a contribution to a better understanding of the past. For some it may sound heretical, but there is, perhaps, something to be said for archivists to stand at one remove from the registrars and record managers. Although nothing should be done during the working and intermediate stages of the lives of records worth keeping which might impede their eventual preservation, the intrusion of the archivist too soon or too obviously can increase the risk of artificiality and distortion.

The Grigg Committee referred to the dangers that might result if an official knew that his papers were to be made available during his lifetime, arguing that his susceptibilities were no less important than the desire of the historian to obtain the material as soon as possible. That argument can perhaps be overstated: it must surely be a rare bird who thinks much beyond the task in hand, let alone dwells on the assumed prejudices of posterity. Moreover, the modern policy process, with many decisions taken by committee and wide consultation with outside interests, tends to make superfluous many of the fears which might at one time have been felt by individual civil servants. Freedom-of-information legislation could have some effect upon official behaviour in that respect, but it must be hoped that, should records thereby be made available to individuals, that should not be allowed to influence the question of permanent preservation. In such matters the democrat within the archivist is occasionally at odds with the professional. The latter, haunted by the chilling spectre of Winston Smith in Orwell's *1984* rewriting history in the Records Department of the Ministry of Truth, can never forget that the Public Records Acts were introduced to secure the archives not just for the observers of the contemporary scene, but for countless future generations. The fears expressed during the Lords debate on the Public Records Bill of 1958 about possible political interference ought never to be forgotten, and in that respect the choice of the lord chancellor as ministerial head of the office has much to be said for it.

The office's record in looking after its users has been good, although conditions for nineteenth-century readers were tolerable only by comparison with the high fees and makeshift facilities of the pre-1838 era. The twentieth century saw a gradual improvement, but it was only after the Second World War that the first signs appeared of the dramatic jump in productions and attendances which were to be a feature of the 1960s and 1970s. That vast leap, which by 1986 resulted in 123,000 readers consulting some three-quarters of a million documents in the reading rooms at Kew, Portugal Street and Chancery Lane, arose mainly from the expansion of higher education in the 1960s and the greater popularity of family history as a leisure pursuit rather than from any particular effort by the office itself to make its contents known to a wider public. The gradual unfolding of more material each year and the reduction from 50 to 30 years of the normal access period also played their part.

It would be wrong to conclude, either from the office's low public profile or from the Treasury investigations into its organisation during the 1950s, that it operated other than effectively so far as most of its users were concerned. It is true that it clung for too long to outmoded working methods and that its assistant keepers were engaged for far too much of their time upon duties which ought to have been carried out at a less exalted level. Steps to remedy those defects began under Evans and gathered momentum thereafter, but it is doubtful whether the searcher using the reading rooms or the enquirer writing to the office for information noticed any dramatic changes, and by general consent the office enjoyed an enviable place in public esteem. Even the Grigg Committee paid tribute to its work for readers, praising its assistant keepers for their extensive knowledge and breadth of understanding of the needs of research students.

The Treasury deserves credit for the action it took in the 1950s to have the management of the departmental records placed upon a more workmanlike footing. The Grigg Committee provided the blue-print, but had its work not been sustained by the Treasury and its recommendations fully supported its efforts would have been of little avail. But just as the nineteenth-century Treasury often displayed a woeful ignorance of record realities, as in its lack of understanding of the enduring nature of the problem facing those charged with the administration of the 1877 act, its twentieth-century successors also revealed, on occasions, a lamentable failure to appreciate the extent to which the Public Record Office's hands were tied by its inadequate accommodation and the limited resources at its disposal. For instance, in an internal Treasury minute to Playfair, when the establishment of the Grigg Committee was being considered at the end of 1951, Johnston stated in all seriousness that 'the Public Record Office have shown no interest in local authority records or in industrial or commercial records. They refuse even to advise about the keeping of records for which they have no statutory responsibility'.[2] Had the office done so in any formal manner the outcry from its Treasury paymasters can be imagined, but in fact it had always been fully supportive

---

2. T 222/538: Johnston to Playfair, 28 December 1951.

of the British Records Association, which existed for that purpose, and many instances of unofficial assistance to local record offices could be quoted.[3] Johnston was also surely on flimsy ground, and most unfair to Greene, when he said that at the time of the repulse of the Public Record Office claim for the records of the British Transport Commission its general policy could not be seen and it was unclear over what fields it thought its writ ought to run. In one sense the problem lay in the difficulty of defining 'public records', but the underlying explanation was that by the early 1950s the Public Record Office had so antagonised the Treasury that any stick was good enough for beating it. On the question of the records of the nationalised industries, the opportunity to rationalise the position was lost at the time of the 1958 act, but any harmful consequences may prove to have been short-lived as a result of the new situation created by the policy of privatisation after 1979 and the decision of the British Railways Board to seek a formal liaison with the office.

What is a matter for rejoicing is that despite Jenkinson's forebodings no attempt was made in the aftermath of the Grigg Report to make a distinction between the legal and the departmental records. Both kinds of records need to be consulted together, particularly because the growth in government activity during the present century has led to increasing recourse to the courts by individuals or groups seeking protection against unlawful use by public authorities of their powers or to expose their failure to fulfil their statutory obligations.[4] If recurring themes can be seen in this History perhaps the most persistent, if not the most edifying, is the pressure of the staff at all levels for more pay. Of all the changes in that area the gradual improvement in the remuneration and status of the craftsmen is probably the most pleasing. The increased flexibility given to office manning as a result of the more open grading structures of the late twentieth-century Civil Service is also to be welcomed. Many examples could be given to illustrate that point. No doubt later chroniclers will deal with the outstanding rise of Alfred Mabbs from clerical officer to keeper and the corresponding openness of the public service as a whole which allowed the appointment to the same post of Stephen Wilson from the Iron and Steel Holding and Realisation Agency in 1960 and that of Professor Geoffrey Martin from the University of Leicester in 1982.

Above all else, accommodation difficulties have always been present to plague the minds of successive deputy keepers. Almost at the end of the period covered by this History, Evans was arguing the case for an expansion of the Chancery Lane site with the Ministry of Works. He wanted a new block at the Fetter Lane end of the building to house office staff and to

---

3. For example, the inspection and report by Evans on the county record offices at Shrewsbury and Truro in 1946 and 1951 respectively: PRO 1/775 and PRO 1/1217.

4. For details concerning this point see John Cantwell, 'The Public Record Office: The Legal and Departmental Records', *The Journal of Legal History*, II (1981), 227–237.

provide search-room, library and technical facilities; flats for one or two resident officers were also requested. Longer term, Evans urged the building of a second repository, outside London but easily accessible to it, preferably to the north or north west. Nothing came of his endeavours or of the scheme for a search room on the roof of the Chancery Lane building, proposed by Keeper Wilson in the early 1960s. Consequently various expedients, such as the removal of the Records Administration Division to Hanover Square in the West End between 1975 and 1977 and the provision of repository, conservation and search-room accommodation from 1968 in the Land Registry building in Portugal Street, had to be adopted. It was fortunate that by the time Ashridge was vacated in 1980 the office had been in occupation of its new purpose-built repository at Kew since 1977. The part played by Lionel Bell, as head of the Research and Planning Unit, in its appearance must await another occasion, as must the industrial troubles which accompanied the transfer of the staff to it and which created so much worry for Keeper Ede and for Gavin, who had the misfortune to be establishment officer at the time. In the nature of things, the housing of the public records, whatever form they may take in the future, will always be at the centre of the office's preoccupations. The time may well come when Hardy's 'searcher at a distance' will be able to view, at the very least, the more popular classes on his own visual display unit, possibly by direct transmission, without the need to order photocopies or make a personal visit. The danger for the Public Record Office is that the charm of the past, to which it is inevitably exposed, may result in an undue attachment to traditional practices as well as a reluctance to explore new technologies. Those temptations must be resisted if the office is to adapt to changes as they occur in the social and economic environment in which it has to operate. The act of 1958 has already been on the statute book for 30 years and seems as secure as that of 1838 did in 1868. Time alone will tell whether it proves as long lasting.

List of Appendixes

Appendix I

Summary of Public Records Bills 1837–1838

	(1) Buller (Cole) Bill February 1837	(2) Palgrave Bill May 1837	(3) Bethune Bill 1837–1838
Central Authority	General Record Office	High Court of Chancery	Public Record Office
Custodian of the Records	Keeper general to be appointed by the crown and to have custody of records specified below from the passing of the act	Master of the rolls to have custody of records in 'A' and 'B' below and to have responsibility for those in 'C' as specified	Master of the rolls to have custody of all records deposited in the PRO when established
Staff	Assistant record keepers, clerks, workmen, messengers and officers, as deemed necessary, appointed by the keeper general, subject to Treasury consent	Assistant record keepers and a secretary of records to be appointed by the master of the rolls, with the proviso that the keepers of the record offices at the Tower of London, Rolls Chapel and Chapter House, Westminster, should be the first assistant record keepers under the act. Master of the rolls to appoint senior clerks, junior clerks, workmen and assistants subject to Treasury direction as to	Keeper of the records to be appointed by the master of the rolls with crown approval. Treasury to appoint assistant record keepers and such other officers, clerks and servants as necessary

	(1)	(2)	(3)
Staff – *contd*		numbers employed but reserving places for persons already employed in such capacity in the three record offices previously named	
General repository	To be provided in London or Westminster	To be provided in London or Westminster upon the Rolls Estate, or elsewhere, if thought by the Treasury fitting and expedient, and advantageous for the public service. Provision to be made for the dwelling and accommodation of such persons as may be resident officers and also for the operations of cleaning, binding and repairing	As in (1).
Salaries	Payable out of Consolidated Fund. Keeper general's salary to be fixed by the Treasury but not to exceed sum determined	Payable out of Chancery Suitors' Fund. Salaries of assistant keepers and secretary of records to be fixed by the	Payable out of Consolidated Fund. Keeper's salary to be fixed by the Treasury but not to exceed sum determined by

512

	(1)	**(2)**	**(3)**
Salaries – *contd*	by Parliament. Other salaries to be fixed by the Treasury in fit proportion	Treasury but not to exceed sum determined by Parliament. Other salaries to be fixed by the Treasury annually upon the report of the master of the rolls	Parliament. Other salaries to be fixed in fit proportion according to duties they may have to perform
Records to be placed in official custody	A. Records of the age of 20 years in: Tower of London Record Office Chapter House of Westminster Record Office Rolls Chapel Record Office Petty Bag Office Offices in the custody of the king's remembrancer of the Exchequer or of any other officer of the Exchequer, Augmentation Office, First Fruits and Tenths Office and Office of the Auditor of the Land Revenues of England and Wales Office of the Pells of the Exchequer in the custody of	A. Records in: Tower of London R. O. Rolls Chapel R. O. Chapter House R. O. Crown Office in Chancery Hanaper Office Petty Bag Office Chancery Register Office Chancery Report Office Six Clerks' Office Chancery Inrolment Office Examiners' Office Clerk of the Dispensations and Faculties Office King's Remembrancer's Office Lord Treasurer's Remembrancer's Office Augmentation Office Chirographer's Office King's Silver Office Pells Office Pipe Office B. Records of the	As in (1) but subject to the fitness of the PRO to receive them and to those in 'A' being 50 years of age

	(1)	(2)	(3)
Records to be placed in official custody – *contd*	HM comptroller general of the Exchequer	Great Sessions of Wales and County Palatine of Chester	
	Courts of Chancery, Exchequer, King's Bench and Common Pleas	C. Records in the following may be transferred to one or more of the three record offices mentioned in 'A' above or to the General Record Office when provided, on the order of the master of the rolls, with the approbation of the Treasury and with the consent of the judges or other functionaries named. In the case of court records judges to retain their present authority after removal:	
	B. Records of the lately abolished courts of the Principality of Wales and the Palatinate of Chester	Parliament Office (lord chancellor after taking directions of the House)	
		Paper Office of the House of Commons (the speaker after taking directions of the House)	
		State Paper Office (home secretary)	
		Privy Council Office	

	(1)	(2)	(3)
Records to be placed in official custody – *contd*		(lord president)	
		Privy Seal Office (lord keeper)	
		Privy Signet (secretaries of state, or any one of them)	
		Board of Green Cloth (lord chamberlain)	
		Land Revenue Office (commissioners)	
		Crown Office, Custos Brevium and Treasury of the King's Bench (justices or the chief and any two)	
		Custos Brevium and Treasury of the Common Pleas (justices or any two)	
		Clerk of the pleas of the Exchequer, auditor of Exchequer (barons or the chief and any two)	
		Clerks of assize in the several circuits (justices of the King's Bench etc.)	
		Admiralty, Appeal and Delegates (lords commissioners of the Admiralty or any three)	

	(1)	(2)	(3)
Power to remove records	Granted to the keeper general subject, as regards accruals, to the consent of the chief judge concerned; if consent not given, the issue to be referred to the Treasury for determination	Granted to the master of the rolls subject to the assent of the judges or other functionaries in respect of those in 'C' above	Accruing records to be removed into the PRO on the certificate of the chief judges of the Courts of Chancery, Exchequer, King's Bench and Common Pleas, when 50 years old, or sooner if thought fit, but the judges able to delay transmissions where thought expedient for the purposes of justice
Records as evidence	No removal under the act to affect the records as evidence	On provision of General Record Office, the master of the rolls to make rules and orders for the authentication of office copies which could then be received in legal evidence	Copies of records made and certified by two assistant record keepers and countersigned by the master of the rolls (or keeper of the records) could be given in evidence, as also could calendars printed by his direction
Public access and fees	To be regulated by the keeper general and the judges. No fees to be levied except for	Subject to rules, orders and regulations made by the master of the rolls with the	To be regulated by the master of the rolls with power to fix fees if thought proper. All

	(1)	(2)	(3)
Public access and fees – *contd*	making of office copies	approval of the Treasury and, as regards court records in 'C', the further assent of the judges	rules to be laid before Parliament
Stamping of records	All records to bear official stamp	As in (1)	No provision
Annual reports	To be made to Parliament by the keeper general	To be made to Parliament but not specified by whom	To be made by the keeper of records, approved and signed by the master of the rolls and laid before Parliament
Disposal of records	Judges to have power to destroy 'worthless' records on application from the keeper general	Master of the rolls to destroy 'useless' records with approval of the Treasury and assent of the judges	No provision
Felony to certify false copies of records	No provision	Erasure or falsification of office copies or counterfeiting the authentication to be a felony	Anyone belonging to or employed in the Public Record Office certifying a copy knowing it to be false to be guilty of a felony
Publication and preservation of records	Keeper general to make such rules and regulations as deemed necessary for preservation, arrangement	Indexing, calendaring, arranging, cleaning, binding and repairing to be regulated by the	Master of the rolls empowered to make orders for the preservation and arrangement of

	(1)	(2)	(3)
Publication and preservation of records – *contd*	and binding, and for the compilation of calendars, catalogues and indexes. Judges to retain their powers of superintendence	master of the rolls, with Treasury approval	records to be deposited in the PRO and for making calendars, catalogues and indexes of them both before and after their delivery into his custody. Such records to be printed as seem to the master of the rolls needful subject to an estimate of cost being laid before Parliament
Private catalogues	Keeper general to have power to purchase with Treasury consent	Clause to empower purchase of indexes	Master of the rolls empowered to purchase for PRO use any private calendar, catalogue or index to the public records subject to Treasury consent. Any calendar, catalogue or index compiled, continued or copied after the passing of the act by any officer of the PRO to be vested in the crown

	(1)	**(2)**	**(3)**
Compensation	Persons whose office, profits or emoluments may be affected to deliver a statement to the keeper general who shall report and give an opinion thereon to the Treasury who shall have power to award such compensation as it deems fit. Account to be taken of such compensation on appointment to any other public office	Treasury to award full and adequate compensation to persons whose offices may be extinguished or whose offices, profits or emoluments may be diminished or affected. Any compensation, if made by annuity, to be set against any subsequent payment on appointment to a public office	Any officers sustaining losses as a result of the act may submit a statement to the master of the rolls or the keeper of the records who shall report and give an opinion thereon for determination by the Treasury. Account to be taken of such compensation in any subsequent appointment in the PRO or elsewhere in crown service
Definition of public records	None, but in the 'General Repository' clause it is stated 'and such General Record Office shall, for all purposes, be the legal Repository of all records, rolls, books, papers and documents at any time therein deposited'	All writs, rolls, enrolments and all other proceedings in or before any civil, criminal, ecclesiastical or other court of justice, whether subsisting, extinct or dissolved. Rolls, bills, journals, petitions and all other proceedings in or before the High Court of	As in (1) but 'Public Record Office' instead of General Record Office

	(1)	(2)	(3)
Definition of public records – *contd*		Parliament or either House thereof, or any committee of either House. Books, minutes, or other documents or proceedings of his majesty's most honourable Privy Council, or any committee thereof or of any public board or commission or belonging to the offices of his majesty's principal secretary of state. Official letters or memorials or other documents relating to public or official business addressed to any secretary of state or to any public board or commission, or to any member or officer thereof in his official capacity. Rolls, books and accounts of	

(1)	(2)	(3)
Definition of public records – *contd*	revenue and expenditure of the crown in all its branches and also all charters, rolls, deeds, books, papers and muniments, now deposited in the several repositories named in the schedules to this bill or which according to the course and order of business in such repositories may have been removed therefrom, or which ought to be, or ought to have been deposited therein	

Appendix II

Memoranda of Sir Francis Palgrave Concerning the Management of the Records

(i) 14 June 1838[1]

I   No small proportion of the defects pointed out (perhaps with some exaggeration) in the management of the public Record Offices, have arisen from the peculiar character of these Repositories, their management being more complicated in its elements than may at first appear.

It must also be recollected that in some of these offices the Principals have treated them as Sinecures, and that in others they have had no other remuneration except that arising from fees. The abolition of the right of the Keepers to the fees, and the consequent payment of them into a general fee fund (subject to the observation XIII) is an indispensable measure of amendment – and that in any attempts to introduce a better system direct *censure* upon the old one should be avoided and that to those Individuals especially those in the *inferior Departments* who have so long continued under the old defective management some degree of consideration is due.

II   A Repository of Records is in the first place a *public Office*, and a department of the general administration of the Law. It deals with the public as Suitors, Clients, or Customers in matters of business. And the Officers as practical Men of Business must perform those duties which are common to all Departments where fees are paid by the Applicant or Suitor as a price for the document which he obtains or sues out, or for the information or services which he receives.

III   A Record Repository is also a *public Library* to which the public are to be permitted to resort under proper restrictions for Literary purposes and without payment of fees. In this branch of duty, the Officer must act as Librarian, he must be somewhat more than a mere Man of business, he must possess the qualifications which may enable him to assist the literary Enquirer.

IV   A Record Repository ought to be *a Workshop*. The several operations of cleaning, stitching, repairing and binding Records should be all carried on within its Walls and, amongst its Officers, there should be a practical Man fully qualified to inspect and direct all the mechanical operations which the Records require: and to be responsible for the due performance of such operations and the safety of the Records whilst under the hands of the Workman as well as for the economy of the expenditure.

---

1. PRO 36/53

V   Record employment in its higher branches is a *Profession* and requiring previous preparation and long practice and experience. Some degree of legal knowledge (differing according to the several grades) is indispensible; a sufficient proficiency in the mediaeval Latin Language, of the old French, of the character and handwriting of Records can only be acquired by continued study and application.

        Much *collateral* information upon matters of History is also highly desirable and unless the employment be taken up and pursued not casually or as a make shift, but steadily and permanently, it will be difficult to find Persons properly qualified.

VI   Lastly – Record employment includes in it a *Trade* for although the repairing of Records is a branch of Bookbinding still, to do the thing well, it requires much care and practice.

VII   Supposing the preceding views to be accurate, it is obvious that it is exceedingly important to effect a proper division of labour amongst the clerks and other persons composing the Record establishment under the Principal so as to use each of your Tools for its proper Work. If you place a Man of literary acquirements in a situation where his time is constantly broken up by attending to the *Customers* of the Office; if you employ a Clerk who is qualified to calendar Records upon the task of paging and numbering them it is obvious that you are frittering away your power. A perfect adaptation of the talent of each Individual to the *whole* of his branch of employment may not be practicable, but at all events an approximation should be made. And the organisation of the Staff or Establishment of a general Record Office (subject however to modification upon certain points) should I think be something like the following Scheme.

VIII   Assuming that the general custody and superintendance of the Records will be vested in the Master of the Rolls and exercised by a Keeper or Keepers responsible to him and that such Keeper or Keepers will be required personally to attend to the duties of the office and to direct all the business and operations thereof I would venture to suggest that the Office be composed of three Departments *viz* (1) 'The Search Department' (2) 'The Library Department' and (3) 'The Binding Department'. Not that the 'Search Department' and the 'Library Department' should be separated by Walls and Partitions, for the more you multiply Rooms and Apartments the more you multiply the difficulties of control and inspection but that they should be distinguished in management (e.g. that the 'Search Department' should be on the right hand side and the 'Library Department' on the left hand side of the Room).

        The establishment or staff of these three Departments under the Chief Keeper or Keepers to be as follows.

IX   Search Department.

One Chief Clerk to attend to all the Suitors or Customers of the Office, Examine Office Copies, Receive fees, Keep the Office Accounts, to keep the Office Keys to open and shut the Office and to be responsible to the principals for the custody of the Records and particularly that no injury is done to them by persons making searches and that all *are put away before the Office is closed*, a piece of *tidiness* which it is very difficult to induce clerks to observe – to superintend the arrangement and marking [*sic*] of the Calendars of the modern (under this term I include all records after the abolition of Court hand) or current Records; and, if he has any spare time, to make Office Copies.

Second Clerk. To perform the duties of the Chief Clerk in case of illness or absence, to make and examine Office Copies, to make fair Copies of Reports, to copy and enter official Letters, his surplus time to be employed upon the arrangement and Calendars of modern Records.

And a sufficient number of Junior Clerks.

X   Library Department.

One Chief clerk.

To receive persons consulting the Records for Literary purposes, to be answerable for the putting away of the Records etc. etc. consulted by them and to be employed generally upon the calendaring and arrangement of the more *antient* i.e. those *before* the abolition of Court hand – Records or Manuscripts for which he would probably have a large proportion of time, as his office duties would be less onerous than those of the Chief Search Clerk.

Second and Junior Clerks as in the 'Search Department'.

XI   Binding Department.

One Superintendent, to receive such Records as are selected for binding or repairing, to keep a Book specifying the nature, description or title of the Record, the dates when received by him and when returned. To direct and inspect all the operations of the Workmen, to act as Store Keeper delivering out not only the Articles required for his own Department, but also the Stationary required for the Search and Library Departments so as to prevent waste, to pay the Workmen their Wages and to keep the Accounts thereof, but I am of opinion that it will be of the greatest importance to connect this Department with Her Majesty's Stationary Office that they should have the direction of all Contracts, and that the Accounts of the Superintendent should be examined by their Controller.

An assistant, and a competent number of Workmen, some of whom should be always at the service of the other Departments when required to assist in dusting or removing Records.

XII   The great secret in the management of Clerks is to give them such a stimulus to Industry as that, in Ordinary cases, the acting principal may have rather to lead than to drive, and that they may in some degree identify their Interests with those of the Concern – In well managed private Concerns – e.g. a good Solicitor's Office or a respectable Bank – this is effected, to a considerable extent, by the wish which the Clerks have to learn the business for the purpose at some future period of Establishing themselves in the same or some similar line; or by the power which the Principal possesses of rewarding them by increase of Salary – In those Public Offices whose main business consists in dealing with the public (e.g. the Custom House) the *pressure from without* goes a long way in Securing attention and activity but in those Public Departments where if I may use the expression the business is done in the back shop, there is always the greatest difficulty in enforcing due diligence without exerting such a degree of control as is equally irksome to both parties and which, after all, is but a poor substitute for the energy excited by cheerfulness and goodwill.

XIII In such Employments as these of Calendering or Indexing Records no kind of inspection can ensure *vigorous* application – you never can prevent the clerk from dawdling over his Work – because, except in the *single* case of mere *dry transcription* you never can calculate the time in which he is really able to perform the Task and after having tried every mode, I feel convinced that a *mixed remuneration* arising partly from Salary and partly from task work e.g. so much for every Roll indorsed ticketed and arranged, so much for every dozen Documents abstracted in the Calendar etc. is the best possible plan and the one which insures the greatest return for the Public Money.

And the search clerks should, in like manner receive a small proportion of the fees and copy money, which should be specified in the table hung up in the office – in the Bank of England the junior clerks have an allowance called *early money*, which they forfeit for the *whole year*, if *once* absent in the course of the year, after the clock has struck – when the small notes were issued, they had so much per hundred (in addition to their salaries) according to the quantity signed.

If you pay *wholly* by task work you tempt the party to haste and sloveliness – if you pay *wholly* by time, you buy the Clerk's time, and as it thus becomes Your Property and not his, he then becomes constantly tempted to waste it like Your Paper and Pens but by a due Combination of both, You will equally secure Economy and diligence – of course the adaptation of this principle requires constant attention on the part of the Principal nor is it universally applicable and there must be a boundary beyond which it ought not to pass; but if adopted, all the details can be arranged without difficulty and they would also be constantly submitted to the approbation of the Master of the Rolls who might vary or regulate them as he may think fit.

XIV A graduated increase of Salary is also indispensible and as far as possible all promotions should take place according to Seniority and no Stranger ever put above the head of an Office Clerk without the strongest reason. Perhaps in these and many other respects the Chancery Register Office will afford the best model. Everything must be done to make the Clerks feel that if they do not misconduct themselves they are settled in their Employment – I used to Article the Record Clerks to me for 5 years and I found that this plan was very influential upon their Conduct and it was also more satisfactory to their friends.

XV   Amongst the regulations of the Office, a Waste or Day Book should be kept in which the Clerks should enter the time of their attendance together with a Note of the Work which they have performed.

I can see no objection to the Office Clerks being employed upon Record Publications, out of Office hours provided the assent of the Principal be first obtained, but I do see the strongest objection to their acting as record agents. It is their duty to be stake holders and not to act for any one particular party.

XVI   Assuming that the Master of the Rolls will until the General Record Office be built, have the power of regulating the existing Record Offices, it would be expedient that he should in the meanwhile place settle and fix the hours of attendance, the duties of the Officers and the Fees upon a uniform footing, (since at present every Office varies in these particulars). And that as far as practicable he should enable the Principals of the several Offices to effect the proper Division of labour so that the different Establishments may be prepared for amalgamation and facilities should be given to those clerks upon the present establishments who might wish to retire – such a proceeding would be the most effectual training and the best and most quiet mode of removing difficulties – with respect to Calendars no plan can be adopted which will suit all classes of records alike – Some are best Calendered in a tabular form others by Abstracts – some by giving the Substance in English, others by giving the Title in Latin – all therefore that can be done, is to settle a Scheme for the Calendering of each particular set of Records (e.g. The post mortem inquisitions which are now in the Tower, the Rolls Chapel, the Chapter House and elsewhere) so that when the Records are brought together the Calendars may be united at the same time – Modern records (I use the term generally i.e. including equity proceedings) will require no calendering except an Order of the Names of the Plaintiffs and Defendants. As to the removal of records it would be advisable to begin with those which at present are without Keepers, e.g. those belonging to the Suppressed Courts of the Great Session of Wales – Of course all operations in the present Record Offices would be directed to an ultimate removal, and it would ultimately save expence if all new presses or racks could be planned with reference to a New Office which if made (as they ought to be) of Iron and Slate could be effected without difficulty. It is I believe quite practicable to construct a record office upon such a plan as, with little comparative waste of rooms in the first instance, shall be calculated to receive the *growing masses* of records. But I will not venture to give the details until I can consult some practical builder.

(ii) 23 October 1838[2]

A considerable space of time must necessarily elapse before a New General Office capable of containing within its Walls the Records now dispersed in the several Repositories can be completed. Nor would it be desirable to proceed to the immediate erection of such a structure. It is therefore expedient in the meanwhile for the purpose of carrying the Act into execution to form a plan for the systematic and orderly transfer of the Records when the proper era shall arrive. And such plan must furthermore afford until the head Office is built as much facility and convenience for use of the Records as can be effected under existing circumstances.

It is proposed therefore for these purposes that the Master of the Rolls having appointed his Deputy, should establish one head or chief Office, in which under the management of the Deputy all such information shall be concentrated as may enable the Applicant to ascertain where the Record which he requires is deposited. In this head Office, the Applicant or Suitor ought to find not merely a General Synopsis of the Records within the purview of the Act but also the particulars of the several series and classes, consequently this Office must possess copies of all the Indexes or Calendars now subsisting in the different Offices or hereafter to be compiled under the direction of the Master of the Rolls, and in short the main object of the Deputy must be to collect whatever Materials, may render the Office a complete Record Repertory. Furthermore so far as is practicable with a due regard to security and economy – keeping in view the ultimate erection of a New General Office – the more important Records required for practical purposes should be gradually collected from the other Offices and united with the Deputy's Office. If these two arrangements can be effected although very much will remain to be done, still a great practical benefit will be immediately attained and the measures requisite for the Classification of the Records will proceed *pari passu* with the encrease of facilities of access and search.

Considering the locality of the Rolls Record Office and the conveniences which the Buildings connected therewith offer even in their present state, it appears highly expedient that the Head or Deputy's Office should be there established, and besides the advantages of the situation (about which professional Men are unanimous) it already possesses several sections of the classes of Records most needed for Evidence of Title and legal enquiries in general vizt., the Post Mortem Inquisitions together with the Patent, Close, Charter and other Chancery Enrolments from the reign of Richard III to the present time. These Classes of Muniments which contain the main and primary Evidence of all Grants emanating from the Crown are not however all at the Rolls, only the latter portions are there, the anterior portions of them viz., from John to Edward V, being in the Tower and if these Tower Enrolments are forthwith transferred to the Rolls the Sections now so inconveniently separated will

---

2. PRO 36/54

be united. And for all practical and legal purposes the materials which furnish at least three fourths of all the Record Business, but which at the same time are the smallest in bulk of any Classes of the Records would be brought under one roof and the *cream* of the Records would be placed in one convenient Repository. The removal thus contemplated can be effected with the greatest cheapness and facility. The Rolls and Inquisitions at the Tower are in good condition and are contained in Pigeon holes on very stout Oaken presses furnished with doors, such presses standing detached from the Walls. A room measuring 25 by 15 would contain the whole of these presses – and nothing more would be required than to have the presses, with their contents, placed bodily in Packing Cases and removed to the Rolls Office. It may be confidently asserted that a sum not exceeding £150 would cover all the expences of the removal of these Records and the refitting of the presses. And for the more immediate accommodation and practical advantage of the legal public the greatest proportion of benefit will be obtained with the smallest outlay.

It must be observed that this proposed transfer of the Tower Rolls would not by any means pledge the Government to erect the General Office upon the Rolls Estate (if they should think any other site more expedient) and that in such case the utmost loss to the Treasury would be measured by the very small expence of removal which it is believed would not exceed the sum of £150 as before mentioned. Of course a vast mass of important Documents will remain to be disposed of, but a great step will have been gained. The Parliamentary Records are excepted from the Act and as they never will come into the New General Office Mr. Barry's Tower may be well appropriated to their reception.

The Rolls Record Office being thus refounded as the Head Office and a centre of information being thus established it must next be considered what measures are to be adopted in relation to the other Offices or Repositories viz., The Tower, the Chapter House, the Augmentation Office, the Carlton Ride, the late Chirographer's Office, the late Pell Office and others of the same description. Of these some are now in charge of Official and permanent keepers, others are under the care of Individuals provisionally appointed by the late Record Board and some are without any keepers at all. With respect to the more important of these Offices it is proposed to reserve them from suppression until the erection of the General Office – to continue an Establishment in each of these and to remove into the Repositories so reserved the contents of those which shall be extinguished or suppressed. In the reserved Repositories so long as they subsist the public will have access to the Records which they contain, the buildings will also be used as Workshops and places of Stowage and the Establishment will be employed besides the current business upon the formation of Calendars and Indexes to be transmitted to the Head Office, and in selecting and sorting the records for the operations of cleaning and binding. In the preparation of the Calendars such a system must however be laid down as will adapt itself to the classification and ultimate arrangement of the Records in the General Office. The Calendars must become Maps if such a term can be employed of the future general Office so that in proportion as the premises become fit for the reception of the Records they may be drafted in, successively and in Sections, Class after Class according to their importance and nature, the more useful classes for practical legal purposes being always preferred to the Classes less useful for practical purposes. In very many instances the Records are equally applicable to practical purposes and to Historical research and this is eminently the case with respect to the Muniments which it is proposed in the first instance to unite in the Head Office. But when otherwise, the precedence of removal of Records to the General Office should be determined by their comparative applicability to legal business, always taking due care that the sorting and calendaring of the unremoved Records keeps pace with the removal of the other classes, so that the applicants at the General Office may either find the Record itself, or an account of it.

It is moreover expedient that as far as is practicable the Records should be sorted, cleaned and secured in covers or bound before their transmission to the future General Office. To fill such an Office with crude Records in a state not fit for perusal would only be a delusive diligence perpetuating the present confusion. A sack or box of crumpled dirty unsorted and unindexed Parchments would be of no more use at the General Office than they are at the Tower.

But by working upon the cleaning and binding of the Records in the reserved Offices in the manner before suggested they will when the New building shall be erected, fit themselves in their places at once in a state of complete availability and whatever interval may elapse between the present time and the erection of the General Office will be most usefully employed.

It appears probable that it will be found advisable in the first instance to reserve the Tower, Chapter House, Augmentation Office, Pells, and Carlton Ride, but with the understanding that they are to be further consolidated and reduced to a smaller number in proportion as the Work advances, and more particularly when the time arrives for clearing them out into the New General Office. But for all these and similar purposes they must be first classed *upon Paper*, by that means alone a proper degree of method can be attained.

With respect to the Establishment at the Head Office or Deputy's Office at the Rolls and also at the other reserved Repositories, it must be observed that as the power of examining and authenticating Office Copies is confirmed by the Act to the Deputy and Assistant Record Keepers there must be a sufficient staff of the latter class of functionaries to perform this duty a duty which if properly executed requires a very great consumption of time and upon a rough estimate it seems that at present, on account of the local disposition of the Records in different parts of the Town, seven assistant Keepers will be required. But when the Records are consolidated in one building it is possible that a smaller number will be sufficient. Such Assistant Keepers to be distributed as follows,

Head Office, Rolls – *Three* – The Business of this Office which is already large will be much increased by the proposed transmission of the Tower Rolls and by the facilities which the new system will afford and if fewer than three were appointed, their time would be so absorbed by examinations of Office Copies as to leave them little leisure (even with the Assistance of the Deputy Keeper) to perform the other duties of their situations.

Tower – Two Assistant Keepers – The Business of this Office will be decreased by the removal of the Chancery Rolls to the Rolls or Head Office. But the Chancery Pleadings which are *very numerous* will remain, and the Tower, affording as it does ample stowage room for bulky records, it will be a most convenient place of deposit for the Records of the suppressed Offices and dissolved Courts of Judicature which the Master of the Rolls will call in. Hence it will become second in importance to the Head Office or Deputy's Office at the Rolls.

Chapter House and Carlton Ride to be united under one Assistant Keeper. The Vicinity of these Repositories will enable the Assistant Keeper attending at the Chapter House to perform the needful duty in respect of Examinations at the Carlton Ride there being a head Clerk to take care of the Records at the latter place.

Augmentation Office and Pell Office Records (Comptroller of the Exchequer) to which would be added the other Exchequer Records in Scotland Yard – One Assistant Keeper attending at the Augmentation Office with proper Clerks to take care of the Records or the other Repositories of the Union.

The Binding Department will constitute a very important Branch of the New Record service. The best mode of conducting this Business will be to entrust the finance and pecuniary control of the operations of cleaning and binding to the Stationery Office, but the operations themselves to be carried on with the Assistance and constant supervision of a Superintendant under the direction of the Deputy. The Stationery Office will make the Contracts, provide the Materials and pay the Workmen or audit the Bills. The Superintendant (who must possess a competent knowledge of Records) will receive the Records from the Deputy or from Assistant Keepers deliver them to the Workmen, receive them when completed and constantly inspect the proceedings of the Workmen so as to ensure the performance of their operations with due correctness and care. By this arrangement the Stationery Office will be responsible for the economy of the Service and the Record Office for the Security and condition of the Records and the careful execution of the Work. If this arrangement be adopted it is assumed that the Stationery Office will find the means of keeping together the experienced Workmen who have been trained by the late Record Commissioners. But it is quite essential that the examination and responsibility of the Binding expenditure should be detached from the Record Service and receive the benefit of the control of the Department to whom the duty properly belongs.

In relation to the funds to be provided for the Record Service, it is submitted that it is reasonable that the Fees arising from searches should be applied towards the Binding and repairing the Records. If the Fees [be] reduced so low as to encourage idle or impertinent applications, detriment and not advantage will ensue to the public service and the time of the Officers will be consumed in satisfying unnecessary requests. But if on the other hand the Fees be fixed according to a moderate scale with the power of making a complete remission in requisite cases, the total amount will from the consolidation of the Records, the additional Calendars and the facilities of access and searches be without doubt much increased, and to that extent the proceeds of the Establishment will relieve the public charge.

The payment of a portion of the expences of the New Record Office and Establishment by the investment of sums taken out of the floating balance of the Suitors Fund has been more than once urged. And with the greatest deference to the opinions of those who have opposed the proposition it is not difficult to find a valid argument against such their opposition both by quotation of precedent and reference to principle. The Six Clerks, and Registers, the Masters, the Cursitors and Examiners have all been furnished either with buildings or provided with salaries by such applications or investments of the Suitors balance.

The New Record Establishment is as much a service provided for the benefit of the public as any of these Departments nor is the money of the Suitors in any degree placed in jeopardy by such an investment. The Act would ensure the repayment of the appropriation if it should be required to be forthcoming. And in what manner are the Suitors placed in a worse situation than they would otherwise have been? If the money be invested in the 3 per cents what security have the Suitors except Parliamentary Security?

Until the main outline is fixed further details as to the organization of the Establishment of Keepers and Clerks would be premature. It is not however irrelevant to observe that the Record service, requiring as it does a knowledge of Law, of Languages, and of General History, must if it is to be rendered efficient be treated as a distinct *profession*.

The Establishment so constructed as to train up and educate within it, a supply of qualified persons. And let it be remarked that the making of Indexes and Calendering under proper superintendence affords the best schooling in the inferior Departments.

It must also be observed that many of the defects and abuses on the management of the Old Offices have arisen from the circumstance that the Officers – Principals as well as Clerks, have been placed in situations in which their interests are directly opposed to their duties. Depending for their living and sustenance either wholly or to a large extent upon the Fees they have been led to consider the Records solely as a source of direct or indirect gain and if the service is to be rendered respectable as well as efficient the regulations for preventing the recurrence of past abuses must be accompanied by a fair remuneration to all the public Servants employed therein. They must be settled in the Record Establishment and induced to consider it as their calling to be followed with the single object of performing their duty and not held as a mere convenience collateral to other Employments or subservient to other plans or avocations.

Appendix III

Patrick Fraser Tytler's Plan, 1838[1]

I

To examine carefully the present state of each separate Record Office inquiring into

1st The security of the documents – Whether in a dry place and well preserved against Fire.

2   Their Arrangement – Whether they are easy of access and of consultation by Indices Nominum Et Locorum – Where such Indices do not exist to be immediately constructed.

3   Fees of Consultation to be made as low as possible.

Having done this the first great point is gained. The Records (under which I include all letters and State Papers) are preserved, and there will be no loss sustained by fire, damp, disarrangement, or careless custody. The public also will have the means of consulting them by good Indices preserved in each Office (or department when all are removed into one great Record Office) and they will be consulted at as cheap a rate as is compatible with safety and the stopping of frivolous enquiry.

II

I would for the present suspend *all printing*, even of those works which have been left incomplete by the late Record Commission whose great error was the beginning by printing the Records themselves. It may be a question, whether under any circumstances large Collections of consecutive Records ought to be printed – but it is also most self evident that none ought to be printed till you know what you possess, and of these what *have* and what *have not* been printed. For this purpose I would

1. Construct a full Index of all documents *which have been already printed* illustrative of the Legal, Civil or Ecclesiastical History of the Country, stating in the Index in what Collection it has been printed, whether it is printed from an Original or from a Copy, and where the original is preserved. To make this Index extensively useful I would make it include not only all that have been printed in any Record publications, but in such Works as Rymer's Foedera, Wharton's Anglia Sacra etc. This having been done I would

2. Construct an Index, on the same plan, of all documents illustrating the Legal, Civil and Ecclesiastical History of the Country, which *have not*

---

1. PRO 1/1: enclosure to Tytler's letter to Langdale, 8 August 1838

been already printed but exist in manuscript, stating where each is to be found.

The completion of two such Indices would be a work of much labour and time, but it is evident it would be facilitated by having the separate MS Indices in each Office; and when completed it would supply the greatest desideratum in our national literature. When these two Indices are finished, I would advise their being immediately printed, published – and sold at as low a price as possible to the public: such is the want daily felt for such a Work, that there can be little doubt their sale would remunerate Government for the expence of their construction.

III

Having done all this we should be possessed of clear data to form a correct judgment on what ought, I think, to be the *last step* viz. to examine Critically, with a reference to its legal or historical value each Work left incomplete by the old Commission, and to decide

1. Whether all or any of such Works ought to be completed and
2. Whether they ought to be completed on their original, or on an altered scale.

Patrick Fraser Tytler

Hampstead
August 8th 1838

Appendix IV

Henry Cole's Scheme, February 1839: The Question of Arrangement, etc.[1]

1. Every Record to be cleansed of dust.

2. Some Records according to their value, their states of preservation, ink, etc. to be washed and repaired; rolls to be ticketted, flat documents to be bound or put in portfolios.

3. Boxes or other means to be adopted to preserve them in order and from future dust and dirt.

4. Lists of the titles of documents to be made *pari passu* with the titles themselves – every box to be labelled with the real nature of its contents and not any artificial title.

5. For the labels and tickets the press to be employed as far as possible – every title to indicate the real nature of the document and to avoid as far as possible such artificial References as Cleopatra A1, Galba B2, – etc.

6. The local arrangement of Records to be as far as possible in classes with an internal chronological arrangement if possible – e.g. All close rolls classed together and in a chronological series – all Parliament Rolls, etc.

7. List of the contents of each box to be affixed inside the box – by these means the existence of every document will be recorded and every document will have its fixed and determined locality.

8. The binding or final local arrangement of the Records to be performed unless the Record or series of Records is obviously complete.

9. These operations to be carried on, without exception throughout the whole of the Records – to begin with the most useful and valuable.

10. Every membrane of a record (at least in the first instance all of the greatest value) to be stamped with two stamps – one indicating the court, etc. to which it may belong and the other bearing the words "Public Records' Office".

Reasons for having a superintendent of the arrangement etc.

11. On an effective arrangement of the Records, their future order and preservation must be founded:- it is desirable that any arrangement which may take place,

---

1. PRO 1/2

534

should be done once for all in the best manner. Judgment is required to determine the mode of arrangement and preservation and convenience of access:- Some Records are best kept in their original shape as rolls, while others owing to their decay must be flattened:- some should be kept in portfolios:- some bound into volumes. To secure economy of space – a very important consideration, records of various sizes and shapes must have appropriate boxes. Simple as this matter seems when done, it requires some judgment in doing it. The intrinsic value of Records varies very much, and care is necessary that the greatest amount of labour and cost is not bestowed on the least valuable. It would not be wise to wash, repair and bind 'coast bonds' and 'portbooks' at the same expense that you would 'Inquisitions post mortem' and 'Wardrobe' accounts, etc., yet such unluckily has been the case. To avoid such errors, both a knowledge of records and some attention to the mere mechanical arrangement and preservation is needed. Heedlessness or ignorance may bind up as complete, volumes which are incomplete, and cause scattered membranes of rolls to be stitched together, which would require to be again unstitched to admit of the insertion of additional materials. Judgment is required in the case of miscellaneous collections to determine merely the order of the pages or membranes – whether they will admit of an internal arrangement – chronological – alphabetical or otherwise for example. A very great number of court rolls were found dispersed through the Miscellaneous Records of the Augmentation office. Before 1833 court rolls when found were bound up with every other class of Records. After that time they were all collected into one series – those belonging to one place were all brought together and then arranged in chronological order, and each Manor or place was arranged in alphabetical order:- e.g. Rolls of *Alton* 1 Hen 7. 3 Hen 8 Wm & Mary. *Banbury* 12 Edw I. 15 Edw III, etc. – thus this arrangement in itself serviced all the purposes of a calendar, which no other arrangement would have done. Some thought is required to settle the style of titles and letterings which cannot be done without a knowledge of the matter to be described. As far as possible uniformity should be preserved in the various stages of arrangement. It is presumed that this work in all its several and minute departments, would be much better executed if superintended by one person, whose sole business the superintendence should be, instead of by a number of persons each necessarily entertaining views more or less different – each with other duties to perform, and each located in different places, with little opportunity of consulting with each other and obtaining hints from the several systems. This work of arrangement, though it seems mechanical is on the contrary, one which requires both a general and specific knowledge of Records, and the work though somewhat manual is chiefly mental.

Increase in the numbers of workmen

12. The numbers of workmen will require very considerable increase, if much way is to be made of this first and most important branch of the service.

Inexpedient to have all the workmen in one place

13. It has been assumed that there will remain until a General Repository is built
     six branches:- The Chapter House – Augmentation Office – and Carlton Ride
     are all nearly in one vicinity – The Rolls Chapel and Rolls House are in another
     quarter of the Town – and the Tower in a third; three miles distant from the
     first named and two miles from the last.

     It has been suggested as being desirable to have all the works of reparation,
     etc. performed in one place, but this is very questionable. It is evident that
     much loss of time would occur in carrying records backwards and forwards
     between the Tower, Chancery Lane and Westminster. If many records are
     centralised at the Tower, there will be ample work for a force of six or eight
     men at that Repository. The Queen's Bench Records, supposing them not to
     be removed from the Rolls House, and the Chancery Records in the Rolls
     Chapel, would give employment to another set of men there. Little time would
     be lost in bringing the Records from the Chapter House, Augmentation Office
     and Carlton Ride to some one spot in the Vicinity, and the rooms in No. 3
     Whitehall Yard being relieved of the Exchequer of Pleas Records would be
     ample and convenient for a work-shop. It is proposed therefore to have three
     sets of workmen – say not less than half a dozen in each – with a head workman
     over each set:- to be placed thus – one set in Whitehall Yard – another in
     Chancery Lane and a third at the Tower. It would be easy to establish a tight
     responsibility over the head workman of these places. If it should be thought
     desirable to have a binding establishment for the Service, it might be placed
     at the most convenient of these three spots, and the Records to be selected for
     binding, which would be comparatively few might be removed thither from
     time to time for that purpose.

Tickets required for almost all documents

14. The very great majority of the records would require ticketting: greater part
     of those which are already ticketted, such as the Patent Rolls, etc., because
     their tickets are worn out – and others because they have no tickets at all – An
     incalculable saving of time and a great promotion of neatness and uniformity
     will accrue from making use of the printing press for tickets, labels etc. Wher-
     ever five and twenty tickets are required for a class of documents the press
     should be employed.

Order in which arrangement may be conducted

15. The repair etc. of the Remembrancer's Miscellaneous Records will not be
     interrupted at all. After certain removals have been done, it would be desirable
     that one man at least should commence sorting and tying up the Modern
     Common Pleas Records in Whitehall Yard. As Mr Gay is familiar with the
     character of the Augmentation Records perhaps it would be well to employ
     him in sorting the Records of the Land Revenue in the Ryde preparatory to

536

their junction with the larger series in the Augmentation Office. The ticketting of the Pipe Rolls and Memoranda Rolls and other which have no tickets at all should be performed before new tickets are placed upon those records which have them already. The Inquisitions post mortem, and Miscellaneous Records at the Tower are among those which require arrangement, etc. in the first instance at that Repository. The miscellaneous Records at the Rolls Chapel will require to be examined, etc. forthwith.

16. Boxes should be prepared for every class of records, as soon as the arrangement and reparation of them are commenced.

Appendix V

Workmen's Petitions for Better Pay, 1840

(i) To Sir Francis Palgrave, 24 February 1840[1]

The undersigned Workmen employed as above [the Augmentation Office] and at the Rolls Chapel very humbly and respectfully hope you will kindly pardon the liberty they have taken in addressing you.

They have long suffered from the low wages they have received and nearly two years ago they presented a memorial to Lord Langdale praying for a suitable advance; they have since waited patiently until the present moment when the permanent arrangements are making for carrying on the Record Service.

You were pleased to say some short time ago to two of the undersigned at the Chapter House that you thought a fairer scale could not be taken relative to their wages than what was paid by Mr Tuckett at the British Museum. They have since been informed by Mr Tuckett as follows, that any scale of payment for this work by piece must necessarily be productive of injustice to the employer or employed; at the same time that it involves the greatest risk of damage or destruction to the instruments.

That he has tried 10 or 12 different persons (Bookbinders) to repair Records and Manuscripts but has always found after a little time a dislike and neglect of the work from its tediousness, and he has been compelled to repair all the most injured documents himself, giving the men only those that were easy, but complaints should be made by the authorities of the establishment of bad and inefficient work.

That the men employed by him earn regularly from £1 12s 0d to £1 16s 0d per week, working 10 hours, and Mr Tuckett gives it as his opinion that where men can only work 7 hours a day and the whole of that time is employed in repairing Manuscripts or Records, they ought from the greater attention exacted in that branch to receive £1 10s 0d per week; and Mr Tuckett also gave permission to make use of his name in stating the preceding particulars and further added that he should be happy to afford any other information or explanation of what is here stated to any Gentleman connected with Records.

We have also included for your kind consideration and information a detail of weekly expenditure for the merest necessities calculated at the lowest scale for a man, his wife and two children, also the eight undersigned Persons have between them Twenty Four Children to maintain.

---

1. PRO 1/3

538

They humbly hope the preceding statements will justify their soliciting your generous and humane support to the prayer of a petition they have this day addressed to Lord Langdale for an advance of Wages, and which they entrust herewith to your kindness to present.

Your very obedient and obliged humble Servants.

Robert Hanney	Richard Toovey
Henry Gay	William Y. Finley
Henry Barber	William Thomas Goodenough
Joseph Blainey	Henry Mogford

Inclosure to the preceding
Estimate of Weekly Necessaries for a
Man, Wife and Two Children

	s	d
Rent	4	0
Coals 1½ Hund^d	2	0
Candles 1½ lb	1	0
Soap 1 lb		7
Meat/1 shilling a day is little enough for 4 persons	7	0
Potatoes, 13 lbs		7½
Bread, or Loaves	3	6
Butter, 1½ lbs	1	6
Milk		7
Tea, 4 lbs	1	0
Sugar, 2 lbs	1	2
Beer, 2 pints daily	1	9
	£1 4	8½

Medicine, Clothes, Shoes, Shoe mending,		
Wear & Tear of Furniture, Table & Bed Linen		
Domestic Utensils, Pepper, Salt, &c.,		3½
Vegetables, Cheese, Fruit, Flour, Fire-wood,		
Schooling for Children &c., &c., &c.		
Weekly Wages	£1 5	0

(ii) To Lord Langdale, 24 February 1840[1]

The undersigned Workmen employed in the Record Service most humbly venture to address your Lordship.

It is nearly two years since we represented to your Lordship in a memorial the inadequacy of our Wages to our support; we have never received any answer and have continued to suffer patiently and cheerfully the severest privations arising from the augmented prices of provisions up to the present period, always relying that the hardship of our position would be taken into consideration at the time your Lordship made the permanent arrangements generally for carrying on the Record Service.

We respectfully found our claims on the comparative Wages paid to other Workmen in occupations analogous to our own, on the fact that the Wages earned in London generally are much higher than what we should be happy to receive, that we have by our diligence and attention arrived at an ability which could not be acquired by new hands for some years, that we are by our proved integrity worthy of confidence in an employment where the want of it would be very disastrous and irreparable, that our position is a fixed one without a gleam of hope for future advancement, and that being almost all married men, while it is a guarantee for steadiness and propriety of conduct, is also accompanied by the circumstances that we have Twenty four Children amongst us dependent for support out of our present very stinted and inadequate Wages.

My Lord, our pretensions are not great; if our Wages were advanced to 5s. per day, which is only an advance of 5s. per week on what we now receive it would still rank with the lowest Wages paid to the Working Classes or even Shopmen; we would then be contented and happy and the whole amount of the advance among us would be but little beyond £100 per annum.

We appeal to your Lordship's humanity to investigate our case; to inquire into our individual character and respectability in our very humble situation in life and we humbly and fervently hope and pray for a favourable result to enable us to exist without disgrace, or the bitter want of the common necessaries of life for ourselves and families.

We are, My Lord, with the highest respect, Your Lordship's very obedient and obliged humble Servants

Robert Hanney	Richard Toovey
Henry Gay	William Y. Finley
Henry Barber	William Thomas Goodenough
Joseph Blainey	Henry Mogford

---

1. PRO 1/3

540

Appendix VI

Summary of Reports made by Sir Henry Ellis and Sir Francis Palgrave in 1840 on the Uncompleted Works of the Record Commission[1]

Publication, Editor, and estimated cost of completion	Recommendations		Outcome
	Sir H. Ellis	Sir F. Palgrave	
Pipe Rolls, 2–4 Hen II, 1 Ric I Rev. J. Hunter £820:15:0	Of considerable interest to the historian, topographer, and genealogist, but the cost may certainly be a ground for delaying immediate publication	Publish	Published 1844
Final Concords, 1195–1214 Rev. J. Hunter £383:7:6	Doubtful: inclined to avoid further cost	Publish: of considerable utility as to the topography of the four counties to which it relates	Published 1844
Docquets of Letters Patent, 1643–1646 Rev. W. H. Black £12:10:0	An acceptable publication though not of first-rate interest in itself	Publish	Although Langdale approved the publication of this work it was not completed by Black during his lifetime. It was eventually published in the 1870s.

---

1. PRO 2/87, pp 211–215, 275–289

Publication, Editor, and estimated cost of completion	Recommendations		Outcome
	Sir H. Ellis	Sir F. Palgrave	
Monumenta Historica Britannica Henry Petrie and Rev. J. Sharpe £428:10:0	Most important work of all considered. Of its value to the historical world there cannot be a doubt	The plan of this work, based on the method of Dom Bouquet, thought intrinsically defective. Has some value but not expedient to do more than print as it stands without incurring the expense of £428:10:0 in adding an introduction and indexes	Petrie died in 1842 and his co-editor declined to continue. The additional work necessary to enable it to be published was undertaken by T. D. Hardy. It appeared in 1848
Foedera Vol. IV, 1377–1383 Dr Adam Clarke and others £1906	Only publish if extended to end of reign of Richard II (1399)	Defects so great as to be irremediable so its continuation cannot be recommended	Langdale decided not to publish but it was eventually run off in 1869
Close Rolls, Vol. II, 1224–1227 T. D. Hardy £1727:8:0	Important and executed with ability and care, but publication recommended only if it is to be extended through the whole reign i.e. to 1272	Highly critical of editorial treatment which thought over-elaborate. With judicious abridgement the work might be rendered in the highest degree useful, but if this be not adopted volume should not extend beyond 1227	Vol. II published in 1844. Series not resumed until end of 19th century

Publication, Editor, and estimated cost of completion	Recommendations		Outcome
	Sir H. Ellis	Sir F. Palgrave	
Rotuli Vasconiae, 26 Hen III T. D. Hardy £1600:9:0	Unnecessary	If continued, should be subject to abridgement and selection. If not, to conclude at 26 Hen III	On Hardy's own recommendation calendar abandoned as the volume could not conveniently be broken off mid-stream, and, in any case, it would not sell in France unless the whole series was published[2]
Liberate etc. Rolls, John T. D. Hardy £305:2:0	Publish: any document connected with the history and manners of the Norman and earliest Plantagenet times a boon to the historian and antiquary	Publish: has its value being illustrative of the finance and manners of the period	Published 1844
Catalogue of Exchequer records; Catalogue or Inventory of Ministers' Accounts; Inventory of Surveys in the Exchequer; Inventory of Surrenders in the	Cost cannot be worth incurring	Abandon not because they are useless but because it would be better to adopt a more general and systematic plan for the formation and publication of the calendars of records	–

---

2. PRO 2/88: Hardy to Langdale, 10 February 1841

Publication, Editor, and estimated cost of completion	Recommendations		Outcome
	Sir H. Ellis	Sir F. Palgrave	
Exchequer; Calendar of Heirs H. Cole £1277:12:6			
Documents illustrative of English History in the 13th and 14th centuries from the Queen's Remembrancer's records in the Exchequer H. Cole £7:10:0	Publish at once – highly interesting both to the historian and antiquary	Publish	Published 1844
Modus tenendi Parliamentum T. D. Hardy	Publish but with a preface	Publish with addition of title page. The work is a curious forgery and a preface would require much investigation and research	Published with preface 1846
Report on Foedera W. H. Black £696:9:6	Most acceptable to the historical world though perhaps too much fault found with the Record Commission edition	Publish though without tables and indexes which might save £200. The Report is wrongly attributed to C. P. Cooper and its real authorship should be made clear	The Report was not published but there is a copy in the PRO Library (Press mark: R 11). The appendixes to it were published in 1869

Publication, Editor, and estimated cost of completion	Recommendations		Outcome
	Sir H. Ellis	Sir F. Palgrave	
General comment	Regrets so much use of 'Domesday' type in the Record Commission publications as even 'fair Latin scholars' can be deterred from consulting them due to the reproduction of the contractions and other flourishes, which makes them doubt whether they are right in explaining these contracted words. Acknowledges that several persons were employed in the very early commissions with insufficient Latin to put the words of a record at length	On completion of unfinished volumes priority should be given to the making of calendars, based upon a judicious selection of records for publication	

Appendix VII

Rules and Orders for Workmen at Carlton Ride Branch Office 1845[1]

	Fines[2]	
	Official	Shop
1. Respecting the Records		
Removing Records – No Records are to be removed by any person whatever from their appointed places in the Treasury without communication with the Registration Officer – Notice of every Record removed from, or restored to its place is to be entered in the proper Register – May 1842.		
Repairs &c. of Records – The Foreman shall as far as practicable, make a note of the name &c. of every Record delivered to a Workman for repair &c. and of its return when done with.		
Return of Records – The Foreman will cause every Record as far as practicable to be returned to the Record Room daily.		
Damages of Records – The Foreman to be responsible for any damages done in Record room to the Covers tickets &c.		
2. Respecting Tools and Materials		
Cartridge Paper – No cartridge paper clean or dirty, to be taken out of the Offices.	6d	
An Account to be kept by Foreman of the Quantity of Cartridge paper held by each man, no fresh supply to be given without producing that which has been used.		
Six sheets wanting	2d	
Twelve sheets wanting	4d	
Every six sheets above	2d	

---

1. PRO 1/9, enclosure in letter from Cole to Palgrave, 15 March 1845.
2. Official fines were stopped from the men's wages; shop fines were distributed among the men themselves.

The men will be called upon to produce their stock occasionally.

Tools – Each man will produce his stock of Tools on the first of each month when called upon – the value of any lost will be deducted.

Value deducted

Stores – All stores received from Mr Bond to be kept by the Foreman, and to be given out by him or his Deputy.

The Foreman to have charge of all printed tickets and to deliver them as required.

Drawers or Boxes of Workmen – No man to go to another workman's Drawer or Drawers, or Box on any pretence whatever. Sixpence to be paid to the person who observes and reports the fact.

Works Books – To be given to the Foreman by 12 o'clock on Monday morning, and if not, during that day – Neglect reported

3d

Work Books to be made up on Monday or fined

3d

Work Papers on the Monday after the last Friday in the month or fined

3d

Presses – Top of Lower Shop
The Large Press – for broads, both wooden and milled boards.
The Second Press – for narrow Boards.
The Light Press – for light work only.

The Saucepan – to be given to P. Paul or deputy when out of use.
The Shop Broom – to be hung on the nail of door, at bottom of shop when out of use.
The Birch Broom – to be placed in privy when out of use.
Fine for inattention – each Offence.

3d

Lanterns – The Lanterns are always to be returned to their place after use – on the shelf by the Foreman's Bench.

	Official	Shop

3. *Respecting Building*

Cooking – Half an hour in the course of the day will be allowed for refreshment, but no Cooking of any kind whatever is to be permitted.

Windows of Treasury – The Foreman to see that the windows of Record Room (Treasury) are opened daily and securely closed – when the Office is shut.

Fire Guards – No person is to open the fire-guards except John Toovey, and except in cases allowed by Mr Cole. For default — **1 hour**

If the door of the Fire guard is found open all the men in that shop will be fined each — **1 hour**

Strangers – Every Stranger must be conducted by the person opening the door to whomsoever he wishes to see – officially.

Any man spilling water and not remedying it will be fined. — *Shop:* **3d**

If slops are found each man in the workshop will be fined. — *Shop:* **3d**

4. *Respecting Attendance*

Time Book – Every workman to sign his name and time of arrival at his work, daily.
Late of a Morning
If after the Time of a morning being
paid 7d or 8d – per hour — *Shop:* **3d**
ditto 5d or 6d – ditto — *Shop:* **2d**
ditto 3d or 4d – ditto — *Shop:* **1½d**
If 10 minutes past the Time to lose — *Official:* **1 hour**

After Lunch – Any one beyond the half hour at lunch, will be subject to the same rule as of a morning.

If any men wish to leave the Office during the half hour, between ½ past 12 and 1 o'clock, they must go out in a body and return together.

	Fines	
	Official	*Shop*

Holidays – The men will be allowed the Holidays named in the Official Rules & Regulations.

The Workmen are to consider themselves engaged from Week to Week.

All Men to be considered 6 hour men – but to be allowed Holidays and Illness the full time they are working whatever that may be.

Illness – When a man stops away from illness he must send a note the first day, expressing that to be the cause of his absence – and also must send a Certificate on or before every Friday, or the time will not be allowed.

If Mr Cole permits a man to go home in consequence of being ill – he admits it for that day only, and the man must send a certificate if away the next.
A man is allowed the day in cases of his Wife's accouchment
> in case of Death
> > of Burial
> > of Marriage

Passes – Every man who leaves the Office during the day (except at Luncheon time) must procure a pass from the Foreman, or his Deputy, which he will deliver to the Doorkeeper upon going out – When he returns he will obtain the pass from the Doorkeeper and bring it back to the Foreman.
> In default   3 hours

The doorkeeper must report the name of any man who comes in after 1 o'clock without a pass – In default   3 hours

The Workmen are to pass in and out always thro' the Lower Work-shop.

The Foreman to see the Men out at Lunch time – as at 4 o'clock.

Any person taking a pass without the Foreman's or his Deputy's knowledge of the same will have to lose   1 day

5. *Respecting General Conduct*

Slovenliness – Any complaints of slovenliness or
Dirtiness observed or reported by Foreman – each
offence

Foreman – Every man to be subjected to the Directions
of the Foreman, who will be held responsible for the
work of every person.

Idleness – Any person whose name shall be entered in
a book as having been found by the assistant keeper
idle or neglecting his work six times in any quarter shall
be suspended for
No appeal against such entry of name allowed.

Perquisites – No perquisites in any case, such as selling
refuse parchment &c. to be allowed.

If any person shall be a party in any way to any
misrepresentation made by the Foreman to the
Assistant Keeper, such party having it in his power to
correct the same shall be suspended for

If any Person or Persons shall combine in any way
whatever to render any decision of the Assistant Keeper
null and void, he or they shall be suspended for

Persons drinking from the pitcher will be fined

Rewards

Men not fined at all by Office or Shop – 3 days holiday.

Men who have not incurred 6 fines – 2 days.

Men who have not incurred 12 fines – 1 day.

The Assistant Keeper will also consider the neatness of
Keeping the Diaries – good conduct &c.

Fines		
	Official	Shop
Slovenliness		3d
Idleness	a week	
Misrepresentation	2 days	
Combine	1 week	
Pitcher		3d

Appendix VIII

Langdale's Letter to the Treasury Objecting to the Deposit of Public Documents in the British Museum, 1849[1]

. . . But it seems to be assumed both by the Trustees and Sir F Madden that records and documents may probably be better arranged and managed and made more easily accessible to the public and literary men in the British Museum than in the Record Department and I conceive this assumption to be so far contrary to the truth that the only effectual mode of realizing it would be, if it were possible, to prevail upon the Government to adopt as a general rule, that adequate means of accommodating and managing such documents should be withheld from the Record Office and afforded to the British Museum.

The proposal of the British Museum should be considered on legal and public grounds only with reference to the determination of their Lordships, approved by Her Majesty's Secretaries of State, to unite the State Paper Office and the Record Office under one system of management.

. . . there are now in the Record Office some writings (not properly called Records) but which have been selected, and are now preserved, for the use of the Government with a view to certain publications recommended either by the House of Commons, such as the 'Materials for the History of Britain', the first volume of which has been recently published; or recommended by the late Record Commission such as the Papers referred to by Sir Fred[k] Madden which were collected for the intended completion of Rymer's *Foedera* by continuation or supplement.

As to Public Records properly so called they are either accessible to the public as of right, such as all judicial records and proceedings, Chancery records, and some others, to which the government and the Public have access equally; or they are kept for the information and use of the Government itself and only made accessible to the Public subject to such regulations as may be directed by the Government or by Parliament.

As a general rule it appears to me very desirable to give great publicity and easy access to all records of every kind – but the Public service or the exigencies or convenience of Government require that some limits should be appointed: those limits must depend mainly, perhaps not entirely, on the dates of the documents and the nature of the subject to which they relate . . . There may be many cases which can only be determined by the authority and discretion of Government exercised on the occasion, and whatever the nature or the age of the records may be, it appears to me to be necessary for the Public interest that the property in them should be

---

1. T 1/5459/8817/1849

vested in the Crown and that the management of them should either remain in the Public or Government Offices, or be committed to a Public Officer responsible to the Crown and to the Public and required to be subservient and auxiliary to the Crown and the Public Offices in the management of all such records as are not accessible to the Public as of right.

It was in consequence and upon the foundation of this opinion that I suggested the duties of the Record Office with reference to such records and public papers in my letter to you of 8th August 1845 which was subsequently approved by their Lordships.

On consideration I am fully persuaded that the British Museum is not and cannot consistently with its proper duties be so constituted as to make the Trustees or any of their Officers, fit agents for the Government in the management of any public records whatever.

The numerous and valuable MSS which the Museum contains are vested in the Trustees as property – they are accessible to the Public according to general rules, and the Crown has no direct authority or control over them – and I have no doubt that the Trustees would now, as upon a former occasion they did, refuse to receive into their charge any documents otherwise than for permanent deposit.

The Trustees have indeed upon the present occasion excepted from their proposal those records which being of legal importance or containing matters of State Policy require to be in the exclusive and immediate custody of Government. But my opinion is that all public records of whatever nature ought to be in the exclusive and immediate custody of the responsible Ministers of the Crown on behalf of the Crown, or of an authorized public Officer acting legally and avowedly in aid of the Crown and its Ministers.

The documents referred to in the Report of Sir Frederick Madden, viz. the transcripts collected for the completion of the collection called Rymer's *Foedera* require other considerations.

. . . Sir F. Madden properly calls them historical documents – and independently of any special use which the Government might desire or intend to make of them – it might at first sight seem that they might be deposited in the British Museum as usefully to the Public and to Literature as in the Public Record Office. But I have great reason to believe that the fact is otherwise and (for example) that portions of the MSS collected for Mr Petrie's 'Materials for the History of Britain' have been very usefully applied for the purposes of literature in a manner which the regulations of the British Museum would not have permitted.

. . . I take the liberty of expressing my hope that the distaste occasioned by the imprudences of the late Record Commission will not always be considered as conclusive reasons for the abandonment of all the Record and Historical Publications which they recommended, and that the time may come when the Government, for its own credit and the advantage of the Public, will think it right to make arrangements for the publication by a duly constituted authority of useful historical documents upon a prudent and economical plan.

In my opinion, if it be not resolved finally to abandon the contemplated completion of Rymer's *Foedera*, the documents now in question ought to remain in the exclusive possession of Government.

. . . Before I conclude this letter I wish to observe that there are in the British Museum many genuine public records acquired by purchase or gift, but which must have been improperly abstracted from the Record Offices to which they properly belonged. These records ought undoubtedly to be either in the General Record Office or in the particular Offices from which they have been improperly abstracted. Among the latter is a volume containing entries of the proceedings in the Privy Council. The absence of it leaves the series in the Council Office imperfect and the late Lord Wharncliffe, when President of the Council, attempted in vain to procure its restoration.

I believe that as the law now stands the Trustees of the British Museum would not be justified in delivering up this volume or the other Public Records which they have, without the authority of an Act of Parliament.

And this consideration appears to me to shew the caution which ought to be used in parting with documents which may be required by Government for the Public use.

Appendix IX

Memorial to the Master of the Rolls Requesting Access to the Records for Literary Purposes Without the Payment of Fees[1]

London, July 7, 1851

Sir

The undersigned historical writers, members of various Literary Societies specially interested in the prosecution of historical inquiry, and persons otherwise engaged in literary pursuits, or connected therewith, beg leave most respectfully to submit to you:

That, by the Statute 1 & 2 Vict. c. 94. s. 9, the Master of the Rolls is empowered to make rules for the admission of such persons as ought to be admitted to the use of the Records, Catalogues, Calendars, and Indexes, and also to make rules for dispensing with the payment of fees in such cases as he shall think fit.

The undersigned would also most respectfully submit to you, that the researches of persons engaged in historical investigation and inquiry would be greatly facilitated, and the welfare of our national historical literature be promoted in a very high degree, if you would be pleased to exercise the power given to you in the Statute before mentioned by making an order that such persons may have permission granted to them to have access to the Public Records, with the Indexes and Calendars thereof, without payment of any fee.

At present any person may search for and inspect any Record on payment of a fee of one shilling for a search in the Calendars, which may be continued for one week, and of another fee of the same amount for the inspection of each Record, or such fees may be commuted at the sum of five shillings per week, provided the search be limited to one family or place, or to a single object of inquiry.

These fees are of no benefit to any individual, but are paid over to the nation, the different officers of the Record Establishment being remunerated by salaries.

When a person desires to inspect one or two specific Records for his own private purposes these fees are unimportant in amount.

But, when a person engaged in historical or antiquarian research wishes to build upon the evidence of Public Documents – the only sure foundation of historical truth – it ordinarily happens that in the progress of his inquiry he is obliged to refer to many Records; the inspection of one almost necessarily leads him on to others, and, as he proceeds, he continually finds references and allusions to many more, all which he ought to inspect, if for no other purpose, in order to be satisfied of their inapplicability to the subject of his research. This is the course of inquiry which in

---

1. PRO 1/15. Printed in *The Thirteenth Report of the Deputy Keeper*, Appendix no. 4.

such cases is absolutely necessary to be adopted for the establishment of historical truth. Under the present practice this course cannot be adopted. Inquirers are deterred from referring to Records by the total amount of the reiterated fees, and are thus compelled to copy erroneous or questionable statements from earlier authors.

The literary men of the present day find it necessary for the establishment of truth to verify the authorities and references of earlier writers, but the amount of the present fees compels inquirers to accept statements professedly built upon the authority of the Records as they find them. Thus doubt and mistake are perpetuated and made part of our national history; and thus time, which ought to be a test of truth, is often made to lend additional authority to error.

The present practice cannot be defended on the ground of its productiveness to the national revenue. The amount received for literary searches is altogether insignificant, except to those who pay it. The attainment of historical truth – an object in which the whole nation is interested – is therefore prejudiced, and in many cases defeated, by the enforcement of fees which produce the nation absolutely nothing.

The exclusion of literary men from the inspection of the Records excites a demand on the part of persons interested in historical literature for the continuance, at the expense of the Government, of works similar to those published by the late Record Commission. If access were freely granted to the Records, such demand would be silenced; for such publications would be undertaken by the numerous existing publishing societies, or by other voluntary associations which would be instituted for the purpose, as well as by individuals. Everything that is historically valuable at the British Museum is published without difficulty as soon as it is discovered.

Even in cases in which free access to manuscripts does not lead to their being printed, it promotes transcription, which tends to preserve valuable information against the unavoidable danger of total loss, to which it is liable whilst existing in a single copy. With a view to this danger, the House of Commons ordered a transcript to be made of the Parliamentary Survey of 1650, a manuscript existing in the library of Lambeth Palace; and examples might be adduced of the contents of Cottonian MSS., destroyed by fire in 1731, having been partially supplied through the means of notes and transcripts previously made by persons who had access to the MSS.

Many of the most valuable historical works of past ages; such works, for example, as Dugdale's Baronage, the foundation of all our books relating to the peerage; Madox's History of the Exchequer, the basis of much of our legal history; Tanner's Notitia Monastica, the groundwork of our monastic history; and Rymer's Foedera, which first enabled historical writers to put general English history upon a sure foundation; – were all compiled principally from the Records. Every page contains many references to them. It is a common complaint that now-a-days no such works are published. Under the present practice such works cannot be compiled, nor can the improved historical criticism of the present age be applied to the correction of the errors which unavoidably crept into such works published in times past.

Lastly, the undersigned desire to state distinctly that they do not solicit this permission on behalf of any persons engaged in Record searches for legal purposes, or for any persons whatever save those who are carrying on researches for historical or other literary objects; and they would most readily acquiesce in and approve of the most stringent precautions against any abuse of the privilege which they solicit on literary grounds solely.

The undersigned therefore beg, with the greatest respect, to solicit your attention to the circumstances they have stated, and to request that you would be pleased to make an order that persons who are merely engaged in historical inquiry, antiquarian research, and other literary pursuits connected therewith, should have permission granted to them to have access to the Public Records, with the Indexes and Calendars, without payment of any fee.

> And the undersigned have the honour to be, Sir,
> > With the greatest respect,
> > > Your most obedient and very humble servants,
> > > > (Signed)

Braybrooke	Mahon	John Bruce
Talbot de Malahide	W. H. Blaauw	J. Y. Akerman
Thomas Carlyle	W. H. Smythe	James Heywood
Londesborough	Henry Ellis	G. A. Hoskins
Chs. Purton Cooper	Albert Way	J. R. Planché
F. Madden	John Holmes	P. Levesque
H. H. Milman	Bolton Corney	W. Harrison Ainsworth
Jas. Prior	Edwd. Foss	F. H. Davis
T. J. Pettigrew	Edward F. Rimbault	T. Crofton Croker
John Lee	Samuel Birch	C. W. Dilke
Alfred White	Augustus W. Franks	Thos. Corser
Strangford	Edwd. Oldfield	Charles Boutell
S. Oxon	Wm. S. W. Vaux	J. O. Halliwell
Octavius Morgan	Jas. Spedding	Lucy Aikin
Fortunatus Dwarris	F. A. Carrington	Charles Roach Smith
Thomas Wright	G. Poulett Scrope	T. K. Hervey
Mary Anne Everett Green	J. B. Nichols	Douglas Jerrold
Philip Hardwicke	John Gough Nichols	Charles Knight
John Forster	Ev. Ph. Shirley	James Crossley
William J. Thoms	Agnes Strickland	Richard Parkinson
Charles Tucker	S. R. Maitland	George L. Craik
John Henry Parker	Hepworth Dixon	Peter Cunningham
Henry Shaw	John Britton	John Doran
Henry Hallam	John Ayre	J. B. Bergne
T. B. Macaulay	Edward Smirke	J. Hamilton Gray
Robert Harry Inglis	Charles Dickens	S. R. Solly
J. Payne Collier	Francis R. Raines	Charles Bailey
R. Neville	Edward Hawkins	

Appendix X

Romilly's and Trevelyan's Letters Concerning the 1855 Reorganisation

(i) Sir John Romilly to Sir George Cornewall Lewis, chancellor of the Exchequer, 9 June 1855[1]

Sir C Trevelyan remarks that it is a cheap & effective mode of remunerating public officers by the expectation of succeeding to a few prizes & that this is constantly met by a continual opposition of the Chiefs of Departments who desire to have the power of disposing of staff appointments to persons out of the office. To whom this passage refers besides myself I am unable to state but I must deny that it has just reference to the present case. . . . The MR for the time being has now the power by statute of appointing whom he pleases to the office of Deputy Keeper when that office is vacant. Until that statute is repealed this power cannot be altered by a Treasury minute. I repeat the expression of my belief that if that office were now vacant it would be injurious to the public service to fill it up by the appointment of any person now in the Record Department. According to my present disposition I should not do so. I have openly stated to [sic] this to all the assistant keepers & I also again express my belief that my successor will entertain the same opinion that I do on this subject. I shall be happy to explain the grounds for this opinion & belief but it would occupy too much time & space to put them down here.

The mode by which Sir C Trevelyan endeavours to carry his plan into execution is in my opinion open to great objection. This is by the creation of a sort of a 2nd Deputy to the Master of the Rolls by raising to the office of Secretary, Registrar and Accountant into the office of Secretary simply & giving him a salary of £200 p.annum above the other officers of the first class with whom till the present time he has always been considered as on an equal footing. What his new duties are to be is not suggested. Mr Thomas is a most excellent, laborious & painstaking officer & well deserves this extra £100 p.annum which he is to receive: but at this moment he is extremely jealous of Sir Francis Palgrave because that gentleman is consulted confidentially respecting the Record Department by the present MR & also because Sir F believes, & Mr Thomas boasts, that he has the ear of the Treasury. The increase of this office without any corresponding increase in the salaries of the other officers of the first class & the placing it on a new footing will in my opinion foment the present & create fresh jealousies extremely injurious to the well working of the Establishment. Unfortunately Sir C T consulted no one connected with the Record Department before he determined on this plan, at least he has not consulted with me, nor as I am informed with Sir F Palgrave or any of the assistant keepers in offices of the 1st class.

---

1. T 1/5968A/19558/1855

. . . The regular record work itself is extremely harassing & requires great care & exercise of judgement & knowledge & I believe produces as much wear & tear & anxiety as belongs to the offices charged with the current business of the government. When I saw Sir C T on this matter he observed to me in conversation that he considered the record business as a mere pastime & that he had formerly indulged in it as a recreation & it is clear that this idea is the foundation of his plan. But it arises in a misconception of what that work consists in. No doubt the pursuit of some literary subject chosen by the person pursuing it amongst old records may be very interesting. But this pleasure is not open to the assistant keepers. The duty which falls on them day after day of sorting, classifying & calendaring with minute accuracy masses of miscellaneous documents of all times and of all kinds is of a very different & of a very irksome character. It leads to no literary result, it requires great knowledge of modern history, of the ancient institutions of the country, of old French & Latin languages together with the knowledge of various other descriptions which will readily occur to you & all this to be applied with judgement on the spur of the moment to enable them to perform this work accurately & efficiently.

. . . It is a mistake also to suppose that this Office is properly a branch of the Civil Service department. So far as it takes care of government papers it is so, but this has been the addition made to it in late years, in all other respects it remains, as it has been from its first existence in the earliest times of our history, a legal Office attached to the Department of the Law . . . But even if regarded as a branch of the united civil service it will I confidently believe be found to be remunerated on a scale far below the other branches of that service. In actual amt. it is confessedly so: in the requirements necessary for the purpose of having the Office properly filled it is difficult without having carefully examined into the nature of the duties belonging to every Office to say correctly whether the requirements of the Record Office stand higher or lower than any other Office. I can only say that (not having had the opportunity of making such an investigation) I believe none to stand higher. Sir C T says that the Establishments are united by a prevailing proportion of duty to salary. If this were really so, that is if the proportion of salary had been fixed after a general examination & comparison of the relative duties of all the Offices taken together & made by competent persons intrusted for that purpose to settle & arrange the salaries there might be some force in this observation. But the fact is I believe certain that no such investigation has ever been made & that no proportion between duty & salary has ever been regulated or attempted to be fixed upon any general and comprehensive examination of the whole of the Offices taken collectively; they have in fact been fixed at different times with a mere vague feeling of acting on this principle according to the views of the Secretary of the Treasury for the time being; and I have heard it frequently regretted that no such investigation had ever taken place & the salaries regulated by a report founded on such an inquiry & that the want of it did in fact occasion the pressure of which Sir Chas T complains: without it, for instance, it is impossible to say whether the establishment of the Registrar General to which Sir C T refers ought or not to be revised as compared with the Record Department.

558

I feel confident that regarding it simply as a Government Office the officers of the Record Department possess high claims to an increase of salary & that if such an increase takes place no inference injurious to the rest of the Offices can fairly be drawn from that circumstance.

But if the Record Department is to be regarded in the light of its original institution & to which its duties principally belong, viz., a legal Office, then it is so far below the scale of remuneration prevailing in all the other legal Offices with which I am acquainted, viz., those connected with the Court of Chancery, as to make a most striking difference. Even in the British Museum which has always been considered to be extremely low (as Offices open to literary men are apt to be) the principal officers below the Head of the Establishment receive £600 p.annum with duties less onerous, & requiring no higher qualification, than those necessary for an assistant keeper.

Whatever may be the course adopted I beg distinctly to express my opinion that . . . in attempting to create a second office in the matter of a 2nd Deputy Keeper or 2nd Secretary, which the Deputy Keeper now is, jealousies will be fostered & created injurious to the well working of the Office which will not cease until either the office of Deputy Keeper or that of Secretary becomes practically a sinecure, which I believe will be the probable result; and this evil will be produced by the attempt to get the services of men for less than their real worth by holding the prospects of advancement which will for the most part prove delusive.

I wish this letter not to be considered official but you are at liberty to make any use of it you may think fit.

(ii) Sir Charles Trevelyan to Sir George Cornewall Lewis, 13 June 1855[1]

. . . There are personal allusions in the Letter from the Master of the Rolls which render it necessary for me to state that Mr Thomas was not consulted in reference to any of the proceedings above described. In what was done I merely applied to this particular case the general rules derived from a constant revision of the Public Establishments for many years past; and I was assisted by Mr Stephenson, who next to myself has had the most extensive experience of this important subject.

. . . I should be unworthy of the confidence which has been reposed in me in making me a Member of the numerous Committees which have been appointed of late years for the revision of the Public Establishments, if I did not state, as the result of my experience, that under various names, and with numerous trifling differences of Salary, there is a prevailing proportion of remuneration to duty which

---

1. T 1/5968A/19558/1855

is well understood throughout the Service – that according to this proportion the Officers of the Record Department are liberally remunerated, the only point on which they fell short of a full equality (the quinquennial instead of the annual rise) having been set right by the recent arrangement – and that an increase of their Salaries would inevitably bring upon the Treasury a pressure from other quarters which it would be impossible to resist.

. . . As I have lately submitted to you my observations on the extremely injurious effect upon the Public interests of the prevailing practice of withholding from the Body of permanent Civil Servants the legitimate prizes of their profession, I will only remark on the present occasion that, however sufficiently & even liberally any particular class of Public Servants may be paid (and in this case their remuneration is ample), they will never, as a class, be what they ought to be, if there is no higher situation to which they can look forward as the reward of superior diligence & self improvement.

In completion of what I have to say on this point, I will quote the following Extract from the Draft of the Treasury Minute which I submitted to you in reference to the last official Letter of the Master of the Rolls.

'In making these observations it was not their Lordships' intention to interfere with the free exercise of the discretion of the Master of the Rolls in the execution of the duty imposed upon him by Parliament of appointing the Deputy Keeper; but they desired to express their opinion that both the Economy & efficiency of the united Establishment would be consulted by selecting one of its Members for that Office **provided one could be found as well qualified for it as any other Person.** The clause in the Record Act, which vests the power of appointment in the . . . Master of the Rolls, prescribes that the Deputy Keeper 'or Chief Record Keeper under the Master of the Rolls', who is to superintend all Persons employed in keeping the Records subject to such directions as he may from time to time receive from the Master of the Rolls, shall be 'a fit Person **duly qualified by his knowledge of Records to be Deputy Keeper of the Records**'; and if it be clearly understood that promotion from the lowest to the highest situations in the Department will depend upon superior fitness, it is probable that besides the intimate practical acquaintance with the Records which is pointed out by the Act of Parliament as the primary qualification, the other qualities required for the Office of Deputy Keeper will be developed in some of the numerous well educated and intelligent gentlemen composing the Establishment. But if, notwithstanding these advantages, a Person better qualified for the Office should be found elsewhere than in the united Public Record Establishment the Master of the Rolls will, of course, exercise the power vested in him by Act of Parliament of the selection of that Person.'

Appendix XI

Sir Thomas Hardy's Paper Concerning the Qualifications and Duties of a Keeper General of the Public Records, 187[3][1]

Qualifications

I   He should have a thorough knowledge of the public muniments and be familiar with their legal, historical, and political bearing, so as to be able to assist and advise the Government and general inquirer in their several objects of investigation. In consequence of the numerous alterations of the law of property the ancient records are not so much used for legal purposes as they were formerly, and legal searchers have consequently much diminished; on the contrary the historical purposes, for which the records are consulted, have become more numerous, and will certainly extend as the facilities for examining the public documents increase and indexes and calendars to their contents become more generally diffused. To all persons interested in general history, biographical, topographical and genealogical researches the public records have become, as might be expected, a subject of the liveliest interest, which is not likely to grow less. In fact scarcely any work now appears, or any article written on these subjects of which the authors have not considered it indispensable to examine what materials can be found among the national archives bearing on their special pursuits. When points affecting claims made on the government, and others of a political aspect arise it is necessary that the Keeper General should be able to assist the government in such inquiries.

II   He should be sufficiently a master of palaeography, in all its branches, to read the documents themselves and see that the officers of the establishment do their duty, when appointed to calendar and index them. This is a difficult task arising partly from the varied and complicated nature of the documents themselves prepared in so many different offices and connected with the multifarious business of the nation in its widest extent. Many, also, of the ancient muniments are written in difficult and perplexing characters with numerous abbreviations, which require a peculiar study and application to master them accompanied by general and critical knowledge.

III   He ought to be acquainted with medieval Latin, Norman French and ancient English, for anterior to the Statute 4 George II. c.26 nearly all legal records (except during the Commonwealth) were written in medieval Latin or Norman French, and those which are in English, are in an obsolete idiom, whilst most of the Foreign papers are in the different languages of Europe, this would

---

1. PRO 1/133

561

suggest the necessity of a good linguist, or at least some acquaintance with such languages.

IV   He should have such a comprehensive knowledge of general and particular history as to be able to select the documents most useful to the public to be calendared as well as the most skilled and experienced scholars to be entrusted with the formation of such Calendars, and if necessary to superintend their operations; for here it may be remarked that the culminating point of proficiency in record knowledge is the power and ability of making a précis of ancient documents, so as to convey a just notion of their contents, by giving all their distinctive characters clearly and concisely. Fact, knowledge and extreme accuracy must be constantly exercised.

V   It is necessary also that he should understand the classification and arrangement of Records so as to avoid confusion and render them easy of access when required for consultation; for it is not possible in the great national Record Office that the papers and muniments should be arranged all alike. Those belonging to each of the several courts and public offices require widely different treatment and adjustment. Some must be arranged according to subject, some chronologically, and in many instances according to size and shape.

Duties

I   To have the direction and superintendence of all officers and persons employed in the Public Record Office (now numbering upwards of one hundred) as well as the general management of the whole Department subordinate to the Treasury.

II   To have the control of the expenditure sanctioned by the Treasury and to prepare the annual estimates for Parliament. To have the power to appoint the Secretary as the public accountant of the Department with the approval of the Treasury.

III   To conduct the correspondence with the Treasury and other public Departments; to prepare public and confidential Reports to the Government and Secretaries of State upon all subjects on which they require information.

IV   To select, and have the sole management of the national publications which have been sanctioned by the Treasury such as Calendars, Chronicles and Memorials.

V   To superintend the formation or collection of Transcripts, under the Sanction of the Treasury of documents relating to British History in France, Spain, Austria, Belgium, Rome, Venice, etc.

VI   To make annual Reports to Parliament of the operations in the Public Record Office.

Appendix XII

Llewelyn-Williams's Letter to Lloyd George, Calling for a Royal Commission on the Public Records, 27 April 1910[1]

The Prime Minister has already done British Archaeology splendid service by appointing Commissions to inquire into and report upon the condition of our Ancient Monuments. The Government would earn the gratitude of all scholars if they completed the work by appointing the Commission for which I now appeal.

I cannot do better than refer you to an able article which appeared in the January number of the *Quarterly Review*, in which the whole subject is broadly and comprehensively treated. It will, I think, convince you.

    a.   that as compared with our predecessors in the 'dark ages' we have grown criminally careless in keeping our national records.

    b.   that most of the continental countries are ahead of us. The French *Ecole des Chartes* was founded a century ago by the great Napoleon, and other countries have based their archivist departments on the French model.

    c.   that though we have made great progress in the last 15 years – thanks largely to the energy of Sir Maxwell Lyte – still more is urgently required to be done and

    d.   that the longer we delay, the greater will be the loss and confusion.

To come down to particulars:

    (1)   The Public Record Office Act (1 & 2 Vic. c.94) was passed in 1838. The Order in Council extending its provisions was issued March 5 1852. No general enquiry as to the making of the Act has ever been held. The only official information available as to the condition of the Records, the Reports of the Deputy Keepers presented in accordance with the Act, has not been published in any detail since the year 1862.

    (2)   It is feared – if not indeed certain – that certain Records, specifically mentioned in the Act and Order have not been transferred to the keeping of the Master of the Rolls. Nor are they under the superintendence of the MR in respect of their arrangement, repair, or made accessible to the public, according to the intention of the Act. Many such documents have been abstracted from official custody – some

---

1. T 172/35

of them have been publicly sold – others have been destroyed or have perished or suffered damage through neglect, while others are still outstanding and are in danger of destruction and deterioration.

(3) Under the Act of 1877 (40 & 41 Vic. c.55) and the amending Act of 1898 (61 & 62 Vic. c.12) there are grounds for apprehending

a. that certain Records of historical value have been destroyed

b. that the safeguards provided by the Acts are illusory without further measures for the publication of schedules of documents proposed to be destroyed and for the consideration of the various historical interests concerned.

(4) A large number of legal records, State Papers, and Departmental Archives, which were transferred to the custody of the MR under the Act of 1838 have remained practically unarranged, unrepaired, and undescribed or, in other cases, the arrangement, repair, description have been inadequate.

(If I were disposed to make a Welsh grievance of this, I could give the glaring instance of the Records of the Courts of Great Sessions (1543–1830), but I wish to put the whole case on broader and more general grounds).

(5) Access to Records has been in certain cases immeasurably impeded by departmental restrictions.

(6) Tho' 300 vols. of English, 70 vols. of Scotch and 40 vols. of Irish Records have been published no such Calendars of Welsh Records have been published in a separate series. It is well-known that the Welsh Records are of great historical value.

(7) No systematic or comprehensive survey of ancient charters, deeds, feudal inquests etc. not yet transferred has been attempted, nor has any professional training been provided or required for the archivists who are engaged in the arrangement or description of the Archives.

I wish to emphasise that there is not the smallest intention to blame the authorities of the Public Record Office, whose zeal and ability are well proved and universally admitted. But we plead for an enquiry which will enable us to make a real advance on the lines already shown by continental countries, particularly France, Belgium, and Holland. The recent discoveries of Professor Wallace with regard to the life of Shakespeare in London illustrate the value of the material which lies hidden – unknown and uncalendared – in the Record Office. Only a week or two ago Mr Jenkinson discovered certain writs of summons which prove that Constitutional

Historians were wrong in calling the 1295 Parliament the 'Model Parliament'. The constitution of the 1275 Parliament was almost identical.

If I were once to embark on the possible – and even probable – discoveries which would throw light on the history of Wales, I would make this letter unendurably long.

I trust I have made out a strong *prima facie* case for such an enquiry, and I would suggest the following subjects should be included within the scope of the reference.

1. The situation, condition, and accessibility of the Records since 1838, including all Records under the charge and superintendence of the MR under that Act and the Order in C. of 1852.

2. Proceedings taken for the disposal of valueless Records under the Acts of 1877 and 1898.

3. Arrangement, classification, and description of the Records since 1838.

4. Record publications (texts, calendars, and lists) since 1838.

5. Present custody and future disposal of the local records of a public nature.

6. Establishment of the Archives.

I regret that my letter should have run to such length: but I have not done more than touch the fringe of the subject. I can assure you that you would confer an unforgettable boon on a body of men who deserve well of their country and who are working for their country's interests, if you could see your way to grant their request for such an enquiry.

Appendix XIII

Public Record Office Staffing
1838–1958

	1838	1848	1858	1868	1878	1888	1898	1908	1918	1928	1938	1948	1958
Administrative and Clerical	24	31	37	45	45	40	43	37	42	38	42	48	60
Support grades	14	47	63	54	55	55	59	68	77	74	85	110	117
Total	38*	78	100+	99	100	95	102	105	119**	112	127	158	177

* Until July 1840 all but two borne on former record service vote.

+ State Paper Office staff taken over in 1854.

** Including staff in HM Forces or on loan to other departments.

Appendix XIV

Expenditure and Receipts
1838–1958

	1838* £	1848 £	1858** £	1868 £	1878 £	1888 £	1898 £	1908 £	1918 £	1928 £	1938 £	1948 £	1958 £
Salaries, etc.	307	9,599	14,450	15,368	16,237	18,344	20,007	20,760	19,770	35,229	37,691	64,989	138,690
Incidental expenses	–	295	120	70	80	60	165	210	180	467	460	750	1,766
Calendars and Historical Documents (payment to editors)	–	–	4,500	6,007	5,560	3,230	3,200	3,850	1,600	2,200	2,500	3,500	Under salaries
Receipts (inspection fees and charges for copies)	–	869	802	543	546	863	675	615	250	700	615	2,150+	19,569+

* Deputy Keeper, Secretary and Housekeeper for part of year only. Other staff borne on record service vote until consolidation in 1840.
** Merger with State Paper Office 1854.
+ Increase following introduction of an official photocopying service.

Appendix XV

Lists of the Holders of Various Offices 1838–1958

1. Keepers of the Records (Masters of the Rolls)

1838–1851	Henry Bickersteth, Lord Langdale	
1851–1873	Sir John Romilly (Baron Romilly, 1865)	
1873–1883	Sir George Jessel	
1883–1897	Sir William Baliol Brett (Baron Esher, 1885)	Viscount, 1895
1897–1900	Sir Nathaniel Lindley (Baron Lindley, 1900)	
1900	Sir Richard Everard Webster, Lord Alverstone	
1900–1901	Sir Archibald Levin Smith	
1901–1907	Sir Richard Henn Collins (Baron Collins, 1907)	
1907–1918	Sir Herbert Hardy Cozens-Hardy (Baron Cozens-Hardy, 1914)	
1918–1919	Sir Charles Swinfen-Eady (Baron Swinfen-Eady, 1919)	
1919–1923	William Pickford, Lord Sterndale	
1923–1935	Sir Ernest Pollock (Baron Hanworth, 1926)	Viscount, 1936
1935–1937	Robert Alderson Wright, Lord Wright of Durley	
1937–1949	Sir Wilfrid Arthur Greene (Baron Greene, 1941)	
1949–1958	Sir (Francis) Raymond Evershed (Baron Evershed, 1956)	Chairman of the Advisory Council on Public Records, 1959–1962

2. Deputy Keepers of the Records (1838 Act)

1838–1861	Sir Francis Palgrave
1861–1878	Thomas Duffus Hardy (Knighted, 1869)
1878–1886	William Hardy (Knighted, 1883)
1886–1926	Henry Churchill Maxwell Lyte, CB (Knighted, 1897)
1926–1938	Alfred Edward Stamp, CB

1938–1947	Cyril Thomas Flower, CB	
	(Knighted, 1946)	
1947–1954	(Charles) Hilary Jenkinson, CBE	
	(Knighted, 1949)	
1954–1958	David Lewis Evans, OBE	Keeper, 1959–1960
	(Knighted, 1958)	

3. Secretaries

1838–1857	Francis Sheppard Thomas	
1857–1866	Charles Roberts	
1866–1887	John Edwards	
1887–1903	James Joel Cartwright	
1903–1912	Samuel Robert Scargill-Bird	
1912–1916	Richard Arthur Roberts	
1916–1918	Harley Rodney	
1918–1926	Alfred Edward Stamp	Deputy keeper, 1926–1938
1926–1938	Cyril Thomas Flower	Deputy keeper, 1938–1947
1938–1947	(Charles) Hilary Jenkinson, CBE	Deputy keeper, 1947–1954
1947–1952	Charles Drew	
1952–1957	Leonard Charles Hector, OBE	Director of publications, 1957–1967
1957–1958	Harold Cottam Johnson, OBE	Deputy keeper, 1959–1966; keeper, 1966–1969

4. Establishment Officers

[Until 1952 establishment duties were undertaken variously by the deputy keeper and the secretary]

1952–1954	David Lewis Evans, OBE	Deputy keeper, 1954–1958; keeper, 1959–1960
1954–1957	Harold Cottam Johnson, OBE	Secretary, 1957–1958; deputy keeper, 1959–1966; keeper, 1966–1969
1957–1960	Oliver George Robert Fox, OBE	

5. Inspecting Officers

(i) Secretaries of committee appointed to review government documents, 1859–1874

| 1859–1866 | W. Lascelles |
| 1866–1874 | J. Redington |

(ii) Members of Committee of Inspecting Officers established under the Public
     Record Office Act 1877, 1881–1958

1881–1886	Sir W. Hardy	
1881–1891	J. Redington	
1881–1899	L. O. Pike	Barrister member
1886–1926	Sir H. C. Maxwell Lyte	
1892–1912	R. F. Isaacson	
1892–1905	G. J. Morris	
1900–1919	R. A. Roberts	Barrister member
1900–1912	S. R. Scargill-Bird	
1905–1921	H. Hall	
1912–1947	Sir C. T. Flower	Barrister member, 1919–1938
1912–1930	C. Johnson	
1919–1929	R. C. Fowler, OBE	
1921–1934	M. S. Giuseppi, ISO	
1925–1946	M. C. B. Dawes	
1926–1938	A. E. Stamp, CB	
1930–1952	P. V. Davies, OBE	Barrister member, 1938–1952
1934–1938	S. C. Ratcliff, ISO	
1938–1954	Sir (C) H. Jenkinson	
1938–1958	J. H. Collingridge, OBE	Barrister member, 1952–1958
1947–1958	Sir D. L. Evans	
1947–1952	C. Drew	
1952–1958	L. C. Hector, OBE	

(From 1952 until the winding-up of the committee in 1958, E. W. Denham
acted as secretary)

(iii) Records Administration Division
Records Administration Officer

1955–1964	J. H. Collingridge, CBE	Re-employed in various dis-established capacities until final retirement in 1973

Assistant Keeper (appraisal)

1956–1959	E. W. Denham	Records administration officer, 1973–1978; deputy keeper, 1978–1982

Inspecting Officers (Senior Executive Officers)

1956–1962	R. D. Farmer, MBE	
1956–1961	K. F. Huggons	Returned to parent department (Ministry of Works) 1961
1956–1966	R. F. Monger, MBE	Assistant keeper, 1966–1971
1956–1967	F. T. Williams, DFM	Establishment officer, 1967–1972

6. Assistant Keepers

[Date of first entry into record service shown in brackets, except for officers recruited directly to the grade]

1840–1851 (1796)	T. Palmer	
1840–1861 (1819)	T. D. Hardy	Deputy keeper, 1861–1878
1840–1850 (1823)	H. Cole	
1840–1861 (1833)	J. Hunter	
1840–1858 (1819)	F. Devon	
1840–1857 (1820)	C. Roberts	Secretary, 1857–1866
1840–1859 (1810)	H. G. Holden	
1840–1853 (1834)	W. H. Black	
1850–1876 (1821)	H. J. Sharpe	
1851–1876 (1832)	J. Burtt	
1853–1862 (1834)	W. Nelson	
1855–1862 (1820)	C. Lechmere	
1855–1866 (1819)	R. Lemon	
1855–1888 (1834)	H. C. Hamilton	
1855–1866 (1837)	W. Lascelles	
1855–1866 (1838)	J. Edwards	Secretary, 1866–1887
1855–1883 (1840)	J. J. Bond	
1857–1891 (1837)	J. Redington	
1859–1893 (1846)	J. Gairdner, CB	
1859–1885 (1840)	W. B. Sanders	

1868–1878 (1823)	W. Hardy	Deputy keeper, 1878–1886
1877–1891 (1841)	P. Turner	
1878–1885 (1844)	A. Kingston	
1885–1891 (1841)	P. B. S. L. Hunt	
1885–1887 (1845)	F. S. Haydon	
1887–1891 (1848)	W. N. Sainsbury	
1888–1906 (1861)	C. T. Martin	
1891–1899 (1862)	L. O. Pike	
1891–1912 (1866)	S. R. Scargill-Bird	
1892–1904 (1868)	R. D. Trimmer	
1892–1902 (1868)	J. M. Thompson	
1893–1912 (1868)	J. E. E. S. Sharp, ISO	
1900–1911 (1868)	G. F. Handcock	
1902–1905 (1872)	G. H. Overend	
1903–1912 (1872)	R. A. Roberts	Secretary, 1912–1916
1904–1912 (1873)	R. F. Isaacson	
1905–1914 (1873)	G. J. Morris	
1906–1916 (1879)	H. Rodney	Secretary, 1916–1918
1911–1921 (1878)	E. Salisbury	
1912–1917 (1874)	E. G. Atkinson	
1912–1924 (1879)	R. H. Brodie, ISO	
1912–1921 (1879)	H. Hall	
1914–1921 (1879)	J. G. Black	

1916–1923 (1888)	C. G. Crump	
1917–1926 (1890)	A. St John Story-Maskelyne	
1918–1929 (1891)	R. C. Fowler, OBE	
1920–1933 (1891)	J. V. Lyle	
1920–1934 (1891)	M. S. Giuseppi, ISO	
1920–1930 (1893)	C. Johnson	
1920–1926 (1893)	A. E. Stamp	Deputy keeper, 1926–1938
1920–1933 (1893)	H. E. Headlam	
1920–1936 (1897)	J. B. W. Chapman	
1920–1926 (1903)	C. T. Flower	Secretary, 1926–1938; deputy keeper, 1938–1947
1920–1938 (1903)	S. C. Ratcliff, ISO	
1920–1946 (1905)	M. C. B. Dawes	
1920–1938 (1906)	(C). H. Jenkinson*	Secretary, 1938–1947; deputy keeper, 1947–1954
1920–1947 (1907)	J. J. O'Reilly*	
1920–1923 (1911)	O. C. Chapman, OBE	
1920–1925 (1912)	W. R. Cunningham	
1920–1954 (1912)	R. L. Atkinson, OBE, MC	Continued as secretary of Historical Manuscripts Commission until 1957
1920–1944	C. S. Buckland	
1921–1928	V. H. Galbraith	
1921–1953	A. C. Wood	
1921–1952	D. L. Evans*	Establishment officer, 1952–1954; deputy keeper, 1954–1958; keeper, 1959–1960
1921–1955	K. H. Ledward	

* Holder of directorial or other senior assistant keeper post.

1924–1953	P. V. Davies, OBE*	
1925–1937	J. R. Crompton	
1925–1928	Miss M. G. Smieton	
1926–1973	J. H. Collingridge*	Records administration officer, 1955–1964
1926–1954	H. C. Johnson*	Establishment officer, 1954–1957; secretary, 1957–1958; deputy keeper, 1959–1966; keeper, 1966–1969
1927–1959	F. H. Slingsby, MC	
1928–1970	H. N. Blakiston, OBE*	
1928–1929	S. S. Wilson	Keeper, 1960–1966
1929–1934	Miss E. S. G. Potter	
1929–1964	D. B. Wardle*	Records administration officer, 1964–1967
1930–1947	C. E. S. Drew	Secretary, 1947–1952
1930–1967	L. C. Hector*	Secretary, 1952–1957
1933–1957	R. H. Ellis*	Secretary, Historical Manuscripts Commission, 1957–1972
1933–1949	R. B. Pugh	
1934–1967	R. E. Latham*	
1937–1943 (1913)	E. W. S. Safford	
1938–1946	R. W. N. B. Gilling	
1938–1946	T. H. Brooke	
1939–1940	Duke of Rutland	Honorary unpaid
1941–1944	Dr A. Guillaume	Honorary unpaid
1947–1974	C. A. F. Meekings, OBE	
1947–1948	A. H. K. Slater	
1947–1978	E. K. Timings, MVO*	
1947–1949	K. G. Davies	
1947–1966	J. R. Ede*	Deputy keeper, 1967–1969; keeper, 1970–1978
1947–1957	J. E. Fagg	
1949–1973	E. W. Denham*	Records administration officer, 1973–1978; deputy keeper, 1978–1982
1949–1982	Miss D. H. Gifford*	
1950–1970 (1938)	A. W. Mabbs*	Records administration officer, 1970–1973; deputy keeper, 1973–1978; keeper, 1978–1982

---

* Holder of directorial or other senior assistant keeper post.

1950–1967	N. J. Williams	Records administration officer, 1967–1970; deputy keeper, 1970–1973
1951–1959	R. A. Brown	
1953–1956	Miss S. B. Challenger	
1953–1988	R. F. Hunnisett*	
1953–1962	R. L. Storey	
1954–1977	L. Bell*	
1954–1978	Miss P. M. Barnes*	Records administration officer, 1978–1982; deputy keeper, 1982–1985
1957–	N. E. Evans*	
1957–1961	J. R. Rea	

[But for the disappearance of the AK II grade between 1860 and 1920 the following clerks would probably have ranked for inclusion in the above list:

T. Ameer Ali, J. R. Atkins, A. E. Bland, J. J. Cartwright, C. A. Cole, A. J. Crosby, F. C. Drake, E. Elgey, A. C. Ewald, M. Fenwick, E. T. Gurdon, W. D. Hamilton, W. H. Hart, F. H. Hohler, H. C. Hollway-Calthrop, A. Hughes, C. Jelf, J. T. Kentish, J. W. King, G. Knight, H. E. Lawrance, E. Lethbridge, J. R. V. Marchant, M. Moloney, A. S. Pattinson, J. Pedder, J. G. Phillimore, A. Purser, E. H. Rhodes, W. D. Selby, H. St James Stephen, E. J. Tabrum, F. C. Thomas and S. Waine.]

---

* Holder of directorial or other senior assistant keeper post.

Select Bibliography

[A set of annual reports of the deputy keepers of the records are preserved in the Public Record Office in PRO 43]

E. Bonython   :   *King Cole* (London, V & A Museum, 1982)

H. Cole   :   *Fifty Years of Public Work* (London, 1884)

R. H. Ellis   :   'The Building of the Public Record Office', in *Essays in Memory of Sir Hilary Jenkinson*, ed. A. E. J. Hollaender (Chichester, 1962)

C. T. Flower   :   'Manuscripts and the War', *Royal Historical Society Transactions*, Fourth Series, XXV (1943)

H. Hall   :   'The National Archives', *The Quarterly Review*, 212 (January 1910)

    :   *British Archives and the Sources for the History of the World War* (Oxford, 1925)

T. D. Hardy   :   *Memoirs of the Life of Henry, Lord Langdale* (London, 1852)

H. Jenkinson   :   *Guide to the Public Records, Part 1, Introductory* (HMSO, London, 1949)

C. Johnson   :   'The Public Record Office', in *Studies presented to Sir Hilary Jenkinson*, ed. J. Conway Davies (Oxford, 1957)

M. D. Knowles   :   'Great Historical Enterprises IV, The Rolls Series', *Royal Historical Society Transactions*, Fifth Series, II (1961)

P. Levine   :   'History in the Archives, the Public Record Office and its Staff, 1838–1886', *English Historical Review*, CI (1986)

E. L. C. Mullins   :   'The Making of the "Return of Members" ', *Bulletin of the Institute of Historical Research*, LVIII (1985)

Report of the Committee on Departmental Records, Cmd. 9163 of 1954

Reports of the Royal Commission on Public Records, I-III, Cd. 6361, Cd. 6395 and Cd. 6396 of 1912; Cd. 7544, Cd. 7545 and Cd. 7546 of 1914; Cmd. 367, Cmd. 368 and Cmd. 369 of 1919

W. Rye   :   *Records and Record Searching* (London, 1897)

A. E. Stamp: :   'The Historical Student and the Public Record Office: A Retrospect', *Royal Historical Society Transactions*, Fourth Series, XI (1928)

R. B. Wernham   :   'The Public Record Office, 1838–1938', *History*, New Series, XXIII (1939)

Index

Most subjects are arranged in groups, the principal groups being under the headings:

Abbot, Charles, Lord Colchester, 2, 494
Mrs E, 460 (n 8)
Aberdare, Lord *see* Bruce
Abraham, H R, 121
Accessions
accommodation difficulties, 160, 264–5,
329, 331–2, 419
arrangement and classification, 38, 53,
67–8, 373, 380–1, 402–3, 502, 527–9,
532, 534–5, 562, 565–6
deferment, 9, 93
detailed in *DK's Reports*, 104, 183, 223,
225
preparation for transfer, 66, 412, 414, 425,
503
processing costs, 62–3
refused by Jenkinson, 478
registration, 410
regulations and warrants, 142–3, 281,
331–2, 411, 491
see also under Departmental records; Legal
records
Accidents *see* Staff and staffing
Acton, Sir John, (*later* Lord Acton), 241,
255, 288–9
Admiralty, 143, 244, 328, 400, 427, 429, 457
dockyards, 368
lords commissioners, 455, 515
records, disposal, 160, 196–7, 208, 221,
355, 374, 394
lent to Festival of Britain, 454–5
public access, 197, 220–1, 329–30,
358–9, 361, 404
transfers, 86, 106, 160, 264, 503
unsuitable storage, 106, 183, 196
reservations about Grigg proposals, 470
see also Navy League; Navy Records
Society
Admiralty Court *see* High Court of Admiralty
Advisory (Consultative) Committee on
Publication, 372, 389, 447, 456, 459,
474, 477–8
Advisory Council on Public Records, 398,
472, 490, 493–5, 569
Agarde, A, 424
Agriculture, Board of, 105, 347
Aikin, L, 556
Ailesbury, Lord *see* Brudenell-Bruce
Ainsworth, W H, 139, 556
Air corporations' records, 441
Air Ministry, 394, 428, 433, 435
Air-raid incidents and precautions, 379–80,
425–32, 439–40, 443, 457–8, 502
Akerman, J Y, 556
Akers-Douglas, A, 342

Albert, prince consort, 1, 82, 121, 123,
219–20, 226, 358–9
Alexander, Albert Victor, Lord Alexander of
Hillsborough, 493–4
Ali, T Ameer, 378, 576
Alienation Office, 45
Aliens, 361, 380
Alington, Richard, 343
Allen, F, 261
J, 6 (n 10), 8 (n 13), 19, 55–6, 59, 224
(n 17b)
M, 119 (n 30a)
Allerton, Lord *see* Jackson
Allied Commission for Austria, 436, 440
Alverstone, Lord *see* Webster
America, Americans *see* United States of
America
Ancient monuments, inquiry, 564
Ancient Monuments Inspectorate, 486
Anderson, Sir John, 403
Anglia Sacra, 532
Anglo-American Conference of Historians,
391
Anglo-German relations, 392, 403
Anglo-Jewish Historical Exhibition, 311
Anglo-Saxon
charters, 217, 230, 281
Chronicle, 191, 202, 217
laws, 61
materials, 499
Angus, W, 452–3
Anne, Queen, 226, 260 (n 8c)
Anne Boleyn, second queen of Henry VIII,
79, 282
Annual reports on work of Public Record
Office, 309, 472, 496, 563–4
modification, 104, 170, 308
new format, 215, 218
no longer printed, 386, 406
printing resumed, 452
repair statistics, 301
statutory proviso, 517
Anslow, R A, 458
Antigua records, 446
Antiquarian and archaeological societies *see*
Societies
Archibald, Sir Thomas Dickson, 276
Archive administration
Agarde's list of perils, 424
campaign for employment of women, 396,
425
changing requirements, 502–3
diploma course, 445, 450, 477
foreign practice, 363, 367, 383, 423, 454,
469, 476–7

Archive administration – *contd*
  foreign practice – *contd*
    see also Ecole des Chartes
  Jenkinson's *Manual* and pioneering, 385,
    388–9, 425, 467–8, 478–9
  modern records, 477, 502–3
  overseas links, 201, 300–1, 446, 497
  palaeography, palaeographers, 68, 77–8,
    188, 193, 198, 203, 212, 248, 267, 297,
    303, 321, 327, 345, 455, 474, 477, 502,
    523, 545, 561–2
  possible course for COs, 438
  PRO seen as centre, 465
  professional nature, 400, 445, 475, 523,
    531
  role of archivists, 445, 467–9, 479, 494,
    504, 558
  technical duties *see* Conservation;
    Photocopying work and services
  training, 363, 367, 382, 455, 477, 565
  UN technical assistance, 483
Archive and record societies *see* Societies
Armstrong, William, (*later* Lord Armstrong),
  461 (n 11)
Army and Ordnance Medical Board, 160
Army List, 94
Army records *see under* War Office
Army Spectacles Depot, 379
Ashridge branch repository *see under* Record
  offices and repositories
Ashworth, W, 479
Asquith, H H, MP, prime minister, 564
Assheton, R, MP, 278, 280
  Lord Clitheroe, 495
Assizes, clerks of, 515
  records *see under* Legal records
Association of Assistant Keepers
  see First Division Association
Atkins, J R, 144–6, 184 (n 21), 220, 238,
  262–3, 270, 282, 399, 576
  wife, 282
Atkinson, E G, 249, 322, 335, 378–80, 389,
  573
  R L, 287 (n 1), 378, 389, 403, 420, 422,
    426, 442, 443 (n 35), 487–9, 574
Attendances *see under* Search
  Department/rooms
Attendants' and Repairers' Association, 401
Audit Office, records, 130–1, 149, 221–2,
  330, 335, 355–6, 420
Auditors of the land revenues, 513
Auerbach, E, 454
Augmentation Office, 4, 16, 37–8, 45, 50–1,
  52 (n 20), 53, 58, 64, 69, 72, 79, 82,
  94, 172, 486, 513, 528–30, 535–8

Augustus Frederick, duke of Sussex, 287
Austin, A, 155 (n 22)
Australia
  accommodation for military authorities,
    379, 435
  convict records, sensitivity, 357
  display of Australian records, 424
  microfilming for, 434, 449
  S Australian Emigration Office, 68
Austria, 435–6, 440
  archives, 241, 255, 562
Ayre, J, 556

Baggallay, Sir Richard, 276
Bailey C, 556
Balfour, A J, MP, 345, 347, 357, 391
  J, MP, 404
Balls, E H, 399, 449
Banham, A E, 412
Bank of England, 441, 525
Barber, H, 17, 539–40
Barham, R H, 3 (n 3)
Baring, F, 14, 71 (n 26)
Barnes, Miss P M, 456, 576
Baronage of England, Dugdale's, 555
Barry, Sir Charles, 60, 120, 528
Baschet, A, 241, 255, 300, 389
Bateman, H M, 400
Bateson, E, 417
Bayley, J, 7 (n 12)
Beaconsfield, Lord *see* Disraeli
Beall, T, 180, 231, 233, 252, 301
Beavan, C, 16
Bede (Beda), Venerable, 246
Bedfordshire records, 442
Beer
  money, 101–2, 138, 180
  supplied to workmen, 69, 266
Belgium, 403
  archives, 241, 255, 368, 405–6, 562, 565
Bell, H E, 409, 417, 435, 486
  L, 456, 507, 576
Bennett, W H, 353–4
Benstead, L, 378
Bentinck *see* Cavendish Bentinck
Bentley, R, 148
Beresford-Hope, W, MP, 280
Bergenroth, G, 201, 216, 240
Bergne, F A'Court, 318 (n 8a), 322–4, 328,
  336, 353
  J B, 556
Bethune, J E Drinkwater, 6, 9, 11, 26,
  511–21
Beveridge, Sir William, 364, 409

Bickersteth, Henry, Lord Langdale, master
of the rolls, 65, 82, 103–6, 111–12,
117, 139–40, 164 (n 3), 167–8, 189,
193, 215, 252, 264, 301–2, 496, 532
(n 1), 569
AKs' farewell address, 132–5, 138, 147
alarmed by mildew problem, 72
assumes charge of record business, 1,
6–7, 482
bust, 185
coat of arms, 226
consideration of organisational, staffing
and pay questions, 8 (n 14), 13–41,
43–58, 63–4, 66–7, 75–8, 81, 86–9,
92–3, 96–102, 125–6, 131, 149
death, 135, 137–8
decision concerning Record Commission
works, 60–2, 541–5
difficulties and differences with
Palgrave, 29, 31, 39–41, 54, 62–3,
70–2, 77–9, 86–90, 96–7, 99, 104,
118, 121–4, 128, 131, 138, 176, 245
'Father of the Records', 12, 499
fellowship controversy, 147
Hardy's Memoirs, 13, 132, 147–8
holds dinner party for senior officers, 54
impending resignation, 124, 131
new repository endeavours, 60, 121,
128, 137–8, 157
Palgrave's appointment, 13–15, 18–32,
78, 148, 285, 443
papers, 13
presses for union of State Paper Office
and Public Record Office, 107–9
recommendations concerning Irish
records, 113–15
record reformer, 1, 7–8, 33–4, 43–5,
59–60, 134–5, 150
releases Cole for Great Exhibition, 121–4
secretary, 8, 17, 70, 136–7
settles PRO regulations, 54–5
states conditions for departmental
transfers, 107–8, 143, 279, 552
supports Cole's Record Society, 73–4
views on Record Bill, 9–12
on records disposal, 130, 196
Jane Elizabeth, Lady Langdale, 124,
147–8, 185
Bickley, F, 389, 405, 486
Binding see Conservation
Birch, S, 556
Bird, W H B, 355, 405, 417
see also Scargill-Bird
Blaas, P B M, 62 (n 8)
Blaauw, W H, 556

Black, J G, 296, 300, 314, 334, 352, 378,
388, 573
W H, 3 (n 3), 4 (nn 4–5), 8, 94, 202, 237,
356
assistant keeper, 65–6, 85, 98, 102–3,
132–4, 144, 233, 572
appointment, 4, 49–50, 53
damage to sight, 112, 150, 197
difficulties with Palgrave, 70, 92,
111–14, 125–6, 129–31, 149–50
pay, 53, 111, 131, 149
retirement, 149–51
work and investigations, 58, 79–80,
86, 107, 111–15, 130–1, 250
death, 249–50
defender of Record Commission, 4
draws up Record Bill, 6–7
editorial work for Record Commission,
112, 151, 541, 544
evidence to Lords' Committee, 49
minister of Mill Yard chapel, 70, 111,
149, 191, 250
'school of transcribers', 50, 151
termination of employment with former
record service, 9
Welsh records surveyed, 46–7, 49–50,
53, 59, 110, 113
Black Book of the Exchequer, 78
Black Prince's Register, 383
Blainey (Blaney), J, 17, 251, 259, 539–40
Blakiston, H N, 406, 423, 427, 429, 437,
489, 497, 575
Bland, A E, 354, 365, 378, 576
Blaney see Blainey
Bliss, W H, 282, 300, 318, 344, 355
Board of Green Cloth, 515
Bodleian Library, 3 (n 3), 80 (n 38), 220,
226, 282, 318, 446, 466
Bogaert, L, 389, 405
Boggis-Rolfe, H, 491
Boleyn see Anne Boleyn
Bond, E A, 16, 73–4, 222, 288–9
J J, 57, 76, 78, 126–7, 156, 169–70, 193,
211, 233, 238, 241 (n 39a), 245, 251,
253, 256, 266–8, 287, 290–1, 296, 302,
547, 572
Booth, J, 244
Borough record offices see under Record
offices and repositories
Bouillon Correspondence, 357
Bouquet, Dom, 61, 116, 173, 542
Bourke, Richard, Lord Naas, (later earl of
Mayo), 30 (n 10), 205, 228
Boutell, C, 556
Bowyer Tower, 85

Boyd-Carpenter, J, MP, 460–1
Bradford, Sir Edward, 365
Bradley, family, 258, 301
  Mrs –, 136
  F, 259
  R H, 259
  T H, 266
  W, 52, 83, 301, 313
Braidwood, J, 85, 93, 129, 155
Brande, W T, 66
Braybrooke, Lord *see* Neville
Brett, R B, 341–2, 345
  Sir William Baliol, Viscount Esher, master
    of the rolls, 243, 302, 317, 333, 569
    appoints Lyte deputy keeper, 303,
      305–6
    considers DK must be member of
      Inspecting Officers' Committee, 319
    decides against continuation of Rolls
      Series, 307
    declines to give public access to office
      garden, 335
    negotiates further development of Rolls
      Estate, 337–8
    opposed to national archive service,
      328–9
    rarely seen by Lyte, 317
    refers question of office organisation to
      Consultative Committee, 323–4,
      327–8
    regulations, rules etc, issued, 308–10,
      320
    succeeded by Lindley, 347
  W G, 140, 243
Brewer, E C, 239
  J S, 60, 116–17, 171–4, 188, 192–3,
    199–200, 206, 212, 214, 226–8, 240,
    242, 245, 262, 274, 282, 288–9
Bridges, Sir Edward, 459–66, 475–6, 482
Bright, Sir Charles, 244
British Academy, 304 (n 15), 348, 447, 456,
  488
British Columbia, exhibition of records, 487
British Empire Exhibition, 389
British Film Institute, 450, 471–2
British Guiana, 357
British Institute of Recorded Sound, 450
British Library, 456
British Museum, 60, 123–4, 141, 172, 229,
  273, 276, 297, 331, 365, 433, 555
  destruction of Exchequer records
    deprecated, 49
  principal librarianship, 20, 222, 288–9
  relations with PRO, 200, 221–2, 309, 348,
    420

British Museum – *contd*
  staff and staffing, 16 (n 2b), 51, 73–4, 103,
    127, 145–6, 153, 180, 243, 258, 288,
    324, 364, 454, 538, 559
  wish to acquire Record Commission
    transcripts, etc, 105–6, 109–10, 142,
    551–3
British Railways Board, 442, 491, 506
British Records Association, 419, 425,
  439–40, 450, 487, 506
British Standards Institution, 456
British Transport Commission, 441, 506
Britton, J, 556
Brodie, J G, 300, 322, 335, 378, 388, 573
Brook, Sir Norman, 464, 480, 498
Brooke, C N L, 147 (n 9)
  T H, 426, 435, 575
Brougham, Henry Peter, Lord Brougham
  and Vaux, 30 (n 8)
Broughton, H, 154 (n 20b)
Brown, H, 318, 355
  P A, 378
  R A, 456, 576
  Rawdon, 217, 255–6, 300
  W J, MP, 399–400
Browning, O, 333
Bruce, Edward, Lord Bruce of Kinloss, 343,
  348
  Henry Austin, Lord Aberdare, 378
  J, 4–5, 139–40, 163 (n 1), 171, 214, 240–1,
    243, 262, 556
Brudenell-Bruce, Henry Augustus, Lord
  Ailesbury, 348–9
Brussels, 241, 255, 405
Bryce, James, (*later* Viscount Bryce), 357
Buckingham Palace, 21
Buckland, C, 148, 381, 395, 408, 432, 435,
  503, 574
Buckley, Denys (*later* Sir Denys), 466, 472,
  482
Bullen, W, 226, 262
Buller, C, MP, 4, 6–7, 9, 36 (n 4), 94, 105,
  120, 150, 278, 499, 511–21
Burrow, J W, 499
Burtt, J, 16, 50, 76, 126, 138, 150, 156, 169,
  190, 193, 201–2, 215, 232–3, 236,
  256–8, 274, 281, 356, 572
Butler, A J, 335, 355
  Joseph, bishop of Durham, 336 (n 21)
  Richard Austen, MP, (*later* Lord Butler),
    442
    chancellor of the Exchequer, 460–1,
      463, 465–6
Butterworth, publishers, 171
Byerley, A, 325 (n 12b), 376, 387

Deptford Dockyard, 106, 221, 503
Deputy keeper's reports *see* Annual reports
Deputy keepership, 1, 71 (n 27), 72, 93
  Acton's views, 288–9
  carries post of inspecting officer *ex officio*, 292, 319
  Esher on qualities needed, 306
  Grigg Committee proposes new role, 471
  increased load, 316
  Ireland, 228–9
  list of appointments, 569–70
  master of the rolls power of nomination, 9–11, 24, 30–1, 166, 168, 186, 252–3, 557, 560
  official designation, 90–1
  pay, 14–15, 23–8, 86–9, 139, 166, 168, 292, 316, 319, 397, 407, 418, 437, 447, 568
  portraits of DKs, 424
  Treasury favour internal appointment, 166, 168, 560
  see also under individual deputy keepers
Derby, Lord *see* Smith-Stanley
Designs, Cole's report for Board of Trade, 118
  see also Schools of design
Destruction of records *see* Disposal of records
Devon, C, 5, 16, 23, 30, 49–50, 58, 71–2, 80, 83, 195, 249, 276
  Frederick
    assistant keeper, 3 (n 3), 56, 66, 72, 76, 80–1, 116–17, 124–5, 134, 138, 159, 186–7, 454, 572
    clerk at Chapter House, 5, 16, 22–3, 30, 47–9, 174, 213
    death, 189–90, 193
    involvement in destruction of Exchequer records, 48–9
    Treasury contacts, 23, 57
    work for Duchy of Cornwall, 16 (n 2a), 57–8
Dialogus de Scaccario, 352
Dicey, A V, 192
Dickens, Charles, 118, 139, 413, 556
Dictionary of National Biography, 13, 285, 364
Dilke, C W, 139, 556
Disposal of records
  BRA leaflet, 450
  by Government Documents Committee, 196–7, 207–8, 210, 214, 220–1, 223, 253, 265–6, 394
  by Inspecting Officers' Committee, 292–4, 317–18, 332–3, 337, 346–7, 356, 362, 369–74, 393–4, 412–14, 432, 437, 443, 450, 457

Disposal of records – *contd*
  by presentation *see* Presentation of records
  criticisms of policy, 265, 274, 356, 371–4, 394, 464, 470, 474, 503, 565–6
  early proposals and proceedings, 5, 9, 11, 60, 66–7, 113–14, 121, 130, 141–2, 160, 183, 227–8, 253, 256, 265–6, 269–70
  governing statutes *see* Public Record Office Acts 1877 and 1898
  Grigg proposals, 467–75
  irregular, 266, 355–6, 363
  Jessel's views, 265–6, 269–70, 278–80, 283–4, 291–4, 318
  Langdale's and Romilly's views, 130, 196, 253
  modern records, 502
  Office History to have chapter about, 423
  policy under 1958 act, 494–5, 503–4
  proposal for selection criteria to be statutorily defined, 496
  public opinion averse, 336
  publication of schedules, 294 (n 8), 374, 565
  Record Bills (1837–8), 517
  robust approach urged, 412–14
  Select Committee inquiry (1840), 49, 65
  war records, 384, 432
Disraeli, Benjamin, Lord Beaconsfield, 234–5, 290, 333
Dixon, W H, 225 (n 20a), 556
Dodwell, Rev H J, 282–3
Domesday Book, 80 (n 38), 163, 226, 439, 456
  anniversary celebrations, 311
  display, 75, 78, 290–1
  evacuation, 379, 428–9
  postcard, 403
  rebinding, 202, 230–1, 473
  reproduction, 202, 215, 230, 290
  research and studies, 320, 473
  storage, 38, 74, 129, 190, 262–3, 299
  use, 89
Domesday (or Norman) Tower, Chancery Lane repository, 224, 262
'Domesday' type, 545
Dominions Office, 435
  raises question of access to Cabinet papers, 415
  relaxes closure rules, 404
Doran, J, 556
Drake, F C, 322, 576
Drew, C, 408, 427, 436 (n 28d), 437, 448–51, 459 (n 7), 465, 473, 570–1, 575
Du Cann, E (*later* Sir Edward), MP, 496
Duckett, Sir George, 327

589

Evans, Sir David Lewis – *contd*
principal assistant keeper,
appointment, 449–50
Edwards anxious to safeguard his
interests, 471
involved in search for branch
repository, 458
involvement in Grigg preliminaries,
465–6
mentioned as Jenkinson's successor,
462, 476
Sir Henry Vincent, 364
N E, 200 (n 44), 456, 576
Evershed, Sir Raymond, *later* Lord
Evershed, 485 (n 25a), 569
appointment as master of the rolls, 450
backs Jenkinson on Ashridge staffing, 458
clash with Treasury, 459–61
concern about Grigg proposals, 476, 482
efforts to obtain branch repository, 458
Grigg Committee, appointed jointly by,
462–3, 465–6
Jenkinson's submission about Grigg
Report, 474
presses for pay increase for deputy keeper,
447
record services acknowledged, 493, 496
remains on good terms with Jenkinson,
478
signs address to Sharp, 455
speech on Public Records Bill, 493–5
views on inspecting officer grading, 484
Ewald, A C, 202, 250–1, 310, 315–16, 321–2,
576
Examiners' Office, 513, 531
Exchequer, 33, 60 (n 7a), 80, 161, 370, 513,
515
chancellor *see* Chancellor of the Exchequer
Court of, 45, 56, 62, 67, 147, 318, 514,
516
King's/Queen's remembrancer, *q.v.*
Madox's *History and Antiquities*, 82, 352,
555
records *see* Legal records
Exchequer and Audit Department, 222
Exchequer of Pleas, 7, 17, 34–5, 37, 41, 47,
53, 56, 83, 95, 515, 536
Exeter, bishop of *see* Stapeldon
Exhibitions (PRO)
Cole's proposals, 219
Collingridge put in charge, 437
special, 311, 339, 389, 416, 462
mentioned
BRA, 487
British Columbia, 487

Exhibitions (PRO) – *contd*
centenary (PRO Act), 423–4
(PRO Building), 454
Chancery, 487
Jamestown, 486–7
mutiny on the *Bounty*, 416
naval records, 454–5
resettlement of Jews, 487
Shakespeare, 378–9
treaties, 454
see also Museum (PRO)

Fagg, J, 437, 456, 575
Falkland Islands, restrictions on records,
357, 393
Family history *see* Historical research
Faraday, M, 66, 236
Farmer, R D, 396, 398–9, 405, 427, 435–6,
438, 440, 448, 457–9, 483–4, 571
Fearnside, T R, 223
Fees and charges, 8, 84, 335
abolition, 225, 263, 272, 500
census returns, 380, 451–2
changes (1949), 451
Devon's attachment to old system, 189
Hardy's and Cole's proposals, 5, 35–41,
54, 139–40
increase (1921), 390
inquiry (1860), 199
legal records, 40–1, 139–40, 272, 308–10,
330, 361, 390, 432, 451
Nicolas's views, 2, 91, 500
Palgrave's proposals, 33, 40–1, 522, 524,
526, 530–1
photocopying, 485
receipts (1838–1958), 568
record searches, 2, 57, 74–5, 530
regulation under original Record Bills, 6,
9, 516–17
regulations, 54, 59, 83–4, 139, 184,
308–10, 361, 390
remission for literary searchers, 91,
139–41, 164, 199, 272 (n 20), 554–6
revision (1938), 432
statement requested by Treasury, 44
suggested appropriation, 33, 530
Treasury views, 330–1
Tytler's view, 532
under 1958 act, 497
Feltham, Midd, 457
Fenian outrages, 232, 312, 403
Fenwick, M, 76–7, 97–8, 126, 143, 152, 176,
194, 210–11, 238, 249–50, 576

Foss, E, 556
Foster, C, 231, 259, 301
Foster and Dicksee, Messrs, 338
Fowler, G H, 442
  R C, 322, 352, 376, 380–1, 383, 386–9,
    394–6, 400, 403, 406, 571, 574
Fox, Henry, Lord Holland, 19–20, 89
  O G R, 399–402, 426, 435, 438, 448–9,
    455, 459, 473, 482–3, 570
France
  ambassador's visit to PRO, 94
  archives, 53, 163, 368, 564–5
  Claims Commission records, 86
  clerk's convalescence in, 144
  disturbances (1871), 255
  Ecole des Chartes, q.v.
  Gascon Rolls project, 319, 447, 543
  Napoleon's captivity, 490
  Paris Exhibition (1867), 234
  record works, 246
  restrictions on access to papers, 270, 330,
    357
  work on documents relating to British
    history, 241, 255, 320, 334, 389, 562
Franks, A, 556
Fraser, Alexander Arthur, Lord Saltoun, 494
Freedom of information, 375, 504
Freeman, E, 192, 273, 289, 307, 320
Fremantle, Sir Charles, 234, 325–7, 354
Froude, J A, 192, 246
Fry, E A, 397
Furnivall, F J, 263, 307
Fyfe, David Patrick Maxwell, Lord Kilmuir,
  493, 495

Gairdner, J, 117, 126, 172, 174, 184 (n 21),
  193–4, 213, 229, 238, 282, 288, 295,
  306, 315, 322, 335, 366, 377–8, 572
Galbraith, V H, 395, 406, 436, 466, 472, 574
Galton, Sir Douglas, 244
Gardiner, S R, 288–9, 318, 331, 334–5
Garnier, J, 67
Gaselee, Sir Stephen, 392–3, 425
Gaskoin, C J B, 486
Gatliff, H E C, 428–30
Gavin, J A, 399, 438, 440, 457, 459, 484,
  507
Gawler, H, 8 (n 13)
Gay C, 8 (n 14), 17, 51–2, 63–4, 69, 75, 154,
  159, 180, 536
  H, junior, 69
  senior, 17, 69, 159, 233, 252, 539–40
  Mrs S, 252
Gayangos, Don Pascual, 240–1, 255, 300, 318

Genealogy see Historical research, family
  history
General Register and Record Office of
  Shipping and Seamen, 332
General Register House, Edinburgh, 229–30,
  420
General Register Office, 94, 142, 418, 479,
  558
General Strike (1926), 395–6
George I, statue, 343
George VI, 416
George Edward Alexander Edmund, duke of
  Kent, 423–4
Germany
  colonial policy, 392
  Control Commission, 435–6, 438
  king of Hanover, 94
  postcard withdrawn in interest of good
    relations, 403
  record works, 246
  restrictive access policy, 432
Gibraltar, restrictions on access to records,
  357, 393
Gibson, J E, 99, 126, 143–4
Gifford, Miss D H, 456, 473, 486, 575
  Robert, Lord Gifford, 338
Gilbert, J T, 227–9, 243, 308
Giles, J A, 116
Gilkes, J, 417–18, 449
Gilling, R W N, 426, 435, 575
Giuseppi, M, 322, 352, 388–90, 394, 396–7,
  417, 424–5, 473, 477, 571, 574
Gladstone, H J, MP, 357–8
  Miss M, 288
  W E, MP
    chancellor of the Exchequer, 119, 212,
      230
    prime minister, 243–5, 252–3, 255, 264,
      291, 307
Glasgow University, 378
Glenelg, Lord see Grant
Glover, W, 78
Golden Grove Book, 262
Gondomar Manuscripts, 319
Gonville and Caius College, 147
Gooch, G P, 393, 398, 415, 480
Goodenough, W T, 17, 539–40
Gorrequer Papers, 490
Goschen, G, chancellor of the Exchequer, 337
Government chemist, 222, 351, 376
Government Documents Committee, 287,
  292
  formation, 196–7
  secretaries, 570
  work see under Disposal of records

Hardy, Sir Thomas Duffus – *contd*
  assistant keeper – *contd*
    correspondence with Palgrave, 42–3,
      117, 127–8, 155 (n 21), 157–8
    designation, 90–1
    difficulties with Chancery records, 67
    friendship with Cole, 55, 94, 97
    influence at Tower, 57, 91–2
    loyalty to Petrie, 61, 116
    Memoirs of Lord Langdale, 13, 132,
      147–8
    move to Chancery Lane, 174
    Palgrave's praise, 82
    plays leading part in drafting address
      to Langdale, 132–4
    readiness to serve in Ireland, 115
    renewed differences with Palgrave,
      97, 117, 188
    report on Durham etc records, 158–9,
      224
    seeks secretaryship, 185–7
    supports workmen's claim, 127, 138
    views on search fees, 139, 199
      on stamping documents, 65–6
    work on inquisitions post mortem, 79,
      82, 117
      on *Monumenta Historica Britannica*,
        115–16, 172–3
  clerk at Tower, 6–7, 34, 41–3, 50, 56,
    281
    comments on Record Bill, 11
    critic of Record Commission, 4
    document believed borrowed by, 497
    editorial work, 3, 7, 43, 61, 542–4
    feud with Palgrave, 3, 23, 32, 56, 174,
      223–4, 285–6, 361
    Palgrave preferred as deputy keeper,
      13, 19–21, 30–2, 115, 252, 285, 500
    record agency, 213
    record plan, 34–6
    transcriber for Palgrave, 2–3
  daughter, 290 (n 5)
  deputy keeper, 30–1, 42 (n 8), 154
    (n 20b), 175, 180, 214, 241 (n 39a),
    300, 303, 307, 309, 350, 448, 507,
    569
    abolition of fees urged, 225
    appointment, 205–6, 219, 222, 252
    assessment of career, 286, 499–501
    assists Stevenson, 255
    Athanasian Creed report, 255–6
    backs Romilly's recommendations for
      promotion, 210–11
    death, 284–5, 289

Hardy, Sir Thomas Duffus – *contd*
  deputy keeper – *contd*
    departmental records assigned
      secondary place, 221, 467, 503
    deprecates Lemon's criticism of
      Hunter, 210
    difficulties, with Burtt, 215, 236,
      256–8, 281
      with C Cole, 234–6
      with Hart, 253–4
    dispute, with Carr, Grove and
      Yeatman, 256–8, 263, 270–7,
      286, 292–3, 348, 500
      with Thorpe, 217
    Domesday Book rebound, 230
    Duchy of Lancaster records secured,
      223–4
    Durham records inspected and
      secured, 224–5
    editorial work, 216, 239–40, 250, 305,
      334
    evidence to Commons on Courts Bill,
      206–7
      to Civil Service Inquiry
        Commission, 266–8
      to Lords on Records Bill, 278–80
    fears too liberal access policy, 271–2,
      333
    feeling age, 246, 272
    forbids candles, 261
    form of *Annual Report*, 215, 218, 223,
      262
    good relations with Bond, 222
    Historical MSS Commission
      activities, 243, 247, 262–3
    honorary degrees, 247
    knighted, 243–5
    Lethbridge tribute, 212
    management of staff, 233–8
    no enthusiasm for record displays, 219
    obtains annuity for Mrs Hood, 251
      grant for Mrs Atkins, 282
    proposes separation of keepership
      from post of master of the rolls,
      252–3, 561–2
    Public Records Bill prepared, 277
    recommends Fenwick for promotion,
      211, 238
    reinstates Lea, 252
    reliance upon Edwards and Kingston,
      245
    report, on editorial works, 215–18,
      246–7
      on other record establishments, etc,
        226–30

595

Huggons, K F, 483, 571
Hughes, A, 320–1, 352, 354, 576
  E, MP, 496
  R, 354
  T, 192
Hume, D, 246
  J, MP, 128
  M, 318–19, 355
Hunnisett, R F, 456, 576
Hunt, G W, 30, 236
  P B S L, 68, 98, 126, 153, 194, 203, 233,
    303, 314, 321, 573
Hunter, F L, 16
  J, 8, 16, 19, 23, 51–4
    assistant keeper, 4, 48–9, 54, 56, 58–9,
      65–7, 69–70, 72, 74, 82, 86–92, 99,
      102–3, 124, 126, 132–4, 144, 151,
      153, 159, 169–70, 178, 186–8, 191–2,
      199, 272, 370, 541, 572
    biographical notice on Palgrave, 13
    comments on Record Bill, 10–11
    death, 203, 209–10
    defender of Record Commission, 4–5
Huntington Library, 385, 419
Hurst, Sir Cecil, 393
Hyde, H Montgomery, MP, 420 (n 20a), 460,
  496
Hylton-Foster, Sir Harry, MP, 495–6

IDS van service, 457
Imperial Airways records, 441
Imperial College of Science, 408
Imperial War Museum, 384
Impey, W, 171, 194–5
India, 212, 226, 231 (n 28a), 241, 451, 491
  Office, 391, 491
Industrial Court, 401
Industrial injuries see Staff and staffing,
  accidents and health hazards
Inglis, Sir Robert Harry, MP, 145–6, 161,
  556
Inland Revenue, 196, 324, 327, 354, 378, 466
Inner Temple, 85
Innes, C, 202
Insolvent debtors' records, 413
Inspecting Officers' Committee, 315, 319,
  353, 377, 388, 484
    appointments, 291–2, 322, 349–50, 354,
      377–8, 394–5, 403, 408–9, 417, 426,
      450, 473–4
    formation, 284, 291–2, 298
    list of members, 571
    work see under Disposal of records

Inspection of records (by public) see Public
  access
  fees see Fees and charges
Institute of British Photographers, 433
Institute of Historical Research, 391, 436,
  442, 447, 466, 502
  see also Historical research
Interdepartmental Committee on Social and
  Economic Research, 450
Intermediate ('Limbo') repositories see under
  Record offices and repositories
International Council on Archives, 446
International Exhibition (1862), 219, 244
Inventions, 97, 419
  see also Patent commissioners and
    documents
Iran, 483
Ireland, 242 (n 40)
  Casement diaries, 496
  coat of arms, 226
  commissariat papers, 149
  Fenians, 232, 312, 403
  HMC inspector, 243
  knights, 244
  neglect of records alleged, 348, 362
  parliamentary criticism of Papal calendar,
    344
  position of records under 1898 act, 347
  Public Record Office, 227–9, 247, 353
    possible oversight, 226
  Public Records Bill, 30–1, 228 (n 24)
  record publications, 161, 226–7, 230,
    238–9, 261–2, 300, 307–8, 334–5, 344,
    565
  records survey, 112–15
  restrictions on access to papers, 270, 333,
    344–5, 357, 403
  return of state papers, 229
  see also Northern Ireland
Irish Manuscripts Commission, 447
Irish Office, 202, 357–8
Irish regiments, servicemen's records, 479
Ironmongers' Company, 310 (n 3)
Isaacson, R F, 249, 322, 334, 352, 354, 377,
  571, 573
Italy, 89, 137, 191, 435, 489
  editorial work, 217, 229, 238, 241, 254–6,
    282, 300, 318, 344, 355, 389, 416–17, 562

Jackson, William, (later Lord Allerton), 336
Jamaica, 319, 446
James, Sir Henry, 202, 230
  M Rhodes, 364
  Sir William Milbourne, 276

598

King's/Queen's Bench, Court of – *contd*
  records *see under* Legal records
  royal portraits from plea rolls, 454
King's/Queen's remembrancer, 513
  books deposited, 370
  purchase of record from clerk in office, 492
  see also under Legal records
King's Silver Office, 513
  books, 85
Kingston, A, 92, 97, 126, 176, 199, 211–12,
    220, 226, 231–2, 245, 264, 267, 281,
    284–5, 288–91, 295–6, 303, 305–6, 312,
    350, 501, 573
  W, 144, 176
Kipling, J, 8 (n 13), 54, 58
Kirby, Miss E, 232, 261
  J, 232
Kirk, R, and wife, 83
Knight, C, 203–4, 556
  G, 112, 126, 144, 176–9, 184 (n 21), 194–5,
    211, 215, 233, 576
Knowles, M D, 173 (n 10a), 300
  R B, 217
Kraus Reprint, 217

La Touche, J J D, 229
Labour, Ministry of, 398
Lake, B G, 329 (n 15a)
Lamb, William, Lord Melbourne, 2, 21–2
Lambeth Palace Library, 172, 226, 262, 555
Lancashire distress fund, 219
Lancaster, county palatine, 266, 331, 369,
    375
  duchy, 10, 19, 25, 71 (n 27), 223–4, 262,
    266, 284, 288, 345, 495
Land Registry, 345, 448–9, 507
Land revenue
  records, 10, 37, 45, 513, 515, 536
  solicitor, 25
Land Revenue Record Office *see under*
    Record offices and repositories
Land tax records, 256, 261, 275
Landed Estates Record Office (Ireland), 229
Lane, R H, 486
Langdale, Lord and Lady *see* Bickersteth
Larken, A S, 218
Lascelles, R, 11, 47, 161
  William
    assistant keeper I, 211, 221, 572
    assistant keeper II, 154, 160, 169,
      176–9, 187, 210
    clerk, 17, 47, 50, 67, 76, 84, 97, 112,
      126
    death, 237

Lascelles, William – *contd*
    secretary of Government Documents
      Committee, 196–7, 210, 214, 394,
      570
Laski, H, 392
Latham, R E, 406 (n 5c), 417, 429, 435–7,
    488, 575
Laughton, Sir John Knox, 394
Law, E, 222
  W, 247 (n 3a), 269 (n 17b)
Law of Property Acts, 347, 389, 408
Law officers, 10, 105, 142, 223, 264, 273,
    383, 441, 490, 492
Law officers' opinions, public access, 270,
    356, 359–61, 392–3, 404
Lawrance, H E, 249, 281, 321, 576
Le Dieu, H F, 146, 259
  T, 147
Le Neve, P, 148
Lea, J T, 251–2
Leach, Sir John, 8 (n 13)
  T, 7–8, 19, 48, 56, 71
Leake Street intermediate repository *see*
    under Record offices and repositories
Lechmere, C, 31, 90 (n 1), 166, 169, 180,
    185–7, 194–5, 209–11, 213, 572
Lecky, W E H, 331, 345
Ledward, K H, 395, 410, 417, 429, 437, 451,
    487, 574
Lee, G A J, 406 (n 5b)
  J, 556
  Sir Sidney, 364
Leeds, duke of *see* Osborne
Legacy Duty Office, 324
Legal records
  cost of processing accessions, 62–3
  covered by original Record Act, 9, 105
  disposal *see* Disposal of records
  fees to searchers *see under* Fees and charges
  filing, 368
  future custody, 109
  Grigg proposals, 472, 482, 490
  guide, 390
  Irish, 228
  location, 529
  modern, 312
  neglect alleged, 565
  new references, 380–1
  Public Records Act, 490
  relationship to departmental records,
    278–9, 490, 499–500, 506
  Second World War arrangements, 430
  Select Committee of inquiry into
    destruction of Exchequer records
    (1840), 49, 65

Mills, Miss M H, 486
Milman, H H, 556
Milne, Sir David, 462
Milner, Alfred (*later* Viscount), 327
Milnes, Richard Monckton, Lord Houghton, 120, 278–9
Milroy, Rev W R, 341
Mitchell, H, 391 (n 22)
Mitchell Library, Sydney, 449
Modern Records Department, 458, 488
Modus tenendi parliamentum, 544
Mogford, E, 63
 H, 8 (n 14), 17, 52, 69–70, 95, 539–40
Molesworth, Sir William, 94
Moloney, M, 247–8, 299–300, 576
Monckton Milnes *see* Milnes
Monger, R F, 399, 438, 448, 456–7, 483, 571
Monger and Marchant, photographers, 390, 419, 433
Monsell, W, MP, 226–7
Montagu, F, 4 (n 5)
Monteagle, Lord *see* Spring Rice
Monumenta Historica Britannica, 60–1, 89, 115–16, 172, 500, 542, 551–2
More, Sir Thomas, 79
Morgan, O, 556
 T J, 449, 485
Morrin, J, 227, 229
Morris, G J, 249, 315, 322, 334, 352, 354–5, 378, 571, 573
Morrison, H, MP, lord president, 441, 458
Mortgage foreclosure business, 335
Mosley, Sir Oswald, MP, 409
Mowatt, Sir Francis, 323 (nn 11–12a), 331, 336, 338 (n 23), 346–7
Mowels, S A, 179–80
Muir-Mackenzie, Sir Kenneth Augustus, 383 (n 16a)
Mullins, E L C, 281 (n 30)
Municipal Corporations Commission, 3, 6 (n 9)
Munitions, Ministry of, 394
Murray, A, 279
 Hon C A, 21
 H, 267 (n 16)
Museum (PRO)
 annual report, 389
 catalogue, 343 (n 1), 352, 486
 closure, 379, 460–2, 486
 foundation, 338–9, 341, 343, 501
 monuments, etc, 343, 348, 486
 officers-in-charge, 403, 437, 450
 opening hours, 420, 495
 Palgrave's proposal, 77–8
 postcards, 403, 416
 preparation of records for display, 351

Museum (PRO) – *contd*
 restoration, 486
 slight air-raid damage, 431
 statistics, 389
 war memorial, 378
 see also Exhibitions

Naas, Lord *see* Bourke
National Benevolent Institution, 251
National Coal Board, 441, 491
National Debt Office, 248, 265
National Film Library, 472
National Gallery, 70, 123
National Library of Wales, 362–4, 376, 495
National Maritime Museum, 449
National Portrait Gallery, 175, 299
National Register of Archives, 442
Nationalised industries
 records liaison and superintendence, 450, 494
 status of records, 441–2, 491, 506
Naval records
 exhibition, 454–5
 Navy Board, 106
 see also under Admiralty
Navy League, 345
Navy Records Society, 348
Nelson, W, 16, 50, 151, 169, 203, 211, 572
Netherlands (*or* Holland), 357, 368, 565
Neville, Richard Cornwallis, 556
 Richard Griffin, Lord Braybrooke, 556
New Palace Yard, Westminster, 33
New South Wales, Australia, 357
New York, USA, 355
New Zealand, 201
New Zealand Company, 356
Newfoundland fisheries, restrictions on access to records, 330, 357
Newton, A P, 417, 451
Nichols, J B, 556
 J G, 556
Nicolas, Sir Nicholas Harris, 2–4, 7, 70, 86, 90–1, 174, 273, 308, 500
Noble, T C, 310
Norfolk assizes circuit, strayed records, 421
Norman Tower *see* Domesday Tower
Normanby, Lord *see* Phipps
North Western Railway Company, 158
Northampton, custos rotulorum, 291
Northcote, Sir Stafford, 168, 188, 212, 247
Northern Ireland
 Public Record Office, 388
 University, 447
 see also Ireland

Palgrave, Sir Francis – *contd*
  deputy keeper – *contd*
    fears creation of second deputy
      keeper, 167, 557, 559
    forbidden to undertake private work,
      34, 122
    gives up outside directorships, 71, 93
    good opinion of Thomas's *Guide*,
      131–2
    Hardy's tribute, 215
    inquiry into missing Shakespearian
      documents, 200
    Irish record arrangements considered,
      113–15
    jest concerning, 192
    Langdale period, 13–135, 245, 302
    literary search fees opposed, 54,
      139–41, 272 (n 20), 500
    management of clerks, 47, 63, 67–9,
      97–9, 126–7, 143–6, 151–3, 166,
      176–9, 188, 193–5, 203, 233, 314,
      523–6, 531
    management of workmen, 8 (n 14),
      46, 51–2, 63–4, 75, 95–7, 99–102,
      127–8, 138–9, 144–7, 154, 179–82,
      219, 260, 522–4, 530, 538–9,
      546–50
    Nicolas corrected, 90–1
    organisational proposals, 33, 44–6, 48,
      77–85, 104–6, 138, 159, 176
    pay, 8–9, 23–8, 55, 71, 86–9, 109,
      131–3, 139, 147, 166, 169
    pessimism, 50, 121
    plans for new building, 60, 120–1,
      127–9, 154–60, 175–6, 184, 201,
      208, 274, 526
    position strengthened under Romilly,
      136–7
    proposals for operation of Record Act,
      23, 33–4, 39, 45–6, 527–31
    publication proposals, 108, 170–4,
      202–3, 334
    recovery of strayed public records
      urged, 33, 103, 492
    refuses to sign farewell address to
      Langdale, 132–4, 138, 147
    reliance on and support for Edwards,
      76, 161, 186–7, 202–3, 236
    reports, etc on unfinished editorial
      works, 60–2, 116, 541–5
    representations about dangerous
      crane, 197–8
    reservations about transfer of Duchy
      of Lancaster records, 223–4
    Romilly period, 136–204

Palgrave, Sir Francis – *contd*
  deputy keeper – *contd*
    secures departmental records, 106–7,
      142–3
    seeks Hardy's advice, 41–3
    settles PRO establishment, 50
    stamping controversy, 64–6
    stationed at Rolls House, 43
    supports staff claim for more pay, 161
    surveys legal records, 66–7, 292
    takes over records at branches, 56–7
    Turnbull petition signed, 192
    unenthusiastic about displays of
      records, 75, 78, 219
    urges union with State Paper Office,
      108, 163–5, 503
    views on Palmer's indexes, 189
    visits Ely, 110
    wishes to see rare works reprinted,
      202–3, 238
  editor of *Parliamentary Writs*, 1–3, 56,
    62, 92, 286 (n 36)
  feud with Hardy brothers, 3, 23, 56,
    223–4, 285–6
  former servant, 214, 312
  health, 123, 147, 161, 175, 191, 203
  historical writings, etc, 62 (n 8), 89, 122,
    165 (n 5b), 175, 273, 300–1, 305, 499
  house at Hampstead, 161, 202 (n 49),
    440
  Jewish ancestry, 7 (n 12), 67–8, 264
  keeper at Chapter House, 3, 16, 23, 26,
    56, 117, 203
  knighthood, 3, 244–5
  makes peace with Nicolas, 7
  marriage, 1
  medallion likeness, 202
  observations on record plans, 1, 4, 6–8,
    18, 23, 522–31
  Record Bill, 6–7, 9, 105, 176, 511–21
  sister, 202 (n 49)
  trustee of National Portrait Gallery, 175
  unsuccessful bids for keeperships, 7, 8
    (n 13)
  views on social and political affairs, 3
    (n 2), 102, 119–20
  will, 202
  F T, 22 (n 4), 119, 139, 226
  G F, 22, (n 4)
  Sir Reginald, 139, 286 (n 36)
  Sir Robert Harry Inglis, 139, 165 (n 5b),
    174–5, 351–2
  W G, 22 (n 4), 119, 139
Palgravians, 281, 361

Palmer, Miss E, 189
T, 8, 48, 54, 56, 58, 65–6, 69–71, 77, 84,
86–9, 91–2, 102, 114, 132–4, 138, 189,
213, 572
V, 486
W, 138–9
Palmerston, Lord *see* Temple
Pandulph, Cardinal, 79
Panizzi, Sir Anthony, 20, 180, 222, 288
Papal letters/registers, calendar, 318, 344,
355, 447
Paper Office (House of Commons), 514
Paper Shortage Committee, 432
Paris, 234, 241, 255, 300, 389, 405
Paris, Matthew, 222, 246
Parish registers, 225, 291
Parker, J H, 556
Parkinson, R, 556
Parliament, 73–4, 107–8, 118 (n 26), 128,
283, 305, 330, 370
annual reports on PRO, 272, 472, 517, 563
census returns in Clock Tower, 332
constitution, 565–6
fire (1834), 85
first writ of summons, 230
history *see* History of Parliament
guarantor of Suitors' Fund, 531
possible records accommodation, 120
power etc under Record Bills, 512–13,
517–20
records, 308, 528, 534
returns, etc, for, 220, 248, 273–5, 292,
309, 562
treaty of union, 453
uninterested in record matters, 121, 356
House of Commons, 139, 209 (n 5), 218,
220, 227, 239, 248, 551
criticism of PRO by Irish and Welsh
MPs, 344, 348, 362–4
debate on PRO manpower cut, 460–1
debates on new building, 120
on Record Bills, 10–11, 277–80, 347,
495–6
examination of PRO work by Select
Committee, 413
Paper Office, 514
questions concerning PRO, 258, 366,
375, 392, 420 (n 20a), 490
Return of Members, 281, 321, 377, 407
Select Committee on Miscellaneous
Expenditure, 108–9, 121, 165
Select Committee on the Courts of
Justice (Money) Bill, 206–7
Select Committee on the Public
Records, 2, 53

Parliament, House of Commons – *contd*
Select Committee on the Record
Commission, 1, 3–5, 6 (n 7), 21, 33,
50 (n 18), 51, 59, 61, 105, 109, 216,
302 (n 13), 501
House of Lords, 364, 492
debates on Record Bills, 10–11, 278–80,
347–8, 493–7, 504
peerage cases, 288
Secret Committee, 92
Select Committee of inquiry into
destruction of Exchequer records, 49,
65
see also Victoria (Barry's) Tower
Parliament Office, 514
Parliamentary counsel, 277–8, 491
Parliamentary Survey (1650), 555
Parliamentary Writs, 2–3, 56, 62, 92, 286
(n 36)
Parratt, G F, 196
Passfield, Lord *see* Webb
Paston Letters, 229, 242
Patent commissioners and documents, 97,
161, 182, 253
Patent Office, 294, 297–8, 448
Patent reform, Cole's interest, 118
Pattinson, A S, 576
Paul, H, 288 (n 3)
P, 17, 69–70, 75, 95–6, 118, 127–8, 159,
233, 547
Paymaster General's Office, 404
Pearson, C, 192
Pedder, J, 322, 576
Peel, B L, 79, 97–8
Sir Robert, 89, 92 (n 3), 97, 119
Pellatt, H, 387, 399
Pells Office, 37, 45, 49, 53, 58, 79, 86, 513,
528–30
Penfold, P A, 399, 438, 483
Peninsular War, 130
Pennell, Sir Charles Henry, 244
Pennethorne, Sir James, 118, 123, 128, 137,
155–7, 185, 247, 336–7, 339, 386 (n 19)
Pensions, Ministry of, 394
Perkins, –, clerk of works, 155
Petrie, H
compensation payable, 71
death, 61
editor *Monumenta Historica Britannica*,
60–1, 89, 115–16, 172–3, 500, 542,
551–2
keeper at Tower, 7, 19, 30, 34, 48, 50, 105
papers, 381 (n 14b)
retirement, 56
Petroleum Department, 435

Rolls Chapel Record Office *see under* Record offices and repositories
Rolls Court, 38, 147, 206–7, 282, 299
Rolls Estate, 190, 210, 215, 291, 299
  plans for Record Office, 5, 34, 44, 120–1, 123, 128–9, 154–8, 424, 512, 528
  police patrol, 160, 176, 226, 232, 264
Rolls Estate Act 1837, 7, 336
Rolls House headquarters *see under* Record offices and repositories
Rolls Office (Ireland), 227
Rolls Room *see* Search Department/rooms, Chancery Lane
Rolls Series *see* Record publications
Rolls Yard, 34, 112, 182, 196, 299, 303, 311–12
  demolition of houses, 281, 335–9
Romaine, W G, 244
Roman Catholics, employment as editors, 192–3, 217–18, 226–7, 240, 243, 254–5, 282, 318–19, 416–17
Rome, editorial work, 241, 255, 282, 300, 318, 344, 355, 389, 416–17, 562
Romilly, Lady Caroline Charlotte, 136–7
  Sir John, *later* Lord Romilly, master of the rolls, 147–8, 174, 179–80, 202, 233, 237, 251, 309, 569
    AKs' and clerks' pay claims backed, 161, 166–70, 207–8, 557–60
    anxious to placate State Paper Office clerks, 195
    appointment, 124, 135–7
    appointments, promotions etc made, 145–6, 151, 169–70, 185–8, 191–5, 203, 205–6, 210–15, 224, 236, 238, 285
    Black's services terminated, 149–51
    bust, 225, 274
    coat of arms, 226
    dealings with Hart, 253–4
    difficulties with staff, 196–7, 256–8
    dispute with Sir Henry James, 230
    Duchy of Lancaster records secured, 223–4
    efforts to secure further building, 160, 195–6, 208–9, 218, 225
    feeling age, 246
    gives more calendaring work to staff, 241
    good opinion of Holden, 138
    Hunter's rules countermanded, 188
    inquires into effect of remission of literary search fees, 199
    insists on wire doors to presses, 156, 175, 208

Romilly, Sir John – *contd*
  institutes examination for clerks, 193–6, 203
  instructions to editors, 216, 240
  joins Rolls Chapel congregation, 137
  lays foundation stone of new building, 137, 454
  literary search fees remitted, 139–41, 500, 554–6
  main administrative burden shouldered, 201
  Museum proposal unlikely to find favour, 219
  no faith in Thorpe's competence, 217
  obtains knighthood for Hardy, 243–5
  opposes removal of Rolls Court, 206–7
  order in council obtained, 142–3
  Palgrave's pay claim supported, 139
  Palgrave's plan of organisation approved, 159
  Palgrave treated with consideration, 161, 186
  presentation of record publications to Philadelphia, 229
  problems with clerks, 144, 151–3
  proposals for dealing with historical manuscripts in private hands, 200–1, 242–3
  publication programme, 170–4, 201, 216–18, 238–40, 255, 263, 273, 334–5, 500
  raised to peerage, 225
  rebukes Thorpe, 191
  relations with British Museum, 200, 222
  reorganises AKs and clerks, 198–9
  repository plans approved, 155–60
  resignation, 263–4
  resists removal of records to Victoria Tower, 208–9
  restrictions placed on Stevenson's calendars, 193, 240, 255
  Rolls Chapel demolition opposed, 247
  Roman Catholic editors, 192–3, 217–18, 240, 243, 254–5
  salary, 167
  services to record searchers, 225
  State Paper Office merger supported, 163–6
  Thomas's *Notes* valued, 185
  time given to record duties, 207, 228
  unlikely to approve records loan, 219
  unwilling to support Mrs Thomas's claim, 248
  views on change of MR's record responsibilities, 252–3

617

Southampton, 202, 215, 230, 262, 281, 288, 290, 303
Spain, editorial work, 201, 216, 238, 240–1, 255, 300, 318–19, 355, 405–6, 562
Sparks, J, MP, 495–6
Spearman, Sir Alexander Young, 13–15, 80
Spedding, J, 556
Spencer, John Poyntz, Earl Spencer, 291
Spring Gardens, Westminster, 33, 345
Spring Rice, E S, 353
 Thomas, Lord Monteagle, 14, 20, 23, 25, 164
Staff and staffing
 accidents and health hazards, 112, 160, 180–1, 197–8, 237, 320, 325, 366
 addresses subscribed, 132–5, 219, 245, 263, 282–3, 302, 396, 455
 complements (1838–1958), 500, 567
 duties during General Strike, 395–6
 former members, 424
 honours and awards, 243–5, 302, 308, 342, 377–8, 380, 388, 390, 398, 426, 439, 443, 446, 473, 488–9
 proposed direction etc, 562
 salaries, etc, 568
 war memorial (1914–1918), 378
 women
  campaign for archival employment, 396, 425
  employment as clerks urged, 314–15
  employment as sewers, 387
  engagement of ladies' attendant, 225
  entry age for charwomen, 248
  first entry to AK grade, 395
  increased role in PRO, 485
  Mrs Green engaged in editorial capacity, 170–1, 334–5
  possible employment on lighter manual work, 64
  PRO's reluctance to employ, 351, 396, 398
  sewing undertaken by workmen's wives, 69
 abstractors *see* clerical grades (pre-1920) *below*
 assistant keepers, 90–1, 103–4, 191, 245, 256, 305
  AK II grade, abolition, 198–9
   reintroduction, 388
  allowance posts, 418, 488
  appointment, by competitive interview, 406–8, 417, 426, 437–8, 456
   by departmental examination, 77–8, 193–6

Staff and staffing, assistant keepers – *contd*
 appointment – *contd*
  by internal promotion, 125, 138, 151, 169, 187, 195, 203, 210–11, 237–8, 290, 303, 322, 353–5, 376, 378–81, 399, 456, 483
  by nomination, 48–50, 53, 56, 58–9, 224
  by transfer, 406
  from administrative class examination, 395, 406
  from reconstruction examination (1920), 395
  honorary (Second World War), 428
  under Record Bills, 11, 34, 511–12
 centenary plans, 421–4
 certification of office copies, 33, 36, 40, 45–6, 77, 151, 388, 516, 529
 comments on organisation, 159, 314–16
 complement, 37–9, 41, 46, 48, 86, 148–9, 166, 198, 294, 353, 408, 436, 459–60, 487, 567
 consulted about regulations for searchers, 54, 184
 director posts, 436–7, 473–4, 488
 eligibility etc for DK post, 166, 168, 285, 557, 560
 employment on routine and non-editorial work, 427, 459, 505
 evidence to outside bodies, 266–8, 365
 executivisation of certain work, 448, 459, 482–3, 489–90
 farewell address to Langdale, 132–5, 138, 147
 form of address, 400
 Fox not popular, 402, 483
 Grigg Report, 468–9, 482, 484, 502
 gulf with rest of staff, 350, 398
 HMC loan, 488
 hours, 320–1, 489
 impatience with troublesome searchers, 199, 272
 inventories prepared by, 77–80
 investigations of work, 294–8, 314–16
 itinerant, 113
 list, 442–3, 572–6
 membership of Inspecting Officers' Committee *see* Inspecting Officers' Committee
 necessary qualities, 46, 54–5, 443 (n 35), 448, 477
 Palgrave's proposed organisation, 77–8, 529–31
 pay, 48, 55, 86–9, 121, 131, 149, 161, 166–70, 207–9, 233, 257, 295–6, 298,

621

Walford, J, 4 (n 4), 197 (n 37)
Wallace, C, 565
Walrond, T, 242 (n 40)
Walsh, J E W, 228
Walton, H O, 402
War memorial (PRO Museum), 378
War Office, 332, 345, 380
  Historical Section, 434
  monuments and fine arts adviser, 435
  records, 264–5, 440
    disposal, 183, 196–7, 208, 293 (n 7a),
      355–6, 394
    official searches, 220, 328, 380
    public access, 220, 270, 330, 358–9, 361,
      393, 404, 451
    transfers, 160, 183, 349
War Records Disposal Committee, 384
Wardle, D B, 397, 400, 406, 411, 428, 433–5,
  437, 439, 449, 458, 474, 481, 485,
  488–9, 497, 575
Wardley, D J, 418 (n 19a)
Wardrobe accounts and books, 348, 535
Wards and Liveries, Court of, 125, 312, 486
Wartime repositories see under Record offices
  and repositories
Warwickshire records, 279
Waterlow, Sir Sydney Hedley, 244
Watson family, 258
  A T, 42 (n 8), 225, 232, 251, 259–60, 266,
    269, 302, 313, 325–6, 350
  J, 259, 313
Way, A, 556
Weatherley, H W, 325 (n 12b), 378
Webb, Mrs B, 3 (n 2), 345, 364
  Sidney, Lord Passfield, 3 (n 2), 345, 364,
    383, 404
Webster, C K, 392
  Sir Richard Everard, Lord Alverstone, 347
    (n 3c), 569
Wedgwood, Col J, MP, 407
Weeding Committee see Inspecting Officers'
  Committee
Welby, Reginald Erle, Lord Welby, 246 (n
  1), 296, 308, 318, 323, 327, 331, 336–7
Welsh
  Guards bands, 424
  heraldry and genealogy, 262
  laws, 61
  office Welshmen, 348, 395
  Reconstruction Advisory Council, 375
  records, 160, 191
    agitation for inquiry, 362–4, 470, 501
    Black's surveys, 46–7, 49–50, 53, 59,
      110, 113

Welsh, records – contd
    former courts, 14, 37–8, 41, 44–5,
      513–14, 526, 565
    land revenue, 513
    Langdale's concern, 22, 34
    List and Index, 375
    neglect alleged, 14, 348, 362, 367, 565–6
    oversight, 226
    purchase of plea rolls, 319
    Royal Commission report, 369, 372–6
    transfer to PRO, 110, 158–9, 376
    witnesses' evidence to Royal Commission,
      366
  see also Wales
Wernham, R B, 409, 424, 447
Westminster, archbishop of see Hinsley
Westminster, 56, 131, 226, 536
  Abbey
    Chapter House see under Record offices
      and repositories
    Cole's Guide, 74–5
    dean of see Stanley
    muniments, 281
    writs, 348
  favoured as site for new Record Office, 60,
    89, 120
  Hall, 45, 82, 93, 176, 311
  Improvement Commission, 121
  provision for building general repository in
    London or, 11, 512
  Queen's Rifles, 232
  records in Treasury, 424
Wetton, Miss C, 485
Wharncliffe, Lord see Stuart-Wortley-
  Mackenzie
Wharton, H, 532
Whistler, W, 234
White, A, 556
  R E, 387
  W L, 398–9, 438–9, 458–9, 485, 489
Whitechapel Association, 129
Whitehall Yard branch see under Record
  offices and repositories
Whitley Council, 399, 401, 418, 443, 486
  establishment, 387
  Staff Side constitution, 489
Whitleyism, 397
Wilberforce, Samuel, bishop of Oxford, 556
Wilde, Oscar, 404
Willett, W, 344
William I, arms, 226
Williams, F T, 483, 571
  N J, 222 (n 16a), 456, 576
Willoughby, Maj Gen M F, 232 (n 30a)

Wills
  British Record Society's work, 328
  deposit desired, 291
  Palgrave's, 202
  Prerogative court of Canterbury, 486
  Probate Division of High Court, 490
  Probate Registry, Canterbury, 405
Wilson, Sir Charles Rivers, 238, 252
  F M, 195, 211–12, 237
  H W, 345
  S S, 161, 406, 441, 452, 478, 498, 506–7,
    575
Winchester, storage of Domesday at, 129
Windsor Castle, 220, 245, 355
Winsford salt mine, 429
Withdrawals of records
  Board of Agriculture, 105
  Charity Commission, 183
  registration, 410
  Royal Archives, 419–20
  Scottish, 420, 452–3
  Welsh, 376
Wood, Miss A see Green
  A C, 395–6, 417, 429, 437, 487–8, 574
Woodcroft, B, 161
Woodruff, C H, 298, 334, 354
Woods, Forests and Land Revenues, Office
  of, 10, 44, 86, 280, 345
Woodward, Sir Llewellyn, 480–1
Woolby, W, 154, 214, 266, 312, 322
Woolner, T, 202
Workers' Educational Association, 378
Workmen see under Staff and staffing,
  support grades
Works departments, 332, 483
  accommodation and building services, 44,
    64, 123, 160, 190, 196–8, 208, 234, 264,
    299, 308, 312, 336–45, 379, 383–4, 386,
    395, 410, 419, 427, 440, 458, 464–5,
    486, 506

Works departments – contd
  difficulties with Jenkinson, 410
  History of the King's Works, 492
  records, public access, 404, 451
  represented on committee to consider
    intermediate storage of departmental
    records, 440
  secretary, 325
  supply services, 119 (n 29), 180–1, 232,
    423, 457
World Congress of Universal
  Documentation, 419
Wright, Robert Alderson, Lord Wright, 417,
  420–1, 425, 569
  T, 556
  W A, 307
  W S, 386–7, 400, 402, 405, 426–7, 429,
    440
Wyatt, W, MP, 460–1
Wynne, W, 103
Wyon, W, 46 (n 11)

Yarmouth, Great
  Palgrave's visit, 22
  return of documents, 215
  Turner family bank, 139
Yeading intermediate repository see under
  Record offices and repositories
Yeatman, J P, 263, 272–7, 282 (n 31), 286,
  292–3, 299, 306, 308, 348, 356, 500
Yong, J, 343, 486
Yonge, H, 126, 153, 212
York, flood damage to records, 326
Young, Sir Charles George, 3, (n 3)

Zinoviev letter, 392, 493